PRAISE FOR
RELIGION AND RESISTANCE IN EARLY JUDAISM:

John Nordling is eminently suited for this task, since he combines classical scholarship with a profound knowledge of New Testament Greek. His selections from 1 Maccabees and Josephus, together with his enlightening grammatical and historical notes, supported by an extensive vocabulary, excel in sustaining reader interest and I am positive that the insights and enthusiasm reflected in this most valuable *vademecum* will rub off on both tutors and students.

—Andrie du Toit, PhD
Emeritus Professor of New Testament
University of Pretoria
Ret. Pres. of *Societas Novi Testamenti Studiorum*

With an impressively clear and hard☐working introduction, excellent selection, and notes that are as historically and culturally rich as they are helpful in matters of vocabulary, grammar and syntax, Religion and Resistance is a sourcebook for scholars as much as it is a handy and informative reader for students of intermediate Greek. For all those many students of antiquity who rightly find the political and religious intrigues of 1 Maccabees and Josephus an Idumaean jungle, overgrown and hard to penetrate, John Nordling has opened a clear and easily traveled path.

—Kirk Freudenburg, PhD
Department of Classics
Yale University

John Nordling's masterful Greek anthology for advanced courses in Greek reading, *Religion and Resistance in Early Judaism*, focuses on selections of the Greek texts of 1 Maccabees and Josephus, with a historical introduction and includes a wealth of detailed notes on the Greek text and vocabulary. Teachers of Greek, particularly in theological institutions and programs, will welcome this Greek reader that provides both a historical background to this crucial period of early Judaism as well as a pedagogically sophisticated tool for introducing students of the New Testament to a more sophisticated form of Greek. This text fills a gap in available Greek readers and should prove useful for the serious study of advance Greek.

—David E. Aune, PhD
Walter Professor of New Testament & Christian Origins
Department of Theology
University of Notre Dame

This book is valuable on several counts. On the one hand, its lexicon and abundance of grammatical explanations will help move students through the reading of simpler texts into much more advanced ones. On the other hand, the passages Nordling has chosen are historically most significant; these selections are indispensible for an in-depth understanding of early Judaism and the milieu of early Christianity. Thus, the author's focus on historical matters within his introductory remarks and textual notes further enhances the book's value.

—Robert A. Sorensen, PhD
Associate Professor of Greek and Theology
Concordia University Chicago

This new text containing selections from 1 Maccabees and excerpts from the writings of Josephus evokes memories of the carefully edited texts from which I studied as an undergraduate nearly fifty years ago. John Nordling's edition contains many outstanding features and meets the needs of college and seminary teachers who enhance New Testament readings by incorporating related Hellenistic texts into the curriculum. Professor Nordling has given us an excellent text to accomplish those goals. . . .

I wholeheartedly endorse his excellent edition and recommend it to teachers eager to enrich their Greek curriculum through serious study of Hellenistic works.

—Brent M. Froberg, PhD
Senior Lecturer in Classics
Baylor University, Waco, TX

Religion and Resistance in Early Judaism

BOOKS BY JOHN G. NORDLING

Concordia Commentary: A Theological Exposition of Sacred Scripture

PHILEMON, 2004

As Article Contributor

THE LUTHERAN STUDY BIBLE

CONCORDIA COMMENTARIES: NEW TESTAMENT

MATTHEW 1:1–11:1, Gibbs, 2006.
MATTHEW 11:2–20:34, Gibbs, December 2010.
LUKE 1:1–9:50, Just, 1996.
LUKE 9:51–24:53, Just, 1997.
1 CORINTHIANS, Lockwood, 2000.
COLOSSIANS, Deterding, 2003.
REVELATION, Brighton, 1999.

ADDITIONAL TITLES FROM CONCORDIA

THE LAND OF MILK AND HONEY: AN INTRODUCTION TO THE GEOGRAPHY OF ISRAEL, BECK

"HEAR THE WORD OF YAHWEH": ESSAYS ON SCRIPTURE AND ARCHAEOLOGY IN HONOR OF HORACE D. HUMMEL, WENTHE, ET AL.

THE LAW IN HOLY SCRIPTURE, GIESCHEN

FUNDAMENTAL GREEK GRAMMAR, VOELZ

CONCORDIA GREEK READER

RELIGION AND RESISTANCE IN EARLY JUDAISM

Readings in First Maccabees and Josephus

JOHN G. NORDLING

Peer Reviewed

CONCORDIA PUBLISHING HOUSE • SAINT LOUIS

ABOUT THE COVER: The Greek text on the cover is based on a stock image of the fourth-century Codex Vaticanus, Matthew 14:35–15:28.

Peer Reviewed
Published by Concordia Publishing House
3558 S. Jefferson Ave., St. Louis, MO 63118-3968

1-800-325-3040 • www.cph.org

Copyright © 2010 John G. Nordling

All rights reserved. No part of this publication may be reproduced, stored in a retrieval system, or transmitted, in any form or by any means, electronic, mechanical, photocopying, recording, or otherwise, without the prior written permission of Concordia Publishing House.

See the Credits and Acknowledgements pages, beginning on page 360, for a complete listing of permissions and attributions.

Unless otherwise indicated, Scripture quotations and translations from the Greek texts are the author's translation.

Manufactured in the United States of America

Library of Congress Cataloging-in-Publication Data

Nordling, John G.

  Religion and resistance in early Judaism : readings in first Maccabees and Josephus / John G. Nordling.

    p. cm. -- (Concordia Greek reader)

  "Religion and resistance in early Judaism prepares advanced students of Greek to read and translate selections from 1 Maccabees and Josephus, with an emphasis on building knowledge of grammar, syntax, and vocabulary. The book also describes the religious and cultural clash between the classical world and early Judaism."–ECIP summary.

  Includes bibliographical references.

  ISBN 978-0-7586-2667-7

  1. Greek language–Grammar. 2. Greek language–Syntax. 3. Greek language–Vocabulary. 4. Bible. O.T. Apocrypha. Maccabees, 1st–Language, style. 5. Josephus, Flavius. Antiquitates Judaicae. I. Title. II. Series.

PA695.N67 2011

425–dc22   2010042080

2 3 4 5 6 7 8 9 10   19 18 17 16 15 14 13 12

Contents

Foreword	ix
Preface	xiii
Bibliography	xv
Introduction	1
Greek Text: 1 Maccabees 1:1–4:61	21
Text Notes: 1 Maccabees	41
Greek Text: Josephus Selections	67
Text Notes: Josephus	107
Vocabulary	289
Credits and Acknowledgments	363

Notice to the reader: An updated version of the Greek Cardo font has been used in this printing to improve the book by eliminating the appearance of spaces that occurred in several Greek words in the first printing. As a result, there has been a slight reflow of the text. This has had no effect on the page numbers in the table of contents, except that the "Credits and Acknowledgments" appear on p. 363 rather than p. 360. Professors or students using different printings of the book in group study should be aware that some pages of this printing may differ in appearance from the first printing.

FOREWORD

Today the world's international language is English. Several centuries ago it was French, at least in diplomatic exchange. For the entire medieval era, of course, it was Latin, but in the ancient Mediterranean world it was Greek. Since this is the area where Jesus and the Apostles lived and the era in which the New Testament was written—*in Greek*—the study of this classical language is of prime importance to any student of antiquity or any seminarian trying to plumb the ultimate meaning of language in the Gospels or the letters of St. Paul and other biblical authors.

When Paul wrote that Jesus arrived "when the fullness of time had come" (Galatians 4:4), many factors are often cited to show that God did indeed have a good sense of timing. Probably the most important of these, however, was that the entire Mediterranean basin now had linguistic unity through common commercial (*koine*) Greek, the language of the New Testament. Small wonder that this linguistic vehicle powerfully enabled the rapid spread of Christianity in the Roman Empire

To be sure, Roman governmental proclamations were often in Latin, but Greek was the tongue spoken in all the Mediterranean ports, even in the West. It was *the* classical language for any educated Roman, and when the emperor Marcus Aurelius (AD 161–180) wrote his masterpiece of Stoic philosophy, *The Meditations*, he used Greek, not Latin. Fully to understand, then, the mind, the culture, and the whole intellectual essence of the ancient Mediterranean, one simply cannot do without Greek.

How sad, then, that Greek is no longer taught on the secondary level in our educational system, and not even offered that often in our colleges and universities. One of the reasons may well be the drudgery of learning Greek grammar, syntax, and vocabulary, and the fact that there are fewer cognates between Greek and English than in the case of Latin, even though many English words do have Greek roots, especially in our more technical and scientific terms.

Foreword

Here is where John G. Nordling's *Religion and Resistance in Early Judaism* provides a valuable service, indeed something of a cure for the malaise just cited. Why not let a student who has ingested the pabulum of Greek basics now cut his teeth on some *real* food? "The farmer is good," or "The army moved ten stadia" may have been fine for early learning purposes, but all ancient texts come to life when they convey real information. For openers, how about some of the action passages in I Maccabees or Flavius Josephus?

In this book, classical scholar and Lutheran theologian John G. Nordling has chosen some of the most interesting or exciting passages from the history of the great Jewish war of liberation from Syrian rule that immediately preceded Jesus, as well as key passages from the works of Josephus for the benefit of both secular and religious students of Greek. These can now learn not only the language but also the history of the times—and have fun in the process.

Nordling begins with a pellucid overview of Mediterranean antiquity in the last two centuries before Christ and the first century after. Clearly providing the context and setting for each of the passages selected, this author-editor does not leave the student to his own devices, especially in the case of the more difficult passages. Much of this book is devoted to linguistic notes on the texts chosen from 1 Maccabees and Josephus, all of which provide ready helps in translation. And finally, a whole Greek-English Vocabulary is also provided at the close, or at least a listing of all the more difficult words in the texts chosen, obviating the need for the usual Greek-English lexicon.

To be sure, the Greek of the New Testament will be easier reading for most students of the language, but this is primarily because they "knew the translation" ahead of time—i.e., the New Testament stories—ever since Sunday School, in many cases. Once these non-biblical texts are mastered, however, the Greek New Testament will take on even more meaning.

Some years ago, a scholar friend of mine said that if there were extraterrestrials on the moon or any other planet in the universe who wanted to exchange information with humanity on Mother Earth, Greek would have to be used because of its precision. This, of course, was exaggeration to prove a point: that Greek has shaped the Western mind more than any other language. In terms of our culture, our institutions, and the way we think and act, we're more Greek than anything else.

This Greek reader will help us return to the mother tongue!

>   Paul L. Maier
>   Russell H. Seibert Professor of Ancient History
>   Western Michigan University

PREFACE

Religion and Resistance in Early Judaism introduces advanced level Greek students to the selections drawn from 1 Maccabees and Josephus and enables them to read this literature with interest and appreciation.

By advanced Greek student I mean a collegian or seminarian who, having spent the first year in grammatical study, has also spent at least one semester reading such authors as Herodotus, Xenophon, or St. Paul in the Greek New Testament. Such a background will have acquainted the student with indirect statement, purpose clauses, the genitive absolute, and the type of vocabulary one frequently encounters in standard Greek prose.

Many students at this level are familiar with Septuagintal and New Testament Greek; 1 Maccabees, which resembles the Septuagint more than incidentally, provides a bridge from the Greek with which students are familiar to the lengthier and more rhetorically sophisticated passages of Josephus. After reading a chapter or two in 1 Maccabees, one is ready to encounter some of the briefer, though still famous, passages in Josephus (his birth and education, John the Baptist, Jesus, etc.), and from there vignettes drawn from the destruction of Jerusalem and the capture of Masada. Almost no class is capable of reading all the Greek contained here in a single term; I would like, therefore, to give Greek instructors the freedom to choose those passages which they know their own students can handle and consistently work up to the lengthier and more difficult passages. They will be delighted to see how much progress can be made as students proceed in this manner.

The in-class goal should be to translate and discuss as much of the Greek text as possible. It is expected that students will have engaged assignments in advance of class time and thus be prepared to translate and explain basic grammatical points. The Vocabulary in the back of the book will enable students to look up unknown words, or words which—while known—have a peculiar meaning in the selections considered. The Text Notes are intended to help students with difficult passages, remind them of grammatical features already encountered, and provide parallel passages so that

PREFACE

they may penetrate the texts more deeply in preparation for oral reports and term projects. I recommend that class members have access to Smyth's *Greek Grammar* (Harvard, 1920; ISBN 0-674-36250-0) and the Perseus Word Study Tool:

http://www.perseus.tufts.edu/hopper/morph

The focus is on Judaism and Hellenism/Romanism in the first century BC and AD, and all the ways—both positive and negative—that the two cultures interacted with each other in antiquity. Translation and analysis of the text selections may well stimulate the following in-class discussions:

- Amid all the heartache and suffering that occurred between Jews, Hellenists, and Romans during the periods represented, what positive developments emerged, if any?

- Which character traits epitomize the Jews? the Hellenists? the Romans? What details do the texts use to bring the character traits home to readers?

- Did the Jews, bound by tradition, scripture, and a covenantal relationship with the monotheistic God of the Old Testament, always reject Hellenism and Greco-Roman culture? In what ways were Jews open to Greco-Roman culture? Likewise, in what ways did Hellenists and Romans accommodate Judaism?

- Does the ancient tension between Judaism and Greco-Roman culture anticipate modern conflicts that occur, for example, in the Middle East?

I would like to thank my wife, Sara A. Nordling, for support in writing most of this book during a difficult time in my life, and Dr. Robert A. Sorensen, Associate Professor of Theology and Greek, Concordia University, Chicago, who has provided much encouragement along the way. I would like to dedicate this book to those hard-working students with whom I had the pleasure of reading many of the selections contained here in the spring of 2002—namely, Megan Gros, John Kinnaird, Sean Mathis, Robert Phillips, Amanda Seamans, Mark Taylor, and Chad Walker.

John G. Nordling

March 2010

BIBLIOGRAPHY

ABBREVIATIONS

Antiq	*Antiquitates Judaicae* (Antiquities of the Jews)
BJ	*Bellum Judaicum* (Jewish War)
BJRL	*Bulletin of the John Rylands University Library of Manchester*
BYU Studies	*Brigham Young University Studies*
CBQ	*Catholic Biblical Quarterly*
Contra Ap	*Contra Apionem* (Against Apion)
CQ	*Classical Quarterly*
GRBS	*Greek, Roman, and Byzantine Studies*
IDB	*The Interpreter's Dictionary of the Bible.* Edited by G. A. Buttrick, 5 vols. Nashville: Abingdon, 1962; 11th printing, 1980
JBL	*Journal of Biblical Literature*
JJS	*Journal of Jewish Studies*
JQR	*Jewish Quarterly Review*
JSJ	*Journal for the Study of Judaism*
JTS	*Journal of Theological Studies*
LCL	the translation is not the author's, but that of the Loeb Classical Library
LSJ	Liddell, H. G., R. Scott, and H. S. Jones. *A Greek-English Lexicon.* Ninth ed. with rev. supplement. Oxford: Clarendon, 1966
LXX	Septuagint
Macc	Maccabees

BIBLIOGRAPHY

NBD	*New Bible Dictionary*. Edited by J. D. Douglas et al. Grand Rapids, MI: Eerdmans, 1962; reprint, 1979
NEA	*Near Eastern Archaeology*
NT	New Testament
OCD	*Oxford Classical Dictionary*. Edited by N. G. L. Hammond and H. H. Scullard. Second Ed. Oxford: Clarendon, 1970
OT	Old Testament
RhM	*Rheinisches Museum*
Smyth	H. W. Smyth. *Greek Grammar*. Cambridge, MA: Harvard University Press, 1920; 1956; 10th printing, 1976
Vita	*Vita Josephi* (Life of Josephus)
§	section (as opposed to page number)

See LSJ (pgs. xvi–xli) for the abbreviations of Greek authors and works not represented above. In this volume, abbreviations of biblical and apocryphal books follow the conventions adopted by the Concordia Commentary Series, published by Concordia Publishing House since 1996. Many (not all) of the bibliographical items below appear in the Introduction, annotations, and Text Notes below. All items have been chosen to provide students with suitable materials for producing oral reports and term projects.

Amaru, Betsy H. 1980–81. "Land Theology in Josephus' *Jewish Antiquities*." *JQR* 71:201–29.

―――. 1987. "Martin Luther and Flavius Josephus." Pages 411–26 in *Josephus, Judaism, and Christianity*. Edited by Louis H. Feldman and Gohei Hada. Detroit: Wayne State University Press.

Atkinson, Kenneth. 2007. "Noble Deaths at Gamla and Masada? A Critical Assessment of Josephus' Accounts of Jewish Resistance in Light of Archaeological Discoveries." Pages 349–71 in *Making History: Josephus and Historical Method*. Edited by Zuleika Rodgers. Leiden: Brill.

Beardslee, William A. 1962. "James." *IDB* 2:790–94.

Birdsall, J. N. 1985. "The Continuing Enigma of Josephus' Testimony about Jesus." *BJRL* 67:609–22.

Black, Matthew. 1962. "Pharisees." *IDB* 3:774–81.

Bowersock, G. W. 2005. "Foreign Elites at Rome." Pages 53–62 in *Flavius Josephus and Flavian Rome*. Edited by Jonathan Edmondson, Steve Mason, and James Rives. Oxford: Oxford.

Bradley, Keith R. 1987. "On the Roman Slave Supply and Slave Breeding." Pages 42–64 in *Classical Slavery*. Edited by Moses I. Finley. London: Frank Cass.

Brownlee, William H. 1962. "Maccabees, Books of." *IDB* 3:201–15.

Bruce, F. F. 1979. "Essenes." *NBD* 391–92.

———. 1979. "Herod." *NBD* 521–22.

———. 1979. "Josephus, Flavius." *NBD* 660–61.

———. 1979. "Procurator." *NBD* 1036.

Burrows, Millar. 1962. "Jerusalem." *IDB* 2:843–66.

Buttrick, George A., ed. 1962, 1976. *The Interpreter's Dictionary of the Bible*. 5 vols. Nashville: Abingdon.

Cadoux, Theodore J. 1970. "Petronius (1)." *OCD* 807.

Chancey, Mark A. and Adam Porter. 2001. "The Archaeology of Roman Palestine." *NEA* 64.4:164–203.

Chapman, Honora H. 2005. "Spectacle in Josephus' *Jewish War*." Pages 289–313 in *Flavius Josephus and Flavian Rome*. Edited by Jonathan Edmondson, Steve Mason, and James Rives. Oxford: Oxford.

———. 2007. "Masada in the 1st and 21st Centuries." Pages 82–102 in *Making History. Josephus and Historical Method*. Edited by Zuleika Rodgers. Leiden: Brill.

Clark, Kenneth W. 1962. "Antonia, Tower of." *IDB* 1:153–54.

Cohen, Shaye J. D. 1982. "Masada: Literary Tradition, Archaeological Remains and the Credibility of Josephus." *JJS* 28:385–405.

_____. 1987. *From the Maccabees to the Mishnah*. Philadelphia: Westminster.

Conybeare, F. C. and St. George Stock. 2001. *Grammar of Septuagint Greek: With Selected Readings, Vocabularies, and Updated Indexes*. Boston: Ginn and Company, 1905. Reprint, Peabody, Mass.: Hendrickson.

Cotton, Hannah M. and Werner Eck. 2005. "Josephus' Roman Audience: Josephus and the Roman Elites." Pages 37–52 in *Flavius Josephus and Flavian Rome*. Edited by Jonathan Edmondson, Steve Mason, and James Rives. Oxford: Oxford.

Cressey, M. H. 1979. "Stoics." *NBD* 1217.

Douglas, J. D. 1962; reprint, 1979. *New Bible Dictionary*. Grand Rapids: Eerdmans.

Ellison, H. L. 1979. "Pharisees." *NBD* 981–82.

Eshel, Hanan. 1999. "Josephus' View on Judaism without the Temple in Light of the Discoveries at Masada and Murabba'at." Pages 229–38 in *Gemeinde ohne Tempel: Zur Substituierung und Transformation des Jerusalemer Tempels und seines Kults im Alten Testament, antiken Judentum und frühen Christentum*. Wissenschaftliche Untersuchungen zum Neuen Testament 118. Edited by Beate Ego, Armin Lange, and Peter Pilhofer. Tübingen: Mohr Siebeck.

Farmer, W. R. 1956. *Maccabees, Zealots, and Josephus: An Inquiry into Jewish Nationalism in the Greco-Roman Period*. New York: Columbia University Press.

Funk, Robert W. 1962. "Masada." *IDB* 3:293–94.

Garrison, James V. 1996–97. "Casting Stones: Ballista, Stones as Weapons, and Death by Stoning." *BYU Studies* 36.3:351–62.

Goldin, Judah. 1962. "Josephus, Flavius." *IDB* 2:987–88.

Grant, Michael. 1984. *The History of Ancient Israel*. New York: Charles Scribner's Sons.

Hall, John F. 1996–97. "The Roman Province of Judea: a Historical Overview." *BYU Studies* 36.3:319–36.

Hamblin, William J. 1996–97. "The Roman Army in the First Century." *BYU Studies* 36.3:337–49.

Hammond, Nicholas G. L. and Howard H. Scullard. 1970. *Oxford Classical Dictionary*. 2nd ed. Oxford: Clarendon.

Harrison, Roland K. 1979. "Antioch (Syrian)." *NBD* 40–41.

―――――. 1979. "Caesarea." *NBD* 174–75.

Holzapfel, Richard N. 1996–97. "King Herod." *BYU Studies* 36.3:35–73.

Huntsman, Eric D. 1996–97. "And They Cast Lots: Divination, Democracy, and Josephus." *BYU Studies* 36.3:365–77.

―――――. 1996–97. "The Reliability of Josephus: Can He be Trusted?" *BYU Studies* 36.3:392–402.

Jackson, Kent P. 1996–97. "Revolutionaries in the First Century." *BYU Studies* 36.3:129–40.

Jacobs, I. 1982. "Eleazar Ben Yair's Sanction for Martyrdom." *JSJ* 13:183–86.

Jones, C. P. 2005. "Josephus and Greek Literature in Flavian Rome." Pages 201–08 in *Flavius Josephus and Flavian Rome*. Edited by Jonathan Edmondson, Steve Mason, and James Rives. Oxford: Oxford.

Josephus. 1926–1965. Translated by Henry St. J. Thackeray et al. 10 vols. LCL. Cambridge, Mass.: Harvard University Press.

Judd, Daniel K. 1996–97. "Suicide at Masada and in the World of the New Testament." *BYU Studies* 36.3:378–91.

Ladouceur, D. J. 1981. "Masada: A Consideration of the Literary Evidence." *GRBS* 21:245–60.

―――――. 1987. "Josephus and Masada." Pages 95–113 in *Josephus, Judaism, and Christianity*. Edited by Louis H. Feldman and Gohei Hada. Detroit: Wayne State University Press.

Liddell, Henry G, Robert Scott, and Henry S. Jones. 1966. *A Greek-English Lexicon*. 9th ed. with revised supplement. Oxford: Clarendon.

Luz, Menahem. 1983. "Eleazar's Second Speech on Masada and its Literary Precedents." *RhM* 126:25–43.

Maier, Paul L. 1988. *Josephus: The Essential Writings*. Grand Rapids: Kregel.

_____. 1991. *In the Fullness of Time: A Historian Looks at Christmas, Easter, and the Early Church*. New York: HarperSanFrancisco.

Macfarlane, Roger T. 1996–97. "Hebrew, Aramaic, Greek, and Latin: Languages of New Testament Judea." *BYU Studies* 36.3: 228–38.

Mason, Steve. 2001. *Life of Josephus: Translation and Commentary*. Vol. 9 of *Flavius Josephus: Translation and Commentary*. Edited by Steve Mason. Leiden: Brill.

_____. 2003. *Josephus and the New Testament*. 2nd ed. Peabody, Mass.: Hendrickson.

_____. 2005. "Figured Speech and Irony in T. Flavius Josephus." Pages 243–88 in *Flavius Josephus and Flavian Rome*. Edited by Jonathan Edmondson, Steve Mason, and James Rives. Oxford: Oxford.

McKelvey, R. J. 1979. "Temple." *NBD* 1242–50.

McLaren, James S. 2001. "Ananus, James, and Earliest Christianity: Josephus' Account of the Death of James." *JTS* 52:1–25.

Millar, Fergas. 2005. "Last Year in Jerusalem: Monuments of the Jewish War in Rome." Pages 101–28 in *Flavius Josephus and Flavian Rome*. Edited by Jonathan Edmondson, Steve Mason, and James Rives. Oxford: Oxford.

Oesterley, William O. E. 1941. "The History of the Jews During the Last Three Pre-Christian Centuries." Pages 16–41 in *The Jews and Judaism During the Greek Period: The Background of Christianity*. London: Society for Promoting Christian Knowledge.

Olson, Ken. 1999. "Eusebius and the *Testimonium Flavianum*." *CBQ* 61:305–22.

Orlinsky, Harry M. 1962. "Maccabees, Maccabean Revolt." *IDB* 3:197–201.

Patterson, J. H. 1979. "Tiberias." *NBD* 1275.

Payne, D. F. 1979. "Jerusalem." *NBD* 614–20.

Peek, Cecilia M. 1996–97. "Alexander the Great Comes to Jerusalem: the Jewish Response to Hellenism." *BYU Studies* 36.3:99–112.

Rajak, Tessa. 2005. "Josephus in the Diaspora." Pages 79–97 in *Flavius Josephus and Flavian Rome*. Edited by Jonathan Edmondson, Steve Mason, and James Rives. Oxford: Oxford.

Richards, G. C. and R. J. H. Shutt. 1937. "Critical Notes on Josephus' Antiquities." *CQ* 31:170–77.

Richardson, Peter. 1996. *Herod: King of the Jews and Friend of the Romans*. Columbia: University of South Carolina Press.

Russell, David S. 1967. *The Jews from Alexander to Herod*. London: Oxford.

Sandmel, Samuel. 1962. "Herod." *IDB* 2:585–94.

Schreckenberg, Heinz. 1987. "The Works of Josephus and the Early Christian Church." Pages 315–24 in *Josephus, Judaism, and Christianity*. Edited by Louis H. Feldman and Gohei Hada. Detroit: Wayne State University Press.

Seely, David R. 1996–97. "The Masada Fragments, the Qumran Scrolls, and the New Testament." *BYU Studies* 36.3:287–301.

Sievers, Joseph. 1998. "Josephus and the Afterlife." Pages 20–34 in *Understanding Josephus: Seven Perspectives*. Journal for the Study of the Pseudepigrapha Supplement Series 32. Edited by Steve Mason. Sheffield: Sheffield Academic Press.

Skinner, Andrew C. 1996–97. "A Historical Sketch of Galilee." *BYU Studies* 36.3:113–25.

Smyth, Herbert Weir. 1920; 1956; revised by Gordon G. Messing, 1984. *Greek Grammar*. Cambridge, Mass.: Harvard University Press.

Spilsbury, Paul. 1998. "God and Israel in Josephus: a Patron-Client Relationship." Pages 172–91 in *Understanding Josephus: Seven Perspectives*. Journal for the Study of the Pseudepigrapha Supplement Series 32. Edited by Steve Mason. Sheffield: Sheffield Academic Press.

Stern, M. 1987. "Josephus and the Roman Empire as Reflected in *The Jewish War*." Pages 71–80 in *Josephus, Judaism, and Christianity*. Edited by Louis H. Feldman and Gohei Hada. Detroit: Wayne State University Press.

Stinespring, W. F. 1962. "Temple, Jerusalem." *IDB* 4:534–60.

Teasdale, Andrew. 1996–97. "Herod the Great's Building Program." *BYU Studies* 36.3:84–98.

Thackeray, Henry St. John. 1956. Introduction. Pages vii–xxxii in *Josephus: The Jewish War, Books I–III*. Edited by Henry St. John Thackeray. LCL. Cambridge, Mass.: Harvard University Press.

_____. 1967. *Josephus: the Man and the Historian*. New York: Ktav.

van Henten, Jan Willem. 2007. "Noble Death in Josephus: Just Rhetoric?" Pages 195–218 in *Making History: Josephus and Historical Method*. Edited by Zuleika Rodgers. Leiden: Brill.

Vardaman, Jerry. 1962. "A New Inscription which Mentions Pilate as 'Prefect'." *JBL* 81:70–71.

Walls, A. F. 1979. "Maccabees." *NBD* 762–64.

Watson, Alan. 1985. *The Digest of Justinian*. Latin text edited by T. Mommsen with the aid of P. Krueger. English translation edited by Alan Watson. 4 vols. Philadelphia: University of Pennsylvania Press.

Whealey, Alice. 2007. "Josephus, Eusebius of Caesarea, and the *Testimonium Flavianum*." Pages 73–116 in *Josephus und das Neue Testament*. Edited by Christfried Böttrich and Jens Herzer. Tübingen: Mohr Siebeck.

Wheaton, D. H. 1979. "Pilate." *NBD* 996–97.

Wilson, E. Jan. 1996–97. "The Masada Synagogue and its Relationship to Jewish Worship during the Second Temple Period." *BYU Studies* 36.3:269–76.

Yadin, Yigael. 1966. *Masada: Herod's Fortress and the Zealots' Last Stand*. New York: Random House.

_____. 1996–97. "Masada: Herod's Fortress and the Zealots' Last Stand." *BYU Studies* 36.3:15–32.

Ziolkowski, Adam. 1993. "*Urbs direpta*, or How the Romans Sacked Cities." Pages 69–91 in *War and Society in the Roman World*. Edited by J. Rich and G. Shipley. London and New York: Routledge.

INTRODUCTION

ISRAEL'S INVOLVEMENT IN INTERNATIONAL AFFAIRS

1. Geographically, Israel serves as a land bridge connecting vast regions in Asia Minor, Mesopotamia, and Africa. It was impossible, therefore, for the ancient inhabitants of Israel to follow strict policies of isolationism. Israel's involvement in international affairs culminated during the Hellenistic period, thanks to the conquests of Alexander the Great (356–323 BC) whose armies ranged over Macedonia, Asia Minor, the Levant, Egypt, Mesopotamia, and India. Hellenism united many disparate peoples and regions under one dominant culture. Emerging Judaism became more involved with Hellenism than any of the other ethnic, religious, or political groups in the area (Orlinsky 1962, 197; Cohen 1987, 34–38).

ALEXANDER THE GREAT AND JUDAISM

2. Alexander was favorably disposed toward the Jews, though later Judaism and Hellenism would clash dramatically. Most Jews lived outside Judea—along the Mediterranean coast of Asia Minor and in Babylonia and Persia—near the end of the fourth-century BC. During his conquests, Alexander favored the Jews in general, and the inhabitants of Judea in particular. Thus Alexander supported Jerusalem as the site of the Temple against the Samaritans' rival shrine at Mount Gerizim, and he added several important cities of Samaria to Judea. According to legend, Alexander turned off to Jerusalem and offered sacrifices in the Temple to Israel's God after having conquered Tyre and while enroute to Egypt (Joseph. *Antiq* 11.317–320, 325–339; cf. Oesterley 1941, 16; Russell 1967, 13–15; Peek 1996–97, 104–108).

THE EMERGENCE OF ANTIOCHUS IV EPIPHANES (CA. 215–163 BC)

3. After Alexander died in 323 BC, the empire was divided among Alexander's "successors" (Gk: ἐπίγονοι): Cassander

(Macedonia), Lysimachus (Thrace), Antigonus (Asia Minor and northern Syria), and Ptolemy (Egypt and southern Syria). Somewhat later Seleucus (Babylonia-Syria) joined this group. Seleucus and Ptolemy joined forces against Antigonus, and in 312 BC overcame the latter's fleet at Gaza. Seleucus then emerged as the pre-eminent ruler, and the year 312—the "year of the Greeks," as it came to be called (Orlinsky 1962, 198)—became the first year of the Seleucid era and the year by which the author of 1 Macc dates several momentous happenings (cf. 1 Macc 4:28 and 52 below).

4. Egypt and Syria vied with each other for hegemony over Judea, a power struggle that ceased in 219 BC with the conquest by Antiochus III of Coele-Syria and the Transjordan. Judea's council of elders (Gerousia) decided in favor of Syria over Egypt in 201; although an Egyptian army briefly re-conquered several Judean cities and punished many pro-Seleucid Jews, Antiochus III of Syria took back these regions in 199, thus expelling the Egyptians (Ptolemies) forever. At a treaty in 192 BC Antiochus III showed his appreciation for Judea by cancelling taxes, compensating cities that had suffered during the wars, and exempting priests, scribes, and temple singers from the poll and crown taxes. Furthermore, Antiochus provided duty-free timber for the reconstruction of Jerusalem's walls, made money available for the sacrifices in the Temple, and restored many Jewish captives to freedom.

5. The bright future that Judea might have enjoyed with Syria ended as a result of Rome's entrance into the Near East (Battle of Magnesia, 190 BC). Assassins toppled Seleucus IV in 175, and Antiochus IV Epiphanes, Seleucus' brother, seized the throne. As a result of having spent time as a hostage in Rome (after Antiochus III's loss in 190), the younger Antiochus realized that Rome would attempt to control western Asia Minor and the east; accordingly, he tried to thwart Roman designs by conquering Egypt and uniting it with Syria (Russell 1967, 33). The Seleucids increased taxes sharply, imposing upon Judea high tributes from which they themselves were obliged to pay Rome (Grant 1984, 205). Antiochus used radical Hellenization as a policy to unite otherwise disparate peoples in the area, deposing from the high-priesthood Onias III (championed Jewish orthodoxy) and elevating his brother Jason (a pro-Syrian who supported Hellenism; cf. Russell 1967, 35–37). Then Menelaus became high priest by a bribe, whose Hellenism was still more

extreme. It seemed clear that Antiochus meant to "exterminate the Jewish religion altogether" (Russell 1967, 41).

THE MACCABEAN REVOLT

6. The Maccabeans (or Hasmoneans) led Judea during the last two centuries BC when Judaism struggled mightily against Hellenism. Judas, son of Mattathias, was nicknamed "Maccabeus" (1 Macc 2:4), perhaps meaning "the hammer-headed" (cf. Aramaic *maqqaba*). Judas' brothers all had nicknames too (cf. 1 Macc 2:2–5), possibly reflecting physical characteristics. The name "Hasmonean," by which the Maccabeans and their descendants are known, derives from "Asmonaeus," the name of an ancestor of Mattathias—either his father or grandfather (Joseph. *BJ* 1.36).

7. The pro-Seleucid Jews increasingly spoke Greek instead of Hebrew and came to adopt Hellenized mannerisms and names. Not only were the traditional laws of Judaism irksome to these elites, but economic interests also motivated Jason (who had supplanted his brother Onias as high priest) to request Antiochus Epiphanes IV for authorization to set up "a gymnasium and a body of youth... and to enroll the people of Jerusalem as citizens of Antioch" (2 Macc 4:9). By this request Jason really was asking for permission to transform the Holy City into a Hellenistic city, with the right to strike coinage and enjoy other Greek amenities. Indeed, Jason did build a gymnasium in Jerusalem (2 Macc 4:12), where the youth—even priests, with naked bodies—took part in the discus and other Greek forms of prestige (2 Macc 4:14; cf. Russell 1967, 28–29, 36). However, the worst affront was the rededication of the Jerusalem Temple as a shrine of the Olympian Zeus (December 167 BC), "the abomination that makes desolate" (Dan 11:31; 12:11; cf. 1 Macc 1:41–64). A Syrian fortress called the Acra was set up to protect high priests appointed directly by the Seleucid king and to watch over sacrifices that accommodated the spirit of Hellenism.

8. While the Judean upper classes did not oppose, but even welcomed, Hellenism, the common people—farmers, craftsmen, menial workers, petty merchants, and the like—did not favor it. Foremost among the opponents was Mattathias and his five sons who had moved from Jerusalem to Modein (1 Macc 2:1) to avoid contamination. This family "rent their clothes, put on sackcloth, and

mourned greatly" (1 Macc 2:14) the profanation of the Temple by the pagans (1 Macc 2:7–12). When Antiochus IV's officers came to Modein to offer pagan rites, Mattathias killed both the king's official and the first Jew who stepped forward to oblige the Gentiles. Then he destroyed the altar and invited anyone "zealous for the law" to follow him (1 Macc 2:27). Mattathias, his sons and many followers fled into the Judean hinterland; thus began the Maccabean revolt.

THE SIGNIFICANCE OF THE MACCABEAN REVOLT

9. Mattathias escaped to the mountains whence his family and followers descended from time to time to harass those Jews who supported Hellenism by pulling down pagan altars, "forcibly circumcising" male babies, and killing any as had partaken in "pagan sacrifices" (Russell 1967, 46). When Mattathias died in 166 BC, his third son Judas assumed leadership, effectively living up to his reputation as "a lion in his deeds, like a lion's cub roaring for prey" (1 Macc 3:4). Although Judas also excelled in hit-and-run tactics (like his father), under his leadership the Maccabees came to stage full-scale war; after defeating three Syrian generals in turn, Judas met the Syrian regent himself, Lysias. After a further battle, the ensuing peace gave to the Jews complete freedom of worship. Judas completely cleared the Temple of idolatry (1 Macc 4:43–46) and instituted the Feast of Lights (Hanukkah) in 164 BC (1 Macc 4:52–59; 2 Macc 10:1–8; Josephus *Antiq* 12:316–25).

10. But the Maccabees did not rest; they meant to help mistreated Jews in many areas of Israel, and the Acra remained inhabited by Syrians in Jerusalem, that symbol of domination (cf. Russell 1967, 40, 49). Lysias eventually settled with Judas on amicable terms, formally rescinding the policies of Antiochus Epiphanes and issuing a general amnesty (2 Macc 13:23). Judas would continue to fight in some manner until his death at Elasa in 161 BC (1 Macc 9:1–22), though at some point the Maccabeans fought no longer for religious liberties alone, but also to sway political matters. The Hasmonean dynasty began in 152 BC when Jonathan—ten years before the Jews gained complete independence—was appointed high priest by the upstart Syrian king, Alexander Balas, in whose reign the Jews often were left undisturbed.

11. Jonathan now aided many Seleucids in struggles for the throne. His army was capable of waging successful battles on behalf of any claimant, but he himself was tricked into capture in 143 BC and put to death. Simon Maccabeus took over as captain and as high priest. Simon's final victory was to overcome the Acra and demand of Demetrius II that at last the Jewish people be free of the yoke of the heathen (1 Macc 13:33–52). Simon showed that the efforts of his father, brothers, and their many followers had not been expended in vain.

THE RULE OF THE HASMONEANS (142–63 BC)

12. In 141, the people granted the title of ethnarch to Simon and the right of hereditary succession (1 Macc 14:41–49). Everything indicated that a new day had come: documents were dated from the accession of Simon, coins struck, and treaties concluded with Rome and Sparta (1 Macc 13:33–52). The Romans at least promised an absolute freedom of worship to Jews throughout their territories (Russell 1967, 60). Although he was not king, a plaque was set up in the Temple declaring Simon to be the Jews' "leader and high priest forever, until a trustworthy prophet should arise" (1 Macc 14:41). Now Simon was to be high priest, military commander, ethnarch, and protector—all rolled into one (1 Macc 14:47). The Maccabeans (Hasmoneans) would secure for the Jewish people a seventy-nine-year period of relative peace and stability, between periods of Syrian/Greek and Roman domination. Hasmonean leaders during this period were Simon Maccabeus (142–134 BC), John Hyrcanus (134–104 BC), Judas Aristobulus I (104–103 BC), Alexander Janneus (103–76 BC), Salome Alexandra (76–67 BC), and Aristobulus II (67–63 BC; cf. dates in Russell 1967, 60–81).

THE ARRIVAL OF POMPEY IN JERUSALEM (63 BC)

13. One of the regents, Salome Alexandra (76–67 BC), had two sons: the elder, Hyrcanus, who (upon his mother's death), would be appointed king and high priest; and a younger, more ambitious son, Aristobulus, who by the permission of his mother had come to occupy military fortresses throughout the land. Both sons strove for supremacy while their aged mother lived, and when she died (67 BC) the two brothers made separate appeals to Rome to decide the dispute.

Pompey had been in the east campaigning against Mithridates (died 63 BC), then set large tracts of Asia, Syria, and Judea under Roman rule. In the dispute, Marcus Scaurus (Pompey's legate in Syria) decided in favor of Aristobulus; supporters of Hyrcanus sent an embassy to Pompey at Damascus in 63. Aristobulus did the same.

14. While Pompey was determining which brother to support, Aristobulus suddenly set off for Judea, taking refuge at the fortress of Alexandrium—an act that Pompey interpreted as a threat (*BJ* 1.133). Then Aristobulus fled to Jerusalem, and would have opened the gates to Pompey's legate Gabinius had not followers kept them shut. Now that Aristobulus was safely in Pompey's hands, the Roman army advanced on Jerusalem and considered how best to take the city (*BJ* 1.141). Though bereft of their leader, Aristobulus' party retreated to the fortified Temple mount and held out against the Romans for three months. Eventually Pompey's forces prevailed, entered the Temple itself, and massacred the priests serving at the altar. Josephus reports that Pompey's men butchered some 12,000 Jews at this time (*BJ* 1.150–151). Pompey entered the Holy of Holies to see its riches: the candelabrum and lamps, the table, vessels and censers, spices, and 2,000 talents of sacred money. Still, he took nothing and even ordered custodians to cleanse the place and resume the sacrifices (*BJ* 1.152–153).

15. So ended the rule of the Hasmoneans. Aristobulus and his family were carried off by Pompey to Rome where, in 61 BC, Aristobulus was forced to take part in Pompey's victory parade. Hyrcanus, the elder brother, was allowed to rule on as high priest and ethnarch (*BJ* 1.153), though without the title king. Pompey set the country and Jerusalem under tribute (*BJ* 1.154), imposed a garrison in the city, and set Judean affairs under supervision of Scaurus, the Roman proconsul of Syria. In 57 BC the Roman senate appointed Gabinius, who had assisted Pompey in the siege of Jerusalem, as governor of Syria (*Antiq* 14.82; Oesterley 1941, 38–39; Chancey and Porter 2001, 165). Gabinius also divided the whole nation into five *synedria* (councils) that met at various points in Israel: at Jerusalem, Gadara, Amathus, Jericho, and Sepphoris (*Antiq* 14.91).

INTRODUCTION

THE FAMILY OF THE HERODS (37 BC–AD 70)

16. Antipater (also known as Antipas), father of Herod the Great (37–4 BC), had supported Hyrcanus against Aristobulus in the earlier struggle (Intro 13–14 above). Since Hyrcanus was psychologically and militarily weaker than Aristobulus, he was open to Antipater's self-seeking suggestions. Hyrcanus' restoration to high priest and ethnarch resulted in Antipater's elevation also. Antipater, an Idumean, had married a woman named Cypros of an illustrious Nabataean family; by her he sired four sons: Phasael, Herod (born 73 BC), Joseph, Pheroras, and a daughter, Salome. Some have stressed Herod's Jewish origins (e.g., Holzapfel 1996–97, 44); the fact that two of Herod's siblings—Joseph and Salome—had Jewish names may indicate that the family actually had close associations with Judaism, in spite of the negativity with which Herod's Jewish subjects would regard his ancestry later (cf. Intro 19 below).

17. Antipater had supported Julius Caesar in that statesman's fight against Pompey's supporters in Alexandria (48–47 BC), and was even wounded on behalf of Caesar. To reward him, Caesar bestowed Roman citizenship on Antipater, appointed him procurator of Judea in 47, and confirmed Hyrcanus as high priest. In turn, Antipater made his son Phasael governor of Jerusalem and Herod governor of Galilee. The Parthians entered political affairs at this time, removing Phasael and Hyrcanus and imposing as king the Hasmonean Antigonus (Chancey and Porter 2001, 165). After escorting his family to Masada and leaving them there, Herod fled to Petra, Alexandria, then Rome, where Antony and Octavian (later Caesar Augustus) graciously received him (probably in Dec. 40; *BJ* 1.285). The Romans opposed Antigonus for having joined their enemies, the Parthians; accordingly, the Senate eventually named Herod king of Judea, Galilee, Perea, and Idumea (Holzapfel 1996–97, 36), a post held until 4 BC. As *rex socius* ("confederate king") Herod was supposed to possess ultimate powers in Palestine, but answered directly to Caesar and the Roman senate (Russell 1967, 90–91).

18. Although Herod at first enjoyed the good will of Mark Antony (originally on the side of Octavian), Antony's consort Cleopatra made precarious Herod's position in Palestine. The Egyptian Cleopatra hoped to see Judaea and Coele-Syria reunited to the Ptolemaic kingdom and used her liaison with Antony to attempt

this objective. Octavian (Augustus) became master of the Roman world at the battle of Actium (September 2, 31 BC), defeating Antony and Cleopatra. Though Herod's reign dates from ca. 37 BC (see date in Russell 1967, 90), the middle-aged regent faced so many challenges in Palestine that he scarcely could come into his kingdom. Holdovers of the Parthian-supported Antigonus opposed Herod at every turn, and remnants of the Hasmoneans resented Herod's Idumean ancestry. Although Herod had married into the Hasmonean family by wedding Mariamme, granddaughter of the former high priest Hyrcanus, his suspicious nature led him to kill off especially those family members who descended from the Hasmoneans, including Mariamme herself in 29 BC (Holzapfel 1996–97, 54–55).

19. Herod engaged in impressive building programs throughout Palestine, deliberately imitating the great building projects of Augustus. Thus Herod completed major building at Sebaste, Caesarea Maritima, Herodium, Machaerus, Masada, Jericho, the Temple complex at Jerusalem (cf. Richardson 1996, 174–215; Teasdale 1996–97) and still other places (see map in Chancey and Porter 2001, 166). However, nothing Herod did—not even vast expenditures lavished upon the Temple—could endear him to his Jewish subjects. The Jews never forgot Herod's Idumean (Edomite) ancestry, nor did rebuilding the Temple in Jerusalem prevent Herod from erecting temples to pagan deities elsewhere (Richardson 1996, 186).

20. Herod possessed many sons and wives, all of whom contended for supremacy in his court. The two sons by Mariamme, Alexander and Aristobulus, were raised at Rome as the designated heirs. Their Hasmonean descent (through Mariamme) would have made them acceptable to the Jewish people; however, Herod's plotting sister Salome and jealous siblings—especially Herod's eldest son Antipater (the issue of Herod's first wife Doris)—set Herod's mind against the two heirs apparent. Both were found guilty of plotting against Herod in 7 BC and executed. Antipater also fell victim to Herod's suspicions and so executed a few days before Herod's own death in 4 BC. In his will, which Augustus ratified, Herod bequeathed his kingdom to three other sons: Archelaus was to receive Judaea, Idumaea and Samaria; Antipas was to receive Galilee and Peraea; and Philip was to receive the north-eastern territories of Batanaea, Trachonitis, Aurantis, and certain portions of the domain of Zeno near Panias (*BJ* 2.94–98).

ARCHELAUS (4 BC–AD 6)

21. Herod Archaelaus, also known as "Herod the ethnarch" on coins, is mentioned only once in the NT: significantly, Joseph (father of Jesus) relocated to Galilee after hearing that Archelaus "was reigning over Judea in place of his father Herod" (Mt 2:22). Although Archelaus was supposed to have been Herod's successor in Judea (see Herod's will, immediately above), he did not actually possess the title king—although Augustus promised to make him king "should he prove his deserts" (*BJ* 2.93 LCL). However, Archelaus gained the worst reputation of all the sons of Herod: he was the son of Herod's wife Malthace, a despised Samaritan; married Glaphyra, widow of another half-brother Alexander; used force of arms to put down rebellions that were aimed originally at his father; and squabbled incessantly with his brother Antipas for the throne. A delegation of Jews warned Augustus that there would be revolt at home unless Archaelaus were deposed. Archaelaus was accordingly put down, banished to Gaul, and his territory (Judea) added to Syria. Henceforth prefects (or procurators) appointed by the emperor would administer Judea directly (see Roman Prefects/Procurators in Palestine, Intro 26 below). Coponius was first to hold this office (*BJ* 2.117–118; cf. Mason 2003, 166).

HEROD ANTIPAS (4 BC–AD 39)

22. Herod Antipas, also known as "Herod the tetrarch" (Lk 3:19), was Herod the Great's younger son by Malthace and inherited the Galilean and Peraean portions of his father's kingdom. The gospel writers remember him for executing John the Baptist (Mk 6:14–28) and challenging Jesus when the latter was sent to him by Pilate (Lk 23:7–12; cf. 13:1–2, 31). He too was a builder whose greatest achievement was Tiberias on the sea of Galilee (AD 22), named in honor of the emperor Tiberius (AD 14–37). Herod Antipas married the daughter of the Nabataean king Aretus IV, but divorced her to marry Herodias, the wife of his half-brother Philip (cf. Intro 23 below). John the Baptist denounced this marriage as unlawful and was executed (Mk 6:17–18); Josephus' telling of the story (cf. *Antiq* 18.118) raises the possibility that John's many followers could have raised a revolt. King Aretas, avenging the insult offered to his daughter, waged war against Herod Antipas in AD 36, defeating him. Josephus reports that many regarded this defeat as "divine

vengeance" for Herod Antipas' killing of John in the first place (*Antiq* 18.116 LCL). In AD 39 Herod Antipas was denounced as a plotter to the emperor Caligula by his nephew Agrippa I (see Intro 24, below); Herod Antipas, deposed from his tetrarchy, was banished to Gaul, and the lands of his tetrarchy were given to Agrippa I.

PHILIP (4 BC–AD 34)

23. Philip, known also as Herod Philip, was a son of Herod the Great by his fifth wife Cleopatra and brought up at Rome. Philip was to receive in the will of Herod the tetrarchy of Gaulanitis, Trachonitis, Auranitis, Batanaea, and Ituraea (cf. Lk 3:1). Philip's long and relatively stable reign indicated to Josephus that Philip ruled more justly and moderately than his brothers (*Antiq* 18.106). Philip rebuilt Panias (modern Banias) as Caesarea Philippi and refurbished Bethsaida Julia; the names of the latter two cities reflect Philip's pro-Roman sympathies. Philip was the first Herod to adorn coins with the heads of Roman emperors. At his death in 34, because he had no children, the territory was incorporated into the province of Syria until AD 37 when the emperor Caligula also granted this territory to Agrippa I (the Herod of Acts 12:1, 19–23).

AGRIPPA I (AD 37–44)

24. Agrippa I (10 BC–AD 44), also known as "Herod the king" (Acts 12:1), was son of that Aristobulus whom Herod the Great had intended would succeed him as a Hasmonean prince until killing him in 7 BC (see Intro 20, above). Like his father, the young Agrippa was raised by the imperial family in Rome where he—like so many others in this position—led a dissolute life and fell into debt. Agrippa received shelter at Tiberias in AD 23 from his uncle Herod Antipas (cf. Intro 22 above), thanks largely to his sister Herodias who had married Antipas. He quarreled with Antipas, however, and so returned to Rome in AD 36 where he offended the emperor Tiberius who threw him into prison. At Tiberius' death (AD 37), however, the new emperor Caligula released Agrippa, bestowed on him the title king, and put him in charge of a kingdom that consisted first of the tetrachies of Philip and Lysanias (cf. Lk 3:1). On Antipas' banishment in AD 39, Agrippa received also Galilee and Peraea, then Judea and Samaria when Claudius became emperor (AD 41). Thus, this former prisoner and debauchee came to rule over almost as vast a kingdom as Herod the Great once ruled. Agrippa courted the goodwill

of his Jewish subjects, who regarded him as a descendant of the Hasmoneans (through his grandmother Mariamme). His horrific death by worms at the age of fifty-four in AD 44 is recorded by Luke (Acts 12:19–23) and Josephus (*Ant.* 19.343–352; cf. Maier 1991, 241–43). According to Josephus *BJ* 2.220, Agrippa left one son, also called Agrippa (cf. Intro 25, below), and two daughters—Berenice (mentioned in Acts 25:13, 23; 26:30) and Drusilla (the eventual wife of the prefect Felix, Acts 24:24).

AGRIPPA II (AD 48–100)

25. Born in AD 27/28, Agrippa II could not take over his father's kingdom when the latter died in 44 because, at seventeen, he was deemed too young; in 48, however, Claudius bestowed on him the title king and various small holdings in the north and east which Nero drastically increased in 56. To compliment the latter emperor Agrippa II changed the name of his capital from Caesarea Philippi to Neronias. From AD 48–66 he appointed the Jewish high priests, doing his best to prevent the outbreak of war against Rome (which began in AD 66). Throughout that war Agrippa remained steadfastly loyal to the Romans (cf. *BJ* 2.345–404; 3.68). In his famous encounter with St. Paul (Acts 25:13–26:32), Agrippa appeared with his sister Berenice, a beautiful Herodian princess with whom Agrippa probably had "an incestuous relationship" (so Maier 1991, 315; cf. Mason 2003, 164). At the climactic point of the apostle's defense Agrippa charged, jokingly, that Paul was persuading him to "be a Christian" (Acts 26:28)—a charge that, apparently, held no weight. As in the case of Jesus (Lk 23:15, 22), the Roman magistrates found in Paul "nothing deserving [of] death" (Acts 25:25; cf. Mason 2003, 176). Josephus claims that Agrippa wrote 62 letters vouching for the truth of Josephus' telling of the Jewish war in the *BJ* (*Vita* 364; cf. Rajak 2005, 89). The dynasty of the Herods ended in about AD 100 when this Agrippa died childless.

Roman Prefects/Procurators in Palestine

26. Since the mismanagement of Archelaus (cf. Intro 21, above), imperial Roman authorities governed Judea through a prefect appointed directly by the emperor. It is sometimes difficult to determine which nomenclature should be used, whether "prefect" or "procurator." Apparently, Roman governors in Judea after Archelaus (4 BC–AD 6) and before Claudius (AD 41–54) were "prefects," not "procurators" (so Maier 1991, 146; cf. note 1 on pg. 346). From Claudius on bearers of this office were known as "procurators." In the NT the same office is described as "governor" (ἡγεμών; cf. Bruce 1979, 1036). Matthew's gospel regularly describes Pontius Pilate as "the governor" (27:2, 11, 14, 15, 21, 27; 28:14; cf. Lk 20:20)—i.e., prefect. The Pontius Pilate inscription (see annotation to the text of Josephus *BJ* 2.169–177, below) provides stunning proof that Pilate at least was known in Judea by speakers of Latin as a "prefect," not a "procurator."

27. The word procurator (Greek ἐπίτροπος, though ἡγεμών occurs in the NT) indicated the financial officer of a province, but could indicate governance of a Roman province of a lesser status, such as Judaea was. Three such "governors" are mentioned in the NT: Pontius Pilate (Mt 27:2; Lk 3:1; Acts 4:27; 1 Tim 6:13), Marcus Antonius Felix (Acts 23:24, 26; 24:3, 22, 24–25, 27; 25:14), and Porcius Festus (Acts 24:27; 25:1, 4, 9, 12–14, 22–24; 26:24–25, 32). Other sources provide the names and years in office for the following prefects/procurators: Coponius (AD 6–9), M. Ambibulus (9–12), Annius Rufus (12–15), Valerius Gratus (15–26), Pontius Pilate (26–36), Marcellus (36–37), Marullus (37?), C. Cuspius Fadus (44–46), Tiberius Julius Alexander (46–48), Ventidius Cumanus (48–52), Antonius Felix (52–58), Porcius Festus (58–62), Albinus (62–64), and Gessius Florus (64–66). Prefects/procurators were generally drawn from the equestrian order (Felix, a freedman, was an exception). Although administrators in this office had auxiliary troops at their disposal (and so were responsible for general military and financial affairs), they answered to the superior command of any propraetor (imperial legate) in the area. Thus governors in Judea yielded to propraetors headquartered in Damascus (Syria). The seat of imperial government in Palestine was Caesarea Maritima, not Jerusalem.

INTRODUCTION

THE TEMPLE: MACCABEAN AND HERODIAN TIMES

28. The exiles who returned to Judah from Babylon (ca. 537 BC) took with them the vessels looted by Nebuchadnezzar (Ezra 1:7), and the authorization of Cyrus for the rebuilding of the Temple (Ezra 1:2–4; McKelvey 1979, 1246; Cohen 1987, 29). Ezra describes how "the children of Israel" cleared the site of rubble, built an altar, began to offer the daily burnt offerings, and made provisions to lay the foundations for the second Temple (Ezra 3:1–10). Some of the people wept, for the very foundations indicated that the second Temple would be inferior to the first (Ezra 3:12). There were other differences too: Solomon's ark was never recovered (2 Chr 5:2, 10); one seven-branched candelabrum stood in the place of the ten lamp stands (1 Ki 7:49; Zech 4:2, 11); and there were diminutions in the Holy Place, Table for Showbread, and the Incense Altar. Part of what precipitated the Maccabean Revolt was Antiochus IV Epiphanes' snatching of the temple furnishings and setting up on the altar a so-called "desolating sacrilege" on 15 December 167 BC (1 Macc 1:54). Judas and his brothers cleansed the Temple from this pollution and resumed the correct sacrifices on the new altar three years later to the day (164 BC; 1 Macc 4:54). There was the restoration of other Temple furnishings then and "very great gladness among the people... [as] the reproach of the Gentiles was removed" (1 Macc 4:58). Later the Hasmoneans fortified the Temple to such an extent that Aristobulus' party was able to withstand Pompey's siege for three months (cf. Intro 14, above).

29. Herod undertook to build the Temple early in 19 BC, more to reconcile his Jewish subjects to an Idumean upstart than glorify the God of Israel sincerely. For scruple's sake, Herod trained some 1,000 priests as masons to build the shrine within the sacred area. Although the main area was finished by 9 BC, work on the massive Temple complex continued unabated until the procurator Albinus (AD 62–65), not long before the outbreak of the first Jewish war itself in AD 66. Indeed, according to Josephus' record (*BJ* 5.5–20, 98–105, 278), the factionalized Jews took up residence within the massive Temple complex itself and from these precincts launched a series of raids and terror plots against the Romans until the destruction of Jerusalem in September AD 70.

30. Herod's Temple consisted of the vast Platform upon which the Temple complex stood, the Royal Portico (across the southern end of the Platform), the Fortress Antonia (adjoining the complex in the north-west corner), and the Temple proper (Teasdale 1996–97, 91–96). There were four courts that surrounded the Temple proper: the Court of the Gentiles, Court of Women, Court of Israel, and Priests' Court. A balustrade separated the Court of Gentiles from the three interior courts, with notices in Greek and Latin warning Gentiles to proceed no farther on pain of death (cf. Joseph. *BJ* 5.194; 6.124–126). The showpiece of the complex was, of course, the Temple itself, a massive structure rising over 200 feet above the surrounding Platform with an exterior covered in pure white marble and gold that dazzled the eyes (Joseph. *BJ* 5.222–223). "The [T]emple's front I was about 172 feet high and 172 feet broad—the same as the length of the [T]emple" (Teasdale 1996–97, 95). The Holy Place contained the Golden Lamp Stand (menorah), the Table of Showbread, and Incense Altar. The Holy Place was separated from the Holy of Holies by a curtain (Mt 27:51; Mk 15:38; Lk 23:45). The Holy of Holies was empty during NT times, though it had held the ark of the covenant during the days of Solomon (1 Ki 6:19; 2 Chr 5:7–9; 35:3; Heb 9:4). Around the Holy of Holies and the Holy Place were storage rooms, a water drain, and a stairway that provided access to the upper floor. Such leaders as Eleazar and John of Giscala headquartered the Jewish resistance to the Romans in 70 AD in the Temple area especially (*BJ* 5.5, 104, 254; 6.249, 251).

THE AUTHORSHIP OF 1 MACCABEES

31. 1 Macc has been transmitted to posterity in Greek, though Jerome testifies that the language was originally Hebrew, and indeed the text of 1 Macc is riddled with idioms, figures of speech, and an entire way of thinking that put one in mind of the OT and Judaism. However, no early form of 1 Macc in Hebrew exists; since 1 Macc 16:23–24 chronicles the achievements of John Hyrcanus I (he served as high priest 134–104 BC), it is possible that 1 Macc was written as early as 104 BC, the year of John's death. Since chapters 14–16 are, on the whole, favorably disposed toward the Romans, it is possible that they were added to 1 Macc not long after AD 70 (destruction of Jerusalem), when Jewish-Roman relations were at an all time low.

32. The author of 1 Macc modeled the book on various historical narratives of the OT, particularly those contained in the books of Kings and Chronicles. Although the book is an excellent historical source, the order of events frequently differs from that presented in 2 Macc, a parallel account of many of the same events (cf. examples in Brownlee 1962, 208–09). There are fewer instances of divine intervention in 1 Macc, although the author obviously sees God's handiwork in the Maccabeans' many victories over Gentile armies. 1 Macc also contains the letters of kings, law decrees, and other writings which may well preserve actual documents the author once had at hand. Such poetic sections as 1 Macc 1:24–28, 36–40; 2:7–13; 3:3–9, 45, and 50–53 provide contemporary perspectives on events described and are reminiscent of the OT.

FLAVIUS JOSEPHUS (AD 37/38–100)

33. Josephus was the son of a priest named Matthias and a mother descended from the Hasmoneans. He was amazingly mature for a boy his age, for he claims that he won great renown for his love of letters by age fourteen, and that the chief priests and city leaders visited him regularly for information on particular aspects of the Jewish law (*Vita* 9). By age sixteen, Josephus began to study the main Jewish sects—Pharisees, Sadducees, and Essenes—favoring the third group when he lived for three years in the wilderness as a disciple of a hermit named Bannus. But after a time of intense rigor, he left Bannus in the wilderness, returned to Jerusalem at age nineteen, and joined the Pharisees (Maier 1988, 10; Mason 2003, 39–40).

34. When he was 26, Josephus traveled to Rome in AD 64 to intercede for some Jewish priests whom Felix, the Judean procurator, had sent to Nero for trial (*BJ* 2.253; *Vita* 13–16; cf. Rahak 2005, 84–86). Josephus succeeded, due to the intervention of Poppaea, mistress of Nero, to whom Josephus was introduced by a Jewish actor named Haliturus (*Vita* 16). Josephus was thoroughly impressed by Rome, and his appreciation for all things Roman must have begun during this visit. Returning to Judea, Josephus found many of his countrymen clamoring for war against Rome; unable to restrain their ardor, he reluctantly joined the revolt, hoping that the governor of Syria, Cestius Gallus, would crush the rebellion quickly (*Vita* 23). But Cestius failed, his army routed (*BJ* 2.499–552); Josephus testifies that he was himself given command over

the two Galilees, with the addition of Gamala, "the strongest city in that region" (*BJ* 2.568 LCL).

35. Josephus had trained an army, secured provisions, and fortified his cities—using Jotapata as his stronghold—when Vespasian entered Galilee with his legions (*BJ* 3.115, 127). Jotapata fell after a siege of forty-seven days (*BJ* 3.339), but Josephus hid in a cave with forty "persons of distinction" who would rather die than surrender (*BJ* 3.342 LCL, cf. 362–3). Drawing lots, all killed each other save Josephus himself and another survivor (for the procedure, see Huntsman 1996–97, 370), who emerged from the cavern and surrendered (*BJ* 3.390–92). Hauled before Vespasian, Josephus would have been sent for judgment to Nero but for his prediction that Vespasian, and his son, Titus, would soon become emperors (*BJ* 3.401; cf. Suetonius *Vesp.* 5; Dio Cassius *Epit.* 66.1). The prophecy may be part of those good omens that were supposed to attend the ascension of a new emperor, or perhaps Josephus possessed keen insight into such mysterious utterances as the vision of the four kingdoms in Daniel 2:31–45 (Mason 2003, 49; cf. *BJ* 3.352). At any rate, Josephus was immediately freed of his chains when Vespasian was elevated to emperor on 1 July AD 69 (*BJ* 4.622–29).

36. For the rest of the war Josephus served the Romans as a go-between, appealing frequently to his countrymen to lay down their arms and thus save Jerusalem and the Temple against the military might of Rome (cf. *BJ* 5.114, 261, 361–420, 541–47; 6.94–112, etc). Due to these intercessions, as well as to the remarkable circumstances surrounding his surrender at Jotapata, many of Josephus' countrymen despised him as a traitorous coward, an opinion that still today carries some weight (cf. Bruce 1979, 660; Maier 1988, 11; Mason [2003] 24–26). Josephus claims, however, that he did everything within his power to save something "from the wreck of [his] country" (*Vita* 417 LCL), once liberating some 190 prisoners from slavery (*Vita* 419) and attempting the rescue of still other acquaintances whom he found affixed to crosses (*Vita* 420–21).

37. After the war, Vespasian's son Titus took Josephus to Rome with himself, bestowing on him many gifts: lodging in Rome at the same house Vespasian occupied before he became emperor; Roman citizenship; a pension that permitted Josephus to follow a literary career; holdings in Judea; freedom from taxation; and many

INTRODUCTION

protections from informers who envied his good fortune (Vita 422–25). Josephus became a client of the Flavian house, adopting that family's name into his own (Titus Flavius Josephus). Indeed, Josephus became one of the "foreign elites at Rome" (Bowersock 2005, 53). Although he left five sons (three of whom he names proudly), he was married to four different women—often unhappily: "at this period I divorced my wife, being displeased at her behavior" (Vita 426 LCL). Eusebius claims (Hist. Eccles. 3.9.2; cf. Jerome de Vir. Illustr. 13) that Josephus was honored with a statue at Rome, perhaps indicating "continuing imperial support" (Mason 2003, 8). The evidence seems overwhelming that Josephus wrote for a gentile audience in Rome that was genuinely interested in his work (cf. Mason 2001, xix–xxi; 2003, 94–98).

38. Josephus' major works are *Bellum Judaicum* (*BJ* = Jewish War, AD 77 or 78; 7 books), *Antiquitates Judaicae* (*Antiq* = Antiquities of the Jews, AD 93–94; 20 books), *Vita Josephi* (*Vita* = Life of Josephus, an appendix to the *Antiquities*, AD 95), and *Contra Apionem* (*Contra Ap* = Against Apion, AD 75). The work most represented in this reader is the *Jewish War*, a revision (or a new edition in Greek) of a work originally composed in Aramaic (*BJ* 1.3). Nevertheless, Josephus' Greek is superb. He claims that his native tongue hindered him from "attaining precision in the pronunciation" of Greek (*Antiq* 20.263 LCL), and clearly his works owe much to the various "assistants" who helped him cast his ideas in a foreign tongue (*Contra Ap* 1.50 LCL; cf. Thackeray 1956, xv); still, it is important to remember that the eastern part of the Roman empire was largely Greek-speaking, and that the "intellectual milieu" wherein Josephus lived and worked in Flavian Rome was thoroughly Greek (Rajak 2005, 80).

39. The *BJ* is divided into seven books, the first book and one half of which is a rapid survey of Jewish history from the earlier capture of the Temple by Antiochus Epiphanes IV down to the outbreak of the war with Rome almost 250 years later (Thackeray 1956, xiii). Remaining books document the story of the revolt against Rome and its aftermath. Here Josephus had not only his own experience to draw upon, but probably also access to records kept by the Roman commanders (Stern 1987, 71; Eshel 1999, 232 n. 22). Dramatic speeches in the mouths of leading personalities, echoes of the Greek tragedians, a flare for the spectacular, and many involved

passages lend to the *BJ* a considerable vigor (for a survey of passages in both Greek and Latin which Josephus may have incorporated into the *BJ* cf. Thackeray 1956, xv–xix; Stern 1987, 78 n. 7). What stands out in the *BJ* especially is its pro-Roman tone; not only was the work produced under his Flavian patrons (e.g., *Contra Ap* 1.50), but the overall effect was to impress on all readers the utter futility of trying to rise up against imperial Rome (Ladouceur 1981, 247). On the other hand, a deeper appreciation of Josephus' work reveals that he was frequently ironic, reserving some of the most extreme examples for Titus (Mason 2005, 262–267).

40. Most historians write with some bias, and the same is true of Josephus whose partiality is easy to detect in many passages (for the difference between modern history and ancient historiography cf. Huntsman 1996–97, 392–395). Maier cites (1988, 11) the following prejudices in Josephus, quite apart from "a lofty appreciation of himself": first, the assumption that the Jews had a glorious history, as well as the purest and highest form of religion on earth; second, that God now favors the Romans on account of the wickedness of the Jewish Zealots whom Josephus regularly calls "revolutionaries" (οἱ στασιῶται). Accordingly, Vespasian and Titus are "heroized as sterling sorts who can do no wrong," and "John of Gischala, Simon bar-Giora, and other rebel leaders are vilified as miscreants who can do no right" (Maier 1988, 11; cf. Ladouceur 1981, 246). Another fault in Josephus is a tendency to exaggerate, especially the numbers: "the reader must... discount such hyperboles as, for example, the claim that so much blood was spilled in Jerusalem during its conquest that streams of gore extinguished fires there" (Maier 1988, 12; cf. *BJ* 6.406).

41. It is nonetheless true, however, that Josephus' positives far outnumber his negatives. He remains our only source for much extra-biblical information often only presumed in the pages of the NT. Josephus also illumines such wide-ranging matters as Roman military and siege tactics, details associated with the Roman emperors, and such amazing stories as, e.g., the desperate Mary who ate her only son (see the text *BJ* 6.201–13 below). Josephus knows how to create and sustain reader interest, involve dialogue, deliver graphic portrayal, and delight the reader with all "the color, drama, and excitement" of everything that happened in Palestine during extraordinary times (Maier 1988, 12). He also excels in geographical and architectural

description, and his accuracy of the land and its structures in ancient times "is being progressively affirmed today by archaeological excavations" (Maier 1988, 12). For good reason Jerome called Josephus "the Greek Livy" (Jerome *Epist.* 22.35; in Huntsman 1996–97, 393, cf. n. 8 on pg. 400).

1 MACCABEES 1:1–4:61

1 Macc has come down to modern times in Greek, although the original version was prob. written in Hebrew just after the death of John Hyrcanus I (high priest, 134–104 BC). The author is believed to have been a Palestinian Jew who modeled his history on such books of the OT as Kings and Chronicles. The author of 1 Macc features the conquests of Alexander the Great (336–323 BC), his death, the accession of Antiochus IV 'Epiphanes' (of Syria, 176–164 BC), victories of Mattathias and Judas Maccabeus over Gentile armies, and the rededication of the Temple on the twenty-fifth day of Chislev 164 BC.

ALEXANDER THE GREAT

1 Macc 1:1–9: The author of 1 Macc holds a jaundiced view of Alexander the Great and Hellenizing successors who came to rule Israel and large portions of the ancient world: "they caused many evils on the earth" (1 Macc 1:9).

Καὶ ἐγένετο μετὰ τὸ πατάξαι Ἀλέξανδρον τὸν Φιλίππου Μακεδόνα, ὃς ἐξῆλθεν ἐκ γῆς Χεττιιμ, καὶ ἐπάταξεν τὸν Δαρεῖον βασιλέα Περσῶν καὶ Μήδων καὶ ἐβασίλευσεν ἀντ' αὐτοῦ, πρότερον ἐπὶ τὴν Ἑλλάδα. 2 καὶ συνεστήσατο πολέμους πολλοὺς καὶ ἐκράτησεν ὀχυρωμάτων καὶ ἔσφαξεν βασιλεῖς τῆς γῆς· 3 καὶ διῆλθεν ἕως ἄκρων τῆς γῆς καὶ ἔλαβεν σκῦλα πλήθους ἐθνῶν. καὶ ἡσύχασεν ἡ γῆ ἐνώπιον αὐτοῦ, καὶ ὑψώθη, καὶ ἐπήρθη ἡ καρδία αὐτοῦ. 4 καὶ συνῆξεν δύναμιν ἰσχυρὰν σφόδρα καὶ ἦρξεν χωρῶν ἐθνῶν καὶ τυράννων, καὶ ἐγένοντο αὐτῷ εἰς φόρον.

5 Καὶ μετὰ ταῦτα ἔπεσεν ἐπὶ τὴν κοίτην καὶ ἔγνω ὅτι ἀποθνῄσκει. 6 καὶ ἐκάλεσεν τοὺς παῖδας αὐτοῦ τοὺς ἐνδόξους τοὺς συνεκτρόφους αὐτοῦ ἐκ νεότητος καὶ διεῖλεν αὐτοῖς τὴν βασιλείαν αὐτοῦ ἔτι αὐτοῦ ζῶντος. 7 καὶ ἐβασίλευσεν Ἀλέξανδρος ἔτη δώδεκα καὶ ἀπέθανεν.

8 Καὶ ἐπεκράτησαν οἱ παῖδες αὐτοῦ, ἕκαστος ἐν τῷ τόπῳ αὐτοῦ. 9 καὶ ἐπέθεντο πάντες διαδήματα μετὰ τὸ ἀποθανεῖν αὐτὸν καὶ οἱ υἱοὶ αὐτῶν ὀπίσω αὐτῶν ἔτη πολλὰ καὶ ἐπλήθυναν κακὰ ἐν τῇ γῇ.

Antiochus Epiphanes (176–164 BC):

1 Macc 1:10–64: Antiochus Epiphanes' policies included the erection of a pagan gymnasium in Jerusalem (1:14), the plundering of the Temple (1:21–23), taxation (1:29), the unification of subject peoples under Hellenism (1:41), and the desecration of the Temple in December in 167 BC (1:54). Many of the Jews were deceived by Antiochus' apparently enlightened policies (e.g., 1:11–13, 30, 43, 52), though some were determined to die than profane their scruples, "and they did die" (1:63).

Καὶ ἐξῆλθεν ἐξ αὐτῶν ῥίζα ἁμαρτωλὸς Ἀντίοχος Ἐπιφανὴς υἱὸς Ἀντιόχου τοῦ βασιλέως, ὃς ἦν ὅμηρα ἐν Ῥώμῃ· καὶ ἐβασίλευσεν ἐν ἔτει ἑκατοστῷ καὶ τριακοστῷ καὶ ἑβδόμῳ βασιλείας Ἑλλήνων.

11 Ἐν ταῖς ἡμέραις ἐκείναις ἐξῆλθον ἐξ Ισραηλ υἱοὶ παράνομοι καὶ ἀνέπεισαν πολλοὺς λέγοντες Πορευθῶμεν καὶ διαθώμεθα διαθήκην μετὰ τῶν ἐθνῶν τῶν κύκλῳ ἡμῶν, ὅτι ἀφ' ἧς ἐχωρίσθημεν ἀπ' αὐτῶν, εὗρεν ἡμᾶς κακὰ πολλά. 12 καὶ ἠγαθύνθη ὁ λόγος ἐν ὀφθαλμοῖς αὐτῶν, 13 καὶ προεθυμήθησάν τινες ἀπὸ τοῦ λαοῦ καὶ ἐπορεύθησαν πρὸς τὸν βασιλέα, καὶ ἔδωκεν αὐτοῖς ἐξουσίαν ποιῆσαι τὰ δικαιώματα τῶν ἐθνῶν. 14 καὶ ᾠκοδόμησαν γυμνάσιον ἐν Ιεροσολύμοις κατὰ τὰ νόμιμα τῶν ἐθνῶν 15 καὶ ἐποίησαν ἑαυτοῖς ἀκροβυστίας καὶ ἀπέστησαν ἀπὸ διαθήκης ἁγίας καὶ ἐζευγίσθησαν τοῖς ἔθνεσιν καὶ ἐπράθησαν τοῦ ποιῆσαι τὸ πονηρόν.

16 Καὶ ἡτοιμάσθη ἡ βασιλεία ἐνώπιον Ἀντιόχου, καὶ ὑπέλαβεν βασιλεῦσαι γῆς Αἰγύπτου, ὅπως βασιλεύσῃ ἐπὶ τὰς δύο βασιλείας. 17 καὶ εἰσῆλθεν εἰς Αἴγυπτον ἐν ὄχλῳ βαρεῖ, ἐν ἅρμασιν καὶ ἐλέφασιν καὶ ἐν ἱππεῦσιν καὶ ἐν στόλῳ μεγάλῳ

18 καὶ συνεστήσατο πόλεμον πρὸς Πτολεμαῖον βασιλέα Αἰγύπτου· καὶ ἐνετράπη Πτολεμαῖος ἀπὸ προσώπου αὐτοῦ καὶ ἔφυγεν, καὶ ἔπεσον τραυματίαι πολλοί. 19 καὶ κατελάβοντο τὰς πόλεις τὰς ὀχυρὰς ἐν γῇ Αἰγύπτῳ, καὶ ἔλαβεν τὰ σκῦλα γῆς Αἰγύπτου.

20 Καὶ ἐπέστρεψεν Ἀντίοχος μετὰ τὸ πατάξαι Αἴγυπτον ἐν τῷ ἑκατοστῷ καὶ τεσσαρακοστῷ καὶ τρίτῳ ἔτει καὶ ἀνέβη ἐπὶ Ισραηλ καὶ ἀνέβη εἰς Ιεροσόλυμα ἐν ὄχλῳ βαρεῖ. 21 καὶ εἰσῆλθεν εἰς τὸ ἁγίασμα ἐν ὑπερηφανίᾳ καὶ ἔλαβεν τὸ θυσιαστήριον τὸ χρυσοῦν καὶ τὴν λυχνίαν τοῦ φωτὸς καὶ πάντα τὰ σκεύη αὐτῆς 22 καὶ τὴν τράπεζαν τῆς προθέσεως καὶ τὰ σπονδεῖα καὶ τὰς φιάλας καὶ τὰς θυΐσκας τὰς χρυσᾶς καὶ τὸ καταπέτασμα καὶ τοὺς στεφάνους καὶ τὸν κόσμον τὸν χρυσοῦν τὸν κατὰ πρόσωπον τοῦ ναοῦ καὶ ἐλέπισεν πάντα· καὶ ἔλαβεν τὸ ἀργύριον καὶ τὸ χρυσίον καὶ τὰ σκεύη τὰ ἐπιθυμητὰ 23 καὶ ἔλαβεν τοὺς θησαυροὺς τοὺς ἀποκρύφους, οὓς εὗρεν· καὶ λαβὼν πάντα ἀπῆλθεν εἰς τὴν γῆν αὐτοῦ.

24 Καὶ ἐποίησεν φονοκτονίαν
  καὶ ἐλάλησεν ὑπερηφανίαν μεγάλην.
25 καὶ ἐγένετο πένθος μέγα ἐπὶ Ισραηλ ἐν παντὶ τόπῳ
  αὐτῶν.
26 καὶ ἐστέναξαν ἄρχοντες καὶ πρεσβύτεροι,
  παρθένοι καὶ νεανίσκοι ἠσθένησαν,
  καὶ τὸ κάλλος τῶν γυναικῶν ἠλλοιώθη.
27 πᾶς νυμφίος ἀνέλαβεν θρῆνον,
  καὶ καθημένη ἐν παστῷ ἐπένθει.
28 καὶ ἐσείσθη ἡ γῆ ἐπὶ τοὺς κατοικοῦντας αὐτήν,
  καὶ πᾶς ὁ οἶκος Ιακωβ ἐνεδύσατο αἰσχύνην.

29 Μετὰ δύο ἔτη ἡμερῶν ἀπέστειλεν ὁ βασιλεὺς ἄρχοντα φορολογίας εἰς τὰς πόλεις Ιουδα, καὶ ἦλθεν εἰς Ιερουσαλημ ἐν ὄχλῳ βαρεῖ. 30 καὶ ἐλάλησεν αὐτοῖς λόγους εἰρηνικοὺς ἐν δόλῳ, καὶ ἐνεπίστευσαν αὐτῷ. καὶ ἐπέπεσεν ἐπὶ τὴν πόλιν ἐξάπινα καὶ ἐπάταξεν αὐτὴν πληγὴν μεγάλην καὶ ἀπώλεσεν λαὸν πολὺν ἐξ Ισραηλ. 31 καὶ ἔλαβεν τὰ σκῦλα τῆς πόλεως καὶ ἐνέπρησεν αὐτὴν πυρὶ καὶ καθεῖλεν τοὺς οἴκους αὐτῆς καὶ τὰ

τείχη κύκλῳ. 32 καὶ ᾐχμαλώτισαν τὰς γυναῖκας καὶ τὰ τέκνα, καὶ τὰ κτήνη ἐκληρονόμησαν. 33 καὶ ᾠκοδόμησαν τὴν πόλιν Δαυιδ τείχει μεγάλῳ καὶ ὀχυρῷ, πύργοις ὀχυροῖς, καὶ ἐγένετο αὐτοῖς εἰς ἄκραν. 34 καὶ ἔθηκαν ἐκεῖ ἔθνος ἁμαρτωλόν, ἄνδρας παρανόμους, καὶ ἐνίσχυσαν ἐν αὐτῇ. 35 καὶ παρέθεντο ὅπλα καὶ τροφὴν καὶ συναγαγόντες τὰ σκῦλα Ιερουσαλημ ἀπέθεντο ἐκεῖ καὶ ἐγένοντο εἰς μεγάλην παγίδα.

    36 Καὶ ἐγένετο εἰς ἔνεδρον τῷ ἁγιάσματι
       καὶ εἰς διάβολον πονηρὸν τῷ Ισραηλ διὰ παντός.
    37 καὶ ἐξέχεαν αἷμα ἀθῷον κύκλῳ τοῦ ἁγιάσματος
       καὶ ἐμόλυναν τὸ ἁγίασμα.
    38 καὶ ἔφυγον οἱ κάτοικοι Ιερουσαλημ δι' αὐτούς,
       καὶ ἐγένετο κατοικία ἀλλοτρίων·
       καὶ ἐγένετο ἀλλοτρία τοῖς γενήμασιν αὐτῆς,
       καὶ τὰ τέκνα αὐτῆς ἐγκατέλιπον αὐτήν.
    39 τὸ ἁγίασμα αὐτῆς ἠρημώθη ὡς ἔρημος,
       αἱ ἑορταὶ αὐτῆς ἐστράφησαν εἰς πένθος,
       τὰ σάββατα αὐτῆς εἰς ὀνειδισμόν,
       ἡ τιμὴ αὐτῆς εἰς ἐξουδένωσιν.
    40 κατὰ τὴν δόξαν αὐτῆς ἐπληθύνθη ἡ ἀτιμία αὐτῆς,
       καὶ τὸ ὕψος αὐτῆς ἐστράφη εἰς πένθος.

    41 Καὶ ἔγραψεν ὁ βασιλεὺς πάσῃ τῇ βασιλείᾳ αὐτοῦ εἶναι πάντας εἰς λαὸν ἕνα 42 καὶ ἐγκαταλιπεῖν ἕκαστον τὰ νόμιμα αὐτοῦ. καὶ ἐπεδέξαντο πάντα τὰ ἔθνη κατὰ τὸν λόγον τοῦ βασιλέως. 43 καὶ πολλοὶ ἀπὸ Ισραηλ εὐδόκησαν τῇ λατρείᾳ αὐτοῦ καὶ ἔθυσαν τοῖς εἰδώλοις καὶ ἐβεβήλωσαν τὸ σάββατον. 44 καὶ ἀπέστειλεν ὁ βασιλεὺς βιβλία ἐν χειρὶ ἀγγέλων εἰς Ιερουσαλημ καὶ τὰς πόλεις Ιουδα πορευθῆναι ὀπίσω νομίμων ἀλλοτρίων τῆς γῆς 45 καὶ κωλῦσαι ὁλοκαυτώματα καὶ θυσίαν καὶ σπονδὴν ἐκ τοῦ ἁγιάσματος καὶ βεβηλῶσαι σάββατα καὶ ἑορτὰς 46 καὶ μιᾶναι ἁγίασμα καὶ ἁγίους, 47 οἰκοδομῆσαι βωμοὺς καὶ τεμένη καὶ εἰδώλια καὶ θύειν ὕεια καὶ κτήνη κοινὰ 48 καὶ ἀφιέναι τοὺς υἱοὺς αὐτῶν ἀπεριτμήτους βδελύξαι τὰς ψυχὰς αὐτῶν ἐν παντὶ ἀκαθάρτῳ καὶ βεβηλώσει 49 ὥστε ἐπιλαθέσθαι τοῦ νόμου καὶ ἀλλάξαι πάντα τὰ δικαιώματα·

50 καὶ ὃς ἂν μὴ ποιήσῃ κατὰ τὸν λόγον τοῦ βασιλέως, ἀποθανεῖται.

51 Κατὰ πάντας τοὺς λόγους τούτους ἔγραψεν πάσῃ τῇ βασιλείᾳ αὐτοῦ καὶ ἐποίησεν ἐπισκόπους ἐπὶ πάντα τὸν λαὸν καὶ ἐνετείλατο ταῖς πόλεσιν Ιουδα θυσιάζειν κατὰ πόλιν καὶ πόλιν. 52 καὶ συνηθροίσθησαν ἀπὸ τοῦ λαοῦ πολλοὶ πρὸς αὐτούς, πᾶς ὁ ἐγκαταλείπων τὸν νόμον, καὶ ἐποίησαν κακὰ ἐν τῇ γῇ 53 καὶ ἔθεντο τὸν Ισραηλ ἐν κρύφοις ἐν παντὶ φυγαδευτηρίῳ αὐτῶν.

54 Καὶ τῇ πεντεκαιδεκάτῃ ἡμέρᾳ Χασελευ τῷ πέμπτῳ καὶ τεσσαρακοστῷ καὶ ἑκατοστῷ ἔτει ᾠκοδόμησεν βδέλυγμα ἐρημώσεως ἐπὶ τὸ θυσιαστήριον. καὶ ἐν πόλεσιν Ιουδα κύκλῳ ᾠκοδόμησαν βωμούς· 55 καὶ ἐπὶ τῶν θυρῶν τῶν οἰκιῶν καὶ ἐν ταῖς πλατείαις ἐθυμίων. 56 καὶ τὰ βιβλία τοῦ νόμου, ἃ εὗρον, ἐνεπύρισαν ἐν πυρὶ κατασχίσαντες. 57 καὶ ὅπου εὑρίσκετο παρά τινι βιβλίον διαθήκης, καὶ εἴ τις συνευδόκει τῷ νόμῳ, τὸ σύγκριμα τοῦ βασιλέως ἐθανάτου αὐτόν. 58 ἐν ἰσχύι αὐτῶν ἐποίουν τῷ Ισραηλ τοῖς εὑρισκομένοις ἐν παντὶ μηνὶ καὶ μηνὶ ἐν ταῖς πόλεσιν. 59 καὶ τῇ πέμπτῃ καὶ εἰκάδι τοῦ μηνὸς θυσιάζοντες ἐπὶ τὸν βωμόν, ὃς ἦν ἐπὶ τοῦ θυσιαστηρίου. 60 καὶ τὰς γυναῖκας τὰς περιτετμηκυίας τὰ τέκνα αὐτῶν ἐθανάτωσαν κατὰ τὸ πρόσταγμα 61 καὶ ἐκρέμασαν τὰ βρέφη ἐκ τῶν τραχήλων αὐτῶν, καὶ τοὺς οἴκους αὐτῶν καὶ τοὺς περιτετμηκότας αὐτούς.

62 Καὶ πολλοὶ ἐν Ισραηλ ἐκραταιώθησαν καὶ ὠχυρώθησαν ἐν αὑτοῖς τοῦ μὴ φαγεῖν κοινὰ 63 καὶ ἐπεδέξαντο ἀποθανεῖν, ἵνα μὴ μιανθῶσιν τοῖς βρώμασιν καὶ μὴ βεβηλώσωσιν διαθήκην ἁγίαν, καὶ ἀπέθανον. 64 καὶ ἐγένετο ὀργὴ μεγάλη ἐπὶ Ισραηλ σφόδρα.

THE REVOLT OF MATTATHIAS

1 Macc 2:1–48: Mattathias, the father of five sons, witnessed the blasphemies being committed in Judah and Jerusalem and seized the moment to revolt when an officer of Antiochus Epiphanes came to force the populace of Modein to offer sacrifice upon a pagan altar. Mattathias publicly defied the order, killed a Jew who was about to comply with Antiochus' directive, then killed Antiochus' officer. Mattathias came to live in the Judean wilderness with his sons and many supporters, there to keep the religious law without compromise and organize resistance to the policies of the Gentiles.

Ἐν ταῖς ἡμέραις ἐκείναις ἀνέστη Ματταθιας υἱὸς Ιωαννου τοῦ Συμεων ἱερεὺς τῶν υἱῶν Ιωαριβ ἀπὸ Ιερουσαλημ καὶ ἐκάθισεν ἐν Μωδεϊν. 2 καὶ αὐτῷ υἱοὶ πέντε, Ιωαννης ὁ ἐπικαλούμενος Γαδδι, 3 Σιμων ὁ καλούμενος Θασσι, 4 Ιουδας ὁ καλούμενος Μακκαβαῖος, 5 Ελεαζαρ ὁ καλούμενος Αυαραν, Ιωναθης ὁ καλούμενος Απφους. 6 καὶ εἶδεν τὰς βλασφημίας τὰς γινομένας ἐν Ιουδα καὶ ἐν Ιερουσαλημ 7 καὶ εἶπεν

Οἴμμοι, ἵνα τί τοῦτο ἐγεννήθην ἰδεῖν
   τὸ σύντριμμα τοῦ λαοῦ μου
   καὶ τὸ σύντριμμα τῆς ἁγίας πόλεως
   καὶ καθίσαι ἐκεῖ ἐν τῷ δοθῆναι αὐτὴν ἐν χειρὶ ἐχθρῶν,
   τὸ ἁγίασμα ἐν χειρὶ ἀλλοτρίων;
8 ἐγένετο ὁ ναὸς αὐτῆς ὡς ἀνὴρ ἄδοξος,
9 τὰ σκεύη τῆς δόξης αὐτῆς αἰχμάλωτα ἀπήχθη,
   ἀπεκτάνθη τὰ νήπια αὐτῆς ἐν ταῖς πλατείαις αὐτῆς,
   οἱ νεανίσκοι αὐτῆς ἐν ῥομφαίᾳ ἐχθροῦ.
10 ποῖον ἔθνος οὐκ ἐκληρονόμησεν βασίλεια
   καὶ οὐκ ἐκράτησεν τῶν σκύλων αὐτῆς;
11 πᾶς ὁ κόσμος αὐτῆς ἀφῃρέθη,
   ἀντὶ ἐλευθέρας ἐγένετο εἰς δούλην.

12 καὶ ἰδοὺ τὰ ἅγια ἡμῶν καὶ ἡ καλλονὴ ἡμῶν
καὶ ἡ δόξα ἡμῶν ἠρημώθη,
καὶ ἐβεβήλωσαν αὐτὰ τὰ ἔθνη.
13 ἵνα τί ἡμῖν ἔτι ζωή;

14 Καὶ διέρρηξεν Ματταθιας καὶ οἱ υἱοὶ αὐτοῦ τὰ ἱμάτια αὐτῶν καὶ περιεβάλοντο σάκκους καὶ ἐπένθησαν σφόδρα.

15 Καὶ ἦλθον οἱ παρὰ τοῦ βασιλέως οἱ καταναγκάζοντες τὴν ἀποστασίαν εἰς Μωδεϊν τὴν πόλιν, ἵνα θυσιάσωσιν. 16 καὶ πολλοὶ ἀπὸ Ισραηλ πρὸς αὐτοὺς προσῆλθον· καὶ Ματταθιας καὶ οἱ υἱοὶ αὐτοῦ συνήχθησαν. 17 καὶ ἀπεκρίθησαν οἱ παρὰ τοῦ βασιλέως καὶ εἶπον τῷ Ματταθια λέγοντες Ἄρχων καὶ ἔνδοξος καὶ μέγας εἶ ἐν τῇ πόλει ταύτῃ καὶ ἐστηρισμένος υἱοῖς καὶ ἀδελφοῖς· 18 νῦν πρόσελθε πρῶτος καὶ ποίησον τὸ πρόσταγμα τοῦ βασιλέως, ὡς ἐποίησαν πάντα τὰ ἔθνη καὶ οἱ ἄνδρες Ιουδα καὶ οἱ καταλειφθέντες ἐν Ιερουσαλημ, καὶ ἔσῃ σὺ καὶ οἱ υἱοί σου τῶν φίλων τοῦ βασιλέως, καὶ σὺ καὶ οἱ υἱοί σου δοξασθήσεσθε ἀργυρίῳ καὶ χρυσίῳ καὶ ἀποστολαῖς πολλαῖς.

19 Καὶ ἀπεκρίθη Ματταθιας καὶ εἶπεν φωνῇ μεγάλῃ Εἰ πάντα τὰ ἔθνη τὰ ἐν οἴκῳ τῆς βασιλείας τοῦ βασιλέως ἀκούουσιν αὐτοῦ ἀποστῆναι ἕκαστος ἀπὸ λατρείας πατέρων αὐτοῦ καὶ ᾑρετίσαντο ἐν ταῖς ἐντολαῖς αὐτοῦ, 20 κἀγὼ καὶ οἱ υἱοί μου καὶ οἱ ἀδελφοί μου πορευσόμεθα ἐν διαθήκῃ πατέρων ἡμῶν· 21 ἵλεως ἡμῖν καταλιπεῖν νόμον καὶ δικαιώματα· 22 τῶν λόγων τοῦ βασιλέως οὐκ ἀκουσόμεθα παρελθεῖν τὴν λατρείαν ἡμῶν δεξιὰν ἢ ἀριστεράν.

23 Καὶ ὡς ἐπαύσατο λαλῶν τοὺς λόγους τούτους, προσῆλθεν ἀνὴρ Ιουδαῖος ἐν ὀφθαλμοῖς πάντων θυσιάσαι ἐπὶ τοῦ βωμοῦ ἐν Μωδεϊν κατὰ τὸ πρόσταγμα τοῦ βασιλέως. 24 καὶ εἶδεν Ματταθιας καὶ ἐζήλωσεν, καὶ ἐτρόμησαν οἱ νεφροὶ αὐτοῦ, καὶ ἀνήνεγκεν θυμὸν κατὰ τὸ κρίμα καὶ δραμὼν ἔσφαξεν αὐτὸν ἐπὶ τὸν βωμόν· 25 καὶ τὸν ἄνδρα τοῦ βασιλέως τὸν ἀναγκάζοντα θύειν ἀπέκτεινεν ἐν τῷ καιρῷ ἐκείνῳ καὶ τὸν βωμὸν καθεῖλεν. 26 καὶ ἐζήλωσεν τῷ νόμῳ, καθὼς ἐποίησεν Φινεες τῷ Ζαμβρι υἱῷ Σαλωμ. 27 καὶ ἀνέκραξεν Ματταθιας ἐν

τῇ πόλει φωνῇ μεγάλῃ λέγων Πᾶς ὁ ζηλῶν τῷ νόμῳ καὶ ἱστῶν διαθήκην ἐξελθέτω ὀπίσω μου. 28 καὶ ἔφυγεν αὐτὸς καὶ οἱ υἱοὶ αὐτοῦ εἰς τὰ ὄρη καὶ ἐγκατέλιπον ὅσα εἶχον ἐν τῇ πόλει.

29 Τότε κατέβησαν πολλοὶ ζητοῦντες δικαιοσύνην καὶ κρίμα εἰς τὴν ἔρημον καθίσαι ἐκεῖ, 30 αὐτοὶ καὶ οἱ υἱοὶ αὐτῶν καὶ αἱ γυναῖκες αὐτῶν καὶ τὰ κτήνη αὐτῶν, ὅτι ἐσκληρύνθη ἐπ' αὐτοὺς τὰ κακά. 31 καὶ ἀνηγγέλη τοῖς ἀνδράσιν τοῦ βασιλέως καὶ ταῖς δυνάμεσιν, αἳ ἦσαν ἐν Ιερουσαλημ πόλει Δαυιδ ὅτι κατέβησαν ἄνδρες, οἵτινες διεσκέδασαν τὴν ἐντολὴν τοῦ βασιλέως, εἰς τοὺς κρύφους ἐν τῇ ἐρήμῳ. 32 καὶ ἔδραμον ὀπίσω αὐτῶν πολλοὶ καὶ κατελάβοντο αὐτοὺς καὶ παρενέβαλον ἐπ' αὐτοὺς καὶ συνεστήσαντο πρὸς αὐτοὺς πόλεμον ἐν τῇ ἡμέρᾳ τῶν σαββάτων 33 καὶ εἶπον πρὸς αὐτούς Ἕως τοῦ νῦν· ἐξελθόντες ποιήσατε κατὰ τὸν λόγον τοῦ βασιλέως, καὶ ζήσεσθε. 34 καὶ εἶπον Οὐκ ἐξελευσόμεθα οὐδὲ ποιήσομεν τὸν λόγον τοῦ βασιλέως βεβηλῶσαι τὴν ἡμέραν τῶν σαββάτων. 35 καὶ ἐτάχυναν ἐπ' αὐτοὺς πόλεμον. 36 καὶ οὐκ ἀπεκρίθησαν αὐτοῖς οὐδὲ λίθον ἐνετίναξαν αὐτοῖς οὐδὲ ἐνέφραξαν τοὺς κρύφους 37 λέγοντες Ἀποθάνωμεν πάντες ἐν τῇ ἁπλότητι ἡμῶν· μαρτυρεῖ ἐφ' ἡμᾶς ὁ οὐρανὸς καὶ ἡ γῆ ὅτι ἀκρίτως ἀπόλλυτε ἡμᾶς. 38 καὶ ἀνέστησαν ἐπ' αὐτοὺς ἐν πολέμῳ τοῖς σάββασιν, καὶ ἀπέθανον αὐτοὶ καὶ αἱ γυναῖκες αὐτῶν καὶ τὰ τέκνα αὐτῶν καὶ τὰ κτήνη αὐτῶν ἕως χιλίων ψυχῶν ἀνθρώπων.

39 Καὶ ἔγνω Ματταθιας καὶ οἱ φίλοι αὐτοῦ καὶ ἐπένθησαν ἐπ' αὐτοὺς σφόδρα. 40 καὶ εἶπεν ἀνὴρ τῷ πλησίον αὐτοῦ Ἐὰν πάντες ποιήσωμεν ὡς οἱ ἀδελφοὶ ἡμῶν ἐποίησαν καὶ μὴ πολεμήσωμεν πρὸς τὰ ἔθνη ὑπὲρ τῆς ψυχῆς ἡμῶν καὶ τῶν δικαιωμάτων ἡμῶν, νῦν τάχιον ὀλεθρεύσουσιν ἡμᾶς ἀπὸ τῆς γῆς. 41 καὶ ἐβουλεύσαντο τῇ ἡμέρᾳ ἐκείνῃ λέγοντες Πᾶς ἄνθρωπος, ὃς ἐὰν ἔλθῃ ἐφ' ἡμᾶς εἰς πόλεμον τῇ ἡμέρᾳ τῶν σαββάτων, πολεμήσωμεν κατέναντι αὐτοῦ καὶ οὐ μὴ ἀποθάνωμεν πάντες καθὼς ἀπέθανον οἱ ἀδελφοὶ ἡμῶν ἐν τοῖς κρύφοις.

42 Τότε συνήχθησαν πρὸς αὐτοὺς συναγωγὴ Ασιδαίων, ἰσχυροὶ δυνάμει ἀπὸ Ισραηλ, πᾶς ὁ ἑκουσιαζόμενος τῷ νόμῳ·

43 καὶ πάντες οἱ φυγαδεύοντες ἀπὸ τῶν κακῶν προσετέθησαν αὐτοῖς καὶ ἐγένοντο αὐτοῖς εἰς στήριγμα. 44 καὶ συνεστήσαντο δύναμιν καὶ ἐπάταξαν ἁμαρτωλοὺς ἐν ὀργῇ αὐτῶν καὶ ἄνδρας ἀνόμους ἐν θυμῷ αὐτῶν· καὶ οἱ λοιποὶ ἔφυγον εἰς τὰ ἔθνη σωθῆναι. 45 καὶ ἐκύκλωσεν Ματταθιας καὶ οἱ φίλοι αὐτοῦ καὶ καθεῖλον τοὺς βωμοὺς 46 καὶ περιέτεμον τὰ παιδάρια τὰ ἀπερίτμητα, ὅσα εὗρον ἐν ὁρίοις Ισραηλ, ἐν ἰσχύι 47 καὶ ἐδίωξαν τοὺς υἱοὺς τῆς ὑπερηφανίας, καὶ κατευοδώθη τὸ ἔργον ἐν χειρὶ αὐτῶν· καὶ ἀντελάβοντο τοῦ νόμου ἐκ χειρὸς τῶν ἐθνῶν καὶ τῶν βασιλέων καὶ οὐκ ἔδωκαν κέρας τῷ ἁμαρτωλῷ.

DEATH OF MATTATHIAS

1 Macc 2:49–70: As death drew near Mattathias summoned to his side his five sons, urged them to remain faithful when tested, and charged Judas Maccabeus to assume command of the army. Mattathias' farewell bears a striking resemblance to similar scenes of farewell and blessing in the OT, e.g., Gen 48:8–20 (Jacob); Gen 49:1–28 (Jacob); Deut 33 (Moses); Josh 23 (Joshua).

Καὶ ἤγγισαν αἱ ἡμέραι Ματταθιου ἀποθανεῖν, καὶ εἶπεν τοῖς υἱοῖς αὐτοῦ Νῦν ἐστηρίσθη ὑπερηφανία καὶ ἐλεγμὸς καὶ καιρὸς καταστροφῆς καὶ ὀργὴ θυμοῦ. 50 νῦν, τέκνα, ζηλώσατε τῷ νόμῳ καὶ δότε τὰς ψυχὰς ὑμῶν ὑπὲρ διαθήκης πατέρων ἡμῶν 51 καὶ μνήσθητε τὰ ἔργα τῶν πατέρων, ἃ ἐποίησαν ἐν ταῖς γενεαῖς αὐτῶν, καὶ δέξασθε δόξαν μεγάλην καὶ ὄνομα αἰώνιον. 52 Αβρααμ οὐχὶ ἐν πειρασμῷ εὑρέθη πιστός, καὶ ἐλογίσθη αὐτῷ εἰς δικαιοσύνην; 53 Ιωσηφ ἐν καιρῷ στενοχωρίας αὐτοῦ ἐφύλαξεν ἐντολὴν καὶ ἐγένετο κύριος Αἰγύπτου. 54 Φινεες ὁ πατὴρ ἡμῶν ἐν τῷ ζηλῶσαι ζῆλον ἔλαβεν διαθήκην ἱερωσύνης αἰωνίας. 55 Ἰησοῦς ἐν τῷ πληρῶσαι λόγον ἐγένετο κριτὴς ἐν Ισραηλ. 56 Χαλεβ ἐν τῷ μαρτύρασθαι ἐν τῇ ἐκκλησίᾳ ἔλαβεν γῆς κληρονομίαν. 57 Δαυιδ ἐν τῷ ἐλέει αὐτοῦ ἐκληρονόμησεν θρόνον βασιλείας εἰς αἰῶνας. 58 Ηλιας ἐν τῷ ζηλῶσαι ζῆλον νόμου ἀνελήμφθη εἰς τὸν οὐρανόν. 59 Ανανιας, Αζαριας, Μισαηλ πιστεύσαντες ἐσώθησαν ἐκ φλογός. 60 Δανιηλ ἐν τῇ ἁπλότητι αὐτοῦ ἐρρύσθη ἐκ στόματος λεόντων.

61 Καὶ οὕτως ἐννοήθητε κατὰ γενεὰν καὶ γενεάν, ὅτι πάντες οἱ ἐλπίζοντες ἐπ' αὐτὸν οὐκ ἀσθενήσουσιν. 62 καὶ ἀπὸ λόγων ἀνδρὸς ἁμαρτωλοῦ μὴ φοβηθῆτε, ὅτι ἡ δόξα αὐτοῦ εἰς κόπρια καὶ εἰς σκώληκας· 63 σήμερον ἐπαρθήσεται καὶ αὔριον οὐ μὴ εὑρεθῇ, ὅτι ἐπέστρεψεν εἰς τὸν χοῦν αὐτοῦ, καὶ ὁ διαλογισμὸς αὐτοῦ ἀπολεῖται. 64 τέκνα, ἀνδρίζεσθε καὶ ἰσχύσατε ἐν τῷ νόμῳ, ὅτι ἐν αὐτῷ δοξασθήσεσθε.

65 Καὶ ἰδοὺ Συμεων ὁ ἀδελφὸς ὑμῶν, οἶδα ὅτι ἀνὴρ βουλῆς ἐστιν, αὐτοῦ ἀκούετε πάσας τὰς ἡμέρας, αὐτὸς ἔσται ὑμῶν πατήρ. 66 καὶ Ιουδας Μακκαβαῖος ἰσχυρὸς δυνάμει ἐκ νεότητος αὐτοῦ, αὐτὸς ἔσται ὑμῖν ἄρχων στρατιᾶς καὶ πολεμήσει πόλεμον λαῶν. 67 καὶ ὑμεῖς προσάξετε πρὸς ὑμᾶς πάντας τοὺς ποιητὰς τοῦ νόμου καὶ ἐκδικήσατε ἐκδίκησιν τοῦ λαοῦ ὑμῶν· 68 ἀνταπόδοτε ἀνταπόδομα τοῖς ἔθνεσιν καὶ προσέχετε εἰς πρόσταγμα τοῦ νόμου. 69 καὶ εὐλόγησεν αὐτούς· καὶ προσετέθη πρὸς τοὺς πατέρας αὐτοῦ. 70 καὶ ἀπέθανεν ἐν τῷ ἕκτῳ καὶ τεσσαρακοστῷ καὶ ἑκατοστῷ ἔτει καὶ ἐτάφη ἐν τάφοις πατέρων αὐτοῦ ἐν Μωδεϊν, καὶ ἐκόψαντο αὐτὸν πᾶς Ισραηλ κοπετὸν μέγαν.

DEFEAT OF APOLLONIUS

1 Macc 3:1–12: A contemporary poem proclaims that Judas Maccabeus was "like a lion in his deeds, like a lion's cub roaring for prey" (3:4). An initial skirmish took place against a certain Apollonius who commanded a Gentile force at Samaria (3:10). In the ensuing rout Judas took possession of the sword of Apollonius and "used it in battle the rest of his life" (3:12).

3.1 Καὶ ἀνέστη Ιουδας ὁ καλούμενος Μακκαβαῖος υἱὸς αὐτοῦ ἀντ' αὐτοῦ. 2 καὶ ἐβοήθουν αὐτῷ πάντες οἱ ἀδελφοὶ αὐτοῦ καὶ πάντες, ὅσοι ἐκολλήθησαν τῷ πατρὶ αὐτοῦ, καὶ ἐπολέμουν τὸν πόλεμον Ισραηλ μετ' εὐφροσύνης.

3 Καὶ ἐπλάτυνεν δόξαν τῷ λαῷ αὐτοῦ
  καὶ ἐνεδύσατο θώρακα ὡς γίγας
  καὶ συνεζώσατο τὰ σκεύη τὰ πολεμικὰ αὐτοῦ
  καὶ πολέμους συνεστήσατο σκεπάζων παρεμβολὴν
  ἐν ῥομφαίᾳ.
4 καὶ ὡμοιώθη λέοντι ἐν τοῖς ἔργοις αὐτοῦ
  καὶ ὡς σκύμνος ἐρευγόμενος εἰς θήραν.
5 καὶ ἐδίωξεν ἀνόμους ἐξερευνῶν
  καὶ τοὺς ταράσσοντας τὸν λαὸν αὐτοῦ ἐφλόγισεν.
6 καὶ συνεστάλησαν ἄνομοι ἀπὸ τοῦ φόβου αὐτοῦ,
  καὶ πάντες οἱ ἐργάται τῆς ἀνομίας συνεταράχθησαν,
  καὶ εὐοδώθη σωτηρία ἐν χειρὶ αὐτοῦ.
7 καὶ ἐπίκρανεν βασιλεῖς πολλοὺς
  καὶ εὔφρανεν τὸν Ιακωβ ἐν τοῖς ἔργοις αὐτοῦ,
  καὶ ἕως τοῦ αἰῶνος τὸ μνημόσυνον αὐτοῦ εἰς
  εὐλογίαν.
8 καὶ διῆλθεν ἐν πόλεσιν Ιουδα
  καὶ ἐξωλέθρευσεν ἀσεβεῖς ἐξ αὐτῆς
  καὶ ἀπέστρεψεν ὀργὴν ἀπὸ Ισραηλ
9 καὶ ὠνομάσθη ἕως ἐσχάτου γῆς
  καὶ συνήγαγεν ἀπολλυμένους.

10 Καὶ συνήγαγεν Ἀπολλώνιος ἔθνη καὶ ἀπὸ Σαμαρείας δύναμιν μεγάλην τοῦ πολεμῆσαι πρὸς τὸν Ισραηλ. 11 καὶ ἔγνω Ιουδας καὶ ἐξῆλθεν εἰς συνάντησιν αὐτῷ καὶ ἐπάταξεν αὐτὸν καὶ ἀπέκτεινεν· καὶ ἔπεσον τραυματίαι πολλοί, καὶ οἱ ἐπίλοιποι ἔφυγον. 12 καὶ ἔλαβον τὰ σκῦλα αὐτῶν, καὶ τὴν μάχαιραν Ἀπολλωνίου ἔλαβεν Ιουδας καὶ ἦν πολεμῶν ἐν αὐτῇ πάσας τὰς ἡμέρας.

The Battle of Beth-Horon

1 Macc 3:13–26: The battle of Beth-Horon became Judas' first great victory over the Gentiles. Beth-Horon connected the coastal plain to the Judean highlands. With a small force Judas defeated Seron, commander of the Syrian army, who supposed that by making war on Judas he would create a name for himself and "win honor in the kingdom" (3:14). However, "in the sight of heaven" (3:18), Judas defeated Seron's army, so that it was Judas' name, and not Seron's, that reached the ears of Antiochus Epiphanes (3:26).

13 Καὶ ἤκουσεν Σήρων ὁ ἄρχων τῆς δυνάμεως Συρίας ὅτι ἤθροισεν Ιουδας ἄθροισμα καὶ ἐκκλησίαν πιστῶν μετ' αὐτοῦ καὶ ἐκπορευομένων εἰς πόλεμον, 14 καὶ εἶπεν Ποιήσω ἐμαυτῷ ὄνομα καὶ δοξασθήσομαι ἐν τῇ βασιλείᾳ καὶ πολεμήσω τὸν Ιουδαν καὶ τοὺς σὺν αὐτῷ τοὺς ἐξουδενοῦντας τὸν λόγον τοῦ βασιλέως. 15 καὶ προσέθετο καὶ ἀνέβη μετ' αὐτοῦ παρεμβολὴ ἀσεβῶν ἰσχυρὰ βοηθῆσαι αὐτῷ ποιῆσαι τὴν ἐκδίκησιν ἐν υἱοῖς Ισραηλ.

16 Καὶ ἤγγισεν ἕως ἀναβάσεως Βαιθωρων, καὶ ἐξῆλθεν Ιουδας εἰς συνάντησιν αὐτῷ ὀλιγοστός. 17 ὡς δὲ εἶδον τὴν παρεμβολὴν ἐρχομένην εἰς συνάντησιν αὐτῶν, εἶπον τῷ Ιουδα Τί δυνησόμεθα ὀλιγοστοὶ ὄντες πολεμῆσαι πρὸς πλῆθος τοσοῦτο ἰσχυρόν; καὶ ἡμεῖς ἐκλελύμεθα ἀσιτοῦντες σήμερον. 18 καὶ εἶπεν Ιουδας Εὔκοπόν ἐστιν συγκλεισθῆναι πολλοὺς ἐν χερσὶν ὀλίγων, καὶ οὐκ ἔστιν διαφορὰ ἐναντίον τοῦ οὐρανοῦ σῴζειν ἐν πολλοῖς ἢ ἐν ὀλίγοις· 19 ὅτι οὐκ ἐν πλήθει δυνάμεως νίκη πολέμου ἐστίν, ἀλλ' ἐκ τοῦ οὐρανοῦ ἡ ἰσχύς. 20 αὐτοὶ ἔρχονται ἐφ' ἡμᾶς ἐν πλήθει ὕβρεως καὶ ἀνομίας τοῦ ἐξᾶραι ἡμᾶς καὶ τὰς γυναῖκας ἡμῶν καὶ τὰ τέκνα ἡμῶν τοῦ σκυλεῦσαι ἡμᾶς, 21 ἡμεῖς δὲ πολεμοῦμεν περὶ τῶν ψυχῶν ἡμῶν καὶ τῶν νομίμων ἡμῶν. 22 καὶ αὐτὸς συντρίψει αὐτοὺς πρὸ προσώπου ἡμῶν, ὑμεῖς δὲ μὴ φοβεῖσθε ἀπ' αὐτῶν.

23 Ὡς δὲ ἐπαύσατο λαλῶν, ἐνήλατο εἰς αὐτοὺς ἄφνω, καὶ συνετρίβη Σήρων καὶ ἡ παρεμβολὴ αὐτοῦ ἐνώπιον αὐτοῦ.

24 καὶ ἐδίωκον αὐτὸν ἐν τῇ καταβάσει Βαιθωρων ἕως τοῦ πεδίου· καὶ ἔπεσον ἀπ' αὐτῶν εἰς ἄνδρας ὀκτακοσίους, οἱ δὲ λοιποὶ ἔφυγον εἰς γῆν Φυλιστιιμ. 25 καὶ ἤρξατο ὁ φόβος Ιουδου καὶ τῶν ἀδελφῶν αὐτοῦ καὶ ἡ πτόη ἐπέπιπτεν ἐπὶ τὰ ἔθνη τὰ κύκλῳ αὐτῶν· 26 καὶ ἤγγισεν ἕως τοῦ βασιλέως τὸ ὄνομα αὐτοῦ, καὶ ὑπὲρ τῶν παρατάξεων Ιουδου ἐξηγεῖτο τὰ ἔθνη.

JUDAS DEFEATS THE ARMY OF LYSIAS

1 Macc 3:27–4:35: Having depleted the treasury, Antiochus Epiphanes turned royal affairs over to Lysias and departed Antioch for Persia in 165 BC. Lysias was supposed to "wipe out and destroy the strength of Israel" (3:35), then settle foreigners in Judea and distribute the resulting land allotments (3:36). In the battles that ensued, however, Judas Maccabeus got the upper hand so that Lysias was forced to retreat, enlist mercenaries to replace troops that had been slaughtered by the Maccabeans, and make plans to invade Judea again with an even larger army.

27 Ὡς δὲ ἤκουσεν ὁ βασιλεὺς Ἀντίοχος τοὺς λόγους τούτους, ὠργίσθη θυμῷ καὶ ἀπέστειλεν καὶ συνήγαγεν τὰς δυνάμεις πάσας τῆς βασιλείας αὐτοῦ, παρεμβολὴν ἰσχυρὰν σφόδρα. 28 καὶ ἤνοιξεν τὸ γαζοφυλάκιον αὐτοῦ καὶ ἔδωκεν ὀψώνια ταῖς δυνάμεσιν εἰς ἐνιαυτὸν καὶ ἐνετείλατο αὐτοῖς εἶναι ἑτοίμους εἰς πᾶσαν χρείαν. 29 καὶ εἶδεν ὅτι ἐξέλιπεν τὸ ἀργύριον ἐκ τῶν θησαυρῶν καὶ οἱ φόροι τῆς χώρας ὀλίγοι χάριν τῆς διχοστασίας καὶ πληγῆς, ἧς κατεσκεύασεν ἐν τῇ γῇ τοῦ ἆραι τὰ νόμιμα, ἃ ἦσαν ἀφ' ἡμερῶν τῶν πρώτων, 30 καὶ εὐλαβήθη μὴ οὐκ ἔχῃ ὡς ἅπαξ καὶ δὶς εἰς τὰς δαπάνας καὶ τὰ δόματα, ἃ ἐδίδου ἔμπροσθεν δαψιλῇ χειρὶ καὶ ἐπερίσσευσεν ὑπὲρ τοὺς βασιλεῖς τοὺς ἔμπροσθεν, 31 καὶ ἠπορεῖτο τῇ ψυχῇ αὐτοῦ σφόδρα καὶ ἐβουλεύσατο τοῦ πορευθῆναι εἰς τὴν Περσίδα καὶ λαβεῖν τοὺς φόρους τῶν χωρῶν καὶ συναγαγεῖν ἀργύριον πολύ.

32 Καὶ κατέλιπεν Λυσίαν ἄνθρωπον ἔνδοξον καὶ ἀπὸ γένους τῆς βασιλείας ἐπὶ τῶν πραγμάτων τοῦ βασιλέως ἀπὸ

τοῦ ποταμοῦ Εὐφράτου καὶ ἕως ὁρίων Αἰγύπτου 33 καὶ τρέφειν Ἀντίοχον τὸν υἱὸν αὐτοῦ ἕως τοῦ ἐπιστρέψαι αὐτόν· 34 καὶ παρέδωκεν αὐτῷ τὰς ἡμίσεις τῶν δυνάμεων καὶ τοὺς ἐλέφαντας καὶ ἐνετείλατο αὐτῷ περὶ πάντων, ὧν ἠβούλετο, καὶ περὶ τῶν κατοικούντων τὴν Ιουδαίαν καὶ Ιερουσαλημ 35 ἀποστεῖλαι ἐπ' αὐτοὺς δύναμιν τοῦ ἐκτρῖψαι καὶ ἐξᾶραι τὴν ἰσχὺν Ισραηλ καὶ τὸ κατάλειμμα Ιερουσαλημ καὶ ἆραι τὸ μνημόσυνον αὐτῶν ἀπὸ τοῦ τόπου 36 καὶ κατοικίσαι υἱοὺς ἀλλογενεῖς ἐν πᾶσιν τοῖς ὁρίοις αὐτῶν καὶ κατακληροδοτῆσαι τὴν γῆν αὐτῶν. 37 καὶ ὁ βασιλεὺς παρέλαβεν τὰς ἡμίσεις τῶν δυνάμεων τὰς καταλειφθείσας καὶ ἀπῆρεν ἀπὸ Ἀντιοχείας ἀπὸ πόλεως βασιλείας αὐτοῦ ἔτους ἑβδόμου καὶ τεσσαρακοστοῦ καὶ ἑκατοστοῦ καὶ διεπέρασεν τὸν Εὐφράτην ποταμὸν καὶ διεπορεύετο τὰς ἐπάνω χώρας.

38 Καὶ ἐπέλεξεν Λυσίας Πτολεμαῖον τὸν Δορυμένους καὶ Νικάνορα καὶ Γοργίαν, ἄνδρας δυνατοὺς τῶν φίλων τοῦ βασιλέως, 39 καὶ ἀπέστειλεν μετ' αὐτῶν τεσσαράκοντα χιλιάδας ἀνδρῶν καὶ ἑπτακισχιλίαν ἵππον τοῦ ἐλθεῖν εἰς γῆν Ιουδα καὶ καταφθεῖραι αὐτὴν κατὰ τὸν λόγον τοῦ βασιλέως. 40 καὶ ἀπῆρεν σὺν πάσῃ τῇ δυνάμει αὐτῶν, καὶ ἦλθον καὶ παρενέβαλον πλησίον Αμμαους ἐν τῇ γῇ τῇ πεδινῇ. 41 καὶ ἤκουσαν οἱ ἔμποροι τῆς χώρας τὸ ὄνομα αὐτῶν καὶ ἔλαβον ἀργύριον καὶ χρυσίον πολὺ σφόδρα καὶ πέδας καὶ ἦλθον εἰς τὴν παρεμβολὴν τοῦ λαβεῖν τοὺς υἱοὺς Ισραηλ εἰς παῖδας. καὶ προσετέθησαν πρὸς αὐτοὺς δύναμις Συρίας καὶ γῆς ἀλλοφύλων.

42 Καὶ εἶδεν Ιουδας καὶ οἱ ἀδελφοὶ αὐτοῦ ὅτι ἐπληθύνθη τὰ κακὰ καὶ αἱ δυνάμεις παρεμβάλλουσιν ἐν τοῖς ὁρίοις αὐτῶν, καὶ ἐπέγνωσαν τοὺς λόγους τοῦ βασιλέως, οὓς ἐνετείλατο ποιῆσαι τῷ λαῷ εἰς ἀπώλειαν καὶ συντέλειαν, 43 καὶ εἶπαν ἕκαστος πρὸς τὸν πλησίον αὐτοῦ Ἀναστήσωμεν τὴν καθαίρεσιν τοῦ λαοῦ ἡμῶν καὶ πολεμήσωμεν περὶ τοῦ λαοῦ ἡμῶν καὶ τῶν ἁγίων. 44 καὶ ἠθροίσθη ἡ συναγωγὴ τοῦ εἶναι ἑτοίμους εἰς πόλεμον καὶ τοῦ προσεύξασθαι καὶ αἰτῆσαι ἔλεος καὶ οἰκτιρμούς.

45 Καὶ Ιερουσαλημ ἦν ἀοίκητος ὡς ἔρημος,
οὐκ ἦν ὁ εἰσπορευόμενος καὶ ἐκπορευόμενος ἐκ τῶν
   γενημάτων αὐτῆς,
   καὶ τὸ ἁγίασμα καταπατούμενον,
καὶ υἱοὶ ἀλλογενῶν ἐν τῇ ἄκρᾳ,
   κατάλυμα τοῖς ἔθνεσιν·
καὶ ἐξήρθη τέρψις ἐξ Ιακωβ,
   καὶ ἐξέλιπεν αὐλὸς καὶ κινύρα.

46 Καὶ συνήχθησαν καὶ ἤλθοσαν εἰς Μασσηφα κατέναντι Ιερουσαλημ, ὅτι τόπος προσευχῆς ἦν ἐν Μασσηφα τὸ πρότερον τῷ Ισραηλ. 47 καὶ ἐνήστευσαν τῇ ἡμέρᾳ ἐκείνῃ καὶ περιεβάλοντο σάκκους καὶ σποδὸν ἐπὶ τὴν κεφαλὴν αὐτῶν καὶ διέρρηξαν τὰ ἱμάτια αὐτῶν. 48 καὶ ἐξεπέτασαν τὸ βιβλίον τοῦ νόμου περὶ ὧν ἐξηρεύνων τὰ ἔθνη τὰ ὁμοιώματα τῶν εἰδώλων αὐτῶν. 49 καὶ ἤνεγκαν τὰ ἱμάτια τῆς ἱερωσύνης καὶ τὰ πρωτογενήματα καὶ τὰς δεκάτας καὶ ἤγειραν τοὺς Ναζιραίους, οἳ ἐπλήρωσαν τὰς ἡμέρας, 50 καὶ ἐβόησαν φωνῇ εἰς τὸν οὐρανὸν λέγοντες

   Τί ποιήσωμεν τούτοις καὶ ποῦ αὐτοὺς ἀπαγάγωμεν,
   51 Καὶ τὰ ἅγιά σου καταπεπάτηνται καὶ βεβήλωνται
      καὶ οἱ ἱερεῖς σου ἐν πένθει καὶ ταπεινώσει;
   52 καὶ ἰδοὺ τὰ ἔθνη συνῆκται ἐφ' ἡμᾶς τοῦ ἐξᾶραι ἡμᾶς·
      σὺ οἶδας ἃ λογίζονται ἐφ' ἡμᾶς.
   53 πῶς δυνησόμεθα ὑποστῆναι κατὰ πρόσωπον αὐτῶν,
      ἐὰν μὴ σὺ βοηθήσῃς ἡμῖν;

54 Καὶ ἐσάλπισαν ταῖς σάλπιγξιν καὶ ἐβόησαν φωνῇ μεγάλῃ. 55 καὶ μετὰ τοῦτο κατέστησεν Ιουδας ἡγουμένους τοῦ λαοῦ, χιλιάρχους καὶ ἑκατοντάρχους καὶ πεντηκοντάρχους καὶ δεκαδάρχους. 56 καὶ εἶπεν τοῖς οἰκοδομοῦσιν οἰκίας καὶ μνηστευομένοις γυναῖκας καὶ φυτεύουσιν ἀμπελῶνας καὶ δειλοῖς ἀποστρέφειν ἕκαστον εἰς τὸν οἶκον αὐτοῦ κατὰ τὸν νόμον. 57 καὶ ἀπῆρεν ἡ παρεμβολή, καὶ παρενέβαλον κατὰ νότον Αμμαους.

58 Καὶ εἶπεν Ιουδας Περιζώσασθε καὶ γίνεσθε εἰς υἱοὺς δυνατοὺς καὶ γίνεσθε ἕτοιμοι εἰς πρωὶ τοῦ πολεμῆσαι ἐν τοῖς ἔθνεσιν τούτοις τοῖς ἐπισυνηγμένοις ἐφ' ἡμᾶς ἐξᾶραι ἡμᾶς καὶ τὰ ἅγια ἡμῶν· 59 ὅτι κρεῖσσον ἡμᾶς ἀποθανεῖν ἐν τῷ πολέμῳ ἢ ἐπιδεῖν ἐπὶ τὰ κακὰ τοῦ ἔθνους ἡμῶν καὶ τῶν ἁγίων. 60 ὡς δ' ἂν ᾖ θέλημα ἐν οὐρανῷ, οὕτως ποιήσει.

4.1 Καὶ παρέλαβεν Γοργίας πεντακισχιλίους ἄνδρας καὶ χιλίαν ἵππον ἐκλεκτήν, καὶ ἀπῆρεν ἡ παρεμβολὴ νυκτὸς 2 ὥστε ἐπιβαλεῖν ἐπὶ τὴν παρεμβολὴν τῶν Ιουδαίων καὶ πατάξαι αὐτοὺς ἄφνω· καὶ υἱοὶ τῆς ἄκρας ἦσαν αὐτῷ ὁδηγοί. 3 καὶ ἤκουσεν Ιουδας καὶ ἀπῆρεν αὐτὸς καὶ οἱ δυνατοὶ πατάξαι τὴν δύναμιν τοῦ βασιλέως τὴν ἐν Αμμαους, 4 ἕως ἔτι ἐσκορπισμέναι ἦσαν αἱ δυνάμεις ἀπὸ τῆς παρεμβολῆς. 5 καὶ ἦλθεν Γοργίας εἰς τὴν παρεμβολὴν Ιουδου νυκτὸς καὶ οὐδένα εὗρεν· καὶ ἐζήτει αὐτοὺς ἐν τοῖς ὄρεσιν, ὅτι εἶπεν Φεύγουσιν οὗτοι ἀφ' ἡμῶν.

6 Καὶ ἅμα ἡμέρᾳ ὤφθη Ιουδας ἐν τῷ πεδίῳ ἐν τρισχιλίοις ἀνδράσιν· πλὴν καλύμματα καὶ μαχαίρας οὐκ εἶχον ὡς ἠβούλοντο. 7 καὶ εἶδον παρεμβολὴν ἐθνῶν ἰσχυρὰν καὶ τεθωρακισμένην καὶ ἵππον κυκλοῦσαν αὐτήν, καὶ οὗτοι διδακτοὶ πολέμου. 8 καὶ εἶπεν Ιουδας τοῖς ἀνδράσιν τοῖς μετ' αὐτοῦ Μὴ φοβεῖσθε τὸ πλῆθος αὐτῶν καὶ τὸ ὅρμημα αὐτῶν μὴ δειλωθῆτε· 9 μνήσθητε ὡς ἐσώθησαν οἱ πατέρες ἡμῶν ἐν θαλάσσῃ ἐρυθρᾷ, ὅτε ἐδίωκεν αὐτοὺς Φαραω ἐν δυνάμει· 10 καὶ νῦν βοήσωμεν εἰς οὐρανόν, εἰ θελήσει ἡμᾶς καὶ μνησθήσεται διαθήκης πατέρων καὶ συντρίψει τὴν παρεμβολὴν ταύτην κατὰ πρόσωπον ἡμῶν σήμερον, 11 καὶ γνώσονται πάντα τὰ ἔθνη ὅτι ἔστιν ὁ λυτρούμενος καὶ σῴζων τὸν Ισραηλ.

12 Καὶ ἦραν οἱ ἀλλόφυλοι τοὺς ὀφθαλμοὺς αὐτῶν καὶ εἶδον αὐτοὺς ἐρχομένους ἐξ ἐναντίας 13 καὶ ἐξῆλθον ἐκ τῆς παρεμβολῆς εἰς πόλεμον· καὶ ἐσάλπισαν οἱ παρὰ Ιουδου 14 καὶ συνῆψαν, καὶ συνετρίβησαν τὰ ἔθνη καὶ ἔφυγον εἰς τὸ πεδίον, 15 οἱ δὲ ἔσχατοι πάντες ἔπεσον ἐν ῥομφαίᾳ. καὶ ἐδίωξαν αὐτοὺς ἕως Γαζηρων καὶ ἕως τῶν πεδίων τῆς Ιδουμαίας καὶ Ἀζώτου καὶ Ιαμνείας, καὶ ἔπεσαν ἐξ αὐτῶν εἰς ἄνδρας τρισχιλίους. 16 1 καὶ ἀπέστρεψεν Ιουδας καὶ ἡ δύναμις ἀπὸ τοῦ διώκειν ὄπισθεν

αὐτῶν 17 καὶ εἶπεν πρὸς τὸν λαόν Μὴ ἐπιθυμήσητε τῶν σκύλων, ὅτι πόλεμος ἐξ ἐναντίας ἡμῶν, 18 καὶ Γοργίας καὶ ἡ δύναμις ἐν τῷ ὄρει ἐγγὺς ἡμῶν· ἀλλὰ στῆτε νῦν ἐναντίον τῶν ἐχθρῶν ἡμῶν καὶ πολεμήσατε αὐτούς, καὶ μετὰ ταῦτα λάβετε τὰ σκῦλα μετὰ παρρησίας.

19 Ἔτι πληροῦντος Ιουδου ταῦτα μέρος τι ὤφθη ἐκκύπτον ἐκ τοῦ ὄρους· 20 καὶ εἶδεν ὅτι τετρόπωνται, καὶ ἐμπυρίζουσιν τὴν παρεμβολήν· ὁ γὰρ καπνὸς ὁ θεωρούμενος ἐνεφάνιζεν τὸ γεγονός. 21 οἱ δὲ ταῦτα συνιδόντες ἐδειλώθησαν σφόδρα· συνιδόντες δὲ καὶ τὴν Ιουδου παρεμβολὴν ἐν τῷ πεδίῳ ἑτοίμην εἰς παράταξιν 22 ἔφυγον πάντες εἰς γῆν ἀλλοφύλων. 23 καὶ Ιουδας ἀνέστρεψεν ἐπὶ τὴν σκυλείαν τῆς παρεμβολῆς, καὶ ἔλαβον χρυσίον πολὺ καὶ ἀργύριον καὶ ὑάκινθον καὶ πορφύραν θαλασσίαν καὶ πλοῦτον μέγαν. 24 καὶ ἐπιστραφέντες ὕμνουν καὶ εὐλόγουν εἰς οὐρανὸν ὅτι καλόν, ὅτι εἰς τὸν αἰῶνα τὸ ἔλεος αὐτοῦ. 25 καὶ ἐγενήθη σωτηρία μεγάλη τῷ Ισραηλ ἐν τῇ ἡμέρᾳ ἐκείνῃ.

26 Ὅσοι δὲ τῶν ἀλλοφύλων διεσώθησαν, παραγενηθέντες ἀπήγγειλαν τῷ Λυσίᾳ πάντα τὰ συμβεβηκότα. 27 ὁ δὲ ἀκούσας συνεχύθη καὶ ἠθύμει, ὅτι οὐχ οἷα ἤθελεν, τοιαῦτα ἐγεγόνει τῷ Ισραηλ, καὶ οὐχ οἷα αὐτῷ ἐνετείλατο ὁ βασιλεύς, ἐξέβη. 28 καὶ ἐν τῷ ἐρχομένῳ ἐνιαυτῷ συνελόχησεν ἀνδρῶν ἐπιλέκτων ἑξήκοντα χιλιάδας καὶ πεντακισχιλίαν ἵππον ὥστε ἐκπολεμῆσαι αὐτούς. 29 καὶ ἦλθον εἰς τὴν Ιδουμαίαν καὶ παρενέβαλον ἐν Βαιθσουροις, καὶ συνήντησεν αὐτοῖς Ιουδας ἐν δέκα χιλιάσιν ἀνδρῶν.

30 Καὶ εἶδεν τὴν παρεμβολὴν ἰσχυρὰν καὶ προσηύξατο καὶ εἶπεν Εὐλογητὸς εἶ, ὁ σωτὴρ Ισραηλ ὁ συντρίψας τὸ ὅρμημα τοῦ δυνατοῦ ἐν χειρὶ τοῦ δούλου σου Δαυιδ καὶ παρέδωκας τὴν παρεμβολὴν τῶν ἀλλοφύλων εἰς χεῖρας Ιωναθου υἱοῦ Σαουλ καὶ τοῦ αἴροντος τὰ σκεύη αὐτοῦ· 31 οὕτως σύγκλεισον τὴν παρεμβολὴν ταύτην ἐν χειρὶ λαοῦ σου Ισραηλ, καὶ αἰσχυνθήτωσαν ἐπὶ τῇ δυνάμει καὶ τῇ ἵππῳ αὐτῶν· 32 δὸς αὐτοῖς δειλίαν καὶ τῆξον θράσος ἰσχύος αὐτῶν, καὶ σαλευθήτωσαν τῇ συντριβῇ αὐτῶν· 33 κατάβαλε αὐτοὺς

ρομφαίᾳ ἀγαπώντων σε, καὶ αἰνεσάτωσάν σε πάντες οἱ εἰδότες τὸ ὄνομά σου ἐν ὕμνοις.

34 Καὶ συνέβαλλον ἀλλήλοις, καὶ ἔπεσον ἐκ τῆς παρεμβολῆς Λυσίου εἰς πεντακισχιλίους ἄνδρας καὶ ἔπεσον ἐξ ἐναντίας αὐτῶν. 35 ἰδὼν δὲ Λυσίας τὴν γενομένην τροπὴν τῆς αὐτοῦ συντάξεως, τῆς δὲ Ιουδου τὸ γεγενημένον θάρσος καὶ ὡς ἕτοιμοί εἰσιν ἢ ζῆν ἢ τεθνηκέναι γενναίως, ἀπῆρεν εἰς Ἀντιόχειαν καὶ ἐξενολόγει πλεοναστὸν πάλιν παραγίνεσθαι εἰς τὴν Ιουδαίαν.

REDEDICATION OF THE TEMPLE

1 Macc 4:36–61: Judas and his brothers resolved, following the victories over Lysias, to cleanse the Temple and rededicate it to the Lord (4:36). Working through priests, the Maccabeans tore down the altar that the Gentiles had defiled, built a new altar and sanctuary, and made new Holy Vessels, Lamp Stand, Incense Altar, Table, and Curtains (4:42–51). Then they rededicated the Temple early on the twenty-fifth day of the month Chislev 164 BC, "at the very season and on the very day that the Gentiles had profaned it" (4:54). The Maccabeans resolved that the dedication of the altar should be observed with regularity for eight days on subsequent years, and this practice eventually became the festival of Hanukkah.

36 Εἶπεν δὲ Ιουδας καὶ οἱ ἀδελφοὶ αὐτοῦ Ἰδοὺ συνετρίβησαν οἱ ἐχθροὶ ἡμῶν, ἀναβῶμεν καθαρίσαι τὰ ἅγια καὶ ἐγκαινίσαι. 37 καὶ συνήχθη ἡ παρεμβολὴ πᾶσα καὶ ἀνέβησαν εἰς ὄρος Σιων. 38 καὶ εἶδον τὸ ἁγίασμα ἠρημωμένον καὶ τὸ θυσιαστήριον βεβηλωμένον καὶ τὰς θύρας κατακεκαυμένας καὶ ἐν ταῖς αὐλαῖς φυτὰ πεφυκότα ὡς ἐν δρυμῷ ἢ ὡς ἐν ἑνὶ τῶν ὀρέων καὶ τὰ παστοφόρια καθῃρημένα. 39 καὶ διέρρηξαν τὰ ἱμάτια αὐτῶν καὶ ἐκόψαντο κοπετὸν μέγαν καὶ ἐπέθεντο σποδὸν 40 καὶ ἔπεσαν ἐπὶ πρόσωπον ἐπὶ τὴν γῆν καὶ ἐσάλπισαν ταῖς σάλπιγξιν τῶν σημασιῶν καὶ ἐβόησαν εἰς

οὐρανόν. 41 τότε ἐπέταξεν Ιουδας ἀνδράσιν πολεμεῖν τοὺς ἐν τῇ ἄκρᾳ, ἕως καθαρίσῃ τὰ ἅγια.

42 Καὶ ἐπελέξατο ἱερεῖς ἀμώμους θελητὰς νόμου, 43 καὶ ἐκαθάρισαν τὰ ἅγια καὶ ἦραν τοὺς λίθους τοῦ μιασμοῦ εἰς τόπον ἀκάθαρτον. 44 καὶ ἐβουλεύσαντο περὶ τοῦ θυσιαστηρίου τῆς ὁλοκαυτώσεως τοῦ βεβηλωμένου, τί αὐτῷ ποιήσωσιν· 45 καὶ ἔπεσεν αὐτοῖς βουλὴ ἀγαθὴ καθελεῖν αὐτό, μήποτε γένηται αὐτοῖς εἰς ὄνειδος ὅτι ἐμίαναν τὰ ἔθνη αὐτό· καὶ καθεῖλον τὸ θυσιαστήριον 46 καὶ ἀπέθεντο τοὺς λίθους ἐν τῷ ὄρει τοῦ οἴκου ἐν τόπῳ ἐπιτηδείῳ μέχρι τοῦ παραγενηθῆναι προφήτην τοῦ ἀποκριθῆναι περὶ αὐτῶν. 47 καὶ ἔλαβον λίθους ὁλοκλήρους κατὰ τὸν νόμον καὶ ᾠκοδόμησαν θυσιαστήριον καινὸν κατὰ τὸ πρότερον. 48 καὶ ᾠκοδόμησαν τὰ ἅγια καὶ τὰ ἐντὸς τοῦ οἴκου καὶ τὰς αὐλὰς ἡγίασαν 49 καὶ ἐποίησαν σκεύη ἅγια καινὰ καὶ εἰσήνεγκαν τὴν λυχνίαν καὶ τὸ θυσιαστήριον τῶν θυμιαμάτων καὶ τὴν τράπεζαν εἰς τὸν ναόν. 50 καὶ ἐθυμίασαν ἐπὶ τὸ θυσιαστήριον καὶ ἐξῆψαν τοὺς λύχνους τοὺς ἐπὶ τῆς λυχνίας, καὶ ἔφαινον ἐν τῷ ναῷ. 51 καὶ ἐπέθηκαν ἐπὶ τὴν τράπεζαν ἄρτους καὶ ἐξεπέτασαν τὰ καταπετάσματα. καὶ ἐτέλεσαν πάντα τὰ ἔργα, ἃ ἐποίησαν.

52 Καὶ ὤρθρισαν τὸ πρωὶ τῇ πέμπτῃ καὶ εἰκάδι τοῦ μηνὸς τοῦ ἐνάτου (οὗτος ὁ μὴν Χασελευ) τοῦ ὀγδόου καὶ τεσσαρακοστοῦ καὶ ἑκατοστοῦ ἔτους 53 καὶ ἀνήνεγκαν θυσίαν κατὰ τὸν νόμον ἐπὶ τὸ θυσιαστήριον τῶν ὁλοκαυτωμάτων τὸ καινόν, ὃ ἐποίησαν. 54 κατὰ τὸν καιρὸν καὶ κατὰ τὴν ἡμέραν, ἐν ᾗ ἐβεβήλωσαν αὐτὸ τὰ ἔθνη, ἐν ἐκείνῃ ἐνεκαινίσθη ἐν ᾠδαῖς καὶ κιθάραις καὶ κινύραις καὶ κυμβάλοις. 55 καὶ ἔπεσεν πᾶς ὁ λαὸς ἐπὶ πρόσωπον καὶ προσεκύνησαν καὶ εὐλόγησαν εἰς οὐρανὸν τὸν εὐοδώσαντα αὐτοῖς. 56 καὶ ἐποίησαν τὸν ἐγκαινισμὸν τοῦ θυσιαστηρίου ἡμέρας ὀκτὼ καὶ προσήνεγκαν ὁλοκαυτώματα μετ' εὐφροσύνης καὶ ἔθυσαν θυσίαν σωτηρίου καὶ αἰνέσεως. 57 καὶ κατεκόσμησαν τὸ κατὰ πρόσωπον τοῦ ναοῦ στεφάνοις χρυσοῖς καὶ ἀσπιδίσκαις καὶ ἐνεκαίνισαν τὰς πύλας καὶ τὰ παστοφόρια καὶ ἐθύρωσαν αὐτά. 58 καὶ ἐγενήθη εὐφροσύνη μεγάλη ἐν τῷ λαῷ σφόδρα, καὶ ἀπεστράφη ὀνειδισμὸς ἐθνῶν.

59 Καὶ ἔστησεν Ιουδας καὶ οἱ ἀδελφοὶ αὐτοῦ καὶ πᾶσα ἡ ἐκκλησία Ισραηλ ἵνα ἄγωνται αἱ ἡμέραι τοῦ ἐγκαινισμοῦ τοῦ θυσιαστηρίου ἐν τοῖς καιροῖς αὐτῶν ἐνιαυτὸν κατ' ἐνιαυτὸν ἡμέρας ὀκτὼ ἀπὸ τῆς πέμπτης καὶ εἰκάδος τοῦ μηνὸς Χασελευ μετ' εὐφροσύνης καὶ χαρᾶς.

60 Καὶ ᾠκοδόμησαν ἐν τῷ καιρῷ ἐκείνῳ τὸ ὄρος Σιων κυκλόθεν τείχη ὑψηλὰ καὶ πύργους ὀχυρούς, μήποτε παραγενηθέντα τὰ ἔθνη καταπατήσωσιν αὐτά, ὡς ἐποίησαν τὸ πρότερον. 61 καὶ ἀπέταξεν ἐκεῖ δύναμιν τηρεῖν αὐτὸ καὶ ὠχύρωσεν αὐτὸ τηρεῖν τὴν Βαιθσουραν τοῦ ἔχειν τὸν λαὸν ὀχύρωμα κατὰ πρόσωπον τῆς Ιδουμαίας.

TEXT NOTES: 1 MACCABEES

1 MACC 1:1–9

1:1 Καὶ ἐγένετο μετὰ τὸ πατάξαι Ἀλέξανδρον: Ἀλέξανδρον represents the subj. accus. of πατάξαι in the articular infin.

1:1 ἐπάταξεν τὸν Δαρεῖον: Alexander (356–323 BC) defeated Darius both at Issus (333 BC) and Gaugamela (331 BC).

1:2 ἕως ἄκρων τῆς γῆς: after taking Egypt, Mesopotamia, and Persia Alexander advanced to Bactria and India.

1:4 καὶ ἐγένοντο αὐτῷ εἰς φόρον: lit. "and they became for him for tribute." Very oft in imitation of Hebrew, clauses and sentences are introduced by appr. forms of γίγνομαι and εἰμί.

1:6 ἔτι αὐτοῦ ζῶντος: gen. abs. The trans. of the pres. ptc. ζῶντος should reflect the aor. tense of διεῖλεν, the principal vb. in the vicinity; thus, "[while] he was still living…"

1:7 ἔτη δώδεκα: accus. of ext. of time. "For twelve years."

1:9 ἐπέθεντο πάντες διαδήματα μετὰ τὸ ἀποθανεῖν αὐτόν: the pron. αὐτόν, which refers to Alexander, is the subj. accus. of the articular infin. Three dynasties had been established by 275 BC, the Antigonids (Macedonia), Ptolemies (Egypt), and Seleucids (Syria).

1:9 καὶ ἐπλήθυναν κακὰ ἐν τῇ γῇ: "and they multiplied evils in the earth." The neg. bias of 1 Macc is evident throughout.

1 MACC 1:10–64

1:10 ῥίζα ἁμαρτωλὸς Ἀντίοχος Ἐπιφανής: the author of 1 Macc refers to Antiochus Epiphanes (175–64 BC) as a "sinful root," possibly in imitation of Is 11:10 and Dan 11:7.

1:10 υἱὸς Ἀντιόχου τοῦ βασιλέως, ὃς ἦν ὅμηρα ἐν Ῥώμῃ: Antiochus the king (223–187 BC), of whom Antiochus Epiphanes was a son, had wrested Palestine from Egypt at the battle of Paneas in 198 BC but lost most of Asia Minor to Rome at the battle of Magnesia in 190 BC (cf. Dan 11:18). It was on account of this defeat that the younger Antiochus "had been a hostage in Rome." As context makes clear, ὅς refers to Antiochus IV and not to the immed. anteced. Antiochus III; it is not clear why 1 Macc uses the neut. plur. ὅμηρα here although the masc. sing. ὅμηρος ("pledge, surety, hostage") could have been used instead (cf. LSJ, pg. 1221).

1:10 ἐν ἔτει ἑκατοστῷ καὶ τριακοστῷ καὶ ἑβδόμῳ: "in the one hundred and thirty-seventh year." Perhaps the time is reckoned from the beg. of Seleucid rule. Thus, 175 BC. Cf. Intro 3 above.

1:11 υἱοὶ παράνομοι: "lawless" in that they were willing to abandon Judaism, though "apostate" is another epithet for Jews of this type (Cohen 1987, 41–42). These Jews were led by Jason whom Antiochus appointed high priest in place of his brother Onias III (2 Macc 4:7) and this party followed a policy of enforced Hellenization (2 Macc 4:11–17).

1:11 διαθώμεθα διαθήκην: "Let's make a covenant." Delib. subjunct. + cogn. accus. The cogn. accus. is highly characteristic of the Greek of 1 Macc, e.g., ἐπάταξεν... πληγὴν μεγάλην "struck a great blow" (1:30); ἐν τῷ ζηλῶσαι ζῆλον "in his great zeal" (2:58); ἐκδικήσατε ἐκδίκησιν "avenge the wrong" (2:67); ἀνταπόδοτε ἀνταπόδομα "pay back in full" (2:68); ἐκόψαντο... κοπετὸν μέγαν "mourned with great lamentation" (2:70); ἐπολέμουν τὸν πόλεμον "fought the war" (3:1); and ἤθροισεν... ἄθροισμα "gathered a company" (3:13), etc. Some Jews were always ready to do away with distinctions between Jew and gentile (cf. Cohen 1987, 42).

1:13 καὶ προεθυμήθησάν τινες... ἐπορεύθησαν πρὸς τὸν βασιλέα: hendiadys and parataxis. Trans. "and some... went eagerly to the king."

1:14 ᾠκοδόμησαν γυμνάσιον ἐν Ιεροσολύμοις κατὰ τὰ νόμιμα τῶν ἐθνῶν: cf. 2 Macc 4:9–10. Antiochus (through Jason, his appointee) was following the Greek way of life wherein young men of Jerusalem were to worship the gods of other nations and cultivate such athletic pursuits as wrestling and throwing the discus. Cf. Intro 7 above.

1:15 καὶ ἐποίησαν ἑαυτοῖς ἀκροβυστίας: most trans., "and they removed the marks of circumcision." Ἀκροβυστία means, lit., a "growth from the top," and so is a perfect word to describe the male foreskin.

1:15 ἐπράθησαν τοῦ ποιῆσαι τὸ πονηρόν: cf. 2 Ki 17:17.

1:16 ὅπως βασιλεύσῃ: a pur. clause, sec. seq. The subjunct. mood does not occur in Koine in violation of the usual rule (Smyth §2196), although the subjunct. may be used in place of the optv., also in Attic Greek for the sake of vividness (Smyth §2197). Also, "the subjunctive is always possible instead of the optative" (Smyth §2198).

1:17 ...ἐν ἅρμασιν καὶ ἐλέφασιν καὶ ἐν ἱππεῦσιν καὶ ἐν στόλῳ μεγάλῳ: here ἐν invades the domain inhabited in purely class. Greek by μετά + gen. and σύν + dat. The so-called "ἐν of Accompanying Circumstances" (Conybeare & Stock, §91) includes the instr. use and in most cases may be rendered by the Engl. "with."

1:18 Πτολεμαῖον βασιλέα Αἰγύπτου: Ptolemy VI Philometor (180–145 BC).

1:20 μετὰ τὸ πατάξαι Αἴγυπτον: note the aor. tense of the infin. and trans. accordingly: "after having crushed Egypt."

1:20 καὶ ἀνέβη εἰς Ιεροσόλυμα ἐν ὄχλῳ βαρεῖ: Having invaded Egypt, Antiochus suspected that Judea would revolt so he took Jerusalem by storm and desecrated the Temple (2 Macc 5:1, 11–26). Cf. 1:17 for the use of ἐν.

1:21 καὶ πάντα τὰ σκεύη αὐτῆς: "and all its vessels." To what does the pron. αὐτῆς refer? To the sanctuary (τὸ ἁγίασμα)? But that is neuter. To the Lamp Stand (τὴν λυχνίαν)? That seems too strictly circumscribed. Perhaps αὐτῆς refers to Jerusalem in gen. or to still other words that might describe the Temple, sanctuary or cult in the fem. gender.

1:24–28. These vss. may constitute a frag. of a contemporary poem, though the imagery associated with mourning and weeping seems typical enough. Cf. Is 1:7; 33:7–9; Lam 1:4; Joel 1:8–13.

1:26 καὶ πρεσβύτεροι, παρθένοι καὶ νεανίσκοι ἠσθένησαν: for a contr. upon the activity of the elders, maidens and young men, cf. Joel 2:28–29; Acts 2:17–18.

1:29 Μετὰ δύο ἔτη ἡμερῶν: for the Semitism, cf. Gen 25:7; 41:1; 47:8; 2 Sam 14:28.

1:29 ἐν ὄχλῳ βαρεῖ: the occurrence of this phrase in 1:17 (of Antiochus Epiphanes who invaded Egypt "with a strong force") seems tantamount to saying that the tax depredations on Jerusalem were as bad as the earlier outright invasion of Egypt.

1:30–31 ἐπέπεσεν ἐπὶ τὴν πόλιν… ἐπάταξεν αὐτὴν πληγὴν μεγάλην… ἐπάταξεν αὐτὴν πληγὴν μεγάλην: the descr. possibly reflects the effects of taxation and what could happen if inhabitants did not comply with the levies.

1:33 καὶ ᾠκοδόμησαν τὴν πόλιν Δαυιδ: there has been a change of subj. from those who fortified the city of David (the Ophel hill, cf. 2 Sam 5:7) and those in 1:32 who took women and children captive. The latter were those who represented the inters. of Aniochus IV, and the former were the city inhabitants whom the author of 1 Macc nonetheless calls "lawless men" in 1:34; cf. 1:43.

1:33 καὶ ἐγένετο αὐτοῖς εἰς ἄκραν: another Semitism involving the appr. form of γίγνομαι; cf. 1:4.

1:34 ἔθνος ἁμαρτωλόν, ἄνδρας παρανόμους: The phrases "sinful nation" and "lawless men" apparently designate those Jews who, in the opinion of the author, were in a cert. sense irrelig. May he have meant those inhabitants who had trusted Aniochus' minister of taxation in 1:30, or who willingly adopted Antiochus' religion and profaned the Sabbath in 1:43?

1:35 καὶ ἐγένοντο εἰς μεγάλην παγίδα: for the Semitism, cf. 1:4. The subj. of ἐγένοντο seems delib. vague. It might refer (1) to the arms, food and spoils of Jerusalem mentioned earlier in the verse, or (2) the irrelig. Jews mentioned in 1:34. The statement reinforces the author's neg. view of the city inhabitants, or even of Jerusalem itself during the dire circums. recounted.

1:36–40. The poet. frag. expatiates upon the idea with which the author concludes 1:35; cf. sim. somber tones in Pss 74 and 79.

1:36 ἐγένετο εἰς ἔνεδρον: the idiom ἐγένετο εἰς (+ accus.), which is exceedingly common in the LXX (cf. Judg 1:29, 30, 35; 11:39; 1 Sam 30:25; 1 Chr 11:6; Jer 3:9; Ezek 17:6), seems to mean "A turned into B"; cf. καὶ ἐγένοντο εἰς μεγάλην παγίδα in 1:35 and εἰς λαὸν ἕνα in 1:41.

1:41 Καὶ ἔγραψεν ὁ βασιλεὺς... εἶναι πάντας εἰς λαὸν ἕνα: note the subj. accus. with an infin. in indir. state. (cf. Smyth §§2016–24). The prep. εἰς ("that all be *into* one people") would not occur in purely class. Greek but does function here in conformity to Semitic idiom; cf. 1:36. Judaism, with its conception of a revealed law and so rejection of other gods, was at odds with the idea of "one people" united in language, religion, culture, and dress.

1:42 καὶ ἐγκαταλιπεῖν ἕκαστον τὰ νόμιμα αὐτοῦ: ἕκαστον represents the subj. accus. here and ἐγκαταλιπεῖν the infin. in indir. state. (cf. 1:41). The 2 aor. tense of the infin. suggs. that Antiochus IV desired the citizens of his realm to comply with his directive at once (punctiliar action). For the tenses of the infin. in indir. state. cf. Smyth §§1866–1867.

1:44 καὶ ἀπέστειλεν... βιβλία... πορευθῆναι ὀπίσω νομίμων ἀλλοτρίων τῆς γῆς: πορευθῆναι represents an infin. of pur. (cf. Smyth §§2008–2009): Antiochus sent letters... "*to journey after laws [that were] strange [to] the land*." The prep. ὀπίσω (+ gen.) patterns naturally with νομίμων and ἀλλοτρίων (modifying νομίμων) patterns with τῆς γῆς.

1:45–49. The verbal struct. of this extended sentence is ἀπέστειλεν βιβλία (the mn. verbal idea) plus a series of dep. verbal ideas in the infinitive coordinated by καί, thus πορευθῆναι... καὶ κωλῦσαι... καὶ βεβηλῶσαι... καὶ μιᾶναι... οἰκοδομῆσαι... καὶ θύειν... καὶ ἀφιέναι... βδέλυξαι... ὥστε ἐπιλαθέσθαι... καὶ ἀλλάξαι. Thus, Antiochus sent letters (for the inhabitants of his realm) to "journey... prevent... profane... befoul... build... sacrifice... leave... make detestable... so that (they) forget... and exchange." Each infin. is integral to its clause, e.g., καὶ κωλῦσαι ὁλοκαυτώματα καὶ θυσίαν καὶ σπονδὴν ἐκ τοῦ ἁγιάσματος: "and *to prevent* burnt offerings and sacrifice and drink offering *from* the sanctuary."

1:49 ὥστε ἐπιλαθέσθαι... καὶ ἀλλάξαι: while dep. upon the overlying struct. (see preced note), these two infins. are also part of a pot. res. clause. For the diff. between ὥστε + infin. (pot. res.) and ὥστε + finite vb. (act. res.), cf. Smyth §§2257–2259.

1:50 καὶ ὃς ἂν μὴ ποιήσῃ... ἀποθανεῖται: ὃς ἂν is equiv. to the clause marker ἐάν. Thus the underlying struct. is ὃς ἂν... ποιήσῃ, ἀποθανεῖται, a modified FmoreV cond.

1:51 καὶ ἐνετείλατο ταῖς πόλεσιν Ιουδα θυσιάζειν...: θυσιάζειν represents an infin. of pur.; cf. 1:44.

1:54 τῇ πεντεκαιδεκάτῃ ἡμέρᾳ Χασελευ τῷ πέμπτῳ καὶ τεσσαρακοστῷ καὶ ἑκατοστῷ ἔτει: The month Chislev is approx. December. The "one hundred and forty-fifth year" is approx. 167 BC. Cf. Intro 3 above.

1:54 βδέλυγμα ἐρημώσεως: cf. Dan 11:31; 12:11 and 2 Macc 6:2 for the "desolating sacrilege." Perhaps the sacrilege consisted of an altar to the Olympian Zeus, and a likeness of this god thereon. Cf. Intro 7 above.

1:57 καὶ εἴ... συνευδόκει, ...ἐθανάτου: a mixed cond. Εἰ... συνευδόκει constitutes the protasis of simp. fact. pres. (SF pres.) and ἐθανάτου (3 sing. impf. indic. act.) the apodosis of a simp. fact. past (SF past). The context is past time, however, so the author obviously used pres. συνευδόκει to convey vividness.

1:58 τῷ Ισραηλ τοῖς εὑρισκομένοις: two clauses in close apposition. Trans. "...to Israel, those found month after month."

1:59 θυσιάζοντες ἐπὶ τὸν βωμόν: the sacrifice prob. consisted of swine; cf. 1:47; 2 Macc 6:4–5.

1:59 ὃς ἦν ἐπὶ τοῦ θυσιαστηρίου: the anteced. of ὃς is evidently τὸν βωμόν of the preced clause. So what the author apparently describes here is a sacrifice of one (lesser) altar (ὁ βωμός) upon the θυσιαστήριον which held always special place within the cultus and religion of Israel; cf. only the evidence in the NT, partic. Heb 7:13 and 13:10. Also, Mt 23:18–20; Lk 1:11; 1 Cor 9:13; 10:18; James 2:21; Rev 6:9; 8:3.

1:60–61. The atrocities recounted here seem comparable to those mentioned in Heb 11:35–38 and the many earlier texts upon which the latter passage is based.

1:62 τοῦ μὴ φαγεῖν κοινά: the articular infin. in the gen. oft signals pur.: "not to eat common things."

1:63 ἵνα μὴ μιανθῶσιν... καὶ μὴ βεβηλώσωσιν διαθήκην: both finite vbs. in the subjunct. express neg. pur.: "not to be defiled... and not profane."

1 Macc 2:1–48

2:1 Μωδεϊν: Modein was on the road to Beth-Horon, about seventeen miles northwest of Jerusalem.

2:2 καὶ αὐτῷ υἱοὶ πέντε: the vb. "to be" (which must be supplied mentally) is ἦσαν; αὐτῷ represents the poss. dat. (Smyth §1476). The correct trans. is "he had five sons," not "there were to him five sons."

2:3 Σιμων: The Hasmonean line would proceed through Simon when the other brothers died (cf. 1 Macc 13:1–6).

2:4 Ιουδας... Μακκαβαῖος: while "Maccabeus" may derive from a Hebr. word mng. "hammer," surnames of the other brothers are of less cert. deriv. Cf. Intro 6 above.

2:6 καὶ εἶδεν τὰς βλασφημίας τὰς γινομένας ἐν Ιουδα καὶ ἐν Ιερουσαλημ: vbs. of seeing, perceiving, and hearing, when they denote phys. (actual) percep., take the ptc. (Smyth §2110, §2112). Thus, "and he saw that the blasphemies *were existing* in Judah and in Jerusalem."

2:7–13. The poet. frag. elaborates upon what the author reveals in 2:6; passages in the OT that convey comparable ideas are Pss 44, 74, 79 and Lamentations.

2:7 ἐν τῷ δοθῆναι αὐτὴν ἐν χειρὶ ἐχθρῶν: here αὐτήν represents the obj. of the vb. δοθῆναι in the articular infin.: "...in her having been given over in the hands of her enemies." Some flex. is essent. in dealing with ἐν here: "as she was given over" seems just as valid as the more wooden "in her having been given over," and "to the hands" seems better than "in the hands" in light of the fact that "in another of its Biblical uses ἐν becomes indistinguishable from εἰς" (Conybeare and Stock § 91.c).

2:9 τὰ σκεύη τῆς δόξης αὐτῆς αἰχμάλωτα ἀπήχθη: αἰχμάλωτα (in the same case, number and gender as τὰ σκεύη) is not essent. to the central idea but reinforces it as a subj. pred.: "the vessels were led away *as booty*." A neut. plur. can serve as the subj. of a vb. in the 3 pers. sing.

2:11 ἐγένετο εἰς δούλην: for the Semitism, cf. καὶ ἐγένετο αὐτοῖς εἰς ἄκραν in 1:33.

2:13 ἵνα τί ἡμῖν ἔτι ζωή: ἐστιν, the appr. form of the vb. "to be," must be supplied mentally, cf. 2:2. What type of dat. is ἡμῖν?, cf. 2:2.

2:14 καὶ διέρρηξεν... τὰ ἱμάτια αὐτῶν: a well-known sign of mourning, cf. Gen 37:34; 44:13; Num 14:6; Jos. 7:6; 2 Sam 1:11; 2 Ki 2:12; 5:7; 11:14; 22:11; Job 1:20.

2:14 καὶ περιεβάλοντο σάκκους: another well-known sign of mourning, cf. Gen 37:34; 2 Sam 3:31; 1 Ki 20:31; 21:27; 2 Ki 6:30; 19:1, 2; Job 16:15; Ps 69:11.

2:15 οἱ καταναγκάζοντες τὴν ἀποστασίαν εἰς Μωδεΐν τὴν πόλιν: the rel. clause reveals the author's bias, cf. 1:9.

2:18 καὶ ἔσῃ σὺ καὶ οἱ υἱοί σου τῶν φίλων τοῦ βασιλέως: the first gen. is part., the second subjv.: "both you and your sons shall be (part of) the friends of the king." οἱ φίλοι τοῦ βασιλέως may refer to a special class of potentates and courtiers whom Antiochus favored by granting them distinctive clothing and insignia. Cf. Intro 7 above.

2:19 ἀκούουσιν αὐτοῦ: for ἀκούω + gen. in the sense of hearken or obey, cf. Smyth §1366.

2:19 ἀποστῆναι... ἀπὸ λατρείας πατέρων αὐτοῦ: compound vbs. typically pattern with the same prep. as occurs within the vb., so "to apostatize from the worship of his fathers."

1 MACCABEES NOTES

2:23 καὶ ὡς ἐπαύσατο λαλῶν: for παύομαι + suppl. ptc. in the nom. case, cf. Smyth §2098; thus, "and when he stopped speaking."

2:24 καὶ ἐτρόμησαν οἱ νεφροὶ αὐτοῦ: not "his heart trembled," but "his kidneys trembled," the latter organ being considered to be the seat of deliberations. Cf. Ps 15:7; 72:21; Lam 3:13.

2:24 καὶ ἀνήνεγκεν θυμὸν κατὰ τὸ κρίμα: trans. the prep. phrase as an adv., thus, "and he became *justifiably* angry." Again the author reveals his bias, cf. 1:9; 2:15.

2:26 καθὼς ἐποίησεν Φινεες τῷ Ζαμβρι υἱῷ Σαλωμ: cf. Num 25:6–8. The zeal of Phinehas for the Lord's honor became the occasion for the Lord's covenanting with him and his descendants as God's true priests, cf. Num 25:11–13.

2:27–28. Mattathias' invitation to be zealous, establish the covenant, and follow Mattathias (cf. 2 Macc 5:27) seems reminiscent of Jesus' invitation to the disciples to leave everything and follow him, cf. Mt 4:19–20; Mk 1:17–18; Lk 5:10–11; Jn 1:39.

2:33 Ἕως τοῦ νῦν·: "enough of this!" For the phrase, cf. LXX Gen 15:16; 18:12; 32:5; 46:34; Num 14:19; Deut 12:9; 2 Sam 19:8; 2 Ki 8:6; Eccl 4:2; Ezek 4:14.

2:37 Ἀποθάνωμεν πάντες ἐν τῇ ἁπλότητι ἡμῶν: the Maccabeans would rather die in innocence than profane the Sabbath, cf. 1 Macc 1:63. It is interesting to compare apostolic usage of ἁπλότης, which seems to mean "sincerity" or "single-hearted devotion" (Rom 12:8; 2 Cor 8:2; 9:11, 13; 11:3; Eph 6:5; Col 3:22), with the innocent zeal of the Maccabeans.

2:40 the underlying struct. is Ἐὰν... ποιήσωμεν... καὶ μὴ πολεμήσωμεν..., ὀλεθρεύσουσιν ἡμᾶς: a FmoreV cond.

2:41 ὃς ἐὰν ἔλθῃ..., πολεμήσωμεν: equiv. to an FmoreV, cf. Smyth §2565.

2:41 οὐ μὴ ἀποθάνωμεν: the neg. particles οὐ and μή + the fut. indic. or aor. subjunct. produce strong fut. neg. (SFN), the strongest type of negation in Greek, cf. Smyth §1919.

RELIGION AND RESISTANCE

2:42 Τότε συνήχθησαν πρὸς αὐτοὺς συναγωγὴ Ἀσιδαίων: The Hasideans, or "pious ones," were a group concerned not for Jewish nationalism as such but for the relig. law. While they at first resisted Hellenism passively (cf. 1 Macc 1:62–63; 2:37), they here turn to more active means.

2:43 καὶ ἐγένοντο αὐτοῖς εἰς στήριγμα: for the by now familiar Semitism, cf. 1:4, 33, 35; 2:11: "they (the Hasideans) became reinforcements for them (αὐτοῖς)." It is evident from context that the pron. αὐτοῖς refers to the Maccabeans, a dat. of adv. (Smyth §1481).

2:44–47. The author refers to the less committed Jews as "sinners" and "lawless men," 2:44. He also justifies the Maccabeans' harsh emotions (ἐν ὀργῇ αὐτῶν, 44; ἐν θυμῷ αὐτῶν, 44) as they "smote" (ἐπάταξαν, 44) the less committed Jews, forced the latter to flee to the Gentiles, and circumcised babies "forcibly" (ἐν ἰσχύι, 46). Cf. Intro 9 above.

1 MACC 2:49–70

2:52 Αβρααμ... ἐν πειρασμῷ εὑρέθη πιστός: Biblically, Abraham is considered the paradigm of faithfulness, cf. Gen 22:15–18; Rom 4:1–25; Gal 3:6–9, 14, 16, 18, 29; 4:22.

2:52 καὶ ἐλογίσθη αὐτῷ εἰς δικαιοσύνην: cf. Gen 15:6; Rom 4:9.

2:53 Ιωσηφ... ἐγένετο κύριος Αἰγύπτου: cf. Gen 39–45.

2:54 Φινεες... ἔλαβεν διαθήκην ἱερωσύνης αἰωνίας: cf. Num 25:6–15; 1 Macc 2:26.

2:55–56. Joshua and Caleb were special instruments whom God used for Israel's good during the conquest, cf. Num 13:1–14:12; 26:65; Josh 1:1–9.

2:57 Δαυιδ... ἐκληρονόμησεν θρόνον βασιλείας εἰς αἰῶνας: cf. 2 Sam 7:16; Pss 89:35–37; 132:11–12.

2:58 Ηλιας... ἀνελήμφθη εἰς τὸν οὐρανόν: cf. 2 Ki 2:9–12.

2:58 ἐν τῷ ζηλῶσαι ζῆλον νόμου: "because of his great zeal for the law." For the cogn. accus. ζηλῶσαι ζῆλον, cf. 1:11. Ηλιας, in the immed. vicinity, is the subj. of this articular infin.; νόμου appears to be an obj. gen., "zeal *for the law*."

2:59 Ανανιας, Αζαριας, Μισαηλ: cf. Dan 3:8–30, though the names in the biblical text are "Shadrach, Meshach, and Abednego."

2:60 Δανιηλ ἐν τῇ ἁπλότητι αὐτοῦ ἐρρύσθη ἐκ στόματος λεόντων: cf. Dan 6:1–24. For ἐν τῇ ἁπλότητι αὐτου, cf. 2:37.

2:62 καὶ ἀπὸ λόγων ἀνδρὸς ἁμαρτωλοῦ μὴ φοβηθῆτε: lit., "flee *from* the words of a sinner." "Ἀπό in the LXX is often little more than a sign of the genitive, like our English 'of,' provided that the genitive be partitive" (Conybeare & Stock §92.a). Μή + aor. subjunct. signifies Prohibition (Smyth §1800).

2:63 οὐ μὴ εὑρεθῇ: strong fut. neg. (SFN), cf. 2:41.

2:64 ἀνδρίζεσθε καὶ ἰσχύσατε: for the refrain, cf. Deut 31:6, 7, 23; Jos. 1:6, 7, 9, 18; 10:25; 1 Chr 22:13; 28:20; 32:7; Dan 10:19; 11:1.

2:65 Συμεων ὁ ἀδελφὸς ὑμῶν: "Simeon" and "Simon" can be variants of the same name (cf. Acts 15:14 and 2 Pet 1:1), so the Συμεων featured here is apparently the same individual as the Σιμων mentioned in 2:3.

2:65 πάσας τὰς ἡμέρας: accus. ext. of time (Smyth §§1582–1583). Thus, "for all your days..."

2:66 αὐτὸς ἔσται ὑμῖν ἄρχων στρατιᾶς: periphrasis (such as ἔσται... ἄρχων = "he will command your army") tends to adjectivize the ptc. and so emphasizes the idea (Smyth §1857). Ὑμῖν is prob. best described as a dat. of adv., "for you."

2:66 καὶ πολεμήσει πόλεμον λαῶν: for the cogn. accus., cf. 1:11. While no parallel expression exists in the LXX, the author plainly means that the war would be waged "with the peoples" (μετὰ λαῶν or σὺν λαοῖς) or "against the peoples" (κατὰ λαῶν). The occurrence of the bare gen. here in lieu of a more complicated struct. in class. Greek seems sugg. of the noun-construct in Hebrew.

2:69 καὶ προσετέθη πρὸς τοὺς πατέρας αὐτοῦ: the phrase "gathered to his fathers" means to be buried with one's ancestors, i.e., to be united with them in death. For the idea in the Bible cf. Gen 15:15; 47:30; 49:29; Deut 31:16; Jg. 2:10; 2 Sam 7:12; 1 Ki 1:21; Ps 49:19.

2:70 ἐκόψαντο αὐτὸν πᾶς Ισραηλ κοπετὸν μέγαν: "all Israel... mourned." Sing. subjs. can pattern with plur. vbs. if the subj. is a collective noun, as here. For the cogn. accus. ἐκόψαντο... κοπετὸν μέγαν, cf. 1:11.

1 Macc 3:1–12

3:1 υἱὸς αὐτοῦ ἀντ' αὐτοῦ: "*his* son and in *his* place" refers to Mattathias.

3:3–9. The poet. frag. reveals the idea contained in 3:2, namely, Judas Maccabeus' joyful and successful waging of war against the enemies of Israel.

3:3 καὶ ἐνεδύσατο θώρακα ὡς γίγας: cf. Ps 93:1.

3:3 ἐν ῥομφαίᾳ: here ἐν + dat. functions instrumentally, "by his sword." Cf. καὶ οὐ σώσω αὐτοὺς ἐν τόξῳ οὐδὲ ἐν ῥομφαίᾳ οὐδὲ ἐν πολέμῳ οὐδὲ ἐν ἅρμασιν οὐδὲ ἐν ἵπποις οὐδὲ ἐν ἱππεῦσιν (Hos 1:7); ὤφθη Ἰούδας... ἐν τρισχιλίοις ἀνδράσιν (1 Macc 4:6).

3:4 καὶ ὡμοιώθη λέοντι: cf. Hos 5:14; 13:7; Job 10:16.

3:6 καὶ συνεστάλησαν ἄνομοι ἀπὸ τοῦ φόβου αὐτοῦ: are the ἄνομοι the same as the "lawless" Jews featured in 1:11, 34; and 2:44? A parallelism such as one frequently finds in the Pss exists between ἄνομοι and οἱ ἐργάται τῆς ἀνομίας in the next strophe. Συστέλλω in the pass. means to become smaller, i.e., shrink. So, "lawless men shrunk out of fear for him." Cf. 2:62 for the use of ἀπό in lieu of gen.; the pron. αὐτοῦ, which plainly refers to Judas Maccabeus, represents an obj. gen., "fear *for* him."

3:7 ἐπίκρανεν... εὔφρανεν: trans. into Eng. obscures the fine antithetical parallelism here: "he *embittered* many kings," but "he *gladdened* Jacob by his deeds." Note also that the vbs. ἐπίκρανεν and εὔφρανεν assume the same pos. in their respective lines and sound identical in the verbs' two final syllables (= Homoiteleuton, Smyth §3026).

3:8 ἐξωλέθρευσεν... ἐξ αὐτῆς, καὶ ἀπέστρεψεν... ἀπὸ Ισραηλ: for the repetition of preps. used in compound vbs. and prep. phrases, cf. 2:19. God used Judas Maccabeus to execute his wrath, cf. 2 Macc 7:38.

3:9 καὶ ὠνομάσθη... καὶ συνήγαγεν: i.e., Judas' renown to the ends of the earth existed in proportion to his marshalling of those who, apart from his influence, would have perished (and so not be able to extol Judas' exploits).

3:9–10 συνήγαγεν... συνήγαγεν: the quick repetition of συνήγαγεν, accompanied by a shift in subj. from Judas Maccabeus to Apollonius, links the poet. frag. to the author's narrative that resumes here. Apollonius was the Seleucid governor of Syria, cf. Joseph. *Antiq* 12.5.5; 12.7.1.

3:11 ἔγνω... ἐξῆλθεν... ἐπάταξεν... ἀπέκτεινεν: the short, choppy style is that of parataxis, not syntaxis, as oft in Septuagintal Greek: "he came to know... went forth... defeated... killed."

3:11 καὶ ἐξῆλθεν εἰς συνάντησιν αὐτῷ: trans. "and he came forth *to meet him*." The subj. of the mn. vb. is Judas Maccabeus, and the pers. pron. αὐτῷ refers to Apollonius, as determined by context. The prep. phrase εἰς συνάντησιν αὐτῷ, virtually equiv. to a pur. clause (ἵνα συναντᾷ αὐτῷ = "in order to meet him"), is a quite common idiom in Septuagintal Greek. For the idea cf. Gen 14:17; 18:2; Ex 4:14; Num 20:18; Deut 1:44; Jos. 8:5; Judg6:35; 1 Ki17:48; 2 Chr 14:9; Judith 2:6; Ps 58:5, etc.

3:11 καὶ ἔπεσον τραυματίαι πολλοί: lit. "and many wounded ones fell," but what the author means, surely, is that many were wounded and then fell = καὶ ἐτραυματίσθησαν καὶ ἔπεσον. Hysteron Proteron ("later earlier") is a device which reverses the order of time wherein events occur naturally in order to give prominence to the more imp. event (Smyth §3030).

3:12 καὶ ἦν πολεμῶν ἐν αὐτῇ πάσας τὰς ἡμέρας: ἦν πολεμῶν = "he was fighting" is an example of an Analytic Tense, a verbal idea formed with auxiliary vb. + ptc. instead of by an inflected form, "as in English '[he] is coming' for '[he] comes'" (Conybeare and Stock, §72). In the expression ἐν αὐτῇ, ἐν functions instrumentally ("by it"), i.e., the sword (τὴν μάχαιραν) mentioned earlier in the verse. For the type of accus. evident in πάσας τὰς ἡμέρας, cf. 2:65.

1 Macc 3:13-26

3:13 ἐκκλησίαν πιστῶν μετ' αὐτοῦ καὶ ἐκπορευομένων εἰς πόλεμον: with the addition of καί, πιστῶν... ἐκπορευομένων cannot constitute a gen. abs. but pertains rather to ἐκκλησίαν, thus, "an assembly of faithful people with him (Judas Maccabeus) and going forth into battle."

3:14 τοὺς σὺν αὐτῷ τοὺς ἐξουδενοῦντας: the prtcl. phrase τοὺς ἐξουδενοῦντας mods. the def. article τούς which functions here as a pers. pron.: "those with him *who think little of* the word of the king."

3:15 ἀνέβη... βοηθῆσαι αὐτῷ ποιῆσαι τὴν ἐκδίκησιν ἐν υἱοῖς Ισραηλ: "came up... to help him (Seron) to exact vengeance upon the sons of Israel." Βοηθέω patterns with an obj. dat. (Smyth §1592); it is unusual to have two infins. of pur. in a row in class. Greek, though occasionally that construction can occur in prose after a vb. signifying to *go* or *come* (Smyth §2009).

3:16 καὶ ἤγγισεν ἕως ἀναβάσεως Βαιθωρων: the ascent of Beth-Horon was a route from the coastal plain to the Judean highlands. The town is about twelve miles northwest of Jerusalem.

3:16 εἰς συνάντησιν αὐτῷ: "to meet him" = ἵνα συναντᾷ αὐτῷ, cf. 3:11; 3:17.

3:17 ὡς δὲ εἶδον τὴν παρεμβολὴν ἐρχομένην: accus. with ptc. after a vb. of percep. (Smyth §2110) = "and when they saw the army advancing..."

3:18 καὶ οὐκ ἔστιν διαφορὰ ἐναντίον τοῦ οὐρανοῦ: "indeed, there is no distinction before heaven." "Heaven" functions here as a metonym for God, e.g., Susanna 9; Lk 15:18. Also, "strength comes from heaven," 1 Macc 3:19; "will in heaven," 3:60; "and now we shall call to heaven," 4:10. Even αὐτός can function as a circumlocution for the divine name: "he himself" (αὐτός = God) shall crush them," 3:22.

3:23 ὡς... ἐπαύσατο λαλῶν: for the idiom, cf. Gen 18:33; Num 16:31; Judg 15:17; 1 Macc 2:23.

3:23 ἐνήλατο εἰς αὐτοὺς ἄφνω: the author cannot mean that Judas Maccabeus alone charged the enemy, but that a force of Maccabeans accomplished the attack wherein Judas played at most a decisive role. The 3 pers. sing. vb. in initial pos. seems to emphasize the most imp. member of a larger group, e.g. διέρρηξεν Ματταθιας καὶ οἱ υἱοὶ αὐτοῦ τὰ ἱμάτια αὐτῶν (1 Macc 2:14), where Mattathias and (all) his sons tore their robes, not just Mattathias; καὶ εἶδεν Ιουδας καὶ οἱ ἀδελφοὶ αὐτοῦ (1 Macc 3:42), where Judas Maccabeus and (all) his brothers saw evils multiply, not just Judas.

3:23 καὶ συνετρίβη Σήρων καὶ ἡ παρεμβολὴ αὐτοῦ ἐνώπιον αὐτοῦ: the first αὐτοῦ refers to Seron, the second to Judas Maccabeus. Again, the true subj. of συνετρίβη is Seron and his entire army, even though the form of the vb. συνετρίβη is sing. not plur.

3:24 ἐν τῇ καταβάσει Βαιθωρων ἕως τοῦ πεδίου... εἰς γῆν Φυλιστιιμ: note that the rout begins on the descent to Beth-Horon (cf. ἕως ἀναβάσεως Βαιθωρων, 3:16), extends to the plain, and then survivors of the Gentile army limped all the way to the "land of Philistines," i.e., the coastal plain.

3:26 ἤγγισεν ἕως τοῦ βασιλέως τὸ ὄνομα αὐτοῦ: the news of the great battle and Judas Maccabeus' role therein reached the ears of "the king," i.e., Antiochus Epiphanes (cf. ὁ βασιλεὺς Ἀντίοχος, 3:27). Now even Gentiles extol Judas' good name, a decided expans. upon 3:9.

1 MACC 3:27–4:35

3:27 ὠργίσθη θυμῷ: the author expresses Antiochus IV's rage at Judas Maccabeus in an idiom that appears in Num 22:22; 25:3; 32:10, 13; Deut 29:26; Judg 2:14, 20; 3:8; 9:30; 10:7; 14:19; 2 Ki 13:3; 2 Chr 35:19c; Judg 5:2; Ps 105:40. Usually the God of Israel (θεός) or Yahweh (κύριος) is the subj. of ὠργίσθη, no mere human.

3:28–30. With the failure of the treasury and internal dissention, the author paints this section as though the Seleucid power was in decline. Sometimes sources outside of 1 Macc sugg. that the relationship between Judaism and Hellenism was actually quite beneficial (so Peek 1996–97).

3:30 καὶ εὐλαβήθη μὴ οὐκ ἔχῃ... εἰς τὰς δαπάνας καὶ τὰ δόματα: "and he feared that he might not have anything... in proportion to his expenditures and gifts." The particle μή sets off a fear clause (Smyth §§2221–24). Tarsus and Mallus revolted because the king had given the two cities as a present to Antiochis, the king's concubine (2 Macc 4:30).

3:31 λαβεῖν τοὺς φόρους τῶν χωρῶν: "to exact tributes *from* the lands" constitutes an ablatival use of the gen. (Smyth §1391) or a gen. of sep. (Smyth §1392–1400). Consider the following examples: λήγειν τῶν πόνων "to cease from toils" (Isocr. 1.14); παύσαντες αὐτὸν τῆς στρατηγίας "having removed him from the office of general" (Xen. *Hiero* 6.2.13); εἴργεσθαι τῆς ἀγορᾶς "to be excluded from the agora" (Lys. 6.24); σῶσαι κακοῦ "to save from evil" (Soph. *Ph.* 919).

3:32 Λυσίαν ἄνθρωπον ἔνδοξον: the adj. ἔνδοξος is a status indicator as parallel passages in 1 Macc sugg.: τοὺς παῖδας αὐτοῦ τοὺς ἐνδόξους, 1:6 (Alexander's officers); καὶ ἔνδοξος καὶ μέγας εἶ ἐν τῇ πόλει ταύτῃ, 2:17 (Mattathias); Ἐλυμαΐς... πόλις ἔνδοξος, 6:1 (Elymais).

3:33 Ἀντίοχον τὸν υἱὸν αὐτοῦ: Antiochus V Eupator, nine years old at the time, would reign 164–162 BC.

3:33 ἕως τοῦ ἐπιστρέψαι αὐτόν: "until he returned." The pron. αὐτόν, the subj. of the articular infin., refers to Antiochus Epiphanes as is evident from context.

3:35–36. Antiochus Epiphanes' plan appears to have been that of removing Jews from their habitual abodes and resettling aliens into the vacated places, a policy followed in Assyrian times, cf. 2 Ki 17:24. Despite such strong-sounding phrases as "banish the memory (of the Jews) from the place" (1 Macc 3:35), it still seems that many of the Jews actually were quite receptive to Hellenic culture and policy (so Peek 1996–97, 101–102).

3:37 τὰς ἡμίσεις τῶν δυνάμεων τὰς καταλειφθείσας: lit., "the half of his forces that remained." The other half Antiochus had turned over to his commander Lysias, cf. τὰς ἡμίσεις τῶν δυνάμεων (3:34).

3:37 καὶ ἀπῆρεν ἀπὸ Ἀντιοχείας ἀπὸ πόλεως βασιλείας αὐτοῦ: for the repetition of preps. used in compound vbs. and in accomp. prep. phrases, cf. 2:19; 3:8. The second prep. phrase is appos. to the first: "from Antioch, from the city of his kingdom." The effect of the repetition is to call attn. to Antioch which had been built by Seleucus I in 300 BC and was expanded upon by Antiochus IV.

3:37 ἔτους ἑβδόμου καὶ τεσσαρακοστοῦ καὶ ἑκατοστοῦ: "during the one hundred and forty-seventh year," i.e., 165 BC. The gen. denotes the time within which the action takes place (Smyth §1444).

3:37 τὰς ἐπάνω χώρας: "upper" lands refers to Persia.

3:38 ἄνδρας δυνατοὺς τῶν φίλων τοῦ βασιλέως: Lysias chooses Ptolemy, Nicanor, and Gorgias, other so-called "friends of the king," cf. 2:18. Cf. 2 Macc 10:12; 8:9; and 10:14 for each individual, respectively.

3:39 καταφθεῖραι αὐτὴν κατὰ τὸν λόγον τοῦ βασιλέως: the huge force was expected to carry out Antiochus' severe policies already mentioned in 3:35–36.

3:40 καὶ ἀπῆρεν σὺν πάσῃ τῇ δυνάμει αὐτῶν, καὶ ἦλθον καὶ παρενέβαλον πλησίον Αμμαους: which commander was it that departed (ἀπῆρεν) "with his entire force"—Lysias or one of the other three mentioned in 3:38? The author is unclear. The plur. vbs. ἦλθον and παρενέβαλον sugg. that the author actually had the entire force of the Gentile invaders in mind, not one individual. The Emmaus mentioned here is prob. not the one in Luke's gospel (Lk 24:13) but another village about twenty-five miles west of Jerusalem on the coastal plain.

3:41. The activities mentioned here—the procurement of money and leg-irons just before battle—sugg. that the native traders (οἱ ἔμποροι τῆς χώρας) were positioning themselves to make a killing off the vast number of slaves that inevitably followed a successful campaign. See Bradley (1987, 45) for the usual procedure, and for a partial list of battles at the conclusions of which prisoners were typically sold into slavery.

3:42 τοὺς λόγους τοῦ βασιλέως, οὓς ἐνετείλατο ποιῆσαι τῷ λαῷ εἰς ἀπώλειαν καὶ συντέλειαν: "...policies of the king which he had commanded to do to the people for their final destruction." Τοὺς λόγους τοῦ βασιλέως recalls the wording of the sim. phrase τὸν λόγον τοῦ βασιλέως in 3:39 which in turn refers to 3:35-36. The dat. in τῷ λαῷ is prob. that of disadv. (Smyth §1481). Εἰς ἀπώλειαν καὶ συντέλειαν represents hendiadys wherein two words connected by καί express a single idea (Smyth §3025), so "final destruction."

3:44 καὶ ἠθροίσθη ἡ συναγωγή: συναγωγή, the distinctive assembly of the Jews, does several times mean "synagogue" in the NT, e.g., Mt 4:23; 6.2, 5; 9:35; Jn 6:59; 18:20; Acts 6:9; 9:2, 20, etc. Here it seems to mean fighting assembly, on par with παρεμβολή, δύναμις, στρατιά and other expressions the author of 1 Macc uses to describe a military force in battle array.

3:44 τοῦ εἶναι ἑτοίμους εἰς πόλεμον καὶ τοῦ προσεύξασθαι καὶ αἰτῆσαι ἔλεος καὶ οἰκτιρμούς: articular infins. in the gen. oft denote pur.: "to be ready for battle and to pray and ask for mercy and acts of compassion." The warfare of the Jews is conceived of as both involvement in battle (ordinary) and engagement with God in prayer for his almighty aid (extraordinary). The plur. οἰκτιρμούς suggs. various *acts of compassion* that God might render, thus an elaboration upon his distinctive and thereby sing. mercy (ἔλεος).

3:45. The poet. frag. draws attn. to the loss of Jerusalem to the Gentiles (note: "it became a lodging place for the Gentiles") to which themes in Ps 74 and Is 24:8 are sim.

3:46 καὶ συνήχθησαν καὶ ἤλθοσαν εἰς Μασσηφα: the gathering at Mizpah had several historically sign. associations of which the Maccabeans were no doubt aware, e.g., Gen 31:49; Judg 10:17; 20:1; 1 Sam 7:5; 2 Ki 25:23; Hos 5:1. A number of places were called Mizpah in ancient Israel, cf. Judg 11:11, 29; Josh 13:26.

3:47 περιεβάλοντο σάκκους... διέρρηξαν τὰ ἱμάτια αὐτῶν: for the wearing of sackcloth and rending of garments, cf. 2:14. Fasting is still another indication of abject humility (Judg 20:26; 1 Sam 7:6; 2 Sam 1:12; 1 Chr 10:12), as is the impos. of ashes (Judg 9:1; Is 58:5).

3:48 καὶ ἐξεπέτασαν τὸ βιβλίον τοῦ νόμου: pagans consult oracles, but Jews behold the book of the Law, cf. Deut 31:26; 1 Esdras 9:45.

3:49 καὶ ἤνεγκαν... τὰς δεκάτας: in addition to the priestly garments and first-fruits, the Maccabeans offer "tenths," i.e., a tithe of ten percent, cf. Neh 10:35. Sim. tithes were used to support the priests and Levites, cf. Ex 23:19; Num 18:13; Deut 26:1–11; Ezek 44:30.

3:49 ἤγειραν τοὺς Ναζιραίους, οἳ ἐπλήρωσαν τὰς ἡμέρας: Why do the Maccabeans rouse Nazirites during this critical time? Perhaps the gesture has to do with the Nazirites' complete sep. from Canaanite culture, particularly viticulture (Num 6:3–4). A Nazirite was a holy pers. who had taken a vow to separate himself to the Lord for a set period of time, cf. Judg 13:5; 1 Sam 1:11; Amos 2:11–12.

3:50–53. Like the earlier poem in 3:45, these verses call God to witness outrages against the sanctuary perpetrated by Gentile aggressors: "Who can stand if you will not help?"

3:53 δυνησόμεθα ὑποστῆναι... ἐὰν μὴ... βοηθήσῃς: the underlying struct. is ἐὰν μή + aor. subjunct. (protasis), fut. indic. (apodosis) = FmoreV cond.

3:54 ἐσάλπισαν ταῖς σάλπιγξιν: the refrain occurs elsewhere at Jos. 6:13, 20; 2 Chr 13:14; 1 Macc 4:40; 5:33; 6:33; 16:8. These passages reveal that trumpet flourishes attended prayers or were used in battle. Trumpets were to be a perpetual statute for the people of Israel, cf. Num 10:8.

3:55 κατέστησεν Ιουδας ἡγουμένους τοῦ λαοῦ: the leaders that Judas Maccabeus appointed assisted in civic administration in Moses' day, cf. Ex 18:25; here they had a military function, cf. 2 Macc 8:22–23.

3:56 καὶ εἶπεν... ἀποστρέφειν ἕκαστον εἰς τὸν οἶκον αὐτοῦ κατὰ τὸν νόμον: for the principle, cf. Deut 20:5–8.

3:58 Καὶ εἶπεν Ιουδας Περιζώσασθε: everywhere else in the LXX the 2 pers. plur. impv. περιζώσασθε means, "gird yourself with sackcloth" (σάκκους). Here Judas Maccabeus says, in effect, "gird yourselves with weaponry and prepare to fight!"

3:58 γίνεσθε εἰς υἱοὺς δυνατούς: "become powerful sons!" For the Semitism that involves γίγνομαι and the prep. εἰς , cf. 1:4, 33, 35; 2:11, 43.

3:60 ὡς δ' ἂν ᾖ θέλημα ἐν οὐρανῷ, οὕτως ποιήσει: the struct. is ὡς ἂν + pres. subjunct. (protasis), fut. indic. (apodosis), equiv. to a FmoreV cond.

4:2 υἱοὶ τῆς ἄκρας ἦσαν αὐτῷ ὁδηγοί: "sons of the citadel" refers to those Jewish refugees who were opp. to the Maccabeans, cf. υἱοὶ παράνομοι, 1:11.

4:4–7. The strategy of both armies was to strike the opposing camp while the fighters were out on maneuvers. Gorgias struck the Maccabeans' camp, found no one there, and so assumed that the Jews had fled (Φεύγουσιν οὗτοι ἀφ' ἡμῶν, 4:5). However, the Maccabeans discovered the Gentile camp to be "strong and fortified" (ἰσχυρὰν καὶ τεθωρακισμένην, 4:7) while they themselves lacked essent. armor and weaponry (4:6). Judas Maccabeus' speech (4:8–11) averts disaster.

4:7 καὶ εἶδον παρεμβολήν... καὶ τεθωρακισμένην καὶ ἵππον κυκλοῦσαν αὐτήν: accus. and ptc. after a vb. of percep. (Smyth §2110, §2112), "and they saw that the camp... had been covered with armor and that cavalry was encircling it." Ἵππον ("cavalry") is here in the fem. gender and the fem. sing. accus. ptc. κυκλοῦσαν mods. ἵππον; the pron. αὐτήν refers to παρεμβολήν.

4:8 Μὴ φοβεῖσθε... μὴ δειλωθῆτε: μή + 2 pers. plur. impv. and μή + aor. subjunct., respectively. Prohibitions refer to fut. time (Smyth §1835, §1840).

4:9 ὅτε ἐδίωκεν αὐτοὺς Φαραω ἐν δυνάμει: for the great deliverance from Pharaoh, cf. Ex 13:17–15:21.

4:11 καὶ γνώσονται πάντα τὰ ἔθνη: even Gentiles shall realize that God has rescued Israel, cf. Ezek 17:24; 39:23.

4:11 ὁ λυτρούμενος: "ransomer" is just one of the God of Israel's several titles, cf. ὁ θεὸς ὁ λυτρούμενός σε, Ισραηλ, Is 41:14; κύριος ὁ θεὸς ὁ λυτρούμενος ὑμᾶς ὁ ἅγιος Ισραηλ, Is 43.14; κύριος ὁ λυτρούμενός σε, Is 44:24; ὁ λυτρούμενος αὐτοὺς ἰσχυρός, κύριος παντοκράτωρ, Jer 27:34.

4:12 ἦραν... τοὺς ὀφθαλμοὺς αὐτῶν: cf. 1 Macc 5:30; 9:39.

4:12 καὶ εἶδον αὐτοὺς ἐρχομένους ἐξ ἐναντίας: accus. with ptc. after a vb. of percep. (Smyth §2110, §2112), "and saw them coming against them."

4:13 καὶ ἐξῆλθον ἐκ τῆς παρεμβολῆς εἰς πόλεμον: "and they went out of the camp into battle." The prep. phrase ἐκ τῆς παρεμβολῆς can depict the Israelites' camp during the wilderness wanderings, e.g., Ex 19:17; Num 2:9; 5:2; 10:36; 14:44; Deut 2:14, 15. Elsewhere, of any military camp, cf. 1 Sam 4:16.; 2 Sam 1:2, 3; 2:8; 2 Ki 7:12; 1 Macc 4:34; 6:48; 2 Macc 15:22; Is 37:36.

4:14 καὶ ἔφυγον εἰς τὸ πεδίον: the rout recalls the dissolution of Seron's forces "into the plain," cf. 3:24.

4:15 οἱ δὲ ἔσχατοι πάντες ἔπεσον ἐν ῥομφαίᾳ: the "last men" (οἱ ἔσχατοι) constitute the rear guard, as in Num 2:31; 10:25. For the instr. use of ἐν in the phrase ἐν ῥομφαίᾳ, cf. 1:17; 3:3.

4:15 καὶ ἐδίωξαν αὐτοὺς ἕως Γαζηρων καὶ ἕως τῶν πεδίων τῆς Ιδουμαίας καὶ Ἀζώτου καὶ Ιαμνείας: the pursuit of Gorgias' force went in all directions, whereas Seron's force had fled mnly. to the coastal plain, cf. 3:24. Gazara, or Gezer (Josh 21:21; 1 Ki 9:17), was five miles northwest of Emmaus; Idumaea is far to the south, between the southern shore of the Dead Sea and the Mediterranean Sea; Azotus and Jamnia lie west and southwest, respectively.

4:16 ἀπὸ τοῦ διώκειν ὄπισθεν αὐτῶν: lit. "from pursuing behind them." This articular infin. does not require a subj. infin. because the first half of the verse reveals who the subjs. are, namely, Judas Maccabeus and his force. Αὐτῶν in the prep. phrase ὄπισθεν αὐτῶν refers to the vanquished Gentile fighters.

RELIGION AND RESISTANCE

4:17 Μὴ ἐπιθυμήσητε τῶν σκύλων: booty motivated most soldiers in antiquity, so Judas presents himself as a successful commander by leading his soldiers past their natural inclinations.

4:18 μετὰ ταῦτα λάβετε τὰ σκῦλα μετὰ παρρησίας: a sign. portion of the spoil would be exacted from those merchants who had intended to reduce prisoners of war to slavery, cf. 3:41; 2 Macc 8:25.

4:19 ἔτι πληροῦντος Ιουδου ταῦτα: gen. abs. (Smyth §2070). The pres. ptc. πληροῦντος indicates that Judas Maccabeus was still speaking while the action described by the mn. vb. (ὤφθη) took place.

4:19 μέρος τι ὤφθη ἐκκύπτον ἐκ τοῦ ὄρους: the pres. act. ptc. ἐκκύπτον mods. μέρος τι, the subj. of ὤφθη = "a cert. portion (of the Gentile army) was seen peeking out of the mountains." Sometimes the sing. "mountain" (ὄρος, ὄρους n.; cf. Lat. *mons montis* m.) refers to a mountainous region—here, the Judean highland.

4:20 καὶ εἶδεν ὅτι τετρόπωνται, καὶ ἐμπυρίζουσιν τὴν παρεμβολήν: three separate subjs. occur here: (1) μέρος τι is the subj. of εἶδεν; (2) Gentiles are the subj. of τετρόπωνται; and (3) the Maccabeans are the subj. of ἐμπυρίζουσιν.

4:21 παρεμβολὴν ἐν τῷ πεδίῳ ἑτοίμην εἰς παράταξιν: "force in the plain prepared for battle array" seems to hint at the way Judas Maccabeus organized his army to meet the Greeks—namely, that he employed Greek battle formations to fight the Greeks.

4:22 ἔφυγον πάντες εἰς γῆν ἀλλοφύλων: in this context, "land of the foreigners" (γῆ ἀλλοφύλων) gen. means "land of the Philistines." Thus, 3:41; 5:66, 68; cf. Χανααν γῆ ἀλλοφύλων, Soph. 2:5. This second rout resembled the one in 3:24 in that the Gentiles headed for the coastal plain, away from Jewish influence.

4:23 τὴν σκυλείαν τῆς παρεμβολῆς: for the greater spoil cf. 4:17; 2 Macc 8:24–29.

4:24 ὕμνουν καὶ εὐλόγουν εἰς οὐρανὸν ὅτι καλόν, ὅτι εἰς τὸν αἰῶνα τὸ ἔλεος αὐτοῦ: amid the rejoicing the Maccabeans were careful not to mention God by name. So their praises reflect God's gracious activity: He is "good" (ὅτι καλόν) and His mercy endures "forever" (εἰς τὸν αἰῶνα τὸ ἔλεος αὐτοῦ). For the first praise, cf. Ps 134:3; the second is the refrain heard so commonly in the Pss, cf. Ps 99:5; 105:1; 106:1; 117 (5 times); 135 (28 times).

4:25 ἐν τῇ ἡμέρᾳ ἐκείνῃ: the victory occurred on a particular "day," as is reflected so oft in the LXX: Gen 15:8 (covenant); Ex 12:51 (Exodus); Lev 27:23 (sacrifice); Num 9:6 (Passover); Josh 8:25 (victory); Judg 3:30 (victory).

4:27 συνεχύθη καὶ ἠθύμει: "he was confounded and discouraged." For the first vb. cf. 2 Macc 13:23; Jonah 4:1; for the second cf. 1 Sam 1:6, 7.

4:27 ὅτι οὐχ οἷα ἤθελεν, τοιαῦτα ἐγεγόνει τῷ Ισραηλ: this correlative consists in the relationship between the prons. οἷα and τοιαῦτα, lit., "because *of what sort* (of things) he did not wish, *of such sort* had happened for Israel."

4:27 καὶ οὐχ οἷα αὐτῷ ἐνετείλατο ὁ βασιλεύς, ἐξέβη: an extension of the correlative, lit., "and not *what sort* (of things) the king ordered him came to pass." The vb. ἐνετείλατο recalls Antiochus IV's commands that were to wreak such havoc in Israel, cf. 1:51; 3:42. Lysias in particular was under orders to the king, cf. 3:34.

4:28 καὶ ἐν τῷ ἐρχομένῳ ἐνιαυτῷ: "in the coming year," so possibly autumn 164 BC, just before the rededication of the Temple.

4:28 συνελόχησεν ἀνδρῶν ἐπιλέκτων ἑξήκοντα χιλιάδας καὶ πεντακισχιλίαν ἵππον: a much larger force than Gorgias had commanded, cf. 4:1.

4:28 ὥστε ἐκπολεμῆσαι αὐτούς: a res. clause + infin. expresses that something may occur in conseq. of an intention, tendency, or capacity—not that it *actually* did occur, as is expressed in a res. clause + indic. mood (Smyth §2257, §2258).

4:29 καὶ ἦλθον εἰς τὴν Ιδουμαίαν καὶ παρενέβαλον ἐν Βαιθσουροις: Beth-zur is located about twenty miles south of Jerusalem, on the road to Hebron. Lysias had decided to attack the Maccabeans, already embedded in Jerusalem, from the south. The 3 pers. plur. aor. indic. form παρενέβαλον rather resembles παρεμβολή, the word 1 Macc uses repeatedly to describe Greek tactical forces, cf. 3:15, 17, 23, 27, 41, 57, 4:1, 4, 7, etc.

4:29 καὶ συνήντησεν αὐτοῖς Ιουδας ἐν δέκα χιλιάσιν ἀνδρῶν: this time the ratio is Lysias' 60,000 infantry + 5,000 cavalry (4:28) vs. Judas Maccabeus' 10,000 men. There is no mention of the Maccabeans' fear of a vastly larger foe, cf. 3:17; perhaps the Maccabeans were more confident, now that they had subdued their enemies several times. What saves the Maccabeans this time is not their commander's speech (cf. 3:18–22), but rather his prayer, cf. 4:30–33.

4:30 Εὐλογητὸς εἶ, ὁ σωτὴρ Ισραηλ: the first two words constitute an exceedingly common prayer formula, cf. 1 Chr 29:10; 1 Esdras 4:60; Judg 13:17; Tobit 3:11; Ps 118.12; Dan 3:26, etc. "Savior of Israel" occurs only here. Judas Maccabeus reminds the Almighty that He had permitted David to triumph over Goliath (1 Sam 17); Jonathan's triumph over the camp of the foreigners (τὴν παρεμβολὴν τῶν ἀλλοφύλων, 4:30) is more diff. to identify.

4:34–35. Striking is Lysias' decision to abort the battle with a loss of 5,000 men. The account in 2 Macc agrees that Judas won the contest, but states that there followed a negotiated peace.

1 Macc 4:36–61

4:36 ἀναβῶμεν καθαρίσαι τὰ ἅγια καὶ ἐγκαινίσαι: the decision to purify the sanctuary and renew the Temple seems to arise spontaneously, though Maccabeans were prob. in charge of Jerusalem by the time Lysias attacked, cf. 4:29.

4:38 καὶ εἶδον... ἠρημωμένον καὶ... βεβηλωμένον καὶ... κατακεκαυμένας καὶ... πεφυκότα... καὶ... καθῃρημένα: accus. and ptcs. after a vb. of percep. (Smyth §2110, §2112).

4:41 τότε ἐπέταξεν Ιουδας ἀνδράσιν πολεμεῖν τοὺς ἐν τῇ ἄκρᾳ: 1:33–35 reveals that "lawless"—i.e., Hellenizing—Jews held the citadel (ἡ ἄκρα) in Jerusalem since Antiochus IV's chief collector of tribute had visited the city. The same citadel would be occupied by a Syrian garrison until the time of Simon Maccabeus, the last remaining brother, cf. 1 Macc 13:49–52. Cf. Intro 11 above.

4:43 τοὺς λίθους τοῦ μιασμοῦ: here the gen. case approx. the noun construct chain in Hebrew. "The stones of defilement" means, more accurately, "the stones which had been defiled."

4:44 καὶ ἐβουλεύσαντο... τί αὐτῷ ποιήσωσιν: indir. quest.: "they deliberated... what they should do for it." The sec. tense ἐβουλεύσαντο may either retain the mood and tense of the dir. form or use the optv. instead (Smyth §2677), a rule little followed in Septuagintal Greek.

4:45 μήποτε γένηται αὐτοῖς εἰς ὄνειδος: the clause marker μήποτε signals a fear clause here—i.e., they destroyed the altar *"lest perchance* it become a reproach for them." For the Semitism that involves γίγνομαι, cf. 1:4; 1:33, 35; 2:11,43; 3:58. Perhaps αὐτοῖς represents the dat. of inter. (Smyth §1474).

4:46 μέχρι τοῦ παραγενηθῆναι προφήτην: it is diff. to know what to make of the prophet who would tell the Jews what to do with the stones stored in the convenient place on the Temple hill. Malachi was regarded as the last prophet (Mal 3:1–2; 4:5); though John Hyrcanus I (134–104 BC) and John the Baptist were believed to have prophetic gifts, such was not universally recognized.

4:47 λίθους ὁλοκλήρους κατὰ τὸν νόμον: cf. Ex 20:25 and Deut 27:5–6 for the injunction against hewn stones in the altar.

4:49 σκεύη ἅγια: even the vessels were to be "holy" to the Lord, cf. 1 Esdras 8:57; 2 Esdras 8:28.

4:49 τὴν λυχνίαν: for the Lamp Stand, cf. Ex 25:31; 26:35; 30:27; 31:8; 35:14; 40:4, 24; Num 4:9; 8:4; 1 Macc 1:21.

4:50 ἐθυμίασαν... καὶ ἐξῆψαν τοὺς λύχνους τοὺς ἐπὶ τῆς λυχνίας: according to Ex 30:7–8, Aaron was resp. for burning incense in lamps before the Lord, though this practice could have been borrowed from the Canaanites.

4:51 ἐπέθηκαν ἐπὶ τὴν τράπεζαν ἄρτους: cf. Ex 25:30 for the practice of setting the Bread of Presence before the Lord.

4:51 καὶ ἐξεπέτασαν τὰ καταπετάσματα: much is made of the veil in Exodus, Leviticus and Numbers.

4:52 τοῦ ὀγδόου καὶ τεσσαρακοστοῦ καὶ ἑκατοστοῦ ἔτους: "in the one hundred and forty-eighth year," i.e., 164 BC. Judas set the rededication exactly three years after the defilement of the Temple (cf. 1 Macc 1:54) and three and a half years after Antiochus' capture of Jerusalem (Dan 7:25; but cf. 2 Macc 10:3).

4:54 ἐν ᾠδαῖς καὶ κιθάραις καὶ κινύραις καὶ κυμβάλοις: The rededication, timed precisely to coincide with the earlier profanation (4:52), is accompanied by distinctive instruments of praise. Cf. ἐν ᾠδαῖς καὶ ἐν κινύραις καὶ ἐν νάβλαις καὶ ἐν τυμπάνοις καὶ ἐν κυμβάλοις καὶ ἐν αὐλοῖς, 2 Sam 6:5; ἐν ᾠδαῖς... καὶ ἐν κινύραις, Eccl 39:15.

4:55 καὶ ἔπεσεν πᾶς ὁ λαὸς ἐπὶ πρόσωπον: the people "fell on their faces" to the true God as had happened after the contest between Elijah and the prophets of Baal, cf. 1 Ki 18:39.

4:55 καὶ εὐλόγησαν εἰς οὐρανὸν: for the circumlocution "heaven" in the place of God's unutterable name, cf. 3:18.

4:56 ἔθυσαν θυσίαν σωτηρίου καὶ αἰνέσεως: for the "sacrifice of deliverance" (θυσία σωτηρίου), cf. Ex 24:5; 32:6; Lev 3:6; 7:29; Num 6:17; 7:17; Deut 27:7; Jos. 22:23; 2 Chr 33:16, etc.; for the "sacrifice of praise" (θυσία αἰνέσεως), cf. Lev 7:3; Ps 49:14, 23; 106:22; 115:8.

4:58 καὶ ἐγενήθη εὐφροσύνη μεγάλη ἐν τῷ λαῷ σφόδρα: for the "great joy" (εὐφροσύνη μεγάλη) cf. 2 Chr 20:27; 30:21, 26.

4:59 καὶ ἔστησεν... ἵνα ἄγωνται: the clause marker ἵνα sets off a pur. clause.

4:59 ἡμέρας ὀκτὼ ἀπὸ τῆς πέμπτης καὶ εἰκάδος τοῦ μηνὸς: the Hanukkah festival, celebrated for eight days (like Hezekiah's reconsecration of the Temple, 2 Chr 29:17), commemorates Judas Maccabeus' rededication of the Temple in 164 BC.

JOSEPHUS SELECTIONS

JOSEPHUS: INTRODUCTION

Josephus may have been born just after the crucifixion of Jesus and died sometime in the early second-century AD. He is one of the most important sources for the great war of the Jews against Rome (AD 66–73), and understood this event from both the Roman and the Jewish perspectives. He was loyal to his Jewish race and religion, and should be considered one of the greatest apologists of Judaism. Josephus' perspective was that of the Jewish aristocrat in a Roman world who desired to defend his nation and people at a time when many Romans—after the fall of Jerusalem in AD 70—looked askance at the history, laws, and seemingly peculiar customs of the Jews. His extant works are: *Bellum Judaicum* (*BJ* = Jewish War, written immediately after the war, originally in Aramaic); *Antiquitates Judaicae* (*Antiq* = Antiquities of the Jews, a history of the Jews from Creation to Josephus' own time, ca. AD 93–94); *Vita Josephi* (*Vita* = Life of Josephus, ca. AD 95); *Contra Apionem* (*Contra Ap* = Against Apion, an apologetic written against anti-Jewish propaganda).

BIRTH AND EDUCATION

> *Vita* 7–12: Josephus preserves a few details about his noble birth, father, education under an early teacher, and the three dominant sects of Judaism in his day. Like most members of the Judean upper class, Josephus lived in several worlds at once. Cf. Mason (2003, 39–41) for various inconsistencies in the account.

7 Ὁ πατὴρ δέ μου Ματθίας οὐ διὰ μόνην τὴν εὐγένειαν ἐπίσημος ἦν, ἀλλὰ πλέον διὰ τὴν δικαιοσύνην ἐπῃνεῖτο, γνωριμώτατος ὢν ἐν τῇ μεγίστῃ πόλει τῶν παρ' ἡμῖν τοῖς Ἱεροσολυμίταις. 8 ἐγὼ δὲ συμπαιδευόμενος ἀδελφῷ Ματθίᾳ τοὔνομα, γεγόνει γάρ μοι γνήσιος ἐξ ἀμφοῖν τῶν γονέων. εἰς μεγάλην παιδείας προύκοπτον ἐπίδοσιν μνήμῃ τε καὶ συνέσει δοκῶν διαφέρειν, 9 ἔτι δ' ἀντίπαις ὢν περὶ τεσσαρεσκαιδέκατον ἔτος διὰ τὸ φιλογράμματον ὑπὸ πάντων ἐπῃνούμην συνιόντων

ἀεὶ τῶν ἀρχιερέων καὶ τῶν τῆς πόλεως πρώτων ὑπὲρ τοῦ παρ' ἐμοῦ περὶ τῶν νομίμων ἀκριβέστερόν τι γνῶναι. 10 περὶ δὲ ἑκκαίδεκα ἔτη γενόμενος ἐβουλήθην τῶν παρ' ἡμῖν αἱρέσεων ἐμπειρίαν λαβεῖν· τρεῖς δ' εἰσὶν αὗται, Φαρισαίων μὲν ἡ πρώτη, καὶ Σαδδουκαίων ἡ δευτέρα, τρίτη δ' Ἐσσηνῶν, καθὼς πολλάκις εἴπομεν· οὕτως γὰρ ᾤμην αἱρήσεσθαι τὴν ἀρίστην, εἰ πάσας καταμάθοιμι. 11 σκληραγωγήσας οὖν ἐμαυτὸν καὶ πολλὰ πονηθεὶς τὰς τρεῖς διῆλθον, καὶ μηδὲ τὴν ἐντεῦθεν ἐμπειρίαν ἱκανὴν ἐμαυτῷ νομίσας εἶναι πυθόμενός τινα Βάννουν ὄνομα κατὰ τὴν ἐρημίαν διατρίβειν, ἐσθῆτι μὲν ἀπὸ δένδρων χρώμενον, τροφὴν δὲ τὴν αὐτομάτως φυομένην προσφερόμενον, ψυχρῷ δὲ ὕδατι τὴν ἡμέραν καὶ τὴν νύκτα πολλάκις λουόμενον πρὸς ἁγνείαν, ζηλωτὴς ἐγενόμην αὐτοῦ. 12 καὶ διατρίψας παρ' αὐτῷ ἐνιαυτοὺς τρεῖς καὶ τὴν ἐπιθυμίαν τελειώσας εἰς τὴν πόλιν ὑπέστρεφον. ἐννεακαιδέκατον δ' ἔτος ἔχων ἠρξάμην τε πολιτεύεσθαι τῇ Φαρισαίων αἱρέσει κατακολουθῶν, ἣ παραπλήσιός ἐστι τῇ παρ' Ἕλλησιν Στωϊκῇ λεγομένῃ.

PONTIUS PILATE

BJ 2.169–177: Judaea became a subordinate province of Rome on account of the mismanagement of Archelaus, a son of Herod the Great and Malthace (cf. Intro 21 above). Roman procurators (or prefects) mentioned in the NT are Pontius Pilate, Felix, and Festus (Intro 27). An inscription discovered at Caesarea Maritima in 1961 provides outside proof that Pilate possessed the title *prefect* (for the following reconstruction of the inscription and free translation cf. Vardaman 1962, 70; for a clear picture cf. Maier 1991, 147):

    ...]S TIBERIÉVM
    ...PON]TIVS PILATUS
    ..PRAEF]ECTVS IVDA[EA]E

    ...

"Tiberium [?of the Caesareans?] Pontius Pilate, Prefect of Judea [...has given]."

Josephus Text

The following selection reveals the tremendous tensions created when Pontius Pilate (prefect, AD 26-36) attempted to impose in Jerusalem military standards upon which likenesses of the emperor Tiberius appeared. Another uproar ensued when the populace discovered that Pilate intended to expend the sacred treasure (called *Corbonas*) upon the construction of an aqueduct. Parallel accounts of both incidents appear in *Antiq* 18.55-62.

Πεμφθεὶς δὲ εἰς Ἰουδαίαν ἐπίτροπος ὑπὸ Τιβερίου Πιλᾶτος νύκτωρ κεκαλυμμένας εἰς Ἱεροσόλυμα εἰσκομίζει τὰς Καίσαρος εἰκόνας, αἳ σημαῖαι καλοῦνται. 170 τοῦτο μεθ' ἡμέραν μεγίστην ταραχὴν ἤγειρεν Ἰουδαίοις· οἵ τε γὰρ ἐγγὺς πρὸς τὴν ὄψιν ἐξεπλάγησαν ὡς πεπατημένων αὐτοῖς τῶν νόμων, οὐδὲν γὰρ ἀξιοῦσιν ἐν τῇ πόλει δείκηλον τίθεσθαι, καὶ πρὸς τὴν ἀγανάκτησιν τῶν κατὰ τὴν πόλιν ἄθρους ὁ ἐκ τῆς χώρας λαὸς συνέρρευσεν. 171 ὁρμήσαντες δὲ πρὸς Πιλᾶτον εἰς Καισάρειαν ἱκέτευον ἐξενεγκεῖν ἐξ Ἱεροσολύμων τὰς σημαίας καὶ τηρεῖν αὐτοῖς τὰ πάτρια. Πιλάτου δὲ ἀρνουμένου περὶ τὴν οἰκίαν πρηνεῖς καταπεσόντες ἐπὶ πέντε ἡμέρας καὶ νύκτας ἴσας ἀκίνητοι διεκαρτέρουν.

172 Τῇ δ' ἑξῆς ὁ Πιλᾶτος καθίσας ἐπὶ βήματος ἐν τῷ μεγάλῳ σταδίῳ καὶ προσκαλεσάμενος τὸ πλῆθος ὡς ἀποκρίνασθαι δῆθεν αὐτοῖς θέλων, δίδωσιν τοῖς στρατιώταις σημεῖον ἐκ συντάγματος κυκλώσασθαι τοὺς Ἰουδαίους ἐν τοῖς ὅπλοις. 173 περιστάσης δὲ τριστιχεὶ τῆς φάλαγγος Ἰουδαῖοι μὲν ἀχανεῖς ἦσαν πρὸς τὸ ἀδόκητον τῆς ὄψεως, Πιλᾶτος δὲ κατακόψειν εἰπὼν αὐτούς, εἰ μὴ προσδέξαιντο τὰς Καίσαρος εἰκόνας, γυμνοῦν τὰ ξίφη τοῖς στρατιώταις ἔνευσεν. 174 οἱ δὲ Ἰουδαῖοι καθάπερ ἐκ συνθήματος ἀθρόοι καταπεσόντες καὶ τοὺς αὐχένας παρακλίναντες ἑτοίμους ἀναιρεῖν σφᾶς ἐβόων μᾶλλον ἢ τὸν νόμον παραβῆναι. ὑπερθαυμάσας δὲ ὁ Πιλᾶτος τὸ τῆς δεισιδαιμονίας ἄκρατον ἐκκομίσαι μὲν αὐτίκα τὰς σημαίας Ἱεροσολύμων κελεύει.

175 Μετὰ δὲ ταῦτα ταραχὴν ἑτέραν ἐκίνει τὸν ἱερὸν θησαυρόν, καλεῖται δὲ κορβωνᾶς, εἰς καταγωγὴν ὑδάτων ἐξαναλίσκων· κατῆγεν δὲ ἀπὸ τετρακοσίων σταδίων. πρὸς

τοῦτο τοῦ πλήθους ἀγανάκτησις ἦν, καὶ τοῦ Πιλάτου παρόντος εἰς Ἱεροσόλυμα περιστάντες τὸ βῆμα κατεβόων. 176 ὁ δέ, προῄδει γὰρ αὐτῶν τὴν ταραχήν, τῷ πλήθει τοὺς στρατιώτας ἐνόπλους ἐσθῆσιν ἰδιωτικαῖς κεκαλυμμένους ἐγκαταμίξας καὶ ξίφει μὲν χρήσασθαι κωλύσας, ξύλοις δὲ παίειν τοὺς κεκραγότας ἐγκελευσάμενος σύνθημα δίδωσιν ἀπὸ τοῦ βήματος. 177 τυπτόμενοι δὲ οἱ Ἰουδαῖοι πολλοὶ μὲν ὑπὸ τῶν πληγῶν, πολλοὶ δὲ ὑπὸ σφῶν αὐτῶν ἐν τῇ φυγῇ καταπατηθέντες ἀπώλοντο. πρὸς δὲ τὴν συμφορὰν τῶν ἀνῃρημένων καταπλαγὲν τὸ πλῆθος ἐσιώπησεν.

PETRONIUS

> *BJ* 2.184-87, 192-203: Pilate's policies were but a prelude to more extreme measures envisioned by the emperor Gaius ("Caligula," AD 37–41) who desired that statues of himself be set up in the Temple at Jerusalem. Gaius was apparently influenced by a certain Greek of Alexandria named Apion who, some time before Gaius' decree, told the emperor that all subject peoples, save the Jews, dedicate altars and temples to Gaius and regard him as a god (*Antiq* 18.257; cf. Cohen 1987, 47). The decree would no doubt have been enacted at Jerusalem also were it not for the heroism of Publius Petronius, Gaius' legate in Syria, who came to favor the position of the Jews against Gaius and helped the Jews to evade Gaius' decree. For parallel accounts of the incident cf. Joseph. *Antiq* 18.261–309; Philo *Leg.* 188, 207–208; and Tac. *Hist.* 5.9.

Γάιος δὲ Καῖσαρ ἐπὶ τοσοῦτον ἐξύβρισεν εἰς τὴν τύχην, ὥστε θεὸν ἑαυτὸν καὶ δοκεῖν βούλεσθαι καὶ καλεῖσθαι τῶν τε εὐγενεστάτων ἀνδρῶν ἀκροτομῆσαι τὴν πατρίδα, ἐκτεῖναι δὲ τὴν ἀσέβειαν καὶ ἐπὶ Ἰουδαίαν. 185 Πετρώνιον μὲν οὖν μετὰ στρατιᾶς ἐπὶ Ἱεροσολύμων ἔπεμψεν ἐγκαθιδρύσοντα τῷ ναῷ τοὺς ἀνδριάντας αὐτοῦ, προστάξας, εἰ μὴ δέχοιντο Ἰουδαῖοι, τούς τε κωλύοντας ἀνελεῖν καὶ πᾶν τὸ λοιπὸν ἔθνος ἐξανδραποδίσασθαι. θεῷ δ' ἄρα τῶν προσταγμάτων ἔμελεν. 186 καὶ Πετρώνιος μὲν σὺν τρισὶ τάγμασι καὶ πολλοῖς ἐκ τῆς

Συρίας συμμάχοις εἰς τὴν Ἰουδαίαν ἤλαυνεν ἐκ τῆς Ἀντιοχείας, 187 Ἰουδαίων δὲ οἱ μὲν ἠπίστουν ἐπὶ ταῖς τοῦ πολέμου φήμαις, οἱ δὲ πιστεύοντες ἦσαν ἐν ἀμηχάνῳ πρὸς τὴν ἄμυναν· ταχὺ δ' ἐχώρει διὰ πάντων τὸ δέος ἤδη παρούσης εἰς Πτολεμαΐδα τῆς στρατιᾶς...

192 Ἰουδαῖοι δὲ μετὰ γυναικῶν καὶ τέκνων ἀθροισθέντες εἰς τὸ πεδίον τὸ πρὸς Πτολεμαΐδι καθικέτευον τὸν Πετρώνιον ὑπὲρ τῶν πατρίων νόμων πρῶτον, ἔπειτα ὑπὲρ αὑτῶν. ὁ δὲ πρός τε τὸ πλῆθος καὶ τὰς δεήσεις ἐνδοὺς τοὺς μὲν ἀνδριάντας καὶ τὰς στρατιὰς ἐν Πτολεμαΐδι λείπει, 193 προελθὼν δὲ εἰς τὴν Γαλιλαίαν καὶ συγκαλέσας τό τε πλῆθος καὶ τοὺς γνωρίμους πάντας εἰς Τιβεριάδα τήν τε Ῥωμαίων διεξῄει δύναμιν καὶ τὰς Καίσαρος ἀπειλάς, ἔτι δὲ τὴν ἀξίωσιν ἀπέφαινεν ἀγνώμονα· 194 πάντων γὰρ τῶν ὑποτεταγμένων ἐθνῶν κατὰ πόλιν συγκαθιδρυκότων τοῖς ἄλλοις θεοῖς καὶ τὰς Καίσαρος εἰκόνας, τὸ μόνους ἐκείνους ἀντιτάσσεσθαι πρὸς τοῦτο σχεδὸν ἀφισταμένων εἶναι καὶ μεθ' ὕβρεως.

195 Τῶν δὲ τὸν νόμον καὶ τὸ πάτριον ἔθος προτεινομένων καὶ ὡς οὐδὲ θεοῦ τι δείκηλον, οὐχ ὅπως ἀνδρός, οὐ κατὰ τὸν ναὸν μόνον ἀλλ' οὐδὲ ἐν εἰκαίῳ τινὶ τόπῳ τῆς χώρας θέσθαι θεμιτὸν εἴη, ὑπολαβὼν ὁ Πετρώνιος "ἀλλὰ μὴν καὶ ἐμοὶ φυλακτέος ὁ τοὐμοῦ δεσπότου νόμος", ἔφη· "παραβὰς γὰρ αὐτὸν καὶ φεισάμενος ὑμῶν ἀπολοῦμαι δικαίως. πολεμήσει δ' ὑμᾶς ὁ πέμψας με καὶ οὐκ ἐγώ· καὶ γὰρ αὐτός, ὥσπερ ὑμεῖς, ἐπιτάσσομαι." 196 πρὸς ταῦτα τὸ πλῆθος πάντ' ἐβόα πρὸ τοῦ νόμου πάσχειν ἑτοίμως ἔχειν. καταστείλας δ' αὐτῶν ὁ Πετρώνιος τὴν βοήν, "πολεμήσετε, εἶπεν, ἄρα Καίσαρι;" 197 καὶ Ἰουδαῖοι περὶ μὲν Καίσαρος καὶ τοῦ δήμου τῶν Ῥωμαίων δὶς τῆς ἡμέρας θύειν ἔφασαν, εἰ δὲ βούλεται τὰς εἰκόνας ἐγκαθιδρύειν, πρότερον αὐτὸν δεῖν ἅπαν τὸ Ἰουδαίων ἔθνος προθύσασθαι· παρέχειν δὲ σφᾶς αὐτοὺς ἑτοίμους εἰς τὴν σφαγὴν ἅμα τέκνοις καὶ γυναιξίν. 198 ἐπὶ τούτοις θαῦμα καὶ οἶκτος εἰσῄει τὸν Πετρώνιον τῆς τε ἀνυπερβλήτου θρησκείας τῶν ἀνδρῶν καὶ τοῦ πρὸς θάνατον ἑτοίμου παραστήματος. καὶ τότε μὲν ἄπρακτοι διελύθησαν.

199 Ταῖς δ' ἑξῆς ἀθρόους τε τοὺς δυνατοὺς κατ' ἰδίαν καὶ τὸ πλῆθος ἐν κοινῷ συλλέγων ποτὲ μὲν παρεκάλει, ποτὲ δὲ συνεβούλευεν, τὸ πλέον μέντοι διηπείλει τήν τε Ῥωμαίων ἐπανατεινόμενος ἰσχὺν καὶ τοὺς Γαΐου θυμοὺς τήν τε ἰδίαν πρὸς τούτοις ἀνάγκην. 200 πρὸς δὲ μηδεμίαν πεῖραν ἐνδιδόντων ὡς ἑώρα καὶ τὴν χώραν κινδυνεύουσαν ἄσπορον μεῖναι, κατὰ γὰρ ὥραν σπόρου πεντήκοντα ἡμέρας ἀργὰ προσδιέτριβεν αὐτῷ τὰ πλήθη, τελευταῖον ἀθροίσας αὐτοὺς καὶ "παρακινδυνευτέον ἐμοὶ μᾶλλον," εἰπών, 201 "ἢ γὰρ τοῦ θεοῦ συνεργοῦντος πείσας Καίσαρα σωθήσομαι μεθ' ὑμῶν ἡδέως ἢ παροξυνθέντος ὑπὲρ τοσούτων ἑτοίμως ἐπιδώσω τὴν ἐμαυτοῦ ψυχήν", διαφῆκεν τὸ πλῆθος πολλὰ κατευχομένων αὐτῷ, καὶ παραλαβὼν τὴν στρατιὰν ἐκ τῆς Πτολεμαΐδος ὑπέστρεψεν εἰς τὴν Ἀντιόχειαν. 202 ἔνθεν εὐθέως ἐπέστελλεν Καίσαρι τήν τε ἐμβολὴν τὴν εἰς Ἰουδαίαν ἑαυτοῦ καὶ τὰς ἱκεσίας τοῦ ἔθνους, ὅτι τε, εἰ μὴ βούλεται πρὸς τοῖς ἀνδράσιν καὶ τὴν χώραν ἀπολέσαι, δέοι φυλάττειν τε αὐτοὺς τὸν νόμον καὶ παριέναι τὸ πρόσταγμα. 203 ταύταις ταῖς ἐπιστολαῖς οὐ σφόδρα μετρίως ἀντέγραψεν ὁ Γάιος, ἀπειλῶν Πετρωνίῳ θάνατον, ὅτι τῶν προσταγμάτων αὐτοῦ βραδὺς ὑπηρέτης ἐγίνετο. ἀλλὰ τοὺς μὲν τούτων γραμματοφόρους συνέβη χειμασθῆναι τρεῖς μῆνας ἐν τῇ θαλάσσῃ, τὸν δὲ Γαΐου θάνατον ἄλλοι καταγγέλλοντες εὐπλόουν. ἔφθη γοῦν τὰς περὶ τούτων Πετρώνιος λαβὼν ἐπιστολὰς ἑπτὰ καὶ εἴκοσιν ἡμέραις ἢ τὰς καθ' ἑαυτοῦ.

Capture of Josephus

BJ 3.392–408: though opposed to fighting, Josephus assumed command of a Jewish army and, according to his own account, fought bravely against the Romans in Jotapata in Galilee (e.g., *BJ* 3.204–206, 222–223, 240). Ultimately Jotapata fell and Josephus hid in a cave with forty holdouts who, drawing lots, put each other to death rather than submit to the Romans. Josephus drew the final lot, and he and the second-to-the-last survivor "decided not to follow through with the suicide pact" (Huntsman 1996–97, 370), turning themselves in to the Romans. Hauled before Vespasian, Josephus received the clemency of Titus who pleaded with Vespasian for the prisoner's life. Something else that assured Josephus' safety was the latter's prediction that Vespasian and Titus would both become emperors one day and so govern the entire Roman world (*BJ* 3.401; cf. Huntsman 1996–97, 397 n. 30, on pgs. 401–402). The town of Jotapata (modern Yodefat) was totally destroyed by the Romans, though a new settlement sprang up afterwards on a nearby plateau. Excavations have recovered arrowheads, ballista stones, a rolling stone, the shaft of an iron spear, and portions of a siege ramp from the battle (Chancey and Porter 2001, 184).

Ὁ μὲν οὖν οὕτως τόν τε Ῥωμαίων καὶ τὸν οἰκείων διαφυγὼν πόλεμον ἐπὶ Οὐεσπασιανὸν ἤγετο ὑπὸ [τοῦ] Νικάνορος. 393 οἱ δὲ Ῥωμαῖοι πάντες ἐπὶ θέαν αὐτοῦ συνέτρεχον, καὶ τοῦ πλήθους συνθλιβομένου περὶ τῷ στρατηγῷ θόρυβος ἦν ποικίλος, τῶν μὲν γεγηθότων ἐπὶ τῷ ληφθέντι, τῶν δ' ἀπειλούντων, τῶν δ' ἐγγύθεν ἰδεῖν βιαζομένων. 394 καὶ οἱ μὲν πόρρωθεν κολάζειν ἐβόων τὸν πολέμιον, τῶν δὲ πλησίον ἀνάμνησις αὐτοῦ τῶν ἔργων εἰσῄει καὶ πρὸς τὴν μεταβολὴν θάμβος, τῶν τε ἡγεμόνων οὐδεὶς ἦν, 395 ὃς εἰ καὶ πρότερον ὠργίζετο, τότε πρὸς τὴν ὄψιν οὐκ ἐνέδωκεν αὐτοῦ. 396 μάλιστα δὲ τὸν Τίτον ἐξαιρέτως τό τε καρτερικὸν ἐν ταῖς συμφοραῖς ᾕρει τοῦ Ἰωσήπου καὶ πρὸς τὴν ἡλικίαν ἔλεος, ἀναμιμνησκομένῳ τε τὸν πάλαι μαχόμενον καὶ τὸν ἐν χερσὶν ἐχθρῶν ἄρτι κείμενον ὁρῶντι παρῆν [δὲ] νοεῖν, ὅσον δύναται τύχη, καὶ ὡς ὀξεῖα μὲν πολέμου ῥοπή, τῶν δ' ἀνθρωπίνων οὐδὲν βέβαιον· 397 παρὸ καὶ τότε συνδιέθηκεν μὲν πλείστους ἑαυτῷ καὶ πρὸς οἶκτον τοῦ Ἰωσήπου, πλείστη δ' αὐτῷ καὶ παρὰ τῷ πατρὶ μοῖρα σωτηρίας ἐγένετο. 398 ὁ μέντοι Οὐεσπασιανὸς φρουρεῖν αὐτὸν μετὰ πάσης ἀσφαλείας προσέταττεν ὡς ἀναπέμψων αὐτίκα Νέρωνι.

399 Τοῦτο ἀκούσας ὁ Ἰώσηπος μόνῳ τι διαλεχθῆναι θέλειν ἔλεγεν αὐτῷ. μεταστησαμένου δ' ἐκείνου πλὴν τοῦ παιδὸς Τίτου καὶ δυοῖν φίλων τοὺς ἄλλους ἅπαντας 400 "σὺ μέν, ἔφη, Οὐεσπασιανέ, νομίζεις αἰχμάλωτον αὐτὸ μόνον εἰληφέναι Ἰώσηπον, ἐγὼ δὲ ἄγγελος ἥκω σοι μειζόνων. μὴ γὰρ ὑπὸ θεοῦ προπεμπόμενος ᾔδειν τὸν Ἰουδαίων νόμον, καὶ πῶς

στρατηγοῖς ἀποθνήσκειν πρέπει. 401 Νέρωνί με πέμπεις· τί γάρ; οἱ μετὰ Νέρωνα μέχρι σοῦ διάδοχοι μενοῦσιν. σὺ Καῖσαρ, Οὐεσπασιανέ, καὶ αὐτοκράτωρ, σὺ καὶ παῖς ὁ σὸς οὗτος. 402 δέσμει δέ με νῦν ἀσφαλέστερον, καὶ τήρει σεαυτῷ· δεσπότης μὲν γὰρ οὐ μόνον ἐμοῦ σὺ Καῖσαρ, ἀλλὰ καὶ γῆς καὶ θαλάττης καὶ παντὸς ἀνθρώπων γένους, ἐγὼ δὲ ἐπὶ τιμωρίαν δέομαι φρουρᾶς μείζονος, εἰ κατασχεδιάζω καὶ θεοῦ." 403 ταῦτ' εἰπόντος παραχρῆμα μὲν Οὐεσπασιανὸς ἀπιστεῖν ἐδόκει καὶ τὸν Ἰώσηπον ὑπελάμβανεν ταῦτα περὶ σωτηρίας πανουργεῖν, 404 κατὰ μικρὸν δὲ εἰς πίστιν ὑπήγετο τοῦ θεοῦ διεγείροντος αὐτὸν εἰς τὴν ἡγεμονίαν ἤδη καὶ τὰ σκῆπτρα δι' ἑτέρων σημείων προδεικνύντος. 405 ἀτρεκῆ δὲ τὸν Ἰώσηπον καὶ ἐν ἄλλοις κατελάμβανεν· τῶν γὰρ τοῖς ἀπορρήτοις παρατυχόντων φίλων ὁ ἕτερος θαυμάζειν ἔφη πῶς οὔτε τοῖς ἐπὶ τῶν Ἰωταπάτων περὶ ἁλώσεως, οὔθ' ἑαυτῷ προμαντεύσαιτο αἰχμαλωσίαν, εἰ μὴ ταῦτα λῆρος εἴη διακρουομένου τὰς ἐπ' αὐτὸν ὀργάς. 406 ὁ δὲ Ἰώσηπος καὶ τοῖς Ἰωταπατηνοῖς ὅτι μετὰ τεσσαρακοστὴν ἑβδόμην ἡμέραν ἁλώσονται προειπεῖν ἔφη, καὶ ὅτι πρὸς Ῥωμαίων αὐτὸς ζωγρηθήσεται. 407 ταῦτα παρὰ τῶν αἰχμαλώτων κατ' ἰδίαν ὁ Οὐεσπασιανὸς ἐκπυθόμενος ὡς εὕρισκεν ἀληθῆ, οὕτω πιστεύειν περὶ τῶν κατ' αὐτὸν ἤρκτο. 408 φρουρᾶς μὲν οὖν καὶ δεσμῶν οὐκ ἀνίει τὸν Ἰώσηπον, ἐδωρεῖτο δ' ἐσθῆτι καὶ τοῖς ἄλλοις κειμηλίοις φιλοφρονούμενός τε καὶ περιέπων διετέλει τὰ πολλὰ Τίτου τῇ τιμῇ συνεργοῦντος.

JOHN THE BAPTIST

Antiq 18.116–119: sometimes Josephus offers interesting tidbits on well-known persons presented differently in the NT. The reference to John the Baptist arises from Josephus' recollection of a border war that occurred between Herod Antipas and King Aretas IV of Petra (Nabataea). Most accept the passage as authentic, though the many textual problems are best resolved if one supposes that Christian scribes were long at work on the passage after Josephus wrote it in the late first-century AD. The biggest difference between Josephus and the gospel accounts appears to be that the historian regarded

John as a famous Jewish teacher in his own right, not as a figure of Christian tradition (Mason 2003, 217).

Τισὶ δὲ τῶν Ἰουδαίων ἐδόκει ὀλωλέναι τὸν Ἡρώδου στρατὸν ὑπὸ τοῦ θεοῦ καὶ μάλα δικαίως τινυμένου κατὰ ποινὴν Ἰωάννου τοῦ ἐπικαλουμένου βαπτιστοῦ. 117 κτείνει γὰρ δὴ τοῦτον Ἡρώδης ἀγαθὸν ἄνδρα καὶ τοῖς Ἰουδαίοις κελεύοντα ἀρετὴν ἐπασκοῦσιν καὶ τὰ πρὸς ἀλλήλους δικαιοσύνῃ καὶ πρὸς τὸν θεὸν εὐσεβείᾳ χρωμένοις βαπτισμῷ συνιέναι· οὕτω γὰρ δὴ καὶ τὴν βάπτισιν ἀποδεκτὴν αὐτῷ φανεῖσθαι μὴ ἐπί τινων ἁμαρτάδων παραιτήσει χρωμένων, ἀλλ᾽ ἐφ᾽ ἁγνείᾳ τοῦ σώματος, ἅτε δὴ καὶ τῆς ψυχῆς δικαιοσύνῃ προεκκεκαθαρμένης. 118 καὶ τῶν ἄλλων συστρεφομένων, καὶ γὰρ ἥσθησαν ἐπὶ πλεῖστον τῇ ἀκροάσει τῶν λόγων, δείσας Ἡρώδης τὸ ἐπὶ τοσόνδε πιθανὸν αὐτοῦ τοῖς ἀνθρώποις μὴ ἐπὶ ἀποστάσει τινὶ φέροι, πάντα γὰρ ἐῴκεσαν συμβουλῇ τῇ ἐκείνου πράξοντες, πολὺ κρεῖττον ἡγεῖται πρίν τι νεώτερον ἐξ αὐτοῦ γενέσθαι προλαβὼν ἀνελεῖν τοῦ μεταβολῆς γενομένης [μὴ] εἰς πράγματα ἐμπεσὼν μετανοεῖν. 119 καὶ ὁ μὲν ὑποψίᾳ τῇ Ἡρώδου δέσμιος εἰς τὸν Μαχαιροῦντα πεμφθεὶς τὸ προειρημένον φρούριον ταύτῃ κτίννυται. τοῖς δὲ Ἰουδαίοις δόξαν ἐπὶ τιμωρίᾳ τῇ ἐκείνου τὸν ὄλεθρον ἐπὶ τῷ στρατεύματι γενέσθαι τοῦ θεοῦ κακῶσαι Ἡρώδην θέλοντος.

JESUS

Antiq 18.63–64. Some have referred to Josephus' remarks about Jesus (the so-called *testimonium flavianum*) as "the most famous passage in Josephus" (so Maier 1988, 265 n.). Many suspect, however, that the *testimonium* represents the work of a much later interpolator or interpolators (cf. Euseb. *Hist. Eccles.* 1.11.7–8; *Dem. Ev.* 3.5.105–106) who either fabricated the material outright, or at least altered a more judicious account (Birdsall 1985; Olson 1999; for countless text variants in the *testimonium* and what they mean, cf. Whealey 2007). The *testimonium* presents Jesus in the best possible light, though it seems unlikely that Josephus was himself a Christian. Most commentators hold to a middle position "between authenticity and inauthenticity, claiming that Josephus wrote *something* about Jesus that was subsequently edited by Christian copyists" (Mason 2003, 235; orig. emphasis).

[63 Γίνεται δὲ κατὰ τοῦτον τὸν χρόνον Ἰησοῦς σοφὸς ἀνήρ, εἴγε ἄνδρα αὐτὸν λέγειν χρή· ἦν γὰρ παραδόξων ἔργων ποιητής, διδάσκαλος ἀνθρώπων τῶν ἡδονῇ τἀληθῆ δεχομένων, καὶ πολλοὺς μὲν Ἰουδαίους, πολλοὺς δὲ καὶ τοῦ Ἑλληνικοῦ ἐπηγάγετο· ὁ χριστὸς οὗτος ἦν. 64 καὶ αὐτὸν ἐνδείξει τῶν πρώτων ἀνδρῶν παρ' ἡμῖν σταυρῷ ἐπιτετιμηκότος Πιλάτου οὐκ ἐπαύσαντο οἱ τὸ πρῶτον ἀγαπήσαντες· ἐφάνη γὰρ αὐτοῖς τρίτην ἔχων ἡμέραν πάλιν ζῶν τῶν θείων προφητῶν ταῦτά τε καὶ ἄλλα μυρία περὶ αὐτοῦ θαυμάσια εἰρηκότων. εἰς ἔτι τε νῦν τῶν Χριστιανῶν ἀπὸ τοῦδε ὠνομασμένον οὐκ ἐπέλιπε τὸ φῦλον.]

JAMES, BROTHER OF JESUS

Antiq 20.200: the following shorter allusion to Jesus consists of a passing reference to James, the brother of Jesus, whom a high priest Ananus accused of transgressing the law. If the passage is authentic, the claim could be made that Josephus at least recognized Jesus to be a figure in history (so observed the following witnesses: Orig. *Comm. Matth.* 10.17; *Contra Cels.* 1.47; 2.13; Euseb. *Hist. Eccles.* 2.23.22). This passage, unlike the preceding example, is "typically Josephan" and "fits into both the larger and smaller contexts of *Ant[iq.]* 20" (Mason 2003, 239). It offers a perspective outside the NT that "confirms James's central role in first-generation Christianity" (Mason 2003, 248).

200 Ἅτε δὴ οὖν τοιοῦτος ὢν ὁ Ἄνανος, νομίσας ἔχειν καιρὸν ἐπιτήδειον διὰ τὸ τεθνάναι μὲν Φῆστον, Ἀλβῖνον δ' ἔτι κατὰ τὴν ὁδὸν ὑπάρχειν, καθίζει συνέδριον κριτῶν καὶ παραγαγὼν εἰς αὐτὸ τὸν ἀδελφὸν Ἰησοῦ τοῦ λεγομένου Χριστοῦ, Ἰάκωβος ὄνομα αὐτῷ, καί τινας ἑτέρους, ὡς παρανομησάντων κατηγορίαν ποιησάμενος παρέδωκε λευσθησομένους.

Josephus: The Destruction of Jerusalem

Josephus was an eyewitness of many events he describes, whether as a general for the Jews or as collaborator for the Romans (cf. Intro 36 above). Following his capture and rescue by Titus (*BJ* 3.392–408), the Romans relied on Josephus as an intermediary between themselves and the Jews, many of whom were predisposed toward the Romans. The following selections focus upon those events that lead up to, and include, the destruction of Jerusalem by the Romans in AD 70. In this struggle Josephus, a Jew, clearly favors the Roman side throughout, though he forthrightly acknowledges certain gruesome atrocities that were inflicted upon his countrymen by the Romans. The Romans, however, were not the problem, in Josephus' opinion; the great disasters that had befallen Jerusalem were caused solely by rancorous Zealots whose self-destructive infighting threatened all Jews and indeed the future of Judaism itself. Josephus' graphic account provides a fit backdrop against which to view such predictions as, e.g., Mt 23:38; 24:2; Mk 13:2; Lk 19:40–44; 21:6, 20–24. Later Christians regarded the Roman victory as Jesus' vindication over the Jews who had rejected him (cf. Schreckenberg 1987, 319).

Three Factions

> *BJ* 5.1–10: Titus led an army from Egypt to Caesarea Maritima to organize Roman forces against the Zealots who had already taken possession of the Temple complex in Jerusalem and were wreaking havoc. The leaders of the three rival factions were Eleazar, John, and Simon. Eleazar took possession of the Temple's inner courts, John of the Temple's outer courts, and Simon of large portions of both Upper and Lower Jerusalem. The three factions attacked each other so ferociously that Josephus suggests that the Zealots were serving the Romans on purpose "...by destroying what the city had provided against a siege and severing the sinews of their own strength" (*BJ* 5.24 LCL).

Ὁ μὲν Τίτος ὃν προειρήκαμεν τρόπον διοδεύσας τὴν ὑπὲρ Αἰγύπτου μέχρι Συρίας ἐρημίαν εἰς Καισάρειαν παρῆν ταύτῃ διεγνωκὼς προσυντάξασθαι τὰς δυνάμεις. 2 ἔτι δ' αὐτοῦ κατὰ τὴν Ἀλεξάνδρειαν συγκαθισταμένου τῷ πατρὶ τὴν ἡγεμονίαν νέον αὐτοῖς ἐγκεχειρισμένην ὑπὸ τοῦ θεοῦ συνέβη καὶ τὴν ἐν [τοῖς] Ἱεροσολύμοις στάσιν ἀνακμάσασαν τριμερῆ γενέσθαι καὶ καθ' αὑτοῦ θάτερον ἐπιστρέψαι μέρος, ὅπερ ἄν τις ὡς ἐν κακοῖς ἀγαθὸν εἴποι καὶ δίκης ἔργον. 3 ἡ μὲν γὰρ κατὰ τοῦ δήμου τῶν ζηλωτῶν ἐπίθεσις, ἥπερ κατῆρξεν ἁλώσεως τῇ πόλει, προδεδήλωται μετὰ ἀκριβείας ὅθεν τε ἔφυ καὶ πρὸς ὅσον κακῶν ηὐξήθη· 4 ταύτην δ' οὐκ ἂν ἁμάρτοι τις εἰπὼν στάσει στάσιν ἐγγενέσθαι, καὶ καθάπερ θηρίον λυσσῆσαν ἐνδείᾳ τῶν ἔξωθεν ἐπὶ τὰς ἰδίας ἤδη σάρκας ὁρμᾷ, 5 οὕτως Ἐλεάζαρος ὁ τοῦ Σίμωνος, ὃς δὴ καὶ τὰ πρῶτα τοῦ δήμου τοὺς ζηλωτὰς ἀπέστησεν εἰς τὸ τέμενος ὡς ἀγανακτῶν δῆθεν ἐπὶ τοῖς ὁσημέραι τῷ Ἰωάννῃ τολμωμένοις, οὐ γὰρ ἀνεπαύετο φονῶν οὗτος, τὸ δ' ἀληθὲς αὐτοῦ μεταγενεστέρῳ τυράννῳ μὴ φέρων ὑποτετάχθαι, 6 πόθῳ τῶν ὅλων καὶ δυναστείας ἰδίας ἐπιθυμίᾳ διίσταται, παραλαβὼν Ἰούδην τε τὸν Χέλικα καὶ Σίμωνα τὸν Ἐσρῶνος τῶν δυνατῶν, πρὸς οἷς Ἐζεκίας Χωβαρεῖ παῖς οὐκ ἄσημος. 7 καθ' ἕκαστον δὲ οὐκ ὀλίγοι τῶν ζηλωτῶν ἠκολούθησαν, καὶ καταλαβόμενοι τὸν ἐνδότερον τοῦ νεὼ περίβολον ὑπὲρ τὰς ἱερὰς πύλας ἐπὶ τῶν ἁγίων μετώπων τίθενται τὰ ὅπλα. 8 πλήρεις μὲν οὖν ἐπιτηδείων ὄντες ἐθάρρουν, καὶ γὰρ ἀφθονία τῶν ἱερῶν ἐγίνετο πραγμάτων τοῖς γε μηδὲν ἀσεβὲς ἡγουμένοις, ὀλιγότητι δὲ τῇ κατὰ σφᾶς ὀρρωδοῦντες ἐγκαθήμενοι τὰ πολλὰ κατὰ χώραν ἔμενον. 9 ὁ δὲ Ἰωάννης ὅσον ἀνδρῶν ὑπερεῖχε πλήθει, τοσοῦτον ἐλείπετο τῷ τόπῳ καὶ κατὰ κορυφὴν ἔχων τοὺς πολεμίους οὔτ' ἀδεεῖς ἐποιεῖτο τὰς προσβολὰς οὔτε δι' ὀργὴν ἠρέμει, 10 κακούμενος δὲ πλέον ἤπερ διατιθεὶς τοὺς περὶ τὸν Ἐλεάζαρον ὅμως οὐκ ἀνίει, συνεχεῖς δ' ἐκδρομαὶ καὶ βελῶν ἀφέσεις ἐγίνοντο, καὶ φόνοις ἐμιαίνετο πανταχοῦ τὸ ἱερόν.

Josephus' Speech

BJ 5.375–400: As Jewish factions skirmished among themselves in and around the Temple, the Romans established a position on the outskirts of the city, mounted a formidable siege, and eventually took back the city by surmounting three defensive walls. When all the walls had been captured save one, Titus delegated Josephus to parley with the besieged in their native tongue, supposing that the hearers might yield to the advice of a fellow-countryman (5.361). What follows is a major address (5.362–419) wherein Josephus— keeping out of the range of missiles occasionally hurled at him from the parapets—implores his fellow Jews to spare themselves and not succumb to self-destruction. Josephus argues that, in any event, the Romans could not be defeated, nor had the Jews ever defeated foreigners in the past by fighting; it was God, not the Jews, who had performed miraculous rescues in history on behalf of a people whom He loved.

Ταῦτα τὸν Ἰώσηπον παραινοῦντα πολλοὶ μὲν ἔσκωπτον ἀπὸ τοῦ τείχους, πολλοὶ δ' ἐβλασφήμουν, ἔνιοι δ' ἔβαλλον. ὁ δ' ὡς ταῖς φανεραῖς οὐκ ἔπειθε συμβουλίαις, ἐπὶ τὰς ὁμοφύλους μετέβαινεν ἱστορίας, 376 "ἆ δειλοί," βοῶν, "καὶ τῶν ἰδίων ἀμνήμονες συμμάχων, ὅπλοις καὶ χερσὶ πολεμεῖτε Ῥωμαίοις; τίνα γὰρ ἄλλον οὕτως ἐνικήσαμεν; 377 πότε δ' οὐ θεὸς ὁ κτίσας ἂν ἀδικῶνται Ἰουδαίων ἔκδικος; οὐκ ἐπιστραφέντες ὄψεσθε πόθεν ὁρμώμενοι μάχεσθε καὶ πηλίκον ἐμιάνατε σύμμαχον; οὐκ ἀναμνήσεσθε πατέρων ἔργα δαιμόνια, καὶ τὸν ἅγιον τόνδε χῶρον ἡλίκους ἡμῖν πάλαι πολέμους καθεῖλεν; 378 ἐγὼ μὲν φρίττω τὰ ἔργα τοῦ θεοῦ λέγων εἰς ἀναξίους ἀκοάς· ἀκούετε δ' ὅμως, ἵνα γνῶτε μὴ μόνον Ῥωμαίοις πολεμοῦντες ἀλλὰ καὶ τῷ θεῷ.

379 βασιλεὺς ὁ τότε Νεχαὼς Αἰγυπτίων, ὁ δ' αὐτὸς ἐκαλεῖτο καὶ Φαραώ, μυρίᾳ χειρὶ καταβὰς ἥρπασε Σάρραν βασιλίδα, τὴν μητέρα τοῦ γένους ἡμῶν. 380 τί οὖν ὁ ταύτης ἀνὴρ Ἀβραάμ, προπάτωρ δὲ ἡμέτερος; ἆρα τὸν ὑβριστὴν

ἠμύνατο τοῖς ὅπλοις, καίτοι ὀκτωκαίδεκα μὲν καὶ τριακοσίους ὑπάρχους ἔχων, δύναμιν δὲ ἐφ' ἑκάστῳ τούτων ἄπειρον; ἢ αὐτοὺς μὲν ἐρημίαν ἡγήσατο μὴ συμπαρόντος θεοῦ, καθαρὰς δ' ἀνατείνας τὰς χεῖρας εἰς ὃν νῦν ἐμιάνατε χῶρον ὑμεῖς τὸν ἀνίκητον αὐτῷ βοηθὸν ἐστρατολόγησεν; 381 οὐ μετὰ μίαν ἑσπέραν ἄχραντος μὲν ἡ βασίλισσα ἀνεπέμφθη πρὸς τὸν ἄνδρα, προσκυνῶν δὲ τὸν ὑφ' ὑμῶν αἱμαχθέντα χῶρον ὁμοφύλῳ φόνῳ καὶ τρέμων ἀπὸ τῶν ἐν νυκτὶ φαντασμάτων ἔφευγεν ὁ Αἰγύπτιος, ἀργύρῳ δὲ καὶ χρυσῷ τοὺς θεοφιλεῖς Ἑβραίους ἐδωρεῖτο;382 εἴπω τὴν εἰς Αἴγυπτον μετοικίαν τῶν πατέρων; οὐ τυραννούμενοι μὲν καὶ βασιλεῦσιν ἀλλοφύλοις ὑποπεπτωκότες τετρακοσίοις ἔτεσι παρὸν ὅπλοις ἀμύνεσθαι καὶ χερσὶ σφᾶς αὐτοὺς ἐπέτρεψαν τῷ θεῷ; 383 τίς οὐκ οἶδεν τὴν παντὸς θηρίου καταπλησθεῖσαν Αἴγυπτον καὶ πάσῃ φθαρεῖσαν νόσῳ, τὴν ἄκαρπον [γῆν], τὸν ἐπιλείποντα Νεῖλον, τὰς ἐπαλλήλους δέκα πληγάς, τοὺς διὰ ταῦτα μετὰ φρουρᾶς προπεμπομένους πατέρας ἡμῶν ἀναιμάκτους ἀκινδύνους, οὓς ὁ θεὸς αὐτῷ νεωκόρους ἦγεν;

384 ἀλλὰ τὴν ὑπὸ Σύρων ἁρπαγεῖσαν ἁγίαν ἡμῖν λάρνακα οὐκ ἐστέναξε μὲν ἡ Παλαιστίνη καὶ Δαγὼν τὸ ξόανον, ἐστέναξε δὲ πᾶν τὸ τῶν ἁρπασαμένων ἔθνος, 385 σηπόμενοι δὲ τὰ κρυπτὰ τοῦ σώματος καὶ δι' αὐτῶν τὰ σπλάγχνα μετὰ τῶν σιτίων καταφέροντες, χερσὶ ταῖς λῃσαμέναις ἀνεκόμισαν κυμβάλων καὶ τυμπάνων ἤχῳ καὶ πᾶσι μειλικτηρίοις ἱλασκόμενοι τὸ ἅγιον; 386 θεὸς ἦν ὁ ταῦτα πατράσιν ἡμετέροις στρατηγῶν, ὅτι τὰς χεῖρας καὶ τὰ ὅπλα παρέντες αὐτῷ κρῖναι τὸ ἔργον ἐπέτρεψαν.

387 βασιλεὺς Ἀσσυρίων Σενναχηρεὶμ ὅτε πᾶσαν τὴν Ἀσίαν ἐπισυρόμενος τήνδε περιεστρατοπεδεύσατο τὴν πόλιν, ἆρα χερσὶν ἀνθρωπίναις ἔπεσεν; 388 οὐχ αἱ μὲν ἀπὸ τῶν ὅπλων ἠρεμοῦσαι ἐν προσευχαῖς ἦσαν, ἄγγελος δὲ τοῦ θεοῦ μιᾷ νυκτὶ τὴν ἄπειρον στρατιὰν ἐλυμήνατο, καὶ μεθ' ἡμέραν ἀναστὰς ὁ Ἀσσύριος ὀκτωκαίδεκα μυριάδας ἐπὶ πεντακισχιλίοις νεκρῶν εὗρε, μετὰ δὲ τῶν καταλειπομένων ἀνόπλους καὶ μὴ διώκοντας Ἑβραίους ἔφυγεν; 389 ἴστε καὶ τὴν ἐν Βαβυλῶνι δουλείαν, ἔνθα μετανάστης ὁ λαὸς ὢν ἔτεσιν

ἑβδομήκοντα οὐ πρότερον εἰς ἐλευθερίαν ἀνεχαίτισεν ἢ Κῦρον τοῦτο χαρίσασθαι τῷ θεῷ· προυπέμφθησαν γοῦν ὑπ' αὐτοῦ, καὶ πάλιν τὸν αὐτῶν σύμμαχον ἐνεωκόρουν. 390 καθόλου δ' εἰπεῖν, οὐκ ἔστιν ὅ τι κατώρθωσαν οἱ πατέρες ἡμῶν τοῖς ὅπλοις ἢ δίχα τούτων διήμαρτον ἐπιτρέψαντες τῷ θεῷ· μένοντες μέν γε κατὰ χώραν ἐνίκων ὡς ἐδόκει τῷ κριτῇ, μαχόμενοι δὲ ἔπταισαν ἀεί.

391 τοῦτο μέν, ἡνίκα βασιλεὺς Βαβυλωνίων ἐπολιόρκει ταύτην τὴν πόλιν, συμβαλὼν Σεδεκίας ὁ ἡμέτερος βασιλεὺς παρὰ τὰς Ἰερεμίου προφητείας αὐτός τε ἑάλω καὶ τὸ ἄστυ μετὰ τοῦ ναοῦ κατασκαπτόμενον εἶδε· καίτοι πόσῳ μετριώτερος ὁ μὲν βασιλεὺς ἐκεῖνος τῶν ὑμετέρων ἡγεμόνων ἦν, ὁ δ' ὑπ' αὐτῷ λαὸς ὑμῶν. 392 βοῶντα γοῦν τὸν Ἰερεμίαν, ὡς ἀπέχθοιντο μὲν τῷ θεῷ διὰ τὰς εἰς αὐτὸν πλημμελείας, ἁλώσοιντο δ' εἰ μὴ παραδοῖεν τὴν πόλιν, οὔθ' ὁ βασιλεὺς οὔθ' ὁ δῆμος ἀνεῖλεν. 393 ἀλλ' ὑμεῖς, ἵν' ἐάσω τἄνδον, οὐ γὰρ ἂν ἑρμηνεῦσαι δυναίμην τὰς παρανομίας ὑμῶν ἀξίως, ἐμὲ τὸν παρακαλοῦντα πρὸς σωτηρίαν ὑμᾶς βλασφημεῖτε καὶ βάλλετε, παροξυνόμενοι πρὸς τὰς ὑπομνήσεις τῶν ἁμαρτημάτων καὶ μηδὲ τοὺς λόγους φέροντες ὧν τἄργα δρᾶτε καθ' ἡμέραν.

394 τοῦτο δ', ἡνίκα Ἀντιόχου τοῦ κληθέντος Ἐπιφανοῦς προσκαθεζομένου τῇ πόλει πολλὰ πρὸς τὸ θεῖον ἐξυβρικότος, οἱ πρόγονοι μετὰ τῶν ὅπλων προῆλθον, αὐτοὶ μὲν ἀπεσφάγησαν ἐν τῇ μάχῃ, διηρπάγη δὲ τὸ ἄστυ τοῖς πολεμίοις, ἠρημώθη δ' ἔτη τρία καὶ μῆνας ἓξ τὸ ἅγιον.

395 καὶ τί δεῖ τἆλλα λέγειν; ἀλλὰ Ῥωμαίους τίς ἐστρατολόγησε κατὰ τοῦ ἔθνους; οὐχ ἡ τῶν ἐπιχωρίων ἀσέβεια; πόθεν δ' ἠρξάμεθα δουλείας; 396 ἆρ' οὐχὶ ἐκ στάσεως τῶν προγόνων, ὅτε ἡ Ἀριστοβούλου καὶ Ὑρκανοῦ μανία καὶ πρὸς ἀλλήλους ἔρις Πομπήιον ἐπήγαγεν τῇ πόλει καὶ Ῥωμαίοις ὑπέταξεν ὁ θεὸς τοὺς οὐκ ἀξίους ἐλευθερίας; 397 τρισὶ γοῦν μησὶ πολιορκηθέντες ἑαυτοὺς παρέδοσαν, οὔθ' ἁμαρτόντες εἰς τὰ ἅγια καὶ τοὺς νόμους ἡλίκα ὑμεῖς καὶ πολὺ μείζοσιν ἀφορμαῖς πρὸς τὸν πόλεμον χρώμενοι.

398 τὸ δ' Ἀντιγόνου τέλος τοῦ Ἀριστοβούλου παιδὸς οὐκ ἴσμεν, οὗ βασιλεύοντος ὁ θεὸς ἁλώσει πάλιν τὸν λαὸν ἤλαυνε πλημμελοῦντα, καὶ Ἡρώδης μὲν ὁ Ἀντιπάτρου Σόσσιον, Σόσσιος δὲ Ῥωμαίων στρατιὰν ἤγαγεν, περισχεθέντες δ' ἐπὶ μῆνας ἓξ ἐπολιορκοῦντο, μέχρι δίκας τῶν ἁμαρτιῶν δόντες ἑάλωσαν καὶ διηρπάγη τοῖς πολεμίοις ἡ πόλις;

399 οὕτως οὐδέποτε τῷ ἔθνει τὰ ὅπλα δέδοται, τῷ δὲ πολεμεῖσθαι καὶ τὸ ἁλώσεσθαι πάντως πρόσεστι. 400 δεῖ γάρ, οἶμαι, τοὺς χωρίον ἅγιον νεμομένους ἐπιτρέπειν πάντα τῷ θεῷ δικάζειν καὶ καταφρονεῖν τότε χειρὸς ἀνθρωπίνης, ὅταν αὐτοὶ πείθωσι τὸν ἄνω δικαστήν..."

The Effect of Josephus' Speech

BJ 5.420–423: Josephus' entreaties had no effect upon the Zealots but did incite a large number of the remaining besieged to defect to Titus who resettled most of the refugees without penalty.

Τοιαῦτα τοῦ Ἰωσήπου μετὰ δακρύων ἐμβοῶντος οἱ στασιασταὶ μὲν οὔτε ἐνέδοσαν οὔτ' ἀσφαλῆ τὴν μεταβολὴν ἔκριναν, ὁ δὲ δῆμος ἐκινήθη πρὸς αὐτομολίαν. 421 καὶ οἱ μὲν τὰς κτήσεις ἐλαχίστου πωλοῦντες, οἱ δὲ τὰ πολυτελέστερα τῶν κειμηλίων, τοὺς μὲν χρυσοῦς, ὡς μὴ φωραθεῖεν ὑπὸ τῶν λῃστῶν, κατέπινον, ἔπειτα πρὸς τοὺς Ῥωμαίους διαδιδράσκοντες, ὁπότε κατενέγκαιεν εὐπόρουν πρὸς ἃ δέοιντο. 422 διηφίει γὰρ τοὺς πολλοὺς ὁ Τίτος εἰς τὴν χώραν ὅποι βούλοιτο ἕκαστος, καὶ τοῦτ' αὐτὸ μᾶλλον πρὸς αὐτομολίαν παρεκάλει τῶν μὲν εἴσω κακῶν στερησομένους, μὴ δουλεύσοντας δὲ Ῥωμαίοις. 423 οἱ δὲ περὶ τὸν Ἰωάννην καὶ τὸν Σίμωνα περιεφύλαττον τὰς τούτων ἐξόδους πλέον ἢ τὰς Ῥωμαίων εἰσόδους, καὶ σκιάν τις ὑπονοίας παρασχὼν μόνον εὐθέως ἀπεσφάττετο.

The Crucifixion of Jewish Prisoners

BJ 5.446–451: Quite a number of the besieged were forced to scrounge for food outside the wall where they were picked off by Roman patrols, subjected to tortures, then crucified within sight of the populace—a procedure that was meant to encourage surrender (cf. *BJ* 7.200–209).

Τίτῳ δὲ τὰ μὲν χώματα προύκοπτεν καίτοι πολλὰ κακουμένων ἀπὸ τοῦ τείχους τῶν στρατιωτῶν, πέμψας δ' αὐτὸς μοῖραν τῶν ἱππέων ἐκέλευσεν τοὺς κατὰ τὰς φάραγγας ἐπὶ συγκομιδῇ τροφῆς ἐξιόντας ἐνεδρεύειν. 447 ἦσαν δέ τινες καὶ τῶν μαχίμων οὐκέτι διαρκούμενοι ταῖς ἁρπαγαῖς, τὸ δὲ πλέον ἐκ τοῦ δήμου πένητες, οὓς αὐτομολεῖν ἀπέτρεπε τὸ περὶ τῶν οἰκείων δέος· 448 οὔτε γὰρ λήσεσθαι τοὺς στασιαστὰς ἤλπιζον μετὰ γυναικῶν καὶ παιδίων διαδιδράσκοντες καὶ καταλιπεῖν τοῖς λῃσταῖς ταῦτα οὐχ ὑπέμενον ὑπὲρ αὐτῶν σφαγησόμενα· 449 τολμηροὺς δὲ πρὸς τὰς ἐξόδους ὁ λιμὸς ἐποίει, καὶ κατελείπετο λανθάνοντας τοὺς πολεμίους ἁλίσκεσθαι. λαμβανόμενοι δὲ κατ' ἀνάγκην ἡμύνοντο, καὶ μετὰ μάχην ἱκετεύειν ἄωρον ἐδόκει. μαστιγούμενοι δὴ καὶ προβασανιζόμενοι τοῦ θανάτου πᾶσαν αἰκίαν ἀνεσταυροῦντο τοῦ τείχους ἀντικρύ. 450 Τίτῳ μὲν οὖν οἰκτρὸν τὸ πάθος κατεφαίνετο πεντακοσίων ἑκάστης ἡμέρας ἔστι δὲ ὅτε καὶ πλειόνων ἁλισκομένων· οὔτε δὲ τοὺς βίᾳ ληφθέντας ἀφεῖναι ἀσφαλὲς καὶ φυλάττειν τοσούτους φρουρὰν τῶν φυλαξόντων ἑώρα· τό γε μὴν πλέον οὐκ ἐκώλυεν τάχ' ἂν ἐνδοῦναι πρὸς τὴν ὄψιν ἐλπίσας αὐτούς, εἰ μὴ παραδοῖεν, ὅμοια πεισομένους. 451 προσήλουν δὲ οἱ στρατιῶται δι' ὀργὴν καὶ μῖσος τοὺς ἁλόντας ἄλλον ἄλλῳ σχήματι πρὸς χλεύην, καὶ διὰ τὸ πλῆθος χώρα τε ἐνέλειπε τοῖς σταυροῖς καὶ σταυροὶ τοῖς σώμασιν.

An Attack Against Battering Rams

> *BJ* 5.473–477: the Romans constructed a series of earthen ramps (τὰ χώματα) against which the Zealots launched several desperate attacks. Here Josephus records a thrilling charge wherein Tephtheos, Magassarus, and Ceagiras—three of Simon of Gischala's faction—plunged through the Roman lines and set fire to the siege equipment.

Μετὰ δ' ἡμέρας δύο καὶ τοῖς ἄλλοις ἐπιτίθενται χώμασιν οἱ περὶ τὸν Σίμωνα· καὶ γὰρ δὴ προσαγαγόντες ταύτῃ τὰς ἑλεπόλεις οἱ Ῥωμαῖοι διέσειον τὸ τεῖχος. 474 Τεφθέος δέ τις ἀπὸ Γάρις πόλεως τῆς Γαλιλαίας, καὶ Μαγάσσαρος τῶν βασιλικῶν Μαριάμμης θεράπων, μεθ' ὧν Ἀδιαβηνός τις υἱὸς Ναβαταίου, τοὔνομα κληθεὶς ἀπὸ τῆς τύχης καὶ Κεάγίρας, ὅπερ σημαίνει χωλός, ἁρπάσαντες λαμπάδας προεπήδησαν ἐπὶ τὰς μηχανάς. 475 τούτων τῶν ἀνδρῶν οὔτε τολμηρότεροι κατὰ τόνδε τὸν πόλεμον ἐκ τῆς πόλεως ἐφάνησαν οὔτε φοβερώτεροι· 476 καθάπερ γὰρ εἰς φίλους ἐκτρέχοντες οὐ πολεμίων στῖφος οὔτ' ἐμέλλησαν οὔτ' ἀπέστησαν, ἀλλὰ διὰ μέσων ἐνθορόντες τῶν ἐχθρῶν ὑφῆψαν τὰς μηχανάς. 477 βαλλόμενοι δὲ καὶ τοῖς ξίφεσιν ἀνωθούμενοι πάντοθεν οὐ πρότερον ἐκ τοῦ κινδύνου μετεκινήθησαν ἢ δράξασθαι τῶν ὀργάνων τὸ πῦρ.

An All-Out Attack

> *BJ* 5.478–485: Inspired by the trio's success (cf. previous selection), Jews watching from the wall came to the aid of the three, pushed the dispirited Romans back, and threatened to overwhelm the Roman camp. Only a few soldiers preferring an heroic death to capital punishment for desertion stood firm and so saved the day for the Romans; even so, a goodly number of Romans became despondent and questioned whether they could ever take Jerusalem by siege.

Σιρομένης δὲ ἤδη τῆς φλογὸς Ῥωμαῖοι μὲν ἀπὸ τῶν στρατοπέδων συνθέοντες ἐβοήθουν, Ἰουδαῖοι δ' ἐκ τοῦ τείχους ἐκώλυον καὶ τοῖς σβεννύειν πειρωμένοις συνεπλέκοντο κατὰ μηδὲν τῶν ἰδίων φειδόμενοι σωμάτων. 479 καὶ οἱ μὲν εἷλκον ἐκ τοῦ πυρὸς τὰς ἑλεπόλεις τῶν ὑπὲρ αὐτὰς γέρρων φλεγομένων, οἱ δ' Ἰουδαῖοι καὶ διὰ τῆς φλογὸς ἀντελαμβάνοντο καὶ τοῦ σιδήρου ζέοντος δρασσόμενοι τοὺς κριοὺς οὐ μεθίεσαν· διέβαινε δ' ἀπὸ τούτων ἐπὶ τὰ χώματα τὸ πῦρ καὶ τοὺς ἀμύνοντας προελάμβανεν. 480 ἐν τούτῳ δ' οἱ μὲν Ῥωμαῖοι κυκλούμενοι τῇ φλογὶ καὶ τὴν σωτηρίαν τῶν ἔργων ἀπογνόντες ἀνεχώρουν ἐπὶ τὰ στρατόπεδα, 481 Ἰουδαῖοι δὲ προσέκειντο πλείους ἀεὶ γινόμενοι τῶν ἔνδοθεν προσβοηθούντων καὶ τῷ κρατεῖν τεθαρρηκότες ἀταμιεύτοις ἐχρῶντο ταῖς ὀργαῖς, προελθόντες δὲ μέχρι τῶν ἐρυμάτων ἤδη συνεπλέκοντο τοῖς φρουροῖς. 482 τάξις ἐστὶν ἐκ διαδοχῆς ἱσταμένη πρὸ τοῦ στρατοπέδου, καὶ δεινὸς ἐπ' αὐτῇ Ῥωμαίων νόμος τὸν ὑποχωρήσαντα καθ' ἣν δήποτ' οὖν αἰτίαν θνῄσκειν. 483 οὗτοι τοῦ μετὰ κολάσεως τὸν μετ' ἀρετῆς θάνατον προκρίναντες ἵστανται, καὶ πρὸς τὴν τούτων ἀνάγκην πολλοὶ τῶν τραπέντων ἐπεστράφησαν αἰδούμενοι. 484 διαθέντες δὲ καὶ τοὺς ὀξυβελεῖς ἐπὶ τοῦ τείχους εἶργον τὸ προσγινόμενον πλῆθος ἐκ τῆς πόλεως, οὐδὲν εἰς ἀσφάλειαν ἢ φυλακὴν τῶν σωμάτων προνοουμένους· συνεπλέκοντο γὰρ Ἰουδαῖοι τοῖς προστυχοῦσι καὶ ταῖς αἰχμαῖς ἀφυλάκτως ἐμπίπτοντες αὐτοῖς τοῖς σώμασι τοὺς ἐχθροὺς ἔπαιον. 485 οὔτε δὲ ἔργοις αὐτοὶ πλέον ἢ τῷ θαρρεῖν περιῆσαν καὶ Ῥωμαῖοι τῇ τόλμῃ πλέον εἶκον ἢ τῷ κακοῦσθαι.

Titus Saves the Day

BJ 5.486–490: Titus appears on the scene. Severely reprimanding the troops for having put themselves into the position of the besieged, he gets around the enemy and attacks the flank. Neither side can distinguish friend from foe. Finally the Jews, sensing the turn in battle, retreat into the city; the Romans, with their earthworks demolished, remain in deep dejection.

Παρῆν δ' ἤδη Τίτος ἀπὸ τῆς Ἀντωνίας, ὅπου κεχώριστο κατασκεπτόμενος τόπον ἄλλοις χώμασι, καὶ πολλὰ τοὺς στρατιώτας φαυλίσας, εἰ κρατοῦντες τῶν πολεμίων τειχῶν κινδυνεύουσι τοῖς ἰδίοις καὶ πολιορκουμένων ὑπομένουσιν αὐτοὶ τύχην, ὥσπερ ἐκ δεσμωτηρίου καθ' αὑτῶν Ἰουδαίους ἀνέντες, περιῄει μετὰ τῶν ἐπιλέκτων κατὰ πλευρὰ τοὺς πολεμίους αὐτός. 487 οἱ δὲ κατὰ στόμα παιόμενοι καὶ πρὸς τοῦτον ἐπιστραφέντες ἐκαρτέρουν. μιγείσης δὲ τῆς παρατάξεως, ὁ μὲν κονιορτὸς τῶν ὀμμάτων, ἡ κραυγὴ δὲ τῶν ἀκοῶν ἐπεκράτει, καὶ οὐδετέρῳ παρῆν ἔτι τεκμήρασθαι τὸ ἐχθρὸν ἢ τὸ φίλιον. 488 Ἰουδαίων δὲ οὐ τοσοῦτον ἔτι κατ' ἀλκὴν ὅσον ἀπογνώσει σωτηρίας παραμενόντων καὶ Ῥωμαίους ἐτόνωσεν αἰδὼς δόξης τε καὶ τῶν ὅπλων καὶ προκινδυνεύοντος

Καίσαρος· 489 ὥστε μοι δοκοῦσι τὰ τελευταῖα δι' ὑπερβολὴν θυμῶν κἂν ὅλον ἁρπάσαι τὸ τῶν Ἰουδαίων πλῆθος, εἰ μὴ τὴν ῥοπὴν τῆς παρατάξεως φθάσαντες ἀνεχώρησαν εἰς τὴν πόλιν. 490 διεφθαρμένων δὲ τῶν χωμάτων Ῥωμαῖοι μὲν ἦσαν ἐν ἀθυμίαις τὸν μακρὸν κάματον ἐπὶ μιᾶς ὥρας ἀπολέσαντες· καὶ πολλοὶ μὲν ταῖς συνήθεσι μηχαναῖς ἀπήλπιζον ἁλώσεσθαι τὴν πόλιν.

A Mother's Desperation

> *BJ* 6.201–213: the following vignette was especially popular with Christians during medieval times. A wealthy Jewish woman named Mary perpetrated an horrific act of cannibalism upon her unnamed infant son during the final days of the siege. The story may have been popular because Christians tended to see the destruction of Jerusalem as God's punishment for the Jews' persistent rejection of Jesus (cf. Schreckenberg 1987, 324 n. 25; Huntsman 1996–97, 398–399; Mason 2003, 11–12). Josephus presents Mary as a pathetic figure who, overcome by rage and hunger pangs, savagely slays her son then offers the brigands a portion of the body to eat which they, in horror, refuse. *Oratio recta* (direct speech) occurs twice in the following passage. Cf. Chapman 2005, 302 for other techniques Josephus uses to heighten the spectacular nature of this account.

201 Γυνή τις τῶν ὑπὲρ τὸν Ἰορδάνην κατοικούντων, Μαρία τοὔνομα, πατρὸς Ἐλεαζάρου, κώμης Βηθεζουβᾶ, σημαίνει δὲ τοῦτο οἶκος ὑσσώπου, διὰ γένος καὶ πλοῦτον ἐπίσημος, μετὰ τοῦ λοιποῦ πλήθους εἰς τὰ Ἱεροσόλυμα καταφυγοῦσα συνεπολιορκεῖτο. 202 ταύτης τὴν μὲν ἄλλην κτῆσιν οἱ τύραννοι διήρπασαν, ὅσην ἐκ τῆς Περαίας ἀνασκευασαμένη μετήνεγκεν εἰς τὴν πόλιν, τὰ δὲ λείψανα τῶν κειμηλίων καὶ εἴ τι τροφῆς ἐπινοηθείη καθ' ἡμέραν εἰσπηδῶντες ἥρπαζον οἱ δορυφόροι. 203 δεινὴ δὲ τὸ γύναιον ἀγανάκτησις εἰσῄει, καὶ πολλάκις λοιδοροῦσα καὶ καταρωμένη τοὺς ἅρπαγας ἐφ' αὑτὴν ἠρέθιζεν. 204 ὡς δ' οὔτε παροξυνόμενός τις

οὔτ' ἐλεῶν αὐτὴν ἀνῄρει, καὶ τὸ μὲν εὑρεῖν τι σιτίον ἄλλοις ἐκοπία, πανταχόθεν δὲ ἄπορον ἦν ἤδη καὶ τὸ εὑρεῖν, ὁ λιμὸς δὲ διὰ σπλάγχνων καὶ μυελῶν ἐχώρει καὶ τοῦ λιμοῦ μᾶλλον ἐξέκαιον οἱ θυμοί, σύμβουλον λαβοῦσα τὴν ὀργὴν μετὰ τῆς ἀνάγκης ἐπὶ τὴν φύσιν ἐχώρει, 205 καὶ τὸ τέκνον, ἦν δὲ αὐτῇ παῖς ὑπομάστιος, ἁρπασαμένη "βρέφος, εἶπεν, ἄθλιον, ἐν πολέμῳ καὶ λιμῷ καὶ στάσει τίνι σε τηρήσω; 206 τὰ μὲν παρὰ Ῥωμαίοις δουλεία, κἂν ζήσωμεν ἐπ' αὐτούς, φθάνει δὲ καὶ δουλείαν ὁ λιμός, οἱ στασιασταὶ δὲ ἀμφοτέρων χαλεπώτεροι. 207 ἴθι, γενοῦ μοι τροφὴ καὶ τοῖς στασιασταῖς ἐρινὺς καὶ τῷ βίῳ μῦθος ὁ μόνος ἐλλείπων ταῖς Ἰουδαίων συμφοραῖς." 208 καὶ ταῦθ' ἅμα λέγουσα κτείνει τὸν υἱόν, ἔπειτ' ὀπτήσασα τὸ μὲν ἥμισυ κατεσθίει, τὸ δὲ λοιπὸν κατακαλύψασα ἐφύλαττεν. 209 εὐθέως δ' οἱ στασιασταὶ παρῆσαν, καὶ τῆς ἀθεμίτου κνίσης σπάσαντες ἠπείλουν, εἰ μὴ δείξειεν τὸ παρασκευασθέν, ἀποσφάξειν αὐτὴν εὐθέως. ἡ δὲ καὶ μοῖραν αὐτοῖς εἰποῦσα καλὴν τετηρηκέναι τὰ λείψανα τοῦ τέκνου διεκάλυψεν. 210 τοὺς δ' εὐθέως φρίκη καὶ παρέκστασις ᾕρει καὶ παρὰ τὴν ὄψιν ἐπεπήγεσαν. ἡ δ' "ἐμόν, ἔφη, τοῦτο τέκνον γνήσιον καὶ τὸ ἔργον ἐμόν. φάγετε, καὶ γὰρ ἐγὼ βέβρωκα. 211 μὴ γένησθε μήτε μαλακώτεροι γυναικὸς μήτε συμπαθέστεροι μητρός. εἰ δ' ὑμεῖς εὐσεβεῖς καὶ τὴν ἐμὴν ἀποστρέφεσθε θυσίαν, ἐγὼ μὲν ὑμῖν βέβρωκα, καὶ τὸ λοιπὸν δὲ ἐμοὶ μεινάτω." 212 μετὰ ταῦθ' οἱ μὲν τρέμοντες ἐξῄεσαν, πρὸς ἓν τοῦτο δειλοὶ καὶ μόλις ταύτης τῆς τροφῆς τῇ μητρὶ παραχωρήσαντες, ἀνεπλήσθη δ' εὐθέως ὅλη τοῦ μύσους ἡ πόλις, καὶ πρὸ ὀμμάτων ἕκαστος τὸ πάθος λαμβάνων ὥσπερ αὐτῷ τολμηθὲν ἔφριττε. 213 σπουδὴ δὲ τῶν λιμωττόντων ἐπὶ τὸν θάνατον ἦν, καὶ μακαρισμὸς τῶν φθασάντων πρὶν ἀκοῦσαι καὶ θεάσασθαι κακὰ τηλικαῦτα.

The Final Assault

BJ 6.403–408: The Romans launched the final assault on Jerusalem on September 25, AD 70. Conflagrations raged throughout the night and so much blood was shed, writes Josephus, that fires were doused by the blood of the slain (*BJ* 6.406). At first the Romans, singing a paean of victory, congratulated each other on how easy it had been to surmount the final wall and plant the standard; then, dropping down into the alleyways, they murdered any inhabitant they came upon and set the torch to houses crammed with refugees. Cf. Ziolkowski (1993) for what typically was involved in the sack of a defeated city.

Ῥωμαῖοι δὲ τῶν τειχῶν κρατήσαντες τάς τε σημαίας ἔστησαν ἐπὶ τῶν πύργων καὶ μετὰ κρότου καὶ χαρᾶς ἐπαιάνιζον ἐπὶ τῇ νίκῃ, πολὺ τῆς ἀρχῆς κουφότερον τοῦ πολέμου τὸ τέλος εὑρηκότες· ἀναιμωτὶ γοῦν τοῦ τελευταίου τείχους ἐπιβάντες ἠπίστουν, καὶ μηδένα βλέποντες ἀντίπαλον ἀληθῶς ἠπόρηντο. 404 εἰσχυθέντες δὲ τοῖς στενωποῖς ξιφήρεις τούς τε καταλαμβανομένους ἐφόνευον ἀνέδην καὶ τῶν συμφευγόντων τὰς οἰκίας αὐτάνδρους ὑπεπίμπρασαν. 405 πολλὰς δὲ κεραΐζοντες ὁπότ' ἔνδον παρέλθοιεν ἐφ' ἁρπαγήν, γενεὰς ὅλας νεκρῶν κατελάμβανον καὶ τὰ δωμάτια πλήρη τῶν τοῦ λιμοῦ πτωμάτων, ἔπειτα πρὸς τὴν ὄψιν πεφρικότες κεναῖς χερσὶν ἐξῄεσαν. 406 οὐ μὴν οἰκτείροντες τοὺς οὕτως ἀπολωλότας ταὐτὸ καὶ πρὸς τοὺς ζῶντας ἔπασχον, ἀλλὰ τὸν ἐντυγχάνοντα διελαύνοντες ἀπέφραξαν μὲν τοὺς στενωποὺς νεκροῖς, αἵματι δὲ ὅλην τὴν πόλιν κατέκλυσαν, ὡς πολλὰ καὶ τῶν φλεγομένων σβεσθῆναι τῷ φόνῳ. 407 καὶ οἱ μὲν κτείνοντες ἐπαύσαντο πρὸς ἑσπέραν, ἐν δὲ τῇ νυκτὶ τὸ πῦρ ἐπεκράτει, φλεγομένοις δ' ἐπανέτειλεν Ἱεροσολύμοις ἡμέρα Γορπιαίου μηνὸς ὀγδόῃ, 408 πόλει τοσαύταις χρησαμένῃ συμφοραῖς κατὰ τὴν πολιορκίαν, ὅσοις ἀπὸ κτίσεως ἀγαθοῖς κεχρημένη πάντως ἂν ἐπίφθονος ἔδοξεν, οὐ μὴν ἀξία κατ' ἄλλο τι τῶν τηλικούτων ἀτυχημάτων ἢ τὸ γενεὰν τοιαύτην ἐνεγκεῖν, ὑφ' ἧς ἀνετράπη.

The Entry of Titus

> *BJ* 6.409–413: Titus entered the city and admired the lofty towers from which, by an inexplicable act of "bad thinking" (φρενοβλάβεια, *BJ* 6.409), the Zealots had come down of their own accord and so became easy targets for Roman artillery barrages (*BJ* 6.399). Of the three towers—Hippicus, Mariamme, and Phasael (*BJ* 5.161–175)—the latter still stands, a monument to Titus' good fortune over men who could not otherwise be captured.
>
> Παρελθὼν δὲ Τίτος εἴσω τά τε ἄλλα τῆς ὀχυρότητος τὴν πόλιν καὶ τῶν πύργων ἀπεθαύμασεν, οὓς οἱ τύραννοι κατὰ φρενοβλάβειαν ἀπέλιπον. 410 κατιδὼν γοῦν τό τε ναστὸν αὐτῶν ὕψος καὶ τὸ μέγεθος ἑκάστης πέτρας τήν τε ἀκρίβειαν τῆς ἁρμονίας, καὶ ὅσοι μὲν εὖρος ἡλίκοι δὲ ἦσαν τὴν ἀνάστασιν, 411 "σὺν θεῷ γε ἐπολεμήσαμεν, ἔφη, καὶ θεὸς ἦν ὁ τῶνδε τῶν ἐρυμάτων Ἰουδαίους καθελών, ἐπεὶ χεῖρες ἀνθρώπων ἢ μηχαναὶ τί πρὸς τούτους τοὺς πύργους δύνανται;" 412 τότε μὲν οὖν πολλὰ τοιαῦτα διελέχθη πρὸς τοὺς φίλους, τοὺς δὲ τῶν τυράννων δεσμώτας, ὅσοι κατελήφθησαν ἐν τοῖς φρουρίοις, ἀνῆκεν. 413 αὖθις δὲ τὴν ἄλλην ἀφανίζων πόλιν καὶ τὰ τείχη κατασκάπτων τούτους τοὺς πύργους κατέλιπε μνημεῖον εἶναι τῆς αὐτοῦ τύχης, ᾗ συστρατιώτιδι χρησάμενος ἐκράτησε τῶν ἁλῶναι μὴ δυναμένων.

The Fate of the Captives

> *BJ* 6.414–420: Wearying of the slaughter, Titus issued orders that the soldiers should kill only those survivors who showed weapons or offered resistance. One of Titus' freedmen guarded the prisoners in the Court of Women in the Temple; there an Alexandrian named Fronto Haterius decided the fates of most, putting known brigands to death yet reserving many for the triumph in Rome or for more varied forms of servitude throughout the empire. Cf. Millar (2005) for the triumph itself and for many structures—such as the Colosseum, Temple of

Peace, and Arch of Titus—that were erected in Rome to commemorate the Jewish war.

Ἐπεὶ δ' οἱ στρατιῶται μὲν ἔκαμνον ἤδη φονεύοντες, πολὺ δέ τι πλῆθος τῶν περιόντων ἀνεφαίνετο, κελεύει Καῖσαρ μόνους μὲν τοὺς ἐνόπλους καὶ χεῖρας ἀντίσχοντας κτείνειν, τὸ δὲ λοιπὸν πλῆθος ζωγρεῖν. 415 οἱ δὲ μετὰ τῶν παρηγγελμένων τό τε γηραιὸν καὶ τοὺς ἀσθενεῖς ἀνήρουν, τὸ δ' ἀκμάζον καὶ χρήσιμον εἰς τὸ ἱερὸν συνελάσαντες ἐγκατέκλεισαν τῷ τῶν γυναικῶν περιτειχίσματι. 416 καὶ φρουρὸν μὲν ἐπέστησε Καῖσαρ ἕνα τῶν ἀπελευθέρων, Φρόντωνα δὲ τῶν φίλων ἐπικρινοῦντα τὴν ἀξίαν ἑκάστῳ τύχην. 417 ὁ δὲ τοὺς μὲν στασιώδεις καὶ λῃστρικοὺς πάντας ὑπ' ἀλλήλων ἐνδεικνυμένους ἀπέκτεινε, τῶν δὲ νέων τοὺς ὑψηλοτάτους καὶ καλοὺς ἐπιλέξας ἐτήρει τῷ θριάμβῳ. 418 τοῦ δὲ λοιποῦ πλήθους τοὺς ὑπὲρ ἑπτακαίδεκα ἔτη δήσας ἔπεμψεν εἰς τὰ κατ' Αἴγυπτον ἔργα, πλείστους δ' εἰς τὰς ἐπαρχίας διεδωρήσατο Τίτος φθαρησομένους ἐν τοῖς θεάτροις σιδήρῳ καὶ θηρίοις· οἱ δ' ἐντὸς ἑπτακαίδεκα ἐτῶν ἐπράθησαν. 419 ἐφθάρησαν δὲ αὐτῶν ἐν αἷς διέκρινεν ὁ Φρόντων ἡμέραις ὑπ' ἐνδείας χίλιοι πρὸς τοῖς μυρίοις, οἱ μὲν ὑπὸ μίσους τῶν φυλάκων μὴ μεταλαμβάνοντες τροφῆς, οἱ δ' οὐ προσιέμενοι διδομένην· πρὸς δὲ τὸ πλῆθος ἦν ἔνδεια καὶ σίτου. 420 τῶν μὲν οὖν αἰχμαλώτων πάντων, ὅσα καθ' ὅλον ἐλήφθη τὸν πόλεμον, ἀριθμὸς ἐννέα μυριάδες καὶ ἑπτακισχίλιοι συνήχθη, τῶν δὲ ἀπολομένων κατὰ πᾶσαν τὴν πολιορκίαν μυριάδες ἑκατὸν καὶ δέκα.

SUMMARY

BJ 6.435–442: Josephus relates the latest capture of Jerusalem to previous conquests of the city and provides a concise chronological record of its history. Some have supposed that Josephus saw Judaism itself—both in Israel itself and in the Diaspora—as having come to an end (Eshel 1999, 233). Others maintain that Josephus wrote as though Jerusalem and its institutions were still intact (e.g., Rajak 2005, 83). Josephus insists that there is no part of the world without Jews (*BJ* 7.43).

Ἑάλω μὲν οὕτως Ἱεροσόλυμα ἔτει δευτέρῳ τῆς Οὐεσπασιανοῦ ἡγεμονίας Γορπιαίου μηνὸς ὀγδόῃ, ἁλοῦσα δὲ καὶ πρότερον πεντάκις τοῦτο δεύτερον ἠρημώθη. 436 Ἀσωχαῖος μὲν γὰρ ὁ τῶν Αἰγυπτίων βασιλεὺς καὶ μετ' αὐτὸν Ἀντίοχος, ἔπειτα Πομπήιος καὶ ἐπὶ τούτοις σὺν Ἡρώδῃ Σόσσιος ἑλόντες ἐτήρησαν τὴν πόλιν. 437 πρὸ δὲ τούτων ὁ τῶν Βαβυλωνίων βασιλεὺς κρατήσας ἠρήμωσεν αὐτὴν μετὰ ἔτη τῆς κτίσεως χίλια τετρακόσια ἑξηκονταοκτὼ μῆνας ἕξ. 438 ὁ δὲ πρῶτος κτίσας ἦν Χαναναίων δυνάστης ὁ τῇ πατρίῳ γλώσσῃ κληθεὶς βασιλεὺς δίκαιος· ἦν γὰρ δὴ τοιοῦτος. διὰ τοῦτο ἱεράσατό τε τῷ θεῷ πρῶτος καὶ τὸ ἱερὸν πρῶτος δειμάμενος Ἱεροσόλυμα τὴν πόλιν προσηγόρευσεν Σόλυμα καλουμένην πρότερον. 439 τὸν μὲν δὴ τῶν Χαναναίων λαὸν ἐκβαλὼν ὁ τῶν Ἰουδαίων βασιλεὺς Δαυίδης κατοικίζει τὸν ἴδιον, καὶ μετὰ τοῦτον ἔτεσι τετρακοσίοις ἑβδομήκοντα καὶ ἑπτὰ μησὶν ἓξ ὑπὸ Βαβυλωνίων κατασκάπτεται. 440 ἀπὸ δὲ Δαυίδου τοῦ βασιλέως, ὃς πρῶτος αὐτῆς ἐβασίλευσεν Ἰουδαῖος, μέχρι τῆς ὑπὸ Τίτου γενομένης κατασκαφῆς ἔτη χίλια καὶ ἑκατὸν ἑβδομήκοντα καὶ ἐννέα. 441 ἀπὸ δὲ τῆς πρώτης κτίσεως ἔτη μέχρι τῆς ἐσχάτης ἁλώσεως δισχίλια ἑκατὸν ἑβδομήκοντα καὶ ἑπτά. 442 ἀλλὰ γὰρ οὔθ' ἡ ἀρχαιότης οὔθ' ὁ πλοῦτος ὁ βαθὺς οὔτε τὸ διαπεφοιτηκὸς ὅλης τῆς οἰκουμένης ἔθνος οὔθ' ἡ μεγάλη δόξα τῆς θρησκείας ἤρκεσέ τι πρὸς ἀπώλειαν αὐτῇ. τοιοῦτο μὲν δὴ τὸ τέλος τῆς Ἱεροσολύμων πολιορκίας.

Josephus: Masada

The final scenes of the Jewish war were enacted in AD 73 at Masada, a spectacular fortress that Herod the Great had made all but impregnable. Excavations by Yigael Yadin uncovered many of the features mentioned by Josephus in *BJ* 7, in addition to dramatic—though mute—evidence of the last tragic days of the struggle by the Zealots against the Romans in AD 73/74 (Yadin 1966; 1996–97). On the other hand, it has been argued that various mistakes in Josephus' account must indicate that the historian had never actually been to Masada himself (Eshel 1999, 231–231). Zealot insurgents had come to occupy Masada in the summer of AD 66, slaying the Roman guards and substituting a garrison of their own (*BJ* 2.408).

Religion and Resistance

The Road to the Top

> *BJ* 7.280–284: Josephus compares the eastern road to the summit of Masada to a writhing snake. The description paints a striking picture of the footpath and the dizzying heights it traverses.

Πέτραν οὐκ ὀλίγην τῇ περιόδῳ καὶ μῆκος ὑψηλὴν πανταχόθεν περιερρώγασι βαθεῖαι φάραγγες κάτωθεν ἐξ ἀοράτου τέρματος κρημνώδεις καὶ πάσῃ βάσει ζῴων ἀπρόσιτοι, πλὴν ὅσον κατὰ δύο τόπους τῆς πέτρας εἰς ἄνοδον οὐκ εὐμαρῆ παρεικούσης. 281 ἔστι δὲ τῶν ὁδῶν ἡ μὲν ἀπὸ τῆς Ἀσφαλτίτιδος λίμνης πρὸς ἥλιον ἀνίσχοντα, καὶ πάλιν ἀπὸ τῆς δύσεως ᾗ ῥᾷον πορευθῆναι. 282 καλοῦσι δὲ τὴν ἑτέραν ὄφιν, τῇ στενότητι προσεικάσαντες καὶ τοῖς συνεχέσιν ἑλιγμοῖς· κλᾶται γὰρ περὶ τὰς τῶν κρημνῶν ἐξοχὰς καὶ πολλάκις εἰς αὑτὴν ἀνατρέχουσα καὶ κατὰ μικρὸν αὖθις ἐκμηκυνομένη μόλις ψαύει τοῦ πρόσω. 283 δεῖ δὲ παραλλὰξ τὸν δι' αὐτῆς βαδίζοντα τὸν ἕτερον τῶν ποδῶν ἐρείδεσθαι. ἔστι δὲ πρόδηλος ὄλεθρος· ἑκατέρωθεν γὰρ βάθος κρημνῶν ὑποκέχηνε τῇ φοβερότητι πᾶσαν εὐτολμίαν ἐκπλῆξαι δυνάμενον. 284 διὰ τοιαύτης οὖν ἐλθόντι σταδίους τριάκοντα κορυφὴ τὸ λοιπόν ἐστιν οὐκ εἰς ὀξὺ τέρμα συνηγμένη, ἀλλ' ὥστ' εἶναι κατ' ἄκρας ἐπίπεδον.

Refinements and Amenities

> *BJ* 7.285–294: Herod the Great had intended to cultivate the fertile summit to alleviate any dearth of provisions that an external enemy might impose. An ingenious system of water-channels and reservoirs guaranteed an abundance of water. Apartments, columns, baths, and mosaics ensured that Masada would be not only a refuge from attack but an oasis of civilization as well.

ἐπὶ ταύτῃ πρῶτον μὲν ὁ ἀρχιερεὺς ᾠκοδομήσατο φρούριον Ἰωνάθης καὶ προσηγόρευσε Μασάδαν, ὕστερον δ' Ἡρώδῃ τῷ βασιλεῖ διὰ πολλῆς ἐγένετο σπουδῆς ἡ τοῦ χωρίου κατασκευή. 286 τεῖχός τε γὰρ ἤγειρε περὶ πάντα τὸν κύκλον τῆς κορυφῆς ἑπτὰ σταδίων ὄντα λευκοῦ μὲν λίθου πεποιημένον, ὕψος δὲ δώδεκα καὶ πλάτος ὀκτὼ πήχεις ἔχον, 287 τριάκοντα δὲ αὐτῷ καὶ ἑπτὰ πύργοι πεντηκονταπήχεις ἀνειστήκεσαν, ἐξ ὧν ἦν εἰς οἰκήματα διελθεῖν περὶ πᾶν τὸ τεῖχος ἔνδον ᾠκοδομημένα. 288 τὴν γὰρ κορυφὴν πίονα καὶ πεδίου παντὸς οὖσαν μαλακωτέραν ἀνῆκεν εἰς γεωργίαν ὁ βασιλεύς, ἵν' εἴ ποτε τῆς ἔξωθεν τροφῆς ἀπορία γένοιτο, μηδὲ ταύτῃ κάμοιεν οἱ τὴν αὑτῶν σωτηρίαν τῷ φρουρίῳ πεπιστευκότες. 289 καὶ βασίλειον δὲ κατεσκεύασεν ἐν αὐτῷ κατὰ τὴν ἀπὸ τῆς ἑσπέρας ἀνάβασιν, ὑποκάτω μὲν τῶν τῆς ἄκρας τειχῶν, πρὸς δὲ τὴν ἄρκτον ἐκκλίνον. τοῦ δὲ βασιλείου τὸ τεῖχος ἦν ὕψει μέγα καὶ καρτερόν, πύργους ἔχον ἑξηκονταπήχεις ἐγγωνίους τέτταρας. 290 ἥ τε τῶν οἰκημάτων ἔνδον καὶ στοῶν καὶ βαλανείων κατασκευὴ παντοία καὶ πολυτελὴς ἦν, κιόνων μὲν ἁπανταχοῦ μονολίθων ὑφεστηκότων, τοίχων δὲ καὶ τῶν ἐν τοῖς οἰκήμασιν ἐδάφων λίθου στρώσει πεποικιλμένων. 291 πρὸς ἕκαστον δὲ τῶν οἰκουμένων τόπων ἄνω τε καὶ περὶ τὸ βασίλειον καὶ πρὸ τοῦ τείχους πολλοὺς καὶ μεγάλους ἐτετμήκει λάκκους ἐν ταῖς πέτραις φυλακτῆρας ὑδάτων, μηχανώμενος εἶναι χορηγίαν ὅση τῷ ἐκ πηγῶν ἐστι χρωμένοις. 292 ὀρυκτὴ δ' ὁδὸς ἐκ τοῦ βασιλείου πρὸς ἄκραν τὴν κορυφὴν ἀνέφερε τοῖς ἔξωθεν ἀφανής. οὐ μὴν οὐδὲ ταῖς φανεραῖς ὁδοῖς ἦν οἷόν τε χρήσασθαι ῥᾳδίως πολεμίους· 293 ἡ μὲν γὰρ ἑῴα διὰ τὴν φύσιν, ὡς προείπαμεν, ἐστὶν ἄβατος, τὴν δ' ἀπὸ τῆς ἑσπέρας μεγάλῳ κατὰ τὸ στενότατον πύργῳ διετείχισεν ἀπέχοντι τῆς ἄκρας πήχεων οὐκ ἔλαττον διάστημα χιλίων, ὃν οὔτε παρελθεῖν δυνατὸν ἦν οὔτε ῥᾴδιον ἑλεῖν· δυσέξοδος δὲ καὶ τοῖς μετὰ ἀδείας βαδίζουσιν ἐπεποίητο. 294 οὕτως μὲν οὖν πρὸς τὰς τῶν πολεμίων ἐφόδους φύσει τε καὶ χειροποιήτως τὸ φρούριον ὠχύρωτο.

Food Stores and Weaponry

> *BJ* 7.295–303: Herod the Great stocked Masada with food stores and weaponry that were still usable at the time of the Roman conquest nearly a century later. Josephus claims that the durability of the foodstuffs was due to the air which was "untainted by all earth-born and foul alloy" (*BJ* 7.298 LCL). Herod hoarded weapons for some 10,000 men and stockpiled an abundance of

unwrought iron, brass, and lead so that future occupants of the citadel could create for themselves the latest in weapons technology.

Τῶν δ' ἔνδον ἀποκειμένων παρασκευῶν ἔτι μᾶλλον ἄν τις ἐθαύμασε τὴν λαμπρότητα καὶ τὴν διαμονήν· 296 σῖτός τε γὰρ ἀπέκειτο πολὺς καὶ πολὺν χρόνον ἀρκεῖν ἱκανώτατος οἶνός τε πολὺς ἦν καὶ ἔλαιον, ἔτι δὲ παντοῖος ὀσπρίων καρπὸς καὶ φοίνικες ἐσεσώρευντο. 297 πάντα δὲ εὗρεν ὁ Ἐλεάζαρος τοῦ φρουρίου μετὰ τῶν σικαρίων ἐγκρατὴς δόλῳ γενόμενος ἀκμαῖα καὶ μηδὲν τῶν νεωστὶ κειμένων ἀποδέοντα· καίτοι σχεδὸν ἀπὸ τῆς παρασκευῆς εἰς τὴν ὑπὸ Ῥωμαίοις ἅλωσιν ἑκατὸν ἦν χρόνος ἐτῶν· ἀλλὰ καὶ Ῥωμαῖοι τοὺς περιλειφθέντας τῶν καρπῶν εὗρον ἀδιαφθόρους. 298 αἴτιον δ' οὐκ ἂν ἁμάρτοι τις ὑπολαμβάνων εἶναι τὸν ἀέρα τῆς διαμονῆς ὕψει τῷ περὶ τὴν ἄκραν πάσης ὄντα γεώδους καὶ θολερᾶς ἀμιγῆ κράσεως. 299 εὑρέθη δὲ καὶ παντοίων πλῆθος ὅπλων ὑπὸ τοῦ βασιλέως ἀποτεθησαυρισμένων, ὡς ἀνδράσιν ἀρκεῖν μυρίοις, ἀργός τε σίδηρος καὶ χαλκὸς ἔτι δὲ καὶ μόλιβος, ἅτε δὴ τῆς παρασκευῆς ἐπὶ μεγάλαις αἰτίαις γενομένης· 300 λέγεται γὰρ αὐτῷ τὸν Ἡρώδην τοῦτο τὸ φρούριον εἰς ὑποφυγὴν ἑτοιμάζειν διπλοῦν ὑφορώμενον κίνδυνον, τὸν μὲν παρὰ τοῦ πλήθους τῶν Ἰουδαίων, μὴ καταλύσαντες ἐκεῖνον τοὺς πρὸ αὐτοῦ βασιλέας ἐπὶ τὴν ἀρχὴν καταγάγωσι, τὸν μείζω δὲ καὶ χαλεπώτερον ἐκ τῆς βασιλευούσης Αἰγύπτου Κλεοπάτρας. 301 αὕτη γὰρ τὴν αὑτῆς γνώμην οὐκ ἐπεῖχεν, ἀλλὰ πολλάκις Ἀντωνίῳ λόγους προσέφερε τὸν μὲν Ἡρώδην ἀνελεῖν ἀξιοῦσα, χαρίσασθαι δ' αὐτῇ τὴν βασιλείαν τῶν Ἰουδαίων δεομένη. 302 καὶ μᾶλλον ἄν τις ἐθαύμασεν, ὅτι μηδέπω τοῖς προστάγμασιν Ἀντώνιος ὑπακηκόει κακῶς ὑπὸ τοῦ πρὸς αὐτὴν ἔρωτος δεδουλωμένος, οὐχ ὅτι περὶ τοῦ μὴ χαρίσασθαι προσεδόκησεν. 303 διὰ τοιούτους μὲν φόβους Ἡρώδης Μασάδαν κατεσκευασμένος ἔμελλεν Ῥωμαίοις ἀπολείψειν ἔργον τοῦ πρὸς Ἰουδαίους πολέμου τελευταῖον.

Eleazar's Speech at Masada

Eleazar had been responsible for getting priests in Jerusalem to stop making sacrifices for Rome and the emperor in the summer of AD 66, an act of defiance that "laid the foundation of the war with the Romans" (*BJ* 2.409 LCL). Now at the end of the war—on the very night before the Romans would mount a final attack against the free Jewish forces at Masada—Eleazar delivered a great speech wherein he argued that the defenders of the citadel should die with nobility and freedom rather than live on as slaves to the enemy. While the speech may contain "views Eleazar might have shared," it is above all else "a literary creation" Josephus himself composed to climax the Masada account (Huntsman 1996–97, 396) and stands in sharp contrast to Josephus' own speech at Jotapata which condemns suicide (*BJ* 3.361–382; Huntsman 1996–97, 372–73). Usually speeches were not strict reproductions of what was said on particular occasions, but an author's own rhetorical creation wherein much freedom was allowed to convey particular points and entertain audiences (Mason 2003, 66). Eleazar's speech owes much not only to Plato, but also to Stoicism and the consolation literature (Ladouceur 1981; Luz 1983).

Preamble

BJ 7.320–336: Josephus perhaps intended that Eleazar's arguments should appear extreme or even dictatorial, since Eleazar himself hatched the idea whereby most of the besieged would die; on the other hand, Eleazar's radical arguments appeal to freedom-loving people everywhere. In Eleazar's bold pronouncements one cannot help but think of Patrick Henry, a hero of the American Revolution, whose rallying cry was "Give me liberty or give me death!"

Οὐ μὴν οὔτε αὐτὸς Ἐλεάζαρος ἐν νῷ δρασμὸν ἔλαβεν οὔτε ἄλλῳ τινὶ τοῦτο ποιεῖν ἔμελλεν ἐπιτρέψειν. 321 ὁρῶν δὲ τὸ μὲν τεῖχος ὑπὸ τοῦ πυρὸς ἀναλούμενον, ἄλλον δὲ οὐδένα σωτηρίας τρόπον οὐδ' ἀλκῆς ἐπινοῶν, ἃ δὲ ἔμελλον Ῥωμαῖοι δράσειν αὐτοὺς καὶ τέκνα καὶ γυναῖκας [αὐτῶν], εἰ κρατήσειαν, ὑπ' ὀφθαλμοὺς αὑτῷ τιθέμενος, θάνατον κατὰ πάντων ἐβουλεύσατο. 322 καὶ τοῦτο κρίνας ἐκ τῶν παρόντων ἄριστον, τοὺς ἀνδρωδεστάτους τῶν ἑταίρων συναγαγὼν τοιούτοις ἐπὶ τὴν πρᾶξιν λόγοις παρεκάλει· 323 "πάλαι διεγνωκότας ἡμᾶς, ἄνδρες ἀγαθοί, μήτε Ῥωμαίοις μήτ' ἄλλῳ τινὶ δουλεύειν ἢ θεῷ, μόνος γὰρ οὗτος ἀληθής ἐστι καὶ δίκαιος ἀνθρώπων δεσπότης, ἥκει νῦν καιρὸς ἐπαληθεῦσαι κελεύων τὸ φρόνημα τοῖς ἔργοις. 324 πρὸς ὃν αὑτοὺς μὴ καταισχύνωμεν πρότερον μηδὲ δουλείαν ἀκίνδυνον ὑπομείναντες, νῦν δὲ μετὰ δουλείας ἑλόμενοι τιμωρίας ἀνηκέστους, εἰ ζῶντες ὑπὸ Ῥωμαίοις ἐσόμεθα· πρῶτοί τε γὰρ πάντων ἀπέστημεν καὶ πολεμοῦμεν αὐτοῖς τελευταῖοι. 325 νομίζω δὲ καὶ παρὰ θεοῦ ταύτην δεδόσθαι χάριν τοῦ δύνασθαι καλῶς καὶ ἐλευθέρως ἀποθανεῖν, ὅπερ ἄλλοις οὐκ ἐγένετο παρ' ἐλπίδα κρατηθεῖσιν. 326 ἡμῖν δὲ πρόδηλος μέν ἐστιν ἡ γενησομένη μεθ' ἡμέραν ἅλωσις, ἐλευθέρα δὲ ἡ τοῦ γενναίου θανάτου μετὰ τῶν φιλτάτων αἵρεσις. οὔτε γὰρ τοῦτ' ἀποκωλύειν οἱ πολέμιοι δύνανται πάντως εὐχόμενοι ζῶντας ἡμᾶς παραλαβεῖν, οὔθ' ἡμεῖς ἐκείνους ἔτι νικᾶν μαχόμενοι. 327 ἔδει μὲν γὰρ εὐθὺς ἴσως ἐξ ἀρχῆς, ὅτε τῆς ἐλευθερίας ἡμῖν ἀντιποιεῖσθαι θελήσασι πάντα καὶ παρ' ἀλλήλων ἀπέβαινε χαλεπὰ καὶ παρὰ τῶν πολεμίων χείρω, τῆς τοῦ θεοῦ γνώμης στοχάζεσθαι καὶ γινώσκειν, ὅτι τὸ πάλαι φίλον αὐτῷ φῦλον Ἰουδαίων κατέγνωστο· 328 μένων γὰρ εὐμενὴς ἢ μετρίως γοῦν ἀπηχθημένος, οὐκ ἂν τοσούτων μὲν ἀνθρώπων περιεῖδεν ὄλεθρον, προήκατο δὲ τὴν ἱερωτάτην αὐτοῦ πόλιν πυρὶ καὶ κατασκαφαῖς πολεμίων. 329 ἡμεῖς δ' ἄρα καὶ μόνοι τοῦ παντὸς Ἰουδαίων γένους ἠλπίσαμεν περιέσεσθαι τὴν ἐλευθερίαν φυλάξαντες, ὥσπερ ἀναμάρτητοι πρὸς τὸν θεὸν γενόμενοι καὶ μηδεμιᾶς μετασχόντες *, οἳ καὶ τοὺς ἄλλους ἐδιδάξαμεν; 330 τοιγαροῦν ὁρᾶτε, πῶς ἡμᾶς ἐλέγχει μάταια προσδοκήσαντας κρείττονα τῶν ἐλπίδων τὴν ἐν τοῖς δεινοῖς ἀνάγκην ἐπαγαγών· 331 οὐδὲ γὰρ ἡ τοῦ φρουρίου φύσις ἀνάλωτος οὖσα πρὸς σωτηρίαν ὠφέληκεν, ἀλλὰ καὶ τροφῆς ἀφθονίαν καὶ πλῆθος ὅπλων καὶ τὴν ἄλλην ἔχοντες παρασκευὴν περιττεύουσαν ὑπ' αὐτοῦ περιφανῶς τοῦ θεοῦ τὴν ἐλπίδα τῆς σωτηρίας ἀφῃρήμεθα. 332 τὸ γὰρ πῦρ εἰς τοὺς πολεμίους φερόμενον οὐκ αὐτομάτως ἐπὶ τὸ κατασκευασθὲν τεῖχος ὑφ' ἡμῶν ἀνέστρεψεν, ἀλλ' ἔστι ταῦτα χόλος πολλῶν ἀδικημάτων, ἃ μανέντες εἰς τοὺς ὁμοφύλους ἐτολμήσαμεν. 333 ὑπὲρ ὧν μὴ τοῖς ἐχθίστοις Ῥωμαίοις δίκας ἀλλὰ τῷ θεῷ δι' ἡμῶν αὐτῶν ὑπόσχωμεν· αὗται δέ εἰσιν ἐκείνων μετριώτεραι· 334 θνησκέτωσαν γὰρ γυναῖκες ἀνύβριστοι καὶ παῖδες δουλείας ἀπείρατοι, μετὰ δ' αὐτοὺς ἡμεῖς εὐγενῆ χάριν ἀλλήλοις παράσχωμεν καλὸν ἐντάφιον τὴν ἐλευθερίαν φυλάξαντες. 335 πρότερον δὲ καὶ τὰ χρήματα καὶ τὸ φρούριον πυρὶ διαφθείρωμεν· λυπηθήσονται γὰρ Ῥωμαῖοι, σαφῶς οἶδα, μήτε τῶν ἡμετέρων σωμάτων κρατήσαντες καὶ τοῦ κέρδους ἁμαρτόντες. 336 τὰς τροφὰς μόνας ἐάσωμεν· αὗται γὰρ ἡμῖν τεθνηκόσι μαρτυρήσουσιν ὅτι μὴ κατ' ἔνδειαν ἐκρατήθημεν, ἀλλ' ὥσπερ ἐξ ἀρχῆς διέγνωμεν, θάνατον ἑλόμενοι πρὸ δουλείας."

The Immortality of the Soul

> *BJ* 7.337–348: Failing to obtain a unanimous response to his initial arguments, Eleazar renewed his appeal by pointing out that death releases the soul from mundane service to the body. The passage is riddled with allusions to Plato and other Greek philosophers, even though Eleazar claims that he had been taught by precepts that were "ancestral and divine" (*BJ* 7.343 LCL). Nevertheless, the passage seems more Greek than Jewish, though the issue is more complex than first seems. Cf. Sievers (1998, 23–24) for other passages where Josephus treated the afterlife, and Luz (1983) for the noble death tradition.

Ταῦτα Ἐλεάζαρος ἔλεγεν. οὐ μὴν κατ' αὐτὸ ταῖς γνώμαις προσέπιπτε τῶν παρόντων, ἀλλ' οἱ μὲν ἔσπευδον ὑπακούειν καὶ μόνον οὐχ ἡδονῆς ἐνεπίμπλαντο καλὸν εἶναι τὸν θάνατον νομίζοντες, 338 τοὺς δ' αὐτῶν μαλακωτέρους γυναικῶν καὶ γενεᾶς οἶκτος εἰσῄει, πάντως δὲ καὶ τῆς ἑαυτῶν προδήλου τελευτῆς εἰς ἀλλήλους ἀποβλέποντες τοῖς δακρύοις τὸ μὴ βουλόμενον τῆς γνώμης ἐσήμαινον. 339 τούτους ἰδὼν

Ἐλεάζαρος ἀποδειλιῶντας καὶ πρὸς τὸ μέγεθος τοῦ βουλεύματος τὰς ψυχὰς ὑποκλωμένους ἔδεισε, μή ποτε καὶ τοὺς ἐρρωμένως τῶν λόγων ἀκούσαντας αὐτοὶ συνεκθηλύνωσι ποτνιώμενοι καὶ δακρύοντες. 340 οὔκουν ἀνῆκε τὴν παρακέλευσιν, ἀλλ' αὑτὸν ἐπεγείρας καὶ πολλοῦ λήματος πλήρης γενόμενος λαμπροτέροις ἐνεχείρει λόγοις περὶ ψυχῆς ἀθανασίας, 341 μέγα τε σχετλιάσας καὶ τοῖς δακρύουσιν ἀτενὲς ἐμβλέψας "ἦ πλεῖστον," εἶπεν, "ἐψεύσθην νομίζων ἀνδράσιν ἀγαθοῖς τῶν ὑπὲρ τῆς ἐλευθερίας ἀγώνων συναρεῖσθαι, ζῆν καλῶς ἢ τεθνάναι διεγνωκόσιν. 342 ὑμεῖς δὲ ἦτε τῶν τυχόντων οὐδὲν εἰς ἀρετὴν οὐδ' εὐτολμίαν διαφέροντες, οἵ γε καὶ τὸν ἐπὶ μεγίστων ἀπαλλαγῇ κακῶν φοβεῖσθε θάνατον δέον ὑπὲρ τούτου μήτε μελλῆσαι μήτε σύμβουλον ἀναμεῖναι. 343 πάλαι γὰρ εὐθὺς ἀπὸ τῆς πρώτης αἰσθήσεως παιδεύοντες ἡμᾶς οἱ πάτριοι καὶ θεῖοι λόγοι διετέλουν ἔργοις τε καὶ φρονήμασι τῶν ἡμετέρων προγόνων αὐτοὺς βεβαιούντων, ὅτι συμφορὰ τὸ ζῆν ἐστιν ἀνθρώποις, οὐχὶ θάνατος. 344 οὗτος μὲν γὰρ ἐλευθερίαν διδοὺς ψυχαῖς εἰς τὸν οἰκεῖον καὶ καθαρὸν ἀφίησι τόπον ἀπαλλάσσεσθαι πάσης συμφορᾶς ἀπαθεῖς ἐσομένας, ἕως δέ εἰσιν ἐν σώματι θνητῷ δεδεμέναι καὶ τῶν τούτου κακῶν συναναπίμπλανται, τἀληθέστατον εἰπεῖν, τεθνήκασι· κοινωνία γὰρ θείῳ πρὸς θνητὸν ἀπρεπής ἐστι. 345 μέγα μὲν οὖν δύναται ψυχὴ καὶ σώματι συνδεδεμένη· ποιεῖ γὰρ αὐτῆς ὄργανον αἰσθανόμενον ἀοράτως αὐτὸ κινοῦσα καὶ θνητῆς φύσεως περαιτέρω προάγουσα ταῖς πράξεσιν· 346 οὐ μὴν ἀλλ' ἐπειδὰν ἀπολυθεῖσα τοῦ καθέλκοντος αὐτὴν βάρους ἐπὶ γῆν καὶ προσκρεμαμένου χῶρον ἀπολάβῃ τὸν οἰκεῖον, τότε δὴ μακαρίας ἰσχύος καὶ πανταχόθεν ἀκωλύτου μετέχει δυνάμεως, ἀόρατος μένουσα τοῖς ἀνθρωπίνοις ὄμμασιν ὥσπερ αὐτὸς ὁ θεός· 347 οὐδὲ γὰρ ἕως ἐστὶν ἐν σώματι θεωρεῖται· πρόσεισι γὰρ ἀφανῶς καὶ μὴ βλεπομένη πάλιν ἀπαλλάττεται, μίαν μὲν αὐτὴ φύσιν ἔχουσα τὴν ἄφθαρτον, αἰτία δὲ σώματι γινομένη μεταβολῆς. 348 ὅτου γὰρ ἂν ψυχὴ προσψαύσῃ, τοῦτο ζῇ καὶ τέθηλεν, ὅτου δ' ἂν ἀπαλλαγῇ, μαρανθὲν ἀποθνῄσκει· τοσοῦτον αὐτῇ περίεστιν ἀθανασίας.

The Analogy of Sleep

> *BJ* 7.349–350: Sleep allows the soul to commune with God, range about the universe unhindered by the constraints of the body, and foretell the future. Why should people who welcome the nightly repose of sleep fear death which represents an eternal freedom from the body?

ὕπνος δὲ τεκμήριον ὑμῖν ἔστω τῶν λόγων ἐναργέστατον, ἐν ᾧ ψυχαὶ τοῦ σώματος αὐτὰς μὴ περισπῶντος ἡδίστην μὲν ἔχουσιν ἀνάπαυσιν ἐφ' αὑτῶν γενόμεναι, θεῷ δ' ὁμιλοῦσαι κατὰ συγγένειαν πάντη μὲν ἐπιφοιτῶσι, πολλὰ δὲ τῶν ἐσομένων προθεσπίζουσι. 350 τί δὴ δεῖ δεδιέναι θάνατον τὴν ἐν ὕπνῳ γινομένην ἀνάπαυσιν ἀγαπῶντας; πῶς δ' οὐκ ἀνόητόν ἐστιν τὴν ἐν τῷ ζῆν ἐλευθερίαν διώκοντας τῆς ἀιδίου φθονεῖν αὑτοῖς;

The Indian Sages

> *BJ* 7.351–357: So unafraid were the Indian sages of death that they foretold their deaths in advance and even conveyed letters from loved ones on earth to relatives on the other side of the grave. The Indians consign bodies to fire to rid the soul of fleshly contagion and even sing hymns to celebrate the soul's release from the body.

351 ἔδει μὲν οὖν ἡμᾶς οἴκοθεν πεπαιδευμένους ἄλλοις εἶναι παράδειγμα τῆς πρὸς θάνατον ἑτοιμότητος· οὐ μὴν ἀλλ' εἰ καὶ τῆς παρὰ τῶν ἀλλοφύλων δεόμεθα πίστεως, βλέψωμεν εἰς Ἰνδοὺς τοὺς σοφίαν ἀσκεῖν ὑπισχνουμένους. 352 ἐκεῖνοί τε γὰρ ὄντες ἄνδρες ἀγαθοὶ τὸν μὲν τοῦ ζῆν χρόνον ὥσπερ ἀναγκαίαν τινὰ τῇ φύσει λειτουργίαν ἀκουσίως ὑπομένουσι, 353 σπεύδουσι δὲ τὰς ψυχὰς ἀπολῦσαι τῶν σωμάτων, καὶ μηδενὸς αὐτοὺς ἐπείγοντος κακοῦ μηδ' ἐξελαύνοντος πόθῳ τῆς ἀθανάτου διαίτης προλέγουσι μὲν τοῖς ἄλλοις ὅτι μέλλουσιν ἀπιέναι, καὶ ἔστιν ὁ κωλύσων οὐδείς, ἀλλὰ πάντες αὐτοὺς εὐδαιμονίζοντες πρὸς τοὺς οἰκείους ἕκαστοι διδόασιν ἐπιστολάς· 354 οὕτως βεβαίαν καὶ ἀληθεστάτην ταῖς ψυχαῖς τὴν μετ' ἀλλήλων εἶναι δίαιταν πεπιστεύκασιν. 355 οἱ δ' ἐπειδὰν

ἐπακούσωσι τῶν ἐντεταλμένων αὐτοῖς, πυρὶ τὸ σῶμα παραδόντες, ὅπως δὴ καὶ καθαρωτάτην ἀποκρίνωσι τοῦ σώματος τὴν ψυχήν, ὑμνούμενοι τελευτῶσιν· 356 ῥᾷον γὰρ ἐκείνους εἰς τὸν θάνατον οἱ φίλτατοι προπέμπουσιν ἢ τῶν ἄλλων ἀνθρώπων ἕκαστοι τοὺς πολίτας εἰς μηκίστην ἀποδημίαν, καὶ σφᾶς μὲν αὐτοὺς δακρύουσιν, ἐκείνους δὲ μακαρίζουσιν ἤδη τὴν ἀθάνατον τάξιν ἀπολαμβάνοντας. 357 ἆρ' οὖν οὐκ αἰδούμεθα χεῖρον Ἰνδῶν φρονοῦντες καὶ διὰ τῆς αὐτῶν ἀτολμίας τοὺς πατρίους νόμους, οἳ πᾶσιν ἀνθρώποις εἰς ζῆλον ἥκουσιν, αἰσχρῶς ὑβρίζοντες;

The Destruction of the Jewish Race

> *BJ* 7.358–374: Now Eleazar shifts from philosophical arguments to consider the unfortunate fate of Jews in contemporary political affairs. Even Jews who had allied themselves with Gentiles against the Zealots discover to their horror that Syrians and Greeks murder all Jews with impunity, not just Zealots. Most pitiable, then, are not those Jews who fall bravely in battle while defending their freedom, but rather once free Jews who, bearing the disgrace of servitude, now pray for death but are denied it.

ἀλλ' εἴ γε καὶ τοὺς ἐναντίους ἐξ ἀρχῆς λόγους ἐπαιδεύθημεν, ὡς ἄρα μέγιστον ἀγαθὸν ἀνθρώποις ἐστὶ τὸ ζῆν συμφορὰ δ' ὁ θάνατος, ὁ γοῦν καιρὸς ἡμᾶς παρακαλεῖ φέρειν εὐκαρδίως αὐτὸν θεοῦ γνώμῃ καὶ κατ' ἀνάγκας τελευτήσαντας· 359 πάλαι γάρ, ὡς ἔοικε, κατὰ τοῦ κοινοῦ παντὸς Ἰουδαίων γένους ταύτην ἔθετο τὴν ψῆφον ὁ θεός, ὥσθ' ἡμᾶς τοῦ ζῆν ἀπηλλάχθαι μὴ μέλλοντας αὐτῷ χρῆσθαι κατὰ τρόπον. 360 μὴ γὰρ αὐτοῖς ὑμῖν ἀνάπτετε τὰς αἰτίας μηδὲ χαρίζεσθε τοῖς Ῥωμαίοις, ὅτι πάντας ἡμᾶς ὁ πρὸς αὐτοὺς πόλεμος διέφθειρεν· οὐ γὰρ ἐκείνων ἰσχύι ταῦτα συμβέβηκεν, ἀλλὰ κρείττων αἰτία γενομένη τὸ δοκεῖν ἐκείνοις νικᾶν παρέσχηκε. 361 ποίοις γὰρ ὅπλοις Ῥωμαίων τεθνήκασιν οἱ Καισάρειαν Ἰουδαῖοι κατοικοῦντες; 362 ἀλλ' οὐδὲ μελλήσαντας αὐτοὺς ἐκείνων ἀφίστασθαι, μεταξὺ δὲ τὴν ἑβδόμην ἑορτάζοντας τὸ πλῆθος τῶν Καισαρέων ἐπιδραμὸν μηδὲ χεῖρας ἀνταίροντας ἅμα γυναιξὶ καὶ τέκνοις κατέσφαξαν, οὐδ' αὐτοὺς Ῥωμαίους ἐντραπέντες, οἳ μόνους ἡμᾶς ἡγοῦντο πολεμίους τοὺς ἀφεστηκότας. 363 ἀλλὰ φήσει τις, ὅτι Καισαρεῦσιν ἦν ἀεὶ διαφορὰ πρὸς τοὺς παρ' αὐτοῖς, καὶ τοῦ καιροῦ λαβόμενοι τὸ παλαιὸν μῖσος ἀπεπλήρωσαν. 364 τί οὖν τοὺς ἐν Σκυθοπόλει φῶμεν; ἡμῖν γὰρ ἐκεῖνοι διὰ τοὺς Ἕλληνας πολεμεῖν ἐτόλμησαν, ἀλλ' οὐ μετὰ τῶν συγγενῶν ἡμῶν Ῥωμαίους ἀμύνεσθαι. 365 πολὺ τοίνυν ὤνησεν αὐτοὺς ἡ πρὸς ἐκείνους εὔνοια καὶ πίστις· ὑπ' αὐτῶν μέντοι πανοικεσίᾳ πικρῶς κατεφονεύθησαν ταύτην τῆς συμμαχίας ἀπολαβόντες ἀμοιβήν· 366 ἃ γὰρ ἐκείνους ὑφ' ἡμῶν ἐκώλυσαν ταῦθ' ὑπέμειναν ὡς αὐτοὶ δρᾶσαι θελήσαντες. μακρὸν ἂν εἴη νῦν ἰδίᾳ περὶ ἑκάστων λέγειν· 367 ἴστε γὰρ ὅτι τῶν ἐν Συρίᾳ πόλεων οὐκ ἔστιν ἥτις τοὺς παρ' αὐτῇ κατοικοῦντας Ἰουδαίους οὐκ ἀνῄρηκεν, ἡμῖν πλέον ἢ Ῥωμαίοις ὄντας πολεμίους· 368 ὅπου γε Δαμασκηνοὶ μηδὲ πρόφασιν εὔλογον πλάσαι δυνηθέντες φόνου μιαρωτάτου τὴν αὐτῶν πόλιν ἐνέπλησαν ὀκτακισχιλίους πρὸς τοῖς μυρίοις Ἰουδαίους ἅμα γυναιξὶ καὶ γενεαῖς ἀποσφάξαντες. 369 τὸ δ' ἐν Αἰγύπτῳ πλῆθος τῶν μετ' αἰκίας ἀνῃρημένων ἓξ που μυριάδας ὑπερβάλλειν ἐπυνθανόμεθα. κἀκεῖνοι μὲν ἴσως ἐπ' ἀλλοτρίας γῆς οὐδὲν ἀντίπαλον εὑράμενοι τοῖς πολεμίοις οὕτως ἀπέθανον, τοῖς δ' ἐπὶ τῆς οἰκείας τὸν πρὸς Ῥωμαίους πόλεμον ἀραμένοις ἅπασί τε τῶν ἐλπίδα νίκης ἐχυρᾶς παρασχεῖν δυναμένων οὐχ ὑπῆρξε; 370 καὶ γὰρ ὅπλα καὶ τείχη καὶ φρουρίων δυσάλωτοι κατασκευαὶ καὶ φρόνημα πρὸς τοὺς ὑπὲρ τῆς ἐλευθερίας κινδύνους ἄτρεπτον πάντας πρὸς τὴν ἀπόστασιν ἐπέρρωσεν. 371 ἀλλὰ ταῦτα πρὸς βραχὺν χρόνον ἀρκέσαντα καὶ ταῖς ἐλπίσιν ἡμᾶς ἐπάραντα μειζόνων ἀρχὴ κακῶν ἐφάνη· πάντα γὰρ ἥλω, καὶ πάντα τοῖς πολεμίοις ὑπέπεσεν, ὥσπερ εἰς τὴν ἐκείνων εὐκλεεστέραν νίκην, οὐκ εἰς τὴν τῶν παρασκευασαμένων σωτηρίαν εὐτρεπισθέντα. 372 καὶ τοὺς μὲν ἐν ταῖς μάχαις ἀποθνήσκοντας εὐδαιμονίζειν προσῆκον· ἀμυνόμενοι γὰρ καὶ τὴν ἐλευθερίαν οὐ προέμενοι τεθνήκασι· τὸ δὲ πλῆθος τῶν ὑπὸ Ῥωμαίοις γενομένων τίς οὐκ ἂν ἐλεήσειε; τίς οὐκ ἂν ἐπειχθείη πρὸ τοῦ ταὐτὰ παθεῖν ἐκείνοις ἀποθανεῖν; 373 ὧν οἱ μὲν στρεβλούμενοι καὶ πυρὶ καὶ μάστιξιν αἰκιζόμενοι τεθνήκασιν, οἱ δ' ἀπὸ θηρίων ἡμίβρωτοι πρὸς δευτέραν αὐτοῖς τροφὴν ζῶντες ἐφυλάχθησαν, γέλωτα καὶ παίγνιον τοῖς πολεμίοις παρασχόντες. 374 ἐκείνων μὲν οὖν ἀθλιωτάτους ὑποληπτέον τοὺς ἔτι ζῶντας, οἳ πολλάκις εὐχόμενοι τὸν θάνατον λαβεῖν οὐκ ἔχουσιν.

The Abandonment of Jerusalem

> *BJ* 7.375–379: What has become of Jerusalem, the city that God founded and inhabited? Would that the Jews had died before seeing Jerusalem so horribly disfigured at the hands of enemies!

ποῦ δ' ἡ μεγάλη πόλις, ἡ τοῦ παντὸς Ἰουδαίων γένους μητρόπολις, ἡ τοσούτοις μὲν ἐρυμνὴ τειχῶν περιβόλοις, τοσαῦτα δ' αὐτῆς φρούρια καὶ μεγέθη πύργων προβεβλημένη, μόλις δὲ χωροῦσα τὰς εἰς τὸν πόλεμον παρασκευάς, τοσαύτας δὲ μυριάδας ἀνδρῶν ἔχουσα τῶν ὑπὲρ αὐτῆς μαχομένων; 376 ποῦ γέγονεν ἡμῖν ἡ τὸν θεὸν ἔχειν οἰκιστὴν πεπιστευμένη; πρόρριζος ἐκ βάθρων ἀνήρπασται, καὶ μόνον αὐτῆς μνημεῖον ἀπολείπεται τὸ τῶν ἀνῃρημένων ἔτι τοῖς λειψάνοις ἐποικοῦν. 377 πρεσβῦται δὲ δύστηνοι τῇ σποδῷ τοῦ τεμένους παρακάθηνται καὶ γυναῖκες ὀλίγαι πρὸς ὕβριν αἰσχίστην ὑπὸ τῶν πολεμίων τετηρημέναι. 378 ταῦτα τίς ἐν νῷ βαλλόμενος ἡμῶν καρτερήσει τὸν ἥλιον ὁρᾶν, κἂν δύνηται ζῆν ἀκινδύνως; τίς οὕτω τῆς πατρίδος ἐχθρός, ἢ τίς οὕτως ἄνανδρος καὶ φιλόψυχος, ὡς μὴ καὶ περὶ τοῦ μέχρι νῦν ζῆσαι μετανοεῖν; 379 ἀλλ' εἴθε πάντες ἐτεθνήκειμεν πρὶν τὴν ἱερὰν ἐκείνην πόλιν χερσὶν ἰδεῖν κατασκαπτομένην πολεμίων, πρὶν τὸν ναὸν τὸν ἅγιον οὕτως ἀνοσίως ἐξορωρυγμένον.

Dying Honorably

> *BJ* 7.380–388: Eleazar's speech did not take at first because some of the more sensitive hearers broke out in tears and acted like women (*BJ* 7.339). Thus, a forthright appeal to the audience's manliness constitutes a major component of the second half of the speech (e.g., ἄνδρες ἀγαθοί, 7.323, 352; ἀνδράσιν ἀγαθοῖς, 7.341; καλῶς ἀποθανεῖν, 7.380; ἐπ' ἀνδρείᾳ, 7.383). By the end of

the speech the Zealots' own wives and children were demanding to die (7.387), nor could Eleazar continue speaking because everyone kept clamoring for the slaughter to begin at once (7.389).

ἐπεὶ δὲ ἡμᾶς οὐκ ἀγεννὴς ἐλπὶς ἐβουκόλησεν, ὡς τάχα που δυνήσεσθαι τοὺς πολεμίους ὑπὲρ αὐτῆς ἀμύνασθαι, φρούδη δὲ γέγονε νῦν καὶ μόνους ἡμᾶς ἐπὶ τῆς ἀνάγκης καταλέλοιπεν, σπεύσωμεν καλῶς ἀποθανεῖν, ἐλεήσωμεν ἡμᾶς αὐτοὺς καὶ τὰ τέκνα καὶ τὰς γυναῖκας, ἕως ἡμῖν ἔξεστιν παρ' ἡμῶν αὐτῶν λαβεῖν τὸν ἔλεον. 381 ἐπὶ μὲν γὰρ θάνατον ἐγεννήθημεν καὶ τοὺς ἐξ αὑτῶν ἐγεννήσαμεν, καὶ τοῦτον οὐδὲ τοῖς εὐδαιμονοῦσιν ἔστι διαφυγεῖν· 382 ὕβρις δὲ καὶ δουλεία καὶ τὸ βλέπειν γυναῖκας εἰς αἰσχύνην ἀγομένας μετὰ τέκνων οὐκ ἔστιν ἀνθρώποις κακὸν ἐκ φύσεως ἀναγκαῖον, ἀλλὰ ταῦτα διὰ τὴν αὐτῶν δειλίαν ὑπομένουσιν οἱ παρὸν πρὸ αὐτῶν ἀποθανεῖν μὴ θελήσαντες. 383 ἡμεῖς δὲ ἐπ' ἀνδρείᾳ μέγα φρονοῦντες Ῥωμαίων ἀπέστημεν καὶ τὰ τελευταῖα νῦν ἐπὶ σωτηρίᾳ προκαλουμένων ἡμᾶς οὐχ ὑπηκούσαμεν. 384 τίνι τοίνυν οὐκ ἔστιν ὁ θυμὸς αὐτῶν πρόδηλος, εἰ ζώντων ἡμῶν κρατήσουσιν; ἄθλιοι μὲν οἱ νέοι τῆς ῥώμης τῶν σωμάτων εἰς πολλὰς αἰκίας ἀρκέσοντες, ἄθλιοι δὲ οἱ παρηβηκότες φέρειν τῆς ἡλικίας τὰς συμφορὰς οὐ δυναμένης. 385 ὄψεταί τις γυναῖκα πρὸς βίαν ἀγομένην, φωνῆς ἐπακούσεται τέκνου πατέρα βοῶντος χεῖρας δεδεμένος. 386 ἀλλ' ἕως εἰσὶν ἐλεύθεραι καὶ ξίφος ἔχουσιν, καλὴν ὑπουργίαν ὑπουργησάτωσαν· ἀδούλωτοι μὲν ὑπὸ τῶν πολεμίων ἀποθάνωμεν, ἐλεύθεροι δὲ μετὰ τέκνων καὶ γυναικῶν τοῦ ζῆν συνεξέλθωμεν. 387 ταῦθ' ἡμᾶς οἱ νόμοι κελεύουσι, ταῦθ' ἡμᾶς γυναῖκες καὶ παῖδες ἱκετεύουσι· τούτων τὴν ἀνάγκην θεὸς ἀπέσταλκε, τούτων Ῥωμαῖοι τἀναντία θέλουσι, καὶ μή τις ἡμῶν πρὸ τῆς ἁλώσεως ἀποθάνῃ δεδοίκασι. 388 σπεύσωμεν οὖν ἀντὶ τῆς ἐλπιζομένης αὐτοῖς καθ' ἡμῶν ἀπολαύσεως ἔκπληξιν τοῦ θανάτου καὶ θαῦμα τῆς τόλμης καταλιπεῖν."

Aftermath

BJ 7.389–401: Josephus claims that "all" the listeners (πάντες, *BJ* 7.389) set about to follow Eleazar's dictates to the letter. Like men possessed (δαιμονῶντες, ibid.) they went their separate ways, each eager to outstrip his neighbor in the task of putting loved ones to death. Then, choosing by lot ten of their number to dispatch the rest, the Zealots lay down beside already dead family members and offered their own throats to the killers. The last one to die set a fire to King Herod's palace before slaughtering himself. Only two women and five children evaded death at Masada, though 960 others perished.

Ἔτι βουλόμενον αὐτὸν παρακαλεῖν πάντες ὑπετέμνοντο καὶ πρὸς τὴν πρᾶξιν ἠπείγοντο ἀνεπισχέτου τινὸς ὁρμῆς πεπληρωμένοι, καὶ δαιμονῶντες ἀπῄεσαν ἄλλος πρὸ ἄλλου φθάσαι γλιχόμενος καὶ ταύτην ἐπίδειξιν εἶναι τῆς ἀνδρείας καὶ τῆς εὐβουλίας νομίζοντες, τὸ μή τις ἐν ὑστάτοις γενόμενος ὀφθῆναι· τοσοῦτος αὐτοῖς γυναικῶν καὶ παιδίων καὶ τῆς αὐτῶν σφαγῆς ἔρως ἐνέπεσεν. 390 καὶ μὴν οὐδ' ὅπερ ἄν τις ᾠήθη τῇ πράξει προσιόντες ἠμβλύνθησαν, ἀλλ' ἀτενῆ τὴν γνώμην διεφύλαξαν οἵαν ἔσχον τῶν λόγων ἀκροώμενοι, τοῦ μὲν οἰκείου καὶ φιλοστόργου πάθους ἅπασι παραμένοντος, τοῦ λογισμοῦ δὲ ὡς τὰ κράτιστα βεβουλευκότος τοῖς φιλτάτοις ἐπικρατοῦντος. 391 ὁμοῦ γὰρ ἠσπάζοντο γυναῖκας περιπτυσσόμενοι καὶ τέκνα προσηγκαλίζοντο τοῖς ὑστάτοις φιλήμασιν ἐμφυόμενοι καὶ δακρύοντες, 392 ὁμοῦ δὲ καθάπερ ἀλλοτρίαις χερσὶν ὑπουργούμενοι συνετέλουν τὸ βούλευμα, τὴν ἐπίνοιαν ὧν πείσονται κακῶν ὑπὸ τοῖς πολεμίοις γενόμενοι παραμύθιον τῆς ἐν τῷ κτείνειν ἀνάγκης ἔχοντες. 393 καὶ πέρας οὐδεὶς τηλικούτου τολμήματος ἥττων εὑρέθη, πάντες δὲ διὰ τῶν οἰκειοτάτων διεξῆλθον, ἄθλιοι τῆς ἀνάγκης, οἷς αὐτοχειρὶ γυναῖκας τὰς αὐτῶν καὶ τέκνα κτεῖναι κακῶν ἔδοξεν εἶναι τὸ κουφότατον. 394 οὔτε δὴ τοίνυν τὴν ἐπὶ τοῖς πεπραγμένοις ὀδύνην ἔτι φέροντες καὶ τοὺς ἀνῃρημένους νομίζοντες ἀδικεῖν εἰ καὶ βραχὺν αὐτοῖς ἔτι χρόνον ἐπιζήσουσι, ταχὺ μὲν τὴν κτῆσιν ἅπασαν εἰς ταὐτὸ σωρεύσαντες πῦρ εἰς αὐτὴν ἐνέβαλον,

395 κλήρῳ δ' ἐξ αὐτῶν ἑλόμενοι δέκα τοὺς ἁπάντων σφαγεῖς ἐσομένους, καὶ γυναικί τις αὐτὸν καὶ παισὶ κειμένοις παραστρώσας καὶ τὰς χεῖρας περιβαλών, παρεῖχον ἑτοίμους τὰς σφαγὰς τοῖς τὴν δύστηνον ὑπουργίαν ἐκτελοῦσιν. 396 οἱ δ' ἀτρέπτως πάντας φονεύσαντες τὸν αὐτὸν ἐπ' ἀλλήλοις τοῦ κλήρου νόμον ὥρισαν, ἵν' ὁ λαχὼν τοὺς ἐννέα κτείνας ἑαυτὸν ἐπὶ πᾶσιν ἀνέλῃ· πάντες οὕτως αὑτοῖς ἐθάρρουν μήτ' εἰς τὸ δρᾶν μήτ' εἰς τὸ παθεῖν ἄλλος ἄλλου διαφέρειν. 397 καὶ τέλος οἱ μὲν τὰς σφαγὰς ὑπέθεσαν, ὁ δ' εἷς καὶ τελευταῖος τὸ πλῆθος τῶν κειμένων περιαθρήσας, μή πού τις ἔτ' ἐν πολλῷ φόνῳ τῆς αὐτοῦ λείπεται χειρὸς δεόμενος, ὡς ἔγνω πάντας ἀνῃρημένους, πῦρ μὲν πολὺ τοῖς βασιλείοις ἐνίησιν, ἀθρόᾳ δὲ τῇ χειρὶ δι' αὐτοῦ πᾶν ἐλάσας τὸ ξίφος πλησίον τῶν οἰκείων κατέπεσε. 398 καὶ οἱ μὲν ἐτεθνήκεσαν ὑπειληφότες οὐδὲν ἔχον ψυχὴν ὑποχείριον ἐξ αὐτῶν Ῥωμαίοις καταλιπεῖν, 399 ἔλαθεν δὲ γυνὴ πρεσβῦτις καὶ συγγενὴς ἑτέρα τις Ἐλεαζάρου, φρονήσει καὶ παιδείᾳ πλεῖστον γυναικῶν διαφέρουσα, καὶ πέντε παιδία τοῖς ὑπονόμοις, οἳ ποτὸν ἦγον ὕδωρ διὰ γῆς, ἐγκατακρυβῆναι τῶν ἄλλων πρὸς τῇ σφαγῇ τὰς διανοίας ἐχόντων, 400 οἳ τὸν ἀριθμὸν ἦσαν ἑξήκοντα πρὸς τοῖς ἐνακοσίοις γυναικῶν ἅμα καὶ παίδων αὐτοῖς συναριθμουμένων. 401 καὶ τὸ πάθος ἐπράχθη πεντεκαιδεκάτῃ Ξανθικοῦ μηνός.

The Admiration of the Romans

BJ 7.402–406: the Romans discover that nearly all the defenders have died. One of the two surviving women provides an account of Eleazar's speech and details pertinent to the mass suicide. Instead of exulting over the slain the Romans admire their enemies' noble character and disdain for death.

Οἱ δὲ Ῥωμαῖοι μάχην ἔτι προσδοκῶντες, ὑπὸ τὴν ἕω διασκευασάμενοι καὶ τὰς ἀπὸ τῶν χωμάτων ἐφόδους ταῖς ἐπιβάθραις γεφυρώσαντες προσβολὴν ἐποιοῦντο. 403 βλέποντες δ' οὐδένα τῶν πολεμίων, ἀλλὰ δεινὴν πανταχόθεν ἐρημίαν καὶ πῦρ ἔνδον καὶ σιωπήν, ἀπόρως εἶχον τὸ γεγονὸς συμβαλεῖν, καὶ τέλος ὡς εἰς ἄφεσιν βολῆς ἠλάλαξαν, εἴ τινα τῶν ἔνδον προκαλέσαιντο. 404 τῆς δὲ βοῆς αἴσθησις γίνεται τοῖς γυναίοις, κἀκ τῶν ὑπονόμων ἀναδῦσαι τὸ πραχθὲν ὡς εἶχε πρὸς τοὺς Ῥωμαίους ἐμήνυον, πάντα τῆς ἑτέρας ὡς ἐλέχθη τε καὶ τίνα τρόπον ἐπράχθη σαφῶς ἐκδιηγουμένης. 405 οὐ μὴν ῥᾳδίως αὐτῇ προσεῖχον τῷ μεγέθει τοῦ τολμήματος ἀπιστοῦντες, ἐπεχείρουν τε τὸ πῦρ σβεννύναι καὶ ταχέως ὁδὸν δι' αὐτοῦ τεμόντες τῶν βασιλείων ἐντὸς ἐγένοντο. 406 καὶ τῷ πλήθει τῶν πεφονευμένων ἐπιτυχόντες οὐχ ὡς ἐπὶ πολεμίοις ἥσθησαν, τὴν δὲ γενναιότητα τοῦ βουλεύματος καὶ τὴν ἐν τοσούτοις ἄτρεπτον ἐπὶ τῶν ἔργων ἐθαύμασαν τοῦ θανάτου καταφρόνησιν.

Text Notes: Josephus

Vita 7–12

7 γνωριμώτατος ὢν ἐν τῇ μεγίστῃ πόλει τῶν παρ' ἡμῖν τοῖς Ἱεροσολυμίταις: the phrase τῇ μεγίστῃ πόλει ("very large city") refers to Jerusalem. Construe the def. article τῶν (part. gen.) with γνωριμώτατος ὤν: "being (one of) the most notable men." Παρ' ἡμῖν is akin to Lat. *nobis iudicibus* = "in our opinion." The prep. phrase παρ' ἡμῖν is in appos. to τοῖς Ἱεροσολυμίταις: "in our opinion—we, the citizens of Jerusalem." For details assoc. with Josephus' parentage, noble birth, sense of justice, and the city of Jerusalem cf. Mason (2001, 11–12).

8 ἐγὼ δὲ συμπαιδευόμενος ἀδελφῷ Ματθίᾳ τοὔνομα: the prep. σύν in the ptc. συμπαιδευόμενος indicates that the compound ptc. construes with ἀδελφῷ Ματθίᾳ τοὔνομα: "being educated with my brother, Matthias by name." Τοὔνομα (crasis of τό + ὄνομα) represents an accus. resp. with a quality or attribute (here the name is conceived of as the quality or attribute, cf. Smyth §1601.b). Matthias prob. was Josephus' *older* brother, given the plupf. in the next clause and the fact that he bears the father's name (so Mason 2001, 12).

8 γεγόνει γάρ μοι γνήσιος ἐξ ἀμφοῖν τῶν γονέων: Josephus' high status is attested to by his use of the adj. γνήσιος ("legitimate, true"), the opposite of νόθος ("bastard," usu. the spawn of a free father and slave mother). Josephus' brother Matthias, however, was the issue of two free-born parents (ἐξ ἀμφοῖν τῶν γονέων), a detail that would have mattered to any status-conscious ancient who fretted about the legitimacy of one's parents and close family members.

8 εἰς μεγάλην παιδείας προύκοπτον ἐπίδοσιν μνήμῃ τε καὶ συνέσει δοκῶν διαφέρειν: προκόπτω may mean make one's way, i.e., "advance" (LSJ II.1), "esp. in Philos., of moral and intellectual progress" (LSJ II.3). E.g., St. Paul writes that he was "advancing [προέκοπτον] in Judaism beyond many of [his] own age" (Gal 1:14), for which cf. Zeno Cit. 1.56; Chrysipp. Stoic. 2.337; Arrian *Epict.* 1.4.1; 3.2.5. The vb. διαφέρω oft means "to be different from a person" (LSJ III.4), espec. in the sense of excelling someone "in a thing" (τινί). Thus, ἀρετῇ τοὺς ἄλλους (Diod. Sic. 11.67; cf. Thuc. 2.39; Alex. Rhet. 36.6; Isoc. 3.39; Plato *Apol.* 35b). In boasting of his superiority in "memory and understanding" (μνήμῃ τε καὶ συνέσει) Josephus likely refers to qualities that distinguished him as a young orator. Cf. *memoria bona* (Cic. *Att.* 8.4.2); *Hortensius... primum memoria tanta* (Cic. *Brut.* 301); *memoria... comprehendere* (Cic. *de Or.* 1.154); *memoriam agitare* (Quint. *Inst.* 1.8.14). For the sign. of memory work in both Greco-Roman and Jewish education, cf. Mason (2001, 12–13 nn. 56, 58).

9 ἔτι δ' ἀντίπαις ὢν περὶ τεσσαρεσκαιδέκατον ἔτος διὰ τὸ φιλογράμματον ὑπὸ πάντων ἐπῃνούμην: ἀντίπαις means "a mere boy" (LSJ II.2; cf. Polyb. 15.33.12; 27.15.4; Dion. Hal. 4.3; Plut. *Aem.* 22), a term well-suited to the fourteen year old Josephus. Not only was he proficient in qualities that distinguished him as an orator (cf. μνήμῃ τε καὶ συνέσει, 8) but he was possessed of a "bookishness" (τὸ φιλογράμματον)—i.e., tech. proficiency—for which he was commended by all. For ἐπῃνούμην ("I was commended") cf. Dem. *De Cor.* 113; Isocr. *Panathen.* 267; Chrys. *Adv. Jud.* vol. 48 pg. 844; Liban. *Or.* 1.224.

9 συνιόντων ἀεὶ τῶν ἀρχιερέων καὶ τῶν τῆς πόλεως πρώτων...: gen. abs. The pres. act. ptc. συνιόντων (from σύνειμι: "to come together, assemble") indicates that the action of coming to the fourteen-year-old Josephus for consultation took place *at the same time as* the action represented in the sentence's mn. vb. ἐπῃνούμην. For the references to the chief priests and leading men of the city cf. Mason (2001, 14 nn. 62–63).

9 ...ὑπὲρ τοῦ παρ' ἐμοῦ περὶ τῶν νομίμων ἀκριβέστερόν τι γνῶναι: note the prepos. ὑπέρ + the articular infin. τοῦ... γνῶναι: "for the purpose [ὑπέρ] of knowing something more accurately from me concerning [περί] usages." Josephus refers to these "usages" (τὰ νόμιμα) elsewhere in *Vita* 74, 191 and 295; cf. τὰ κοινὰ τῶν Ἑλλήνων νόμιμα (Thuc. 3.59). Also in the sense of "legal rights" (LSJ II.2): νόμιμα καὶ φιλάνθρωπα (*BGU* 1074.2 [AD 1 cent.]); ἄνευ νομίμων ἀπωθεῖσθαι (= "to be illegally

ejected," *Pfay* 124.18 [AD 2 cent.]). For further details cf. Mason (2001, 14–15 nn. 64–66).

10 περὶ δὲ ἑκκαίδεκα ἔτη γενόμενος ἐβουλήθην τῶν παρ' ἡμῖν αἱρέσεων ἐμπειρίαν λαβεῖν: for the idiom περί + accus. of time (LSJ C.II.1) cf. περὶ λύχνων ἁφάς (= "about the time of lamp-lighting," Hdt. 7.215); περὶ μέσας νύκτας (= "about midnight," Xen. *Ana.* 1.7.1); περὶ τούτους τοὺς χρόνους (= "at about these times," Thuc. 3.89). Thus, περὶ... ἑκκαίδεκα ἔτη γενόμενος means, "when I came to be *about* sixteen years old" (cf. Lat. *annos prope sedecim natus*). Note ἐβουλήθην ("I desired"), not "I was forced"; Josephus takes pride in his willing submission to learning. Thus, he did not hate his studies as so many of the boys did, e.g., *graecas litteras oderam, quibus puerulus imbuebar* (Augustine, *Conf.* 1.13.20). Here αἵρεσις means (philosophical) "sect" or "school" (LSJ B.II.2), espec. the relig. parties into which the Jews were divided (LSJ B.II.2). Cf. Acts 5:17; 15:5; 26:5 (also of the Christians: Acts 24:5, 14; 28:22). For παρ' ἡμῖν cf. *Vita* 7 above. For Josephus' age and submission to what was essentially a philosophical regimen cf. Mason (2001, 15 nn. 67, 69).

10 τρεῖς δ' εἰσὶν αὗται, Φαρισαίων μὲν ἡ πρώτη, καὶ Σαδδουκαίων ἡ δευτέρα, τρίτη δ' Ἐσσηνῶν: the demonst. pron. αὗται ("these") refers to the sects mentioned in the prev clause (τῶν... αἱρέσεων). Likewise, the ordinals ἡ πρώτη... ἡ δευτέρα... τρίτη presume the noun ἡ αἵρεσις in each case: "the first [sect]..., the second [sect]..., and a third [sect]..." The placement of the particles μέν and δέ suggs. that, in Josephus' mind, the Pharisees and Sadducees were somewhat distinct from the third group, the Essenes; generally, the first two groups represented the establishment in first-cent. Judaism (cf. Ellison 1979, 981), whereas the Essenes were a rigorist group who lived in separate communities "dr[awn] aside from the main stream of Jewish life" (Bruce 1979, 392). For further details on the three sects cf. Mason (2001, 15–16 nn. 71–73).

10 καθὼς πολλάκις εἴπομεν: = "as we said oft" Prob. Josephus alludes to descrs. of the three sects in *Antiq* 13.171; 18.11 and *BJ* 2.119–166.

10 οὕτως γὰρ ᾤμην αἱρήσεσθαι τὴν ἀρίστην, εἰ πάσας καταμάθοιμι: the vb. ᾤμην (1 sing. impf. indic. act. of οἴομαι) sets off accus. with infin. in indir. state. (Smyth §1867). A subj. accus. is not needed when the subj. of the infin. and finite vb. are the same, as here: "for thus I supposed that I would choose the best if I learned them all." The vb. καταμάθοιμι in the dep. clause is in the optv. mood because the mn. vb. ᾤμην is in a sec. tense (Smyth §2621). Young male elites were somewhat expected to have studied various philosophies in search of the truth (cf. Mason 2001, 18 n. 75, and passages there).

11 σκληραγωγήσας οὖν ἐμαυτὸν καὶ πολλὰ πονηθεὶς τὰς τρεῖς διῆλθον...: the circumst. ptcs. σκληραγωγήσας ("having brought myself up hardy") and πονηθεὶς ("having toiled much") in the aor. tense describe action that occurs before that mentioned in the mn. vb. διῆλθον ("I passed through"). It seems incredible that Josephus "passed through" (διῆλθον, cf. *Vita* 365) the training regimens of all three (τὰς τρεῖς) sects in so short a time! Just the Essenes' initiation procedure required a three year novitiate (cf. Joseph. *BJ* 2.137–138); at the end of the first year the novice was admitted to the ritual purification in water, but two more years had to elapse before admission to the common meal, and still more before the solemn oaths (Bruce 1979, 392; Mason 2003, 41).

11 καὶ μηδὲ τὴν ἐντεῦθεν ἐμπειρίαν ἱκανὴν ἐμαυτῷ νομίσας εἶναι...: the aor. act. ptc. νομίσας sets off accus. with infin. in indir. state. (Smyth §1867): "nor had I even supposed [νομίσας] that the experience from this was sufficient for myself." The adv. ἐντεῦθεν ("from this") refers to the self-imposed rigors Josephus describes in the prev clause.

11 πυθόμενός τινα Βάννουν ὄνομα κατὰ τὴν ἐρημίαν διατρίβειν, ἐσθῆτι μὲν ἀπὸ δένδρων χρώμενον, τροφὴν δὲ τὴν αὐτομάτως φυομένην προσφερόμενον, ψυχρῷ δὲ ὕδατι τὴν ἡμέραν καὶ τὴν νύκτα πολλάκις λουόμενον πρὸς ἁγνείαν, ζηλωτὴς ἐγενόμην αὐτου: the words πυθόμενος... ζηλωτὴς ἐγενόμην αὐτου ("upon discovering that... I became his devoted [disciple]") constitute the mn. clause, the subj. of which is Josephus; the infin. διατρίβειν and ptcs. χρώμενον..., προσφερόμενον...,

λουόμενον ("...that he was spending time..., wearing..., eating..., and washing himself") depend on πυθόμενος and refer to Bannus. For ὄνομα as an accus. resp. cf. *Vita* 8 above; for the prep. phrase κατὰ τὴν ἐρημίαν ("throughout the wilderness") cf. Joseph. *Antiq* 3.315; 4.1; 4.239; for πρὸς ἁγνείαν ("for purity") cf. Joseph. *BJ* 2.138; for προσφέρω in the mid. voice with the mng. "to take of food and drink" (LSJ C.1) cf. Xen. *Cyr.* 4.2.41; Aesch. 1.145; Plut. *Dem.* 30; *Cic.* 3. Bannus seems to have been an independently minded ascetic, so not attached to the three sects mentioned; he rather resembles John the Baptist who likewise dressed and ate peculiarly (Mt 3:4; Mk 1:6) and held an assoc. with water (Mt 3:11; Mk 1:8; Lk 3:16; Jn 1:26). The teacher's name Bannus may well involve a word-play on the Lat. *balneum* ("bath"; cf. Mason 2001, 18 n. 78). He is otherwise unknown.

12 καὶ διατρίψας παρ' αὐτῷ ἐνιαυτοὺς τρεῖς...: the aor. ptc. διατρίψας recalls διατρίβειν in *Vita* 11 and indicates a further link between the master Bannus and his disciple Josephus. The three years mentioned here "in his presence" (παρ' αὐτῷ) sugg. that the young Josephus' asceticism transpired with Bannus alone, casting further doubt on the assertion that Josephus "passed through" (διῆλθον) the three sects mentioned in *Vita* 11.

12 ...καὶ τὴν ἐπιθυμίαν τελειώσας εἰς τὴν πόλιν ὑπέστρεφον: the expression "having achieved my desire" (τὴν ἐπιθυμίαν τελειώσας) recalls Josephus' willingness to gain pers. experience with the three sects in Judaism (cf. ἐβουλήθην τῶν... αἱρέσεων ἐμπειρίαν λαβεῖν, *Vita* 10). Josephus got what he needed from Bannus, then returned to normal life. Upper-class Romans were expected to be enamored of philosophy, but not too enamored (cf. Mason 2003, 40–41).

12 ἐννεακαιδέκατον δ' ἔτος ἔχων ἠρξάμην τε πολιτεύεσθαι τῇ Φαρισαίων αἱρέσει κατακολουθῶν: for the temp. expression ἐννεακαιδέκατον... ἔτος ἔχων ("being now in my nineteenth year") cf. *Vita* 10. Some mss. omit τε which seems problematic here. For πολιτεύεσθαι ("take part in government," LSJ B.II.1) cf. Critias 45 D; Nausiph. 2; Hyp. *Eux.* 27; Dem. 18.18; for κατακολουθῶν ("follow a historical or philosophical authority," LSJ I.1) cf. Philod.

Rhet. 2.146S; Polyb. 2.56.2. Josephus, fresh from the wilderness (cf. κατὰ τὴν ἐρημίαν, *Vita* 11), possibly joined the Pharisaic sect at the conclusion of his quest because it seemed to possess an urbane sophistication:

> By the first century AD (before the fall of Jerusalem) Pharisaism had become a bourgeois rather than a popular movement, a predominantly Jerusalem "city" party. No doubt the Jerusalem Pharisees also had their followers in the country districts, but their attitude to the *'am ha'ares* ["people of the land"] suggests that the gulf between the Pharisees and the peasants who formed the bulk of the population was as great as that between the Sadducees and the small traders in the cities from whom the Pharisees drew their main support (Black 1962, 781).

Young men typically entered public life at age nineteen (cf. Mason 2001, 20 n. 90).

12 ἣ παραπλήσιός ἐστι τῇ παρ' Ἕλλησιν Στωϊκῇ λεγομένῃ: the rel. pron. ἥ refers to τῇ Φαρισαίων αἱρέσει ("the sect of Pharisees") in the prev clause; the adj. παραπλήσιος ("closely resembling") freq patterns with the dat. case (LSJ I.2), which explains why the phrase τῇ παρ' Ἕλλησιν Στωϊκῇ λεγομένῃ appears in the dat. = "the [sect] called 'Stoic' among the Greeks." Stoicism derived its name from the Stoa Poikile, the portico in Athens where Zeno of Citium (335–263 BC) first taught its doctrines. The Stoics sought to align the human will with the inherent Reason of the universe (Logos); man becomes happy by virtue of cultivating "a willing acceptance" of the way things are (cf. Cressey 1979, 1217). Josephus mentions Stoicism because it was better known to his readers than Pharisaism, yet close enough to permit the comp. Cf. also Joseph. *BJ* 2.162–163.

BJ 2.169–177

2.169 Πεμφθεὶς δὲ εἰς Ἰουδαίαν ἐπίτροπος ὑπὸ Τιβερίου Πιλᾶτος: for πεμφθείς (aor. pass. ptc. of πέμπω) cf. *BJ* 1.35, 160, 261, 272, 288, 290; 2.277. It is tempting to trans. ἐπίτροπος as "procurator" (cf. *per procuratorem Pontium Pilatum*, Tac. *Ann.* 15.44), but cf. Intro 26 for the alternative term "prefect."

JOSEPHUS NOTES

Either term referred to an officer of the Roman empire entrusted with financial and administrative affairs, usu. answerable to the emperor. Cf. ἐπίτροποι τοῦ Καίσαρος (Strabo 3.4.20); ἐπιτρόποις Καίσαρος (Plut. *Praec. ger. reip.* 813E). Tiberius appointed Pilate to be the fifth prefect/procurator (ἐπίτροπος) of Judea in AD 26, a pos. that gave him control over the army of occupation at Caesarea, with a garrison stationed in Jerusalem at the Fortress Antonia:

> The procurator had full powers of life and death, and could reverse capital sentences passed by the Sanhedrin, which had to be submitted to him for ratification. He also appointed the high priests and controlled the Temple and its funds: the very vestments of the high priest were in his custody and were released only for festivals, when the procurator took up residence in Jerusalem and brought additional troops to patrol the city (Wheaton 1979, 996).

2.169 νύκτωρ κεκαλυμμένας εἰς Ἱεροσόλυμα εἰσκομίζει τὰς Καίσαρος εἰκόνας, αἳ σημαῖαι καλοῦνται: the adv. νύκτωρ construes with the pf. pass. ptc. κεκαλυμμένας ("under cover of night"), a detail that puts Pilate in a bad light. The σημαῖαι ("military standard[s]," LSJ I.1; cf. Polyb. 2.32.6; LXX Is 30:17; "image of Emperor on standard," Joseph. *BJ* 2.9.2 [= 2.169–171]) were actually busts or medallions of Caesar attached to standards (Joseph. *Antiq* 18.55). Previous procurators/prefects avoided the offensive ornamentation (Joseph. *Antiq* 18.56), so one's impression must be that Pilate "antagonize[d] the Jews by setting up the Roman standards" (Wheaton 1979, 996). On another occasion Tiberius ordered Pilate to remove to Caesarea some golden shields on which no likeness, but only an inscription to Caesar appeared (Philo *De Leg. ad Gaium* 38).

2.170 τοῦτο μεθ' ἡμέραν μεγίστην ταραχὴν ἤγειρεν Ἰουδαίοις: the pron. τοῦτο refers to the incident mentioned in *BJ* 2.169. The offense, perpetrated at night (νύκτωρ), provoked all the more consternation for the Jews "after day break" (μεθ' ἡμέραν).

2.170 οἵ τε γὰρ ἐγγὺς πρὸς τὴν ὄψιν ἐξεπλάγησαν...: the rel. pron. οἵ refers to the Jews (Ἰουδαίοις, *BJ* 2.170). Josephus emphasizes the visual offense done to the Jews: ἐγγὺς πρὸς τὴν ὄψιν ("near to the image," cf. *BJ* 3.396; 5.52, 290, 451, 547; 6.406); ἐξεπλάγησαν ("they were panic-stricken," cf. Isocr. 5.18; Lk 2:48; Plut. *Dion* 23.1; Polyaen. *Str*. 8.23.5; Thuc. 5.66.2; Xen. *Hellen*. 3.3.8).

2.170 ...ὡς πεπατημένων αὐτοῖς τῶν νόμων: gen. abs. Oft the particle ὡς provides the ground on which an assertion takes place (Smyth §2086), e.g., ἐνταῦθ' ἔμενον ὡς τὸ ἄκρον κατέχοντες = "they remained there *on grounds that* they were in possession of the summit" (Xen. *Ana*. 4.2.5). The Jews' consternation rested on the idea that their scruples had been violated (πεπατημένων = "trampled upon"), the reason for which Josephus does not share. Nevertheless, the abhorrence of visual images seems well substantiated in the OT, e.g., Ex 20:4; 32:8; 34:17; Lev 19:4; 26:1; Deut 4:15–19, 23; 27:15; 1 Ki 14:9; 2 Ki 17:12; Is 40:18–20; 44:9, etc. Αὐτοῖς, a dat. of agent, refers to the Romans.

2.170 οὐδὲν γὰρ ἀξιοῦσιν ἐν τῇ πόλει δείκηλον τίθεσθαι: the subj. of the vb. ἀξιοῦσιν ("they deem worthy") is the laws (cf. τῶν νόμων) mentioned in the prev clause; ἀξιοῦσιν sets off accus. with infin. in indir. state. (Smyth §1867): "...that no image be set up in the city." By its assoc. with the Temple, Jerusalem was supposed to be the abode of God (cf. Deut 12:11; 1 Ki 9:3; 11:13; 2 Ki 19:34; 21:7; Ps 132:13). For δείκηλον ("sculpted figure," LSJ II.2) cf. Lycoph. 1179; Euseb. *Praep. Ev*. 3.9.

2.170 καὶ πρὸς τὴν ἀγανάκτησιν τῶν κατὰ τὴν πόλιν ἄθρους ὁ ἐκ τῆς χώρας λαὸς συνέρρευσεν: construe συνέρρευσεν ("drew together," from συνερύω) with ἄθρους: "the people of the country drew together crowds..." The prep. phrase πρὸς τὴν ἀγανάκτησιν functions virtually as a pur. clause: "to provoke..."; the noun τὴν ἀγανάκτησιν patterns with τῶν (obj. gen.): "...those throughout the city." The prep. phrase κατὰ τὴν πόλιν ("throughout the city") occurs twenty-eight times in the *BJ*; for ἐκ τῆς χώρας ("from the country") cf. *BJ* 1.276; 2.10; 3.199; 4.261, 561. All Judea looked to Jerusalem, the site of the Temple.

2.171 ὁρμήσαντες δὲ πρὸς Πιλᾶτον εἰς Καισάρειαν ἱκέτευον ἐξενεγκεῖν ἐξ Ἱεροσολύμων τὰς σημαίας...: though Jews "rushed" (ὁρμήσαντες, cf. *BJ* 2.495; 6.358) to Pilate in Caesarea, they adopted a suppliant tone (ἱκέτευον, cf. 2.237, 280, 292, 295, 322; 3.202; 6.119, 322, 378): "they *implored* him to carry the standards from Jerusalem." Caesarea Maritima was located some 65 miles north-west of Jerusalem, on a coastal highway that connected Tyre to Egypt. Built in honor of Caesar Augustus by Herod the Great (dedicated 10 BC), Caesarea became "the Roman metropolis of Judea and the official residence both of the Herodian kings and the Roman procurators" (Harrison 1979, 174). Cf. Intro 19 for the building projects of Herod the Great.

2.171 ...καὶ τηρεῖν αὐτοῖς τὰ πάτρια: Αὐτοῖς represents the dat. of adv. (Smyth §1481): "and to keep *for them* their ancestral customs." Here "ancestral customs" (τὰ πάτρια) refers to the Jews' scruples against images (cf. 2.170), but cf. also κατὰ τὰ πάτρια (Aristoph. *Ach.* 1000; Epict. *Ench.* 31.5; Euseb. *Praep. Ev.* 7.9.2; Hdt. 6.60; Thuc. 2.2); παρὰ τὰ πάτρια (App. *Bell. Civ.* 1.4.30; Aristot. *Polit.* 1268b); ποίειν πρὸς τὴν πόλιν τὰ πάτρια (Isocr. 4.31).

2.171 Πιλάτου δὲ ἀρνουμένου...: gen. abs. The pres. tense of the ptc. emphasizes Pilate's obstinacy: "and as Pilate *continued to deny* their request..." To remove the images would have been an outrage to the emperor (Joseph. *Antiq* 18.57).

2.171: ...περὶ τὴν οἰκίαν πρηνεῖς καταπεσόντες ἐπὶ πέντε ἡμέρας καὶ νύκτας ἴσας ἀκίνητοι διεκαρτέρουν: the aor. ptc. καταπεσόντες (*BJ* 2.174; 7.87) represents the ingress. aor. (Smyth §1924): "they *began to fall* headlong around his house." The "house" (τὴν οἰκίαν) represents Pilate's official residence in Caesarea. Both the length of time (ἐπὶ πέντε ἡμέρας καὶ νύκτας ἴσας = "for five whole days and nights") and the Jews' intransigence (ἀκίνητοι διεκαρτέρουν = "they remained immovable") sugg. that Pilate and the Jews were involved in a major contest of wills. Pilate would lose (*BJ* 2.174).

2.172 Τῇ δ' ἑξῆς ὁ Πιλᾶτος καθίσας ἐπὶ βήματος ἐν τῷ μεγάλῳ σταδίῳ: the time referent τῇ δ' ἑξῆς ("and on the ensuing day," cf. *BJ* 1.277; 2.425, 430; 3.206; 4.450; 6.363) indicates that Pilate sat down upon the tribunal *on the day after* the five days already mentioned in 2.171, hence *on the sixth day*. Tensions were growing high and Pilate thought he could resolve matters by transferring them to the great stadium (cf. ἐν τῷ μεγάλῳ σταδίῳ) which, Josephus adds in the parallel account, "provided concealment for the army" (*Antiq* 18.57 LCL).

2.172 καὶ προσκαλεσάμενος τὸ πλῆθος ὡς ἀποκρίνασθαι δῆθεν αὐτοῖς θέλων: the pron. αὐτοῖς ("to them") refers to the Jews. For the aor. mid. ptc. προσκαλεσάμενος cf. *BJ* 1.481, 596, 660; 2.344; 3.161; 4.624. The ὡς clause reveals the alleged ground of Pilate's action: "and having summoned the populace *on grounds that he was willing to answer them*..." Pilate made use of the ploy to lure the Jews into the stadium.

2.172 ...δίδωσιν τοῖς στρατιώταις σημεῖον ἐκ συντάγματος κυκλώσασθαι τοὺς Ἰουδαίους ἐν τοῖς ὅπλοις: the mid. infin. κυκλώσασθαι represents the infin. of pur. (Smyth §2008): "...he gives a signal to the soldiers of the battalion *to surround* the Jews in full weaponry." For ἐκ συντάγματος ("of the battalion") cf. *BJ* 2.290; for κυκλώσασθαι ("to surround") cf. *Vita* 114; *BJ* 4.12; 5.496; for ἐν τοῖς ὅπλοις ("in full weaponry") cf. *BJ* 1.76; 2.452; 4.282; 6.132, 219.

2.173 περιστάσης δὲ τριστιχεὶ τῆς φάλαγγος: gen. abs. The word φάλαγξ brings to mind the Macedonian phalanx (cf. Polyb. 18.29–31). Evidently the crowd had gathered on the stadium floor to await Pilate's verdict; soldiers blocked the entrances and assumed the formation Josephus describes.

2.173 Ἰουδαῖοι μὲν ἀχανεῖς ἦσαν πρὸς τὸ ἀδόκητον τῆς ὄψεως: note the μέν... δέ construction: Ἰουδαῖοι μέν... vs. Πιλᾶτος δέ (next clause). The adj. ἀχανεῖς (from adj. ἀχανής, -ές) means either "not opening the mouth" (LSJ I.1, "of one mute with astonishment"), "yawning" (LSJ II.1), as in ἀχανές χάσμα = "gaping chasm" (Parmen. 1.18). For "the unexpectedness of the sight" (πρὸς τὸ ἀδόκητον τῆς ὄψεως) cf. πρὸς τὸ ἀδόκητον αὐτῶν (*BJ* 4.293).

2.173 Πιλᾶτος δὲ κατακόψειν εἰπὼν αὐτούς, εἰ μὴ προσδέξαιντο τὰς Καίσαρος εἰκόνας: the aor. ptc. εἰπών sets off accus. with infin. in indir. state. (Smyth §1867). A subj. accus. is not needed when the subj. of the infin. and finite vb. are the same, as here: "and Pilate, having said that he would cut them down..." The vb.

προσδέξαιντο in the dep. clause is in the optv. mood because the aor. ptc. εἰπών sets off sec. seq. (Smyth §2621): "...unless they accepted the likenesses of Caesar." For τὰς Καίσαρος εἰκόνας cf. 2.169.

2.173 γυμνοῦν τὰ ξίφη τοῖς στρατιώταις ἔνευσεν: for the idiom "motion to someone to do something" (ἔνευσε τινι + infin.) cf. Joseph. *Antiq* 16.126; *BJ* 1.629. For γυμνοῦν τὰ ξίφη ("to draw the sword") cf. τὰ ξίφη γυμνοῦντας (Joseph. *BJ* 2.619); ἀπογυμνοῦντα τὸ ξίφος (Origen *Ex. in Ps.* Vol. 17 pg. 129).

2.174 οἱ δὲ Ἰουδαῖοι καθάπερ ἐκ συνθήματος ἀθρόοι καταπεσόντες...: the Jews' answer to the Romans' drawing of swords in 2.173 was to "fall down in heaps" (ἀθρόοι καταπεσόντες) on the ground. For ἐκ συνθήματος ("by a pre-concerted signal") cf. Joseph. *Antiq* 5.225; 7.13; 20.78.

2.174 ...καὶ τοὺς αὐχένας παρακλίναντες ἑτοίμους ἀναιρεῖν σφᾶς ἐβόων μᾶλλον ἢ τὸν νόμον παραβῆναι: the act of extending the neck (τοὺς αὐχένας παρακλίναντες) to the Romans calls Pilate's bluff. The Jews suspected that Pilate would not want his first public act to consist of slaughtering hundreds of Jews! The vb. ἐβόων ("they were shouting," cf. *BJ* 2.4, 622; 3.356, 394; 4.592; 5.111, 322) sets off accus. with infin. in indir. state. (Smyth §1867): "they were shouting that they were prepared to kill themselves rather than transgress the law." For ἀναιρεῖν ("to kill") cf. *BJ* 1.255, 360, 441; 2.4, 494; 4.145, 587, 603; 6.126; for παραβῆναι ("to transgress") cf. *BJ* 4.102, 182).

2.174 ὑπερθαυμάσας δὲ ὁ Πιλᾶτος τὸ τῆς δεισιδαιμονίας ἄκρατον ἐκκομίσαι μὲν αὐτίκα τὰς σημαίας Ἱεροσολύμων κελεύει: Pilate was "amazed" (ὑπερθαυμάσας) at the Jews' intense relig. zeal and ordered that the standards should be removed immediately from Jerusalem. Josephus adds in the parallel account that the images were brought to Caesarea (*Antiq* 18.59). Τό... ἄκρατον (from adj. ἄκρατος, -ον = "pure, untempered, absolute" LSJ I.4) represents a substant. noun: "purity"; ἡ δεισιδαιμονία (lit. "fear of the gods") may be either pos. ("religious feeling," LSJ I.1; cf.

Polyb. 6.56.7; Philod. *Herc.* 1251.10; Diod. Sic. 1.70) or neg. ("superstition," LSJ I.2; cf. Polyb. 12.24.5; Diod. Sic. 1.83).

2.175 μετὰ δὲ ταῦτα ταραχὴν ἑτέραν ἐκίνει...: the pron. ταῦτα in the expression "and after this" (μετὰ δὲ ταῦτα) refers to the affair of the standards just described; "fresh disturbance" (ταραχὴν ἑτέραν) refers to the next vignette that Josephus here begins. For ἐκίνει ("he provoked") cf. Joseph. *BJ* 1.297, 332; 3.184; 6.366.

2.175 ...τὸν ἱερὸν θησαυρόν, καλεῖται δὲ κορβωνᾶς, εἰς καταγωγὴν ὑδάτων ἐξαναλίσκων: the vb. ἐξαναλίσκω means either "spend entirely" (LSJ I.1, cf. Plut. *Pomp.* 20; Dem. 50.15) or "exhaust" (LSJ I.2, cf. Theophr. *Vent.* 15; Plut. *Cat. Min.* 20). An aqueduct bringing fresh water to the city provided Pilate a pretext for the grab, though he could not have taken such funds without cooperation from Caiaphas and the priests. In AD 66 the procurator Gessius Florus would compromise "the sacred treasury" (τὸν ἱερὸν θησαυρόν, *BJ* 2.293) to settle an old score. For κορβωνᾶς ("devoted, taboo") cf. τὸν κορβανᾶν (Mt 27:6), oft trans. "treasury" (ESV). Mishnahic sources sugg. that the money was spent on sacrificial animals; hence Pilate was expropriating for secular purposes monies dedicated by the Jews for sacrificial purposes.

2.175 κατῆγεν δὲ ἀπὸ τετρακοσίων σταδίων: the vb. κατάγω can mean "bring down a river or canal" (LSJ. I.1); here, of the aqueduct itself. In place of 400 (τετρακοσίων) cf. τριακοσίων (Lat. Euseb.) and διακοσίων (A).

2.175 πρὸς τοῦτο τοῦ πλήθους ἀγανάκτησις ἦν: the pron. τοῦτο refers to Pilate's act of having purloined the treasury (2.175). Trans. τοῦ πλήθους as a subjv. gen. (Smyth §1330): "the populace was angry." In the parallel account Josephus mentions that "tens of thousands" of people assembled and were hurling the type of abuse against Pilate that a throng commonly engages in (*Antiq* 18.60).

2.175 καὶ τοῦ Πιλάτου παρόντος εἰς Ἱεροσόλυμα: gen. abs. = "while Pilate was on a visit to Jerusalem." The detail suggs. that Pilate had pillaged the Temple treasury through intermediaries from Caesarea. At any rate, Pilate was actually in Jerusalem on the occasion described.

2.175 περιστάντες τὸ βῆμα κατεβόων: prob. the meeting took place in the large royal palace on the west side of the city (referred to in the NT as "the praetorium," Jn 18: 28, 33; 19:9). Complaining Jews were the ones "surrounding" (περιστάντες, cf. *BJ* 1.234; 3.356; 6.86) Pilate on the tribunal and "shouting" (κατεβόων; cf. ἐβόων in 2.174).

2.176 ὁ δέ, προῄδει γὰρ αὐτῶν τὴν ταραχήν: the words ὁ δέ ("and he") refer to Pilate. Pilate was determined to teach the Jews a lesson in hard knocks, an opportunity denied him in Caesarea (cf. *BJ* 2.174).

2.176 τῷ πλήθει τοὺς στρατιώτας ἐνόπλους ἐσθῆσιν ἰδιωτικαῖς κεκαλυμμένους ἐγκαταμίξας: the subj. of the aor. act. ptc. ἐγκαταμίξας ("had interspersed") is Pilate. For ἐνόπλους ("armed") cf. *BJ* 2.445; 6.414; for κεκαλυμμένους ("hidden") cf. 3.284. The soldiers were disguised by "ordinary clothes" (ἐσθῆσιν ἰδιωτικαῖς, cf. 5.228)—i.e., they were not wearing the distinctive garb of a Roman soldier.

2.176 ξίφει μὲν χρήσασθαι κωλύσας, ξύλοις δὲ παίειν τοὺς κεκραγότας ἐγκελευσάμενος: note the μέν... δέ construction (ξίφει μέν vs. ξύλοις δέ). The vb. χράομαι usu. patterns with an obj. in the dat. case (Smyth §1509), e.g., τούτοις χρῶνται δορυφόροις = "they make use of them as body guards" (Xen. *Hiero* 5.3); τί χρησόμεθα τούτῳ = "what use shall we make of it?" (Dem. 3.6). Pilate forbade (κωλύσας, cf. *Vita* 121) the use of swords, even though he had threatened to cut down the Jews at Caesarea unless they accepted the standards (2.173). Far better, thought Pilate, to beat (παίειν, cf. *Vita* 303) those who were abusing him now (τοὺς κεκραγότας, cf. *BJ* 1.245).

2.176 σύνθημα δίδωσιν ἀπὸ τοῦ βήματος: the expression σύνθημα δίδωσιν ("he gave the pre-arranged signal") recalls ἐκ συνθήματος in *BJ* 2.174 above (also *Antiq* 5.225; 7.13; 20.78). Pilate could play the same game as the Jews had played earlier, and so flashed some type of signal to the undercover soldiers from the tribunal.

2.177 τυπτόμενοι δὲ οἱ Ἰουδαῖοι πολλοὶ μὲν ὑπὸ τῶν πληγῶν, πολλοὶ δὲ ὑπὸ σφῶν αὐτῶν ἐν τῇ φυγῇ καταπατηθέντες ἀπώλοντο: for τυπτόμενοι ("being beaten") cf. *BJ* 2.326; 4.165; 6.394. "Many" (πολλοὶ μέν... πολλοὶ δέ) were killed either by the blows Pilate's undercover soldiers inflicted or were trampled upon (καταπατηθέντες) in the ensuing rout. For ὑπὸ σφῶν αὐτῶν ("by one another") cf. *BJ* 1.383; 6.430; for ἐν τῇ φυγῇ ("in the rout") cf. *Antiq* 13.383; for ἀπώλοντο ("they were killed") cf. *BJ* 3.298; 4.643, 651. The soldiers inflicted harsher blows on an unprotected populace than Pilate had ordered (*Antiq* 18.62).

2.177 πρὸς δὲ τὴν συμφορὰν τῶν ἀνῃρημένων καταπλαγὲν τὸ πλῆθος ἐσιώπησεν: the populace, "cowed" (καταπλαγέν, cf. *BJ* 1.372; 2.300) at the fate "of the dead" (τῶν ἀνῃρημένων, cf. *BJ* 1.552, 564, 607; 2.464; 5.553; 7.376), kept silence. The parallel account adds, "thus ended the uprising" (καὶ οὕτω παύεται ἡ στάσις, *Antiq* 18.62 LCL).

BJ 2.184–87, 192–203

2.184 Γάιος δὲ Καῖσαρ ἐπὶ τοσοῦτον ἐξύβρισεν εἰς τὴν τύχην: in the *BJ* the title Καῖσαρ occurs 73 times in the nom. sing. masc. to designate "Caesar," a title of the Roman emperor, e.g., Καῖσαρ Τίτος (1.10); Καῖσαρ (= Julius Caesar, 1.183, 199, 200; = Augustus, 1.242, 285, 386); Καῖσαρ... Οὐεσπασιανέ (3.401), etc. The only other emperor who acted insolently "against fortune" according to Josephus was Nero (ἐξύβρισεν εἰς τὴν τύχην, *BJ* 2.250). Josephus would have supposed, like other Roman historians, that Rome's current greatness was subject to the caprice of fortune (Mason 2003, 71–72).

2.184 ἐπὶ τοσοῦτον... ὥστε θεὸν ἑαυτὸν καὶ δοκεῖν βούλεσθαι καὶ καλεῖσθαι...: pot. res. clause (Smyth §2257, §2258): "to such an extent.... that he wished himself both to seem and to be called a god." For βούλεσθαι ("to wish") cf. *BJ* 2.182; 5.373; for καλεῖσθαι ("to be called") cf. *Antiq* 8.110, 403; 13.45, 146; 18.186; 20.173. For Gaius' pretensions at divinity cf. Suet. *Cal.* 22.2–3; 33.1; 52.1.

2.184 ...τῶν τε εὐγενεστάτων ἀνδρῶν ἀκροτομῆσαι τὴν πατρίδα, ἐκτεῖναι δὲ τὴν ἀσέβειαν καὶ ἐπὶ Ἰουδαίαν: the infins. ἀκροτομῆσαι and ἐκτεῖναι continue the pot. res. clause identified in the preced note: "...and to cut the fatherland off from the most noble men and extend his impiety even to Judea." The phrase τῶν... εὐγενεστάτων ἀνδρῶν represents a gen. of sep. (Smyth §1392). For ἐκτεῖναι ("to extend") cf. *Antiq* 15.411; *BJ* 3.183; for ἐπὶ Ἰουδαίαν ("to Judea") cf. *BJ* 2.185. Gaius' outrages were by no means restricted to "the most noble men" but, in many resps., were imposed on all Romans (cf. Suet. *Cal.* 14.1; 18.2; 28.1; 30.2).

2.185 Πετρώνιον μὲν οὖν μετὰ στρατιᾶς ἐπὶ Ἱεροσολύμων ἔπεμψεν ἐγκαθιδρύσοντα τῷ ναῷ τοὺς ἀνδριάντας αὐτοῦ: the subj. of the vb. ἔπεμψεν is Gaius. The fut. ptc. ἐγκαθιδρύσοντα after a vb. of sending may indicate pur. (Smyth §2065): "[Gaius] sent Petronius... *to install* statues of himself." The installation was to take place "in the Temple" (τῷ ναῷ, cf. *BJ* 1.149, 352, 416; 5.564; 6.164, 280, 309, 322), nor can there be any doubt that these "statues" (τοὺς ἀνδριάντας, cf. ἀνήρ) were in the actual likeness of Gaius (cf. Pind. *Pyth.* 5.40; Hdt. 1.183; 2.91; Aristoph. *Pax* 1183; Thuc. 1.134). Contr. this specificity with the more generic "effigies of Caesar" (τὰς Καίσαρος εἰκόνας, *BJ* 2.169, 173) that Pilate attempted to impose in Jerusalem earlier. For μετὰ στρατιᾶς ("with an army") cf. *BJ* 1.92, 144, 213, 236, 334; 2.296, 334; 3.299; for ἐγκαθιδρύσοντα ("to install") cf. *BJ* 2.197, 267; 6.47. Publius Petronius, of senatorial family, had been a proconsul of Asia (AD 29–35?) and *legatus* of Syria (AD 39–42).

2.185 ...προστάξας, εἰ μὴ δέχοιντο Ἰουδαῖοι, τούς τε κωλύοντας ἀνελεῖν καὶ πᾶν τὸ λοιπὸν ἔθνος ἐξανδραποδίσασθαι: the subj. of the ptc. προστάξας ("having ordered," cf. *BJ* 1.75, 170, 245, 264, 327, 442, 664; 2.11, 67, 507, 551) is Gaius. The vb. in the dep. clause δέχοιντο ("they received," cf. *BJ* 7.195) occurs in the optv. mood because the aor. ptc. προστάξας introduces sec. seq. (Smyth §2621). Trans. τούς... κωλύοντας ("the recalcitrants") as the dir. obj. of the 2 aor. infin. ἀνελεῖν ("to kill"); both ἀνελεῖν (30 times in *BJ*) and ἐξανδραποδίσασθαι ("reduce to utter slavery," LSJ I.1) represent the infin. of pur. (Smyth §2008). Did Gaius intend by these harsh measures to succeed where Pilate had failed (see *BJ* 2.169–177) or was he just a madman?

2.186 θεῷ δ' ἄρα τῶν προσταγμάτων ἔμελεν: the impers. vb. μέλει construes with the dat. of pers. and gen. of thing (Smyth §1467): "God then cared for these orders." Cf. ᾧ μέλει μάχας (Aesch. *Ch.* 946); θεοῖσιν εἰ δίκης μέλει (Soph. *Phil.* 1036); Ζηνὶ τῶν σῶν μέλει πόνων (Eur. *Heracl.* 717).

2.186 καὶ Πετρώνιος μὲν σὺν τρισὶ τάγμασι καὶ πολλοῖς ἐκ τῆς Συρίας συμμάχοις εἰς τὴν Ἰουδαίαν ἤλαυνεν ἐκ τῆς Ἀντιοχείας: Petronius "marched" (ἤλαυνεν, cf. *BJ* 1.274, 290, 320, 343; 3.120, 243, 487, 490; 4.516; 5.62; 7.87) to Judea from Syrian Antioch, located some 300 miles north of Jerusalem, with a population of over 500,000, and the third largest city of the Roman empire after Rome and Alexandria (Harrison 1979, 40–41). "With three legions" (σὺν τρισὶ τάγμασι), though in the parallel account Josephus mentions only two (*Antiq* 18.262). By the statement, "with many allies" (σύν... πολλοῖς... συμμάχοις) Josephus means the auxiliary troops with which the Romans oft augmented their legions. For ἐκ τῆς Συρίας ("from Syria") cf. *Antiq* 13.58, 154, 351; 14.156; *BJ* 1.134, 201, 225, 324; 5.520; for ἐκ τῆς Ἀντιοχείας ("from Antioch") cf. *Antiq* 12.367, 421; 13.112, 123, 188; *BJ* 3.29.

2.187 Ἰουδαίων δὲ οἱ μὲν ἠπίστουν ἐπὶ ταῖς τοῦ πολέμου φήμαις, οἱ δὲ πιστεύοντες ἦσαν ἐν ἀμηχάνῳ πρὸς τὴν ἄμυναν: the μέν... δέ construction establishes a contr. between those Jews who "disbelieved" (οἱ μὲν ἠπίστουν) the rumors and others who, though "believing" (οἱ δὲ πιστεύοντες), were without means of mounting a defense. For ἐν ἀμηχάνῳ ("without means") cf. App. *Bell. Civ.* 2.6.43; Hippocr. *de Arte* 12.14; Philo *de Abr.* 175; Polyaen. *Str.* 4.6.4; Xenoph. *Eph.* 2.3.5; 5.7.4; for πρὸς τὴν ἄμυναν ("for defense") cf. Joseph. *BJ* 2.394; 4.162, 175, 306; 6.253.

2.187 ταχὺ δ' ἐχώρει διὰ πάντων τὸ δέος...: τὸ δέος ("dread") represents the subj. of the vb. ἐχώρει ("to be spread abroad," of rumors, LSJ II.4). Cf. ἡ φάτις κεχώρηκε = "a report spread" (Hdt. 1.122); κλαυθμὸς διὰ πάντων ἐχώρει = "everyone was weeping" (Plut. *Rom.* 19).

2.187 ...ἤδη παρούσης εἰς Πτολεμαΐδα τῆς στρατιᾶς: gen. abs. = "now that the army had already [ἤδη] reached Ptolemais." What would have frightened the inhabitants of Jerusalem was how quickly the Roman army traversed the distance between Syrian Antioch and Ptolemais, a sea port on the north side of the Bay of Acre some 80 miles north-west of Jerusalem.

2.192 Ἰουδαῖοι δὲ μετὰ γυναικῶν καὶ τέκνων ἀθροισθέντες εἰς τὸ πεδίον τὸ πρὸς Πτολεμαΐδι: just as Jews had "rushed" (ὁρμήσαντες, *BJ* 2.171) to Caesarea to supplicate Pilate in the affair of the standards, so Jews on this occasion "assembled" (ἀθροισθέντες, cf. *Antiq* 5.150; 6.325; *BJ* 2.5; 3.9, 307; 4.135) on the plain near Ptolemais to supplicate Petronius. The appeal made with women and children (μετὰ γυναικῶν καὶ τέκνων, cf. *Antiq* 1.74; 10.230; 11.110; 13.200; 14.260; *Vita* 207, 230; *BJ* 6.351) was intended to elicit sympathy from Petronius.

2.192 καθικέτευον τὸν Πετρώνιον ὑπὲρ τῶν πατρίων νόμων πρῶτον, ἔπειτα ὑπὲρ αὐτῶν: Jews had "supplicated" Pilate (ἱκέτευον, *BJ* 2.171) in Caesarea; here they "earnestly beseech" (καθικέτευον, cf. *Antiq* 19.234) Petronius (note shared stem -ικετευ-). For the "ancestral laws" on behalf of which (ὑπὲρ τῶν πατρίων νόμων, cf. *Antiq* 12.267; *BJ* 2.7) the Jews had supplicated Pilate on the earlier occasion cf. the Scripture citations in 2.170 above. How might the Jews have appealed to Petronius "on behalf of themselves" (ὑπὲρ αὐτῶν, *BJ* 3.198, 473; 4.288; 5.190, 449)? Possibly the Jews were clients of Petronius. Jews had prospered in Syrian Antioch since the days of Seleucus I in ca. 300 BC (Harrison 1979, 40).

2.192 ὁ δὲ πρός τε τὸ πλῆθος καὶ τὰς δεήσεις ἐνδοὺς τοὺς μὲν ἀνδριάντας καὶ τὰς στρατιὰς ἐν Πτολεμαΐδι λείπει: the words ὁ δέ ("and he") refer to Petronius. Having "give[n] way" (ἐνδοὺς = 2 aor. ptc. of ἐνδίδωμι, LSJ V.1) to the common people (τὸ πλῆθος) and their entreaties, Petronius "leaves" (λείπει) the statues and armies in Ptolemais in order to parley with Jews in Tiberias, a city on the western shore of the Sea of Galilee. Contr. Petronius' humane behavior with that of Pilate who twice resorted to violence in order to silence the Jews (cf. *BJ* 2.172, 176).

2.193 προελθὼν δὲ εἰς τὴν Γαλιλαίαν καὶ συγκαλέσας τό τε πλῆθος καὶ τοὺς γνωρίμους πάντας εἰς Τιβεριάδα: most editors prefer the variant προελθὼν ("he went on ahead," C) to προσελθὼν ("he entered," remaining mss). Petronius could have "gone on ahead" to Tiberias because, as a thoroughly Roman city, Tiberias would have presented itself as an ideal place to parley with the Jews. Herod Antipas had built Tiberias on the Sea of Galilee in AD 22 (cf. Intro 22 above), though it was considered "unclean in Jewish eyes" (Patterson 1979, 1275). Petronius invited (συγκαλέσας, *BJ* 2.341; 5.535, 554) both the commons (τό πλῆθος) and more notable citizens (τοὺς γνωρίμους) to the meeting place. The word πάντας ("all") likewise suggs. that the meeting was open to all concerned.

2.193 τήν τε Ῥωμαίων διεξῄει δύναμιν καὶ τὰς Καίσαρος ἀπειλάς: the vb. διεξῄει (from διέξειμι) means, "to go through in detail, relate circumstantially" (LSJ II.1). Cf. Dem. *De Cor.* 13, 14, 22; Joseph. *BJ* 3.347; 4.339, 347; Plut. *Pel.* 17.8; *Dem.* 8.1; Thuc. 2.49.7; Xen. *Mem.* 4.7.9. What "threats" of Caesar (τὰς Καίσαρος ἀπειλάς) did Petronius share with the petitioners? Perhaps Gaius' earlier statement that Petronius should kill any Jews as resisted the decree and enslave the rest (cf. *BJ* 2.185); the Romans' "power" (τήν... Ῥωμαίων... δύναμιν) refers to the latters' ability actually to stand by Caesar's decree and carry it out.

2.193 ἔτι δὲ τὴν ἀξίωσιν ἀπέφαινεν ἀγνώμονα: Josephus places for emphasis the adj. ἀγνώμονα after the noun τὴν ἀξίωσιν (pred. pos.) and the governing vb. ἀπέφαινεν (cf. *Antiq* 7.377; 17.326; 18.288; *Vita* 194; *BJ* 5.496): "and he was showing their demand (to be) unreasonable"—namely, the Jews' insistence that no image be set up in Jerusalem (cf. 2.170 above).

2.194 πάντων... τῶν ὑποτεταγμένων ἐθνῶν κατὰ πόλιν συγκαθιδρυκότων...: gen. abs. The ptc. συγκαθιδρυκότων signifies a causal relationship (Smyth §2070.b): "*Since* all the (other) subj. nations have erected throughout their cities..." Petronius refers to what was the usu. practice of setting up temples to Rome or to the current emperor in the leading cities of the eastern provinces. There was, e.g., "a huge temple dedicated to Caesar and Rome" in Caesarea

(Harrison 1979, 174); it was only "reasonable," then, that a sim. service be instituted in Jerusalem, the most imp. city in Israel.

2.194 ...τοῖς ἄλλοις θεοῖς καὶ τὰς Καίσαρος εἰκόνας: Caesar's images would join the august panoplies of subj. peoples everywhere, taking a pos. next to the tutelary deities of the city (τοῖς ἄλλοις θεοῖς). Surely the Jews could accommodate themselves to the custom observed everywhere else in the empire!

2.194 τὸ μόνους ἐκείνους ἀντιτάσσεσθαι πρὸς τοῦτο σχεδὸν ἀφισταμένων εἶναι καὶ μεθ' ὕβρεως: the words μόνους ἐκείνους refer to the Jews who "alone" were "set against" (ἀντιτάσσεσθαι) "this" (πρὸς τοῦτο, cf. *BJ* 1.76, 159; 2.175, 225, 233, 273, 403)—namely, the practice of adding the emperor's images to a city's pantheon. The infin. εἶναι completes the indir. state., and the ptc. ἀφισταμένων represents the poss. gen. (Smyth §1305): "...and that it was almost of [men who were] rebellious and [aggravated] by insult."

2.195 τῶν δὲ τὸν νόμον καὶ τὸ πάτριον ἔθος προτεινομένων...: τῶν... προτεινομένων constitutes a gen. abs. Here the pres. ptc. προτεινομένων signifies a temp., ongoing relationship in past time: "and *while* they [the Jews] were maintaining as an excuse..." On the occasion with Pilate the Jews had appealed to their laws (*BJ* 2.170, 174) and "ancestral custom" (*BJ* 2.171) as reasons why they could not permit the impos. of the emperor's images.

2.195 ...καὶ ὡς οὐδὲ θεοῦ τι δείκηλον, οὐχ ὅπως ἀνδρός, οὐ κατὰ τὸν ναὸν μόνον ἀλλ' οὐδὲ ἐν εἰκαίῳ τινὶ τόπῳ τῆς χώρας θέσθαι θεμιτὸν εἴη: the reader must supp. the idea of "saying" before the clause marker ὡς and ὅπως, both of which look ahead to the clause θέσθαι θεμιτὸν εἴη. The vb. εἴη occurs in the optv. mood because the idea of "saying" (though unexpressed) establishes sec. seq. (Smyth §1862, §1863); the same idea of "saying" introduces accus. with infin. in indir. state. (Smyth §1867): "(saying) that it was lawful neither that any representation of god, nor still less of man, be set up—not only in the Temple but also not in any ordinary place of the region." For δείκηλον... θέσθαι ("set up a representation") cf. δείκηλον τίθεσθαι (*BJ* 2.170); for κατὰ τὸν ναόν ("throughout the temple") cf. *Antiq* 14.483; *BJ* 1.354, 650; 6.388.

2.195 ὑπολαβὼν ὁ Πετρώνιος "ἀλλὰ μὴν καὶ ἐμοὶ φυλακτέος ὁ τοὐμοῦ δεσπότου νόμος", ἔφη: oft ὑπολαβών (cf. *BJ* 1.42, 95, 215; 2.593) means to take up a conversation, i.e., "make reply." The editors have placed Petronius' impassioned response in quote marks (*oratio recta*). Ancient historians used dir. speech at emotional or highly climactic points in a narrative. The Jews have just mentioned "the law" (τὸν νόμον, *BJ* 2.195) as a basis of rejecting Gaius' decree; Petronius uses τὸν νόμον, then, as a point of departure in his reply to the Jews: "*the law* of my master has to be guarded by me!" The pers. pron. ἐμοί represents the dat. of agent with the vb. adj. –τεος (Smyth §1488): "*has to be guarded* [φυλακτέος] by me."

2.195 "παραβὰς γὰρ αὐτὸν καὶ φεισάμενος ὑμῶν ἀπολοῦμαι δικαίως": the subj. of the aor. ptcs. παραβάς ("transgressed," cf. *Antiq* 7.168, 385; 9.243; 12.146; 14.109, 167) and φεισάμενος ("sparing," cf. *Antiq* 6.261; 7.296; 8.95; 9.231; 15.307; 17.134; *BJ* 4.543) is Petronius; the pron. αὐτὸν refers to the law.

2.195 "πολεμήσει δ' ὑμᾶς ὁ πέμψας με καὶ οὐκ ἐγώ": the phrase ὁ πέμψας ("he who sent me," cf. *Antiq* 12.397) refers to Gaius who, as emperor, possessed powers of sending lesser men wherever he wished. Thus Pilate had been "sent" by Tiberius to Judea (πεμφθείς... ὑπὸ Τιβερίου Πιλᾶτος, *BJ* 2.169) even as Gaius had "sent" Petronius to Jerusalem (ἔπεμψεν, *BJ* 2.185). Not Petronius, then, but Gaius would be the one to "make war" (πολεμήσει, cf. *Antiq* 10.104) on the Jews; the comment anticipates Petronius' eventual defiance of Gaius' decree.

2.195 "καὶ γὰρ αὐτός, ὥσπερ ὑμεῖς, ἐπιτάσσομαι": the pers. pron. αὐτός intensifies the subj. of the vb. ἐπιτάσσομαι, Petronius himself: "for indeed *I myself* am under orders, just as you are!" Petronius recognized that even as he answered to Gaius, so the Jews answered to God.

2.196 πρὸς ταῦτα τὸ πλῆθος πάντ' ἐβόα πρὸ τοῦ νόμου πάσχειν ἑτοίμως ἔχειν: the pron. ταῦτα ("these things") refers to Petronius' pronouncement in the preced clause. The vb. ἐβόα (cf. *BJ* 1.500, 544, 584; 4.195; 5.546; 6.309; 7.452) sets off accus. with infin.

in indir. state. (Smyth §1867): "the crowd *kept shouting* that it was prepared to suffer everything on behalf of the law." Ἔχω + adv. is oft used as a periphrasis for an adj. with εἶναι or for a vb. (Smyth §1438), e.g., ἔχειν κακῶς = "to be bad"; ἔχειν ἑτοίμως = "to be prepared."

2.196 καταστείλας δ' αὐτῶν ὁ Πετρώνιος τὴν βοήν, "πολεμήσετε," εἶπεν, "ἄρα Καίσαρι;": the aor. act. ptc. καταστείλας (cf. *BJ* 2.281, 611; 4.271) signifies a gesture speakers used to quell the hubbub of a crowd, e.g., ἀναβὰς γὰρ ἐπὶ τὸ τέγος καὶ τῇ δεξιᾷ καταστείλας τὸν θόρυβον αὐτῶν... ἔφη = "having climbed onto the roof and *having quelled* their clamor with his hand, he said..." (Joseph. *BJ* 2.611; cf. 2 Macc 4.31; Acts 19:35). Petronius had just said that Gaius, and not he, would "make war on" the Jews (πολεμήσει, *BJ* 2.195); now he asks, with palpable irony, whether the Jews shall "make war on" Caesar ("πολεμήσετε...ἄρα Καίσαρι;"). In later usage ἄρα possesses inferential force (LSJ B); oft it expresses the anxiety of the questioner (LSJ B.I.2; Smyth §2793).

2.197 καὶ Ἰουδαῖοι περὶ μὲν Καίσαρος καὶ τοῦ δήμου τῶν Ῥωμαίων δὶς τῆς ἡμέρας θύειν ἔφασαν: the vb. ἔφασαν (3 plur. aor. indic. act. of φημί) sets off accus. with infin. in indir. state. (Smyth §1867). A subj. accus. is not needed when the subj. of the finite vb. and the infin. are the same, as here: "for the Jews said that they sacrificed..." Petronius could not fault the Jews for having failed to make sacrifices for Caesar and the Romans; here the Jews point out that they offered twice-daily sacrifices (prob. at the morning and evening sacrifices, cf. Ex 29:39, 41; Num 28:4, 8; 2 Ch. 13:11; Ezra 3:3) for Caesar and the Romans. Jews had prayed for their captors during the exile (Jer 29:7), and Paul would charge Christian congregations to pray for "kings and for all who are in authority" (1 Tim 2:2; cf. Rom 13:6–7).

2.197 εἰ δὲ βούλεται τὰς εἰκόνας ἐγκαθιδρύειν, πρότερον αὐτὸν δεῖν ἅπαν τὸ Ἰουδαίων ἔθνος προθύσασθαι: the particle δέ represents an adversative clause marker ("but"), and εἰ a simp. fact. cond. within indir. state. (Smyth §2298): "*but if* he wishes to plant the images..." The pers. pron. αὐτόν, which refers to Petronius, serves as the subj. accus. of the infin. δεῖν: "...he would first have to sacrifice all the race of the Jews." The utterance is strikingly sim. to what the Jews told Pilate when he attempted to impose images of Tiberius in Jerusalem (cf. *BJ* 2.174). The infin. ἐγκαθιδρύειν ("to set up") repeats the charge that Gaius put earlier to Petronius in *BJ* 2.185.

2.197 παρέχειν δὲ σφᾶς αὐτοὺς ἑτοίμους εἰς τὴν σφαγὴν ἅμα τέκνοις καὶ γυναιξίν: accus. with infin. in indir. state. (Smyth §1867), dep. on the vb. ἔφασαν. Not only was the mention of wives and children intended to arouse Petronius' sympathies (cf. μετὰ γυναικῶν καὶ τέκνων, 2.192), but it presages ominously the death of many women and children at Masada at the conclusion of the Jewish War (cf. *BJ* 7.334, 382, 400 below).

2.198 ἐπὶ τούτοις θαῦμα καὶ οἶκτος εἰσῄει τὸν Πετρώνιον τῆς τε ἀνυπερβλήτου θρησκείας τῶν ἀνδρῶν καὶ τοῦ πρὸς θάνατον ἑτοίμου παραστήματος: the phrase ἐπὶ τούτοις refers to the heroic, if rash, statements the Jews had uttered in the preced clause. The noun οἶκτος patterns oft with the obj. gen. (LSJ I.1), e.g., App. *Lib.* 383; Eur. *Hipp.* 1089; *Elect.* 1330; Hdt. 1.165; Joseph. *Antiq* 14.381; *BJ* 1.58; 3.204; 5.433; Plut. *Tim.* 7.1; Soph. *Elect.* 100; *Phil.* 965, etc; here οἶκτος patterns with τῆς... θρησκείας... καὶ τοῦ... παραστήματος: "pity *for* the Jews' incomparable devotion... and courage prepared even for death." Pilate's reaction to the Jews had been comparable to Petronius' (cf. *BJ* 2.174). In Jewish literature the word θρησκεία (occurs 22 times in the *BJ*) represents devotion or "service of God" (LSJ I.2, cf. LXX *Wisd.* 14:18; Acts 26:5; Col 2:18); παράστημα (16 times in the *BJ*) represents a form of "desperate courage, exaltation" (LSJ II.1).

2.198 καὶ τότε μὲν ἄπρακτοι διελύθησαν: for διελύθησαν ("part company, be dismissed") cf. *BJ* 1.121, 243; 2.238; 4.321, 517; 6.147; 7.234. The adj. ἄπρακτος means either "unavailing," and "unsuccessful" (LSJ I.1, 2) or "against which nothing can be done" (LSJ II.1). Josephus has just said that amazement and pity seized Petronius, ruling out the first possibility; what Josephus means, then, is that the Jews were ἄπρακτοι in the sense of being "left undone" (LSJ II.3)—i.e., Petronius could not reach a verdict.

2.199 Ταῖς δ' ἑξῆς...: the article ταῖς indicates that Josephus has dropped for stylistic reasons a word, prob. ἡμέραις: "and on successive days..." Indeed, Petronius would spend 50 days remonstrating with the Jews (*BJ* 2.200; only 40 days according to *Antiq* 18.272). Contr. this with the "five whole days and nights" during which Pilate had countenanced the Jews in Caesarea (*BJ* 2.171).

2.199 ...ἀθρόους τε τοὺς δυνατοὺς κατ' ἰδίαν καὶ τὸ πλῆθος ἐν κοινῷ συλλέγων: Petronius did not simply issue orders from on high (as Gaius expected, cf. *BJ* 2.185) but devoted time and attn. to both the aristocracy (τοὺς δυνατοὺς) and the commons (τὸ πλῆθος). Meetings were both public (ἐν κοινῷ) and private (κατ' ἰδίαν) events.

2.199 ποτὲ μὲν παρεκάλει, ποτὲ δὲ συνεβούλευεν, τὸ πλέον μέντοι διηπείλει: note the struct. (ποτὲ μέν..., ποτὲ δέ..., τὸ πλέον μέντοι), an elaboration upon the μέν... δέ construction. Petronius did, to be sure, "threaten" the Jews (διηπείλει, cf. *BJ* 1.58); nevertheless, he also "encouraged" (παρεκάλει, cf. *BJ* 1.481, 655, 668; 2.9, 493; 3.314; 4.195; 5.319, 361, 422; 7.323) and "advised" (συνεβούλευεν, cf. *BJ* 1.266; 3.319; 6.397) them.

2.199 τήν τε Ῥωμαίων ἐπανατεινόμενος ἰσχὺν καὶ τοὺς Γαΐου θυμοὺς τήν τε ἰδίαν πρὸς τούτοις ἀνάγκην: the pres. mid. ptc. ἐπανατεινόμενος ("holding over them") mods. Petronius, the subj. of the vb. διηπείλει (preced clause). The double compound vb. ἐπανατείνομαι means "brandish threateningly" (LSJ II.1, cf. ἐπανατείνεσθαι σίδηρόν τινι, *P.Hal* 1.186 [3d cent. BC]; βάκτρον τινι, Luc. *Cat.* 13; φόβους τινι, Polyb. 2.44.3, etc.); thus, Petronius was attempting to browbeat the Jews with the "might of the Romans" (cf. Ῥωμαίων... δύναμιν, *BJ* 2.193), Gaius' temper tantrums (τοὺς Γαΐου θυμοὺς) and his private compulsion (τήν... ἰδίαν... ἀνάγκην). For the possibility that Petronius possessed Jewish clients cf. *BJ* 2.192 above.

2.200 πρὸς δὲ μηδεμίαν πεῖραν ἐνδιδόντων: gen. abs. Supp. αὐτῶν to the ptc. ἐνδιδόντων: "and *since* they were yielding to not a single one of his attempts..." The arguments Petronius used to sway the Jews are presented in the preced clause.

2.200 ὡς ἑώρα καὶ τὴν χώραν κινδυνεύουσαν ἄσπορον μεῖναι: the conjunction ὡς + a vb. in the indic. mood oft means "when" (Smyth §3000). Ἑώρα + κινδυνεύουσαν represents the accus. with ptc. after a vb. of percep. (Smyth §2110, §2112): "and when he saw that the land was at risk of remaining unsown..." Cf. these additional examples: εἶδε Κλέαρχον διελαύνοντα = "he saw Clearchus riding through" (Xen. *Ana*. 1.5.12); ἤκουσαν αὐτοῦ φωνήσαντος = "they heard him speaking" (Xen. *Symp*. 3.13); ὡς εἶδεν ἔλαφον ἐκπηδήσασαν... ἐδίωκεν = "when he saw a hind break cover he gave chase" (Xen. *Cyr*. 1.4.8).

2.200 κατὰ γὰρ ὥραν σπόρου πεντήκοντα ἡμέρας ἀργὰ προσδιέτριβεν αὐτῷ τὰ πλήθη: for κατά + ὥραν σπόρου ("throughout the time of sowing") cf. κατὰ πλοῦν = "during the voyage" (Thuc. 3.32); κατ' ἐκεῖνον τὸν χρόνον = "at that time" (Thuc. 1.139); οἱ καθ' ἑαυτόν = "his contemporaries" (Dem. 20.73). Construe ἀργά (nom. neut. plur. of the adj. ἀεργός -όν, from ἀ- + *ἔργω = "not working, idle") with τὰ πλήθη, the neut. plur. subj. of the vb. προσδιέτριβεν: "the crowds were idly engaged with him for fifty days." According to Joseph. *Antiq* 18.272, the crowds were idle for 40 days.

2.200 τελευταῖον ἀθροίσας αὐτοὺς καὶ "παρακινδυνευτέον ἐμοὶ μᾶλλον," εἰπών: trans. τελευταῖον as an adv. accus. (Smyth §1606): "at last." For ἀθροίσας ("having gathered," cf. *BJ* 1.118, 214, 571; 2.618) cf. the "crowded" (ἀθρόους, *BJ* 2.199) private conferences Petronius held with the Jews in Tiberias. Presumably, Petronius gathered both types of Jews—the aristocracy and the commons (cf. *BJ* 2.199)—into a central meeting place where he addressed them all at once. That situation would have made his remarks all the more poignant (note the renewed use of *oratio recta*, on which cf. *BJ* 2.195 above). The words παρακινδυνευτέον ἐμοὶ μᾶλλον constitute the dat. of agent with the vb. adj. -τεος (Smyth §1488): "better it be risked *by me*..."

2.201 "ἢ γὰρ τοῦ θεοῦ συνεργοῦντος πείσας Καίσαρα σωθήσομαι μεθ' ὑμῶν ἡδέως ἢ παροξυνθέντος ὑπὲρ τοσούτων ἑτοίμως ἐπιδώσω τὴν ἐμαυτοῦ ψυχήν": the sentence, an "either...

or" (ἤ... ἤ), consists of 3 balanced pairs: 1) τοῦ θεοῦ συνεργοῦντος vs. (τοῦ Καίσαρος) παροξυνθέντος; 2) σωθήσομαι vs. ἐπιδώσω; 3) μεθ᾽ ὑμῶν vs. ὑπὲρ τοσούτων. Petronius, the speaker, pits the Jews' God against the emperor Gaius and reasons either that he will be safe with the Jews or become a willing sacrifice to be expended for the many. For τοῦ θεοῦ συνεργοῦντος ("if God aids me") cf. *Antiq* 4.315; for πείσας ("persuading") cf. *BJ* 1.61, 575; 3.390; 5.502; for παροξυνθέντος ("provoked") cf. *Vita* 298; for ἐπιδώσω τὴν ἐμαυτοῦ ψυχήν ("I shall give up my own life") cf. *BJ* 4.164.

2.201 διαφῆκεν τὸ πλῆθος πολλὰ κατευχομένων αὐτῷ: construe κατευχομένων as a part. gen. with τὸ πλῆθος, the dir. obj. of διαφῆκεν (cf. *Antiq* 10.123; 14.411; *BJ* 1.267, 302, 666; 2.528; 6.386): "he dismissed the crowd of those [who were] making many prayers for him." Πολλά represents the cogn. accus. (Smyth §1573), e.g., μεγάλ᾽ ἁμαρτάνειν = "to commit grave errors" (Dem. 5.5); δεινὰ ὑβρίζειν = "to maltreat terribly" (Xen. *Ana*. 6.4.2); ταὐτὰ ἐπρεσβεύομεν = "we were ambassadors in the same way" (Dem. 19.32). Petronius' magnanimity (cf. prev note) left an impression on the Jews.

2.201 καὶ παραλαβὼν τὴν στρατιὰν ἐκ τῆς Πτολεμαΐδος ὑπέστρεψεν εἰς τὴν Ἀντιόχειαν: Petronius got the army and returned to Antioch as abruptly as he had come (cf. *BJ* 2.186–187). For εἰς τὴν Ἀντιόχειαν ("to Antioch") cf. *BJ* 7.106.

2.202 ἔνθεν εὐθέως ἐπέστελλεν Καίσαρι τήν τε ἐμβολὴν τὴν εἰς Ἰουδαίαν ἑαυτοῦ καὶ τὰς ἱκεσίας τοῦ ἔθνους: trans. the adv. ἔνθεν as "whence"—i.e., from Antioch. Petronius had been under Gaius' orders (*BJ* 2.185), and so some type of written explanation of how Petronius had managed the campaign was apparently expected. Petronius began, diplomatically, by describing his "expedition to Judea" (τήν... ἐμβολὴν τὴν εἰς Ἰουδαίαν ἑαυτοῦ)—though it would have been diff. for him not to mention that actually he left the army in Ptolemais (*BJ* 2.192) to remonstrate with Jews in Tiberias (*BJ* 2.193). For ἐπέστελλεν ("he sent a note") cf. *BJ* 1.200, 299, 308, 398; 2.333; 5.557); for τὴν ἐμβολήν ("the expedition") cf. *BJ* 1.367, 372; 4.422; 5.69, 313; 6.167, 245.

2.202 ...ὅτι τε, εἰ μὴ βούλεται πρὸς τοῖς ἀνδράσιν καὶ τὴν χώραν ἀπολέσαι, δέοι φυλάττειν τε αὐτοὺς τὸν νόμον καὶ παριέναι τὸ πρόσταγμα: the words ὅτι τε continue the indir. state. after the vb. ἐπέστελλεν (preced clause): "and he informed him that unless..." Petronius, whistling in the dark, let on that surely Gaius would not desire "to destroy the region in addition to the people"; but such was to ascribe to Gaius an humanity that the emperor did not possess. The pers. pron. αὐτούς refers to the Jews who constantly brought up "the law" (τὸν νόμον) in this context (cf. *BJ* 2.170, 174, 192, 195, 196); the suggestion that the Jews should themselves "revoke the order" (παριέναι τὸ πρόσταγμα) can only have been most unwelcome to Gaius whose designs had been quite explicit (*BJ* 2.185). The optv. δέοι occurs here because the mn. vb. ἐπέστελλεν (impf. tense) establishes sec. seq. (Smyth §2621).

2.203 ταύταις ταῖς ἐπιστολαῖς οὐ σφόδρα μετρίως ἀντέγραψεν ὁ Γάιος: Lat. and Gk. use the plur. where Eng. uses the sing.: "and in response *to this dispatch* [ταύταις ταῖς ἐπιστολαῖς]... Gaius replied." οὐ σφόδρα μετρίως = "in no measured terms" (Litotes)—i.e., Gaius' written response, unlike Petronius', was quite to the point and in effect would have said, "kill yourself."

2.203 ἀπειλῶν Πετρωνίῳ θάνατον...: for the idiom ἀπειλέω + accus. of the thing threatened cf. θάνατον (Hdt. 4.81); ξίφος (Plut. *Pomp.* 47); ζημίας (Plut. *Cam.* 49), etc. More than a "threat" in the modern sense, Petronius would have been expected to comply with the emperor Gaius' wishes immediately.

2.203 ...ὅτι τῶν προσταγμάτων αὐτοῦ βραδὺς ὑπηρέτης ἐγίνετο: the clause marker ὅτι supplies Gaius' reason for the thinly veiled death warrant: "*because* he [Petronius] was a slow executor of his orders." Petronius, in relation to the emperor, was nothing but an "underling, servant, attendant" (LSJ II.1); "slowness" had not been what prevented Petronius from complying with the emperor's orders so much as disobedience, as Petronius himself recognized (cf. ἀπολοῦμαι δικαίως, *BJ* 2.195).

2.203 ἀλλὰ τοὺς μὲν τούτων γραμματοφόρους συνέβη χειμασθῆναι τρεῖς μῆνας ἐν τῇ θαλάσσῃ: the impers. construction συνέβη ("it came to pass that...," Smyth §1985) occurs 34 times in the *BJ*. The pron. τούτων refers to the content of Gaius' message: "the people carrying *this message*." The vb. χειμασθῆναι apparently means "pass the winter" (LSJ I.2), rather than "to be driven by a storm" (LSJ III.1). Storms at sea could, to be sure, last for weeks (cf. Acts 27:27, 33) though one lasting "for three months" (τρεῖς μῆνας = accus. ext. of time, Smyth §1580) strains credulity. Clearly what happened was that the emperor's envoys, having begun their long journey, were forced to winter mid-route in a suitable harbor for three months until spring came with its favorable sailing season.

2.203 τὸν δὲ Γαΐου θάνατον ἄλλοι καταγγέλλοντες εὐπλόουν: the pron. ἄλλοι refers to "other" γραμματόφοροι who proclaimed the death of Gaius and experienced smooth sailing (εὐπλόουν). For καταγγέλλοντες ("proclaiming") cf. *BJ* 6.286.

2.203 ἔφθη γοῦν τὰς περὶ τούτων Πετρώνιος λαβὼν ἐπιστολὰς ἑπτὰ καὶ εἴκοσιν ἡμέραις ἢ τὰς καθ' ἑαυτοῦ: the prep. phrase περὶ τούτων ("about these things") refers to the announcement of Gaius' death. Φθάνω + suppl. ptc. means, "to be... [ptc.] beforehand," where the ptc. contributes the mn. verbal idea (Smyth §2096). E.g., οὐ φθάνει ἐξαγόμενος ὁ ἵππος = "the horse *is no sooner led out*" (Xen. *Eq.* 5.10); οὐκ ἔφθασαν πυθόμενοι τὸν πόλεμον καὶ ἧκον = "*scarcely had they heard* of the war when they came" (Isocr. 4.86). So ἔφθη... Πετρώνιος λαβὼν means, "Petronius got the letter... *before* the one concerning himself." For the dat. of time at which an action occurs (Smyth §1539) cf. τῇ προτεραίᾳ = "the day before"; τῇ δευτέρᾳ = "the second day"; τρίτῳ μηνί = "in the third month" (Lys. 21.1); ἑξηκοστῷ ἔτει = "in the sixtieth year" (Thuc. 1.12). So ἑπτὰ καὶ εἴκοσιν ἡμέραις ἢ = "27 days before." The parallel account in Joseph. *Antiq* 18.261–309 goes into greater detail than the account presented here. Outstanding additions are the providential rainfall that attended Petronius' statement that he would represent the Jews before Gaius (*Antiq* 18.285–286) and the intercession of Herod Agrippa with Gaius at Rome on behalf of the Jews (*Antiq* 18.289–302).

BJ 3.392-408

3.392 Ὁ μὲν οὖν οὕτως τόν τε Ῥωμαίων καὶ τὸν οἰκείων διαφυγὼν πόλεμον ἐπὶ Οὐεσπασιανὸν ἤγετο ὑπὸ [τοῦ] Νικάνορος: ὁ μέν refers to Josephus. Trans. the adv. οὕτως ("thus") with the aor. ptc. διαφυγών: "[Josephus] who had in this manner evaded both the war with the Romans and that with his own friends..." What Josephus here describes as a "war" with friends actually refers to tense moments at the conclusion of the suicide pact (cf. *BJ* 3.387-391). For Nicanor cf. *BJ* 3.346-55; 5.261.

3.393 οἱ δὲ Ῥωμαῖοι πάντες ἐπὶ θέαν αὐτοῦ συνέτρεχον...: for the expression ἐπὶ θέαν αὐτου ("to catch a glimpse of him") cf. ἐπὶ θέαν τοῦ... ἱεροῦ καὶ τῶν... ἁγίων (*BJ* 1.354). Josephus presents himself as the object of the Romans' hostile gaze, a place fraught with danger (cf. Chapman 2005, 294). For συνέτρεχον ("they rushed together") cf. *Antiq* 3.6; 11.142.

3.393 ...καὶ τοῦ πλήθους συνθλιβομένου περὶ τῷ στρατηγῷ θόρυβος ἦν ποικίλος: construe τοῦ πλήθους συνθλιβομένου with θόρυβος ἦν ποικίλος: "the hubbub of the crowd pressing around the general was of varied hue." The one referred to as "the general" is of course Vespasian.

3.393 τῶν μὲν γεγηθότων ἐπὶ τῷ ληφθέντι, τῶν δ' ἀπειλούντων, τῶν δ' ἐγγύθεν ἰδεῖν βιαζομένων: gen. abs. Note the elaboration upon the μέν... δέ construction: "some boasting..., some threatening..., and some forcing their way in to take a look." The prepos. phrase ἐπὶ τῷ ληφθέντι ("at the one who had been captured") refers to Josephus. The phraseology creates a riot of motion and color, rather like a complicated painting.

3.394 καὶ οἱ μὲν πόρρωθεν κολάζειν ἐβόων τὸν πολέμιον...: trans. κολάζειν as an obj. inf. after ἐβόων (Smyth §1992.c): "those who were further away kept shouting *to punish* the enemy..."

3.394 τῶν δὲ πλησίον ἀνάμνησις αὐτοῦ τῶν ἔργων εἰσῄει καὶ πρὸς τὴν μεταβολὴν θάμβος: mere sight of Josephus unleashed in viewers the memory of what had been the vanquished general's impressive accomplishments. For the heroics of Josephus and his men just before the fall of Jotapata cf. *BJ* 3.258–75. For πρὸς τὴν μεταβολὴν ("at the change in fortune") cf. *Antiq* 14.481; *BJ* 1.282, 353; 4.501. Josephus presents himself as a tragic figure.

3.394–395 τῶν τε ἡγεμόνων οὐδεὶς ἦν, ὃς εἰ καὶ πρότερον ὠργίζετο, τότε πρὸς τὴν ὄψιν οὐκ ἐνέδωκεν αὐτοῦ: members of the Roman officer corps, who doubtless knew Josephus through his liaison with Titus, relented at the mere sight of Josephus. The words εἰ καὶ πρότερον ὠργίζετο (protasis of a simp. fact. cond.) seem hypothetical. For the telling phrase πρὸς τὴν ὄψιν ("at the sight") cf. *BJ* 2.170; 5.52, 290, 451, 547; 6.406.

3.396 μάλιστα δὲ τὸν Τίτον ἐξαιρέτως τό τε καρτερικὸν ἐν ταῖς συμφοραῖς ᾕρει τοῦ Ἰωσήπου καὶ πρὸς τὴν ἡλικίαν ἔλεος…: two factors in particular affected (ᾕρει) Titus: 1) Josephus' stick-to-itiveness (τό καρτερικόν, coined from the adj. καρτερικός, -ή, όν = "enduring, patient") amid his misfortunes; and 2) pity for Josephus' age. Josephus, born in AD 37 (*Vita* 5), would now have been about thirty years old. In place of ἐξαιρέτως ("espec.," "remarkably") some mss. read ἐξ ἀρετῆς ("valorously").

3.396 ἀναμιμνησκομένῳ τε τὸν πάλαι μαχόμενον καὶ τὸν ἐν χερσὶν ἐχθρῶν ἄρτι κείμενον ὁρῶντι παρῆν [δὲ] νοεῖν: the pres. act. ptcs. ἀναμιμνησκομένῳ and ὁρῶντι, which refer to Titus, are in the dat. case to construe with the compound vb. παρῆν: "it was in the power of (Titus) as he was recalling… and seeing to consider…" The words τὸν… μαχόμενον and τὸν… κείμενον refer to Josephus.

3.396 ὅσον δύναται τύχη, καὶ ὡς ὀξεῖα μὲν πολέμου ῥοπή, τῶν δ' ἀνθρωπίνων οὐδὲν βέβαιον: the clause markers ὅσον and ὡς demarcate indir. quest. Titus, like a character in a Greek drama, is led to reflect upon the power of fate (τύχη cf. *BJ* 1.431; 2.360; 3.25, 354, 359, 389; 4.40; 5.121, 122, 548) and thus empathizes with Josephus. Battles oft came down to a decisive outcome (referred to here as πολέμου ῥοπή; cf. *BJ* 2.52, 410; 5.66); for the frailty of human affairs cf. espec. Hdt. 1.32.

3.397 παρὸ καὶ τότε συνδιέθηκεν μὲν πλείστους ἑαυτῷ καὶ πρὸς οἶκτον τοῦ Ἰωσήπου: the rare double compound vb.

συνδιέθηκεν (from συνδιατίθημι = "to help in arranging," LSJ I.1) seems to describe Titus' persuasiveness in bringing "many" (πλείστους) of his fellows to share in his compassion for Josephus.

3.397 πλείστη δ' αὐτῷ καὶ παρὰ τῷ πατρὶ μοῖρα σωτηρίας ἐγένετο: the superl. adj. πλείστη mods. μοῖρα; the pers. pron. αὐτῷ refers to Josephus; τῷ πατρί refers to Vespasian.

3.398 ὁ μέντοι Οὐεσπασιανὸς φρουρεῖν αὐτὸν μετὰ πάσης ἀσφαλείας προσέταττεν ὡς ἀναπέμψων αὐτίκα Νέρωνι: Vespasian was the one on whom Josephus' fate most depended, but here (μέντοι = "however") Vespasian issues orders to guard Josephus "with every precaution" (μετὰ πάσης ἀσφαλείας, cf. *Antiq* 15.178, 291; *Vita* 330; *BJ* 6.116). The fut. ptc. (here ἀναπέμψων) oft denotes pur. (Smyth §2065); with ptcs. of pur. the particle ὡς denotes the presumed intention of the subj. of the principal vb., without implicating the writer (Smyth §2086). Cf. συλλαμβάνει Κῦρον ὡς ἀποκτενῶν = "he seized Cyrus for the pur. (as he declared) of putting him to death" (Xen. *Ana.* 1.1.3). The vb. ἀναπέμπω may have the tech. mng. of referring someone "to a higher authority" (LSJ I.3). Thus, ψήφισμα πρὸς βασιλέα (*OGI* 329.51); τινὰ πρός τινα (Lk 23:7); τινά τινι (Philemon 12).

3.399 τοῦτο ἀκούσας ὁ Ἰώσηπος μόνῳ τι διαλεχθῆναι θέλειν ἔλεγεν αὐτῷ: the demonst. pron. τοῦτο refers to what Josephus has revealed in the preced. sentence. The vb. ἔλεγεν sets off indir. state. (Smyth §1867); a subj. accus. is not needed when the subj. of the infin. and finite vb. are the same, as here: "Josephus said that *he* desired to have a conversation with him alone." The words μόνῳ and αὐτῷ refer to Vespasian.

3.399 μεταστησαμένου δ' ἐκείνου πλὴν τοῦ παιδὸς Τίτου καὶ δυοῖν φίλων τοὺς ἄλλους ἅπαντας: the words μεταστησαμένου... ἐκείνου constitute a gen. abs.: "and when he [= Vespasian] had removed all the others [from the room]..." In granting Josephus his wish of a private audience Vespasian excepted Titus and the two friends on whom he relied, perhaps, as witnesses. Josephus must have known at least one of these friends in advance for the second of them (ὁ ἕτερος, *BJ* 3.405) claims that he had never heard Josephus predict the fall of Jotapata nor his own captivity.

3.400 "σὺ μέν," ἔφη, "Οὐεσπασιανέ, νομίζεις αἰχμάλωτον αὐτὸ μόνον εἰληφέναι Ἰώσηπον, ἐγὼ δὲ ἄγγελος ἥκω σοι μειζόνων": the editors have placed Josephus' impassioned remarks in quote marks (*oratio recta*, cf. *BJ* 2.195 above), indicating a moment of high drama. Note also the marked contr. between σὺ μέν and ἐγὼ δέ: "you (for your part)..., but I (for mine)..." The vb. νομίζεις sets off indir. state. (Smyth §1867); a subj. accus. is not needed when the subj. of the infin. and finite vb. are the same, as here: "you suppose that *you* have captured Josephus, a mere captive." The word Ἰώσηπον, the dir. obj. of εἰληφέναι, is in appos. with the phrase αἰχμάλωτον αὐτὸ μόνον.

3.400 "μὴ γὰρ ὑπὸ θεοῦ προπεμπόμενος ᾔδειν τὸν Ἰουδαίων νόμον...": trans. μή... προπεμπόμενος as though it were the protasis of past contr. fact cond. (Smyth §2303): "for *unless* I had been sent forth by God." The words ᾔδειν τὸν Ἰουδαίων νόμον function as what in effect becomes the apodosis: "...I would have known the law of the Jews." Which "law of the Jews" does Josephus have in mind? Possibly Josephus alludes to "the laws of our fathers" (οἱ πάτριοι νόμοι, *BJ* 3.356) which fellow Jewish captives supposed Josephus violated when he contemplated surrender to the Romans at the fall of Jotapata (cf. *BJ* 3.355–360).

3.400 "...καὶ πῶς στρατηγοῖς ἀποθνῄσκειν πρέπει": indir. quest., prim. seq.: "and how it befits generals to die." Josephus, himself a general, had spoken of himself as "destined to die" (τεθνηξομένου καὶ τοῦ στρατηγοῦ, *BJ* 3.390); nevertheless, the lots had favored him so that he did not commit suicide with the others, eventually persuading another sole survivor to remain alive (cf. *BJ* 3.390–391). Cf. Huntsman (1996–97) 370 n. 27 for the possibility that Josephus somehow "fixed" the lots.

3.401 "Νέρωνί με πέμπεις· τί γάρ;": some versions mention Nero's impending death after the words τί γάρ. That omission would explain the next clause which assumes that Nero has already died.

3.401 "οἱ μετὰ Νέρωνα μέχρι σοῦ διάδοχοι μενοῦσιν": this phrase is not represented in all versions. Josephus applies the word διάδοχοι ("successors") to Alexander the Great in *Contra Ap* 1.200; to Julius Caesar in *Antiq* 19.174.

3.401 "σὺ Καῖσαρ, Οὐεσπασιανέ, καὶ αὐτοκράτωρ, σὺ καὶ παῖς ὁ σὸς οὗτος": only Οὐεσπασιανε is in the vocative case; the titles Καῖσαρ and αὐτοκράτωρ represent statements of fact. Josephus mentions several who claimed the title Καῖσαρ at Rome: Titus (*BJ* 1.10); Julius Caesar (*BJ* 1.183, 199, 200); Sextus Caesar (*BJ* 1.211); and Octavian (*BJ* 1.242). For the title αὐτοκράτωρ, cf. *Antiq* 4.329; 5.273; 14.190, 192, 199; 18.32, 33, 177; 20.11; *Vita* 363; *BJ* 1.24; 4.494, 495, 546, etc. The words, "both you and your son here" (σὺ καὶ παῖς ὁ σὸς οὗτος), indicate that Josephus' predication applied not only to Vespasian but also to Titus.

3.402 δέσμει δέ με νῦν ἀσφαλέστερον, καὶ τήρει σεαυτῷ: the compar. adj. ἀσφαλέστερον mods. the pers. pron. με: "bind me more securely and keep me for yourself!" Josephus remained a client of the Flavian emperors from the time of his surrender in spring AD 67 to the end of his life (hence the adoption of the name Flavius). When the prediction was fulfilled in 69, Vespasian made Josephus a free man. Cf. Intro 37 above for Josephus' relationship with the Flavians.

3.402 δεσπότης μὲν γὰρ οὐ μόνον ἐμοῦ σὺ Καῖσαρ, ἀλλὰ καὶ γῆς καὶ θαλάττης καὶ παντὸς ἀνθρώπων γένους: not only would Vespasian be the master (δεσπότης) of Josephus personally, but also of the earth, the sea, and all its peoples. For the statement "earth and sea" (καὶ γῆς καὶ θαλάττης) cf. καὶ διὰ γῆς καὶ διὰ θαλάττης (*Antiq* 11.53); τοὺς μὲν ὑπὸ γῆν, τοὺς δὲ ἐν θαλάττῃ (*Contra Ap* 2.240); for "every race of men" (παντὸς ἀνθρώπων γένους) cf. *Antiq* 4.262; 8.121.

3.402 ἐγὼ δὲ ἐπὶ τιμωρίαν δέομαι φρουρᾶς μείζονος, εἰ κατασχεδιάζω καὶ θεοῦ: As before (cf. δέσμει δέ με νῦν ἀσφαλέστερον, καὶ τήρει σεαυτῷ, *BJ* 3.402), Josephus asks for a still more restrictive custody—even one leading to punishment (ἐπὶ τιμωρίαν, *Antiq* 19.329; *BJ* 3.346, 348)—if his prediction does not come to pass. The rare vb. κατασχεδιάζω ("affirm rashly of," LSJ I.1) apparently means to trifle with the words of God—i.e., misrepresent him.

3.403 ταῦτ' εἰπόντος παραχρῆμα μὲν Οὐεσπασιανὸς ἀπιστεῖν ἐδόκει: the pron. ταῦτα refers to the overall content of

Josephus' speech, just ended (cf. *BJ* 3.400–402). The ptc. εἰπόντος constitutes a gen. abs. (the gen. ptc. may stand without its corresponding pron.—here ἐμοῦ—when it may be supplied from context, Smyth §2072.a). The statement that Vespasian "seemed to disbelieve" (ἀπιστεῖν ἐδόκει) lends to Vespasian an aloofness that arises, perhaps, from the colossal stature of the man.

3.403 καὶ τὸν Ἰώσηπον ὑπελάμβανεν ταῦτα περὶ σωτηρίας πανουργεῖν: the vb. ὑπελάμβανεν (occurs 17 times in the *BJ*) sets off indir. state.: "and he suspected that Josephus was playing the knave in this way for his safety." For the phrase περὶ σωτηρίας ("for his safety") cf. *Antiq* 3.190; 11.17; *BJ* 3.346; 6.387; for πανουργεῖν ("to play the knave") cf. *BJ* 2.278.

3.404 κατὰ μικρὸν δὲ εἰς πίστιν ὑπήγετο τοῦ θεοῦ διεγείροντος αὐτὸν εἰς τὴν ἡγεμονίαν ἤδη καὶ τὰ σκῆπτρα δι' ἑτέρων σημείων προδεικνύντος: note the contr. between παραχρῆμα μέν ("straight away," *BJ* 3.403) and κατὰ μικρὸν δέ ("but gradually"). For ὑπήγετο ("he was led") cf. *Antiq* 12.398; for εἰς πίστιν ("to a belief"—namely, in Josephus' prediction) cf. *Antiq* 12.150; 15.201; 17.327; *BJ* 1.485; 2.341. Here the two gen. abs. (τοῦ θεοῦ διεγείροντος and [τοῦ θεοῦ] προδεικνύντος) account for the *cause* of Vespasian's belief (Smyth §2070.b): "*because* God was already rousing in him thoughts of empire and foreshadowing the throne by other tokens." According to the testimonies of Tacitus (*Hist.* 5.13) and Suetonius (*Vesp.* 4), persons "proceeding from Judaea" were to become masters of the world.

3.405 ἀτρεκῆ δὲ τὸν Ἰώσηπον καὶ ἐν ἄλλοις κατελάμβανεν: Vespasian had discovered Josephus to be "true" (ἀτρεκῆ, from ἀτρεκής, -ές) in "other matters" (ἐν ἄλλοις, cf. *BJ* 1.286; 2.78, 340) that become clear in the following words. For κατελάμβανεν ("discovered") cf. *Antiq* 2.293; 11.241; 14.399; 17.269; *BJ* 3.527; 4.313.

3.405 τῶν γὰρ τοῖς ἀπορρήτοις παρατυχόντων φίλων ὁ ἕτερος θαυμάζειν ἔφη πῶς οὔτε τοῖς ἐπὶ τῶν Ἰωταπάτων περὶ ἁλώσεως, οὔθ' ἑαυτῷ προμαντεύσαιτο αἰχμαλωσίαν...: construe the phrase τῶν... παρατυχόντων φίλων with ὁ ἕτερος: "for the second of the friends [who] happened to be pres. at the private interview…" The words τοῖς ἀπορρήτοις mean "private interview" in this context. The vb. ἔφη sets off indir. state. (Smyth §1867): "said that he was surprised…" The aor. tense of the mn. vb. ἔφη requires that the depending vb. προμαντεύσαιτο ("he predicted") be in the optv. mood. The clause marker πῶς ("how") sets off indir. quest. sec. seq.

3.405 …εἰ μὴ ταῦτα λῆρος εἴη διακρουομένου τὰς ἐπ' αὐτὸν ὀργάς: εἰ μή demarcates the protasis of a pres. contr. fact (the vb. εἴη has been changed to the optv. mood because the mn. vb. ἔφη establishes sec. seq.): "unless these things were [the] rubbish of someone delaying the fits of anger against him." Thus the so-called "friends" (cf. δυοῖν φίλων, *BJ* 3.399) provide incriminating evidence against Josephus at the private interview: their argument is that if Josephus really did have the gift of prophecy, he would have predicted (προμαντεύσαιτο) the fall of Jotapata and his own capture. But he did neither.

3.406 ὁ δὲ Ἰώσηπος καὶ τοῖς Ἰωταπατηνοῖς ὅτι μετὰ τεσσαρακοστὴν ἑβδόμην ἡμέραν ἁλώσονται προειπεῖν ἔφη, καὶ ὅτι πρὸς Ῥωμαίων αὐτὸς ζωγρηθήσεται: Follow this order of trans.: ὁ δὲ Ἰώσηπος… ἔφη προειπεῖν… ὅτι… ἁλώσονται… καὶ ὅτι… ζωγρηθήσεται. Remember that there is no accus. subj. when the mn. vb. and infin. have the same subj., as here. The inhabitants of Jotapata constitute the subj. of the vb. ἁλώσονται; Josephus constitutes the subj. of the vb. ζωγρηθήσεται. Josephus' reply undermines what the two friends had just said about his inability to predict the fut. (cf. prev note). For ἁλώσονται ("they shall be captured") cf. *BJ* 1.374; for προειπεῖν ("to tell the fut.") cf. *BJ* 1.234; 7.42.

3.407 ταῦτα παρὰ τῶν αἰχμαλώτων κατ' ἰδίαν ὁ Οὐεσπασιανὸς ἐκπυθόμενος ὡς εὕρισκεν ἀληθῆ, οὕτω πιστεύειν περὶ τῶν κατ' αὐτὸν ἦρκτο: trans. the clause that begins with ὡς first; note that ἀληθῆ mods. ταῦτα: "when Vespasian discovered (to be) true those things that he had inquired privately from the captives…" Πιστεύειν ("to believe") recalls εἰς πίστιν ὑπήγετο in *BJ* 3.404. For ἦρκτο ("he began") cf. *Antiq* 5.87; 18.317.

3.408 φρουρᾶς μὲν οὖν καὶ δεσμῶν οὐκ ἀνίει τὸν Ἰώσηπον, ἐδωρεῖτο δ' ἐσθῆτι καὶ τοῖς ἄλλοις κειμηλίοις...: here the vb. ἀνίει (3 pers. sing. impf. of ἀνίημι) patterns with the ablatival gens. φρουρᾶς and δεσμῶν: "so he did not release Josephus *from* custody and bonds, but..." For ἐδωρεῖτο in the middle voice ("but he presented [Josephus] with" + dat.) cf. *Antiq* 15.6, 327; 16.128; 17.173; 20.212; *BJ* 2.215; 5.381. The descr. is reminiscent of the imprisoned St. Paul who lived in Rome for two years yet received visitors and taught the Gospel "with all boldness and without hindrance" (Acts 28:31).

3.408 ...φιλοφρονούμενός τε καὶ περιέπων διετέλει τὰ πολλὰ Τίτου τῇ τιμῇ συνεργοῦντος: trans. τὰ πολλά as an adv. accus. ("quite"). Construe the finite vb. διετέλει with the two suppl. ptcs. φιλοφρονούμενος and περιέπων: "he was continuing to deal affectionately and take care [of Josephus]." The words Τίτου... συνεργοῦντος consist of a gen. abs.: "[while] Titus was cooperating [with him]." For φιλοφρονούμενός ("deal affectionately") cf. *Antiq* 10.168; 15.53; 16.61; *BJ* 1.608; for διετέλει ("he was continuing") cf. *BJ* 2.483, 583; 3.408; 6.303. Τῇ τιμῇ prob. refers to *the expense* of the captivity (cf. LSJ III.1), espec. in light of the clothing and other gifts (ἐσθῆτι καὶ τοῖς ἄλλοις κειμηλίοις, *BJ* 3.408) with which Vespasian favored Josephus during his imprisonment.

ANTIQ 18.116–119

18.116 Τισὶ δὲ τῶν Ἰουδαίων ἐδόκει ὀλωλέναι τὸν Ἡρώδου στρατόν: trans. the first words as follows: "it seemed to some of the Jews that..." The pf. act. infin. ὀλωλέναι ("to have perished," from ὄλλυμι) serves as the subj. of the finite vb. ἐδόκει; τὸν... στρατόν serves as the subj. of ὀλωλέναι. The Herod here mentioned is Herod Antipas (see Intro 22) whose army was beaten by Aretas IV, king of Petra, in a boundary dispute (*Antiq* 18.113). In the ensuing battle, the whole army of Herod Antipas was destroyed when some refugees, who had come from the region of Herod Philip, played Herod Antipas false.

18.116 ὑπὸ τοῦ Θεοῦ καὶ μάλα δικαίως τινυμένου κατὰ ποινὴν Ἰωάννου τοῦ ἐπικαλουμένου βαπτιστοῦ: the variant τιννυμένου (in place of τινυμένου) reflects a later spelling. For καὶ μάλα δικαίως ("even very justly") cf. Joseph. *Contra Ap* 2.51; for κατὰ ποινήν ("for recompense") cf. Anton. Lib. *Meta.* 38.4; Euseb. *Hist. Eccles.* 1.11.4; *Dem. Ev.* 9.5.15; Salam. Hermias *Hist. Eccles.* 9.6.5. According to the NT, John the Baptist had incurred the wrath of Herod Antipas for denouncing the marriage to Herodias as unlawful (Mt 14:4; Mk 6:18; Lk 3:19).

18.117 κτείνει γὰρ δὴ τοῦτον Ἡρώδης ἀγαθὸν ἄνδρα καὶ τοῖς Ἰουδαίοις κελεύοντα ἀρετὴν ἐπασκοῦσιν καὶ τὰ πρὸς ἀλλήλους δικαιοσύνῃ καὶ πρὸς τὸν Θεὸν εὐσεβείᾳ χρωμένοις βαπτισμῷ συνιέναι: the words τοῦτον... ἀγαθὸν ἄνδρα and κελεύοντα refer to John the Baptist. Construe κελεύοντα with τοῖς Ἰουδαίοις and ptcs. ἐπασκοῦσιν... χρωμένοις: "...ordering the Jews to enter into baptism as they were practicing virtue toward each other... and employing righteousness [δικαιοσύνῃ]... and piety [εὐσεβείᾳ]." Mason believes (2003, 214–215) that Josephus reduced the content of John's preaching to "piety toward God and justice toward one's fellows."

18.117 οὕτω γὰρ δὴ καὶ τὴν βάπτισιν ἀποδεκτὴν αὐτῷ φανεῖσθαι...: the pers. pron. αὐτῷ refers to John the Baptist: "for in this way [οὕτω] indeed did baptism appear acceptable to him..." The two apparently interchangeable words for baptism—ὁ βαπτισμός (prev sentence) and ἡ βάπτισις—occur nowhere else in the Josephan corpus.

18.117 μὴ ἐπί τινων ἁμαρτάδων παραιτήσει χρωμένων...: trans. the prep. ἐπί with the noun παραιτήσει in the dat. case: "not with a view to supplication for cert. sins [already] perpetrated." In place of the more usu. word for "sin" (ἡ ἁμαρτία) Josephus here prefers ἡ ἁμαρτάς (cf. *Antiq* 18.350), an Ionic and later Greek form.

18.117 ...ἀλλ' ἐφ' ἁγνείᾳ τοῦ σώματος, ἅτε δὴ καὶ τῆς ψυχῆς δικαιοσύνῃ προεκκεκαθαρμένης: "...but with a view to a purification of the body, since in fact the soul has already been purified by righteousness." Might this emphasis on the soul's righteousness (τῆς ψυχῆς δικαιοσύνῃ) be related to Jesus' statement in Matthew's gospel that, by being baptized by John, it was necessary "to fulfill all righteousness" (πληρῶσαι πᾶσαν δικαιοσύνην, Mt 3:15)?

18.118 καὶ τῶν ἄλλων συστρεφομένων: gen. abs.: "and while others were joining together..." In the pass. the vb. συστρέφω can mean "club together, conspire" (LSJ III.1), e.g., ἐπ' ἐμέ συστράφεντες ἥκουσι (Aesch. 2.178). Also, Thuc. 4.68; 8.54.

18.118 καὶ γὰρ ἥσθησαν ἐπὶ πλεῖστον τῇ ἀκροάσει τῶν λόγων: in place of ἥσθησαν ("they rejoiced"), which could represent a Christian interpolation, some versions prefer ἤρθησαν ("they were aroused"). Ἐπὶ πλεῖστον means "to the greatest extent." An ἀκρόασις represents a "hearing, hearkening, or listening to" (LSJ I.1) or that to which one listens, a "recitation, lecture" (LSJ II.1). The passage indicates that John was popular with the crowds and a good speaker. The NT records, moreover, that "all" (πάντες, Mk 1:5) the inhabitants of Jerusalem went out to John in the wilderness and were baptized by him.

18.118 δείσας Ἡρώδης τὸ ἐπὶ τοσόνδε πιθανὸν αὐτοῦ τοῖς ἀνθρώποις μὴ ἐπὶ ἀποστάσει τινὶ φέροι: the aor. act. ptc. δείσας (from δείδω) construes with the prep. ἐπί; trans. τό... πιθανὸν as a substant. noun: "such great persuasiveness with the people..." The words μή... φέροι constitute a fear clause, sec. seq. (Smyth §2221). Occasionally the vb. φέρω means "lead to..., be conducive to" (LSJ A.VII.3). Thus Herod Antipas was afraid that John's persuasiveness would lead to some type of sedition (ἐπὶ ἀποστάσει τινί).

18.118 πάντα γὰρ ἐῴκεσαν συμβουλῇ τῇ ἐκείνου πράξοντες: the pers. pron. ἐκείνου refers to John. Trans. ἐῴκεσαν and πράξοντες together: "for they seemed about to do everything by his [John's] will." According to the NT, John was imprisoned because he questioned Herod Antipas' right to marry his sister-in-law Herodias (Mk 6:17–21). Thus, the NT emphasizes the moral charges that John brought against Herod Antipas, whereas Josephus stresses political fears that John possibly aroused in the ruler.

18.118 πολὺ κρεῖττον ἡγεῖται πρίν τι νεώτερον ἐξ αὐτοῦ γενέσθαι...: the adv. accus. πολύ mods. the adv. κρεῖττον: "much better." When the clause marker πρίν patterns with an infin. the translation is "before" (Smyth §2434). The adj. νέος, -α, -ον (of which the compar. form νεώτερον occurs here) may mean "unexpected, strange, untoward, evil" (LSJ II.2). Thus Herod Antipas thought he should act decisively before something more "unexpected" came "from him" (ἐξ αὐτοῦ)—that is, from John—in the form of a political upheaval.

18.118 ...προλαβὼν ἀνελεῖν τοῦ μεταβολῆς γενομένης [μὴ] εἰς πράγματα ἐμπεσὼν μετανοεῖν: the aor. act. ptc. προλαβών mods. Herod Antipas, subj. of the vb. ἡγεῖται in the prev clause: "he thought it much better... [to] arrest him and kill him." The def. article τοῦ presents a problem. However, the version in Euseb. *Hist. Eccles.* 1.11.6 reads ἤ (instead of τοῦ) which makes for a better comp. with the πρίν clause. Eusebius also omits μή (bracketed in our version) which, owing to the first change, is not necessary. Note also the gen. abs. (μεταβολῆς γενομένης) and the idiom ἐμπίπτω... εἰς + accus. (LSJ I.4.b): "he thought it much better to arrest and kill him before, when a change had occurred, he fall into problems and repent [of not having dealt with John earlier]." The textual difficulties may be due to later changes by Christians who desired to avoid connecting John with political insurrection.

18.119 καὶ ὁ μὲν ὑποψίᾳ τῇ Ἡρώδου δέσμιος: "a prisoner, then, by Herod's suspicions..." In the NT the word δέσμιος ("prisoner") is used espec. of St. Paul, e.g., ἐγὼ Παῦλος ὁ δέσμιος τοῦ Χριστοῦ Ἰησοῦ (Eph 3:1). Cf. Acts 23:18; 25:14; 28:17; Eph 4:1; 2 Tim 1:8; Philemon 1, 9.

18.119: ...εἰς τὸν Μαχαιροῦντα πεμφθεὶς τὸ προειρημένον φρούριον ταύτῃ κτίννυται: Josephus has just mentioned Machaerus (*Antiq* 18.111-112), the fortress Herod the Great built and developed into one of his strategic centers. Three such fortresses—Machaerus, Masada and Herodium—held out against the Romans after the destruction of Jerusalem in AD 70. Trans. the fem. sing. pron. ταύτῃ as "there"—namely, at Machaerus. The NT relates, more generally, that Herod had seized John and "put him in prison" (Mt 14:3); there

JOSEPHUS NOTES

is, nonetheless, a much fuller account of the circums. surrounding John's death in Mt 14:1–12.

18.119 τοῖς δὲ Ἰουδαίοις δόξαν ἐπὶ τιμωρίᾳ τῇ ἐκείνου τὸν ὄλεθρον ἐπὶ τῷ στρατεύματι γενέσθαι: the particle δέ possesses adversative force ("but") and the pron. ἐκείνου refers to John. Trans. τοῖς... Ἰουδαίοις as a poss. dat. (Smyth §1476): "the Jews were of the opinion that..." The words τὸν ὄλεθρον... γενέσθαι constitute accus. with infin. in indir. state.: "...that the destruction upon [Herod's] army was a vindication of John." For ἐπὶ τιμωρίᾳ cf. Joseph. *Antiq* 7.181; 17.254; *BJ* 1.217, 227; 2.277; for τὸν ὄλεθρον cf. *Antiq* 2.301, 328; 19.127, 190; *BJ* 7.112.

18.119 τοῦ θεοῦ κακῶσαι Ἡρώδην θέλοντος: gen. abs.: "[since] God wished to harm Herod."

ANTIQ 18.63–64:

18.63 Γίνεται δὲ κατὰ τοῦτον τὸν χρόνον Ἰησοῦς σοφὸς ἀνήρ, εἴγε ἄνδρα αὐτὸν λέγειν χρή: for the expression κατὰ τοῦτον τὸν χρόνον ("at about this time") cf. Joseph. *Antiq* 13.46; 17.19; 18.39, 80. Josephus has just described a riot that broke out in Jerusalem, a riot that Pilate put down by force (*Antiq* 18.60–62). Others referred to as a "wise man" (σοφὸς ἀνήρ) include Aesop (Plut. *Crass.* 32.5), Aristobolos (Euseb. *Praep. Ev.* 7.13.7), Socrates (Plato *Apol.* 18b), and Lycurgus (Plato *Ep.* 354b), though the NT does not once refer to Jesus in that manner. Do the words "if it be lawful to call him a man" (εἴγε ἄνδρα αὐτὸν λέγειν χρή) repres. a genuine observation from Josephus or a pious disclaimer from a later interpolator? It is impossible to tell.

18.63 ἦν γὰρ παραδόξων ἔργων ποιητής: the adj. παράδοξος, -ον means "contrary to expectation, incredible" (LSJ I.1). Onlookers used this word to describe Jesus' healing of a paralyzed man in Luke's gospel: "we have seen *extraordinary things* [παράδοξα] today" (Lk 5:26). For ποιητής ("doer") cf. ποιητὴς ἔργου (James 1:25) and ποιητὴς νόμου (James 4:11); also Rom 2:13; James 1:22.

18.63 διδάσκαλος ἀνθρώπων τῶν ἡδονῇ τἀληθῆ δεχομένων: the NT refers many times to Jesus as a "teacher" (διδάσκαλος, cf. Mt 8:19; 9:11; 12:38; 17:24; 19:16; 22:16, 24, 36; 26:18, in Matthew's gospel alone). Ἡδονῇ ("gladly") represents the dat. of accomp. circum. (Smyth §1527). Cf. βίᾳ ("by force"), δίκῃ ("justly"), δόλῳ ("by guile"), ἔργῳ ("in fact"), ἡσυχῇ ("quietly"), and κύκλῳ ("round about"). Some versions—accentuating the idea that Jesus was a miracle worker—read τὰήθη ("unusual things") in place of τἀληθῆ ("true things").

18.63 καὶ πολλοὺς μὲν Ἰουδαίους, πολλοὺς δὲ καὶ τοῦ Ἑλληνικοῦ ἐπηγάγετο: note the μέν... δέ construction. For the idea that Jesus "won over to himself" (ἐπηγάγετο, cf. *Antiq* 8.167, 380; 17.327) many Jews and Gentiles cf. Mt 2:2; 21:41; Lk 2:31; 4:26-27; Jn 12:32. For τὸ Ἑλληνικόν as a designation of the Greeks collectively cf. Hdt. 1.4; 7.139; Plut. *Arist*. 19.8; *Tit. Flam.* 9.7; Thuc. 3.82; Xen. *Hellen.* 3.2.4; *Anab.* 1.2.1.

18.63: ὁ χριστὸς οὗτος ἦν: some prefer the emendation Χριστὸς λεγόμενος (Richards and Shutt, 1937, 176). However, Josephus plainly uses χριστός elsewhere in a tech., non-theological sense: μέχρι τῆς στέγης χριστὸν (*"plastered over* as far as the roof," *Antiq* 8.137). Many dismiss the remaining occurrences of ὁ χριστός in Josephus as so many interpolations: τῶν Χριστιανῶν (*Antiq* 18.64); Ἰησοῦ τοῦ λεγομένου Χριστοῦ (*Antiq* 20.200). But such "anointings" were extremely signif. in the OT (cf. Ex 28:41; 29:7, 21; 30:30-31; 40:9; Lev 21:10 1 Sam 10:1; 1 Ki 1:39; Ps 89:20; 133:2, etc), so they need not be restricted to Jesus.

18.64 καὶ αὐτὸν ἐνδείξει τῶν πρώτων ἀνδρῶν παρ' ἡμῖν σταυρῷ ἐπιτετιμηκότος Πιλάτου: the pron. αὐτόν refers to Jesus. The words ἐπιτετιμηκότος Πιλάτου constitute a gen. abs.: "although Pilate, by an indictment of the leading men among us, had penalized him with crucifixion…" According to the NT, however, Pilate found "no guilt" in Jesus (Jn 18:38; 19:4, 6; cf. Mt 27:23; Mk 15:14; Lk 23:4, 14). For παρ' ἡμῖν ("among us") cf. *Antiq* 1.5, 9; 3.172, 248, 318, 320; 5.95, 96; 8.46, etc; for σταυρῷ cf. *BJ* 2.308.

18.64 οὐκ ἐπαύσαντο οἱ τὸ πρῶτον ἀγαπήσαντες: the expression "those who first loved him" (οἱ τὸ πρῶτον ἀγαπήσαντες) refers to the devotees of Jesus. For ἐπαύσαντο cf. *Antiq* 5.161; 9.266, 290; 15.80; 19.152; *BJ* 1.18, 94, 569; 2.498; 5.295; 6.407, 433.

18.64 ἐφάνη γὰρ αὐτοῖς τρίτην ἔχων ἡμέραν πάλιν ζῶν: for Jesus' resurrection from the dead the NT prefers ὤφθη ("he appeared," so Lk 24:34; Acts 13:31; 1 Cor 15:5, 6, 7, 8; 1 Tim 3:16), though ἐφάνη ("he appeared") appears once at Mk 16:9. Trans. ἔχων as "continually" (Smyth §2062.a); ζῶν describes the resurrected Jesus only in Mt 27:63.

18.64 τῶν θείων προφητῶν ταῦτά τε καὶ ἄλλα μυρία περὶ αὐτοῦ θαυμάσια εἰρηκότων: gen. abs.: "[since] the divine prophets had spoken both these and countless other marvelous things about him." Prophecies about the coming messiah constitute a major theme in the OT. For a select few of the "countless marvelous things" (μυρία... θαυμάσια) that feature the messiah in the OT cf. Is 52:13–53:12; Jer 23:5–6; Lam 1:12; 2:15–16; 3:19; Dan 9:26; 10:5–9; Hos 6:1–2; Amos 9:11–12; Micah 5:2; Nah 1:15; Hag 2:6–7; Zech 3:8; 11:12–13; 12:10; and 13:7. The case can be made, however, that Josephus himself "feared and despised the messianism of the Zealots" (Amaru 1980–81, 229) with all its revolutionary implications.

18.64 εἰς ἔτι τε νῦν τῶν Χριστιανῶν ἀπὸ τοῦδε ὠνομασμένον οὐκ ἐπέλιπε τὸ φῦλον: the subj. of the vb. ἐπέλιπε (cf. *Antiq* 2.189; 8.323; 9.62; 15.2; *BJ* 3.276; 4.50) is τῶν Χριστιανῶν... τὸ φῦλον ("the tribe of the Christians"); the pf. pass. ptc. ὠνομασμένον ("has been named," cf. *Antiq* 11.125; 19.8; *Contra Ap* 1.245) mods. τὸ φῦλον; the prep. phrase ἀπὸ τοῦδε ("from him") refers to Jesus who, according to the phrase in 18.63 (ὁ χριστὸς οὗτος ἦν), was the Christ.

ANTIQ 20.200

20.200 Ἄτε δὴ οὖν τοιοῦτος ὢν ὁ Ἄνανος: the Ananus here mentioned was one of five sons of another Ananus who had served as high priest (*Antiq* 20.198). The statement "since, therefore, he was of such a sort" (ἄτε δὴ οὖν τοιοῦτος ὢν) looks back to Josephus' earlier observations that the younger Ananus was insolent (*Antiq* 20.199) and among those Sadducees who were "very rigid in judging offenders" (ibid.). Josephus has already presented the Sadducees in less than favorable terms (cf. *Antiq* 13.293–298; 18.17; McLaren 2001, 4–5, 12). The episode shows one man acting rashly, "on a vendetta" (Mason 2003, 241). In other passages, however, Josephus presents Ananus in a more positive light (cf. McLaren 2001, 3–4).

20.200 νομίσας ἔχειν καιρὸν ἐπιτήδειον διὰ τὸ τεθνάναι μὲν Φῆστον, Ἀλβῖνον δ' ἔτι κατὰ τὴν ὁδὸν ὑπάρχειν: the subj. of the aor. ptc. νομίσας is Ananus (cf. preced note). Festus and Albinus were two of several Roman prefects/procurators who governed Judea (see Intro 27). Ananus supposed he had a "proper opportunity" (καιρὸν ἐπιτήδειον) because both procurators were, at the moment, conveniently out of the way: Festus had just died (AD 62) and Albinus was in transit from Alexandria to assume command. For κατὰ τὴν ὁδὸν ("on the way") cf. *Antiq* 1.254; 5.294; 8.240, 295; 10.114; 11.134; 12.170; 14.355, 360, 436, 446.

20.200 καθίζει συνέδριον κριτῶν καὶ παραγαγὼν εἰς αὐτὸ τὸν ἀδελφὸν Ἰησοῦ τοῦ λεγομένου Χριστοῦ, Ἰάκωβος ὄνομα αὐτῷ, καί τινας ἑτέρους: for καθίζει ("he assembled") cf. *Antiq* 19.97; *BJ* 3.532. The Sanhedrin was comprised of chief priests, elders, and teachers of the law (cf. Mk 14:55), so of what did the body called here συνέδριον κριτῶν ("council of judges") consist? The phrase would seem to describe a lesser, perhaps hastily contrived council—not the famed Sanhedrin (McLaren 2001, 6; Mason 2003, 241). Consider that Ananas perpetrated an illegality by even convening the assembly (*Antiq* 20.201), an offense for which he was subsequently removed from office (*Antiq* 20.203). It seems, nevertheless, that James, the brother of Jesus, "and certain others" (καί τινας ἑτέρους) were condemned at this council, wrongly convened though it was. There seems no doubt that James was put to death by the priestly authorities in the early sixties AD, "perhaps as part of a wider move of opposition to Christianity" (Beardslee 1962, 793; but McLaren 2001, 14–19 disagrees). Mention of "the Christ" here assumes the earlier passage (*Antiq* 18.63–64; so Mason 2003, 233, 243).

20.200 ὡς παρανομησάντων κατηγορίαν ποιησάμενος παρέδωκε λευσθησομένους: Ananus is the subj. of the ptc. ποιησάμενος and vb. παρέδωκε; the fut. pass. ptc. λευσθησομένους refers to James and the "certain others" (τινας ἑτέρους) mentioned in the prev clause: "Ananus handed them over *to be stoned*." Did the accusation for "having broken the law" (παρανομησάντων κατηγορίαν) involve James and the others' participation in Christianity? That possibility, though attractive, cannot be proven; the real conflict may have been that which transpired between rival parties of the Pharisees and Sadducees who constantly jostled for position, but even this possibility "is, at best, questionable" (cf. McLaren 2001, 8). It seems ironic that James, the one so "scrupulous about legal observance" (Mason 2003, 247; cf. Gal 2:11–13), should have been accused by Ananus of "breaking laws."

BJ 5.1–10

5.1 Ὁ μὲν Τίτος ὃν προειρήκαμεν τρόπον διοδεύσας τὴν ὑπὲρ Αἰγύπτου μέχρι Συρίας ἐρημίαν εἰς Καισάρειαν παρῆν ταύτῃ διεγνωκὼς προσυντάξασθαι τὰς δυνάμεις: trans. the rel. pron. ὃν with τρόπον: "whose *manner* we have described above..." The rel. clause refers to *BJ* 3.658–663 which provides a complete itinerary of Titus' march from Alexandria to Caesarea. Note the curious use of the preps. ὑπέρ, μέχρι, and εἰς: "having traversed the wilderness *over* Egypt *until* Syria, he arrived *at* Caesarea." For the idiom παρεῖναι εἰς ("to have arrived at") cf. Hdt. 1.9; 8.60; Xen. *Anab.* 7.1.11. The pron. ταύτῃ ("here") refers to Καισάρειαν, Caesarea Maritima, the staging area for the Roman forces in Palestine. For the pf. act. ptc. διεγνωκὼς ("having resolved") cf. *Antiq* 5.148; 10.84; 13.186; 14.466; *BJ* 3.445; 4.663; 6.249; 7.117.

5.2 ἔτι δ' αὐτοῦ κατὰ τὴν Ἀλεξάνδρειαν συγκαθισταμένου τῷ πατρὶ τὴν ἡγεμονίαν νέον αὐτοῖς ἐγκεχειρισμένην ὑπὸ τοῦ θεοῦ...: the words αὐτοῦ... συγκαθισταμένου constitute a gen. abs.: "[while] he was still in Alexandria, helping to establish for his father the empire which God had recently [νέον] committed to their hands..." The pronouncement corroborates Josephus' earlier prediction that Vespasian and Titus would become emperors over the Roman world (cf. *BJ* 3.401 above). For ὑπὸ τοῦ θεοῦ cf. *BJ* 6.39, 108, 401.

5.2 συνέβη καὶ τὴν ἐν [τοῖς] Ἱεροσολύμοις στάσιν ἀνακμάσασαν τριμερῆ γενέσθαι...: the word συνέβη ("it came to pass") occurs 34 times in the *BJ*. Στάσις ("party formed for seditious purposes, faction," LSJ B.III.1) refers most oft in the *BJ* to the rebellion of the Jews; by "break out afresh" (ἀνακμάσασαν) Josephus refers to the influx of fighting that had taken place when the Zealots occupied the Temple (*BJ* 4.151). Eleazar, son of Simon, John of Gischala, and Simon, son of Giora were the three mn. rebels (cf. *BJ* 5.5; 5.11), accounting for Josephus' statement that the rebellion had "became triangular" (τριμερῆ γενέσθαι).

5.2 καὶ καθ' αὑτοῦ θάτερον ἐπιστρέψαι μέρος, ὅπερ ἄν τις ὡς ἐν κακοῖς ἀγαθὸν εἴποι καὶ δίκης ἔργον: the infin. ἐπιστρέψαι depends on the finite vb. συνέβη earlier in the sentence: "it came to pass that... one of the parties turned against itself." The pron. ὅπερ refers not to μέρος (as one might reasonably suspect), but rather to the self-defeating nature of the rebellion itself—"a thing which [ὅπερ], as among evil deeds, one could say was a blessing and an act of justice." Josephus never tires of pointing out the faults of the Zealots whom he held resp. for the Jewish War. The words ἄν + εἴποι constitute a potent. optv. (Smyth §1824); for ἐν κακοῖς cf. *Antiq* 1.218; 3.34; 11.265; 12.274; *Vita* 14.

5.3 ἡ μὲν γὰρ κατὰ τοῦ δήμου τῶν ζηλωτῶν ἐπίθεσις, ἥπερ κατῆρξεν ἁλώσεως τῇ πόλει, προδεδήλωται μετὰ ἀκριβείας ὅθεν τε ἔφυ καὶ πρὸς ὅσον κακῶν ηὐξήθη: the rel. pron. ἥπερ refers to ἡ... τῶν ζηλωτῶν ἐπίθεσις ("the Zealots' attack") in the prev clause; the clause markers ὅθεν ("whence") and πρὸς ὅσον ("to how great") demarcate indir. quest.. Thus it was not the Romans who brought about the city's destruction (ἁλώσεως τῇ πόλει, cf. *BJ* 1.35), but rather the rebels. Josephus claims to have already given a "precise account" (μετὰ ἀκριβείας, *Antiq* 1.325; 20.147; *Vita* 358; *BJ* 1.22; 2.162; 3.138) of the events described. The best parallel is *BJ* 4.128, 135–37, where rival factions enter Jerusalem from outlying areas and turn first against the populace of the city, then each other.

5.4 ταύτην δ᾽ οὐκ ἂν ἁμάρτοι τις εἰπὼν στάσει στάσιν ἐγγενέσθαι: potent. optv. (Smyth §1824), suppl. ptc. (Smyth §2098), and accus. with infin. in indir. state. (Smyth §1867): "and one would not be wrong in saying that this faction had been bred within a faction..." For the factionalism that bred factionalism cf. espec. *BJ* 4.128-134.

5.4 καὶ καθάπερ θηρίον λυσσῆσαν ἐνδείᾳ τῶν ἔξωθεν ἐπὶ τὰς ἰδίας ἤδη σάρκας ὁρμᾷ: for the aor. act. ptc., nom. neut. sing. λυσσῆσαν ("raging," from λυσσάω) cf. τὸ ζῷον... λυσσῆσαν (Panarion, *Adv. Haer.* vol. 3 pg. 118); and τὸν τῇ κοίτῃ τοῦ πατρὸς ἐπιλυσσήσαντα (Greg. Nys. *Orat. viii de beat.* vol. 44 pg. 1221). The reason why τῶν and τὰς ἰδίας... σάρκας are in the plur. is because Josephus conceives of multiple feedings: "by a lack of the [flesh = τῶν] outside itself it [the ravening beast] preys at length upon its own flesh [ἐπὶ τὰς ἰδίας... σάρκας]." Of course Josephus has the self-destructive feuding of the Zealots in mind.

5.5 οὕτως Ἐλεάζαρος ὁ τοῦ Σίμωνος: the adv. οὕτως demonstrates that Eleazar in particular exemplifies the aforementioned self-destructive characteristics. "Son of Simon" has been corrupted to "son of Gion" (υἱὸς Γίωνος) in *BJ* 4.225, though remaining mss. read υἱὸς Σίμωνος, affording a likely link to the Eleazar mentioned here.

5.5 ὃς δὴ καὶ τὰ πρῶτα τοῦ δήμου τοὺς ζηλωτὰς ἀπέστησεν εἰς τὸ τέμενος ὡς ἀγανακτῶν δῆθεν ἐπὶ τοῖς ὁσημέραι τῷ Ἰωάννῃ τολμωμένοις: the rel. pron. ὅς refers to Eleazar son of Simon (cf. prev note); Eleazar's anger at John of Gischala was nothing but a pretext for his own crimes, particularly the one of coaxing members of his party to withdraw to the inner recesses of the Temple (*BJ* 4.128-154, espec. 153). The particle ὡς in front of ἀγανακτῶν ("ostensibly angry") suggs. Eleazar's anger was more contrived than real: a John "son of Dorcas" had slaughtered some prisoners suspected of pro-Roman tendencies (*BJ* 4.145–146), though still another John—of Gischala—was accorded a splendid reception at Jerusalem (*BJ* 4.121–127) and, perhaps more than Eleazar, influenced the hot-headed youth of Jerusalem (cf. *BJ* 4.128, 133).

5.5 οὐ γὰρ ἀνεπαύετο φονῶν οὗτος: the demonst. pron. οὗτος ("this one") refers to the last-named individual—i.e., John (cf. prev note). Trans. φονῶν as a suppl. ptc. (Smyth §2098): "...took no rest in his murderous career." Elsewhere Josephus refers to the same John as "the most handy assassin among them" (Ἰωάννην... τὸν ἐξ αὐτῶν εἰς φόνους προχειρότατον, *BJ* 4.145).

5.5 τὸ δ' ἀληθὲς αὐτοῦ μεταγενεστέρῳ τυράννῳ μὴ φέρων ὑποτετάχθαι: the subj. of the ptc. φέρων and finite vb. (διίσταται, 5.6) is Eleazar. Here is "the real reason" (τὸ... ἀληθὲς) why, in Josephus' mind, Eleazar was angry (ἀγανακτῶν) at John and seceded from the latter's faction (διίσταται): because he could not bear to be subj. to John, a younger "tyrant" than himself. For John's popularity with the youth cf. 5.5 above.

5.6 πόθῳ τῶν ὅλων καὶ δυναστείας ἰδίας ἐπιθυμίᾳ διίσταται: the phrases sugg. that John enjoyed "abs. mastery" and a "despotism of his own," not Eleazar. Therefore, Eleazar seceded (διίσταται), himself drawing influential leaders of the Zealots to the innermost courts of the Temple.

5.6 παραλαβὼν Ἰούδην τε τὸν Χέλικα καὶ Σίμωνα τὸν Ἐσρῶνος τῶν δυνατῶν, πρὸς οἷς Ἐζεκίας Χωβαρεῖ παῖς οὐκ ἄσημος: the subj. of the aor. act. ptc. παραλαβὼν is Eleazar. The men listed here—Judes the (son) of Chelcias, Simon the (son) of Esron, and Ezechias child/slave to Chobareus—are otherwise unknown, even though Josephus calls the first two "powerful" (τῶν δυνατῶν) and the third "a man of some distinction" (οὐκ ἄσημος, cf. *Antiq* 16.301; *BJ* 6.81). The first two names are in the accus. case; the phrase "in addition to whom" sets off a third name ("Ezekias, son/slave to Chobareus") in the nom. case. for effect. At any rate, these renowned persons were on Eleazar's side, and so against John.

5.7 καθ' ἕκαστον δὲ οὐκ ὀλίγοι τῶν ζηλωτῶν ἠκολούθησαν: the pron. ἕκαστον ("each") refers to each of the three individuals just mentioned—and, of course, to Eleazar, for whom Judes, Simon, and Ezechias appear to have been clients. Οὐκ ὀλίγοι (Litotes) indicates that a goodly number of Zealots supported Eleazar's party after all, in spite of John's popularity with the youth.

5.7 καὶ καταλαβόμενοι τὸν ἐνδότερον τοῦ νεὼ περίβολον ὑπὲρ τὰς ἱερὰς πύλας ἐπὶ τῶν ἁγίων μετώπων τίθενται τὰ ὅπλα: the subjs. of the aor. plur. ptc. καταλαβόμενοι are Judes, Simon and Ezechias, followers of Eleazar (*BJ* 5.6). The ground plan of the inner courts of the Temple remains controversial in details, though not in general conception:

> There was first the balustrade or fence, beyond which Gentiles could not go. Then a stair-way on all sides except the W[est], then first on the E[ast] the large Women's Court, which all Jews could enter. Following that, at a slightly higher level, reached by a semicircular flight of steps, came the Court of Israel (i.e., Jewish men), perhaps surrounding the sanctuary on three sides. Finally, in front of and on both sides of the building was the Court of Priests (Stinespring 1962, 556).

By the expression "above the holy gates" (ὑπὲρ τὰς ἱερὰς πύλας) Josephus possibly had in mind a series of sanctuary gates located within the Court of Priests (cf. fig. 7 in diagram 34, Stinespring 1962, 556); by "upon the sacred façade" (ἐπὶ τῶν ἁγίων μετώπων) Josephus prob. meant the eastern exterior of the Temple, towering to a height of ninety cubits (172 ft.) and overlaid with gold, a delight to the eye (cf. *BJ* 5.208, 210). Cf. Intro 30 above for the Temple precints.

5.8 πλήρεις μὲν οὖν ἐπιτηδείων ὄντες ἐθάρρουν: the Zealots' courage (ἐθάρρουν, cf. *BJ* 2.543; 4.307; 5.544; 7.396) consisted in the abundance of supplies to which they had access in the sacred precincts. There was, e.g., the Bread of Presence (Ex 25:30; 1 Sam 21:4, 6), placed in the Holy Place as a thank offering to the Lord, which David and his men once had consumed because there was no other food (1 Sam 21:6). Jesus used the incident to illustrate that "the Sabbath was made for man, not man for the Sabbath" (Mk 2:27; cf. Mt 12:3-8; Lk 6:3-5).

5.8 καὶ γὰρ ἀφθονία τῶν ἱερῶν ἐγίνετο πραγμάτων τοῖς γε μηδὲν ἀσεβὲς ἡγουμένοις: the Temple contained an abundance of precious items such as Pompey beheld when he penetrated the Holy Place in 63 BC (*BJ* 1.152; cf. Intro 14 above). Elsewhere the noun ἀφθονία patterns with (τῶν) ἐπιτηδείων ("necessities," *BJ* 1.299; 1.304; 5.520; 7.278), ὕλης ("wood," *BJ* 3.505), and τροφῆς ("food," *BJ* 7.331). As the desperados considered nothing ἀσεβές ("impious") they were at liberty of exploiting any means—fair or foul—to maintain their pos. against the rival Jewish factions and the Romans. For ἀσεβές ("impious") cf. *Antiq* 4.31; 7.284; 10.37; 11.300; 15.275; 16.331; 20.37; *BJ* 3.536.

5.8 ὀλιγότητι δὲ τῇ κατὰ σφᾶς ὀρρωδοῦντες ἐγκαθήμενοι τὰ πολλὰ κατὰ χώραν ἔμενον: elsewhere the pres. act. ptc. ὀρρωδοῦντες means to be intimidated at someone or something, e.g. ὀρρωδοῦντες τὰς φυλακὰς τῶν στασιαστῶν ("intimidated at the rebels' guards," *BJ* 6.113); πρὸς τὸ τῶν ἀπολωλότων πάθος ὀρρωδοῦντες ("intimidated at the fate of the fallen," *BJ* 6.226). Here Eleazar's followers were intimidated at "the paucity of their own numbers" (ὀλιγότητι... τῇ κατὰ σφᾶς, *BJ* 5.8; cf. ὀλιγότητι τῶν ὠνουμένων = "dearth of purchasers," *BJ* 6.384); therefore they "hunkered down" (ἐγκαθήμενοι) and kept their pos. (κατὰ χώραν ἔμενον). For the tech. expression "keep one's position" = κατὰ χώραν + μένειν, cf. κατὰ χώραν μένειν (*BJ* 2.551); κατὰ χώραν μένοντες (*BJ* 3.150); κατὰ χώραν... ἔμενον (*BJ* 3.307); κατὰ χώραν μένοντες (*BJ* 3.430). Context suggs. that by "position" (κατὰ χώραν) Josephus means the inner sanctuaries of the Temple.

5.9 ὁ δὲ Ἰωάννης ὅσον ἀνδρῶν ὑπερεῖχε πλήθει, τοσοῦτον ἐλείπετο τῷ τόπῳ...: the anteced. of the demonst. pron. τοσοῦτον is the clause signified by the correlative pron. ὅσον (Smyth §340): "*by as much as* [ὅσον] John was superior in quantity of men, *so much* [τοσοῦτον] was he inferior in pos..." For intrans. ὑπερεῖχε (from ὑπερέχω = to "overtop, be prominent above," LSJ II.2) cf. *BJ* 2.43; 5.156, 287; for ἐλείπετο (from λείπω [pass.] = "come short of, be inferior to," LSJ B.II.3) cf. *BJ* 5.113; 7.179. Eleazar's men would have had a more commanding pos. than John's, inasmuch as they had set their weapons "above the holy gates on the sacred façade" (ὑπὲρ τὰς ἱερὰς πύλας ἐπὶ τῶν ἁγίων μετώπων τίθενται τὰ ὅπλα, BJ 5.7).

5.9 ...καὶ κατὰ κορυφὴν ἔχων τοὺς πολεμίους οὔτ' ἀδεεῖς ἐποιεῖτο τὰς προσβολὰς οὔτε δι' ὀργὴν ἠρέμει: the enemies over John's head (κατὰ κορυφήν, cf. BJ 4.23, 34, 44; 5.224; 6.45) were Eleazar's followers who actually planted weaponry over the gates leading to the inner courts of the Temple (cf. prev note). Thus John could neither launch attacks against Eleazar's forces "with impunity" (ἀδεεῖς, cf. 4.242, 254; 7.206) nor could he, in spite of his rage, "remain inactive" (ἠρέμει, cf. 1.5, 47, 301, 303; 2.231; 3.89, 212; 5.255, 265, 267). In his anger (δι' ὀργὴν) John was anything but a philosophically enlightened man and so his repeated forays did more harm than good. Interestingly, Josephus uses a form of the vb. ἠρεμέω which, in the appr. context, means "to be still, keep quiet, be at rest" (in a philosophical sense, cf. LSJ I.1–2), e.g., ἐν τοῖς νόμοις ἠρεμοῦντες διαμένειν (Xen. Ages. 7.3); μόνος οὗτος ἠρεμεῖ ὁ λόγος (Plato Gorg. 527b).

5.10 κακούμενος δὲ πλέον ἤπερ διατιθεὶς τοὺς περὶ τὸν Ἐλεάζαρον ὅμως οὐκ ἀνίει: the reason why—in Josephus' mind—John did not "relent" (ἀνίει, cf. BJ 1.484, 578; 3.408; 5.541) in his incessant attacks on Eleazar's pos. is because John was a fool, a danger both to himself and to those around him. For κακούμενος ("harmed") cf. κακουμένου (BJ 5.528); κακούμενοι (BJ 2.537; 3.212; 5.274; 6.164); κακουμένων (BJ 3.207; 5.446); κακουμένοις (BJ 4.135); κακουμένους (BJ 3.280). For διατιθεὶς ("wreak havoc" on someone) cf. δεινὰ τοὺς Ῥωμαίους διατιθείς ("wreak a frightful havoc upon the Romans," BJ 7.197).

5.10 συνεχεῖς δ' ἐκδρομαὶ καὶ βελῶν ἀφέσεις ἐγίνοντο, καὶ φόνοις ἐμιαίνετο πανταχοῦ τὸ ἱερόν: the adj. συνεχεῖς ("continuous") mods. both ἐκδρομαί ("sallies," cf. BJ 3.157; 5.307) and βελῶν ἀφέσεις ("showers of missiles," cf. 2.423). The res. of John's incessant attacks was that the Temple was completely defiled by "carnage" (φόνοις, cf. 5.265, 402), a picture Josephus develops espec. in BJ 5.18–19.

BJ 5.375–400

5.375 Ταῦτα τὸν Ἰώσηπον παραινοῦντα πολλοὶ μὲν ἔσκωπτον ἀπὸ τοῦ τείχους, πολλοὶ δ' ἐβλασφήμουν, ἔνιοι δ' ἔβαλλον: note the tri-partite division of the sentence (πολλοὶ μέν... πολλοὶ δέ... ἔνιοι δέ), an elaboration upon the μέν... δέ construction: "many were mocking..., many were defaming..., and some [ἔνιοι] were even shooting missiles." Josephus has just concluded a lengthy exhortation (BJ 5.362–374) delivered within ear-shot of hostile Zealots on the wall. For ἔσκωπτον ("they were mocking") cf. 4.317; 5.120; for ἐβλασφήμουν ("they were defaming") cf. 2.406, 493, 602; 5.458; 6.320. The prep. phrase ἀπὸ τοῦ τείχους ("from the wall") occurs 23 times in the BJ.

5.375 ὁ δ' ὡς ταῖς φανεραῖς οὐκ ἔπειθε συμβουλίαις, ἐπὶ τὰς ὁμοφύλους μετέβαινεν ἱστορίας: the words ὁ δ' refer to Josephus. Trans. the particle ὡς as a causal clause marker (Smyth §2240, §3000): "*because* he did not persuade them..." By "the dir. counsels" (ταῖς φανεραῖς... συμβουλίαις) Josephus means those clear proofs in his speech up to this point that the Romans—all but invincible—are lenient in victory (5.372), so the Zealots should surrender at once. That message had merely fired up the Zealots against Josephus, however, and so the orator passes on from current events to "reminiscences of their nation's history" (ἐπὶ τὰς ὁμοφύλους... ἱστορίας)—i.e., miraculous stories of rescue wherein God saved the Jews from hostile enemies quite apart from the Jews' own abilities to save themselves. The message is clear: the Zealots should quit kicking against the pricks by opposing the Romans, God's instr., and appeal to Titus' (and God's) mercy.

5.376 "ἆ δειλοί," βοῶν, "καὶ τῶν ἰδίων ἀμνήμονες συμμάχων, ὅπλοις καὶ χερσὶ πολεμεῖτε Ῥωμαίοις;": Josephus records the bulk of this speech in *oratio recta* ("dir. disc."), a device used in ancient historiography to signify a speaker's emotionally charged thoughts and sentiments (cf. note on BJ 2.195, above). The word βοῶν ("while shouting," cf. BJ 2.112; 3.173; 4.359, 436; 5.571; 6.183, 303; 7.16) functions as a stage direction; something else that reveals the highly rhet. nature of the passage are the many forms of dir. address Josephus scatters liberally throughout the address, e.g., πολεμεῖτε (5.376); ὄψεσθε... μάχεσθε... ἐμιάνατε... ἀναμνήσεσθε (5.377); ἀκούετε... γνῶτε (5.378), etc. It is not clear who Josephus means by the expression "your own allies" (τῶν ἰδίων... συμμάχων, but cf. *BJ* 1.96, 327, 346, 354; 2.76, 555; 4.228, 265, 351, 355; 5.554; 6.330; 7.236); Josephus refers several times to God as an "ally" (note sing.) whom the Zealots, in their stubbornness, offend (cf. *BJ* 5.377, 403, 389, 459).

5.376 "τίνα γὰρ ἄλλον οὕτως ἐνικήσαμεν;": by οὕτως ("in this way") Josephus means ὅπλοις καὶ χερσί ("by weapons and by [force of] hands," prev clause). The implicit answer to the question Josephus poses here is that the Jews have conquered *no one* by force of arms because all Israel's victories—throughout history—have been achieved by God himself, without the agency of the Jews. The Jews, by contr., have been on the receiving end of God's mercies.

5.377 "πότε δ' οὐ θεὸς ὁ κτίσας ἂν ἀδικῶνται Ἰουδαίων ἔκδικος;": the clause ἂν ἀδικῶνται is equiv. to ἐὰν ἀδικῶνται ("if ever they are wronged"), the protasis of a pres. gen. cond. A vb. such as ἐστιν has dropped out of the clause οὐ θεὸς ὁ κτίσας... Ἰουδαίων ἔκδικος which functions as the sentence's apodosis: "when has God our creator not been the avenger of Jews?" Again, the implicit answer to the question is, "At no time has this happened!"

5.377 "οὐκ ἐπιστραφέντες ὄψεσθε πόθεν ὁρμώμενοι μάχεσθε καὶ πηλίκον ἐμιάνατε σύμμαχον;": construe the suppl. ptc. ἐπιστραφέντες with the finite vb. ὄψεσθε: "will you not *turn round* and see...?" Both πόθεν and πηλίκον signify indir. quest.: "...*whence* you rush out [and] fight and *how great* an ally you defile?" The area that the Zealots "rush out from" is the Temple; Josephus argues that in the past the Temple and its precincts quelled hostility, but these Zealots actually have launched their raids from the Temple complex, thus defiling this sacred area. The "ally" mentioned (σύμμαχον) is God (cf. note on *BJ* 5.376 above).

5.377 "οὐκ ἀναμνήσεσθε πατέρων ἔργα δαιμόνια, καὶ τὸν ἅγιον τόνδε χῶρον ἡλίκους ἡμῖν πάλαι πολέμους καθεῖλεν;": Josephus employs the language of remembrance (here ἀναμνήσεσθε), met occasionally in the LXX, e.g., ἀναμνηθήσεσθε

(Ex 23:13; Num 10:9); ἀναμνήσθητε (4 Macc 16:18); ἀναμνησθείη (Ps 108:14); ἀναμνήσθωσιν (Ezek 33:13, 16). The phrase "this holy place" (τὸν ἅγιον τόνδε χῶρον) recalls Josephus' usu. designation of the Temple's "Holy Place" (τὸ ἅγιον, cf. *Antiq* 9.106; *BJ* 1.26; 4.150, 151, 160; 5.207, 386, 394; 6.73, 95, 99, 260). Josephus maintains that the Temple itself had "defeated" (καθεῖλεν, cf. *BJ* 1.10; 7.172) Israel's enemies in the past, a claim nowhere corroborated in the OT.

5.378 ἐγὼ μὲν φρίττω τὰ ἔργα τοῦ θεοῦ λέγων εἰς ἀναξίους ἀκοάς: trans. the suppl. ptc. λέγων with the finite vb. φρίττω: "I shudder to speak..." For the construction cf. οὐπώποτε διέλειπον ζητῶν = "I never left off seeking" (Xen. *Apol.* 16); ἀνέχου πάσχων = "support your sufferings" (Eur. frag. 1090); μὴ κάμῃς φίλον ἄνδρα εὐεργετῶν = "don't grow weary of doing good to your friend" (Plato *Gorg.* 470C).

5.378 ἀκούετε δ' ὅμως, ἵνα γνῶτε μὴ μόνον Ῥωμαίοις πολεμοῦντες ἀλλὰ καὶ τῷ Θεῷ: for the idiom "be at war or make war... with one" (πολεμέω τινι, LSJ I.1), cf. Ἀννίβᾳ πολεμοῦντες (App. *Hann.* 110); αὐτοῖς (App. *Illyr.* 13); τοῖς ἐπιοῦσι (App. *Bell. Civ.* 2.8.50); ἡμῖν (App. *Bell. Civ.* 4.12.98); ἀλλήλοις (Dem. *in Theocrin.* 44); δήμῳ (Dion. Hal. *Antiq Rom.* 8.5.5); ταῖς δυναστείαις (Isocr. *Panegy.* 105).

5.379 βασιλεὺς ὁ τότε Νεχαὼς Αἰγυπτίων, ὁ δ' αὐτὸς ἐκαλεῖτο καὶ Φαραώ: the narrative seems to be a curious blend of biblical record and Jewish legend. Abram (later Abraham) went down to Egypt and inflicted serious harm on Pharaoh on account of Sarai (later Sarah) in the biblical account (Gen 12:10–20); here Pharaoh Necho invades Palestine, as indeed a later Pharaoh by that name did to establish entry bases into Palestine (Jer 47:1, 5; cf. 46:2). Hence, Necho is the name of a much later Pharaoh (cf. 2 Ki 23:29; 2 Ch. 35:20), whereas no Egypt. monarch by that name is known in patriarchal times.

5.379 μυρίᾳ χειρὶ καταβὰς ἥρπασε Σάρραν βασιλίδα, τὴν μητέρα τοῦ γένους ἡμῶν: here μυρίᾳ χειρί ("with a huge band") holds the tech. mng. "band, body of men" (LSJ V.1). Thus, χεὶρ μεγάλῃ (Hdt. 7.157); οὐ σὺν μεγάλῃ χειρί (Hdt. 5.72); πολλῇ χειρί (Hdt. 1.174; Thuc. 3.96; Eur. *Heracl.* 337). The words Σάρραν βασιλίδα constitute a pun on Sarah's name which, in Hebrew, can mean princess or lady. As the word for "father" lurks in Abraham's name (cf. Gen 17:5; Rom 4:17), Josephus' claim that Sarah, Abraham's wife, should be "the mother of our [Jewish] race" is at least logical, although it too lacks biblical attestation.

5.380 τί οὖν ὁ ταύτης ἀνὴρ Ἀβραάμ, προπάτωρ δὲ ἡμέτερος;: the pron. ταύτης refers to Sarah: "Abraham, *her* husband..." The reader must supp. a vb.: "What, then, did Abraham... *do*?"

5.380 ἆρα τὸν ὑβριστὴν ἠμύνατο τοῖς ὅπλοις, καίτοι ὀκτωκαίδεκα μὲν καὶ τριακοσίους ὑπάρχους ἔχων: although the particle ἆρα introduces questions asking merely for information (not for a *yes* or *no* answer, Smyth §2650), Josephus plainly requires a response to this question: Abraham used no force against *the ravisher* (τὸν ὑβριστὴν) of his wife. Abraham used 318 retainers to rescue Lot (Gen 14:14)—a separate biblical story Josephus runs together as one.

5.380 δύναμιν δὲ ἐφ᾽ ἑκάστῳ τούτων ἄπειρον: this phrase is appos. to the one that precedes (cf. prev note). The pron. ἑκάστῳ represents a poss. dat. (Smyth §1476); note also the effect of the pred. pos. of the adj. ἄπειρον: "and for each of these there was a force that was boundless."

5.380 ἢ αὐτοὺς μὲν ἐρημίαν ἡγήσατο μὴ συμπαρόντος θεοῦ...: the pron. αὐτοὺς refers to the 318 retainers mentioned earlier; Abraham regarded these as "nothing" (ἐρημίαν) "...if God was not pres." (μὴ συμπαρόντος θεοῦ = gen. abs.).

5.380 ...καθαρὰς δ᾽ ἀνατείνας τὰς χεῖρας εἰς ὃν νῦν ἐμιάνατε χῶρον ὑμεῖς τὸν ἀνίκητον αὐτῷ βοηθὸν ἐστρατολόγησεν;: Josephus portrays Abraham as "lifting holy hands" (ἀνατείνας τὰς χεῖρας, cf. *Antiq* 11.143; *BJ* 2.179; 5.519) to the Temple—the place which the Zealots have, by their villainy, defiled. Scripture records that Abraham nearly sacrificed his son Isaac on Mt. Moriah (Gen 22:2), a region elsewhere identified as the Temple mount in Jerusalem (2 Chr 3:1). That prayer, then, had the effect of "enrolling" (ἐστρατολόγησεν, cf. *BJ* 1.550; 5.395) God as Abraham's unconquerable "helper" (βοηθὸν), another title Josephus uses occasionally as a circumlocution for God (cf. *Antiq* 2.172, 331).

5.381 οὐ μετὰ μίαν ἑσπέραν ἄχραντος μὲν ἡ βασίλισσα ἀνεπέμφθη πρὸς τὸν ἄνδρα, προσκυνῶν δὲ τὸν ὑφ' ὑμῶν αἱμαχθέντα χῶρον ὁμοφύλῳ φόνῳ καὶ τρέμων ἀπὸ τῶν ἐν νυκτὶ φαντασμάτων ἔφευγεν ὁ Αἰγύπτιος, ἀργύρῳ δὲ καὶ χρυσῷ τοὺς θεοφιλεῖς Ἑβραίους ἐδωρεῖτο;: attn. to the μέν... δέ construction helps one to see that Josephus has effected a contr. between Sarah "the queen" and "the Egyptian" (i.e., Pharaoh), both of whom remained pure and thus evaded (ἔφευγεν) God's wrath—unlike the Zealots who, according to Josephus' caricature, have profaned the holy spot with the blood of their own countrymen. The adj. ἄχραντος ("undefiled") occurs elsewhere in Josephus in *BJ* 5.219, of the Holy of Holies. Abimelech, not Pharaoh, bestowed gifts on Abraham under sim. circums. (Gen 20:14–16); there is no biblical evidence that Pharaoh trembled at visions in the night. For the adj. θεοφιλής, -ές ("beloved by God") cf. *Antiq* 1.106, 346; 6.280; 9.183; 10.215, 264; 14.22, 455.

5.382 εἴπω τὴν εἰς Αἴγυπτον μετοικίαν τῶν πατέρων;: what began as two journeys to Egypt to buy grain during famine (Gen 42:3; 43:15; Acts 7:12–13) ended up as a protracted stay in Egypt as slaves of the Egyptians (Gen 15:13).

5.382 οὐ τυραννούμενοι καὶ βασιλεῦσιν ἀλλοφύλοις ὑποπεπτωκότες τετρακοσίοις ἔτεσι παρὸν ὅπλοις ἀμύνεσθαι καὶ χερσὶ σφᾶς αὐτοὺς ἐπέτρεψαν τῷ θεῷ;: trans. οὐ with the finite vb. ἐπέτρεψαν: "did they not... turn themselves to God?" During their servitude the Israelites had been oppressed (τυραννούμενοι) and subj. to foreign kings (βασιλεῦσιν ἀλλοφύλοις ὑποπεπτωκότες)—i.e., the pharaohs of Egypt. The expression "for four hundred years" (τετρακοσίοις ἔτεσι) represents the round number followed in Gen 15:13; Acts 7:6; and Joseph. *Antiq* 2.204; the more precise "430 years" occurs in Ex 12:40. Trans. the ptc. παρόν concessively (Smyth §2060): "*although* it was possible to avenge themselves..." For the phrase ὅπλοις... καὶ χερσί ("by weapons and hands") cf. *BJ* 1.373; 5.376.

5.383 τίς οὐκ οἶδεν τὴν παντὸς θηρίου καταπλησθεῖσαν Αἴγυπτον καὶ πάσῃ φθαρεῖσαν νόσῳ, τὴν ἄκαρπον [γῆν], τὸν ἐπιλείποντα Νεῖλον, τὰς ἐπαλλήλους δέκα πληγάς...: The vb. οἶδεν sets off accus. with ptc. after a vb. of percep. (Smyth §2110): "who has not heard of the land of Egypt overrun... and wasted..., a barren land, the failing Nile, the ten successive plagues...?" For the well-known stories cf. Ex 7:14–11:10. For plagues involving animals cf. Ex 7:25–8:15 (frogs); 8:16–19 (gnats); 8:20–32 (flies); 9:1–7 (livestock); 10:1–20 (locusts). For plagues involving disease cf. Ex 9:8–12 (boils). For the fruitlessness of the land cf. Ex 9:25 (hail); 10:15 (locusts). Although the Bible does not mention the failing Nile, cf. Ex 7:18, 21.

5.383 ...τοὺς διὰ ταῦτα μετὰ φρουρᾶς προπεμπομένους πατέρας ἡμῶν ἀναιμάκτους ἀκινδύνους, οὓς ὁ θεὸς αὐτῷ νεωκόρους ἦγεν;: the words τίς οὐκ οἶδεν govern this portion of the sentence also, and the words in the accus. case repres. accus. with ptc. after a vb. of percep. (prev note): "who has not heard... of our fathers set forth under guard on this account without bloodshed, without risk...?" While the Bible does not mention that the Egyptians led the Israelites forth "under guard" (μετὰ φρουρᾶς), Pharaoh did insist that Moses and the Israelites leave Egypt immediately at the culmination of the plagues, the death of the firstborn (Ex 12:31–32). The point of the adjs. ἀναιμάκτους ("without bloodshed," cf. *BJ* 3.333; 6.52) and ἀκινδύνους ("without risk," cf. *BJ* 4.368; 5.357; 7.197, 324) is that God himself had intervened for the Israelites keeping the latter pure—unlike the Zealots who, in their wickedness, have polluted the Temple.

5.383 οὓς ὁ θεὸς αὐτῷ νεωκόρους ἦγεν: the anteced. to the rel. pron. οὓς is τοὺς... πατέρας in the preced clause. A νεωκόρος is one who sweeps a temple, then (in a derived sense) the keeper of a shrine (e.g., Joseph. *BJ* 1.153; 5.390; also Acts 19:35; Philo *Vit. Mos.* 1.316; Plut. *Rom.* 5.1).

RELIGION AND RESISTANCE

5.384 ἀλλὰ τὴν ὑπὸ Σύρων ἁρπαγεῖσαν ἁγίαν ἡμῖν λάρνακα οὐκ ἐστέναξε μὲν ἡ Παλαιστίνη καὶ Δαγὼν τὸ ξόανον: trans. Δαγὼν τὸ ξόανον as "the image of Dagon." Philistines captured the ark of God at the culmination of a disastrous battle (1 Sam 4:17). First the sorrow was Israel's (1 Sam 4:21–22) but soon the Philistines cried out against the ark and all the damage it caused in several Philistine cities (1 Sam 5:7, 9, 11). Indeed, Dagon, a high god in Canaanite mythology, fell prostrate twice before the ark (1 Sam 5:3, 4). No "Syrians" (cf. ὑπὸ Σύρων) are mentioned in the biblical record. For ἐστέναξε ("rued," lit. "groaned") cf. *BJ* 5.385, 519 (cf. κατεστέναξεν, *BJ* 6.7).

5.384 ἐστέναξε δὲ πᾶν τὸ τῶν ἁρπασαμένων ἔθνος: "all the race of those who plundered these things" (πᾶν τὸ τῶν ἁρπασαμένων ἔθνος) refers to the Philistines (cf. prev note).

5.385 σηπόμενοι δὲ τὰ κρυπτὰ τοῦ σώματος καὶ δι' αὐτῶν τὰ σπλάγχνα μετὰ τῶν σιτίων καταφέροντες: τὰ κρυπτά represents the accus. resp. (Smyth §1601.a): "rotten *with resp. to* the hidden parts of the body..." The statement represents a rhet. amplification of 1 Sam 5.6, 12 which mentions merely that the Philistines were afflicted with tumors as a res. of being in proximity to the ark. The prep. phrase δι' αὐτῶν ("through them") refers to τὰ κρυπτὰ τοῦ σώματος: "and *through them* [= the body's inner parts] they excreted their guts along with their food." More rhet. expans.

5.385 ...χερσὶ ταῖς λῃσαμέναις ἀνεκόμισαν κυμβάλων καὶ τυμπάνων ἤχῳ καὶ πᾶσι μειλικτηρίοις ἱλασκόμενοι τὸ ἅγιον;: together with the finite vb. ἀνεκόμισαν understand τὴν... ἁγίαν... λάρνακα (cf. *BJ* 5.384 above): "they returned [the holy ark]." The Philistines did indeed return the ark of the covenant to Israel (cf. 1 Sam 6:7–12) but the Bible does not mention "the sound of cymbals and tympany" (κυμβάλων καὶ τυμπάνων ἤχῳ). The Philistines sent a guilt offering along with the ark consisting of 5 golden tumors and 5 golden rats (1 Sam 6:4, 8, 11). The expression "propitiating the Holy Place" (ἱλασκόμενοι τὸ ἅγιον) represents another addition to the biblical story.

5.386 θεὸς ἦν ὁ ταῦτα πατράσιν ἡμετέροις στρατηγῶν: the pron. ταῦτα ("these things") refers to the remarkable accomplishments recounted in *BJ* 5.383–384. We have seen how Josephus describes Israel's God as an "ally" (*BJ* 5.376) and "helper" (*BJ* 5.380); here he adds to the descr. by characterizing God as a "general" (ὁ… στρατηγῶν).

5.386 …ὅτι τὰς χεῖρας καὶ τὰ ὅπλα παρέντες αὐτῷ κρῖναι τὸ ἔργον ἐπέτρεψαν: the aor. ptc. παρέντες mods. the subj. of the vb. ἐπέτρεψαν, the Israelites: "because, without resort to hand or weapon, they entrusted the task to him to judge." For the expression "hands and weapons" (τὰς χεῖρας καὶ τὰ ὅπλα) cf. ὅπλοις… καὶ χερσί (*BJ* 5.382 above). The pron. αὐτῷ refers to God; κρῖναι represents an infin. of pur. (Smyth §§2008–2010). Cf. ταύτην τὴν χώραν ἐπέτρεψε διαρπάσαι τοῖς Ἕλλησιν = "he gave this land over to the Greeks *to plunder*" (Xen. *Ana*. 1.2.19); τὸ ἥμισυ (τοῦ στρατεύματος) κατέλιπε φυλάττειν τὸ στρατόπεδον = "he left half (of the army) behind *to guard* the camp" (Xen. *Ana*. 5.2.1).

5.387 βασιλεὺς Ἀσσυρίων Σενναχηρεὶμ ὅτε πᾶσαν τὴν Ἀσίαν ἐπισυρόμενος τήνδε περιεστρατοπεδεύσατο τὴν πόλιν, ἆρα χερσὶν ἀνθρωπίναις ἔπεσεν;: trans. ὅτε ("when") first, a clause marker Josephus postpones for rhet. purposes. For the amazing deliverance from Sennacherib cf. 2 Ki 19:35–36; Is 37:36–37; 2 Chr 32:20–21. The detail that Sennacherib came "with all Asia in his train" (πᾶσαν τὴν Ἀσίαν ἐπισυρόμενος) represents rhet. expans. On the other hand, the traditional site where Sennacherib's army encamped was well-known (cf. 2 Ki 18:17; 19:35), and Titus utilized this area when he occupied the city (*BJ* 5.303). The Bible places the destruction of Sennacherib's forces within or on the outskirts of Jerusalem (cf. Ps 76:2–3), though Herodotus states (2.141) that the disaster occurred at Pelusium (north-east Egypt).

5.388 οὐχ αἱ μὲν ἀπὸ τῶν ὅπλων ἠρεμοῦσαι ἐν προσευχαῖς ἦσαν: trans. οὐχ ("not") with this and the next three clauses and keep each as a question: "were not the hands, free from weaponry, [raised] in prayers…?" Josephus uses the plur. ἐν προσευχαῖς ("in prayers," cf. NT ἐν ταῖς προσευχαῖς, Rom 15:30; Col 4:12) because he conceives of a process of continuous, repetitive praying. In Josephus' opinion, lifting up one's hands to pray—and not the taking up weapons with one's hands—was God-pleasing.

5.388 ἄγγελος δὲ τοῦ θεοῦ μιᾷ νυκτὶ τὴν ἄπειρον στρατιὰν ἐλυμήνατο: the three biblical accounts mention the so-called "angel of the Lord" (LXX ἄγελλος κυρίου) through whom God destroyed the Assyrians. Oft the angel of the Lord functions in the OT as the manifestation of God himself, e.g., Gen 16:7, 11; 21:17; 22:11, 15; 24:7, 40; 31:11; 48:16; Ex 3:2; 14:19; 23:20, 23; 32:34; 33:2; Num 22:22; Jdg. 2:1; 6:11; 13:3; 2 Sam 24:16; 1 Ki 19:5; 2 Ki 1:3; Ps 34:7; Zech 1:11. For the phrase μιᾷ νυκτί ("in one night") cf. *Antiq* 10.19; *BJ* 5.404; for ἐλυμήνατο (2 aor. of λυμαίνομαι = "to outrage, despoil") cf. *BJ* 2.259; 6.8.

5.388 καὶ μεθ' ἡμέραν ἀναστὰς ὁ Ἀσσύριος ὀκτωκαίδεκα μυριάδας ἐπὶ πεντακισχιλίοις νεκρῶν εὗρε: the expression "the Assyrian" (ὁ Ἀσσύριος, cf. *Antiq* 10.15) refers to Sennacherib, just as "the Egyptian" (ὁ Αἰγύπτιος) refers to Pharaoh Necho (cf. *BJ* 5.381 above). Josephus states that Sennacherib woke to find thousands of corpses, whereas the biblical witnesses state that the besieged themselves made that discovery (thus 2 Ki 19:35; Is 37:36). A μυριάς represents a unit of 10,000; thus, 18 X 10,000 + 5,000 = 185,000.

5.388 μετὰ δὲ τῶν καταλειπομένων ἀνόπλους καὶ μὴ διώκοντας Ἑβραίους ἔφυγεν;: the biblical witnesses do not state that there were "survivors" (cf. τῶν καταλειπομένων), but only that Sennacherib himself withdrew and returned in disgrace to Nineveh where he was assassinated in the temple of Nisroch by his sons Adrammelech and Sharezer (2 Ki 19:37; 2 Chr 32:21; Is 37:38). The detail that the Hebrews were "neither armed nor pursuing" (ἀνόπλους καὶ μὴ διώκοντας) represents rhet. expans.

5.389 ἴστε καὶ τὴν ἐν Βαβυλῶνι δουλείαν, ἔνθα μετανάστης ὁ λαὸς ὢν ἔτεσιν ἑβδομήκοντα οὐ πρότερον εἰς ἐλευθερίαν ἀνεχαίτισεν ἢ Κῦρον τοῦτο χαρίσασθαι τῷ θεῷ: for the 70 year period of the Babylonian captivity cf. Jer 25:11–12 and 29:10. For μετανάστης ("one who has left his home, wanderer, migrant," LSJ I.1) cf. μεταναστήσας (Joseph. *Antiq* 10.149). Trans. οὐ πρότερον... ἢ as "not... before." For ἀνεχαίτισεν (from ἀναχαιτίζω = "throw the mane back, rear up," LSJ I.1) cf. ἀναχαιτίσαντες (Joseph. *BJ* 2.370, of the freedom-loving

Dalmatians). The pron. τοῦτο refers to Israel's freedom. Cyrus issued a decree guaranteeing the restoration of the Temple in Jerusalem (2 Ch. 36:22-23; Ezra 1:1-4).

5.389 προυπέμφθησαν γοῦν ὑπ' αὐτοῦ, καὶ πάλιν τὸν αὐτῶν σύμμαχον ἐνεωκόρουν: the pron. αὐτοῦ refers to Cyrus (see preced note); Josephus uses the title "ally" (ὁ σύμμαχος) for God (thus, *BJ* 2.391; 4.366; 5.377, 403, 459; 6.99, 101). The expression πάλιν τὸν αὐτῶν σύμμαχον ἐνεωκόρουν means lit. "honor [God] with a Temple"—i.e., the Israelites, returned from Babylon in ca. 538 BC, would worship the Lord in a second, restored Temple. The biblical books of Ezra and Nehemiah recount the return from exile and restoration of the Temple.

5.390 καθόλου δ' εἰπεῖν, οὐκ ἔστιν ὅ τι κατώρθωσαν οἱ πατέρες ἡμῶν τοῖς ὅπλοις ἢ δίχα τούτων διήμαρτον ἐπιτρέψαντες τῷ θεῷ: for the expression καθόλου... εἰπεῖν ("to speak in general") cf. Aristot. *De Part. Animal.* 697b; *Rhet.* 1374a; 1390b; 1395a. Trans. the words οὐκ ἔστιν ὅ τι as "it is not the case that..." For the vb. κατώρθωσαν ("were set aright") cf. *Antiq* 13.411; 20.265; *Contra Ap* 2.231; *BJ* 5.257; for the prep. phrase δίχα τούτων ("apart from them," i.e., the weapons) cf. *BJ* 5.493; for the vb. διήμαρτον ("they made a mistake") cf. *Antiq* 6.279; 20.217; *Vita* 131, 362; *Contra Ap* 1.217, 218; *BJ* 1.18, 596. Josephus' argument that the Israelites had never been saved by force of arms may seem incorrect in light of Ex 17:9; Deut 2:33; 20:10; Josh 10:25; 19:47; Jdg. 1:1, 3, 9; 11:6; 12:1, 3; 20:20; 1 Sam 8:20; 15:18; 18:17; 29:8 and other passages which show that the Israelites waged battle against enemies. Still other passages reveal, however, that Yahweh, the God of Israel, fought for his people (e.g., Ex 14:14; Deut 1:30; 3:22; Neh 4:20). Indeed, Yahweh was known as a "man of war" (Ex 15:3; Is 42:13) and as Captain headed up the army (2 Ch. 13:12), set ambushes (2 Ch. 20:22), led the people forth in battle (2 Ch. 6: 34), and taught the psalmist to fight (Ps 144:1). There could be no victory for Israel without God's dir. intervention (2 Ch. 20:17).

5.390 μένοντες μέν γε κατὰ χώραν ἐνίκων ὡς ἐδόκει τῷ κριτῇ, μαχόμενοι δὲ ἔπταισαν ἀεί: note the contr. between μένοντες μέν ("if they sat still") and μαχόμενοι δέ ("if they fought").

The title "Judge" (τῷ κριτῇ) refers to God. Trans. the vb. ἔπταισαν intrans.: "they always fell." Not completely true (as the preced note illustrates), but Josephus takes a strategic liberty to maintain—as is correct—that the Israelites fought in vain (and always lost) without God's intervention in battle.

5.391 τοῦτο μέν, ἡνίκα βασιλεὺς Βαβυλωνίων ἐπολιόρκει ταύτην τὴν πόλιν, συμβαλὼν Σεδεκίας ὁ ἡμέτερος βασιλεὺς παρὰ τὰς Ἰερεμίου προφητείας αὐτός τε ἑάλω καὶ τὸ ἄστυ μετὰ τοῦ ναοῦ κατασκαπτόμενον εἶδε: coordinate the first three words (τοῦτο μέν, ἡνίκα...) with τοῦτο μέν, ἡνίκα... in *BJ* 5.394: "and with resp. to this [τοῦτο], on the one hand [μέν], when..." Josephus now turns to former captures of Jerusalem; he begins with Nebuchadnezzar's investiture of the city in 588 BC and its capture in 586 (Jer 39:1–2). Cf. Cohen (1987, 28) for the idea that Nebuchadnezzar served God's will. Zedekiah, though sometimes friendly to Jeremiah, was on the whole a weak and vacillating ruler who allowed the prophet's enemies to mistreat and imprison Jeremiah (Jer 37–38). For the aor. ptc. συμβαλών cf. the tech. expression συμβάλλειν μάχην or πόλεμον = "to engage in war" (LSJ II.2). Jeremiah had urged Zedekiah to bow his neck willingly under the yoke of Nebuchadnezzar (Jer 27:8, 12) but Zedekiah listened instead to false prophets (Jer 27:8–15). Zedekiah could not have "seen" (εἶδε) the destruction of Jerusalem and its Temple because he was blinded first (Jer 39:6), then taken in shackles to Babylon (Jer 39:7). The Temple and principal buildings of the city were destroyed ten years later (Jer 52:12–14).

5.391 καίτοι πόσῳ μετριώτερος ὁ μὲν βασιλεὺς ἐκεῖνος τῶν ὑμετέρων ἡγεμόνων ἦν, ὁ δ' ὑπ' αὐτῷ λαὸς ὑμῶν: Bitterly ironic. Πόσῳ represents the dat. of degr. of diff. (Smyth §1513); "that king" (ὁ βασιλεὺς ἐκεῖνος) refers to Zedekiah, as does the pron. αὐτῷ. Both τῶν ὑμετέρων ἡγεμόνων and ὑμῶν repres. the gen. of comparison (Smyth §1401): "*than your leaders... than you.*"

5.392 βοῶντα γοῦν τὸν Ἰερεμίαν, ὡς ἀπέχθοιντο μὲν τῷ θεῷ διὰ τὰς εἰς αὐτὸν πλημμελείας, ἁλώσοιντο δ' εἰ μὴ παραδοῖεν τὴν πόλιν, οὔθ' ὁ βασιλεὺς οὔθ' ὁ δῆμος ἀνεῖλεν: the words βοῶντα... Ἰερεμίαν serve as the dir. obj. of the vb. ἀνεῖλεν:

"neither did the king nor the people destroy Jeremiah as he was shouting [i.e., prophesying] that..." The vbs. ἀπέχθοιντο and ἁλώσοιντο depend on the pres. act. ptc. βοῶντα: "shouting that [ὡς] they were hateful... and that they would be captured unless..." Jeremiah's consistent prophecy had been that the Israelites were to "hand over the city [παραδοῖεν τὴν πόλιν]" to Nebuchadnezzar and his descendants until still others would subjugate him (Jer 27:7). Zedekiah, however, had not heeded the prophecy.

5.393 ἀλλ' ὑμεῖς, ἵν' ἐάσω τἄνδον, οὐ γὰρ ἂν ἑρμηνεῦσαι δυναίμην τὰς παρανομίας ὑμῶν ἀξίως, ἐμὲ τὸν παρακαλοῦντα πρὸς σωτηρίαν ὑμᾶς βλασφημεῖτε καὶ βάλλετε: note the Aposiopesis (ἀποσιώπησις = "becoming silent," Smyth §3015) after the words ἀλλ' ὑμεῖς: "but *you*...!" The device conveys the idea that a speaker is completely overwhelmed by an emotion and so must stop momentarily (cf. Smyth §2352.d for examples). The pur. clause ἵν' ἐάσω τἄνδον... gives vent to the repressed emotion: "to pass over those things within..." (τἄνδον = τά + ἔνδον). Josephus confesses himself unable (ἂν + δυναίμην = potent. optv., Smyth §1824) to put into words the Zealots' villainies. The mn. clause resumes with the words ...ἐμὲ τὸν παρακαλοῦντα πρὸς σωτηρίαν ὑμᾶς βλασφημεῖτε καὶ βάλλετε: "but *you*... assail me with abuse and missiles as I exhort you to save yourselves!" The words βλασφημεῖτε and βάλλετε convey the impression that Josephus was interrupted by the taunts of onlookers or even by an occasional projectile shot in his direction.

5.393 ...παροξυνόμενοι πρὸς τὰς ὑπομνήσεις τῶν ἁμαρτημάτων καὶ μηδὲ τοὺς λόγους φέροντες ὧν τἄργα δρᾶτε καθ' ἡμέραν: the clause beg. with the pres. pass. ptc. παροξυνόμενοι is appos. to ἀλλ' ὑμεῖς (cf. preced note): "but *you*... provoked at [my] reminders of your crimes..." Oft the vb. φέρω has the sense of enduring something painful or unpleasant, e.g., λύγρα (*Ody.* 18.135); ἄτην (Hdt. 1.32); ζυγόν (Aeschy. *Ag.* 1226); τύχας (Eur. *Or.* 1024); ξυμφοράς (Thuc. 2.60). Hence, μηδὲ τοὺς λόγους φέροντες means, "nor putting up with [my] mentions of what [evil] deeds you do daily." Τἄργα represents the crasis of τά + ἔργα.

5.394 τοῦτο δ', ἡνίκα Ἀντιόχου τοῦ κληθέντος Ἐπιφανοῦς προσκαθεζομένου τῇ πόλει πολλὰ πρὸς τὸ θεῖον ἐξυβρικότος...: for τοῦτο δ', ἡνίκα cf. *BJ* 5.391 above. The expression denotes another division in Josephus' speech—namely, the capture of Jerusalem by Antiochus Epiphanes in 169 BC (cf. 1 Macc 1:20–40; *Antiq* 12.246–47, 248–53). For the expression πρὸς τὸ θεῖον ("against the divine") cf. *Antiq* 1.85, 194; 3.97; 4.326; 5.339; 8.280, 290, 316; 9.16, 276; 12.290; 13.242; 14.257; 16.173; 18.128; *BJ* 1.150. Antiochus Epiphanes' offence consisted of his efforts toward creating "one people" (1 Macc 1:41), unified in language, culture, dress and espec. religion (cf. 1 Macc 1:43–50; cf. Intro 7 above). Antiochus Epiphanes twice captured Jerusalem—once without a battle (ἀμαχατί, *Antiq* 12.246) and once by treachery (ἀπάτῃ, *Antiq* 12.248).

5.394 οἱ πρόγονοι μετὰ τῶν ὅπλων προῆλθον, αὐτοὶ μὲν ἀπεσφάγησαν ἐν τῇ μάχῃ, διηρπάγη δὲ τὸ ἄστυ τοῖς πολεμίοις, ἠρημώθη δ' ἔτη τρία καὶ μῆνας ἓξ τὸ ἅγιον: for the expression μετὰ τῶν ὅπλων ("with weapons") cf. *Contra Ap* 2.231; *BJ* 1.75, 77, 388; 2.212; 4.258, 292, 349, 514, 641; 5.244; 6.122, 348); for ἐν τῇ μάχῃ ("in battle") cf. *Antiq* 4.258; 5.14; 7.113; 8.386, 405; 10.86; 12.304; 13.80, 100, 117; *Contra Ap* 1.301; 2.212; *BJ* 1.324; 2.59). Josephus implies that the desolation occurred because the Maccabeans took up arms to fight, whereas the author of 1 Macc (2:32–38) states that Maccabeans perished because they refused to fight during the Sabbath day. Dan 12:11 mentions that the sanctuary was desolate for 1290 days so the desolation during Maccabean times has been calculated from Dec. 168 to June 164 BC, a period of three and a half years. A time period of three years appears in 1 Macc 1:54 and 4:52 (until Dec. 165 BC).

5.395 καὶ τί δεῖ τἆλλα λέγειν;: the phrase καὶ τί δεῖ τἆλλα λέγειν; ("what need is there of mentioning more?") represents another division in the speech—namely, the capture of Jerusalem by Pompey in 63 BC (cf. Intro 14 above).

5.395 ἀλλὰ Ῥωμαίους τίς ἐστρατολόγησε κατὰ τοῦ ἔθνους;: on ἐστρατολόγησε ("enlisted") cf. *BJ* 5.381 above. The ones chiefly resp. for "enlisting" the Romans at this time were the feuding brothers Hyrcanus and Aristobulus who made separate appeals to Rome against each other. Cf. Intro 13 above.

5.395 οὐχ ἡ τῶν ἐπιχωρίων ἀσέβεια;πόθεν δ' ἠρξάμεθα δουλείας;: the neg. particle οὐ in a question anticipates the answer Yes (Smyth §2651.a), e.g., οὐχ οὕτως ἔλεγες = "did you not say so?" (Plato *Rep.* 334b—i.e., "you did say so, *did you not?*"). To be sure, Pompey had entered the Temple and beheld the Holy of Holies (cf. Intro 14). This would not have happened, however, had Aristobulus' party not retreated to the fortified Temple mount in the first place, obliging the Romans to attack. History, then, was repeating itself. Josephus dates the Jews' "slavery" to Rome from that time.

5.396 ἆρ' οὐχὶ ἐκ στάσεως τῶν προγόνων;...: the particles ἆρ' οὐχί in a question anticipates the answer Yes (Smyth §2651.a), e.g., ἆρ' οὐχ ὕβρις τάδε; = "is not this insolence?" (Soph. *Oed. Col.* 883). The violation of the Temple had not been Pompey's fault but had been the res. of Jewish factionalism (ἐκ στάσεως). A στάσις represents a "party formed for seditious purposes, a faction" (LSJ B.III.1); also the word applies to the "faction, sedition," and "discord" itself (LSJ B.III.2). For ἡ στάσις cf. *Antiq* 9.282; 18.9, 62; 20.63; *BJ* 1.467; 2.490; 5.99, 257.

5.396 ...ὅτε ἡ Ἀριστοβούλου καὶ Ὑρκανοῦ μανία καὶ πρὸς ἀλλήλους ἔρις Πομπήϊον ἐπήγαγεν τῇ πόλει καὶ Ῥωμαίοις ὑπέταξεν ὁ θεὸς τοὺς οὐκ ἀξίους ἐλευθερίας;: for the intense feuding between Aristobulus and Hyrcanus cf. *BJ* 1.131–32. The men "unworthy of freedom" (τοὺς οὐκ ἀξίους ἐλευθερίας) were Aristobulus and Hyrcanus who both appealed to Pompey separately (*BJ* 1.128), thereby drawing the Romans into Palestine. It was espec. Aristobulus who drew Pompey to Jerusalem (cf. Intro 14–15 above).

5.397 τρισὶ γοῦν μησὶ πολιορκηθέντες ἑαυτοὺς παρέδοσαν, οὔθ' ἁμαρτόντες εἰς τὰ ἅγια καὶ τοὺς νόμους ἡλίκα ὑμεῖς καὶ πολὺ μείζοσιν ἀφορμαῖς πρὸς τὸν πόλεμον χρώμενοι: that the siege lasted for three months (τρισὶ... μησί) is corroborated by περὶ τρίτον μῆνα (*Antiq* 14.66). It is hard to reconcile the benign "they gave themselves up" (ἑαυτοὺς παρέδοσαν, cf. *BJ* 4.553) with the hard fighting—and dying—that Josephus elsewhere reveals accompanied Pompey's occupation of the Temple in 63 BC (cf. *BJ* 1.149–51; *Antiq* 14.66–67). On the prev occasion the Jews had died while continuing their sacred ministrations in the Temple, whereas the Zealots to whom Josephus addresses this speech were themselves guilty of bloodshed.

5.398 τὸ δ' Ἀντιγόνου τέλος τοῦ Ἀριστοβούλου παιδὸς οὐκ ἴσμεν, οὗ βασιλεύοντος ὁ θεὸς ἁλώσει πάλιν τὸν λαὸν ἤλαυνε πλημμελοῦντα: trans. τὸ... τέλος as "fate": "or know we not *the fate* of Antigonus, the son of Aristobulus...?" Antigonus had been a younger son of the Aristobulus whom Pompey had sent in chains to Rome (cf. Intro 15) and for this reason could be characterized as an enemy of Rome, the son of a fugitive, and one who had inherited from his father a passion for revolution and sedition (*BJ* 1.198). Herod enjoyed the backing of Julius Caesar and his successors (*BJ* 1.242, 282–83) but the Parthians—and sometimes even the Jews—backed Antigonus, even setting him up as a king in Jerusalem (*BJ* 1.273, 284). Antigonus besieged Herod's family in Masada (*BJ* 1.286, 294) though the climactic battle occurred at Jerusalem (*BJ* 1.342–46).

5.398 καὶ Ἡρώδης μὲν ὁ Ἀντιπάτρου Σόσσιον, Σόσσιος δὲ Ῥωμαίων στρατιὰν ἤγαγεν, περισχεθέντες δ' ἐπὶ μῆνας ἓξ ἐπολιορκοῦντο, μέχρι δίκας τῶν ἁμαρτιῶν δόντες ἑάλωσαν καὶ διηρπάγη τοῖς πολεμίοις ἡ πόλις;: for the complex events upon which these details are based cf. *BJ* 1.345–346; *Antiq* 14.468. Sossius, the governor of Syria, assisted Herod in capturing Jerusalem in 37 BC. The siege lasted 5 months according to *BJ* 1.351 and less than two months according to *Antiq* 14.476. As in the days of Pompey, fighting was fiercest around the Temple (*BJ* 1.351; *Antiq* 14.477), nor was any quarter given to the weak and helpless (*BJ* 1.352; *Antiq* 14.480). Herod kept Roman combatants from pilfering the holy contents of the sanctuary by distributing the rewards of victory out of his own resources (*BJ* 1.356; *Antiq* 14.485).

5.399 οὕτως οὐδέποτε τῷ ἔθνει τὰ ὅπλα δέδοται, τῷ δὲ πολεμεῖσθαι καὶ τὸ ἁλώσεσθαι πάντως πρόσεστι: for Josephus' point that arms have never "been given" (δέδοται) to the race of the Jews cf. *BJ* 5.390 above. The compound vb. πρόσεστι patterns with τῷ πολεμεῖσθαι, an articular infin. in the dat. (Smyth §1544). Another articular infin., τὸ ἁλώσεσθαι ("being captured"), serves as the subj. of the vb. πρόσεστι: "completely does their *being captured* attend their going to war."

5.400 δεῖ γάρ, οἶμαι, τοὺς χωρίον ἅγιον νεμομένους ἐπιτρέπειν πάντα τῷ θεῷ δικάζειν καὶ καταφρονεῖν τότε χειρὸς ἀνθρωπίνης, ὅταν αὐτοὶ πείθωσι τὸν ἄνω δικαστήν: the expression χωρίον ἅγιον ("holy place") refers to the Temple. Josephus seems to have in mind the pious Jews who attended to libations and incense rather than defend themselves while the soldiers of Pompey were ransacking the Temple (*BJ* 1.150; *Antiq* 14.66). Some 12,000 perished (*BJ* 1.151). The factionalized Jews, by contr., befoul the Temple by taking up arms against each other and the Romans. They neither scorn the aid of human hands nor appease "the Arbiter above"—i.e., God. The clause ὅταν... πείθωσι is equiv. to ἐάν... πείθωσι, the protasis of a pres. gen. cond. (Smyth §2567). Persuading "the Arbiter above" could only be done by prayer, not force of arms.

BJ 5.420–423

5.420 τοιαῦτα τοῦ Ἰωσήπου μετὰ δακρύων ἐμβοῶντος: gen. abs. Trans. the pres. ptc. ἐμβοῶντος (cf. *BJ* 4.111) as a temp. clause: "*while* Josephus was shouting such things with tears..." For μετὰ δακρύων ("with tears") cf. *Antiq* 7.153; 11.259; 14.354; 15.36; 16.208; 17.179; 19.141; *Vita* 421; *BJ* 1.636; 5.420; 6.119.

5.420 οἱ στασιασταὶ μὲν οὔτε ἐνέδοσαν οὔτ' ἀσφαλῆ τὴν μεταβολὴν ἔκριναν, ὁ δὲ δῆμος ἐκινήθη πρὸς αὐτομολίαν: note the contr. between the factionalized Jews (οἱ στασιασταὶ μέν) who would not yield (ἐνέδοσαν, cf. *BJ* 2.410; 4.35; 6.394) to Josephus' entreaties and the populace (ὁ δὲ δῆμος) who were moved (ἐκινήθη, cf. *Antiq* 3.297; *BJ* 7.76) to desert (πρὸς αὐτομολίαν, cf. *BJ* 5.30, 422) to the Romans.

5.421 καὶ οἱ μὲν τὰς κτήσεις ἐλαχίστου πωλοῦντες, οἱ δὲ τὰ πολυτελέστερα τῶν κειμηλίων...: this clause represents an elaboration upon the populace (cf. ὁ... δῆμος above) who heeded Josephus' speech and thus defected to the Romans: some (οἱ μέν) sold possessions for the least amount (ἐλαχίστου represents the gen. of price, Smyth §1372), others (οἱ δέ) sold their most valuable treasures. For τὰς κτήσεις ("possessions") cf. *Antiq* 11.132; 12.301; 20.97; *Vita* 77; *BJ* 1.205; 2.494; 3.492; 4.488; 5.334, 427; 6.115, 358. The noun τὸ κειμήλιον (from κεῖμαι) means "anything stored up as valuable," thus "treasure, heirloom" (LSJ I.1). Cf. τῶν ἱερῶν κειμηλίων (*BJ* 1.53); τὰ λαμπρότατα τῶν κειμηλίων (*BJ* 1.268); παντοίων κειμηλίων (*BJ* 1.302); ἄλλα... πολλὰ τῶν κειμηλίων (*BJ* 1.605).

5.421 ...τοὺς μὲν χρυσοῦς, ὡς μὴ φωραθεῖεν ὑπὸ τῶν λῃστῶν, κατέπινον, ἔπειτα πρὸς τοὺς Ῥωμαίους διαδιδράσκοντες, ὁπότε κατενέγκαιεν εὐπόρουν πρὸς ἃ δέοιντο: trans. τοὺς μὲν χρυσοῦς with κατέπινον: "and some *gulped down* their golden coins so that they would not be discovered by the brigands..." For ὑπὸ τῶν λῃστῶν ("by the brigands") cf. *Antiq* 20.185, 256; *BJ* 4.555; for κατέπινον ("they gulped down") cf. *BJ* 4.561; 6.373; for πρὸς τοὺς Ῥωμαίους ("to the Romans") cf. *Antiq* 1.4; *Vita* 34; *BJ* 5.112, 548; 6.114, 119, 169; 7.285, 404; for διαδιδράσκοντες ("escaping") cf. *BJ* 4.378, 397; 5.448. Josephus weaves the following dep. clauses into the narrative: ὡς μὴ φωραθεῖεν (neg. pur.), ὁπότε κατενέγκαειεν (indir. quest.), and ἃ δέοιντο (indir. quest.). The optv. mood is necessary because the mn. vbs. κατέπινον and εὐπόρουν set off sec. seq. For the cruel nemesis which befell 2,000 of those who gulped down gold coins before crossing over to the Roman side cf. *BJ* 5.550–52.

5.422 διηφίει γὰρ τοὺς πολλοὺς ὁ Τίτος εἰς τὴν χώραν ὅποι βούλοιτο ἕκαστος: here Josephus claims Titus discharged (διηφίει = impf. indic. act. of διαφίημι) those inhabitants who crossed the lines, though later in the campaign survivors were sent as hostages to Rome (cf. *BJ* 6.357), sold into slavery (*BJ* 6.384, 386, 418), slaughtered outright (*BJ* 6.404, 406, 414), or even set free (*BJ* 6.386).

5.422 καὶ τοῦτ' αὐτὸ μᾶλλον πρὸς αὐτομολίαν παρεκάλει τῶν μὲν εἴσω κακῶν στερησομένους, μὴ δουλεύσοντας δὲ Ῥωμαίοις: the prons. τοῦτ' αὐτό refer to Titus' generosity toward the refugees (cf. prev note), a generosity all the more remarkable in light of the usual practice of enslaving or putting to death prisoners-of-war. Titus' mercy toward the vanquished ran out when he felt obligated to submit to torture—and crucify—desperados caught in the ravines outside the city who resisted Roman patrols after it seemed too late to sue for mercy (*BJ* 5.449–51).

5.423 οἱ δὲ περὶ τὸν Ἰωάννην καὶ τὸν Σίμωνα περιεφύλαττον τὰς τούτων ἐξόδους πλέον ἢ τὰς Ῥωμαίων εἰσόδους, καὶ σκιάν τις ὑπονοίας παρασχὼν μόνον εὐθέως ἀπεσφάττετο: for the idiom οἱ... περί + accus. ("the partisans of so-and-so") cf. *BJ* 1.172, 296; 2.443, 445, 446; 3.97, 227, 302; 4.204, 217, 226; 5.330; 6.32, etc. Josephus has already explained the fierce rivalries between the Zealot leaders John of Gischala and Simon bar Giora (cf. note on *BJ* 5.2 above). For the counterproductive infighting that epitomized relations between the three Zealot factions cf. note on *BJ* 5.3 above.

BJ 5.446–451

5.446 Τίτῳ δὲ τὰ μὲν χώματα προύκοπτεν καίτοι πολλὰ κακουμένων ἀπὸ τοῦ τείχους τῶν στρατιωτῶν...: the noun Τίτῳ represents either the poss. dat. ("*Titus'* earthworks were progressing...") or the dat. of inter. ("The earthworks were progressing *for Titus*..."). Either way, the neut. plur τὰ χώματα serves as the subj. of the vb. προύκοπτεν. The "earthworks" (τὰ χώματα, cf. *BJ* 3.228, 284, 317; 4.52; 5.264, 274, 359; 6.5, 19, 71, etc.) formed the mainstay of the Romans' siege fortifications in the Jewish War. Note that κακουμένων... τῶν στρατιωτῶν represents the gen. abs.: "*although* the soldiers were suffering many (misfortunes) from the wall..."

5.446 ...πέμψας δ' αὐτὸς μοῖραν τῶν ἱππέων ἐκέλευσεν τοὺς κατὰ τὰς φάραγγας ἐπὶ συγκομιδῇ τροφῆς ἐξιόντας ἐνεδρεύειν: the pron. αὐτός refers to Titus. Trans. πέμψας as a finite vb.: "and he sent..." Inhabitants of Jerusalem went out (ἐξιόντας) "along the ravines" (κατὰ τὰς φάραγγας, cf. *BJ* 5.259) to scavenge inaccessible areas where Roman patrols ranged. The noun συγκομιδή ("ingathering") has an association with the harvest, cf. *Antiq* 2.18; 6.14; *BJ* 3.162; 6.5, 153.

5.447 ἦσαν δέ τινες καὶ τῶν μαχίμων οὐκέτι διαρκούμενοι ταῖς ἁρπαγαῖς, τὸ δὲ πλέον ἐκ τοῦ δήμου πένητες, οὓς αὐτομολεῖν ἀπέτρεπε τὸ περὶ τῶν οἰκείων δέος: Josephus effects a contr. between some (τινες) combatants no longer subsisting on what they could plunder (ταῖς ἁρπαγαῖς, cf. *BJ* 2.506, 593; 4.409; 5.431; 6.373) and more (πλέον) of the populace (ἐκ τοῦ δήμου, cf. *Antiq* 12.395; 15.424; *Vita* 279; *BJ* 5.99) who were indigent. Concern for family members (περὶ τῶν οἰκείων, cf. *Ant*. 3.292) deterred the latter from deserting (αὐτομολεῖν, *BJ* 4.380, 490, 565; 5.440, 454, 544; 6.117, 352, 367, 385).

5.448 οὔτε γὰρ λήσεσθαι τοὺς στασιαστὰς ἤλπιζον μετὰ γυναικῶν καὶ παιδίων διαδιδράσκοντες...: the subj. of the vb. ἤλπιζον are the indigent members of the populace who were afraid to desert (cf. prev note). For λήσεσθαι ("to elude") cf. *Antiq* 2.219; 5.76, 123; 9.120; 11.274; for τοὺς στασιαστάς ("the revolutionaries") cf. *BJ* 2.538; 5.518; 6.119; for μετὰ γυναικῶν καὶ παιδίων ("with wives and children") cf. *Antiq* 5.29; *BJ* 4.107, 110; 7.389; for διαδιδράσκοντες ("escaping") cf. *BJ* 4.378, 397; 5.421.

5.448 ...καὶ καταλιπεῖν τοῖς λῃσταῖς ταῦτα οὐχ ὑπέμενον ὑπὲρ αὐτῶν σφαγησόμενα: the pron. ταῦτα refers to the women and children mentioned earlier in the sentence (cf. prev note). Josephus explains why many honorable inhabitants remained behind in the doomed city: because they could not bear to leave wives and children behind "to be slaughtered" (σφαγησόμενα). For ὑπὲρ αὐτῶν ("on their behalf") cf. *BJ* 2.192; 3.198, 473; 4.288; 5.190.

5.449 τολμηροὺς δὲ πρὸς τὰς ἐξόδους ὁ λιμὸς ἐποίει, καὶ κατελείπετο λανθάνοντας τοὺς πολεμίους ἁλίσκεσθαι: Josephus explains why the indigents ventured out to forage: because hunger (ὁ λιμός, cf. *Antiq* 2.93; *BJ* 5.512, 515; 6.157, 204, 206) made them bold. There is confusion as to whether τοὺς πολεμίους should function as the subj. or dir. obj. of the ptc. λανθάνοντας. Some mss. add μή before the ptc. and εἰς before τοὺς πολεμίους. Trans.: "and it remained that those not escaping the enemy were captured." For τολμηροὺς ("bold") cf. *Antiq* 8.358; for κατελείπετο ("it remained") cf. *Antiq* 3.116; 18.206; 19.259; *BJ* 2.328; 4.84, 379, 537; 5.343; for ἁλίσκεσθαι ("to be captured") cf. *Antiq* 5.13.

5.449 λαμβανόμενοι δὲ κατ' ἀνάγκην ἡμύνοντο, καὶ μετὰ μάχην ἱκετεύειν ἄωρον ἐδόκει: in the mid. voice the vb. ἀμύνω means "defend oneself, act in self-defense" (LSJ B.I.4). Josephus explains why the foragers "of necessity" (κατ' ἀνάγκην, cf. *BJ* 5.198, 339, 497) defended themselves when set upon (λαμβανόμενοι, cf. *Antiq* 15.287) by the Romans: because it seemed ill-timed (ἄωρον, cf. *BJ* 2.355; 4.502) to play the suppliant after fighting. In other words, what happened to the arrested foragers was an exigency of warfare, not the deliberate design of the Romans who, to be sure, carried out the scourges, tortures, and crucifixion on those whom they captured.

5.449 μαστιγούμενοι δὴ καὶ προβασανιζόμενοι τοῦ θανάτου πᾶσαν αἰκίαν ἀνεσταυροῦντο τοῦ τείχους ἀντικρύ: in addition to whipping the poor prisoners (μαστιγούμενοι, cf. *Antiq* 12.256) the Romans inflicted on them "every torment" (πᾶσαν αἰκίαν, cf. *Antiq* 7.52; 10.115; 15.289; *BJ* 3.321)—i.e., Josephus leaves to his reader's imagination the other unspeakable details associated with capture and execution. For ἀνεσταυροῦντο ("they were crucified") cf. *Antiq* 12.256.

5.450 Τίτῳ μὲν οὖν οἰκτρὸν τὸ πάθος κατεφαίνετο πεντακοσίων ἑκάστης ἡμέρας, ἔστι δὲ ὅτε καὶ πλειόνων ἁλισκομένων...: note the μέν... δέ construction: Τίτῳ μέν vs. ἔστι δέ. Trans. Τίτῳ as a dat. of inter. with the adj. οἰκτρὸν in the pred. pos.: "thus the suffering of five hundred men during each day appeared piteous *to Titus*." For κατεφαίνετο ("appeared") cf. *Antiq* 15.275; *BJ* 2.212, 344; 3.18; 5.67, 208, 223; 6.32. Trans. ἔστι δὲ ὅτε as "it sometimes happened." Thus, "it sometimes happened [that] even more [than 500] were captured."

5.450 ...οὔτε δὲ τοὺς βίᾳ ληφθέντας ἀφεῖναι ἀσφαλὲς καὶ φυλάττειν τοσούτους φρουρὰν τῶν φυλαξόντων ἑώρα: by normal grammatical rules, the vb. ἑώρα (3 pers. sing. impf. indic. act. of ὁράω) should set off accus. with ptc. after a vb. of percep. (Smyth §2110). Add, therefore, the neut. sing. ptc. ὄν to ἀσφαλές and the fem. sing. ptc. οὖσαν to φρουρὰν: "[Titus] saw that it was not safe [(ὄν) ἀσφαλές] to free those who had been violently arrested and that the guarding of such ones was an imprisonment [(οὖσαν) φρουράν] of those who would guard them." The arrests are described in *BJ* 5.449 (cf. λαμβανόμενοι there). For ληφθέντας ("caught") cf. *Antiq* 9.58; 10.187; 17.257; 20.209; *BJ* 1.238; 3.452.

5.450 τό γε μὴν πλέον οὐκ ἐκώλυεν τάχ' ἂν ἐνδοῦναι πρὸς τὴν ὄψιν ἐλπίσας αὐτούς, εἰ μὴ παραδοῖεν, ὅμοια πεισομένους: the neut. def. article τό seems akin to *quod* in Lat. (Smyth §2494): "and *as to the fact that* [Titus] did not prevent [the crucifixions]..." Go next to the aor. act. ptc. ἐλπίσας which sets off accus. with infin. in indir. state. (Smyth §1867): "...having hoped that they [αὐτούς] would quickly surrender at the sight." Finally, pick up the last two clauses: "...they would suffer sim. things unless they surrendered." For πρὸς τὴν ὄψιν ("at the sight") cf. *Antiq* 2.55; 3.38; 4.53; 6.332; 9.55; 11.265; 19.36; *BJ* 2.170; 3.396; 5.52, 290, 547; 6.406; for εἰ μὴ παραδοῖεν ("unless they surrendered") cf. *BJ* 5.392.

5.451 προσήλουν δὲ οἱ στρατιῶται δι' ὀργὴν καὶ μῖσος τοὺς ἁλόντας ἄλλον ἄλλῳ σχήματι πρὸς χλεύην: Josephus' earlier statement that the crucified were "subjected to torture of every descr." (προβασανιζόμενοι... πᾶσαν αἰκίαν, *BJ* 5.449) may allude to the gruesome practice mentioned here of nailing prisoners to crosses in varying poses. The clause ἄλλον ἄλλῳ σχήματι is in appos. to the words τοὺς ἁλόντας: "...the prisoners, *one in one guise, another in another (guise)*." The pron. ἄλλος followed by another pron. in a different case does not require the second half of the statement to be expressed (Smyth §1274); so ἄλλος ἄλλα λέγει = "one says one thing, another says another" (Xen. *Ana.* 2.1.15).

5.451 καὶ διὰ τὸ πλῆθος χώρα τε ἐνέλειπε τοῖς σταυροῖς καὶ σταυροὶ τοῖς σώμασιν: the number of crucified—500 or even more per day (*BJ* 5.450)—was huge: there was not room enough for all the crosses, nor crosses enough for the bodies. For διὰ τὸ πλῆθος ("because of the amount") cf. *Antiq* 4.11; 11.316; 13.66; *BJ* 2.1, 431, 654.

BJ 5.473-477

5.473 Μετὰ δ' ἡμέρας δύο καὶ τοῖς ἄλλοις ἐπιτίθενται χώμασιν οἱ περὶ τὸν Σίμωνα: for the expression μετὰ δ' ἡμέρας δύο ("and after two days") cf. BJ 6.68, 166. The Romans had completed four enormous earthworks in 17 days (BJ 5.466-68), and John of Gischala had burned the earthworks in the vicinity of the Fortress Antonia (BJ 5.469). The attack mounted by Simon bar Giora on "the other earthworks" (τοῖς ἄλλοις... χώμασιν) can be dated to 18 June 70 AD. For the vb. ἐπιτίθενται ("they attacked") cf. Antiq 16.292; 17.282; BJ 5.336; 6.157, 251; for the idiom οἱ + accus. ("partisans of so-and-so") cf. BJ 5.423 (above).

5.473 καὶ γὰρ δὴ προσαγαγόντες ταύτῃ τὰς ἑλεπόλεις οἱ Ῥωμαῖοι: the word ταύτῃ ("here," cf. Smyth §346) indicates the three other earthworks described in BJ 5.467-68. Josephus uses two words to describe the battering-ram, an offensive weapon the Romans used to great effect in siege warfare: 1) αἱ ἑλεπόλεις (lit. "city-destroyers," from ἑλεῖν and πόλις; cf. Aesch. Ag. 689 and Eur. Iph. Aul. 1476, 1511), cf. BJ 2.553; 3.121; 5.276, 279, 282, 479; 6.23, 26, 393; and 2) ὁ κριός ("the ram"), cf. BJ 3.214, 215, 220, 223, 233, 235, 241; 4.20; 5.276, 282, 319, 479; 6.16, 220, 394; 7.310. For προσαγαγόντες ("bringing up") cf. BJ 3.219.

5.474 Τεφθέος δέ τις ἀπὸ Γάρις πόλεως τῆς Γαλιλαίας...: this Tephtheos is otherwise unknown. Some mss. read Γεφθέος here (a Jewish champion listed in BJ 6.92, 148).

5.474 καὶ Μαγάσσαρος τῶν βασιλικῶν Μαριάμμης θεράπων...: this is the only mention of Magassarus, a "henchman of Mariamme's royal [henchmen]." Since Marriamme is almost certainly the daughter of Herod Agrippa I and a sister of Herod Agrippa II (cf. BJ 2.220), it seems plausible that Magassarus was a deserter to the Jewish side.

5.474 μεθ' ὧν Ἀδιαβηνός τις υἱὸς Ναβαταίου, τοὔνομα κληθεὶς ἀπὸ τῆς τύχης καὶ Κεαγίρας, ὅπερ σημαίνει χωλός...: the rel. pron. ὧν in the prep. phrase μεθ' ὧν ("with whom") refers to Tephtheos and Magassarus. Both Ἀδιαβηνός and Ναβάταιος are adjs. which, in the course of time, have been turned into Gentilics: "a *cert. man of* Adiabene, the son *of a* Nabataean." Adiabene represents a region of Persia to the north-east of the Tigris and Euphrates rivers; Nabataea, a region to the east of the Dead Sea. For υἱὸς Ναβαταίου ("son of a Nabataean") cf. *Antiq* 8.205. The word τοὔνομα (crasis of τό + ὄνομα) represents the accus. resp. (Smyth §1601.b): "called *with resp. to* his name indeed Ceagiras from his misfortune." Other possibilities for the name Κεαγίρας include Ἀγίρας, Ἀγήρας, and Χαγείρας; possibly these variants, which are uncert. in Greek, were intended to replicate the Aramaic *haggera'* ("lame man").

5.474 ἁρπάσαντες λαμπάδας προεπήδησαν ἐπὶ τὰς μηχανάς: for ἁρπάσαντες ("having seized") cf. *Antiq* 13.136; 19.357; *Vita* 97; *BJ* 2.225, 291, 445, 451; 4.259, 405; 5.75, 115. Attackers flung torches (λαμπάδας, cf. *Antiq* 5.223, 295; *BJ* 2.492; 7.315) at wooden structs. to set them ablaze. Here "the engines" (τὰς μηχανάς, cf. *BJ* 3.267; 4.18, 19, 127; 5.286, 477; 6.392) repres. the battering rams described in *BJ* 5.473.

5.475 τούτων τῶν ἀνδρῶν οὔτε τολμηρότεροι κατὰ τόνδε τὸν πόλεμον ἐκ τῆς πόλεως ἐφάνησαν οὔτε φοβερώτεροι: the words τούτων τῶν ἀνδρῶν ("than these men") constitute the gen. of comp. (Smyth §1069). In the entire course of the war (κατὰ τόνδε τὸν πόλεμον, cf. *Antiq* 14.460) Josephus had found fighters no more bold (τολμηρότεροι, cf. *BJ* 5.280; 6.153) nor more frightening (φοβερώτεροι, cf. *BJ* 3.103) than Tephtheos, Magassarus, and Ceagiras. Josephus may be commenting more on the three rebels' rashness than on their bravery. For ἐκ τῆς πόλεως ("out of the city," i.e., Jerusalem) cf. *BJ* 1.114, 294; 2.557; 4.31, 52, 353, 416; 5.22, 484; 7.200; for ἐφάνησαν ("they appeared") cf. *Contra Ap* 2.289; *BJ* 3.233; 5.101.

5.476 καθάπερ γὰρ εἰς φίλους ἐκτρέχοντες οὐ πολεμίων στῖφος οὔτ' ἐμέλλησαν οὔτ' ἀπέστησαν...: the trio "ran out from" (ἐκτρέχοντες, cf. *Antiq* 12.362; *BJ* 2.423; 3.169; 4.202; 5.269) the city, or rather the walls that kept the Romans from interior parts of the city where the rebels had taken up residence. It was as though the three were running "to friends" (εἰς φίλους), not into the πολεμίων στῖφος ("mass of enemies"). A στῖφος represents a "body of men in close array" (LSJ I.1). Cf. νεῶν στῖφος ("the close array of ships,"

Aesch. *Pers.* 366); στῖφος ποιήσασθαι (Hdt. 9.70); νεανιῶν στῖφος (Aristoph. *Eq.* 852). They neither "delayed" (ἐμέλλησαν, from μέλλω; cf. LSJ III.1) nor "turned aside" (ἀπέστησαν, 2 aor. of ἀφίστημι; cf. LSJ B.I.1) from their desperate mission.

5.476 ἀλλὰ διὰ μέσων ἐνθορόντες τῶν ἐχθρῶν ὑφῆψαν τὰς μηχανάς: the aor. ptc. ἐνθορόντες (from ἐνθρῴσκω = "to leap in, on, or among," LSJ) describes precisely the way the trio broke in upon the Romans who surrounded the battering rams. Cf. the colorful use of ἐνθρῴσκω elsewhere: ἔνθορε μέσσῳ (ποταμῷ) (Hom. *Il.* 21.233); ἔνθορ᾽ ὁμίλῳ (Hom. *Il.* 15.623); ὡς δὲ λέων ἐν βουσὶ θορών (Hom. *Il.* 5.161); ἐνθρῴσκει τάφῳ (Eur. *Elect.* 327). For ὑφῆψαν ("they set fire to") cf. *BJ* 3.234; 6.355; for τὰς μηχανάς cf. *BJ* 5.474.

5.477 βαλλόμενοι δὲ καὶ τοῖς ξίφεσιν ἀνωθούμενοι πάντοθεν οὐ πρότερον ἐκ τοῦ κινδύνου μετεκινήθησαν ἢ δράξασθαι τῶν ὀργάνων τὸ πῦρ: trans. the ptcs. βαλλόμενοι ("shot at," cf. *BJ* 1.551; 2.548; 4.19; 5.275; 6.23, 26) and ἀνωθούμενοι ("pushed at, buffeted," cf. *Antiq* 19.264) concessively: "and *though* shot at and buffeted by swords on all sides..." The noun τὸ πῦρ serves as the subj. of the articular infin. δράξασθαι; the clause marker πρότερον... ἢ + infin. δράξασθαι is equiv. to *antequam* + indic. in Lat.: "...they were not moved from the danger [of attacking the Romans] *before* the fire caught hold of the implements."

BJ 5.478–485

5.478 αἰρομένης δὲ ἤδη τῆς φλογὸς...: gen. abs. The scene plays vividly upon the reader's imagination: "now that the flame was *being lifted* [into the sky]..." For the expression αἰρομένης... τῆς φλογὸς cf. *BJ* 6.180, 253.

5.478 Ῥωμαῖοι μὲν ἀπὸ τῶν στρατοπέδων συνθέοντες ἐβοήθουν, Ἰουδαῖοι δ᾽ ἐκ τοῦ τείχους ἐκώλυον καὶ τοῖς σβεννύειν πειρωμένοις συνεπλέκοντο κατὰ μηδὲν τῶν ἰδίων φειδόμενοι σωμάτων: note how tightly interwoven the clauses are that pertain to the Romans (Ῥωμαῖοι μέν) and the Jews (Ἰουδαῖοι δ'). Like a catalyst, the burning siege engine brought Roman soldiers on the run to help their comrades (ἐβοήθουν, cf. *Antiq* 11.9); the Jews from the wall (ἐκ τοῦ τείχους, cf. *Antiq* 233) sought to hinder them (ἐκώλυον, cf. *Antiq* 11.301; 15.100; *BJ* 2.287; 4.21; 5.298, 346; 6.25). The vb. συνεπλέκοντο (lit. "were weaving themselves among," cf. *BJ* 5.34, 269, 482, 484; 6.75, 136) captures precisely the fierce hand-to-hand fighting that transpired between the two sides. For σβεννύειν ("to quench") cf. *BJ* 6.234, 236, 243, 256, 262; for κατὰ μηδὲν ("in no wise") cf. *BJ* 5.34, 269, 482, 484; 6.75, 136); for φειδόμενοι ("sparing" + obj. gen.) cf. *Antiq* 4.298; 11.110; *BJ* 4.64.

5.479 καὶ οἱ μὲν εἷλκον ἐκ τοῦ πυρὸς τὰς ἑλεπόλεις τῶν ὑπὲρ αὐτὰς γέρρων φλεγομένων...: again note the tightly interwoven struct. (cf. prev note). The conative imperfs εἷλκον ("they *attempted to* drag...," cf. *Antiq* 3.221; *BJ* 5.561) and ἀντελαμβάνοντο ("they were *attempting* to hold on [to them]") convey the idea that the outcome of the two competing actions remained uncert.. For ἐκ τοῦ πυρός ("from the fire") cf. *Antiq* 2.269; *BJ* 1.28; 2.58; for the "city destroyers" (τὰς ἑλεπόλεις) cf. *BJ* 5.473 above. The words τῶν ὑπὲρ αὐτὰς γέρρων φλεγομένων comprise the gen. abs.: "[now that] the wicker-work above them [i.e., the battering rams] was ablaze..." For the wicker-work (τά γέρρα) that covered the mantelets protecting the teams driving the battering rams, cf. *BJ* 3.163, 169, 220, 227, 240; 5.269, 280.

5.479 οἱ δ' Ἰουδαῖοι καὶ διὰ τῆς φλογὸς ἀντελαμβάνοντο καὶ τοῦ σιδήρου ζέοντος δρασσόμενοι τοὺς κριοὺς οὐ μεθίεσαν: the vibrant images continue to unfold: first, that the Jews were "grasping hold of" (for ἀντιλαμβάνω, in mid. voice) the siege engines "through the flame" (διὰ τῆς φλογός, cf. *BJ* 5.330); second, that they "caught hold of" (δρασσόμενοι, cf. *BJ* 3.385; 5.479) "the seething iron" (τοῦ σιδήρου ζέοντος = the metallic tip of the battering ram, cf. *Antiq* 10.209; *BJ* 5.517); third, that they did not relinquish [οὐ μεθίεσαν, from μεθίημι] the rams to the Romans. The vb. δράσσομαι patterns with an obj. gen.: τοῦ δὲ δρασσόμενος τῆς δεξιᾶς (*BJ* 3.385); δρασσόμενοι τοῦ συνεστῶτος (*BJ* 4.480); δραξάμενος ἐκ τοῦ σφυροῦ (*BJ* 6.161).

5.479 διέβαινε δ' ἀπὸ τούτων ἐπὶ τὰ χώματα τὸ πῦρ καὶ τοὺς ἀμύνοντας προελάμβανεν: the noun τὸ πῦρ ("the fire") serves as the subj. of the vb. διέβαινε ("passed to," cf. *Contra Ap* 1.173; *BJ* 1.380; 5.171; 7.22); the pron. τούτων ("from them") refers to the battering-rams. The fire passed from the rams to the earthen ramps, outstripping the defenders. For ἐπὶ τὰ χώματα ("to the earthen ramps") cf. *BJ* 5.264; 6.71.

5.480 ἐν τούτῳ δ' οἱ μὲν Ῥωμαῖοι κυκλούμενοι τῇ φλογὶ καὶ τὴν σωτηρίαν τῶν ἔργων ἀπογνόντες ἀνεχώρουν ἐπὶ τὰ στρατόπεδα: for ἐν τούτῳ ("in this matter," "at this moment"), cf. *BJ* 1.78, 637; 4.454; 5.325, 430; 6.149. Josephus usu. reserves the pass. ptc. κυκλούμενοι ("surrounded") for the besieged (cf. *BJ* 3.18; 5.295; 6.181); here, ironically, it describes the Romans. For ἀπογνόντες ("give up as hopeless or desperate," LSJ II.2) cf. *BJ* 6.222. Soldiers had come at the run from the camps (ἀπὸ τῶν στρατοπέδων, *BJ* 5.478) when the first battering-ram caught fire; now that the whole area was ablaze they retreated (ἀνεχώρουν, cf. *Antiq* 5.158; 13.240; *BJ* 2.231, 329, 453, 529; 4.20, 528; 5.77, 301, 338, 465; 6.22, 116, 227, 266, 364, 392) to the camps which typically surrounded the circumvallation of a city. For τὰ στρατόπεδα ("camps") cf. *BJ* 2.72; 5.284, 295, 338, 551.

5.481 Ἰουδαῖοι δὲ προσέκειντο πλείους ἀεὶ γινόμενοι τῶν ἔνδοθεν προσβοηθούντων καὶ τῷ κρατεῖν τεθαρρηκότες ἀταμιεύτοις ἐχρῶντο ταῖς ὀργαῖς...: in a complete turnabout, Jews were pursuing (προσέκειντο, cf. *BJ* 1.292; 2.450; 3.212; 5.90, 117, 286; 6.179, 248) Romans. There were always "more" Jews (πλείους = Attic variant of πλέονες, nom. plur.) as compatriots from "inside" (ἔνδοθεν) came to the aid (προσβοηθούντων) of those fighting outside, an intensification of what the Romans had done earlier (cf. ἐβοήθουν, *BJ* 5.478). The Jews were of good courage (τεθαρρηκότες, cf. *BJ* 1.339, 367; 4.433; 5.78) because they had prevailed (τῷ κρατεῖν, cf. *Antiq* 16.49; *BJ* 5.78, 372), whereas the Romans had withdrawn to their camps (ἀνεχώρουν ἐπὶ τὰ στρατόπεδα, *BJ* 5.480). For ἐχρῶντο ("yielded to" + dat.) cf. *BJ* 2.423; 4.28, 200, 311, 356; 5.94, 228, 268, 526; 6.12, 138, 258.

5.481 ...προελθόντες δὲ μέχρι τῶν ἐρυμάτων ἤδη συνεπλέκοντο τοῖς φρουροῖς: some editors prefer προσελθόντες ("attacking," cf. *BJ* 1.582; 2.301; 7.31, 70) in place of προελθόντες ("outstripping," cf. *BJ* 1.66; 2.318; 4.113, 553; 5.110; 6.16, 18, 371; 7.27). By the prep. phrase μέχρι τῶν ἐρυμάτων ("as far as the trenches") Josephus alludes to the system of palisades and trenches (*valla et fossae*) with which the Romans surrounded their every camp in hostile territory. Here Jews fought hand-to-hand (συνεπλέκοντο, cf. *BJ* 5.478) with Roman sentries.

5.482 τάξις ἐστὶν ἐκ διαδοχῆς ἱσταμένη πρὸ τοῦ στρατοπέδου...: the Roman army was drawn up in battle array (τάξις... ἱσταμένη) to thwart the Jews who now appeared at the camp. For ἐκ διαδοχῆς ("in shifts") cf. *Antiq* 18.112; *BJ* 2.357; 3.212.

5.482 ...καὶ δεινὸς ἐπ' αὐτῇ Ῥωμαίων νόμος τὸν ὑποχωρήσαντα καθ' ἣν δήποτ' οὖν αἰτίαν θνήσκειν: the pron. αὐτῇ in the prep. phrase ἐπ' αὐτῇ ("against it") refers to the battle array mentioned in the prev clause (τάξις... ἱσταμένη). The law was "frightful" (δεινός, cf. *BJ* 1.529; 2.327, 586; 4.85, 321, 391; 5.558) because it stipulated instant death for any soldier who deserted his post. Here the word νόμος ("law") sets off accus. with infin. in indir. state. (Smyth §1867): "...law that the one who withdrew for whatever reason accordingly dies."

5.483 οὗτοι τοῦ μετὰ κολάσεως τὸν μετ' ἀρετῆς θάνατον προκρίναντες ἵστανται...: the demonst. pron. οὗτοι refers to those soldiers who comprised the τάξις, mentioned in *BJ* 5.482; the ptc. προκρίναντες ("preferring") patterns with the def. article in the gen. case τοῦ (which here functions as a pron. in place of τοῦ θανάτου): "preferring death with valor to (death) with punishment..." By "chastisement" (μετὰ κολάσεως, cf. *BJ* 5.355) Josephus envisions some form of capital punishment—a severe flogging, perhaps. For ἵστανται ("they took a stand") cf. *Antiq* 5.161.

5.483 ...καὶ πρὸς τὴν τούτων ἀνάγκην πολλοὶ τῶν τραπέντων ἐπεστράφησαν αἰδούμενοι: the pron. τούτων refers to those determined soldiers mentioned in *BJ* 5.482. Trans. τὴν... ἀνάγκην (lit. "necessity," cf. *BJ* 6.433) as "resolve"; what turned the tide of battle was the resolve of perhaps only a few firmly planted legionnaires who were prepared to die rather than retreat, as indeed had already happened (cf. ἀνεχώρουν, BJ 5.480). Now "many" (πολλοί) of those who had retreated "turned themselves around" (ἐπεστράφησαν = tech. term, of wheeling soldiers) to confront the enemy, thoroughly "ashamed" of themselves (αἰδούμενοι, cf. BJ 2.83; 5.556). Their burning embarrassment provided a powerful stimulus to fight bravely.

5.484 διαθέντες δὲ καὶ τοὺς ὀξυβελεῖς ἐπὶ τοῦ τείχους εἶργον τὸ προσγινόμενον πλῆθος ἐκ τῆς πόλεως, οὐδὲν εἰς ἀσφάλειαν ἢ φυλακὴν τῶν σωμάτων προνοουμένους: Roman soldiers wrestled into pos. (διαθέντες, cf. BJ 5.104) the ὀξυβελεῖς, an engine for "throwing sharp-pointed bolts" (LSJ); elsewhere Josephus links this contrivance to stone-throwers and other apparatus, e.g., τούς τε ὀξυβελεῖς καὶ καταπέλτας καὶ λιθοβόλα (BJ 3.80); ὀξυβελεῖς τε καὶ λιθοβόλους μηχανὰς τούς τε τοξότας καὶ σφενδονήτας (BJ 4.583); ὀξυβελεῖς... καὶ καταπέλται... καὶ λιθοβόλοι (BJ 5.14). By the phrase ἐπὶ τοῦ τείχους ("upon the wall," cf. BJ 1.57; 3.167, 219, 287, 487; 5.85, 111, 261, 267, 270, 292; 7.198) Josephus envisions the camp wall; from this the Roman soldiers warded off (εἶργον, cf. Antiq 14.375; 15.154; 16.17; BJ 1.190, 348; 2.536, 547; 5.274, 358; 6.72, 158) the populace as it boiled up from the city (ἐκ τῆς πόλεως, cf. BJ 1.114, 294; 2.557; 4.31, 52, 353, 416; 5.22, 475; 7.200). The subj. of the pres. mid. ptc. προνοουμένους ("taking thought") was the Jews who "took no thought" for safety nor personal defense.

5.484 συνεπλέκοντο γὰρ Ἰουδαῖοι τοῖς προστυχοῦσι καὶ ταῖς αἰχμαῖς ἀφυλάκτως ἐμπίπτοντες αὐτοῖς τοῖς σώμασι τοὺς ἐχθροὺς ἔπαιον: for συνεπλέκοντο ("they fought hand-to-hand") cf. BJ 5.478 and 481 above. Though brave, the Jewish fighters were no match for their Roman opponents. Their fighting was hit-and-miss (τοῖς προστυχοῦσι = "those they happened upon," cf. Plato Leg. 914b; Thuc. 1.97; Hdt. 3.36) and unarmed men fell against (ἐμπίπτοντες, cf. Antiq 15.359; BJ 3.294; 6.257) the brandished spears of the Romans. The adv. "unguardedly" (ἀφυλάκτως, cf. Antiq 5.173; BJ 1.475; 3.335) recalls οὐδέν... φυλακὴν τῶν σωμάτων προνοουμένους of the preced clause; Jews lashed out (ἔπαιον, cf. *Antiq* 7.12; *BJ* 2.326; 3.169, 525; 6.87) not with weapons but with their very bodies.

5.485 οὔτε δὲ ἔργοις αὐτοὶ πλέον ἢ τῷ θαρρεῖν περιῆσαν καὶ Ῥωμαῖοι τῇ τόλμῃ πλέον εἶκον ἢ τῷ κακοῦσθαι: only in rashness (τῷ θαρρεῖν, cf. *BJ* 1.375; 2.538; 3.114; 5.265; 6.30, 145) were the Jews "superior" (περιῆσαν, cf. *Antiq* 17.102; *BJ* 1.348, 182; 2.47; 4.202; 5.306) to the Romans; in actual deeds (ἔργοις) they could not measure up, whereas the Romans yielded more to boldness (τῇ τόλμῃ, cf. *Antiq* 6.184; 17.46, 160; 19.304; *BJ* 1.617) than to phys. harm (τῷ κακοῦσθαι, cf. *Antiq* 20.185; *BJ* 2.543; 4.409).

BJ 5.486–490

5.486 παρῆν δ᾽ ἤδη Τίτος ἀπὸ τῆς Ἀντωνίας, ὅπου κεχώριστο κατασκεπτόμενος τόπον ἄλλοις χώμασι: Titus appeared (παρῆν = 36 times in the *BJ*) from the Fortress Antonia (ἀπὸ τῆς Ἀντωνίας, cf. *BJ* 5.246; 6.23, 86, 135, 145, 246) where he had repaired to select a site for additional earthworks. For the earthworks (τὰ χώματα) upon which the Roman siege depended cf. *BJ* 5.446 above. Herod the Great had built the Fortress Antonia early in his career and named it after his friend and patron Mark Antony (83–31 BC); later the fortress—at the northwest corner of the Temple complex—would serve as an official residence for the Roman procurator in Jerusalem and a quarters for soldiers (cf. Clark 1962; Teasdale 1996–97, 92–94).

5.486 καὶ πολλὰ τοὺς στρατιώτας φαυλίσας...: trans. πολλά as an adv. accus. (Smyth §1607): "having *severely* chastised the soldiers..." Titus engages here in a motivational harangue; for the Romans' use of shame to motivate soldiery cf. *BJ* 5.483 above.

5.486 εἰ κρατοῦντες τῶν πολεμίων τειχῶν κινδυνεύουσι τοῖς ἰδίοις καὶ πολιορκουμένων ὑπομένουσιν αὐτοὶ τύχην, ὥσπερ ἐκ δεσμωτηρίου καθ᾽ αὑτῶν Ἰουδαίους ἀνέντες...: these clauses provide the gist of Titus' remarks (cf. prev note). Trans. εἰ as "whether": "*whether* by seizing the enemies' walls they ran a risk with their own..." The Romans were themselves enduring "the fate of the besieged" (πολιορκουμένων... τύχην) by having—as it were (ὥσπερ)—released the Jews from their prison house. For κρατοῦντες ("seizing") cf. *Antiq* 15.248, 387; 16.34, 161; *Contra Ap* 1.277; *BJ* 4.200, 278; for κινδυνεύουσι ("to be at risk" + dat.) cf. *Antiq* 12.409; for ὑπομένουσιν ("they endure") cf. *Antiq* 2.208; 11.405; *Contra Ap* 2.234; *BJ* 2.118, 373; 7.353, 382.

5.486 περιῄει μετὰ τῶν ἐπιλέκτων κατὰ πλευρὰ τοὺς πολεμίους αὐτός: having completed the motivational harangue, Titus engages in a flanking maneuver (περιῄει, cf. *BJ* 1.554; 5.167; 6.302; κατὰ πλευρά, cf. *BJ* 4.6) with picked men (μετὰ τῶν ἐπιλέκτων, cf. *BJ* 6.247). The pron. αὐτός refers to Titus, as elsewhere in the narrative (cf. *BJ* 5.446, 458, 500, 503, 504, 510).

5.487 οἱ δὲ κατὰ στόμα παιόμενοι καὶ πρὸς τοῦτον ἐπιστραφέντες ἐκαρτέρουν: οἱ δέ refers to the Jews; πρὸς τοῦτον refers to Titus. For κατὰ στόμα ("in front"), cf. *BJ* 1.306; 3.490; 4.425; 5.89, 313. Trans. the pres. pass. ptc. παιόμενοι concessively: "*though* they were being struck in the face..." The Jews wheel about (ἐπιστραφέντες, cf. *Antiq*; 5.161; *BJ* 4.174; 5.377; 6.64) to face Titus just as the Romans did at the camp wall (cf. *BJ* 5.483 above). For ἐκαρτέρουν ("they remained steadfast") cf. *Antiq* 5.321.

5.487 μιγείσης δὲ τῆς παρατάξεως, ὁ μὲν κονιορτὸς τῶν ὀμμάτων, ἡ κραυγὴ δὲ τῶν ἀκοῶν ἐπεκράτει...: the words μιγείσης... τῆς παρατάξεως constitute a gen. abs. (temp.): "*when the battle-line had been formed.*" Construe the vb. ἐπεκράτει (cf. *BJ* 4.133; 6.235, 260, 407; 7.419) with τῶν ὀμμάτων and τῶν ἀκοῶν (compound vb. + obj. gen.): "dust *prevailed over* the eyes, and shouting *prevailed over* the ears..."

5.487 οὐδετέρῳ παρῆν ἔτι τεκμήρασθαι τὸ ἐχθρὸν ἢ τὸ φίλιον: it was not possible to determine (τεκμήρασθαι, cf. *BJ* 2.385) friend from foe by the usu. means. Ancient armies used the placement of standards and trumpet flourishes to dir. troops in battle (cf. *conversa signa*, Caes. *BG* 1.25.7; 2.26.2; *signa inferre*, Caes. *BG* 2.25.2; 2.26.2; *tuba signum*, Caes. *BG* 2.20.1; 7.81.3; *BC* 3.46.4; 3.90.3), yet such means were ineffectual here.

5.488 Ἰουδαίων δὲ οὐ τοσοῦτον ἔτι κατ' ἀλκὴν ὅσον ἀπογνώσει σωτηρίας παραμενόντων...: gen. abs. within which a correlative clause occurs (οὐ τοσοῦτον... ὅσον): "the Jews still held out, (though) not so much... as from..." Unlike the Romans, the Jews fought out of desperation, not battle "prowess" (for κατ' ἀλκὴν, cf. *BJ* 5.462). For ἀπογνώσει σωτηρίας ("desperation of safety") cf. *BJ* 3.149; 6.5.

5.488 ...καὶ Ῥωμαίους ἐτόνωσεν αἰδὼς δόξης τε καὶ τῶν ὅπλων καὶ προκινδυνεύοντος Καίσαρος: the word αἰδὼς represents the soldiers' awe—verging on fear—not only for the renown (δόξης) they hoped their own weapons would garner, but also for Caesar "foremost in danger" (προκινδυνεύοντος, Titus had used the same epithet of himself in *BJ* 3.483). For ἐτόνωσεν ("they braced up") cf. Greg. Nys. *De Op. Hom.* pg. 165 ln. 20; John Damasc. *Sac. Par.* vol. 96 pg. 376; *Encom. in Joann. Chrys.* vol. 96 pg. 773.

5.489 ὥστε μοι δοκοῦσι τὰ τελευταῖα δι' ὑπερβολὴν θυμῶν κἂν ὅλον ἁρπάσαι τὸ τῶν Ἰουδαίων πλῆθος...: the subj. of the vb. δοκοῦσι is the Romans; the particle κἂν (= καί + ἄν) makes potential the aor. infin. ἁρπάσαι: "so that they seem to me, in the excess of their fury, ultimately [τὰ τελευταῖα] to have wiped out the Jewish host..." For τὰ τελευταῖα ("finally") cf. *BJ* 5.408; 7.383; for τῶν Ἰουδαίων πλῆθος ("mass of the Jews") cf. *Antiq* 11.67; 17.254; *BJ* 3.152.

5.489 εἰ μὴ τὴν ῥοπὴν τῆς παρατάξεως φθάσαντες ἀνεχώρησαν εἰς τὴν πόλιν: the words εἰ μὴ... ἀνεχώρησαν constitute the protasis of a past contr. fact cond. (Smyth §2302): "unless they [= the Jews] had withdrawn." The Jews' withdrawal "into the city" (εἰς τὴν πόλιν, 39 times in the *BJ*) mirrors that of the Romans' earlier retreat into the camps (cf. ἀνεχώρουν, *BJ* 5.480). The Jews "anticipated" (φθάσαντες, cf. *BJ* 1.156; 2.343, 547, 631; 3.234; 4.503; 7.222) the neg. turn of battle and acted accordingly.

5.490 διεφθαρμένων δὲ τῶν χωμάτων Ῥωμαῖοι μὲν ἦσαν ἐν ἀθυμίαις τὸν μακρὸν κάματον ἐπὶ μιᾶς ὥρας ἀπολέσαντες: the words διεφθαρμένων... τῶν χωμάτων constitute a gen. abs. (temp.): "[now] that the earth-works had been destroyed." Cf. *BJ* 5.466–471 for an earlier loss of the earth-works to Jews, with deleterious effects upon the morale of the Romans. For ἀπολέσαντες ("having lost") cf. *Antiq* 12.410; for ἐπὶ μιᾶς ὥρας ("in one hour") cf. *BJ* 3.228.

5.490 καὶ πολλοὶ μὲν ταῖς συνήθεσι μηχαναῖς ἀπήλπιζον ἁλώσεσθαι τὴν πόλιν: the adj. πολλοί ("many") refers to the Romans. The vb. ἀπήλπιζον sets off accus. with infin. in indir. state. (Smyth §1867): "they lost hope that the city would [ever] be captured..." Resist the temptation to trans. ταῖς συνήθεσι μηχαναῖς as "by the usu. means"; τὰς μηχανάς means "siege engine" in *BJ* 5.475 and 477.

BJ 6.201-213

6.201 Γυνή τις τῶν ὑπὲρ τὸν Ἰορδάνην κατοικούντων, Μαρία τοὔνομα, πατρὸς Ἐλεαζάρου, κώμης Βηθεζουβᾶ, σημαίνει δὲ τοῦτο οἶκος ὑσσώπου, διὰ γένος καὶ πλοῦτον ἐπίσημος, μετὰ τοῦ λοιποῦ πλήθους εἰς τὰ Ἱεροσόλυμα καταφυγοῦσα συνεπολιορκεῖτο: a lot of space separates the subj. Γυνή τις... ("a certain woman") from its governing vb. συνεπολιορκεῖτο ("she was besieged with [the other inhabitants]"). In between Josephus presents a number of specific details about Mary, such as her name, father, city of origin, exalted status, and the fact that she had come to Jerusalem as a refugee "with the rest of her people" (μετὰ τοῦ λοιποῦ πλήθους). Likely Mary's arrival in Jerusalem post-dated the subjugation of areas beyond the Jordan by Vespasian in June AD 68 (cf. *BJ* 4.450); Bethezuba (which has not been identified) apparently fell within the region marked Peraea on most maps, and so would have been within the proximity of such towns as Amathus, Gedor, Abila, Beth-ramatha, or Machaerus. The word τοὔνομα (a contraction of τό + ὄνομα) represents an accus. resp., employed of qualities and attributes (nature, form, size, name, birth, number, Smyth §1601.b), e.g., ποταμός, Κύδνος ὄνομα, εὖρος δύο πλέθρων = "a river, Cydnus by name, two plethra in width" (Xen. *Ana*. 1.2.23). For σημαίνει ("it means") cf. *BJ* 5.51, 474; for ἐπίσημος ("illustrious") cf. *Antiq* 4.174; 10.264; *Vita* 7; *BJ* 5.315; for μετὰ τοῦ λοιποῦ πλήθους ("with the rest of the populace") cf. *BJ* 1.666; for εἰς τὰ Ἱεροσόλυμα ("into Jerusalem") cf. *BJ* 3.432; 4.136.

6.202 ταύτης τὴν μὲν ἄλλην κτῆσιν οἱ τύραννοι διήρπασαν, ὅσην ἐκ τῆς Περαίας ἀνασκευασαμένη μετήνεγκεν εἰς τὴν πόλιν...: the pron. ταύτης refers to Mary; the correlative pron. ὅσην refers to τὴν... ἄλλην κτῆσιν—namely, to the property Mary had packed up and brought with her to the city from Peraea which "the tyrants" (οἱ τύραννοι, another term Josephus reserves for the Zealots, cf. *BJ* 1.24; 6.409) had "plundered" (διήρπασαν, cf. *BJ* 1.302; 2.50, 70, 228, 468, 509; 4.430, 578; 6.359). For Peraea cf. *BJ* 6.201.

6.202 ...τὰ δὲ λείψανα τῶν κειμηλίων καὶ εἴ τι τροφῆς ἐπινοηθείη καθ' ἡμέραν εἰσπηδῶντες ἥρπαζον οἱ δορυφόροι: the brutish "spearmen" (οἱ δορυφόροι, cf. *BJ* 1.672; 2.564; 5.439, 531; 6.229) abused Mary because she was rich, "bursting in" (εἰσπηδῶντες, cf. *BJ* 6.196) on her "daily" (καθ' ἡμέραν) and plundering her goods. Mary possessed mere "remnants" (τὰ... λείψανα, cf. *BJ* 1.29; 2.90; 3.466; 4.411, 484, 556, 657; 5.522; 6.210, 281) of her former treasure and whatever food (τι τροφῆς = part. gen.) she could "contrive" for herself (ἐπινοηθείη, cf. Euseb. *Praep. Ev.* 3.10.2; 3.11.3; *Hist. Eccles.* 2.13.8; 3.6.22; Iambl. *De Myst.* 1.9; Sext. Emp. *Adv. Math.* 9.286). For τῶν κειμηλίων ("treasures") cf. *BJ* 1.268, 605; 2.100; 5.421; 6.432).

6.203 δεινὴ δὲ τὸ γύναιον ἀγανάκτησις εἰσῄει, καὶ πολλάκις λοιδοροῦσα καὶ καταρωμένη τοὺς ἅρπαγας ἐφ' αὑτὴν ἠρέθιζεν: the "dreadful vexation" (δεινή... ἀγανάκτησις) consisted of Mary's anger at the Zealots who plundered her goods and denied her even a morsel of food (cf. prev note); it was an emotion that "entered into" (εἰσῄει, cf. *BJ* 1.58, 438; 2.198, 310, 496; 3.329, 394; 4.31, 116; 5.236, 324; 6.89, 183; 7.338) the poor woman, causing her to "antagonize" (ἠρέθιζεν, cf. *Antiq* 17.16) her persecutors by railing at, and cursing, them "frequently" (πολλάκις). For the metaphorical use of the vb. εἴσειμι of emotions that "come into one's mind" (LSJ IV.1) cf. Ἀστυάγεα ἀνάγνωσις ἐσῄιε (Hdt. 1.116); καίτοι μ' ἐσῄει δεῖμα (Eur. *Orest.* 1668); ἔλεος ἐσῄει με (Plato *Phaed.* 58e); ἄλγος εἰσῄει φρενί (Eur. *Iph. Aul.* 1580); δέος τινὶ εἰσῄει περί τινος (Plato *Rep.* 330d).

6.204 ὡς δ' οὔτε παροξυνόμενός τις οὔτ' ἐλεῶν αὐτὴν ἀνῄρει...: the pron. αὐτήν refers to Mary. Though provoked (παροξυνόμενος), no one "out of pity" (ἐλεῶν, cf. *Antiq* 9.91; 12.30) killed Mary. For ἀνῄρει ("kills") cf. *Antiq* 5.67; 12.343; 20.161; *BJ* 1.319, 338, 358, 493; 2.470; 3.490; 4.26, 427, 433, 584; 5.15, 89, 424; 7.263.

6.204 καὶ τὸ μὲν εὑρεῖν τι σιτίον ἄλλοις ἐκοπία, πανταχόθεν δὲ ἄπορον ἦν ἤδη καὶ τὸ εὑρεῖν...: Mary serves as the subj. of the vb. ἐκοπία (3 sing. impf. indic. act. of κοπιάω): "she *grew weary* of finding any food for others." The next clause explains Mary's particular burden: "for at this point, in fact [καί], the finding [of food] was impossible anywhere..."

6.204 ὁ λιμὸς δὲ διὰ σπλάγχνων καὶ μυελῶν ἐχώρει καὶ τοῦ λιμοῦ μᾶλλον ἐξέκαιον οἱ θυμοί: the famine "coursed through" (ἐχώρει cf. *BJ* 1.77, 218, 222; 2.187, 516, 573; 4.211, 444, 489; 6.58, 131, 205, 422) Mary's guts and bone marrow; but her bouts of anger (οἱ θυμοί, cf. *BJ* 4.314; 6.138, 263) burned even more intensely than the famine did (τοῦ λιμοῦ = gen. of comp.). Hence, it was anger against her persecutors, mingled with hunger, that compelled Mary to take the subsequent course of action. For ὁ λιμός ("the famine") cf. *Antiq* 2.93; *BJ* 5.449, 512, 515; 6.157, 206.

6.204 σύμβουλον λαβοῦσα τὴν ὀργὴν μετὰ τῆς ἀνάγκης ἐπὶ τὴν φύσιν ἐχώρει...: the subj. of the fem. sing. nom. aor. act. ptc. λαβοῦσα (cf. *Antiq* 2.232; 3.155; 4.230; 5.326; 6.308; 17.73; 18.70; *BJ* 1.582) is Mary. Mary's rage (τὴν ὀργὴν) became for her a type of "counselor" (σύμβουλον, cf. *Antiq* 2.141; 6.224; 15.191; *Contra Ap* 2.156, 160; *BJ* 1.113; 3.271; 4.16; 5.530; 7.343); she "necessarily" (μετὰ τῆς ἀνάγκης) proceeded upon an act of outrage "against nature" (ἐπὶ τὴν φύσιν). For ἐχώρει cf. prev note.

6.205 ...καὶ τὸ τέκνον, ἦν δὲ αὐτῇ παῖς ὑπομάστιος, ἁρπασαμένη "βρέφος, εἶπεν, ἄθλιον, ἐν πολέμῳ καὶ λιμῷ καὶ στάσει τίνι σε τηρήσω;": for the significance of dir. speech (*oratio recta*) cf. *BJ* 2.195 above. The pron. αὐτῇ ("her" = poss. dat.) refers to Mary; Mary's "child" (τὸ τέκνον, cf. *Antiq* 19.11; *BJ* 6.210) was a "boy" (παῖς) at Mary's breast—indeed, a wretched "infant" (βρέφος, cf. *Antiq* 2.220, 233; 20.18; *BJ* 3.247). Trans. τίνι as a dat. of adv. (Smyth §1481): *"for what* shall I keep you in war, famine, and revolution?" The question seems purely rhet. For τηρήσω ("I shall keep") cf. *BJ* 6.128.

6.206 "τὰ μὲν παρὰ Ῥωμαίοις δουλεία, κἂν ζήσωμεν ἐπ' αὐτούς, φθάνει δὲ καὶ δουλείαν ὁ λιμός, οἱ στασιασταὶ δὲ ἀμφοτέρων χαλεπώτεροι: the first clause requires a verbal pred.: "for affairs [τὰ μὲν = "things"] among the Romans *shall be* a slavery..." The word κἂν (= καί + ἐάν) sets off the protasis of an FmoreV cond. (Smyth §2565): *"if indeed* we shall live among them [αὐτούς = the Romans]." But the so-called "revolutionaries" (οἱ στασιασταί, cf. *BJ* 2.9, 325, 423, 441, 525, 534; 5.34, 72, 345, 354, 420, 431, 452; 6.72, 316, 207) were worse (χαλεπώτεροι, cf. *Antiq* 16.292; *BJ* 4.558; 5.516) than the Romans and the hunger were. For παρὰ Ῥωμαίοις ("among the Romans") cf. *BJ* 2.117, 390, 524; 3.137, 438; 4.397; 5.126, 355, 445, 536, 549; 6.90, 304); for φθάνει ("preempts") cf. *BJ* 1.116, 121, 184; 2.263, 621; 3.142; 4.499; 6.265, 361; 7.200).

6.207 "ἴθι, γενοῦ μοι τροφὴ καὶ τοῖς στασιασταῖς ἐρινὺς καὶ τῷ βίῳ μῦθος ὁ μόνος ἐλλείπων ταῖς Ἰουδαίων συμφοραῖς": Mary decides that her child shall become 1) food (τροφή, cf. *BJ* 2.425; 4.53; 5.21, 429; 6.198; 7.28, 278) for her; 2) an avenging fury (ἐρινύς) for the so-called revolutionaries; and 3) the only tale (μῦθος ὁ μόνος) in the world that has not been told about Jewish suffering. For ἴθι (= 2 sing. pres. impv. of εἶμι: "come on!") cf. *Antiq* 19.56, 220; *BJ* 1.618; for γενοῦ (= 2 sing. aor. impv. of γίγνομαι: "become!") cf. *Antiq* 2.141; 4.42; 6.234, 304; *Vita* 172. The word ἐρινύς ("avenging fury") occurs only here in the Josephan corpus, though it is one of several words in this section that Josephus seems to have borrowed from literature influenced by tragic drama, e.g., δεινή... ἀγανάκτησις (6.203, cf. Thuc. 2.41); ἠρέθιζεν (6.203; cf. Hom. *Il.* 1.32; Soph. *Antig.* 965; Aesch. *Prom.* 183); λαβοῦσα τὴν ὀργήν (6.204; cf. Hom. *Il.* 23.468; Soph. *Trach.* 446); μετὰ τῆς ἀνάγκης (6.204; cf. Aesch. *Pers.* 569; Soph. *Phil.* 73; Eur. *Med.* 1013; *Hec.* 396); and ἐπὶ τὴν φύσιν (6.204; cf. Soph. *Oed.* 740; *Trach.* 379; Eur. *Bacch.* 1358). The noun ὁ βίος ("life," or "livelihood") occasionally has the mng., "the world we live in, 'the world'" (LSJ III.1). Thus, οἱ ἀπὸ τοῦ βίου ("those of this world," i.e., not philosophers), Sext. Empir. *adv. Mathem*. 11.49; ὁ βίος ὁ κοινός ("the common world"), Sext. Empir. Πυρρ. Ὑποτυπ. 1.237.

6.208 καὶ ταῦθ' ἅμα λέγουσα κτείνει τὸν υἱόν, ἔπειτ' ὀπτήσασα τὸ μὲν ἥμισυ κατεσθίει, τὸ δὲ λοιπὸν κατακαλύψασα ἐφύλαττεν: the adv. ἅμα, while strictly mod. the mn. vb., is oft placed next to a ptc. which it mods. in a sense (Smyth §2081): "saying this, she slew her son..." For κτείνει ("she kills") cf. *BJ* 1.49, 72, 85, 87, 130, 312, 385; 4.448; 6.309. The vb. ὀπτάω ("roast, broil," LSJ) is used "of all kinds of cooking by means of fire or dry heat" (LSJ I.1), as opp. to boiling in water (= ἕψω). Mary's acute hunger (cf. *BJ* 6.204) accounts for her "devouring" (κατεσθίει, cf. *Antiq* 2.83; 12.213; *Contra Ap* 1.261) "half" her son, possibly a sizable amount of flesh; then she covered up and "guarded" (ἐφύλαττεν, cf. *Antiq* 1.321; 8.241; 10.51; 13.17; 15.87; *BJ* 7.31) the rest.

6.209 εὐθέως δ' οἱ στασιασταὶ παρῆσαν, καὶ τῆς ἀθεμίτου κνίσης σπάσαντες ἠπείλουν, εἰ μὴ δείξειεν τὸ παρασκευασθέν, ἀποσφάξειν αὐτὴν εὐθέως: for εὐθέως ("immediately"), cf. *BJ* 209, 210, 212; for the Zealots' tendency to barge in on Mary "daily" cf. *BJ* 6.202; for Josephus' freq use of the term "revolutionaries" (= οἱ στασιασταί) cf. *BJ* 6.206. The aor. act. ptc. σπάσαντες (cf. *BJ* 1.378; from σπάω = "to draw, drain, quaff") patterns here with the obj. gen. (Smyth §1354): "and when they *had drawn* the ungodly odor..." But the odor would have been "ungodly" only to Josephus and his readers; the Zealots did not yet know the source of the smell, and their threat to slaughter Mary unless she showed them "what had been prepared" leads one to suspect that the smell compelled them to assuage their hunger pangs (cf. *BJ* 6.202). For ἀθεμίτου ("unholy") cf. *BJ* 1.659.

6.209 ἡ δὲ καὶ μοῖραν αὐτοῖς εἰποῦσα καλὴν τετηρηκέναι τὰ λείψανα τοῦ τέκνου διεκάλυψεν: the aor. act. ptc. εἰποῦσα ("having said," cf. *Antiq* 1.293; 5.11; 6.301; 7.291; 13.430; 17.77; *BJ* 1.598) sets off accus. with infin. in indir. state. (Smyth §1867): "but *having said* that she had kept a fine portion for them, she uncovered the remains of her son." The unveiling of the murdered child (διεκάλυψεν, cf. κατακαλύψασα, *BJ* 6.208) corresponds to the point in a Greek drama where a protagonist discovers the true nature of a dramatic situation (Anagnorisis); likewise ironic are τετηρηκέναι (cf. σε τηρήσω, *BJ* 6.205) and τὰ λείψανα (cf. τὰ λείψανα, *BJ* 6.202).

6.210 τοὺς δ' εὐθέως φρίκη καὶ παρέκστασις ᾕρει καὶ παρὰ τὴν ὄψιν ἐπεπήγεσαν: the effect of the Anagnorisis. The def. article τοὺς refers to the Zealots. For the adv. εὐθέως cf. *BJ* 6.209 above; for φρίκη ("shuddering") cf. Galen *De sanit. tuend.* vol. 6 pg. 278; *De sympt. caus.* vol. 7 pg. 147; *De tremore* vol. 7 pg. 632; Hippocr. *De humor.* 2; *De morb.* 1.24; 3.11, 16; Plut. *Public.* 7.1; *Tim.* 22.6; *Aem.* 17.8; Soph. *frag.* 875; for παρὰ τὴν ὄψιν ("at the sight") cf. Alex. Aphrod. *De Anima* pg. 60, ln. 18; *Schol. in Odyss.* 15.88.1; for ἐπεπήγεσαν ("they stood rooted," from ἐπιπήγνυμι) cf. Cass. Dio *Hist. Rom.* 62.15.3.1; Euseb. *Hist. Eccles.* 3.6.26.2; Iambl. *Babylon.* frag. 125.3). The word παρέκστασις ("amazement") occurs nowhere else. The vb. αἱρέω is freq used of passions that "come upon" one suddenly (LSJ A.II.1), e.g., χόλος (Hom. *Il.* 18.322); ἵμερος (Hom. *Il.* 3.446); ὕπνος (Hom. *Il.* 10.193).

6.210 ἡ δ' "ἐμόν," ἔφη, "τοῦτο τέκνον γνήσιον καὶ τὸ ἔργον ἐμόν. φάγετε, καὶ γὰρ ἐγὼ βέβρωκα": for the significance of dir. speech (*oratio recta*) cf. *BJ* 2.195 above. The demonst. pron. τοῦτο has a deictic function (Smyth §1240): "*this* [pointing] is my legitimate child and my handiwork." The adj. γνήσιος −α −ον means "lawfully begotten, born in wedlock" (LSJ I.1); it applies espec. to legitimate children as opp. to bastards, e.g., νόθον καὶ γνήσιον (Hom. *Il.* 11.102). For this significance cf. also *Ody.* 14.202; Hdt. 3.2; *Leg. Gort.* 10.41; Aristoph. *Av.* 1665; Andoc. 1.127; Dem. 44.49. For βέβρωκα ("I have eaten") cf. Aesop *Fab.* 177; Euseb. *Hist. Eccles.* 3.6.26; Ezek 4:14.

6.211 μὴ γένησθε μήτε μαλακώτεροι γυναικὸς μήτε συμπαθέστεροι μητρός: Mary chides the ruffians for their less-than-manly behavior; she, on the other hand, had shown herself to be almost anything but a woman and a mother. For μαλακώτεροι ("softer") cf. *BJ* 4.281; for συμπαθέστεροι ("more affected by like feeling") cf. Eus. *Hist. Eccles* 3.6.26.

6.211 "εἰ δ' ὑμεῖς εὐσεβεῖς καὶ τὴν ἐμὴν ἀποστρέφεσθε θυσίαν, ἐγὼ μὲν ὑμῖν βέβρωκα, καὶ τὸ λοιπὸν δὲ ἐμοὶ μεινάτω": the clause marker εἰ sets off the protasis of a simp. fact. cond. (Smyth §2298): "but *if* you shrink piously from my sacrifice..." These phrases contain two ironies: 1) that Mary's tormentors were εὐσεβεῖς ("pious," cf. *Antiq* 7.224, 341; *BJ* 2.128); 2) that the destruction of her son was an "offering" (τὴν ἐμὴν... θυσίαν, cf. *BJ* 1.380; 2.12, 409 [twice]; 6.292, 423). Mary's eating (cf. ἐγὼ βέβρωκα, *BJ* 6.210) seems ritualized, an eating "for you" (ὑμῖν). Since the squeamish Zealots reject her sacrifice, Mary proposes that the rest (of the body) remain for her to eat. The words τὸ λοιπόν ("the remainder") refer elsewhere to the uneaten portion of Mary's son in *BJ* 6.208.

6.212 μετὰ ταῦθ' οἱ μὲν τρέμοντες ἐξῄεσαν, πρὸς ἓν τοῦτο δειλοὶ καὶ μόλις ταύτης τῆς τροφῆς τῇ μητρὶ παραχωρήσαντες...: the ptc. τρέμοντες ("trembling," cf. *BJ* 1.341) recalls the shuddering and amazement that seized the Zealots in *BJ* 6.210. For ἐξῄεσαν ("they stumbled away") cf. *BJ* 1.234, 285; 2.438; 5.516; 6.156, 406. Only with resp. to "this one thing" (ἓν τοῦτο, cf. *BJ* 4.344; 6.134; 7.418)—the gruesome act of cannibalism—were the Zealots "cowards" (δειλοί, cf. *BJ* 5.376); wicked in all other resps., these "cowardly" Zealots scarcely yielded to Mary this "food" she wanted (cf. *BJ* 6.211)—mng. that the Zealots almost did give in to her. The vb. παραχωρέω sometimes patterns with the dat. of pers. and gen. of thing (LSJ I.3), e.g., ὁ ποταμὸς ἡμῖν παρακεχώρηκε τῆς ὁδοῦ = "the river has kept us from the road" (Xen. *Cyr.* 7.5.20); Φιλίππῳ... Ἀμφιπόλεως παρακεχωρήκαμεν = "we have given up Amphipolis to Philip" (Dem. 5.25); τῇ πόλει παραχωρῶ τῆς τιμωρίας = "I leave the task of punishing to the state" (Dem. 21.28).

6.212 ἀνεπλήσθη δ' εὐθέως ὅλη τοῦ μύσους ἡ πόλις...: the gen. is used with vbs. signifying to fill, or to be full of something (Smyth §1369), e.g., οὐκ ἐμπλήσετε τὴν θάλατταν τριήρων; = "won't you fill the sea with your triremes?" (Dem. 8.74); τριήρης σεσαγμένη ἀνθρώπων = "a trireme packed with men" (Xen. *Oec.* 8.8); ὕβρεως μεστοῦσθαι = "to be filled with pride" (Plato *Leg.* 713c). Josephus claims that Mary's gruesome act had filled the whole of Jerusalem (ὅλη) with μύσος ("uncleanness, defilement," LSJ; cf.

Soph. *Oed.* 138; Eur. *Her. Fur.* 1155; Hippocr. *Morb. Sacr.* 1). For ἀνεπλήσθη ("[the city] was filled") cf. *Antiq* 5.357; 16.71; 18.7; 20.160; *BJ* 5.107.

6.212 ...καὶ πρὸ ὀμμάτων ἕκαστος τὸ πάθος λαμβάνων ὥσπερ αὐτῷ τολμηθὲν ἔφριττε: the reason why everyone "shuddered at" (ἔφριττε, cf. φρίκη in *BJ* 6.210) Mary's deed was because it was within the capacity of each to have acted sim. For πρὸ ὀμμάτων ("before one's eyes") cf. Aristot. *De Anima* 427b.18; *Rhet.* 1386a.34; Dion. Hal. *Ant. Rom.* 9.7.3.9; Emped. *Frag.* 139.3. The most basic mng. of τὸ πάθος is "incident, accident" (LSJ I.1), or "what has been suffered" (from πάσχω). The pron. αὐτῷ represents the dat. of agent (Smyth §1499): "as though it had been dared *by him.*"

6.213 σπουδὴ δὲ τῶν λιμωττόντων ἐπὶ τὸν θάνατον ἦν, καὶ μακαρισμὸς τῶν φθασάντων πρὶν ἀκοῦσαι καὶ θεάσασθαι κακὰ τηλικαῦτα: trans. the noun σπουδή with the prepos. phrase ἐπὶ τὸν θάνατον—lit., "the starving peoples' zeal was *for death.*" Likewise, trans. μακαρισμὸς with τῶν φθασάντων: "and a pronouncement of blessedness [belonged to] those who [who were] overtaking [death]." After an affirmative clause πρίν usu. patterns with the infin. and means *before* (Smyth §2431): "...*before* [they had] heard and seen such great evils." For ἀκοῦσαι ("to have heard") cf. *Antiq* 1.286; 6.285; 7.250; 8.218, 276; 9.111, 120; 13.75; 16.29, 113, 217; *Contra Ap* 1.178; 2.13, 124; *BJ* 6.200; for θεάσασθαι ("to have beheld") cf. *Antiq* 1.164; 6.302; 7.191; 8.34; 9.55; 10.270; 16.6; 18.272; *Vita* 204; *BJ* 2.180; 4.260.

BJ 6.403–408

6.403 Ῥωμαῖοι δὲ τῶν τειχῶν κρατήσαντες τάς τε σημαίας ἔστησαν ἐπὶ τῶν πύργων καὶ μετὰ κρότου καὶ χαρᾶς ἐπαιάνιζον ἐπὶ τῇ νίκῃ: trans. κρατήσαντες (*Antiq* 4.191, 300; 6.30; 14.321; *BJ* 2.410; 4.182; 5.302, 342; 7.336) with the obj. gen. τῶν τειχῶν: "and [when] the Romans had *got possession* of the walls..." The Zealots depended upon a series of walls which the Romans, in the course of the siege, had captured one by one. The Romans were understandably happy at the culmination of their task (for the hendiadys μετὰ κρότου καὶ χαρᾶς = "with joyful applause," cf. *Antiq* 7.352), and so sang a song of triumph (ἐπαιάνιζον). Cf. μετὰ παιάνων (*BJ* 2.554), of the Zealots' victory over the Romans at an earlier stage in the war. The Romans planted (ἔστησαν, cf. *Antiq* 5.19, 105; 8.104; 10.6; 11.108; *BJ* 5.88; 7.153) standards atop towers which Titus had supposed were impregnable (cf. *BJ* 6.411). For ἐπὶ τῇ νίκῃ ("in honor of the victory") cf. *Antiq* 4.9; 6.116; 7.252.

6.403 πολὺ τῆς ἀρχῆς κουφότερον τοῦ πολέμου τὸ τέλος εὑρηκότες: trans. πολύ (adv. accus.) with κουφότερον: "much more easily." Τῆς ἀρχῆς represents a compar. gen. (Smyth §1431): "...*than* the beginning." The ptc. εὑρηκότες mods. the subj. of the vb. ἐπαιάνιζον, the Romans.

6.403 ἀναιμωτὶ γοῦν τοῦ τελευταίου τείχους ἐπιβάντες ἠπίστουν, καὶ μηδένα βλέποντες ἀντίπαλον ἀληθῶς ἠπόρηντο: for the adv. ἀναιμωτί ("bloodlessly") cf. *Antiq* 19.116; *BJ* 2.495; 4.40, 415, 529; 5.74. Ἐπιβάντες ("tread upon," cf. *Antiq* 6.364; *BJ* 6.240, 241) and βλέποντες ("seeing," cf. *Antiq* 10.251; 11.195; 12.257, 376; 13.5, 138; *BJ* 1.150; 4.171, 172; 5.572; 7.403) repres. circumstantial ptcs. (Smyth §2054), e.g. γελῶν εἶπε = "he said laughingly" (Aesop *Fab*. 275). In place of the adv. ἀληθῶς ("truly") some mss. read ἀήθως ("unexpectedly"). For ἠπίστουν ("they disbelieved") cf. *Antiq* 18.76; *BJ* 2.187; 3.432; 5.539; 6.214; for ὁ ἀντίπαλος ("opponent," "rival") cf. *BJ* 1.352, 569; 2.442; 3.476, 605; 7.369.

6.404 εἰσχυθέντες δὲ τοῖς στενωποῖς ξιφήρεις τούς τε καταλαμβανομένους ἐφόνευον ἀνέδην...: the substant. noun ἡ στενωπός (from adj. στενωπός, -όν) means "narrow way," "byway" (cf. Lat. *angiportus*). The aor. pass. ptc. εἰσχυθέντες patterns with τοῖς στενωποῖς in the dat. because εἰσχέω ("to pour into") is a compound vb. (Smyth §1545), e.g., ἐμβλέψας αὐτῷ = "looking *at him*" (Plato *Charm*. 162D); ἐλπίδας ἐμποιεῖν ἀνθρώποις = "to create expectations *in people*" (Xen. *Cyr*. 1.6.19); αὐτοῖς ἐπέπεσε τὸ Ἑλληνικόν = "the Greek force fell *upon them*" (Xen. *Ana*. 4.1.10); ἐπέκειντο αὐτοῖς = "they pressed hard *upon them*" (Xen. *Ana*. 5.2.5). For ξιφήρεις ("with sword in hand") cf. *BJ*

1.150, 234, 338; 3.262, 384, 526; 4.145, 603; 5.371; for ἀνέδην ("without restraint") cf. *BJ* 1.32, 101,443, 625; 2.328, 496; 4.92, 334; 5.103; 6.140, 372. Josephus records here the indiscriminate slaughter of the vanquished, although Titus put an end to the killing in *BJ* 6.414. Usu. the general's signal marked both the end of the slaughter and the beginning of the pillage (cf. Ziolkowski 1993, 78-79).

6.404 ...καὶ τῶν συμφευγόντων τὰς οἰκίας αὐτάνδρους ὑπεπίμπρασαν: the adj. αὐτάνδρους, mod. τὰς οἰκίας, means "men and all." Josephus calls attn. to the fact that the Roman soldiers set fire to (ὑπεπίμπρασαν, cf. *BJ* 2.496; 3.228) the refugees' houses when they were crammed with people.

6.405 πολλὰς δὲ κεραΐζοντες ὁπότ᾽ ἔνδον παρέλθοιεν ἐφ᾽ ἁρπαγήν, γενεὰς ὅλας νεκρῶν κατελάμβανον καὶ τὰ δωμάτια πλήρη τῶν τοῦ λιμοῦ πτωμάτων: the adj. πολλὰς mods. "houses" (cf. τὰς οἰκίας in 6.404). Κεραΐζω ("to ravage," "plunder") occurs only here in the Josephan corpus, though cf. Hom. *Il.* 2.861; 5.557; 16.752; 21.129; 22.63; 24.245; *Ody.* 8.516; and Hdt. 1.88, 159; 2.121; 7.125; 8.86, 91. For παρέλθοιεν ("they came inside") cf. *Antiq* 18.17; for ἐφ᾽ ἁρπαγήν ("for plunder") cf. *BJ* 1.268; 2.528; 4.569. The plundering soldiers captured (κατελάμβανον, cf. *Antiq* 1.120; 4.92; *BJ* 2.440, 554) not booty but entire families and rooms stuffed with corpses. The neut. plur. τὰ δωμάτια ("rooms") represents the dimin. of τὰ δώματα ("houses," "dwellings"). Trans. τῶν τοῦ λιμοῦ πτωμάτων as "the corpses that [came from] the famine." Cf. Ziolkowski (1993, 76) for provisions the Romans followed in both the looting and disposal of booty.

6.405 ἔπειτα πρὸς τὴν ὄψιν πεφρικότες κεναῖς χερσὶν ἐξῄεσαν: for the "shuddering" (πεφρικότες) that horrific sights inspire in the timorous cf. *BJ* 6.210 and 212 above; for πρὸς τὴν ὄψιν ("at the sight") cf. *Antiq* 2.55; 3.38; 4.53; 6.332; 9.55; 11.265; 19.36; *BJ* 2.170; 3.396; 5.52, 290, 451, 547; for ἐξῄεσαν ("they withdrew") cf. *Antiq* 2.315; 5.19, 53; 14.388; 17.330; *Vita* 210; *Contra Ap* 1.231; *BJ* 1.234, 285; 2.438; 5.516; 6.156, 212.

6.406 οὐ μὴν οἰκτείροντες τοὺς οὕτως ἀπολωλότας ταὐτὸ καὶ πρὸς τοὺς ζῶντας ἔπασχον: trans. οὐ μήν ("indeed not") with the finite vb. ἔπασχον, not with the circumstantial ptc. οἰκτείροντες. Trans. the latter concessively (cf. Smyth §2055, §2060): "[although] pitying those who had perished thus..." For οἰκτείροντες ("pitying") cf. *Antiq* 2.148; for τοὺς... ἀπολωλότας ("the deceased") cf. *Antiq* 4.258; 16.350; *BJ* 2.85, 320; for ταὐτό ("in the same way") cf. *BJ* 2.63, 411; 5.353, 533; 6.33; 7.395; for πρὸς τοὺς ζῶντας ("toward the living") cf. *BJ* 5.33; for ἔπασχον ("they were disposed") cf. *Antiq* 4.189; 5.187; 6.6; 13.327; *BJ* 5.439.

6.406 ἀλλὰ τὸν ἐντυγχάνοντα διελαύνοντες ἀπέφραξαν μὲν τοὺς στενωποὺς νεκροῖς, αἵματι δὲ ὅλην τὴν πόλιν κατέκλυσαν...: the expression ὁ ἐντύγχων represents the "chance pers." (cf. Thuc. 4.132; Isocr. 18.63); so the Roman soldiers were "running through with a sword" (διελαύνοντες) anyone they came upon. Josephus' rhetorically astute readership would have appreciated the contr. between stopping up (ἀπέφραξαν, cf. *BJ* 1.390) the narrow alleys with corpses and flooding (κατέκλυσαν) the whole city with blood (μέν... δέ construction). For the narrow alleys (τοὺς στενωπούς, cf. *BJ* 2.105, 329; 5.188, 336; 6.301) cf. *BJ* 6.404; for the expression ὅλην τὴν πόλιν ("all the city") cf. *BJ* 2.6; 5.499.

6.406 ...ὡς πολλὰ καὶ τῶν φλεγομένων σβεσθῆναι τῷ φόνῳ: pot. res. clause. Ὡς can take the place of ὥστε in a res. clause (Smyth §2260). Trans. πολλὰ καὶ τῶν φλεγομένων as "many of the fires." Cf. Intro 40 for the tendency of Josephus to exaggerate.

6.407 καὶ οἱ μὲν κτείνοντες ἐπαύσαντο πρὸς ἑσπέραν, ἐν δὲ τῇ νυκτὶ τὸ πῦρ ἐπεκράτει, φλεγομένοις δ' ἐπανέτειλεν Ἱεροσολύμοις ἡμέρα Γορπιαίου μηνὸς ὀγδόη...: the μέν... δέ construction features a contr. between the cessation of killing "toward evening" (πρὸς ἑσπέραν, cf. *Antiq* 5.195; *BJ* 1.340; 2.363; 3.47, 107; 5.130, 238) and the increased ferocity of the fire "in the night" (ἐν... τῇ νυκτί, cf. *Antiq* 15.358). Κτείνοντες represents the suppl. ptc. ("they stopped killing"), e.g. οὔποτ' ἐπαυόμην ἡμᾶς οἰκτίρων = "I never ceased pitying ourselves" (Xen. *Ana.* 3.1.19); τοὺς πένητας ἔπαυσ' ἀδικουμένους = "I put a stop to the poor being wronged" (Dem. 18.102); ἀδικοῦντα Φίλιππον ἐξήλεγξα = "I proved that Philip was acting unjustly" (Dem. 18.136). For ἐπεκράτει ("prevailed") cf. *BJ* 4.133; 5.487; 6.235, 260; 7.419; for the compound vb. ἐπανέτειλεν (ἐπί + ἀνατέλλω) that construes with φλεγομένοις... Ἱεροσολύμοις in the dat. case cf. *BJ* 6.404 above. The date ἡμέρα Γορπιαίου μηνὸς ὀγδόῃ ("the eighth day of the month Gorpiaeus ") represents 26 September AD 70.

6.408 πόλει τοσαύταις χρησαμένῃ συμφοραῖς κατὰ τὴν πολιορκίαν...: note the highly interlocked word order (Synchesis). Trans. χρησαμένῃ (mod. πόλει, which in turn is in appos. to φλεγομένοις... Ἱεροσολύμοις, *BJ* 6.407) as "suffer": "...a city that *had suffered* such great evils throughout the siege." The vb. χράομαι oft means "employ oneself with," "get something done with" + dat. (Smyth §1509). For κατὰ τὴν πολιορκίαν ("throughout the siege") cf. *BJ* 6.308.

6.408 ...ὅσοις ἀπὸ κτίσεως ἀγαθοῖς κεχρημένη πάντως ἂν ἐπίφθονος ἔδοξεν: this clause provides still another perspective on Jerusalem (cf. φλεγομένοις... Ἱεροσολύμοις, *BJ* 6.407; πόλει... χρησαμένῃ, *BJ* 6.408), although the ptc. κεχρημένη (mod. "city," or "Jerusalem") occurs in the nom. case. Trans. the circumst. ptc. κεχρημένη as though it were a cond. clause (Smyth §2060): "[if] [Jerusalem] had enjoyed as many blessings, she would have seemed altogether enviable." The particle ἂν + past indic. (here ἔδοξεν) represents the apodosis of a past contr. fact cond. (Smyth §2292). The point is that Jerusalem's fate was *not* enviable—although, to be sure, she had enjoyed her fair share of blessings since her "foundation" (ἀπὸ κτίσεως, cf. ἀπὸ τῆς κτίσεως in *BJ* 4.533).

6.408 ...οὐ μὴν ἀξία κατ' ἄλλο τι τῶν τηλικούτων ἀτυχημάτων ἢ τὸ γενεὰν τοιαύτην ἐνεγκεῖν, ὑφ' ἧς ἀνετράπη: for the expression οὐ μήν ("indeed not") cf. *BJ* 6.406 above. The adj. ἀξία ("worthy") refers to Jerusalem (as do φλεγομένοις... Ἱεροσολύμοις, πόλει... χρησαμένῃ and κεχρημένη in the preced clauses). Supp. mentally the infin. πάσχειν to complete the idea that the adj. ἀξία requires: "[Jerusalem] was by no means worthy [of suffering] anything other of such great misfortunes than that..." Hence the "misfortune" that Jerusalem was indeed worthy of was to have produced (ἐνεγκεῖν, cf. *Antiq* 2.163; 3.20, 170; 7.5; 8.321;

17.131; 19.269, 362; *Vita* 154) the very generation (γενεὰν τοιαύτην) by which the city would be overthrown (ἀνετράπη, cf. *BJ* 2.295, 331; 6.87). Cf. Intro 40 for Josephus' bias against the leaders of the Zealots—who, in his opinion, were dir. resp. for the suffering of the Jews.

BJ 6.409-413

6.409 παρελθὼν δὲ Τίτος εἴσω τά τε ἄλλα τῆς ὀχυρότητος τὴν πόλιν καὶ τῶν πύργων ἀπεθαύμασεν, οὓς οἱ τύραννοι κατὰ φρενοβλάβειαν ἀπέλιπον: the aor. act. ptc. παρελθών ("having come in") occurs 51 times in the Josephan corpus; trans. as though it were a temp. clause (Smyth §2054): "now Titus, *when he had come in* [to Jerusalem] admired..." The pron. ἄλλος (in the expression τά... ἄλλα) can occur idiomatically, standing before the clause with which the mn. clause is contrasted (Smyth §1273), e.g., τά τε ἄλλα ἐτίμησε καὶ μυρίους ἔδωκε δαρεικούς = "he gave ten thousand darics besides honoring [me] in other ways" (Xen. *Ana.* 1.3.3). Here trans.: "[Titus] admired the city both as to its firmness and espec. its towers..." The anteced. of the rel. pron. οὕς is τῶν πύργων: "which [towers] the tyrants had abandoned on account of their damaged understanding." For the "tyrants" (οἱ τύραννοι) to whom Josephus refers in unmistakably neg. terms cf. *Antiq* 11.287; 19.230; *BJ* 1.24; 4.564, 566, 573; 6.202, 399, etc. By "damaged understanding" (κατὰ φρενοβλάβειαν, cf. *BJ* 1.620; 2.105, 251; 6.398) Josephus alludes to the Zealots' apparently irrational decision to come down from the towers of their own accord and so become susceptible to the rigors of the siege:

> The tyrants [οἱ τύραννοι] stripped themselves of their security and descended of their own accord [ἑκόντες] from those towers, whereon they could never have been overcome by force, and famine alone could have subdued them (*BJ* 6.399 LCL).

6.410 κατιδὼν γοῦν τό τε ναστὸν αὐτῶν ὕψος καὶ τὸ μέγεθος ἑκάστης πέτρας τήν τε ἀκρίβειαν τῆς ἁρμονίας, καὶ ὅσοι μὲν εὖρος ἡλίκοι δὲ ἦσαν τὴν ἀνάστασιν: the subj. of the aor. act. ptc. κατιδών ("having noticed," cf. *Antiq* 4.113; 8.257; 15.331,

373; *BJ* 1.408, 504; 2.523; 3.130; 4.635; 5.59; 7.171) is Titus; the dir. objs. are τό... ναστόν ("their substance"), τὸ μέγεθος ("their size"), τήν... ἀκρίβειαν ("their accuracy"), and ὅσοι... ἡλίκοι ("how great... how vast"). The words ὕψος, εὖρος and τὴν ἀνάστασιν repres. the accus. resp. (Smyth §1601): "in height... in breadth... in stature." In other words, the towers were utterly impressive—even to Titus—by the standards of the day.

6.411 "σὺν θεῷ γε ἐπολεμήσαμεν," ἔφη, "καὶ θεὸς ἦν ὁ τῶνδε τῶν ἐρυμάτων Ἰουδαίους καθελών, ἐπεὶ χεῖρες ἀνθρώπων ἢ μηχαναὶ τί πρὸς τούτους τοὺς πύργους δύνανται;": Only "with God's help" (σὺν θεῷ, cf. *Antiq* 16.318) were the Romans able to defeat the Zealots. God it was had "dragged down" (καθελών, cf. *Antiq* 5.209; 8.146; 9.170; 12.271, 318; *Contra Ap* 1.118) renegade Jews from the fortifications (cf. *BJ* 6.399 where Josephus writes that the Zealots "willingly" came down from the towers). Human weaponry and contrivances were as nothing in comp. with such great towers, so only God could have favored the Romans over the Zealots. Josephus was ever of the opinion that it was God, not the Romans, that brought the Zealots down. For the significance of dir. speech (*oratio recta*) cf. *BJ* 2.195 above.

6.412 τότε μὲν οὖν πολλὰ τοιαῦτα διελέχθη πρὸς τοὺς φίλους, τοὺς δὲ τῶν τυράννων δεσμώτας, ὅσοι κατελήφθησαν ἐν τοῖς φρουρίοις, ἀνῆκεν: oft διελέχθη (aor. pass. of διαλέγω, cf. Joseph. *Antiq* 3.93; 7.342, 383; 8.282; 13.405; 14.47) is depon. (LSJ B.1): "Titus *engaged in* many conversations of this sort with his friends." For πολλὰ τοιαῦτα ("many such things") cf. *Antiq* 4.218; 13.416; 19.258; *BJ* 1.508; 2.33, 64, 583, 594; 3.383; 4.639; for πρὸς τοὺς φίλους ("with his friends") cf. *Antiq* 1.208; 7.345; 12.168; 13.43; 16.84; 18.333; 19.347; *Vita* 205; for ἐν τοῖς φρουρίοις ("in the forts") cf. *Antiq* 12.336; 13.415; for ἀνῆκεν ("he set free") cf. *Antiq* 1.32; 11.61; 14.97; 15.65, 298; 18.246; 19.299; *BJ* 7.288, 340, 430. Among the prisoners whom Titus possibly liberated were Josephus' own father (*BJ* 5.533) and mother (*BJ* 5.544) whom Josephus, in the ardor of a speech, urged the besieged to kill if, by so doing, they would attain unto wisdom (*BJ* 5.419).

Josephus Notes

6.413 αὖθις δὲ τὴν ἄλλην ἀφανίζων πόλιν καὶ τὰ τείχη κατασκάπτων τούτους τοὺς πύργους κατέλιπε μνημεῖον εἶναι τῆς αὐτοῦ τύχης...: the adv. αὖθις means "hereafter" when it refers to the fut. (LSJ II.3). The passage recounts a time later when Titus, to prevent fut. insurrections, would raze portions of the city and dig up the walls (*BJ* 6.434). The vb. ἀφανίζω (lit., "cause to disappear") possesses the tech. mng. "destroy," as in destroy a city (LSJ I.3, on the basis of Xen. *Ana.* 3.2.11; Polyb. 1.81.6; Dem. 21.147); likewise, κατασκάπτω means "dig down" (LSJ I)—i.e., "destroy utterly, raze to the ground" (LSJ II, on the basis of Hdt. 7.156; Soph. *Phil.* 998; *Oed. Col.* 1421; Aesch. *Ag.* 525; Eur. *Her. Fur.* 566). For the three walls upon which the Zealots relied during the siege, cf. *BJ* 5.136, 142, 146, 147. The tower named Phasael still stands (Hippicus and Mariamme no longer do); all three had been part of Herod's building projects (Russell 1967, 98; Holzapfel 1996–97, 50; cf. Intro 19 above). In spite of Titus' statement that he could not have captured Jerusalem without God's help (*BJ* 6.411), the Roman general attached great significance to his personal fate (τῆς αὐτοῦ τύχης), the memorial to which would consist of the remaining towers. Josephus too takes fate into account in his narratives, e.g., *BJ* 1.28, 45, 68, 341, 353, 374; 2.184, 207, 213, 250, 360, 373; 3.9, 25, 72, 100, 106, etc. For τούτους τοὺς πύργους ("these walls") cf. *BJ* 6.412.

6.413 ...ᾗ συστρατιώτιδι χρησάμενος ἐκράτησε τῶν ἁλῶναι μὴ δυναμένων: the anteced. of the rel. pron. ᾗ is fate (cf. τῆς αὐτοῦ τύχης, preced clause). Note that the noun συστρατιώτιδι occupies the pred. pos.: "...which [fate] having utilized [as a] bulwark." For the rare συστρατιῶτις, -ιδος f. ("bulwark") cf. Themistius *Or.* 15.197C. The aor. mid. ptc. χρησάμενος occurs 53 times in the Josephan corpus; for the significance of χράομαι + dat. cf. *BJ* 6.408 above. For ἐκράτησε ("gain possession" + gen.) cf. *BJ* 1.108, 352, 366, 429, 665; 4.530; 5.529; 6.64, 244; 7.3, 440.

BJ 6.414–420

6.414 Ἐπεὶ δ' οἱ στρατιῶται μὲν ἔκαμνον ἤδη φονεύοντες, πολὺ δέ τι πλῆθος τῶν περιόντων ἀνεφαίνετο...: the vb. κάμνω patterns regularly with a suppl. ptc. (Smyth §2098): "and since the soldiers were at this point *growing weary* of inflicting slaughter..."

Cf. μὴ κάμῃς φίλον ἄνδρα εὐεργετῶν = "do not *grow weary* of doing good to your friend" (Plato *Gorg.* 470C). The phrase οἱ στρατιῶται ("the soldiers") occurs 20 times in the Josephan corpus. For ἔκαμνον ("they grew weary") cf. *Antiq* 4.91, 92; 10.132; *BJ* 1.350; 3.157, 184, 270; 5.299; for φονεύοντες ("slaughtering") cf. *Antiq* 13.343; *BJ* 2.255; 4.312. The expression οἱ περίοντες refers to "the survivors"; Josephus records that there was a certain "great crowd" (πολύ... τι πλῆθος) of them that "kept appearing" (ἀνεφαίνετο, cf. *BJ* 4.377).

6.414 κελεύει Καῖσαρ μόνους μὲν τοὺς ἐνόπλους καὶ χεῖρας ἀντίσχοντας κτείνειν, τὸ δὲ λοιπὸν πλῆθος ζωγρεῖν: for the extremely weighty phrase κελεύει Καῖσαρ ("Caesar commands") cf. *BJ* 7.1; oft in the Josephan corpus the subj. of κελεύει is a Roman commander or procurator, e.g., *BJ* 1.344; 2.174, 231; 3.338; 4.626; 6.322; 7.240. Here the finite vb. κελεύει governs the infins. κτείνειν and ζωγρεῖν: "Caesar orders [the soldiers] to kill..., and to enslave..." Generals were expected to give a signal to stop the killing since it was not self-evident that an enemy was incapable of further resistance (Ziolkowski 1993, 79). The killing was to be selective: only those who were "armed" (τοὺς ἐνόπλους) and "offered resistance" (for the idiom χεῖρας ἀντίσχοντας = "offer resistance" cf. *BJ* 2.446; 3.290) would be killed. The vb. ζωγρέω (from ζωός, -ή, -όν + ἀγρέω) means to "take, save alive, take captive instead of killing" (LSJ I.1; cf. *BJ* 1.163; 2.241, 253, 263, 448; 3.351, 407; 5.191, 289; 6.359; 7.134, 441). Though Josephus doubtless includes the enslavement of prisoners to portray Titus favorably, it seems Roman generals usu. enslaved prisoners instead of killing them:

> Slaves (*servi*) are so-called, because generals have a custom of selling their prisoners and thereby *preserving* [*servare*] rather than killing them: and indeed they are said to be *mancipia*, because they are *captives* in the hand (*manus*) of their enemies (Justinian *Digest* 1.5.4.2–3, citing Florentinus, AD 193–224; in Watson 1985, 1:15; orig. emphasis).

6.415 οἱ δὲ μετὰ τῶν παρηγγελμένων τό τε γηραιὸν καὶ τοὺς ἀσθενεῖς ἀνῄρουν: the expression οἱ δέ refers to the Roman soldiers. The prepos. phrase μετὰ τῶν παρηγγελμένων ("with what had been instructed") refers to Titus' directives in *BJ* 6.414; along with the overtly hostile prisoners the soldiers "put to death" (ἀνήρουν, cf. *BJ* 1.114; 2.235, 265, 453; 3.17, 185; 4.23, 654; 5.30, 103, 533; 6.224; 7.194) the most pitiable prisoners—the old (τό... γηραιὸν) and the weak (τοὺς ἀσθενεῖς, cf. *Antiq* 8.293; *BJ* 3.63). Such would bring no profit in the slave markets.

6.415 τὸ δ' ἀκμάζον καὶ χρήσιμον εἰς τὸ ἱερὸν συνελάσαντες ἐγκατέκλεισαν τῷ τῶν γυναικῶν περιτειχίσματι: already Josephus uses the neuter gender to refer as a collective whole to those who would be enslaved: τό... ἀκμάζον (those "in full bloom, at the prime," cf. *Antiq* 2.202; 13.3; *BJ* 1.4) and (τὸ) χρήσιμον ("the useful, serviceable," cf. *BJ* 2.127; 3.71, 91; 5.36). What had made the Temple ideal for keeping out the Romans during the siege served the Romans well for containing the prisoners of war; the latter herded them all together (συνελάσαντες, cf. *Antiq* 9.244) into the Temple (εἰς τὸ ἱερόν) and locked them up (ἐγκατέκλεισαν) in the Court of Women (cf. Intro 30 above). A περιτείχισμα (cf. *BJ* 6.158, 351, 396, 402) represents a type of wall, circumvallation, or stoa.

6.416 καὶ φρουρὸν μὲν ἐπέστησε Καῖσαρ ἕνα τῶν ἀπελευθέρων, Φρόντωνα δὲ τῶν φίλων ἐπικρινοῦντα τὴν ἀξίαν ἑκάστῳ τύχην: for Καῖσαρ ("Caesar") as a designation of Titus cf. *BJ* 6.414 above. Nothing else is known about the anonymous freedman whom Titus appointed (ἐπέστησε, cf. *Antiq* 7.335; 8.71, 98; *BJ* 1.64; 2.551; 3.285; 6.385; 7.196) guardian (φρουρόν, cf. Eur. *Ion.* 22; *Rhes.* 506). However, Fronto Haterius of Alexandria had been among Titus' most trusted friends and advisors (cf. *BJ* 6.238, 243, 419); he it was would determine a fate appr. to each prisoner. His method of arriving at justice is elaborated upon in *BJ* 6.417.

6.417 ὁ δὲ τοὺς μὲν στασιώδεις καὶ ληστρικοὺς πάντας ὑπ' ἀλλήλων ἐνδεικνυμένους ἀπέκτεινε: the expression ὁ δέ refers to Fronto Haterius. By "all" (πάντας) Josephus means as many of the prisoners as Fronto deemed deserving of death by information put forward by the prisoners themselves. These Fronto "killed" (ἀπέκτεινε, *BJ* 1.192, 246; 2.178, 237; 3.315; 6.114; 7.33). For τούς... στασιώδεις ("the seditious") cf. *Antiq* 14.141; 17.314; *Vita*

17; *BJ* 2.91, 493; for ληστρικοὺς ("piratical") cf. Strabo 7.2.2; Plut. *Sert*. 18.

6.417 τῶν δὲ νέων τοὺς ὑψηλοτάτους καὶ καλοὺς ἐπιλέξας ἐτήρει τῷ θριάμβῳ: only the tallest and fairest (τοὺς ὑψηλοτάτους καὶ καλούς) young prisoners would do for the triumph which would be celebrated in AD 71; Titus conveyed some 700 captives to Rome for this pur. (*BJ* 7.118). The Roman triumph would be an espec. lavish affair (*BJ* 1.29; 6.434; 7.36, 118, 121, 131, 158; cf. Millar 2005, 103–107); for ἐπιλέξας ("he selected") cf. *BJ* 2.270, 570; 3.540; 4.70; 5.43, 106; 6.131; 7.118; for ἐτήρει ("he reserved") cf. *Antiq* 19.331.

6.418 τοῦ δὲ λοιποῦ πλήθους τοὺς ὑπὲρ ἑπτακαίδεκα ἔτη δήσας ἔπεμψεν εἰς τὰ κατ' Αἴγυπτον ἔργα: from the great crowd (τοῦ... λοιποῦ πλήθους, cf. *Antiq* 17.157; *BJ* 5.288; 6.201) in the Court of Women Fronto chained together (δήσας, cf. *BJ* 1.49, 71; 6.357, 361) and sent (ἔπεμψεν) an undisclosed number of prisoners older than 17 yrs. These apparently toiled away the rest of their lives in so-called "works" (τά... ἔργα = "mines"?) throughout Egypt (κατ' Αἴγυπτον); for Fronto's connections in Egypt, cf. *BJ* 6.238. Vespasian's sending of prisoners to work on the canal near Corinth (*BJ* 3.540) represents a comp. servitude.

6.418 πλείστους δ' εἰς τὰς ἐπαρχίας διεδωρήσατο Τίτος φθαρησομένους ἐν τοῖς θεάτροις σιδήρῳ καὶ θηρίοις: the designation "most" (πλείστους) renders Titus' gift of prisoners more magnanimous than Fronto's (cf. preced phrase). An ἐπαρχία (Lat. *provincia*) represents a district governed by an ἔπαρχος (= *praefectus*, cf. Polyb. 11.27.2). For the rare διαδωρέομαι ("distribute in presents," LSJ) cf. Xen. *Cyr*. 3.3.6. The prisoners "would be destroyed" (φθαρησομένους, cf. Euseb. *Hist. Eccles*. 3.7.2; Plut. *De Stoic. Rep*. 1052A; *De Comm. Not. adv. Stoic*. 1075C) in the combats and beast hunts conducted in amphitheaters.

6.418 οἱ δ' ἐντὸς ἑπτακαίδεκα ἐτῶν ἐπράθησαν: those less than 17 yrs. old enjoyed the best prospects; the others, as we have seen, were either killed outright (*BJ* 6.414) or reduced to servitudes that were virtual death sentences. For ἐπράθησαν ("they were sold") cf. *Antiq* 14.313.

6.419 ἐφθάρησαν δὲ αὐτῶν ἐν αἷς διέκρινεν ὁ Φρόντων ἡμέραις ὑπ' ἐνδείας χίλιοι πρὸς τοῖς μυρίοις: trans. the pron. αὐτῶν (which refers to the prisoners) with χίλιοι πρὸς τοῖς μυρίοις: "and 11,000 *of them* perished by want in the days wherein Fronto administered justice…" For ἐφθάρησαν ("they perished") cf. *Antiq* 4.56, 155; 5.157; 15.122; 17.276; 20.105; for διέκρινεν ("administered justice") cf. *Antiq* 3.259. By the expression ὑπ' ἐνδείας ("by lack," cf. *Antiq* 2.143; 4.270; 6.360; 20.51, 181; *BJ* 5.426; 6.196, 367) Josephus means hunger, as successive clauses reveal.

6.419 οἱ μὲν ὑπὸ μίσους τῶν φυλάκων μὴ μεταλαμβάνοντες τροφῆς, οἱ δ' οὐ προσιέμενοι διδομένην: the μέν… δέ construction provides a contr. between two categories of prisoners who died by hunger: first, those who were starved by their jailers "out of hatred" (ὑπὸ μίσους, *Antiq* 20.29; *Contra Ap* 2.233); second, those who, out of a broken spirit, refused (οὐ προσιέμενοι: lit., "did not approach") the food offered (διδομένην, cf. *Antiq* 13.168; 19.235) to them.

6.419 πρὸς δὲ τὸ πλῆθος ἦν ἔνδεια καὶ σίτου: for the great "throng" (τὸ πλῆθος) of prisoners involved cf. τό… λοιπὸν πλῆθος (*BJ* 6.414). There was a dearth "even of grain" (καὶ σίτου, cf. *Antiq* 9.238; *BJ* 1.388) for so vast a multitude. Possibly Josephus envisioned the corn dole (Lat. *frumentatio*, cf. Arr. *Epict.* 1.10.2), a portion of which could have been diverted from the soldiery to feed the prisoners.

6.420 τῶν μὲν οὖν αἰχμαλώτων πάντων, ὅσα καθ' ὅλον ἐλήφθη τὸν πόλεμον, ἀριθμὸς ἐννέα μυριάδες καὶ ἑπτακισχίλιοι συνήχθη: trans. τῶν… αἰχμαλώτων πάντων with ἀριθμός: "(the) number… of all the prisoners (that) was gathered together was…" The anteced. of the rel. pron. ὅσα is τῶν… αἰχμαλώτων πάντων: "which (prisoners) were caught throughout the entire war…" For ἐλήφθη ("caught") cf. *Antiq* 10.247; 13.186; 14.71; *Contra Ap* 1.208; *BJ* 1.154; 6.362; 7.148; for συνήχθη ("gathered together") cf. *Antiq* 12.366; *BJ* 2.308; 3.68, 337; 7.160.

6.420 τῶν δὲ ἀπολομένων κατὰ πᾶσαν τὴν πολιορκίαν μυριάδες ἑκατὸν καὶ δέκα: trans. τῶν... ἀπολομένων with ἀριθμός (preced clause): "and (the) number of those who perished throughout the entire siege was..." Josephus means the siege of Jerusalem, of course, the topic of *BJ* 5–6; cf. Intro 40 for the possibility that Josephus exaggerated the numbers.

BJ 6.435–442

6.435 Ἑάλω μὲν οὕτως Ἱεροσόλυμα ἔτει δευτέρῳ τῆς Οὐεσπασιανοῦ ἡγεμονίας Γορπιαίου μηνὸς ὀγδόῃ: for ἑάλω ("[Jerusalem] was captured," from ἁλίσκομαι) cf. *Antiq* 5.48; *BJ* 1.190; 3.339, 429; 4.83, 120, 253, 439; 5.391. Elsewhere Josephus dates the destruction of Jerusalem to the eighth day of the month Gorpiaeus (ἡμέρα Γορπιαίου μηνὸς ὀγδόῃ, *BJ* 6.407) = 26 September AD 70. Here Josephus dates the destruction to the second year of Vespasian's reign. The dat. fixes the time explicitly (Smyth §1540), e.g., τῇ προτεραίᾳ = "the day before"; τῇ δευτέρᾳ = "the second day"; Ἐλαφηβολιῶνος μηνὸς ἕκτῃ (ἡμέρᾳ) = "on the sixth (day) of the month Elaphebolion" (Aeschines *De Fals. Leg.* 90); τρίτῳ μηνί = "in the third month" (Lys. 21.1).

6.435 ἁλοῦσα δὲ καὶ πρότερον πεντάκις τοῦτο δεύτερον ἠρημώθη: the aor. act. ptc. ἁλοῦσα ("[though] captured") mods. Jerusalem (cf. Ἱεροσόλυμα, preced clause). In its long history Jerusalem was captured five times (ἁλοῦσα... πεντάκις, cf. the names in *BJ* 6.436) but sacked (ἠρημώθη, lit. "made desolate") only twice—the time here recounted (70 AD) and then again in 586 BC by the Babylonians (2 Ki 25; 2 Chr 36:17–20; Is 24:10, 12; 25:2; 26:5; 27:10–11; Jer 39:1–10; 52:4–27).

6.436 Ἀσωχαῖος μὲν γὰρ ὁ τῶν Αἰγυπτίων βασιλεὺς καὶ μετ' αὐτὸν Ἀντίοχος, ἔπειτα Πομπήιος καὶ ἐπὶ τούτοις σὺν Ἡρώδῃ Σόσσιος ἑλόντες ἐτήρησαν τὴν πόλιν: the name Ἀσωχαῖος, an Egyptian king, represents the biblical Shishak, who plundered Jerusalem and the Temple in ca. 960 BC (1 Ki 14:25–26; 2 Chr 12:2–4, 9). For Antiochus (Epiphanes) cf. 1 Macc 1:20–24; *BJ* 5.394; for Pompey's capture of Jerusalem in 63 BC, cf. *BJ* 1.141–153. The prepos. phrase ἐπὶ τούτοις means "in addition to these things," i.e., "subsequently." For Sossius' capture of Jerusalem in 37 BC with the assistance of Herod the Great cf. *BJ* 1.345; for ἐτήρησαν ("they held") cf. *Antiq* 8.220.

6.437 πρὸ δὲ τούτων ὁ τῶν Βαβυλωνίων βασιλεὺς κρατήσας ἠρήμωσεν αὐτὴν μετὰ ἔτη τῆς κτίσεως χίλια τετρακόσια ἑξηκονταοκτὼ μῆνας ἕξ: the prep. phrase πρό... τούτων ("before them") refers to Antiochus, Sossius, and Herod, but not to Asochaeus (for his much earlier date cf. *BJ* 6.436). The "king of the Babylonians" who seized possession (κρατήσας, cf. *BJ* 1.50, 183, 265; 2.262; 4.549, 606, 652; 5.347) of Jerusalem and despoiled the city (ἠρήμωσεν, cf. *Contra Ap* 1.154) refers to Nebuchadrezzar (var. Nebuchadnezzar) whose capture of the city is recorded in 2 Ki 24–25 (cf. 1 Chr 6:15; 2 Chr 36:6–7; Ezra 1:7; 2:1; Neh 7:6; Jer 27:6, 8, etc). Josephus claims this destruction occurred "fourteen hundred and sixty-eight years and six months after its [Jerusalem's] foundation." If Babylonians destroyed Jerusalem in 586 BC (a secure date), then the foundation of the city—according to the chronology represented here—would be 2054 BC. Josephus' chronological system is by no means clear.

6.438 ὁ δὲ πρῶτος κτίσας ἦν Χαναναίων δυνάστης ὁ τῇ πατρίῳ γλώσσῃ κληθεὶς βασιλεὺς δίκαιος: for κτίσας ("founder") cf. *Antiq* 4.314; 9.217; 17.341; *BJ* 1.417, 418; 3.356; 5.377; for δυνάστης ("chief") cf. *Antiq* 7.230; 13.118; 14.129; 16.325; for τῇ πατρίῳ γλώσσῃ ("[in] the native language") cf. *BJ* 3.92; 5.272, 361; for ὁ... κληθείς ("who was called") cf. *Antiq* 7.315; 12.234, 266, 267; 13.131, 213, 365; 19.347; *Contra Ap* 2.45, 51; *BJ* 1.19, 31; 2.167; 7.44. The name Melchizedek (Gen 14:18; Heb 7:2) means "king of righteousness" in Hebrew—or, as some scholars suppose, "my king is Zedek" (the latter name being that of a Phoenician deity). Cf. Adonizedek = "my lord is Zedek" (Josh 10:1).

6.438 ἦν γὰρ δὴ τοιοῦτος: Josephus reacts to the mng. of this Canaanite king's name: "indeed, he was righteous."

6.438 διὰ τοῦτο ἱεράσατό τε τῷ θεῷ πρῶτος καὶ τὸ ἱερὸν πρῶτος δειμάμενος Ἱεροσόλυμα τὴν πόλιν προσηγόρευσεν Σόλυμα καλουμένην πρότερον: the prep. phrase διὰ τοῦτο ("on this account") refers to the significance of Melchizedek's name. Josephus reports that Melchizedek had been "first" (πρῶτος... πρῶτος) to serve God as priest (for ἱεράομαι cf. Hdt. 2.35; Dion. Hal. 2.19; Paus. 6.11.2; Thuc. 2.2), build the Temple (δειμάμενος, cf. *BJ* 1.402), and refer to (προσηγόρευσεν, cf. *BJ* 1.402, 416, 419; 7.285) the city as Jerusalem—a pun for "holy Peace" (ἱερός, -ά, -όν + Σόλυμα = Hebr. *shalom*). Scarcely less fanciful is the Bible's interpretation of Melchizedek: the silence of Genesis 14:18 about this priest's genealogy makes it possible for the author of Hebrews to portray Melchizedek as a prefiguration of Christ himself (Heb 7:1-3).

6.439 τὸν μὲν δὴ τῶν Χαναναίων λαὸν ἐκβαλὼν ὁ τῶν Ἰουδαίων βασιλεὺς Δαυίδης κατοικίζει τὸν ἴδιον, καὶ μετὰ τοῦτον ἔτεσι τετρακοσίοις ἑβδομήκοντα καὶ ἑπτὰ μησὶν ἓξ ὑπὸ Βαβυλωνίων κατασκάπτεται: the Canaanite people whom David dislodged were the Jebusites (2 Sam 5:6–10). The pron. τοῦτον refers to David. For ἐκβαλὼν ("driving out") cf. *Antiq* 7.65, 67, 247; 8.128; 12.278; 17.350; *Contra Ap* 1.94, 231, 296; *BJ* 1.39, 280; for κατοικίζει ("established") cf. *Antiq* 1.124. By adding 586 (the year the Babylonians destroyed Jerusalem) to the figure mentioned here one arrives at ca. 1063 BC for the Davidic establishment of the city (although this date does not square with the interval Josephus provides in *BJ* 6.440).

6.440 ἀπὸ δὲ Δαυίδου τοῦ βασιλέως, ὃς πρῶτος αὐτῆς ἐβασίλευσεν Ἰουδαῖος, μέχρι τῆς ὑπὸ Τίτου γενομένης κατασκαφῆς ἔτη χίλια καὶ ἑκατὸν ἑβδομήκοντα καὶ ἐννέα: for Δαυίδου τοῦ βασιλέως ("David the king") cf. *Antiq* 7.360; 8.12; 9.155; 10.49; *BJ* 5.137; for the epithet "first" (πρῶτος) applied to Melchizedek cf. *BJ* 6.438; David, however, had been "first" actually to rule as king (ἐβασίλευσεν, cf. *BJ* 2.222) as a Jew (unlike Melchizedek who had been a Canaanite). The two secure dates for the destruction of Jerusalem—586 BC and 70 AD—do not quite match up with the 1,179 years Josephus posits here. Again, the chronological system is by no means clear.

6.441 ἀπὸ δὲ τῆς πρώτης κτίσεως ἔτη μέχρι τῆς ἐσχάτης ἁλώσεως δισχίλια ἑκατὸν ἑβδομήκοντα καὶ ἑπτά: according to Josephus' chronology, Jerusalem was founded in ca. 2107 BC.

6.442 ἀλλὰ γὰρ οὔθ' ἡ ἀρχαιότης οὔθ' ὁ πλοῦτος ὁ βαθὺς οὔτε τὸ διαπεφοιτηκὸς ὅλης τῆς οἰκουμένης ἔθνος οὔθ' ἡ μεγάλη δόξα τῆς θρησκείας ἤρκεσέ τι πρὸς ἀπώλειαν αὐτῇ: Josephus mentions Jerusalem's antiquity, vast wealth, people spread out over the entire habitable world, and glory of its relig. rites as factors that could not avert Jerusalem's ruin. The repetition of οὔτε, with obvious emphasis, represents Anaphora (Smyth §3010); the statement functions not only as an acknowledgment of Jerusalem's complicity in her own destruction (cf. *BJ* 6.408 above), but registers Josephus' pride in Jerusalem's—or rather Judaism's—ancient and impressive accomplishments. For ὁ πλοῦτος ("wealth") cf. *Antiq* 5.96; 8.378; 14.110; *BJ* 2.218; 6.282; for διαπεφοιτηκός ("wide-ranging") cf. *Antiq* 3.82; *Contra Ap* 1.166; 2.282; for ὅλης τῆς οἰκουμένης ("entire habitable world") cf. *BJ* 1.426; for τῆς θρησκείας ("of her worship") cf. *Antiq* 1.234; 5.98; 8.225, 279; 11.85; 12.324; 13.198, 244; 15.248; 16.45, 174; 18.287; *BJ* 1.148, 150; 2.391, 425; 5.229; for ἤρκεσε ("availed" + dat.) cf. *Antiq* 6.80; 9.266; *BJ* 1.34, 48, 238; 2.110, 375; for πρὸς ἀπώλειαν ("for destruction") cf. *Antiq* 11.262, 278, 279; *BJ* 3.293; 4.76, 364; 5.364, 424.

6.442 τοιοῦτο μὲν δὴ τὸ τέλος τῆς Ἱεροσολύμων πολιορκίας: "such indeed [was] the end of the siege of Jerusalem." Josephus records the beg. of the siege in *BJ* 5.262.

BJ 7.280–284

7.280 πέτραν οὐκ ὀλίγην τῇ περιόδῳ καὶ μῆκος ὑψηλὴν πανταχόθεν περιερρώγασι βαθεῖαι φάραγγες κάτωθεν ἐξ ἀοράτου τέρματος κρημνώδεις καὶ πάσῃ βάσει ζῴων ἀπρόσιτοι: the words πέτραν οὐκ ὀλίγην and μῆκος ὑψηλὴν serve as the dir. obj. of the vb. περιερρώγασι ("they break round about"). The phrase οὐκ ὀλίγην represents Litotes (Smyth §3032) and τῇ περιόδῳ represents the dat. of descr.: "a rock not small *in circumference*." Μῆκος mods. ὑψηλὴν as an adv. accus. (Smyth §1607) and the latter word in turn mods. πέτραν: "[a rock] lofty *in height*." No fewer than three adjs. mod. φάραγγες ("ravines," cf. *BJ* 2.549; 7.169), the subj. of the vb. περιερρώγασι: 1) βαθεῖαι ("deep"); 2) κρημνώδεις ("precipitous," "steep"); and 3) ἀπρόσιτοι ("unapproachable," cf. *Antiq* 3.77; *BJ* 7.435). Two of the adjs. are themselves modified by short phrases: 1) κάτωθεν ἐξ ἀοράτου τέρματος ("down below from an unseen base"); and 2) πάσῃ βάσει ζῴων ("for living creatures' every tread").

7.280 πλὴν ὅσον κατὰ δύο τόπους τῆς πέτρας εἰς ἄνοδον οὐκ εὐμαρῆ παρεικούσης: the gen. abs. consists of τῆς πέτρας and παρεικούσης: "...save only as much as *the rock provides* in two places for a way up [εἰς ἄνοδον] by no means convenient." The words οὐκ εὐμαρῆ (mod. ἄνοδον) repres. litotes (Smyth §3032). For πλὴν ὅσον ("save only as much") cf. *Antiq* 10.225; *BJ* 1.215.

7.281 ἔστι δὲ τῶν ὁδῶν ἡ μὲν ἀπὸ τῆς Ἀσφαλτίτιδος λίμνης πρὸς ἥλιον ἀνίσχοντα: the words τῶν ὁδῶν constitute a part. gen.: "of the [two] tracks the one [ἡ μέν] goes from..." Trans. πρὸς ἥλιον ("towards the sun," cf. Hdt. 3.98; Joseph. *Antiq* 4.305) with the pres. act. ptc. ἀνίσχοντα ("rising"): "toward the rising sun," i.e., east. Josephus refers to what we call the Dead Sea as ἡ Ἀσφαλτῖτις λίμνη ("Bituminous Lake"): *Antiq* 1.175; 4.85; 9.7, 207; 15.168; *Contra Ap* 1.174; *BJ* 1.657; 3.515; 4.438, 453, 456, 474, 476; 7.168.

7.281 καὶ πάλιν ἀπὸ τῆς δύσεως ᾗ ῥᾷον πορευθῆναι: for ἀπὸ τῆς δύσεως ("from the west") cf. *BJ* 3.35, 377; 6.298, 301. The anteced. of the rel. pron. ᾗ is an understood ἡ δέ (cf. ἡ μέν in the preced clause) which Josephus omits for reasons of stylistic economy: "and again a western road by means of which (it was) easier to proceed."

7.282 καλοῦσι δὲ τὴν ἑτέραν ὄφιν, τῇ στενότητι προσεικάσαντες καὶ τοῖς συνεχέσιν ἑλιγμοῖς: "the other" (τὴν ἑτέραν) path—namely, the one whose approach is from the east— was the more diff. of the two. The ancients called it, appropriately, "snake" (ὄφιν, cf. *Antiq* 1.50; 2.287), likening its narrowness and continuous switchbacks to a serpent. Note the idiom: to compare (προσεικάζειν) something (τι) to something else (τινι). The vb. καλοῦσι ("they call") occurs 43 times in the Josephan corpus; for τῇ στενότητι ("narrowness") cf. *BJ* 4.23.

7.282 κλᾶται γὰρ περὶ τὰς τῶν κρημνῶν ἐξοχὰς καὶ πολλάκις εἰς αὐτὴν ἀνατρέχουσα: the path is "broken" (κλᾶται) in that it skirts jutting crags (περὶ τὰς τῶν κρημνῶν ἐξοχὰς) and freq doubles back on itself (πολλάκις εἰς αὐτὴν ἀνατρέχουσα). Josephus describes the serpentine switchbacks of the more diff. footpath. For τάς... ἐξοχάς ("the eminences") cf. *Antiq* 3.231; 3.243; *BJ* 5.108; for τῶν κρημνῶν ("of the crags") cf. *Antiq* 3.76; *BJ* 1.150; for εἰς αὐτήν ("to itself") cf. *Antiq* 2.338; 4.52.

7.282 καὶ κατὰ μικρὸν αὖθις ἐκμηκυνομένη μόλις ψαύει τοῦ πρόσω: this phrase describes those portions of the path that gradually "lengthen out" again (αὖθις ἐκμηκυνομένη) after a tight curve: like a snake, the path scarcely "feels its way" (ψαύει) forward. For κατὰ μικρόν ("gradually") cf. *BJ* 1.75, 111, 210; 2.651; 3.404; 4.31, 203; 5.149, 359; for ψαύει ("feels") cf. *Antiq* 2.58; for the idiomatic use of πρόσω + τοῦ ("forward") cf. ἰέναι τοῦ πρόσω (Xen. *Ana.* 1.3.1).

7.283 δεῖ δὲ παραλλὰξ τὸν δι' αὐτῆς βαδίζοντα τὸν ἕτερον τῶν ποδῶν ἐρείδεσθαι: the subj. of δεῖ... ἐρείδεσθαι is τὸν δι' αὐτῆς βαδίζοντα: "the one proceeding along through it [δι' αὐτῆς]"—i.e., through the path. The adj. ἕτερος, -α, -ον possesses an attributive sense (Smyth §1271), so what Josephus means is that the traveler is obliged "prop himself" (mid. and pass. of ἐρείδεσθαι, cf. LSJ III.1) first on one foot, then on the other, "alternatively" (παραλλὰξ) as he inches along the path.

7.283 ἔστι δὲ πρόδηλος ὄλεθρος: the view afforded by the height presented a picture of imminent destruction. For πρόδηλος ("clear, manifest") cf. *Antiq* 17.223; *BJ* 7.182, 236, 326, 384; for ὄλεθρος ("destruction") cf. *Antiq* 4.127; 17.3, 262; *BJ* 2.496; 4.110.

7.283 ἑκατέρωθεν γὰρ βάθος κρημνῶν ὑποκέχηνε τῇ φοβερότητι πᾶσαν εὐτολμίαν ἐκπλῆξαι δυνάμενον: the subj. of the vb. ὑποκέχηνε (from ὑποχαίνω = to "gape," "yawn") is βάθος... ἐκπλῆξαι δυνάμενον ("height... able to astonish"). Trans. τῇ φοβερότητι with ἐκπλῆξαι: "to astonish *with its terribleness.*" The dizzying height had a deleterious effect upon the most intrepid traveler. For ἑκατέρωθεν ("on both sides") cf. *Antiq* 3.54, 112; 12.130, 371; 15.151, 326, 416; *BJ* 1.413; 2.270; 3.60, 216, 420; 5.141; 6.76; 7.102; for πᾶσαν εὐτολμίαν ("all manner of boldness") cf. *Antiq* 6.250; *BJ* 7.342; for ἐκπλῆξαι ("to astonish") cf. *Antiq* 15.61; 19.88; for δυνάμενον ("able" + infin.) cf. *BJ* 1.324; 2.211; 3.4; 4.403; 5.154; 7.67, 177, 305, 312.

7.284 διὰ τοιαύτης οὖν ἐλθόντι σταδίους τριάκοντα κορυφὴ τὸ λοιπόν ἐστιν: trans. the aor. act. ptc. ἐλθόντι (cf. *Antiq* 2.55; 6.168, 277; 7.191) as a dat. of the observer (Smyth §1497): "*for the one who had come* through such [a path]..." The words σταδίους τριάκοντα ("for 30 stades") constitute an accus. ext. of space (Smyth §1581), e.g., ἄγειν (στρατιὰν) στενὰς ὁδούς = "to lead an army *over narrow roads*" (Xen. *Cyr.* 1.6.43); ἐξελαύνει σταθμοὺς τρεῖς, παρασάγγας εἴκοσι καὶ δύο = "he advances *3 stages, 22 parasangs*" (Xen. *Ana.* 1.2.5); ἀπέχει ἡ Πλάταια τῶν Θηβῶν σταδίους ἑβδομήκοντα = "Plataea is *70 stades* distant from Thebes" (Thuc. 2.5).

7.284 ...οὐκ εἰς ὀξὺ τέρμα συνηγμένη, ἀλλ' ὥστ' εἶναι κατ' ἄκρας ἐπίπεδον: the pf. pass. ptc. συνηγμένη mods. κορυφή in the preced clause: "...a summit *gathered* not into a sharp peak, but so as to be level along the heights." Any aerial photograph of Masada corroborates Josephus' observation. For τέρμα ("peak") cf. *BJ* 7.170; for συνηγμένη ("gathered") cf. Chrysipp. *Frag. Mor.* 323; Diod. Sic. 3.4.3; Philo *De Josepho* 38; Judg 7:22; for κατ' ἄκρας ("along the heights") cf. *BJ* 3.330; 7.144; for ἐπίπεδον ("level") cf. *Antiq* 3.158; 13.238; *BJ* 5.215.

BJ 7.285–294

7.285 ἐπὶ ταύτῃ πρῶτον μὲν ὁ ἀρχιερεὺς ᾠκοδομήσατο φρούριον Ἰωνάθης καὶ προσηγόρευσε Μασάδαν: the pron. ταύτῃ in the prep. phrase ἐπὶ ταύτῃ refers to κορυφή in *BJ* 7.284: "on this (summit)." However, as Josephus has just explained (*BJ* 7.284), the top of the rock was a level plateau, not a peak. Jonathon, brother of Judas Maccabaeus and his successor (161–143 BC; cf. *BJ* 1.48–49; Intro 10–11) built first upon the eminence described and called it Masada ("mountain stronghold"). For ᾠκοδομήσατο ("built") cf. *Antiq* 8.135; 17.26; 20.189; *BJ* 7.175; for προσηγόρευσε ("called") cf. *BJ* 1.402, 416, 419; 6.438; for Μασάδαν ("Masada") cf. *Antiq* 14.296, 358; *BJ* 1.237, 264, 267; 2.408, 434, 447; 4.405, 505, 507; 7.275, 303.

7.285 ὕστερον δ' Ἡρώδῃ τῷ βασιλεῖ διὰ πολλῆς ἐγένετο σπουδῆς ἡ τοῦ χωρίου κατασκευή: the words Ἡρώδῃ τῷ βασιλει repres. the poss. dat. (Smyth §1476); trans. the prep. phrase διὰ πολλῆς... σπουδῆς as "considerable attentions": "later the development [ἡ... κατασκευή] of the site engaged *the considerable attentions* of king Herod..." By the noun ἡ κατασκευή (*BJ* 1.424; 2.606; 4.90, 375; 5.36, 152, 177; 6.267; 7.45, 115, 139, etc.) Josephus intends "permanent or fixed assets" on a site (LSJ II.1), to be distinguished from that which is "movable or temporary" (= ἡ παρασκευή). For the ambitious building projects of Herod the Great (which included Masada) cf. Intro 19.

7.286 τεῖχός τε γὰρ ἤγειρε περὶ πάντα τὸν κύκλον τῆς κορυφῆς ἑπτὰ σταδίων ὄντα λευκοῦ μὲν λίθου πεποιημένον: note the interlocked word order (Synchesis). Trans. in the following order: ἤγειρε... τεῖχος πεποιημένον... λευκοῦ λίθου... περὶ πάντα τὸν κύκλον τῆς κορυφῆς... ὄντα ἑπτὰ σταδίων. The subj. of the vb. ἤγειρε ("he raised") is Herod who fortified Masada sometime after the Roman senate acclaimed him king of Judaea in 40 BC (he returned to Palestine in 39); the purpose of Herod's wilderness retreats—which included the Fortress Antonia in Jerusalem, Masada, Cypros, Docus, Alexandreion, Hyrcania, Machaerus, and perhaps Herodium East (in Peraea)—was to serve as places of refuge to Herod and his family in times of emergency (Richardson 1996, 180). For ἤγειρε ("he raised") cf. *Antiq* 8.199; 10.17, 131; 15.298, 391; 20.229; *BJ* 1.99; 2.170; 3.22; 4.56; for πεποιημένον ("made") cf. *Antiq* 2.284; 3.49, 113, 159; 8.64; 10.264; 17.201; *Contra Ap* 1.206; *BJ* 2.564; 7.221, 316.

7.286 ...ὕψος δὲ δώδεκα καὶ πλάτος ὀκτὼ πήχεις ἔχον: the neut. sing. ptc. ἔχον continues to mod. τεῖχος, the dir. obj. of the vb. ἤγειρε (preced clause). The word πήχεις constitutes an accus. ext. of space (Smyth §1581), and ὕψος and πλάτος repres. the accus. resp.

(Smyth §1601): "a wall... *being* [ἔχον] twelve cubits in height and eight cubits in width." For the intrans. use of ἔχω (= "to be") cf. Smyth §1709.b.

7.287 τριάκοντα δὲ αὐτῷ καὶ ἑπτὰ πύργοι πεντηκονταπήχεις ἀνειστήκεσαν: the pron. αὐτῷ ("upon it") refers to the wall (τεῖχος... πεποιημένον, cf. *BJ* 7.286). In the plupf. tense the vb. ἀνειστήκεσαν (from ἀνίστημι; cf. ὑπερανειστήκεσαν, *BJ* 7.1) is intrans.: "...and 37 towers 50 cubits high *stood* upon it." Even apart from the towers, the sheer rock face of Masada rises some 820 ft. on the east and 600 ft. on the west (so Funk 1962, 294).

7.287 ἐξ ὧν ἦν εἰς οἰκήματα διελθεῖν περὶ πᾶν τὸ τεῖχος ἔνδον ᾠκοδομημένα: the rel. pron. ὧν refers to the towers (πύργοι, preced clause). The usu. idiom is ἦν + δυνατόν + infin.: "it was possible to [infin.]." Here Josephus omits δυνατόν for the pur. of stylistic economy: "from which (towers) *it was possible* to pass through to the apartments..." Clearly, then, the wall and its 37 towers were interconnected; the dwelling-chambers (τὰ οἰκήματα, *Antiq* 8.134, 137, 138) were built into the wall on the inner side (ἔνδον). The aor. act infin. διελθεῖν ("to pass through") occurs 20 times in the Josephan corpus.

7.288 τὴν γὰρ κορυφὴν πίονα καὶ πεδίου παντὸς οὖσαν μαλακωτέραν ἀνῆκεν εἰς γεωργίαν ὁ βασιλεύς: for Herod's title "king" (ὁ βασιλεύς = 47 times in the *BJ*) cf. espec. 13 Lat. inscriptions on wine jugs delivered to Herod in Masada in 19 BC bearing the inscription "king" (*regi herodi iudaico* = "to king Herod the Jew," Richardson 1996, 203; Holzapfel 1996–97, 67). The ptc. οὖσαν connects μαλακωτέραν to τὴν... κορυφὴν. The words πεδίου παντὸς constitute a gen. of comp. (Smyth §1431): "being more fertile *than* any plain." There are 20 arable acres atop Masada (so Funk 1962, 294).

7.288 ...ἵν' εἴ ποτε τῆς ἔξωθεν τροφῆς ἀπορία γένοιτο, μηδὲ ταύτῃ κάμοιεν οἱ τὴν αὑτῶν σωτηρίαν τῷ φρουρίῳ πεπιστευκότες: the clause marker ἵνα patterns not with the vb γένοιτο (εἰ represents its clause marker), but κάμοιεν (pur., sec. seq.): "...*in order that*, if ever there was a dearth of food outside, those who had entrusted their own safety to the fort would not be exhausted by it." The words εἰ... γένοιτο constitute the protasis of a past gen. cond. (Smyth §2340); the pron. ταύτῃ ("by this") refers to ἀπορία ("dearth"). For τροφῆς ἀπορία ("dearth of food") cf. *Antiq* 1.204; 3.3, 20; 20.207; for γένοιτο ("there was") cf. *BJ* 1.168, 259, 274; 2.206, 226, 482; 3.91; 4.294, 640; 5.64; 6.7, 52; 7.71. Josephus identifies Masada as a "fort" (τῷ φρουρίῳ) in *BJ* 7.285 above.

7.289 καὶ βασίλειον δὲ κατεσκεύασεν ἐν αὐτῷ κατὰ τὴν ἀπὸ τῆς ἑσπέρας ἀνάβασιν, ὑποκάτω μὲν τῶν τῆς ἄκρας τειχῶν, πρὸς δὲ τὴν ἄρκτον ἐκκλῖνον: the substant. noun τὸ βασίλειον (from adj. βασίλειος, -α, -ον) means "palace" (cf. Lat. *regia*, from *regius, -a, -um*). Herod built (κατεσκεύασεν, cf. *BJ* 1.410, 416, 421; 5.37; 6.190, 191; 7.176) the palace along the approach from the west (ἀπὸ τῆς ἑσπέρας, *BJ* 7.168, 293). It was lower than the wall around the summit (for which cf. *BJ* 7.286), and inclined (ἐκκλῖνον, cf. *BJ* 5.145) toward the north (τὴν ἄρκτον, cf. *Antiq* 2.305; 9.206; *BJ* 7.180).

7.289 τοῦ δὲ βασιλείου τὸ τεῖχος ἦν ὕψει μέγα καὶ καρτερόν, πύργους ἔχον ἑξηκονταπήχεις ἐγγωνίους τέτταρας: the wall of the palace had to be "great in height" (ὕψει μέγα) and "stout" (καρτερόν, *Antiq* 6.370; *BJ* 1.105; 4.509) because it was positioned on the west (ἀπὸ τῆς ἑσπέρας, *BJ* 7.289), the "easier" (ῥᾷον, *BJ* 7.281) of the two approaches. The four corner towers of the palace were 60 cubits (ἑξηκονταπήχεις), ten cubits higher than the towers on the summit which were 50 cubits high (, *BJ* 7.287). For ἐγγωνίους ("corner") cf. *Antiq* 3.119.

7.290 ἥ τε τῶν οἰκημάτων ἔνδον καὶ στοῶν καὶ βαλανείων κατασκευὴ παντοία καὶ πολυτελὴς ἦν: for the significance of the noun ἡ... κατασκευή ("fixed building") cf. *BJ* 7.285 above. The fixed building of the palace—apartments, colonnades, and baths—were "of manifold variety" (παντοία, cf. *Antiq* 3.57; 18.148) and "very costly" (πολυτελής, cf. *Antiq* 7.379; 17.6; 18.144; *Contra Ap* 2.191). The palace would have been the portion of Masada which Herod and his family occupied; Herod had left his family under guard at Masada when he had been forced to flee to Rome by way of Petra and

Alexandria in 40 BC (cf. Richardson 1996, 126). Other structures suited to religious purposes have been found atop Masada: a synagogue, ritual bathing facility, and possibly a study hall (cf. Chancey and Porter 2001, 185).

7.290 ...κιόνων μὲν ἀπανταχοῦ μονολίθων ὑφεστηκότων, τοίχων δὲ καὶ τῶν ἐν τοῖς οἰκήμασιν ἐδάφων λίθου στρώσει πεποικιλμένων: the gens. depend on ἡ... κατασκευή in the earlier clause: *"the fixed building...* of the columns supporting [the struct.] everywhere [were] of a single block, and that of the walls and flooring in the apartments [were] embroidered with a covering of stone." Josephus leaves to his reader's imagination how single-blocked (μονολίθων) columns and mosaics in the Jewish manner came to exist in the inaccessible fortress (cf. Yadin 1996–97, 26–27); archaeological investigation has revealed three distinct levels of occupation in the northern complex where the palace was situated:

> The Northern Palace at Masada... occupied a knife-edge with three platforms spread over a thirty-five meter (110 foot) vertical drop—the top platform being semi-circular, the middle circular, and the lowest rectangular. It opened out on a view as spectacular as any villa anywhere in the Roman world, looking north up the Rift valley, east to the Dead Sea, and west to the wilderness (Richardson 1996, 182).

7.291 πρὸς ἕκαστον δὲ τῶν οἰκουμένων τόπων ἄνω τε καὶ περὶ τὸ βασίλειον καὶ πρὸ τοῦ τείχους πολλοὺς καὶ μεγάλους ἐτετμήκει λάκκους ἐν ταῖς πέτραις φυλακτῆρας ὑδάτων: the so-called "settled regions" (τῶν οἰκουμένων τόπων) of the fortress comprised three separate areas: 1) the area "above" (ἄνω), consisting of the apartments built inside the wall encircling the summit (οἰκήματα... περὶ πᾶν τὸ τεῖχος ἔνδον ᾠκοδομημένα, *BJ* 7.287); 2) the area surrounding Herod's palace (περὶ τὸ βασίλειον); and 3) a hitherto unmentioned area "in front of the wall" (πρὸ τοῦ τείχους; Josephus prob. means the great tower on the western approach, cf. *BJ* 7.293 below). In proximity to these areas Herod bored (ἐτετμήκει = plupf. of τέμνω) "many and great" (πολλοὺς καὶ μεγάλους, cf. *BJ* 4.176) cisterns in the rock to be what Josephus calls "guardians of waters" (φυλακτῆρας ὑδάτων: φυλακτήρ = "poet. for φύλαξ," espec. "in plur.," LSJ).

7.291 ...μηχανώμενος εἶναι χορηγίαν ὅση τῷ ἐκ πηγῶν ἐστι χρωμένοις: Herod represents the subj. of the ptc. μηχανώμενος (cf. *Vita* 53; *BJ* 4.210). The more well-known mng. of ἡ χορηγία was the office of defraying a public expense, such as, e.g., equipping a trireme or paying for a tragic chorus. However, the word could mean also an "abundance" of something, and so here the word possibly construes with the phrase ἐκ πηγῶν: "*an abundance* of springs." The pron. ὅση refers to χορηγίαν and should construe with χρωμένοις (*Antiq* 2.317; 4.183; 5.294, 349; 18.117, 250): "contriving that there be *as great* an abundance of springs *as* there is for those using it [τῷ]." The def. article τῷ remains problematic: does it serve as the dat. obj. of χρωμένοις ("for those using *it* [τῷ = the water]") or should we—with some mss.—read τῶν (the def. article of πηγῶν)?

7.292 ὀρυκτὴ δ' ὁδὸς ἐκ τοῦ βασιλείου πρὸς ἄκραν τὴν κορυφὴν ἀνέφερε τοῖς ἔξωθεν ἀφανής: the words ὀρυκτή... ὁδός ("sunken road") repres. the subj. of the intrans. vb. ἀνέφερε ("led"). The adj. ὀρυκτός, -ή, -όν means "dug, formed by digging" (LSJ I.1, from ὀρύσσω), e.g., λίμνη (Hdt. 2.149); τάφος (Eur. *Troad.* 1153); εἴσοδοι (Xen. *Ana.* 4.5.25). The sunken road, which was "invisible" (ἀφανής) to observers outside, would provide safety and privacy to the inhabitants of the palace. For ἐκ τοῦ βασιλείου ("from the palace") cf. *Antiq* 9.150; *BJ* 4.651; for ἀνέφερε ("led") cf. *Antiq* 16.306; 17.40; 20.40; *Contra Ap* 2.162; for ἀφανής ("invisible") cf. *Antiq* 6.64, 215; 18.69; 20.172; *Contra Ap* 1.154.

7.292 οὐ μὴν οὐδὲ ταῖς φανεραῖς ὁδοῖς ἦν οἷόν τε χρήσασθαι ῥᾳδίως πολεμίους: for the emphatic neg. οὐ μὴν ("indeed not") cf. *BJ* 6.406 above. The idiom οἷόν τε + infin. ("be able to") occurs 22 times in the Josephan corpus; the adv. ῥᾳδίως ("easily") occurs 71 times. Ταῖς φανεραῖς ὁδοῖς functions as the obj. of χρήσασθαι (Smyth §1509); πολεμίους serves as the subj. of χρήσασθαι: "nor was it at all easy for enemies to make use of the visible approaches." By the expression ταῖς φανεραῖς ὁδοῖς ("the visible approaches") Josephus means the two roads described in *BJ* 7.281. For χρήσασθαι ("to make use of" + dat.) cf. *BJ* 1.73, 311, 528; 2.176, 320, 395, 615; 5.499, 564; 7.24.

7.293 ἡ μὲν γὰρ ἑῴα διὰ τὴν φύσιν, ὡς προείπαμεν, ἐστὶν ἄβατος: the expression ἡ μὲν... ἑῴα refers to the eastern road (ὁδός has been omitted). Josephus states that the eastern approach is impassable (ἄβατος) "on account of its nature" (διὰ τὴν φύσιν; cf. τὴν φύσιν, *BJ* 1.22, 410, 544; 4.476; 6.205; 7.171, 176, 279)—i.e., no man-made contrivances were needed to protect the fortress on that quarter. For Josephus' earlier observation cf. *BJ* 7.281-83; for the expression ὡς προείπαμεν ("as we have said before") cf. *Antiq* 9.29; *BJ* 1.668; 7.304.

7.293 τὴν δ' ἀπὸ τῆς ἑσπέρας μεγάλῳ κατὰ τὸ στενότατον πύργῳ διετείχισεν ἀπέχοντι τῆς ἄκρας πήχεων οὐκ ἔλαττον διάστημα χιλίων, ὃν οὔτε παρελθεῖν δυνατὸν ἦν οὔτε ῥᾴδιον ἑλεῖν: Herod fortified (διετείχισεν) the western approach at its narrowest point by means of a great tower (μεγάλῳ... πύργῳ). The dat. sing. ptc. ἀπέχοντι (cf. *Antiq* 7.34; 12.369) mods. πύργῳ; the vb. ἀπέχω oft means to be distant from τινος (here τῆς ἄκρας = "from the top"). The noun διάστημα represents an accus. ext. of space (Smyth §1581): "an *interval* not less than a thousand cubits." The anteced. of the rel. pron. ὅν is πύργῳ ("tower"). For the idiom ἦν δυνατόν + infin. cf. *BJ* 7.287 above. The aor. infin. ("to pass by") occurs 32 times in the Josephan corpus; ἑλεῖν (2 aor. act. infin. of αἱρέω = "to capture") occurs 15 times. For ἀπὸ τῆς ἑσπέρας ("from the west") cf. *BJ* 7.168, 298.

7.293 δυσέξοδος δὲ καὶ τοῖς μετὰ ἀδείας βαδίζουσιν ἐπεποίητο: even travelers who "had no cause for alarm" (μετὰ ἀδείας, cf. *Antiq* 12.261) would have to pass by the tower. Hence, the western passage had become a "diff. egress" (δυσέξοδος). For τοῖς... βαδίζουσιν ("for those travelling") cf. *Antiq* 8.187; *Contra Ap* 2.24; for ἐπεποίητο ("had been made") cf. *Antiq* 3.258; 14.122, 326; *BJ* 7.304, 432.

7.294 οὕτως μὲν οὖν πρὸς τὰς τῶν πολεμίων ἐφόδους φύσει τε καὶ χειροποιήτως τὸ φρούριον ὠχύρωτο: Josephus refers to Masada as a fort (τὸ φρούριον) in *BJ* 7.285 and 288 above. He has demonstrated the impassableness of both approaches: the east "on account of nature" (διὰ τὴν φύσιν, *BJ* 7.293; cf. φύσει here), the west by virtue of the great tower (μεγάλῳ... πύργῳ, *BJ* 7.293; cf. χειροποιήτως here). The word φύσει ("by nature") occurs 29 times in the *BJ*. For τὰς... ἐφόδους ("attacks") cf. *BJ* 3.88; 4.268; 7.402; for χειροποιήτως ("artificially") cf. Polyb. *Hist.* 10.10.13; for ὠχύρωτο ("it was fortified") cf. Cass. Dio *Hist. Rom.* 37.1.4; 37.16.2; 49.37.5; 56.15.1; 74.10.3.

BJ 7.295–303

7.295 Τῶν δ' ἔνδον ἀποκειμένων παρασκευῶν ἔτι μᾶλλον ἄν τις ἐθαύμασε τὴν λαμπρότητα καὶ τὴν διαμονήν: for the distinction between ἡ κατασκευή (permanent assets: buildings, walls, towers, etc.) and ἡ παρασκευή (that which is prepared: equipage, armament, provisions, etc.) cf. *BJ* 7.285 above. Here Josephus effects a transition from ἡ κατασκευή (the subj. of *BJ* 7.285–94 above) to ἡ παρασκευή (the subj. of *BJ* 7.295–99 below). The words ἄν τις ἐθαύμασε (cf. *BJ* 7.302) repres. the past pot. (Smyth §1784): "someone *could wonder* all the more at the splendor and durability of the stores that had been packed away inside." The expression ἔτι μᾶλλον ("all the more") occurs 37 times in the Josephan corpus. For τὴν λαμπρότητα ("the splendor") cf. *Antiq* 12.81; for τὴν διαμονήν ("the durability") cf. *BJ* 2.166.

7.296 σῖτός τε γὰρ ἀπέκειτο πολὺς καὶ πολὺν χρόνον ἀρκεῖν ἱκανώτατος οἶνός τε πολὺς ἦν καὶ ἔλαιον: note the emphatic repetition: πολύς... πολύν... πολύς (anaphora). Also, the vb. ἀπέκειτο ("was packed away," cf. *Antiq* 17.271; *Vita* 119; *BJ* 6.390) is sing., although there are three collective nouns that serve as subj.: σῖτος ("grain"), οἶνος ("wine"), ἔλαιον ("olive oil"). Trans. the superl. adj. ἱκανώτατος with the infin. ἀρκεῖν (cf. *Antiq* 3.106; 13.115; *BJ* 4.329): "most sufficient to last." The words πολὺν χρόνον (cf. *BJ* 1.142, 265; 4.494) repres. the accus. ext. of time (Smyth §1582): "for a long time." Josephus has designed the rhetorically expansive sentence to reinforce the bountifulness of the food stores in real life.

7.296 ἔτι δὲ παντοῖος ὀσπρίων καρπὸς καὶ φοίνικες ἐσεσώρευντο: the words παντοῖος ("of every sort," cf. *Vita* 264; *BJ* 2.496) and ἐσεσώρευντο ("had been heaped up") create a powerful image of abundance: in addition to the three staples of Mediterranean society represented above—grain, wine, olive oil—there had been "heaped up" at Masada "besides" (ἔτι) every variety of pulse (τὸ ὄσπριον) and dates. For φοίνικες ("dates") cf. *Antiq* 3.9; 8.84, 262; *Contra Ap* 1.28, 63, 169; 2.17; *BJ* 3.517.

7.297 πάντα δὲ εὗρεν ὁ Ἐλεάζαρος τοῦ φρουρίου μετὰ τῶν σικαρίων ἐγκρατὴς δόλῳ γενόμενος ἀκμαῖα καὶ μηδὲν τῶν νεωστὶ κειμένων ἀποδέοντα: for the name Eleazar (Ἐλεάζαρος, here with the def. article) cf. *BJ* 1.42; 2.235, 409, 447, 565; 3.229; 4.225; 5.5; 6.227; 7.196, 203, 253, 320, 337, 339. This Eleazar, son of Ananias the high-priest, persuaded those who officiated in the Temple to accept no gift or sacrifice from a foreigner—an act, claims Josephus, that "laid the foundation of the war with the Romans" (*BJ* 2.409). At about the same time (summer 66 AD) Jewish insurgents captured Masada, slew the Roman guards there, and put a garrison of their own in place (*BJ* 2.408). Josephus alludes to these events in his statement that Eleazar had become master of the fortress "with the Sicarii" (μετὰ τῶν σικαρίων, cf. *Antiq* 20.205, 210; *BJ* 2.425; 7.410, 412, 438, 444) and "by guile" (δόλῳ, cf. *BJ* 1.49, 218; 2.635; 3.277, 319). Then it was that Eleazar had found "everything" (πάντα, i.e., the perishable goods described in *BJ* 7.296) to be "in mint cond." (ἀκμαῖα) and in no whit "inferior" (ἀποδέοντα, cf. *BJ* 4.115) to goods more recently laid in. For εὗρεν ("he found") cf. *BJ* 1.164, 369; 2.587; 3.514; 4.541; 5.388; for ἐγκρατὴς ("master") cf. *Antiq* 12.5, 247; 13.121, 185, 220; 15.248; 16.276; *Vita* 353, 396; *Contra Ap* 1.186; *BJ* 4.577; for ἀποδέοντα ("inferior") cf. *BJ* 4.115.

7.297 καίτοι σχεδὸν ἀπὸ τῆς παρασκευῆς εἰς τὴν ὑπὸ Ῥωμαίοις ἅλωσιν ἑκατὸν ἦν χρόνος ἐτῶν: by "equipage" (τῆς παρασκευῆς, cf. *Antiq* 8.169; *BJ* 7.299) Josephus means the orig. stocking of the fortress under king Herod (for which cf. *BJ* 7.295), in perhaps 31 BC, the year Herod became espec. vulnerable to the designs of Cleopatra (cf. *BJ* 7.300 below). The Romans took final control of Masada in AD 73.

7.297 ἀλλὰ καὶ Ῥωμαῖοι τοὺς περιλειφθέντας τῶν καρπῶν εὗρον ἀδιαφθόρους: note the pred. pos. of the adj. ἀδιαφθόρους: "but [the] Romans also discovered that the left-over fruits [were] *not decayed*." By the aor. pass. ptc. περιλειφθέντας ("left-over," cf. *Antiq* 5.228; 10.112; *BJ* 2.90) Josephus means those perishables that had not been consumed by the Zealots at the time of the Roman conquest. There were, of course, still other goods that had been "more recently laid in" (τῶν νεωστὶ κειμένων, *BJ* 7.297). The subj. Ῥωμαῖοι ("Romans") occurs 94 times in the *BJ*; the vb. εὗρον ("they found") occurs 22 times in the Josephan corpus.

7.298 αἴτιον δ' οὐκ ἂν ἁμάρτοι τις ὑπολαμβάνων εἶναι τὸν ἀέρα τῆς διαμονῆς, ὕψει τῶν περὶ τὴν ἄκραν πάσης ὄντα γεώδους καὶ θολερᾶς ἀμιγῆ κράσεως: note the interlocked word order (Synchesis). Trans. in the following order: αἴτιον... τῆς διαμονῆς ("cause of the durability"); τὸν ἀέρα... ὄντα... ἀμιγῆ ("air unmixed with" + gen.). The words οὐκ ἂν ἁμάρτοι τις repres. the potent. optv. (Smyth §1824): "one could not be wrong..."; the pres. act. ptc. ὑπολαμβάνων sets off accus. with infin. in indir. state. (Smyth §1867): "...*in supposing that* the cause of the durability was the air to the height of the things around the summit unmixed with any earth-born and foul alloy." For the expression οὐκ ἂν ἁμάρτοι τις ("one could not be wrong") cf. *Antiq* 3.174; *BJ* 3.75; 5.4; for ὑπολαμβάνων ("in supposing") cf. *BJ* 1.62, 212, 355; 7.66; for περὶ τὴν ἄκραν ("around the summit") cf. *Antiq* 15.398.

7.299 εὑρέθη δὲ καὶ παντοίων πλῆθος ὅπλων ὑπὸ τοῦ βασιλέως ἀποτεθησαυρισμένων, ὡς ἀνδράσιν ἀρκεῖν μυρίοις: in addition to the "discoveries" of food-stuffs (cf. εὗρεν and εὗρον in *BJ* 7.297 above) there "was discovered" (εὑρέθη, cf. *BJ* 2.387; 5.445; 7.393) all manner of weaponry that had been "hoarded up" (ἀποτεθησαυρισμένων) by king Herod, enough for about 10,000 men. Indeed, some Zealots used the weaponry at Masada to conduct a siege against a Roman garrison trapped in Herod's palace in Jerusalem in the summer of AD 66 (*BJ* 2.433–34). The phrase ὑπὸ τοῦ βασιλέως ("by the king") refers to Herod elsewhere at *BJ* 1.381.

7.299 ...ἀργός τε σίδηρος καὶ χαλκὸς ἔτι δὲ καὶ μόλιβος, ἅτε δὴ τῆς παρασκευῆς ἐπὶ μεγάλαις αἰτίαις γενομένης: as if the mass of every type of weapon (παντοίων πλῆθος ὅπλων, *BJ* 7.299) were not enough, Herod's stocking of iron, bronze and lead at Masada made it possible for later inhabitants of Masada to forge the metals for defensive purposes. For the adj. ἀεργός, -ή, -όν ("unwrought," from ἀ-privative + ἔργον) cf. Isocr. 4.132; Xen. *Cyr.* 3.2.19, of land that is fallow. The words τῆς παρασκευῆς... γενομένης constitute a gen. abs. (the particle ἅτε + ptc. denotes Cause, so Smyth §2085): "*since* the equipage had been brought about for grave reasons." These are explained in the next sentence (cf. γάρ in *BJ* 7.300).

7.300 λέγεται γὰρ αὐτῷ τὸν Ἡρώδην τοῦτο τὸ φρούριον εἰς ὑποφυγὴν ἑτοιμάζειν διπλοῦν ὑφορώμενον κίνδυνον: the impers. vb. λέγεται ("it is said") sets off accus. with infin. in indir. state. (Smyth §1867): "for *it is said* that Herod was preparing this fort for himself as a refuge, suspecting a double danger." For earlier refs. to Masada as a fort (τὸ φρούριον) cf. *BJ* 7.285, 288, 294; for the pres. act. infin. ἑτοιμάζειν ("to prepare") cf. *Antiq* 12.94; 20.70; for ὑφορώμενον ("suspecting") cf. *Antiq* 7.362.

7.300 ...τὸν μὲν παρὰ τοῦ πλήθους τῶν Ἰουδαίων, μὴ καταλύσαντες ἐκεῖνον τοὺς πρὸ αὐτοῦ βασιλέας ἐπὶ τὴν ἀρχὴν καταγάγωσι: both τὸν μὲν and τὸν μείζω δέ καὶ χαλεπώτερον (in the next clause) refer to the double danger (διπλοῦν... κίνδυνον, *BJ* 7.300) Herod suspected. The clause marker μή ("lest") and vb. καταγάγωσι constitute a fear clause in prim. seq. (Smyth §2221): "...lest having deposed that one [ἐκεῖνον = Herod] they restore to power those who were kings before him [πρὸ αὐτοῦ = Herod]." Herod, an Idumean (for his ancestry cf. Intro 16), had been imposed by the Romans on Judea by virtue of his father Antipater's loyalty to Julius Caesar. Judeans were more inclined to favor aspirants to power who were of the Hasmonean line—such as, Antigonus Mattathias, a Hasmonean, who owed his pos. to Parthia, not Rome:

> Antigonus's pact with the Parthians was as much responsible for Herod's elevation as were his own abilities. Antigonus had strong support from among his people, as almost the last Hasmonean, but he had bad

political instincts and bad advice... Had Antigonus avoided entanglements with Parthia and remained on the Caesarian side, Judean history might have been very different. In some respects, Herod's most brilliant decision was to oppose Parthia vigorously (Richardson 1996, 128).

7.300 ...τὸν μείζω δὲ καὶ χαλεπώτερον ἐκ τῆς βασιλευούσης Αἰγύπτου Κλεοπάτρας: as the most powerful woman of the age and Antony's lover, Cleopatra, queen of Egypt, represented a great danger to Herod in the mid to late 30s BC (cf. Richardson 1996, 165–69). The peril was removed by Augustus' victory at the battle of Actium, and Cleopatra's subsequent suicide, in 31 BC.

7.301 αὕτη γὰρ τὴν αὑτῆς γνώμην οὐκ ἐπεῖχεν, ἀλλὰ πολλάκις Ἀντωνίῳ λόγους προσέφερε τὸν μὲν Ἡρώδην ἀνελεῖν ἀξιοῦσα, χαρίσασθαι δ' αὐτῇ τὴν βασιλείαν τῶν Ἰουδαίων δεομένη: the demonst. pron. αὕτη ("she") refers to Cleopatra. The vb. ἐπεῖχεν (from ἐπέχω) may mean "hold back, keep in check" (LSJ IV.1): "for she did not *keep in check* her intention, but..." For the idiom προσφέρειν λόγους ("address proposals," LSJ A.I.4) cf. Hdt. 3.134; 5.30; Dem. 48.6; Thuc. 3.4. The fem. sing. ptcs. ἀξιοῦσα ("demanding," cf. *Antiq* 1.269; 13.431; 15.44, 92) and δεομένη ("begging," *Antiq* 5.291, 312; 9.65; 15.63; *BJ* 2.606; 7.279) delineate what were Cleopatra's frequent proposals to M. Antony, first, that he "do away with" (ἀνελεῖν, cf. *BJ* 1.177, 223, 245; 2.186, 245, 296; 3.331, 368, 540; 4.640; 5.118, 531; 6.187, 362; 7.110) Herod; second, that the kingdom of the Jews be given (χαρίσασθαι, cf. *BJ* 4.99; 5.127, 389; 7.303) to her as a gift. Indeed, Antony forced Herod to cede some of his territory—Ituraea, Samaritis, parts of Nabataea, and the coast land—to Cleopatra in 37 BC; and in 34 BC Cleopatra lay before Antony calumnious charges against Syrian officials in the belief that she could appropriate their possessions, contriving also for the ruin of Herod and Malchus, kings of Judea and Arabia, respectively (*BJ* 1.360). Cf. Intro 18 above for Herod's relationship to Mark Antony and Cleopatra.

7.302 καὶ μᾶλλον ἄν τις ἐθαύμασεν, ὅτι μηδέπω τοῖς προστάγμασιν Ἀντώνιος ὑπακηκόει κακῶς ὑπὸ τοῦ πρὸς αὐτὴν ἔρωτος δεδουλωμένος, οὐχ ὅτι περὶ τοῦ μὴ χαρίσασθαι προσεδόκησεν: the expression μᾶλλον ἄν τις ἐθαύμασεν ("one could the more wonder," cf. *BJ* 7.295) sets off the two ὅτι-clauses, first, "*that* [ὅτι] Antony had not yielded to her behests..."; second, "*that* he not [οὐχ ὅτι] harbor an expectation about it not being given as a gift." In other words, given his great infatuation for Cleopatra (cf. espec. *BJ* 1.359), it was a wonder that M. Antony had not more completely yielded to Cleopatra's charms and suggestions. But Herod was a favored client and Antony protected him. For κακῶς ὑπὸ τοῦ πρὸς αὐτὴν ἔρωτος δεδουλωμένος ("basely enslaved by his passion toward her") cf. τῷ Κλεοπάτρας ἔρωτι διεφθαρμένος Ἀντώνιος ("Antony, demoralized by his love toward Cleopatra," *BJ* 1.359). The name Ἀντώνιος ("Antony") occurs 25 times in the *BJ*. For τοῖς προστάγμασιν ("[her] behests") cf. *Contra Ap* 2.235; for προσεδόκησεν ("harbored an expectation") cf. *BJ* 5.546.

7.303 διὰ τοιούτους μὲν φόβους Ἡρώδης Μασάδαν κατεσκευασμένος ἔμελλεν Ῥωμαίοις ἀπολείψειν ἔργον τοῦ πρὸς Ἰουδαίους πολέμου τελευταῖον: preoccupied with "such great fears" (τοιούτους... φόβους) as those as have been divulged in 7.301–302, Herod "fortified" (κατεσκευασμένος, cf. *Antiq* 8.82, 134; 17.117) Masada. This act was destined to leave to the Romans the "final task" (ἔργον... τελευταῖον) of their war with the Jews. For κατεσκευασμένος ("fortified") cf. κατασκευή (*BJ* 7.285, 290) and κατεσκεύασεν (*BJ* 7.289); for ἀπολείψειν ("to leave") cf. *Antiq* 6.165, 305; 18.38; *BJ* 1.572; 4.16.

BJ 7.320–336:

7.320 Οὐ μὴν οὔτε αὐτὸς Ἐλεάζαρος ἐν νῷ δρασμὸν ἔλαβεν οὔτε ἄλλῳ τινὶ τοῦτο ποιεῖν ἔμελλεν ἐπιτρέψειν: the neg. οὐ μήν means "indeed not." The word δρασμόν ("flight") connects this statement to what immed. precedes (cf. *BJ* 7.319): the Romans, about to attack the wall, mounted watch lest any of the besieged "secretly escape" (λάθωσιν ἀποδράντες, 7.319; cf. δρασμόν here). For the assoc. of the word ἀποδιδράσκω with runaway slaves, cf. Xen. *Ana.* 1.4.8; *IG* 2^2.584; for the word's assoc. with the desertion of soldiers, cf. Xen. *Ana.* 5.6.34; Plato *Protag.* 317a. Construe ἐπιτρέψειν with ἔμελλεν (complementary infin.) and ποιεῖν as an pur. infin. (Smyth §2008): "nor did he intend to entrust to anyone else to do this"—i.e., to run away. Josephus presents Eleazar throughout this section as a man intent not only upon his own death, but upon the demise of many others. Cf. van Henten (2007, 197–199) for other noble death passages in Josephus.

7.321 ὁρῶν δὲ τὸ μὲν τεῖχος ὑπὸ τοῦ πυρὸς ἀναλούμενον...: the ptc. ὁρῶν initiates an accus. with ptc. after a vb. of perception (ACP, Smyth §2110). The ptc. ἀναλούμενον ("being destroyed," from ἀναλόω) represents an alternative form of ἀναλίσκω (in mid. "to be consumed, destroyed"). Note how the pres. ptcs. ὁρῶν..., ἐπινοῶν... and τιθέμενος build tension throughout the period, followed by ἐβουλεύσατο ("he plotted"), which concludes the tension quickly. Eleazar is of course the subj.

7.321 ἄλλον δὲ οὐδένα σωτηρίας τρόπον οὐδ' ἀλκῆς ἐπινοῶν...: for σωτηρίας τρόπον ("method of safety") cf. Ephraem Syrus *Precationes* 6.339.9; Julianus *Comm. in Job* 46.5; for the pres. act. ptc. ἐπινοῶν ("devising") cf. Joseph. *Antiq* 17.114; 19. 30; *Contra Ap* 2.252; *BJ* 2.640; 5.356.

7.321 ἃ δὲ ἔμελλον Ῥωμαῖοι δράσειν αὐτοὺς καὶ τέκνα καὶ γυναῖκας [αὐτῶν], εἰ κρατήσειαν, ὑπ' ὀφθαλμοὺς αὐτῷ τιθέμενος: begin with the ptc. clause ὑπ' ὀφθαλμοὺς αὐτῷ τιθέμενος ("setting before his eyes..."); this idea provides the anteced. upon which the rel. pron. ἅ is based: "...what things [ἅ] the Romans were intending to do..." etc. The reflex. pron. αὐτῷ repres. a poss. dat. (Smyth §1476). The fut. infin. δράσειν (from δράω, "to do, accomplish") has no relation to δρασμόν ("flight," 7.320), even though the two words seem etymologically related. The words εἰ κρατήσειαν (cf. Joseph. *BJ* 6.20) repres. the protasis of a fut. less vivid cond. (Smyth §2329): "if they [the Romans] should prevail..."

7.321 θάνατον κατὰ πάντων ἐβουλεύσατο: the prepos. κατά + gen. can mean "down upon" (LSJ A.II.1), i.e., "against everyone"; in the mid. voice the vb. βουλεύω ("take counsel," "consider") may mean "have designs against" (cf. *BJ* 1.590) or "plot against" (1.596). For Josephus' uniformly neg. opinion of the leaders of the Zealot faction, cf. Intro 40.

7.322 καὶ τοῦτο κρίνας ἐκ τῶν παρόντων ἄριστον: the pron. τοῦτο refers to θάνατον κατὰ πάντων in the prev clause. In Josephus' opinion, Eleazar's baseness consists in the Zealot's determination of what was "best" (ἄριστον) for himself and others, without taking into consideration what could have been the Romans' fair and equitable terms.

7.322 τοὺς ἀνδρωδεστάτους τῶν ἑταίρων συναγαγὼν τοιούτοις ἐπὶ τὴν πρᾶξιν λόγοις παρεκάλει: Josephus admits that Eleazar's henchmen were "most manly" (τοὺς ἀνδρωδεστάτους), generally a pos. descr.: Diog. Laert. *Vit. Phil.* 6.14; Hist. Alex. Magn. Recens. 1.41.12; Polyaen. *Str.* 4.9.3; Polyb. 2.1.8; 3.18.2; Xen. *Ana.* 4.8.2. Perhaps Eleazar's villainy consisted in his "drawing together" (συναγαγών, cf. Joseph. *BJ* 1.41, 160, 372; 3.347, 646; 4.346, 636; 6.33; 7.164, 253) the most courageous of his companions, but not all. Of course, "the deed" (τὴν πρᾶξιν; cf. πρὸς τὴν πρᾶξιν, *BJ* 7.389; τῇ πράξει προσιόντες, 7.390) represents the suicide.

7.323 "πάλαι διεγνωκότας ἡμᾶς, ἄνδρες ἀγαθοί, μήτε Ῥωμαίοις μήτ' ἄλλῳ τινὶ δουλεύειν ἢ θεῷ, μόνος γὰρ οὗτος ἀληθής ἐστι καὶ δίκαιος ἀνθρώπων δεσπότης, ἥκει νῦν καιρὸς ἐπαληθεῦσαι κελεύων τὸ φρόνημα τοῖς ἔργοις": Eleazar's great speech extends to *BJ* 7.388, with a brief pause in 7.337–340. Translators would do well to begin with the phrase ἥκει νῦν καιρὸς ἐπαληθεῦσαι κελεύων... ("now the time has come, bidding us to verify..."); the subj. of the infin. ἐπαληθεῦσαι is διεγνωκότας ἡμᾶς... δουλεύειν: "we who have for a long time decided... to be slaves to [+ dat.]..." For διεγνωκότας ("have decided") cf. Joseph. *Antiq* 2.102; 5.204; 7.200; for ἄνδρες ἀγαθοί ("my brave fellows") cf. Joseph. *Antiq* 12.54; 14.146; 19.17; *BJ* 7.352; for δουλεύειν ("to be slave to τινι) cf. Joseph. *BJ* 1.132; 2.265, 349, 350; 3.313; 5.365; 6.42; 7.78; for τοῖς ἔργοις ("by deeds") cf. Joseph. *BJ* 1.98, 376, 482; 3.234; 4.185; 5.115, 284; 6.16, 374; 7.269. For another place where Jews express the idea that they had been enslaved to no one, cf. Jn 8:33.

7.324 πρὸς ὃν αὐτοὺς μὴ καταισχύνωμεν...: the anteced. of the rel. pron. ὅν is καιρός in 7.323. "Let us not disgrace ourselves." Eleazar appeals to the honor of his listeners who, as we have seen, repres. the "most manly" of his companions (cf. τοὺς ἀνδρωδεστάτους τῶν ἑταίρων, *BJ* 7.322) and "brave fellows" (cf. ἄνδρες ἀγαθοί, *BJ* 7.323).

7.324 πρότερον μηδὲ δουλείαν ἀκίνδυνον ὑπομείναντες, νῦν δὲ μετὰ δουλείας ἑλόμενοι τιμωρίας ἀνηκέστους, εἰ ζῶντες ὑπὸ Ῥωμαίοις ἐσόμεθα: trans. the 2 aor. mid. ptc. ἑλόμενοι (from αἱρέω) as though it were a hortatory subjunct. (Smyth §1797): "we who formerly did not await a slavery that was without danger, let us [not] now, along with slavery, choose [ἑλόμενοι] penalties that are irreparable..." Eleazar represents the view that slavery is a fate worse than death, an irredeemable penalty, a type of living death under the tyranny of the Romans. This argument flatly contradicts Josephus' own when he spoke against suicide at Jotapata (*BJ* 3.368; Ladouceur 1981, 251 n. 16). For ὑπομείναντες ("enduring") cf. Joseph. *Antiq* 4.89; 11.46; 15.139, 289; 17.292; *Contra Ap* 2.123; for μετὰ δουλείας ("with slavery") cf. Joseph. *Antiq* 17.45; for ἑλόμενοι ("having chosen") cf. Joseph. *BJ* 7.336, 395); for ἀνηκέστους ("irreparable") cf. Joseph. *Antiq* 1.14; 16.188; 19.181; *BJ* 2.455. Espec. sinister is the phrase ὑπὸ Ῥωμαίοις ("under the Romans"), for which cf. *Antiq* 15.405; 18.120; 19.288; 20.176; *Vita* 269, 350; *BJ* 1.11; 3.29, 429; 4.134; 5.461; 7.255, 297, 372.

7.324 πρῶτοί τε γὰρ πάντων ἀπέστημεν καὶ πολεμοῦμεν αὐτοῖς τελευταῖοι: apparently there were at Masada Zealots who had revolted from the Romans at the first (πρῶτοί), and the same persons would constitute the "last" fighters as well (τελευταῖοι). In *BJ* 7.303 Josephus refers to Masada as the Romans' "final task" (ἔργον... τελευταῖον) in their war against the Jews. For ἀπέστημεν ("we have revolted") cf. Joseph. *BJ* 7.383.

7.325 νομίζω δὲ καὶ παρὰ θεοῦ ταύτην δεδόσθαι χάριν τοῦ δύνασθαι καλῶς καὶ ἐλευθέρως ἀποθανεῖν: the vb. νομίζω ("I believe," cf. Joseph. *BJ* 2.347; 3.482) sets off accus. with infin. in indir. state. (Smyth §1867): "I believe that this favor has been given by God." The articular infin. τοῦ δύνασθαι ("of being able," cf.

Joseph. *Antiq* 6.295; 13.426; 15.30, 36; 16.102; *BJ* 2.161) patterns with ταύτην... χάριν: "...this favor *of being able* to die well and freely." For ἀποθανεῖν ("to die") cf. Joseph. *BJ* 2.227; 3.313; 5.322; 7.373, 380, 383, 410.

7.325 ὅπερ ἄλλοις οὐκ ἐγένετο παρ' ἐλπίδα κρατηθεῖσιν: the rel. pron. ὅπερ ("a thing which") refers to the prospect of being able to die well and freely alluded to in the preced clause. In what sense had the Zealots' defeat had been "unexpected" (παρ' ἐλπίδα, cf. *BJ* 1.34, 123, 192; 3.183, 316; 4.644, 657; 6.30, 31, 57)? Here Eleazar engages in braggadocio for the sake of his audience (referred to in *BJ* 7.322 as τοὺς ἀνδρωδεστάτους = "most doughty"). Most Zealots, in fact, died horribly at the hands of the Romans (e.g., *BJ* 6.420).

7.326 ἡμῖν δὲ πρόδηλος μέν ἐστιν ἡ γενησομένη μεθ' ἡμέραν ἅλωσις, ἐλευθέρα δὲ ἡ τοῦ γενναίου θανάτου μετὰ τῶν φιλτάτων αἵρεσις: Eleazar develops the idea that a "free choice" (ἐλευθέρα... ἡ... αἵρεσις) of a noble death with one's loved ones was preferable to the "clear capture" (πρόδηλος... ἡ... ἅλωσις) that awaited the besieged at daybreak. The μέν... δέ construction clarifies the distinction between the two alternatives, the one inevitable and base, the other deliberate and noble. Construe ἡμῖν (poss. dat.) with both πρόδηλος... ἅλωσις and ἐλευθέρα... αἵρεσις. The prep. phrase μεθ' ἡμέραν (*BJ* 1.492; 2.29, 170, 254; 3.62, 150, 246; 4.112, 139, 209; 5.31, 67, 274; 6.301) means "by day"—so here, "at daybreak." Cf. δι' ἡμέρας (*BJ* 3.148, 154, 174, 312; 4.517; 5.307) "all day long"; ἐφ' ἡμέραν (*Antiq* 18.93) "sufficient for the day"; καθ' ἡμέραν (*BJ* 1.32, 85, 148; 2.256, 265, 283; 3.177, 288, 431; 4.187, 375, 405; 5.359, 394, 414; 6.100, 177, 202) "day by day"; πρὸς ἡμέραν (*Antiq* 3.261; 17.165) "towards day."

7.326 οὔτε γὰρ τοῦτ' ἀποκωλύειν οἱ πολέμιοι δύνανται πάντως εὐχόμενοι ζῶντας ἡμᾶς παραλαβεῖν: the pron. τοῦτο refers to what Eleazar calls "the free choice" (ἐλευθέρα... ἡ... αἵρεσις) of dying nobly with one's loved ones. The Romans, on the other hand, pray (εὐχόμενοι, *Antiq* 7.357; 11.119; *BJ* 7.374) to capture the besieged alive (ζῶντας, cf. *BJ* 1.589, 655; 2.492; 4.385; 5.33, 517, 518; 6.406; 7.374). Roman commanders and soldiers hoped to become wealthy off the sale of captured prisoners-of-war. For οἱ πολέμιοι ("our enemies") cf. Joseph. *Antiq* 1.305, 330, 339, 374; 3.293, 295, 487; 4.35, 268; 6.343; for πάντως ("fervently") cf. Joseph. *BJ* 1.388, 510, 539; 4.171, 321; 5.34, 400; 6.120, 408; 7.338; for παραλαβεῖν ("capture") cf. Joseph. *Antiq* 5.146, 238; 6.224; 7.296, 345, 355; 8.390; 13.388; 16.92, 97; 17.95, 136; 19.13; 20.93, 153.

7.326 οὔθ' ἡμεῖς ἐκείνους ἔτι νικᾶν μαχόμενοι: the pron. ἐκείνους refers to the Romans. Josephus has omitted for reasons of stylistic economy the finite vb. upon which the complementary infin. νικᾶν depends (cf. δύνανται in the prev clause). Trans. the ptc. μαχόμενοι (Joseph. *Antiq* 7.303; 8.414; 17.276; *Contra Ap* 2.23; *BJ* 3.304; 5.122, 304, 359, 390; 6.77, 80) concessively (Smyth §2060): "*although* we fight."

7.327 ἔδει μὲν γὰρ εὐθὺς ἴσως ἐξ ἀρχῆς...: the infins. that depend on the impers. vb. ἔδει ("it was necessary") are στοχάζεσθαι and γινώσκειν below, not ἀντιποιεῖσθαι (which depends on ἡμῖν... θελήσασι in the ὅτε-clause). For ἐξ ἀρχῆς ("from the beg.") cf. Joseph. *BJ* 1.109; 7.336, 358.

7.327 ὅτε τῆς ἐλευθερίας ἡμῖν ἀντιποιεῖσθαι θελήσασι πάντα καὶ παρ' ἀλλήλων ἀπέβαινε χαλεπὰ καὶ παρὰ τῶν πολεμίων χείρω...: the ὅτε-clause ("when...") interrupts the idea posed by the mn. sentence whose verbal struct. is ἔδει... στοχάζεσθαι καὶ γινώσκειν ("it was necessary... to take aim at and know"). The 3 pers. sing. impers. vb. ἀπέβαινε ("it happened," cf. Joseph. *Antiq* 1.163; 16.304) resembles Lat. *evenit*: "when all manner of difficulties *were happening* to us who had wished [θελήσασι]..." The infin. ἀντιποιεῖσθαι ("to contend," cf. Joseph. *Antiq* 19.251; *BJ* 2.366; 7.410) patterns with τῆς ἐλευθερίας: "to contend for freedom." Eleazar admits that the Jews had experienced difficulties amongst themselves (παρ' ἀλλήλων), yet worse (χείρω) difficulties had befallen them from their enemies.

7.327 τῆς τοῦ θεοῦ γνώμης στοχάζεσθαι καὶ γινώσκειν, ὅτι τὸ πάλαι φίλον αὐτῷ φῦλον Ἰουδαίων κατέγνωστο: the vb. στοχάζομαι means to take aim at something (+ obj. gen.). The stem of the infin. στοχάζεσθαι ("to take aim at τινος") is στόχος ("target"). Cf. ἄλλου στοχαζόμενος ἔτυχε τούτου (Antiph. 2.1.4). Josephus presents Eleazar as a kind of desperado whose thinking is hopelessly defeatist: had the Jews "taken aim" at God's pur. (τῆς τοῦ Θεοῦ γνώμης) at the very beg. they would have discovered that their race, once "dear to God" (φίλον αὐτῷ), had been "condemned" (κατέγνωστο = plupf. indic. pass. of καταγιγνώσκω).

7.328 μένων γὰρ εὐμενὴς ἢ μετρίως γοῦν ἀπηχθημένος: trans. the ptcs. conditionally (Smyth §2060): "for *if* he [God] were remaining kindly or, at any rate, were but lightly incensed..." For εὐμενής ("kindly") cf. Joseph. *Antiq* 1.225, 227, 230, 273; 2.162; 3.84; 4.122, 180, 292, 318; 6.20, 304, 305; 9.200; 16.55, 353; 19.345; for ἀπηχθημένος ("incensed") cf. Joseph. *Antiq* 19.329.

7.328 οὐκ ἂν τοσούτων μὲν ἀνθρώπων περιεῖδεν ὄλεθρον: the subj. of the vb. περιεῖδεν is God. The words ἄν... περιεῖδεν constitute the apodosis of a past contr. fact cond. (Smyth §2305): "he would not have overlooked..." For the prob. inflated numbers of persons who perished in the siege of Jerusalem alone cf. Joseph. *BJ* 6.420.

7.328 προήκατο δὲ τὴν ἱερωτάτην αὐτοῦ πόλιν πυρὶ καὶ κατασκαφαῖς πολεμίων: the particle δέ connects this clause to that which precedes so that προήκατο (like περιεῖδεν in the prev clause) continues the past contr. fact cond.: "...nor would he have abandoned [προήκατο] his most holy city to fire and to the demolishments of enemies." Perhaps the word κατασκαφαῖς ("demolishments") is in the plur. because Eleazar conceives of the several acts of destruction to which Jerusalem was subj. (e.g., cf. Joseph. *BJ* 6.440; 7.145).

7.329 ἡμεῖς δ' ἄρα καὶ μόνοι τοῦ παντὸς Ἰουδαίων γένους ἠλπίσαμεν περιέσεσθαι τὴν ἐλευθερίαν φυλάξαντες...;: in Attic usage the particle ἄρα functions much like οὖν ("then," "therefore"); the same particle can intensify questions, e.g., τίς ἄρα ῥύσεται; = "who then is there to save?" (Aesch. *Sept. contra Theb.* 93). The infin. περιέσεσθαι (fut. mid. infin. of περίειμι) has the same subj. as that of the mn. vb. ἠλπίσαμεν: "did we expect that *we would survive*...?" Trans. the circumst. ptc. φυλάξαντες as though it were a conditional clause (Smyth §2060): "...*if* we had guarded our freedom." For περιέσεσθαι cf. Joseph. *Antiq* 1.185; 4.96; 9.60, 189; for φυλάξαντες cf. Joseph. *Antiq* 1.130; 4.193; 16.49; *BJ* 7.335.

7.329 ὥσπερ ἀναμάρτητοι πρὸς τὸν θεὸν γενόμενοι καὶ μηδεμιᾶς μετασχόντες παρανομίας...;: the particle ὥσπερ ("as though") denotes that the action of the mn. vb. is compared with an assumed case (Smyth §2097): "*as though* we had been faultless before God..." The aor. act. ptc. μετασχόντες (from μετέχω) patterns with μηδεμιᾶς... παρανομίας (obj. gen.): "...as having shared in *no transgression.*" For πρὸς τὸν θεόν ("towards God") cf. Joseph. *BJ* 7.267.

7.329 οἳ καὶ τοὺς ἄλλους ἐδιδάξαμεν;: the rel. pron. οἵ refers to the subj. of the finite vb. ἠλπίσαμεν and continues the idea stated in the prev clause: "we... *who* had taught the others [to rebel]?" Although framed in the form of a question, Eleazar reveals in this admission that Zealots were *not* "faultless before God" and that they *had* partaken of all manner of "lawlessness" in times past. The defeatist attitude of Eleazar remains unabated, a tension that shall be resolved only in group suicide. For ἐδιδάξαμεν ("we taught") cf. Joseph. *Antiq* 14.236.

7.330 τοιγαροῦν ὁρᾶτε, πῶς ἡμᾶς ἐλέγχει μάταια προσδοκήσαντας κρείττονα τῶν ἐλπίδων τὴν ἐν τοῖς δεινοῖς ἀνάγκην ἐπαγαγών: the adv. τοιγαροῦν ("therefore") occurs 28 times in the Josephan corpus. The clause marker πῶς ("how") demarcates a subordinate clause in indir. quest., prim. seq.: "therefore, consider *how* he chastises us." The ptc. προσδοκήσαντας mods. the pers. pron. ἡμᾶς: "we... [who] *awaited* vanities." The compar. adj. κρείττονα is in the accus. sing. (not neut. plur.), so mods. τὴν... ἀνάγκην, not μάταια: "having brought on [ἐπαγαγών] the necessity in dire cir.s [that was] *more powerful* than our hopes." Eleazar as much admits that he and the Zealots had been self-deceived by their earlier victories—or rather, that God had brought the destructive self-deception upon the Zealots. For ὁρᾶτε ("consider") cf. Joseph. *Antiq* 6.66; 19.80; for ἐλέγχει ("he chastises") cf. Joseph. *Antiq* 4.216; *Contra Ap* 1.73; for ἐπαγαγών ("having brought on") cf. Joseph. *Antiq* 18.277; 19.111; *Contra Ap* 1.275; *BJ* 1.19; 5.39.

7.331 οὐδὲ γὰρ ἡ τοῦ φρουρίου φύσις ἀνάλωτος οὖσα πρὸς σωτηρίαν ὠφέληκεν...: Josephus uses the word ἡ φύσις ("nature") to describe the eastern approach to Masada, impassable "on account of its nature" (διὰ τὴν φύσιν, *BJ* 7.293); here the "nature" of the entire fort, impregnable though it had been (ἀνάλωτος οὖσα), had not resulted in the Zealots' safety—another telling admission on Eleazar's part. For τὸ φρούριον ("fort") applied to Masada cf. Joseph. *BJ* 7.252, 253, 276, 277, 279, 285, 294, 297, 300, 335, 407.

7.331 ἀλλὰ καὶ τροφῆς ἀφθονίαν καὶ πλῆθος ὅπλων καὶ τὴν ἄλλην ἔχοντες παρασκευὴν περιττεύουσαν...: trans. the pres. act. ptc. ἔχοντες concessively (Smyth §2060): *"though we had..."* No amount of food, weaponry, or "equipage" (cf. ἀπὸ τῆς παρασκευῆς, *BJ* 7.297) could reverse the disastrous outcome at Masada since God, as Eleazar admits, was on the Romans' side. The clause looks back to the plentitude of food stuffs and weaponry at Masada that Josephus describes in *BJ* 7.299. For ἀφθονία ("plentitude") cf. Joseph. *BJ* 1.299, 304; 3.505; 5.8, 520; 7.278, 430; for πλῆθος ὅπλων ("throng of arms") cf. Joseph. *Antiq* 13.47; *BJ* 7.299.

7.331 ὑπ' αὐτοῦ περιφανῶς τοῦ θεοῦ τὴν ἐλπίδα τῆς σωτηρίας ἀφῃρήμεθα: it was "manifestly" the case (περιφανῶς, cf. *Antiq* 5.259; 15.236; *Contra Ap* 1.252) that the Zealots had been deprived by God of any hope of safety. For the vb. ἀφαιρέω ("to take from") in the mid./pass. voice, cf. Joseph. *Antiq* 8.399; 15.159, 187; 16.170, 269, 293; 18.93; 19.45; *BJ* 1.588; 3.53; 4.50, 490; 5.267; for the phrase τὴν ἐλπίδα τῆς σωτηρίας ("the hope of safety") cf. Joseph. *Antiq* 1.327; 15.153.

7.332 τὸ γὰρ πῦρ εἰς τοὺς πολεμίους φερόμενον οὐκ αὐτομάτως ἐπὶ τὸ κατασκευασθὲν τεῖχος ὑφ' ἡμῶν ἀνέστρεψεν: on the occasion to which Eleazar alludes (cf. *BJ* 7.317–18) the wind had shifted "as if by divine providence" (καθάπερ ἐκ δαιμονίου προνοίας, 7.318; cf. θύελλα δαιμόνιος, *BJ* 4.76 for another disastrous weather change). The words οὐκ αὐτομάτως ("not of its own accord," cf. Joseph. *BJ* 1.378; 3.386; 5.292; 6.293, 295) repres. another admission on Eleazar's part that God, not mere happenstance, supported the Romans and opposed the Zealots. The "wall" (τὸ...

τεῖχος) to which Eleazar refers (cf. *BJ* 7.286–87) was 12 cubits high and 8 cubits wide. For εἰς τοὺς πολεμίους ("against the enemies") cf. Joseph. *Antiq* 5.300; 6.195; 8.414; 13.161; *BJ* 1.261; 3.484, 487; 4.48; 6.44, 181, 273; for ἀνέστρεψεν ("it turned back") cf. Joseph. *BJ* 1.89, 658.

7.332 ἀλλ' ἔστι ταῦτα χόλος πολλῶν ἀδικημάτων, ἃ μανέντες εἰς τοὺς ὁμοφύλους ἐτολμήσαμεν: the pron. ταῦτα ("these things") refers to the content of the prev clause. The "wrath at many injustices" (χόλος πολλῶν ἀδικημάτων) refers to God's wrath toward the same; cf. χόλον... θεῖον, Joseph. *Antiq* 2.292; χόλος τοῦ θεου, *Antiq* 6.16; τὸν τοῦ θεοῦ χόλον, *Antiq* 9.249; χόλον τῶν θεῶν, *Contra Ap* 1.236; θεοῦ χόλον, *BJ* 7.34. The rel. clause ἃ μανέντες εἰς τοὺς ὁμοφύλους ἐτολμήσαμεν ("which we madly dared [to inflict] against our countrymen") may refer to the rabid infighting that prevailed among the Zealot factions in Jerusalem (cf. e.g. Joseph. *BJ* 5.1–11). For μανέντες ("madly") cf. Joseph. *Antiq* 5.108; *BJ* 2.395; for εἰς τοὺς ὁμοφύλους ("against the countrymen") cf. Joseph. *BJ* 2.483; for ἐτολμήσαμεν ("we dared") cf. Joseph. *Antiq* 13.198.

7.333 ὑπὲρ ὧν μὴ τοῖς ἐχθίστοις Ῥωμαίοις δίκας ἀλλὰ τῷ θεῷ δι' ἡμῶν αὐτῶν ὑπόσχωμεν: the anteced. of the rel. pron. ὧν is ταῦτα and ἃ in the two preced clauses. For the idiom ὑπέχειν δίκην [τινος] ("to have to give an account of a thing, or suffer a penalty," LSJ II.3) cf. espec. δίκην ὑπόσχες αἵματος... Εὐμενίσι (Eur. *Orest.* 1649). Also, Plato *Laws* 872c; Eur. *Elect.* 1318; Dem. 19.95; Soph. *Oed.* 552; Eur. *Hec.* 1253; Plato *Phaed.* 99a; Thuc. 3.53. Trans. the prepos. phrase δι' ἡμῶν αὐτῶν (cf. παρ' ἡμῶν αὐτῶν, *BJ* 7.380) as "through the act of our own hands." The vb. ὑπόσχωμεν ("let us pay") represents the hortatory subjunct. (Smyth §1797).

7.333 αὗται δέ εἰσιν ἐκείνων μετριώτεραι: the demonst. pron. αὗται refers to the "penalties" (δίκας, prev clause) that Eleazar admits the Zealots should pay to God for their crimes rather than to the hateful Romans. The pron. ἐκείνων represents the gen. of comparison (Smyth §1069c; 1431): "for these [αὗται = the penalties to God] shall be more tolerable than those [ἐκείνων = penalties to the Romans]."

7.334 θνησκέτωσαν γὰρ γυναῖκες ἀνύβριστοι καὶ παῖδες δουλείας ἀπείρατοι: better the women and children should die (cf. ἀποθνησκέτωσαν, Athanasius *Hom. in Sanct. Patr.* Vol. 28 pg. 1069) than experience the indignities of sexual molestation and slavery. For the adj. ἀνύβριστοι ("not insulted") cf. Joseph. *Antiq* 1.208, 209; 17.309; *Vita* 80, 259; for ἀπείρατοι ("unacquainted with τινος") cf. *BJ* 3.63, 307; 5.365; 7.262.

7.334 μετὰ δ' αὐτοὺς ἡμεῖς εὐγενῆ χάριν ἀλλήλοις παράσχωμεν καλὸν ἐντάφιον τὴν ἐλευθερίαν φυλάξαντες: the pron. αὐτούς refers to the afore-mentioned women and children. "Generous service" (εὐγενῆ χάριν) is a euphemism for death. An ἐντάφιον is the "shroud, winding-sheet" used in burial (LSJ II.1); Josephus' "noble shroud" (καλὸν ἐντάφιον) possibly recalls the identical phrase in Diod. Sic. 14.8.5; 20.78.3; Heliod. *Aeth.* 1.8.3; Isocr. 6.45; Procop. 1.24.37, or even κάλλιστον ἐντάφιον ἕξουσι τὸν ὑπὲρ τῆς πατρίδος θάνατον (Polyb. 15.10.3). For the phrase τὴν ἐλευθερίαν φυλάξαντες cf. Joseph. *BJ* 7.329; for παράσχωμεν ("let us render") cf. App. *Lib.* 370.7; Isocr. 8.20; Plut. *De Facie* 937D.

7.335 πρότερον δὲ καὶ τὰ χρήματα καὶ τὸ φρούριον πυρὶ διαφθείρωμεν·: as an adv. πρότερον means "before, earlier" (LSJ IV). Eleazar's proposal that the Zealots destroy personal possessions and the fort "by fire" (πυρί, cf. Joseph. *BJ* 7.355, 373) would be fulfilled in part by the end of the account (cf. Joseph. *BJ* 7.397). For τὰ χρήματα ("personal possessions") cf. Joseph. *BJ*. 1.220, 524; 2.404, 605, 606; 6.359; for τὸ φρούριον ("fort") applied to Masada cf. *BJ* 7.331 above; for διαφθείρωμεν ("let us destroy") cf. Joseph. *Contra Ap* 2.209.

7.335 λυπηθήσονται γὰρ Ῥωμαῖοι, σαφῶς οἶδα, μήτε τῶν ἡμετέρων σωμάτων κρατήσαντες καὶ τοῦ κέρδους ἁμαρτόντες: for λυπηθήσονται ("they will be grieved") cf. LXX Tobit 13:16; Is 19.10; for σαφῶς οἶδα ("well I know") cf. Aeschines *De Fals. Leg.*

44; *Frag.* 35; Dem. *Olynth.* 3.17; Gorg. *Frag.* 11a; Philo *De Abrah.* 204; Xen. *Mem.* 4.3.15; *Ana.* 2.5.4. Trans. the aor. ptc. κρατήσαντες and pres. act. ptc. ἁμαρτόντες conditionally (Smyth §2060): "*if* they do not *gain control* [μήτε... κρατήσαντες] over our bodies"; and "*if* they *miss out on* [ἁμαρτόντες] gain." Τὰ σώματα ("bodies") occurs freq as a tech. expression for slaves (LSJ II.2); here τὸ κέρδος ("gain," cf. *BJ* 2.63, 141, 305, 346, 581, 587, 605; 4.102; 5.311, 555, 561; 6.324, 432; 7.87) refers to the wealth the Romans hope to acrue by reducing the besieged to slavery.

7.336 τὰς τροφὰς μόνας ἐάσωμεν·: the only thing the besieged should spare was the food supply (τὰς τροφάς, cf. Joseph. *Antiq* 1.106; 4.137; 15.309, 310, 312; 17.13; *BJ* 5.356, 430), the reason for which is provided in the next clause. For ἐάσωμεν ("let us spare") cf. Dem. *De Chers.* 50; *Phil.* 4.26; *Pro Meg.* 5; *Adv. Lept.* 60; Plut. *Ar.* 13.4; *Art.* 15.7; Soph. *Phil.* 826.

7.336 αὗται γὰρ ἡμῖν τεθνηκόσι μαρτυρήσουσιν ὅτι μὴ κατ' ἔνδειαν ἐκρατήθημεν: the demonst. pron. αὗται ("these") refers to τὰς τροφὰς μόνας in the preced clause. Trans. the pf. act. ptc. τεθνηκόσι (from θνήσκω) temporally (Smyth §2060): "to us *[when] we have died.*" The full food lockers atop Masada would bear eloquent witness that the besieged had not died "by hunger" (κατ' ἔνδειαν); nevertheless, hunger (ἡ ἔνδεια) played a role at several critical junctures during the revolt, e.g., *BJ* 1.631, 662; 2.432, 590; 3.181, 184, 188; 4.53; 5.5, 344, 427, 549; 6.196, 367, 419.

7.336 ἀλλ' ὥσπερ ἐξ ἀρχῆς διέγνωμεν, θάνατον ἑλόμενοι πρὸ δουλείας: construe the particle ὥσπερ with the 2 aor. ptc. ἑλόμενοι, not with διέγνωμεν (2 aor. indic. of διαγιγνώσκω): "but that we made our decision from the beg. as though [ὥσπερ] we had preferred death to slavery." During the siege of Jerusalem the Zealots had preferred death "to slavery" (πρὸ δουλείας, Joseph. *BJ* 5.458), by which they meant Titus' clemency. For ἐξ ἀρχῆς ("from the beg.") cf. Joseph. *BJ* 1.109; 7.327, 358; for ἑλόμενοι ("preferred") cf. Joseph. *Antiq* 4.222; 16.37; *Contra Ap* 2.172; *BJ* 7.324, 395.

BJ 7.337–348:

7.337 Ταῦτα 'Ελεάζαρος ἔλεγεν: the demontr. pron. ταῦτα ("these things") refers to the initial portion of Eleazar's speech (*BJ* 7.323-336). The brief pause (*BJ* 7.337-340) allows Josephus to mention the varied reaction Eleazar's arguments received by those who first heard the speech.

7.337 οὐ μὴν κατ' αὐτὸ ταῖς γνώμαις προσέπιπτε τῶν παρόντων: the subj. of the compound vb. προσέπιπτε is ταῦτα: "these [arguments = ταῦτα] did not strike the thoughts of those pres. in the same way." The compound vb. προσέπιπτε (προσπίπτω = to "fall upon, strike against" τινι, LSJ I.1) patterns with ταῖς γνώμαις in the dat. case (Smyth §1545). Cf. ἐμβλέψας αὐτῷ = "having looked *at him*" (Plato *Charm*. 162d); ἐλπίδας ἐμποιεῖν ἀνθρώποις = "to create expectations *in people*" (Xen. *Cyr*. 1.6.19); αὐτοῖς ἐπέπεσε τὸ Ἑλληνικόν = "the Greek force fell upon *them*" (Xen. *Ana*. 4.1.10). For προσέπιπτε ("struck against") cf. Joseph. *Antiq* 16.200; 20.113.

7.337 ἀλλ' οἱ μὲν ἔσπευδον ὑπακούειν καὶ μόνον οὐχ ἡδονῆς ἐνεπίμπλαντο καλὸν εἶναι τὸν θάνατον νομίζοντες: the phrase οἱ μέν represents those eager to comply with the import of Elezar's speech, to be constrasted with τοὺς δ' in the following clause (*BJ* 7.338) who were more reluctant. The idiom μόνον οὐ means "well nigh," or "all but"; the ptc. νομίζοντες (cf. Joseph. *BJ* 2.152; 7.50, 61, 64, 191, 271, 389, 394) sets off accus. with infin. in indir. state. (Smyth 1867): "*supposing* that the death was noble." For ἔσπευδον ("they were eager") cf. Joseph. *BJ* 7.69, 100.

7.338 τοὺς δ' αὐτῶν μαλακωτέρους γυναικῶν καὶ γενεᾶς οἶκτος εἰσῄει: for the contr. between τοὺς δ' here and οἱ μέν in *BJ* 7.337 cf. preced note. Construe the compar. adj. μαλακωτέρους with αὐτῶν (gen. of comp.) "more gentle *than them*"—i.e., the ones featured in *BJ* 7.337 who were eager to comply with Eleazar's proposal. Further, οἶκτος ("pity") patterns oft with the obj. gen. (Smyth §1331): "pity *for* wives and family." For the expression γυναικῶν καὶ γενεᾶς οἶκτος ("pity for wives and family") cf. οἶκτος... τέκνων καὶ γυναικῶν (*BJ* 2.400); ὁ τῶν ὀδυρομένων...

οἶκτος (BJ 3.203); οἶκτος πολιᾶς ἢ νηπίων (BJ 5.433); οἶκτος... τῶν ἀνδρῶν (BJ 6.182); for the vb. εἰσῄει ("entered into") cf. BJ 1.58, 438; 2.198, 310, 496; 3.329, 394; 4.31, 116; 5.236, 324; 6.89, 183, 203.

7.338 πάντως δὲ καὶ τῆς ἑαυτῶν προδήλου τελευτῆς εἰς ἀλλήλους ἀποβλέποντες τοῖς δακρύοις τὸ μὴ βουλόμενον τῆς γνώμης ἐσήμαινον: the subj. of the vb. ἐσήμαινον ("they kept signalling," cf. Joseph. Antiq 9.11) are those softer-hearted ones featured in the preced clause. Trans. the phrase τῆς ἑαυτῶν προδήλου τελευτῆς as an obj. gen. with τὸ μὴ βουλόμενον τῆς γνώμης: "...the unwillingness of their resolve *for* their own quite evident end." Here καί is intensive (Smyth §2881), not connective. The phrase εἰς ἀλλήλους ἀποβλέποντες indicates that some of Eleazar's hearers looked sadly away (ἀποβλέποντες) from the speaker. For ἀποβλέποντες ("looking away") cf. Joseph. Antiq 1.72; 8.80; 12.84; Vita 232.

7.339 τούτους ἰδὼν Ἐλεάζαρος ἀποδειλιῶντας καὶ πρὸς τὸ μέγεθος τοῦ βουλεύματος τὰς ψυχὰς ὑποκλωμένους...: the aor. act. ptc. ἰδών sets off an accus. with ptc. after a vb. of perception (ACP, cf. Smyth §2110): "and *when he saw* that these [men] were playing the coward... and breaking down..." For the pres. act. ptc. ἀποδειλιῶμτας ("playing the coward") cf. Plut. Solon 30.4; Crass. 19.7; Caes. 19.3; Polyb. 1.40.1; the pres. act. ptc. ὑποκλωμένους ("breaking down") occurs nowhere else. Τὰς ψυχάς represents an accus. resp. with a body part (Smyth §1601.a): "and breaking down *with resp. to* their spirits..." For the construction cf. ὁ ἄνθρωπος τὸν δάκτυλον ἀλγεῖ = "the man has a pain *in his finger*" (Plato Rep. 462d); τυφλὸς τά τ' ὦτα τόν τε νοῦν τά τ' ὄμματ' εἶ = "you are blind *in ears, and mind, and eyes*" (Soph. Oed. 371); πόδας ὠκὺς Ἀχιλλεύς = "Achilles swift *with resp. to* his feet" (Hom. Il. 1.58, 84, 148, 215, 364, 489, etc.).

7.339 ἔδεισε, μή ποτε καὶ τοὺς ἐρρωμένως τῶν λόγων ἀκούσαντας αὐτοὶ συνεκθηλύνωσι ποτνιώμενοι καὶ δακρύοντες: the vb. ἔδεισε sets off a fear clause (Smyth §2221), the depending vb. of which is συνεκθηλύνωσι ("they unman"). Josephus' casting of the latter vb. into the subjunct. mood indicates that the fear clause is vivid, whereas one would expect that because the mn. vb. ἔδεισε occurs in the aor.—that is, in a sec. tense—the depending vb. ought by the normal rule to occur in the optv. (Smyth §2226). For the vb. συνεκθηλύνωσι ("they unman") cf. τῆς ψυχῆς... τεθηλυσμένης (Joseph. *Antiq* 4.291); ἐθηλύνετο (*BJ* 1.59); θηλύνοιεν (*BJ* 3.263); and ἐνεθηλυπάθουν (*BJ* 4.561). The ptcs. ποτνιώμενοι ("crying aloud") and δακρύοντες ("weeping") modify the pusilanimous subjs. of the vb. συνεκθηλύνωσι: "lest they [by] *crying aloud* and *weeping* become effeminate..." For ποτνιώμενοι (from ποτνιάομαι: "cry aloud in horror or indignation," LSJ I.1) cf. Euseb. *Hist. Eccles.* 4.69.2; Eust. *De Capt. Thess.* pg. 38 line 8; Chryst. *in Psalm.* 101–107 [sp.] vol. 55 pg. 667; Joseph. *Antiq* 19.141; Philo *De Ebr.* 224; *De Abr.* 6; for δακρύοντες cf. Joseph. *Antiq* 2.159; 4.133, 324; *Vita* 210; *BJ* 7.392.

7.340 οὔκουν ἀνῆκε τὴν παρακέλευσιν...: the adv. οὔκουν means "not therefore," "so not" (Lat. *non igitur*). For the vb. ἀνῆκε ("he slackened") cf. Joseph. *BJ* 6.413; 7.288, 430; for τὴν παρακέλευσιν ("the exhortation") cf. Joseph. *Antiq* 5.116. The less-than-enthusiastic response of some of Eleazar's listeners fired the speaker to an even more impassioned rhetoric.

7.340 αὐτὸν ἐπεγείρας καὶ πολλοῦ λήμματος πλήρης γενόμενος λαμπροτέροις ἐνεχείρει λόγοις περὶ ψυχῆς ἀθανασίας: for the aor. act. ptc. ἐπεγείρας ("having roused") cf. Anax. *Test.* Frag. 1; Diog. Laert. *Vit. Phil.* 2.6; Hippol. *Refut.* 5.16; Luc. *Symp.* 32; *Timon* 36; Plut. *Brut.* 1.3. Some mss. read πολλοῦ λήματος πλήρης ("full of much profit"). However, the better reading is πολλοῦ λήμματος πλήρης ("full of much zeal"). One may compare this speech at the close of the war to that of king Herod Agrippa II at the beginning of the war (*BJ* 2.345–401; cf. Stern 1987, 75–76); also, Eleazar's speech in favor of suicide ought to be weighed against Josephus' arguments against the same in *BJ* 3.362–82 (for which see Ladouceur 1981, 250). For the vb. ἐνεχείρει ("he undertook [a speech]") cf. Joseph. *BJ* 7.304. By dropping the well-known phrase "immortality of the soul" Josephus lets the reader understand that Eleazar engages in commonplaces drawn from the Greek tradition.

7.341 μέγα τε σχετλιάσας καὶ τοῖς δακρύουσιν ἀτενὲς ἐμβλέψας...: μέγα ("greatly") and ἀτενές ("fixedly") repres. adv. accus. (Smyth §1607). For the aor. act. ptc. σχετλιάσας ("having inveighed bitterly") cf. Joseph. *Antiq* 5.170; *BJ* 5.325. For the aor. act. ptc. ἐμβλέψας ("having gazed upon") as a characteristic pose of Jesus cf. Mt 19:26; Mk 10:21, 27; Lk 20:17; Jn 1:43. It was not only Eleazar's rhetorically ornate words that held the audience transfixed, but the speaker's posture of indignation and his piercing gaze which must have left an impression.

7.341 "ἦ πλεῖστον," εἶπεν, "ἐψεύσθην νομίζων ἀνδράσιν ἀγαθοῖς τῶν ὑπὲρ τῆς ἐλευθερίας ἀγώνων συναρεῖσθαι, ζῆν καλῶς ἢ τεθνάναι διεγνωκόσιν: the particle ἦ ("verily"), oft strengthened by other particles (here πλεῖστον), confirms an assertion: "*verily* was I *quite* deceived in supposing..." The pres. act. ptc. νομίζων ("supposing") sets off indir. state.: "*supposing* that I would take part [συναρεῖσθαι] in the struggles for freedom with good men..." The word συναρεῖσθαι represents the fut. act. infin. of συναίρω; other mss. feature the variants συναιρεῖσθαι (pres. mid. infin. of συναιρέω) or συναίρεσθαι (pres. mid. infin. of συναίρω). The pf. act. ptc. διεγνωκόσιν (from διαγιγνώσκω) patterns with ἀνδράσιν ἀγαθοῖς: "with good men... *who have decided* to live bravely or die." The orator's mockery of the fear of death and the hearers' pusillanimity are additional commonplaces that Eleazar's speech betrays (so Luz 1983, 32–33).

7.342 ὑμεῖς δὲ ἦτε τῶν τυχόντων οὐδὲν εἰς ἀρετὴν οὐδ᾽ εὐτολμίαν διαφέροντες: the adv. accus. οὐδέν represents Litotes (Smyth §3032): "not at all different." Oft the vb. διαφέρω means "to be different from a person" (LSJ III.4)—so τῶν τυχόντων here: "...from persons of happenstance," i.e., commoners (= οἱ τύχοντες). For εἰς ἀρετήν ("for valor") cf. Joseph. *Antiq* 18.264; for εὐτολμίαν ("daring") cf. Joseph. *Antiq* 4.298; 6.250; *BJ* 3.25, 232; 5.324; 7.284.

7.342 οἵ γε καὶ τὸν ἐπὶ μεγίστων ἀπαλλαγῇ κακῶν φοβεῖσθε θάνατον...: note the four interlocked pairs (Synchesis): 1) οἵ γε... φοβεῖσθε; 2) τὸν... θάνατον; 3) ἐπί... ἀπαλλαγῇ; 4) μεγίστων... κακῶν. The prep. phrase ἐπί... ἀπαλλαγῇ means "for a departure from something [gen.]." The theme for the remainder of this lengthy speech shall be that death represents the soul's departure from all kinds of troubles, particularly troubles connected to the body. It is unclear whether suicide presented a legitimate way out for Jews at this time (Huntsman 1996-97, 372).

7.342 δέον ὑπὲρ τούτου μήτε μελλῆσαι μήτε σύμβουλον ἀναμεῖναι: Josephus has suppressed the vb. ἐστιν upon which the neut. ptc. δέον (from δέομαι) depends. The structure of the sentence is quite loose: "you ought neither to [+ infin.]... nor to [+ infin.]..." The demonst. pron. τούτου refers to τὸν... θάνατον in the prev clause. That hearers need not wait for the promptings of an "advisor" (σύμβουλον) to end one's life is paralleled in Stoic literature (e.g., Seneca *Ep.* 58.34) which likewise exhorts hearers to assuage one's fears and submit to a noble suicide (Ladouceur 1981, 253-255; Luz 1983, 29).

7.343 πάλαι γὰρ εὐθὺς ἀπὸ τῆς πρώτης αἰσθήσεως...: ordinarily the noun ἡ αἴσθησις means "sense-perception, sensation" (LSJ I.1); here the phrase ἀπὸ τῆς πρώτης αἰσθήσεως seems to mean "from our first inkling...," or "from the dawn of intelligence." Very close is ἀπὸ τῆς πρώτης εὐθὺς αἰσθήσεως (Joseph. *Contra Ap* 2.178). Perhaps Josephus borrowed the phrase from a Platonic dialogue. Cf. δι' αἰσθήσεως (Plato *Phaed.* 79c; *Theaet.* 161d; *Soph.* 248a; 264a); περὶ αἰσθήσεως (Plato *Theaet.* 182d; *Laws* 902c); ἐν τῇ συνάψει αἰσθήσεως (*Theaet.* 195d); ὑπὸ τῆς αἰσθήσεως (*Rep.* 523b); μετ' αἰσθήσεως (*Rep.* 546b; *Tim.* 28a; 28c; 52a). In Platonism, the soul regards the body as an instrument of perception (Luz 1983, 28 n. 17).

7.343 παιδεύοντες ἡμᾶς οἱ πάτριοι καὶ θεῖοι λόγοι διετέλουν ἔργοις τε καὶ φρονήμασι τῶν ἡμετέρων προγόνων αὐτοὺς βεβαιούντων: for the suppl. ptc. παιδεύοντες with the finite vb. διετέλουν (*"continuing* to teach us," cf. Smyth §2098) cf. ἄρξομαι... λέγων = "I will begin my speech" (Stobaeus *Anth.* 1.9.15); παύσω τοῦτο γιγνόμενον = "I will put a stop to this happening" (Plato *Gorg.* 523c); παῦσαι λέγουσα = "stop talking" (Eur. *Hipp.* 706). The pron. αὐτούς refers to λόγοι ("doctrines"). It may seem that Greco-Roman thinking inspired this speech, not Jewish thinking (so Luz 1983, 36; Ladouceur 1987, 98). On the other hand, there was the claim—widespread in the Diaspora—that Judaism was in some sense a "philosophy," and so something which "cultivated pagans could appreciate and admire" (Cohen 1987, 44; cf. Philo *de Vita Mos.* 2.12–44). Josephus must have crafted the speech with the philosophically astute audiences of Flavian Rome in mind (Ladouceur 1981, 256–257). Luz (1983, 37 n. 53) denies the possibility that Eccl 4:1–5; 9:4 reflects a similar pessimism in Judaism.

7.343 ὅτι συμφορὰ τὸ ζῆν ἐστιν ἀνθρώποις, οὐχὶ θάνατος: the noun ἡ συμφορά commonly means "event, circumstance, chance, hap" (LSJ II.1, from συμφέρω LSJ A.III.4 and B.III), then "mishap, misfortune" (LSJ II.2), the mng. it has here. For τὸ ζῆν ("living") cf. Joseph. *BJ* 1.44, 85, 520, 572; 2.109; 3.370, 438; 4.604; 6.350; 7.358; for θάνατος cf. Joseph. *BJ* 1.98, 138, 546; 2.442; 3.372; 4.365, 383; 5.315; 7.182, 358. The following fragment attributed to Euripides seems pertinent to this portion of Eleazar's speech: Τίς οἶδεν, εἰ τὸ ζῆν μέν ἐστι κατθανεῖν, τὸ κατθανεῖν δὲ ζῆν κάτω νομίζεται (Dindorf *Frag.* 634). Luz (1983, 34–35) attempts to connect the idea to Plato, the Academy, and Crantor of Soli.

7.344 οὗτος μὲν γὰρ ἐλευθερίαν διδοὺς ψυχαῖς εἰς τὸν οἰκεῖον καὶ καθαρὸν ἀφίησι τόπον ἀπαλλάσσεσθαι πάσης συμφορᾶς ἀπαθεῖς ἐσομένας...: the demonst. pron. οὗτος refers to θάνατος. The vb. ἀπαλλάσσεσθαι (mid.) oft has the sense "to remove, depart from" (LSJ B.II.1); so ἐκ τῆς χώρης (Hdt. 1.61); ἐξ Αἰγύπτου (Hdt. 2.139); ἀπαλλάσσεσθαι τοῦ βίου (Eur. *Hel.* 102; *Hipp.* 356). For the phrase εἰς τὸν οἰκεῖον καὶ καθαρὸν... τόπον ("into its own pure abode") cf. εἰς τὸν οἰκεῖον τόπον, Aristot. *Cael.* 279b.2; *De Gen. Anim.* 737b.29; *Phys.* 215a.17; *Prob.* 915a.22; Chrys. *In Act Apost. [hom. 1–55]* vol. 60 pg. 134; Plotinus *Enn.* 3.2.17; 6.3.24. The words πάσης συμφορᾶς repres. the gen. of separ. (Smyth §1392): "...to be free *from every misfortune.*" Again, the Stoics—in addition to Plato—shared this pessimistic view of corporeal life (cf. Seneca *Ep.* 58.26–27; Luz 1983, 30).

7.344 ἕως δ' εἰσιν ἐν σώματι θνητῷ δεδεμέναι καὶ τῶν τούτου κακῶν συναναπίμπλανται, τἀληθέστατον εἰπεῖν, τεθνήκασι: trans. ἕως either as "so long as" or "while" (Smyth §2383.a): "so long as" the souls are "imprisoned" (εἰσιν... δεδεμέναι) in the mortal body and "infected with" (συναναπίμπλανται) its ills, they are "dead" (τεθνήκασι, cf. Joseph. *Antiq* 7.255; 16.351; *BJ* 1.623; 7.361, 372, 373). Cf. Luz (1983) 30–31 nn. 24–27 for additional correspondences to Plato and the consolation literature. The pron. τούτου refers to σώματι θνητῷ: "with *its* [the mortal body's] ills." In general, the thinking here is opposed to that presented in the NT where the believer in Christ shall live, even though he die: ὁ πιστεύων εἰς ἐμὲ κἂν ἀποθάνῃ ζήσεται (Jn 11:25; cf. 5:24). And on the last day "the body shall be raised" (1 Cor 15:35–44).

7.344 κοινωνία γὰρ θείῳ πρὸς θνητὸν ἀπρεπής ἐστι: trans. κοινωνία with πρὸς θνητὸν and ἀπρεπής with θείῳ (Synchesis): "for assoc. with what is mortal ill-befits what is divine." One of Socrate's rivals claims that mortality has a share of immortality (θνητὸν ἀθανασίας μετέχει, Plato *Symp.* 208b); usu., however, the assoc. with the material world should be avoided, e.g., οὐσίας... κοινωνία (Plato *Parm.* 152a); ὀργάνων... βελτίων ἡ κοινωνία (Plato *Hipp. Min.* 374e); ἡ... ἡδονῆς τε καὶ λύπης κοινωνία (Plato *Rep.* 462b); ἡ κοινωνία ἡ κατὰ τὸ σῶμα (Plato *Rep.* 462c). In place of πρὸς θνητόν cf. τὸ θνητόν (Plato *Phaedo* 80a; 106e; *Soph.* 219a; *Symp.* 208a, etc); for θείῳ cf. Plato *Phaedo* 80a,b; 95a; *Polit.* 309c; *Symp.* 206d, etc. Cf. Luz (1983) 31; and Sievers (1998) 31 for Josephus' obvious dependence on multiple sources.

7.345 μέγα μὲν οὖν δύναται ψυχὴ καὶ σώματι συνδεδεμένη·: trans. μέγα as an adv. accus. (Smyth §1607) and καί as intensive: "a soul is *hugely* powerful, *even* [when] it has been tied to a body." Josephus has treated the same idea in *BJ* 7.344 above; so has Plato: τὴν ψυχήν... διαδεδεμένην ἐν τῷ σώματι (*Phaedo* 82e). For μέγα... δύναται cf. Plato *Gorg.* 508a; also μέγα δύνασθαι (Plato *Gorg.* 468e).

7.345 ποιεῖ γὰρ αὐτῆς ὄργανον αἰσθανόμενον...: the pron. αὐτῆς refers to the soul (cf. ψυχή... σώματι συνδεδεμένη, prev phrase). The soul makes the body its so-called "organ of perception" (ὄργανον αἰσθανόμενον). Plato had developed the same doctrine, e.g., ὄργανα δι' ὧν αἰσθάνεται ἡμῶν τὸ αἰσθανόμενον (Plato *Theaet.* 185c); ὅσον αἰσθητικὸν ἐν τῷ σώματι (Plato *Tim.* 70b).

7.345 ...ἀοράτως αὐτὸ κινοῦσα καὶ θνητῆς φύσεως περαιτέρω προάγουσα ταῖς πράξεσιν: the fem. sing. ptcs. κινοῦσα and προάγουσα modify soul (ψυχή), the subj. of the vb. ποιεῖ. The pron. αὐτό refers to the body which serves as the soul's organ of perception (cf. ὄργανον αἰσθανόμενον, preced phrase). For the idea of the soul "moving" the body, cf. ψυχή... κινοῦσα (Plato *Rep.* 524e); for ἀοράτως ("imperceptibly"), cf. Athan. *De Incarn.* 30.4; 42.6; 53.1; Chrys. *in Joannem* vol. 59 pg. 84, 280; Origen *Contra Cels.* 5.1; Philo *De Cherub.* 98; *De Somn.* 1.71, 90, 148; 2.2, 213; for προάγουσα ("leading forward") cf. Plot. *Enn.* 4.8.4; for ταῖς πράξεσιν ("in its actions") cf. Plato *Soph.* 234e; 262a; *Pol.* 258d; *Phile.* 24c; Aristot. *Nich. Eth.* 1104a; 1107a 1108b; 1109a; Plot. *Enn.* 1.3.6; 1.5.10; 1.6.6; 2.4.12. Such phrases never seem to be too far removed from Plato.

7.346 οὐ μὴν ἀλλ' ἐπειδὰν ἀπολυθεῖσα τοῦ καθέλκοντος αὐτὴν βάρους ἐπὶ γῆν καὶ προσκρεμαμένου χῶρον ἀπολάβῃ τὸν οἰκεῖον: trans. οὐ μὴν ἀλλά as "nevertheless" or "notwithstanding." Construe ἐπειδὰν with ἀπολάβῃ (equiv. to the protasis of a pres. gen. cond.): "whenever it [the soul] assumes its proper sphere." The fem. sing. ptc. ἀπολυθεῖσα (referring to the soul) patterns with the phrase τοῦ καθέλκοντος... βάρους... καὶ προσκρεμαμένου (ablatival gen.): "having been released from a weight dragging it down... and attaching itself." For ἀπολυθεῖσα cf. ψυχαί... ἀπολυθεῖσαι (Plato *Phaed.* 81d); for προσκρεμαμένου cf. προσκρεμάμενον (Aristot. *Mech.* 856a); for χῶρον... τὸν οἰκεῖον ("its proper sphere") cf. εἰς τὸν οἰκεῖον καὶ καθαρόν... τόπον ("to its own pure abode") Joseph. *BJ* 7.344 above.

7.346 τότε δὴ μακαρίας ἰσχύος καὶ πανταχόθεν ἀκωλύτου μετέχει δυνάμεως...: released (ἀπολυθεῖσα) from the body, the soul "shares" those qualities which it could not while burdened by carnal encumbrances. The mn. vb. μετέχει patterns with the obj. gens. μακαρίας ἰσχύος and ἀκωλύτου... δυνάμεως: "shares in blessed might... and power untrammelled on every side." Cf. ἁρμονίας μετέχει (Plato *Phaedo* 93d); μετέχει ἐκείνου τοῦ καλοῦ (Plato *Phaedo* 100c); τοῦ ὄντος μετέχει (Plato *Soph.* 256d; 256e); αὐτῆς ἐπιστήμης μετέχει (Plato *Parm.* 134c), etc.

7.346 ἀόρατος μένουσα τοῖς ἀνθρωπίνοις ὄμμασιν ὥσπερ αὐτὸς ὁ θεός: the fem. sing. ptc. μένουσα refers to the soul (cf. ψυχή). For the the soul's "invisibility" cf. ἀοράτως in Joseph. *BJ* 7.345 above and οὐδέ... θεωρεῖται, ἀφανῶς and μὴ βλεπομένη in Joseph. *BJ* 7.347 below. Also Luz (1983) 31 and passages there. For the phrase "God himself" (αὐτὸς ὁ θεός) cf. Plato *Polit.* 269c; *Epin.* 980c; Joseph. *Antiq* 3.190.

7.347 οὐδὲ γὰρ ἕως ἐστὶν ἐν σώματι θεωρεῖται: trans. ἕως as "while" or "so long as" (Smyth §2422). Eleazar has just stated that, in life, souls are "locked up" in the body (ἐν σώματι... δεδεμέναι, Joseph. *BJ* 7.344); now he says that the soul is not beheld while "in the body." For ἐν σώματι ("in the body") cf. Joseph. *BJ* 4.406; 7.344; for θεωρεῖται ("is perceived") cf. Plato *Phaedo* 65e; Aristot. *De Color.* 792a; *Meta.* 1064a; *De Mundo* 395b, 399b; *Oec.* 1343a; Plot. *Enn.* 4.6.2; 5.3.15; 6.4.1; 6.5.8.

7.347 πρόσεισι γὰρ ἀφανῶς καὶ μὴ βλεπομένη πάλιν ἀπαλλάττεται: the vb. πρόσεισι ("comes forward," cf. Joseph. *Antiq* 3.277; 6.50; 8.243, 389; 10.197; 14.349; *BJ* 1.387; 2.138, 152) refers to the birth of a soul into a body; by ἀπαλλάττεται ("departs," Joseph. *Antiq* 8.6; 16.266) Eleazar refers to death or the separ. of a soul from a body (cf. ἀπαλλάσσεσθαι, Joseph. *BJ* 7.344; ἀπαλλαγῇ, Joseph. *BJ* 7.348).

7.347 μίαν μὲν αὐτὴ φύσιν ἔχουσα τὴν ἄφθαρτον...: the pers. pron. αὐτή refers to the soul. The soul's one nature (μίαν... φύσιν) has no admixture; the Pharisees also supposed that every soul in a reincarnated body is "imperishable" (ψυχήν... πᾶσαν... ἄφθαρτον, Joseph. *BJ* 2.163). Cicero holds forth eloquently on the simplicity and unconfounded nature of the soul (*Tusc.* 1.70–71; additional passages in Luz 1983, 32 n. 29).

7.347 αἰτία δὲ σώματι γινομένη μεταβολῆς: imperishable itself, Josephus states that the soul is the body's "cause of change" (αἰτία... μεταβολῆς), a concept that seems to be known in Plato and in the Greek philosophical tradition, e.g., τῆς μεταβολῆς τὴν αἰτίαν (Plato *Laws* 676c); μεταβολῆς τε καὶ κινήσεως... αἰτία (Plato *Laws* 896b); τὴν τῆς μεταβολῆς αἰτίαν (Plato *Laws* 904c); ἡ τῆς μεταβολῆς αἰτία (Plot. *Enn.* 2.1.4).

7.348 ὅτου γὰρ ἂν ψυχὴ προσψαύσῃ, τοῦτο ζῇ καὶ τέθηλεν...: the pron. ὅτου represents the alternative form of οὗτινος (gen. sing. of the indefin. rel. pron. ὅστις, ἥτις, ὅ τι). Sophocles seems to have provided the inspiration for the terminology used here. For προσψαύσῃ ("it seizes hold of") cf. προσψαύσητ' (Soph. *Phil.* 1054) and πρόσψαυσον (Soph. *Oed. Col.* 330); for ζῇ καὶ τέθηλεν ("it lives and flourishes") cf. καὶ ζῶντα καὶ θάλλοντα (Soph. *Trach.* 235).

7.348 ὅτου δ' ἂν ἀπαλλαγῇ, μαρανθὲν ἀποθνήσκει: for ἀπαλλαγῇ ("it abandons" cf. ἀπαλλάσσεσθαι (Joseph. *BJ* 7.344) and ἀπαλλάττεται (Joseph. *BJ* 7.347). Trans. μαρανθὲν ἀποθνήσκει as "it shrivels up and dies." For μαρανθὲν (neut. sing. aor. pass. ptc. of μαραίνω) cf. *Anth. Graec.* 12.234.2; Cyril *De Adorat.* vol. 68 pg.821; Ephraem *Chron.* 7503; Heracl. *Alleg.* 26.16.4; Lycoph. *Alex.* 1127, 1231.

7.348 τοσοῦτον αὐτῇ περίεστιν ἀθανασίας: the pron. αὐτῇ (poss. dat.) refers to the soul. Trans. the vb. περίεστιν with αὐτῇ: "so much is her [the soul's] wealth of immortality." For περίεστιν cf. Joseph. *Antiq* 2.137; 6.237; 15.387; *Vita* 426; *Contra Ap* 2.235; *BJ* 2.396.

BJ 7.349-350:

7.349 ὕπνος δὲ τεκμήριον ὑμῖν ἔστω τῶν λόγων ἐναργέστατον: Josephus' τεκμήριον... ἐναργέστατον ("brightest proof") seems akin to the "vivid proof" (ἐναργές... τὸ τεκμήριον) Ion describes in Plato *Ion* 535c. For ὕπνος ("sleep") cf. Joseph. *BJ* 3.319; for τεκμήριον ("proof") cf. Joseph. *BJ* 1.401; 2.318; 3.50, 123; 4.337, 347; 5.426; 6.328; 7.50, 453.

7.349 ἐν ᾧ ψυχαὶ τοῦ σώματος αὐτὰς μὴ περισπῶντος ἡδίστην μὲν ἔχουσιν ἀνάπαυσιν ἐφ' αὐτῶν γενόμεναι...: the rel. pron. ᾧ refers to ὕπνος; the pers. pron. αὐτάς refers to "souls" (ψυχαί), the dir. obj. of the pres. act. ptc. περισπῶντος. Trans. the gen. abs. τοῦ σώματος... μὴ περισπῶντος concessively (Smyth §2060): "*although* the body does not strip them [the souls] off..." Through sleep souls obtain the "most pleasant" rest (ἡδίστην...

ἀνάπαυσιν; for ἀνάπαυσιν cf. Joseph. *Antiq* 1.29, 33; 3.281; 7.231; *BJ* 1.106; 4.88; 5.454; 7.350). The somnolent state enables souls to "come to themselves" (ἐφ᾽ αὑτῶν γενόμεναι), or to become indep. of the body. The ideas are more Platonic than anything else (so Luz 1983, 39).

7.349 θεῷ δ᾽ ὁμιλοῦσαι κατὰ συγγένειαν πάντη μὲν ἐπιφοιτῶσι, πολλὰ δὲ τῶν ἐσομένων προθεσπίζουσι: for the expression θεῷ... ὁμιλοῦσαι ("holding converse with God") cf. ὁμιλεῖ τῷ θεῷ (*Acta Philip.* 46.9); ὁμιλῶν τῷ θεῷ (Aster. *Frag. in Ps.* 17.30); ὁμιλεῖν τῷ Θεῷ (Basil *De Virg.* MPG 692.20); ὁμιλοῦντος τῷ θεῷ (Euseb. *Hist. Eccles.* 5.1.51), etc. For the dreams by which the soul holds converse with God cf. Cic. *De Div.* 1.64; Luz (1983) 37–38. For the phrase "right of kinship" (κατὰ συγγένειαν) cf. Joseph. *Antiq* 2.94; 3.64; 12.260; *Contra Ap* 2.210. For ἐπιφοιτῶσι ("they [the souls] flit about") cf. Joseph. *Antiq* 2.11; 3.100; 17.43; 18.82, 241, 368; 19.197, 223; for τῶν ἐσομένων ("of the things that will be") cf. Joseph. *Antiq* 1.243; 2.27, 84; 4.36, 213, 303; 6.38, 44; 7.72, 383; 18.218; *Vita* 73; *Contra Ap* 1.233; for προθεσπίζουσι ("they foretell the future") cf. Did. Caec. *Comm. in Zach.* 2.47; 4.177; Nicephor. *Hist. Rom.* vol. 2 pg. 1032; Procop. *Comm. in Isaiam.* pg. 2181; Strabo *Geograph.* 14.5.19.

7.350 τί δὴ δεῖ δεδιέναι θάνατον τὴν ἐν ὕπνῳ γινομένην ἀνάπαυσιν ἀγαπῶντας;: the word δεδιέναι (Joseph. *Antiq* 1.209; 2.116, 308; 3.21; 6.332; 7.213; 9.55; 10.127, 165; 14.172; 19.35; *Vita* 337; *Contra Ap* 2.278; *BJ* 1.611; 4.265; 5.498) represents the 2 pf. infin. act. of δέδια "I fear" (Smyth §703). The pres. act. ptc. ἀγαπῶντας (Joseph. *Antiq* 7.254; *BJ* 1.171) serves as the subj. of the impers. vb. δει: "why ought those who love... to fear death?" Trans. τὴν ἐν ὕπνῳ γινομένην ἀνάπαυσιν as "the repose that happens in sleep." For ἀνάπαυσιν cf. Joseph. *BJ* 7.349 above.

7.350 πῶς δ᾽ οὐκ ἀνόητόν ἐστιν τὴν ἐν τῷ ζῆν ἐλευθερίαν διώκοντας τῆς ἀιδίου φθονεῖν αὐτοῖς;: again, the pres. act. ptc. διώκοντας serves as the subj. of the impers. expression οὐκ ἀνόητόν ἐστιν: "how is it not foolish that those pursuing... begrudge themselves?" Eleazar has characterized sleep as "the freedom in life" (τὴν ἐν τῷ ζῆν ἐλευθερίαν); by such reasoning death represents "the eternal [freedom]" (τῆς ἀιδίου [ἐλευθερίας]). For ἀνόητον ("foolish") cf. Joseph. *Antiq* 2.113, 307; 6.43; 7.185; 10.15; for ἐν τῷ ζῆν ("in life") cf. Joseph. *Antiq* 15.179; 17.152; *BJ* 2.157; for διώκοντας ("pursuing") cf. Joseph. *Antiq* 6.119; 14.358; *BJ* 4.60, 420; 5.389; for φθονεῖν ("to begrudge") cf. Joseph. *Antiq* 4.131, 235; 16.248; *Vita* 230; *Contra Ap* 1.224.

BJ 7.351-357:

7.351 ἔδει μὲν οὖν ἡμᾶς οἴκοθεν πεπαιδευμένους ἄλλοις εἶναι παράδειγμα τῆς πρὸς θάνατον ἑτοιμότητος: the Jews—far from being pusillanimous about death (cf. *BJ* 7.338-339 above)—should be an "example to others" (ἄλλοις... παράδειγμα) in how to die nobly. They had been "educated at home" (οἴκοθεν πεπαιδευμένους) in how to die—a ref., perhaps, to the innate philosophical inclinations of the Jews for which cf. *BJ* 7.343 above. For πεπαιδευμένους ("taught") cf. Joseph. *BJ* 1.479; 5.460; for παράδειγμα ("example") cf. Joseph. *Antiq* 17.103, 249, 313; for ἑτοιμότης ("preparation") cf. Joseph. *Antiq* 6.134; 16.253; *Vita* 120.

7.351 οὐ μὴν ἀλλ' εἰ καὶ τῆς παρὰ τῶν ἀλλοφύλων δεόμεθα πίστεως, βλέψωμεν εἰς Ἰνδοὺς τοὺς σοφίαν ἀσκεῖν ὑπισχνουμένους: trans. the first five words as "truly not, but if indeed..." The words εἰ... δεόμεθα constitute the protasis of a simp. fact. cond. (Smyth §2298). The vb. δεόμεθα (cf. Joseph. *Antiq* 8.54) means to "lack, miss, stand in need of something" + gen. case (LSJ δέω B.I.1)—here an "assurance" (πίστεως, cf. Joseph. *BJ* 1.94, 207; 2.104, 106, 135, 476; 3.6; 4.96, 417; 5.46, 113, 510; 6.297) from foreigners. The vb. βλέψωμεν represents the Horatory subjunct. (Smyth §1797): "*let us look* at the Indians who..." The vb. ὑπισχνέομαι + pres. infin. means "*profess* to do a thing" (LSJ I.2)— here *profess* to "practice wisdom" = σοφίαν ἀσκεῖν; cf. ἀσκ. τέχνην (Hdt. 3.125); ἀσκ. πεντάεθλον (Hdt. 9.33); ἀσκ. παγκράτιον (Plato *Theag.* 128e). For the notion that the Jews were descended from Indian sages, cf. Joseph. *Contra Ap* 1.179. For possible sources Joseph. used cf. Luz (1983) 40-42.

7.352 ἐκεῖνοί τε γὰρ ὄντες ἄνδρες ἀγαθοὶ τὸν μὲν τοῦ ζῆν χρόνον ὥσπερ ἀναγκαίαν τινὰ τῇ φύσει λειτουργίαν ἀκουσίως ὑπομένουσι: the pron. ἐκεῖνοι refers to the Indians. These highly philosophical Indians are "good" (ἀγαθοί)—i.e., brave—in that they do not fear death. Only "unwillingly" (ἀκουσίως, cf. Joseph. *Antiq* 18.17, 246) do they "put up with" (ὑπομένουσι, cf. Joseph. *Antiq* 2.208; 11.45; *Contra Ap* 2.234; *BJ* 2.118, 373; 5.486; 7.382) their time of life (τὸν... τοῦ ζῆν χρόνον, cf. Joseph. *Antiq* 8.387), regarding this as a kind of necessary service due to nature (ἀναγκαίαν τινὰ τῇ φύσει λειτουργίαν, cf. Porph. *Abst*. 4.18).

7.353 σπεύδουσι δὲ τὰς ψυχὰς ἀπολῦσαι τῶν σωμάτων...: cf. σπεύδειν δὲ τὰς ψυχὰς ἀπολῦσαι τῶν σωμάτων (Porph. *Abst*. 4.18). The words τῶν σωμάτων repres. a gen. of separ. (Smyth §1392): "they hasten to release their souls *from* their bodies." For representative gens. of separ. cf. ἐπιστήμη χωριζομένη δικαιοσύνης = "knowledge divorced *from* justice" (Plato *Menex*. 246e); μεταστὰς τῆς 'Αθηναίων ξυμμαχίας = "withdrawing *from* the alliance with the Athenians" (Thuc. 2.67); παύσαντες αὐτὸν τῆς στρατηγίας = "removing him *from* his office of general" (Xen. *Hell*. 6.2.13); εἴργεσθαι τῆς ἀγορᾶς = "to be excluded *from* the forum" (Lys. 6.24). For σπεύδουσι ("they hasten") cf. Joseph. *Antiq* 2.30; 6.39; *BJ* 2.638; for ἀπολῦσαι ("to release") cf. Joseph. *Antiq* 2.311; 6.128; 7.274; 8.380; 9.189, 249; 12.88; 13.190; 14.170 (twice), 175, 223, 304; 20.209. This view of death may draw upon Orphic notions (so Sievers 1998, 27; cf. Plato *Crat*. 400c).

7.353 μηδενὸς αὐτοὺς ἐπείγοντος κακοῦ μηδ' ἐξελαύνοντος πόθῳ τῆς ἀθανάτου διαίτης προλέγουσι μὲν τοῖς ἄλλοις ὅτι μέλλουσιν ἀπιέναι...: trans. the gen. abs. μηδενὸς... ἐπείγοντος κακοῦ μηδ' ἐξελαύνοντος concessively (Smyth §2060): "*although* no calamity impels nor drives them..." The pers. pron. αὐτούς refers to the Indian sages. Trans. πόθῳ (cf. Joseph. *Antiq* 1.8 4.298; 6.11; 7.273; 13.258; 15.77; *Vita* 207; *BJ* 1.513; 4.414, 575; 5.6) as a dat. of means/instr. ("*by* a desire...," cf. Smyth §1507). Πόθος patterns oft with an obj. gen.: "by a desire *for* the immortal mode of life..." The latter expression reaffirms Eleazar's contention that the soul is indeed immortal and so must be released from the body to depart to its own pure abode (cf. εἰς τὸν οἰκεῖον καὶ καθαρὸν... τόπον, Joseph. *BJ* 7.344). The vb. προλέγω means "foretell," and "predict, of an oracle" (LSJ II.1.a, based on Hdt. 1.53; 8.136; Aesch. *Prom.* 1071; Soph. *Oed.* 973; Plato *Euth.* 3c, etc.). The pron. τοῖς ἄλλοις refers to the Indian philosophers' many admirers, some of whom—as we shall see—shall request the sages to convey letters from this life to departed relatives! For μέλλουσιν ἀπιέναι ("they are about to depart") cf. Chrys. *In Joannem* vol. 59 pg. 344; Plato *Phaed.* 85a.

7.353 πάντες αὐτοὺς εὐδαιμονίζοντες πρὸς τοὺς οἰκείους ἕκαστοι διδόασιν ἐπιστολάς: the pron. αὐτούς refers to the Indian sages. The pres. act. ptc. εὐδαιμονίζοντες parallels διδόασιν: "count them blessed and each gives them letters for their relatives." Sometimes the word ἐπιστολαί (in the plur.) means a sing. epistle or letter (τὰ γράμματα; Lat. *litterae*); for this mng. cf. Eur. *Iph. Aul.* 111, 314; Thuc. 1.132; 1 Cor 16:3, etc. For εὐδαιμονίζοντες ("counting [them] blessed") cf. Eustr. *in Arist. Eth. Nich.* pg. 106; Lib. *Or.* 43.20; 46.31; Lucian *Somn.* 12; Philostr. *Vita Ap.* 3.50; Porph. *Abstin.* 4.18; for the phrase πρὸς τοὺς οἰκείους ("for their relatives") cf. Plato *Rep.* 329d, 376c; *Laws* 754b; for the expression διδόασιν ἐπιστολάς ("they offer letters") cf. τὰς ἐπιστολὰς ἀποδίδωσιν (Joseph. *Antiq* 11.168); διδόναι τὰς ἐπιστολάς (Joseph. *Antiq* 16.333); τὰς ἐπιστολὰς ἀπεδίδου (Joseph. *Antiq* 18.248).

7.354 οὕτως βεβαίαν καὶ ἀληθεστάτην ταῖς ψυχαῖς τὴν μετ' ἀλλήλων εἶναι δίαιταν πεπιστεύκασιν: the adjs. βεβαίαν and ἀληθεστάτην modify the noun τὴν... δίαιταν ("mode of life"); the phrase ταῖς ψυχαῖς constitutes a poss. dat. (Smyth §1476); the vb. πεπιστεύκασιν (cf. Joseph. *Antiq* 6.263) sets off accus. and infin. in indir. state. (Smyth §1867): "so confirmed and most true have they believed that the souls' mode of life is with one another." Hence in their souls the Indian sages experience a δίαιτα ("way of living, mode of life," LSJ I.1) "with one another" (μετ' ἀλλήλων); earlier Josephus said of the δίαιτα that it is "immortal" (τῆς ἀθανάτου διαίτης, Joseph. *BJ* 7.353).

7.355 οἱ δ' ἐπειδὰν ἐπακούσωσι τῶν ἐντεταλμένων αὐτοῖς, πυρὶ τὸ σῶμα παραδόντες, ὅπως δὴ καὶ καθαρωτάτην ἀποκρίνωσι τοῦ σώματος τὴν ψυχήν, ὑμνούμενοι τελευτῶσιν·: with the particle δέ the def. article οἱ functions as a demonstr. (Smyth §1106): "and they [the Indian sages]..." Note the structure of the complex sentence: ἐπειδάν... ἐπακούσωσι... τελευτῶσιν (equiv. to the protasis of a pres. gen. cond., cf. Smyth §2567) and ὅπως... ἀποκρίνωσι (pur., prim. seq., cf. Smyth §2193). For ἐπακούσωσι ("they hearken") cf. Aristoph. *Av.* 205; Plato *Protag.* 317d. The "directives" (τῶν ἐντεταλμένων) refer to the instructions given in Joseph. *BJ* 7.353 above. The pur. for consigning (παραδόντες, cf. Joseph. *Antiq* 4.139; 6.191; 10.9 *BJ* 2.358; 5.537) the body to flames is to "separate" (ἀποκρίνωσι) a purified soul *from* the body (τοῦ σώματος represents a gen. of separ., Smyth §1392). As they die (τελευτῶσιν, cf. Joseph. *Antiq* 2.199; 5.320; 18.139; *Vita* 421; *BJ* 1.650) the Indian sages are "celebrated in song" (ὑμνούμενοι, cf. Hippolytus *De Univers.* 24; John Damasc. *Sac. Par.* vol. 96 pg. 544; Justin. *Nov.* pg. 36; Prodic. *Frag.* 2; Xen. *Mem.* 2.1.33), apparently by the comrades mentioned in Joseph. *BJ* 7.353 above. This passage has been taken over nearly word for word by Porphyry of Tyre (*De Abstentia.* 4.18; 3d cent. AD).

7.356 ῥᾷον γὰρ ἐκείνους εἰς τὸν θάνατον οἱ φίλτατοι προπέμπουσιν ἢ τῶν ἄλλων ἀνθρώπων ἕκαστοι τοὺς πολίτας εἰς μηκίστην ἀποδημίαν: the pron. ἐκείνους refers to the Indian sages. Trans. ῥᾷον with the compar. particle ἤ: "for it is easier... than..." The vb. προπέμπω possesses the tech. mng. "conduct, escourt, esp. a departing traveler" (LSJ II.1; cf. Hdt. 1.111; 3.50; Soph. *Oed. Col.* 1667; Antiph. 1.16; Theophr. *Char.* 5.2). For οἱ φίλτατοι ("their dearest friends") cf. Joseph. *BJ* 4.132; 6.194; for προπέμπουσιν ("they escourt") cf. Joseph. *BJ* 1.279; 4.4.

7.356 σφᾶς μὲν αὐτοὺς δακρύουσιν, ἐκείνους δὲ μακαρίζουσιν ἤδη τὴν ἀθάνατον τάξιν ἀπολαμβάνοντας: the prons. σφᾶς... αὐτοὺς refer to the mourners; ἐκείνους to the departed. For δακρύουσιν ("they weep") cf. Joseph. *BJ* 7.341; for μακαρίζουσιν ("they esteem") cf. Aristot. *Pol.* 1324a; Porph. *Abstin.* 4.18; LXX Gen 30:13; for ἀθάνατον τάξιν ("immortal rank") cf.

Anth. Graec. 7.61.2; Diog. Laert. *Vit. Phil.* 3.44; Speuss. Frag. 87a.2; for ἀπολαμβάνοντας ("get back") cf. Joseph. *Antiq* 2.325; 6.366; 15.167; 18.312.

7.357 ἆρ' οὖν οὐκ αἰδούμεθα χεῖρον Ἰνδῶν φρονοῦντες καὶ διὰ τῆς αὐτῶν ἀτολμίας τοὺς πατρίους νόμους, οἳ πᾶσιν ἀνθρώποις εἰς ζῆλον ἥκουσιν, αἰσχρῶς ὑβρίζοντες;: the interrog. particle ἆρ' οὐ anticipates an affirm. answer to the quest. (Smyth §2651). Trans. φρονοῦντες (cf. Joseph. *Antiq* 4.297; 7.22; 12.392; 14.58, 124; 15.2; 20.176; *Contra Ap* 2.281; *BJ* 1.140, 201; 3.31; 7.383) as a suppl. ptc. with αἰδούμεθα (Smyth §2100, §2126): "Are we not ashamed of being more mean-spirited than the Indians...?" The conjunction καί links οὐκ αἰδούμεθα to αἰσχρῶς ὑβρίζοντες (also a suppl. ptc.): "and won't we be ashamed... to outrage shamefully?" It is a bit hard to see that the reflex. pron. αὐτῶν refers to the 1 pers. plur. subj. of the vb. αἰδούμεθα:"and through *our own* timidity..." (we might have expected Josephus to use ἡμῶν instead of αὐτῶν). The anteced. of the rel. pron. οἵ is τοὺς πατρίους νόμους ("ancestral laws," cf. οἱ πάτριοι... λόγοι, Joseph. *BJ* 7.343 above).

BJ 7.358–374:

7.358 ἀλλ' εἴ γε καὶ τοὺς ἐναντίους ἐξ ἀρχῆς λόγους ἐπαιδεύθημεν, ὡς ἄρα μέγιστον ἀγαθὸν ἀνθρώποις ἐστὶ τὸ ζῆν συμφορὰ δ' ὁ θάνατος...: the words εἴ γε... ἐπαιδεύθημεν constitute the protasis of a past contr. fact cond. (Smyth §2297): "but even if we were taught the opposite doctrines [but we were not]..." Since the words ὁ... καιρός... παρακαλεῖ (in the next clause, see below) constitute the apodosis of a simp. fact. cond. (Smyth §2297), we are dealing with a mixed cond. The particle ὡς provides the content of what the protasis offers—namely, that living (τὸ ζῆν) represents the greatest good for people, and death (ὁ θάνατος) a misfortune (συμφορά). Cf. Luz (1983) 35–36 for the occurrence of this commonplace elsewhere. Eleazar makes essentially the same claim in Joseph. *BJ* 7.343 above. For ἐξ ἀρχῆς ("from the beg.") cf. Joseph. *BJ* 1.109; 7.327, 336; for μέγιστον ἀγαθόν ("greatest good") cf. Joseph. *Antiq* 1.326; for τὸ ζῆν ("living") cf. Joseph. *BJ* 1.44, 85, 520, 572; 2.109; 3.370, 438; 4.604; 6.350; 7.343; for ὁ θάνατος ("death") cf. Joseph. *Antiq* 5.252; 6.127, 155, 210; 15.60; 17.176, 194; 19.15, 17; *Contra Ap* 2.215, 268.

7.358 ὁ γοῦν καιρὸς ἡμᾶς παρακαλεῖ φέρειν εὐκαρδίως αὐτὸν θεοῦ γνώμῃ καὶ κατ' ἀνάγκας τελευτήσοντας·: by the expression ὁ... καιρός ("opportune moment," cf. Joseph. *BJ* 1.5, 179, 649; 2.55; 3.204, 494; 5.20, 29, 66; 7.79, 194, 323) Josephus refers to the crisis at hand. The pron. αὐτὸν refers to death (cf. ὁ θάνατος in the preced clause). The fut. act. ptc. τελευτήσοντας mods. ἡμᾶς: "that we *shall die* by God's will and of necessity." Thus Eleazar repeats his earlier conviction that it was God's pur. (τῆς τοῦ θεοῦ γνώμης) that the Jewish race, once beloved of God, was doomed to perdition (Joseph. *BJ* 7.327)—an idea, indeed, that Eleazar shall bring to fullest expression in what follows. For εὐκαρδίως ("stout heartedly") cf. Joseph. *Antiq* 12.373.

7.359 πάλαι γάρ, ὡς ἔοικε, κατὰ τοῦ κοινοῦ παντὸς Ἰουδαίων γένους ταύτην ἔθετο τὴν ψῆφον ὁ θεός: how far back in history does Josephus mean by the expression "for long ago" (πάλαι γάρ, cf. Joseph. *Antiq* 11.32; 13.423; *BJ* 1.520; 7.343)? For the expression ὡς ἔοικε ("as it seems") cf. Joseph. *Contra Ap* 2.124; *BJ* 1.392, 593, 609; 5.558; for the idiom ψῆφον τίζεσθαι ("cast the ballot against") cf. Hdt. 6.57; 8.123; Aesch. *Ag.* 816; for ἔθετο ("he cast") cf. Joseph. *Antiq* 1.28, 62; 2.228; 3.273; 5.31; 16.22; *Contra Ap* 1.239.

7.359 ...ὥσθ' ἡμᾶς τοῦ ζῆν ἀπηλλάχθαι μὴ μέλλοντας αὐτῷ χρῆσθαι κατὰ τρόπον: ὥστε signals a poten. res. clause. The aor. mid./pass. infin. ἀπηλλάχθαι patterns with the articular infin. τοῦ ζῆν (gen. of separ., Smyth §1392): "that we must depart [from] life." For τοῦ ζῆν ἀπηλλάχθαι cf. ἀπαλλάσσεσθαι πάσης συμφορᾶς, Joseph. *BJ* 7.344. Trans. the circumst. ptc. μέλλοντας (mod. ἡμᾶς) conditionally (Smyth §2060): "unless we intend to..." The vb. χράομαι patterns with a dat. obj. (Smyth §1509): "...to use it [αὐτῷ]" (the pron. αὐτῷ refers to τοῦ ζῆν). For κατὰ τρόπον ("fitly, duly") cf. Joseph. *Antiq* 12.242.

7.360 μὴ γὰρ αὐτοῖς ὑμῖν ἀνάπτετε τὰς αἰτίας μηδὲ χαρίζεσθε τοῖς Ῥωμαίοις, ὅτι πάντας ἡμᾶς ὁ πρὸς αὐτοὺς πόλεμος διέφθειρεν: the particle μή + the impvs. ἀνάπτετε and χαρίζεσθε represents Prohibition (Smyth §1840): "don't attach blame to yourselves nor credit the Romans..." In other words, God calls the shots—not the freedom-loving Jews, nor even the Romans. The clause marker ὅτι provides the reason why Eleazar's hearers should not blame themselves nor credit the Romans (Smyth §2240): "*because* the war against them [the Romans] was destroying us all." For τὰς αἰτίας ("blame") cf. Joseph. *BJ* 1.503, 539; 2.73, 77, 296; 4.364, 391, 498; for χαρίζεσθε ("credit") cf. Joseph. *Antiq* 4.28; for τοῖς Ῥωμαίοις ("the Romans") cf. Joseph. *Antiq* 17.257; *Vita* 132; *BJ* 1.146, 332, 350; 2.320, 518, 521; 3.17, 112, 152; 4.424; 5.84, 291, 359; 6.248, 251; 7.317, 333; for διέφθειρεν ("destroyed") cf. Joseph. *BJ* 1.307, 370; 2.260, 272, 483; 4.25, 128, 327, 430, 541, 558, 564.

7.360 οὐ γὰρ ἐκείνων ἰσχύι ταῦτα συμβέβηκεν, ἀλλὰ κρείττων αἰτία γενομένη τὸ δοκεῖν ἐκείνοις νικᾶν παρέσχηκε: the pron. ἐκείνων refers to the Romans: "for not by *their* might..." For the expression ἐκείνων ἰσχύι cf. ἐν τῇ ἐκείνων ἰσχύι (Cass. Dio. *Hist. Rom.* 4.2.4; Constant. VII *De Virt. et Vit.* vol. 2 pg. 383). For the expression ταῦτα συμβέβηκεν ("these things have happened") cf. Joseph. *Antiq* 7.84; Aristot. *Analyt.* 83b.12; *Top.* 152a.34. The so-called "cause that became the stronger" (κρείττων αἰτία γενομένη) refers to the divine intervention that favored the Romans, not the Jews; yet even this "better cause" granted the Romans only an apparent victory (τὸ δοκεῖν... νικᾶν = "the seeming... to conquer"). For παρέσχηκε ("has offered") cf. Joseph. *Antiq* 4.318; 7.95, 300.

7.361 ποίοις γὰρ ὅπλοις Ῥωμαίων τεθνήκασιν οἱ Καισάρειαν Ἰουδαῖοι κατοικοῦντες;: technically it was Syrian arms, not Roman, that brought about the slaughter of the Jews in Caesarea in AD 66 (cf. Joseph. *BJ* 2.457), the event that began the war. The Jews had claimed that Caesarea was a Jewish city because its founder, king Herod, was a Jew (Joseph. *BJ* 2.266); however, the Syrians maintained that Herod would never have erected the statues and temples in Caesarea had he intended that city to be for the Jews (ibid.; cf. Joseph. *Antiq* 20.173). According to Josephus, the Jews massacred the Roman garrison in Jerusalem "the same day and hour" the Syrians in Caesarea slaughtered the Jews (Joseph. *BJ* 2.457). For τεθνήκασιν ("they died") cf. Joseph. *Antiq* 7.255; 16.351; *BJ* 1.623; 7.344, 372, 373; for κατοικοῦντες ("inhabiting") cf. *BJ* 2.369; 7.244.

7.362 ἀλλ' οὐδὲ μελλήσαντας αὐτοὺς ἐκείνων ἀφίστασθαι, μεταξὺ δὲ τὴν ἑβδόμην ἑορτάζοντας τὸ πλῆθος τῶν Καισαρέων ἐπιδραμὸν μηδὲ χεῖρας ἀνταίροντας ἅμα γυναιξὶ καὶ τέκνοις κατέσφαξαν...: the subj. of this complicated sentence is τὸ πλῆθος τῶν Καισαρέων ἐπιδραμόν ("the mob of Caesareans... rushed against"); the vb. is κατέσφαξαν ("they slaughtered"); the dir. objs. (mod. the Jews) are μελλήσαντας αὐτούς... ἑορτάζοντας... χεῖρας ἀνταίροντας. For another example of a sing. collective noun that patterns with a plur. vb. (Smyth §950) cf. τοιαῦτα ἀκούσασα ἡ πόλις 'Αγησίλαον εἵλοντο βασιλέα = "the city, after hearing such arguments, chose Agesilaus king" (Xen. *Hell*. 3.3.4). Trans. the aor. ptc. μελλήσαντας concessively (Smyth §2060): "but *though* they [the Jews] had not been willing to revolt from them [the Romans]..." For the idiom ἀφίστασθαι ἀπό τινος (or just τινος) cf. Hdt. 1.95, 130; 2.113; also Joseph. *Antiq* 1.266; 8.209; *Vita* 93, 159, 185, 391; *BJ* 7.221. Trans. μεταξύ as an adv. here, not a prepos.: "and *during* the seventh [day] as they were feasting..."—i.e., the slaughter was perpetrated against the Jews as they were celebrating the Sabbath. For ἑορτάζοντας ("feasting") cf. Joseph. *Antiq* 20.133; for ἅμα γυναιξὶ καὶ τέκνοις ("with women and children") cf. Joseph. *Antiq* 5.250; for κατέσφαξαν ("they slaughtered") cf. Joseph. *Antiq* 9.102, 138; *BJ* 2.430.

7.362 οὐδ' αὐτοὺς 'Ρωμαίους ἐντραπέντες, οἳ μόνους ἡμᾶς ἡγοῦντο πολεμίους τοὺς ἀφεστηκότας: the subj. of the aor. nom. plur. ptc. ἐντραπέντες ("having respected," cf. Joseph. *Antiq* 15.288) is the Syrian inhabitants of Caesarea. They are the ones who, having "disrespected the Romans" (οὐδέ... ἐντραπέντες), considered the Jews to be rebellious hostiles. Cf. Joseph. *BJ* 2.457–60 where Josephus documents a massacre of Jews at Caesarea by Syrians, then fierce Jewish reprisals in Philadelphia, Heshbon, Gerasa, Scythopolis, Gadara—and, ultimately, Caesarea. Cf. Joseph. *BJ* 2.461–462 for the equally hostile Syrian backlash against the Jews.

7.363 ἀλλὰ φήσει τις, ὅτι Καισαρεῦσιν ἦν ἀεὶ διαφορὰ πρὸς τοὺς παρ' αὐτοῖς, καὶ τοῦ καιροῦ λαβόμενοι τὸ παλαιὸν μῖσος ἀπεπλήρωσαν: Eleazar introduces the fictive interlocutor's objection (ἀλλὰ φήσει τις = "but someone shall say...," cf. Joseph. *BJ* 3.368) to dispel the notion that the Syrian inhabitants of Caesarea—admittedly a quarrelsome folk—treated all residents shabbily. Eleazar suggests that what had happened to the Jews at Caesarea far transcended mere quarrelsomeness. Καισαρεῦσιν represents a poss. dat. (Smyth §1476); the phrase τοὺς παρ' αὐτοῖς means "those who reside among them"—i.e., the Jews and any other guests. The words καὶ τοῦ καιροῦ λαβόμενοι... ("and having got opportunity...") = obj. gen.) continue the fictive interlocutor's objection. For the aor. mid. ptc. λαβόμενοι ("having got") cf. Joseph. *Antiq* 4.88; 5.134; *Vita* 375.

7.364 τί οὖν τοὺς ἐν Σκυθοπόλει φῶμεν: the vb. φῶμεν represents the deliberative subjunct. (Smyth §1805): "What then *shall we say*...?" As Eliazar explains, the Jewish residents of Scythopolis—true to the constitution and laws of that city—had warred against their Jewish kinsmen when the latter attacked Scythopolis (Joseph. *BJ* 2.466). Once again, loyalty on the part of the Jews had been rewarded by an undeserved slaughter perpetrated by non-Jews (Joseph. *BJ* 2.468; cf. *Vita* 26). Such perfidiousness proved, in Eleazar's mind, that God was opposed to all Jews.

7.364 ἡμῖν γὰρ ἐκεῖνοι διὰ τοὺς Ἕλληνας πολεμεῖν ἐτόλμησαν, ἀλλ' οὐ μετὰ τῶν συγγενῶν ἡμῶν Ῥωμαίους ἀμύνεσθαι: the passage pulsates with rhetorical energy. The Jews of Scythopolis (ἐκεῖνοι) "dared" (ἐτόλμησαν, cf. Joseph. *Antiq* 1.17; 2.99; 6.72; *Contra Ap* 1.68, 269; 2.169; *BJ* 2.63; 4.264) to make war against Eleazar and the freedom-loving Jews at Masada (here ἡμῖν), but they did not "defend themselves" (ἀμύνεσθαι, cf. Joseph. *BJ* 1.236, 296; 2.48; 3.287; 4.403; 5.383) against the Romans with their "kinsmen" (μετὰ τῶν συγγενῶν, cf. Joseph. *Antiq* 5.317; 10.190, 197, 199)—namely, with Eleazar and the Zealots (here ἡμῶν).

7.365 πολὺ τοίνυν ὤνησεν αὐτοὺς ἡ πρὸς ἐκείνους εὔνοια καὶ πίστις: πολύ ("quite") represents the adv. accus. (Smyth §1607). The postpos. particle τοίνυν is either transitional ("now then," "further") or inferential ("therefore," "accordingly"). The statement drips with irony: "a lot of good did the εὔνοια and πίστις toward the Scythopolitans do those particular Jews in the end—those Jews who were so brutally murdered!" Εὔνοια means "good will" or "kindliness," espec. in a political context; πίστις could mean here "political protection or suzerainty" (LSJ IV.1)—or even *fides* ("faithfulness," "loyalty"), one of the building-blocks of Greco-Roman society. Eleazar maintains that not even these foundational virtues had availed the Jews in the past when they had attempted to play ball with Hellenism; an honorable suicide, then, represented the best way out—not base servitude to the Romans. For ὤνησεν ("availed") cf. Joseph. *Antiq* 9.98; 15.311; *BJ* 1.533; for ἡ... εὔνοια ("goodwill") cf. Joseph. *Antiq* 4.134; 5.96; 16.51, 105; 17.31, 329; 18.254; *Vita* 84; for ἡ... πίστις ("faithfulness") cf. Joseph. *Antiq* 2.111; 10.101; 15.134; 16.51; 18.14; *Vita* 84; *BJ* 1.601; 2.257; 4.418; 6.195, 231.

7.365 ὑπ' αὐτῶν μέντοι πανοικεσίᾳ πικρῶς κατεφονεύθησαν ταύτην τῆς συμμαχίας ἀπολαβόντες ἀμοιβήν: the pron. αὐτῶν represents the Scythopolitans; for the adv. πανοικεσίᾳ ("with all the household," cf. Joseph. *Antiq* 19.177; *BJ* 7.220). This adv. recalls ἅμα γυναιξὶ καὶ τέκνοις in Joseph. *BJ* 7.362 above. The adv. πικρῶς ("bitterly," cf. *Antiq* 3.13; 5.320; 8.220; 9.118, 169; 12.5, 122; 17.205; *Vita* 339; *BJ* 2.41; 7.32) completes the picture. For ἡ ἀμοιβή ("requital, recompense," LSJ I.1) cf., e.g., σοὶ δ' ἄξιόν ἐστιν ἀμοιβῆς (Hom. *Ody.* 1.318); χαρίεσσαν ἀμοιβήν (*Ody.* 3.58); κακήν... ἀμοιβήν (Thgn. 1263); γλυκεῖν... ἀμοιβήν (Pind. *Nem.* 5.48). For ἀπολαβόντες ("having received back") cf. Joseph. *Antiq* 14.252; 17.255.

7.366 ἃ γὰρ ἐκείνους ὑφ' ἡμῶν ἐκώλυσαν ταῦθ' ὑπέμειναν ὡς αὐτοὶ δρᾶσαι θελήσαντες: it is a little hard to see who does what to whom in this closely argued sentence. The pron. ἐκείνους refers to the Greek citizens of Scythopolis; the subj. of the vb. ἐκώλυσαν ("they prevented," cf. Joseph. *BJ* 5.56; 7.310) represents the Jewish residents of Scythopolis; the pron. ἡμῶν represents Eleazar and the Zealots. Eleazar refers again to the war wherein the Jews of Scythopolis kept "them" (ἐκείνους, the Greeks) from difficulties which the Jewish citizens had experienced from the Zealots (cf. Joseph. *BJ* 7.364 above). Indeed, the Scythopolitan Jews "endured" (ὑπέμειναν, cf. Joseph. *Antiq* 1.173; 7.77, 310; 8.220; 10.134; 12.6, 123; 13.161, 258; 15.10; *BJ* 2.152, 479; 6.247; 7.52, 272) these things as though "they had themselves wished to do them"—i.e., suffer the contempt of kinsmen for fighting against fellow Jews. Eleazar's point is that the act of loyalty to the Greeks had been rewarded by the Scythopolitans with treachery.

7.366 μακρὸν ἂν εἴη νῦν ἰδίᾳ περὶ ἑκάστων λέγειν: the vb. εἴη ("it would be") represents the pot. optv. (Smyth §1824). The adv. ἰδίᾳ means "privately," or "on its own account." By the prep. phrase περὶ ἑκάστων ("concerning each [instance]") Eleazar means other examples of the sort he has elaborated in *BJ* 7.364–366.

7.367 ἴστε γὰρ ὅτι τῶν ἐν Συρίᾳ πόλεων οὐκ ἔστιν ἥτις τοὺς παρ' αὐτῇ κατοικοῦντας Ἰουδαίους οὐκ ἀνῄρηκεν, ἡμῖν πλέον ἢ Ῥωμαίοις ὄντας πολεμίους·: for the vb. ἴστε ("you know") cf. Joseph. *BJ* 1.379; 3.374, 483; 5.389, 410; 6.331; for the pres. act. ptc. κατοικοῦντας ("inhabiting") cf. κατοικοῦντες in Joseph. *BJ* 7.361 above; for the 3 pers. sing. pf. vb. ἀνῄρηκεν ("slew") cf. Joseph. *BJ* 1.209; for the adj. πολεμίους ("hostile") cf. Joseph. *BJ* 1.150, 202, 250; 2.34, 466, 476; 3.130, 262, 288; 4.26, 48, 185; 5.9, 30,97; 6.44, 62, 181; 7.332, 368, 380. What Eleazar deems noteworthy is the Greeks' invariable butchery of Jews, even though the latter were in fact—as Eleazar acknowledges—more hostile to one another than they were to the Romans.

7.368 ὅπου γε Δαμασκηνοὶ μηδὲ πρόφασιν εὔλογον πλάσαι δυνηθέντες φόνου μιαρωτάτου τὴν αὐτῶν πόλιν ἐνέπλησαν...: trans. the subordinating conjunction ὅπου as "since" (cf. Smyth §2240, §2770): "*since* the men of Damascus, not having been able to contrive a reasonable pretext..." The citizens of Damascus had decided to kill resident Jews when news of the uprising of the Zealots in Jerusalem reached their ears (cf. Joseph. *BJ* 2.559). They had acted, maintains Eleazar, without any reasonable "pretext" (πρόφασιν, cf. Joseph. *Antiq* 2.145; 4.167; 8.369; 10.76, 252; 14.397, 408; 15.365; 16.89; 19.252, 311; 20.162; *Contra Ap* 1.72; *BJ* 1.292; 2.285; 4.177, 394; 7.240, 258). For the aor. act. ptc.

δυνηθέντες ("having been able") cf. Joseph. *Antiq* 3.319; 10.168; *Vita* 252; for the vb. ἐνέπλησαν ("they filled") cf. Joseph. *Antiq* 18.9; *BJ* 2.598; for the idiom "fill something [accus.] with something else [gen.]," cf. ἐμπίπληθι ῥέεθρα ὕδατος (Hom. *Il*. 21.311); ἐ. δέπας ὕδατος (Hom. *Ody*. 9.209); ἐ. ἵππων τὸν ἱππόδρομον (Xen. *Eq. Mag.* 3.10).

7.368 ὀκτακισχιλίους πρὸς τοῖς μυρίοις Ἰουδαίους ἅμα γυναιξὶ καὶ γενεαῖς ἀποσφάξαντες: elsewhere Josephus claims some 10,500 Jews died in this incident, not 18,000 (Joseph. *BJ* 2.561). For the phrase ἅμα γυναιξί ("with women") cf. Joseph. *Antiq* 5.250; *BJ* 7.70, 362; for ἀποσφάξαντες ("having slaughtered") cf. Joseph. *Antiq* 15.136; *BJ* 3.325; 6.68, 359.

7.369 τὸ δ' ἐν Αἰγύπτῳ πλῆθος τῶν μετ' αἰκίας ἀνῃρημένων ἓξ που μυριάδας ὑπερβάλλειν ἐπυνθανόμεθα: trans. first the finite vb. ἐπυνθανόμεθα ("we learned") which sets off accus. with infin. in indir. state. (Smyth §1867): "we learned that the mass... surpassed, I suppose, 60,000." That the mass (τό... πλῆθος) of those who died in Egypt perished "with torture" (μετ' αἰκίας, cf. Joseph. *Antiq* 11.330; 13.232; *BJ* 2.180, espec. διὰ... τῆς βασάνου καὶ τῆς αἰκίας, Joseph. *Antiq* 16.389) seems to repres. rhetorical license on Eleazar's part, although in Joseph. *BJ* 7.373 (below) Eleazar says of the subj. Jews that some are perishing "on the rack" (στρεβλούμενοι) and others are "tortured" (αἰκιζόμενοι) by fire and the scourge—referring, apparently, to the spectacles wherein the Jewish captives died (see e.g. Joseph. *BJ* 6.418; 7.24). The killing which Eleazar describes here was due to the "incessant strife" (ἀεί... στάσις) that existed between Jews and the native populace in Alexandria (Joseph. *BJ* 2.487). Some 50,000 Jews perished at the hands of the Romans in still another massacre (cf. Joseph. *BJ* 2.494) that Eleazar leaves unmentioned.

7.369 κἀκεῖνοι μὲν ἴσως ἐπ' ἀλλοτρίας γῆς οὐδὲν ἀντίπαλον εὑράμενοι τοῖς πολεμίοις οὕτως ἀπέθανον...: the pron. κἀκεῖνοι (= καί + ἐκεῖνοι: "and those") refers to the Jews who perished "in Egypt" (cf. ἐν Αἰγύπτῳ immed. above). Just those Jews had "died thus" (οὕτως ἀπέθανον, cf. Joseph. *Antiq* 3.210) "in a foreign land" (ἐπ' ἀλλοτρίας γῆς, cf. Ps. Luc. *Am*. 31; Theoph. Conf. *Chron*. pg. 286; Theoph. *Hist*. 7.7.4), found to be no "wrestling match" (ἀντίπαλον, cf. Joseph. *Antiq* 14.480; 15.123; *BJ* 1.352; 2.442; 3.476; 4.605; 6.404) for their enemies. For the aor. pass. ptc. εὑράμενοι ("having been found") cf. Joseph. *BJ* 7.87.

7.369 τοῖς δ' ἐπὶ τῆς οἰκείας τὸν πρὸς Ῥωμαίους πόλεμον ἀραμένοις ἅπασι τί τῶν ἐλπίδα νίκης ἐχυρᾶς παρασχεῖν δυναμένων οὐχ ὑπῆρξε;: the subj. of the vb. ὑπῆρξε is τί: "but what [τί] of those things that are able to offer hope of trustworthy victory *was not lacking* [οὐχ ὑπῆρξε] to all those who on their own territory [ἐπὶ τῆς οἰκείας (sc. γῆς)] picked up the battle against the Romans?" The Zealots had lacked none of the things that seemed to guarantee sure victory. And yet they had lost because God was on the side of the Romans. The phrase πρὸς Ῥωμαίους ("against the Romans") occurs 37 times in the *BJ*. For πόλεμον ἀραμένοις ("having taken up war") cf. Joseph. *BJ*. 2.638; for ἐλπίδα νίκης ("hope of victory") cf. Joseph. *Antiq* 12.300; 13.93; for παρασχεῖν ("to offer") cf. Joseph. *BJ* 1.190, 395, 612, 621; 2.105, 615; 5.373; 7.3, 165, 177, 203; for ὑπῆρξε ("was lacking") cf. Joseph. *Antiq* 3.56, 317; 4.99; 5.95; 7.388; 12.21; 13.214; 14.73; *Vita* 41; *Contra Ap* 2.127; *BJ* 7.451.

7.370 καὶ γὰρ ὅπλα καὶ τείχη καὶ φρουρίων δυσάλωτοι κατασκευαί καὶ φρόνημα πρὸς τοὺς ὑπὲρ τῆς ἐλευθερίας κινδύνους ἄτρεπτον πάντας πρὸς τὴν ἀπόστασιν ἐπέρρωσεν: weapons, walls, all but impregnable forts, and (espec.) the implacable will for freedom against all dangers encouraged freedom-loving Jews to revolt. For δυσάλωτοι ("difficult to capture") cf. Joseph. *BJ* 1.411; 3.26, 61, 157, 285, 290; 5.142; 7.177; for ἡ κατασκευή as a permanent or fixed asset cf. Joseph. *BJ* 7.295; for φρόνημα... ἄτρεπτον ("implacable will") cf. Himerius *Declam. et Or*. 32.55; Photius *Bibl*. 243.376a; for the prep. phrase ὑπὲρ τῆς ἐλευθερίας ("on behalf of freedom") cf. Joseph. *Antiq* 4.42; *BJ* 2.373, 374; 3.365; 4.228, 274; 7.341; for the prep. phrase πρὸς τὴν ἀπόστασιν ("to rebellion") cf. Joseph. *BJ* 7.412; for the vb. ἐπέρρωσεν ("steeled," from ἐπιρρώνυμι) cf. Joseph. *BJ* 1.167, 193.

7.371 ἀλλὰ ταῦτα πρὸς βραχὺν χρόνον ἀρκέσαντα καὶ ταῖς ἐλπίσιν ἡμᾶς ἐπάραντα μειζόνων ἀρχὴ κακῶν ἐφάνη: the pron. ταῦτα ("these things") refers to the items listed immed. above. Eleazar can say—from the perspective of hindsight—that the advantages mentioned "availed" (ἀρκέσαντα, cf. Joseph. *Antiq* 16.288) for only a short time and were, in fact, but the beg. of their problems. The neut. plur. (ταῦτα... ἀρκέσαντα... ἐπάραντα) serves as the subj. of the sing. vb. ἐφάνη: "they... *appeared* as the beg. of greater evils." For the prep. phrase πρὸς βραχὺν χρόνον ("for a brief time") cf. Joseph. *Antiq* 4.129; for ἀρχὴ κακῶν ("beg. of woes") cf. *Antiq* 8.229. Some editors prefer ἀνεφάνη ("came to light," cf. Joseph. *BJ* 7.30) to ἐφάνη ("appeared," cf. Joseph. *BJ* 5.407; 6.55).

7.371 πάντα γὰρ ἥλω, καὶ πάντα τοῖς πολεμίοις ὑπέπεσεν...: the neut. plur. πάντα ("everything") serves as the subj. of the sing. vbs. ἥλω ("were captured" = 3 pers. sing. 2 aor. of ἁλίσκομαι, cf. Joseph. *Antiq* 8.294; 15.119; *Vita* 352; *BJ* 7.441) and ὑπέπεσεν ("succumbed," cf. Joseph. *BJ* 2.120; 5.209, 329). The expansive πάντα ("everything") refers to the items catalogued in Joseph. *BJ* 7.370 above.

7.371 ...ὥσπερ εἰς τὴν ἐκείνων εὐκλεεστέραν νίκην, οὐκ εἰς τὴν τῶν παρασκευασαμένων σωτηρίαν εὐτρεπισθέντα: the pron. ἐκείνων ("their") refers to the Romans (cf. πρὸς Ῥωμαίους, Joseph. *BJ* 7.369 above). The aor. pass. ptc. εὐτρεπισθέντα ("were well prepared") mods. the two πάντας mentioned in the prev clause. For the splendid triumphal procession in Rome at the conclusion of the Jewish War cf. Joseph. *BJ* 7.123–157; for the Zealots' "preparations" (παρασκευασαμένων) at Masada in particular cf. Joseph. *BJ* 7.295, 297 above.

7.372 καὶ τοὺς μὲν ἐν ταῖς μάχαις ἀποθνῄσκοντας εὐδαιμονίζειν προσῆκον: Josephus omits for reasons of stylistic economy the finite vb. ἐστίν upon which the neut. sing. ptc. προσῆκον ("it is meet") depends. For προσῆκον ("it is meet") cf. Joseph. *Antiq* 12.30; 20.224; *BJ* 1.153; 7.271; for ἐν ταῖς μάχαις ("in the battles") cf. Joseph. *Antiq* 4.301; 5.37; 13.379; 15.125, 146; *BJ*

3.98; 7.93; for εὐδαιμονίζειν ("to esteem blessed") cf. Joseph. *BJ* 1.667; 7.353.

7.372 ἀμυνόμενοι γὰρ καὶ τὴν ἐλευθερίαν οὐ προέμενοι τεθνήκασι: trans. the finite vb. τεθνήκασι ("they died") before the circumst. ptcs. ἀμυνόμενοι and προέμενοι (aor. mid./pass. ptc. of προίημι): "for they died defending..., not betraying..." By committing suicide the holdouts at Masada would emulate those who died fighting for liberty. For the pres. mid. ptc. ἀμυνόμενοι ("defending") cf. Joseph. *Antiq* 13.363; *BJ* 3.270, 303; 4.282; 5.346; 6.177, 360; for τὴν ἐλευθερίαν ("liberty") cf. Joseph. *BJ* 2.349; 4.178; 7.329, 335.

7.372 τὸ δὲ πλῆθος τῶν ὑπὸ Ῥωμαίοις γενομένων τίς οὐκ ἂν ἐλεήσειε;: the phrase τίς οὐκ ἂν ἐλεήσειε; represents the pot. optv. (Smyth §1824): "who could not pity...?" (cf. ἂν εἴη... λέγειν = "one may say," Joseph. *BJ* 7.366 above). The prep. ὑπό + dat. expresses subjection or dependence on someone else (LSJ B.II.2), e.g., ὑπό τινι = "under one's power"; εἶναι ὑ. τισί = "to be subordinate, subject to them" (Thuc. 1.32); ἔχειν ὑφ' ἑαυτῷ = "to have under one, at one's command" (Xen. *Cyr.* 2.1.26); ὑ. τινὶ στρατεύσασθαι = "to campaign under someone's command" (Plut. *Cic.* 44). Hence Eleazar acknowledges that the vast majority of Jews (τὸ... πλῆθος) were subj. to Romans (ὑπὸ Ῥωμαίοις) by this final stage in the war.

7.372 τίς οὐκ ἂν ἐπειχθείη πρὸ τοῦ ταὐτὰ παθεῖν ἐκείνοις ἀποθανεῖν;: the phrase τίς οὐκ ἂν ἐπειχθείη constitutes another poten. optv. (cf. prev sentence). The vb. ἐπείγω in the pass. oft means "hurry oneself, haste to do" + infin. (LSJ III.3): "who would not haste to die...?" The prep. πρό ("before") patterns with the defin. article τοῦ of the articular infin. τοῦ... παθεῖν ("suffering," cf. Joseph. *Antiq* 4.13; *BJ* 2.276; 5.315); construe ταὐτα (crasis for τὰ + αὐτά = "the same things") with ἐκείνοις: "...before suffering *the same things* as *them* [= the Jews who had submitted to the Romans]." For the aor. act. infin. ἀποθανεῖν ("to die") cf. Joseph. *BJ* 2.227; 3.313; 5.322; 7.325, 380, 383.

7.373 ὧν οἱ μὲν στρεβλούμενοι καὶ πυρὶ καὶ μάστιξιν αἰκιζόμενοι τεθνήκασιν: the anteced. of the rel. pron. ὧν ("of whom") is ἐκείνοις in the prev sentence—i.e., the subj. Jews. Note the struct.: οἱ μέν... τεθνήκασιν vs. οἱ δ'... ζῶντες (next clause). For στρεβλούμενοι ("stretched on the wheel," oft of slaves, Aristoph. *Nub.* 620; *Ran.* 620; Antiph. 5.32; Hdt. 2.89) cf. Joseph. *BJ* 2.152; 4.329; for αἰκιζόμενοι ("to be tortured") cf. μετ' αἰκίας (*BJ* 7.369 above); for τεθνήκασιν ("they died") cf. Joseph. *Antiq* 7.255; 16.351; *BJ* 1.623; 7.344, 361, 372.

7.373 οἱ δ' ἀπὸ θηρίων ἡμίβρωτοι πρὸς δευτέραν αὐτοῖς τροφὴν ζῶντες ἐφυλάχθησαν: for the epithet ἡμίβρωτοι ("half eaten") cf. τοῖς ἡμιβρώτοις θηριομάχοις (Marc. Aur. 10.8.2); ἡμιβρώτοις σώμασιν (Philostr. *Vita Ap.* 6.24; Photius 241.330a). Recall that Titus had consigned many of the prisoners who had survived the destruction of Jerusalem to be destroyed in amphitheaters "by the sword and by wild beasts" (φθαρησομένους ἐν τοῖς θεάτροις σιδήρῳ καὶ θηρίοις, Joseph. *BJ* 6.418). Some of these same prisoners apparently perished in Caesarea Philippi, having been "flung to wild beasts" (θηρίοις παραβληθέντες, Joseph. *BJ* 7.24) by Titus who staged magnificent spectacles there. The graphic expression "second food for them" (δευτέραν αὐτοῖς τροφήν) likewise signifies the perverse use to which prisoners could be put for the sport and amusement (γέλωτα καὶ παίγνιον) of spectators. For the pres. act. ptc. ζῶντες ("alive") cf. Joseph. *Antiq* 11.339; 12.256; 15.344; *Contra Ap* 2.148, 174; *BJ* 7.324; for the vb. ἐφυλάχθησαν ("they were guarded") cf. Joseph. *Vita* 245; *Contra Ap* 2.134, 295; *BJ* 6.434.

7.374 ἐκείνων μὲν οὖν ἀθλιωτάτους ὑποληπτέον τοὺς ἔτι ζῶντας, οἳ πολλάκις εὐχόμενοι τὸν θάνατον λαβεῖν οὐκ ἔχουσιν: the vb. adj. ὑποληπτέον [ἐστίν] ("one must assume...") sets off accus. with infin. in indir. state. (Smyth §1867): *"one must assume that the most wretched of them are those still living."* The anteced. of the rel. pron. οἵ is τοὺς ἔτι ζῶντας ("those still living"). For the pres. mid. ptc. εὐχόμενοι ("praying") cf. Joseph. *Antiq* 7.357; 11.119; 16.65; *BJ* 7.326; for the idiom ἔχω + infin. ("be able to," Smyth §2000.a): "who, while praying oft for death, *are not able to* receive it." Thus, in Eleazar's reasoning, noble suicide would be far more preferable to the kind of living death here described.

BJ 7.375-379

7.375 ποῦ δ' ἡ μεγάλη πόλις, ἡ τοῦ παντὸς Ἰουδαίων γένους μητρόπολις, ἡ τοσούτοις μὲν ἐρυμνὴ τειχῶν περιβόλοις...;: Rhet. quest.. For Jerusalem as the "mother city" (ἡ μητρόπολις) of the Jews cf. Joseph. *BJ* 2.400, 421, 517, 554, 627; 4.123, 181, etc.; for the fem. sing. adj. ἐρυμνή ("fenced, fortified, strong," LSJ I.1) cf. Joseph. *Antiq* 14.296, 433; 15.148; 16.275; 17.290; *BJ* 2.55, 70; 3.34; for the substant. noun ὁ περίβολος ("circuit") in the expression τοσούτοις... τειχῶν περιβόλοις ("by such great circuits of walls") cf. Joseph. *BJ* 1.104; 4.586; 5.19.

7.375 τοσαῦτα δ' αὐτῆς φρούρια καὶ μεγέθη πύργων προβεβλημένη...: trans. first the pf. pass. ptc. προβεβλημένη ("screened," from προβάλλω; cf. Joseph. *BJ* 4.608) which mods. πόλις; the expression τοσαῦτα... φρούρια καὶ μεγέθη represents accuss. of resp. (Smyth §1600): "screened *with resp. to* its such great forts and magnitudes of towers..." For φρούρια ("forts") cf. *BJ* 1.167, 237, 316; 3.339; 4.1, 447; 5.508; for the towers that had so amazed Titus upon his entry into Jerusalem cf. *BJ* 6.409-10. Jerusalem, like Masada, had been well fortified against invaders long before the Romans came.

7.375 μόλις δὲ χωροῦσα τὰς εἰς τὸν πόλεμον παρασκευάς, τοσαύτας δὲ μυριάδας ἀνδρῶν ἔχουσα τῶν ὑπὲρ αὐτῆς μαχομένων;: by μόλις ("scarcely," used in the Litotes) Eleazar apparently indicates that Jerusalem was so ready for war that it could "scarcely" contain its defensive apparatus and the thousands of men who would fight for her (ὑπὲρ αὐτῆς, cf. Joseph. *Antiq* 1.279; 2.212; 3.20, 182; 5.184; 7.25; 11.228; *BJ* 3.159; 4.264; 5.210; 7.380). The pres. act. ptcs. χωροῦσα and ἔχουσα ("containing... and holding...") mod. ἡ μεγάλη πόλις, ἡ... μητρόπολις immed. above. What is of concern to Eleazar, therefore, are the defensive munitions of the city (for which cf. τῶν ἀποκειμένων παρασκευῶν, *BJ* 7.295[Masada]) and the many persons who died or were captured in Jerusalem at war's end (cf. *BJ* 6.420-428). For the prep. phrase εἰς τὸν πόλεμον ("for the battle") cf. Joseph. *Antiq* 6.325; 7.121; *Vita* 338; *BJ* 2.651; for τάς... παρασκευάς ("the fortifications") cf. Joseph. *BJ* 4.513; 5.104; for μυριάδας ἀνδρῶν ("myriads of men") cf. Joseph. *Antiq* 12.313; *Contra Ap* 1.63, 78, 243, 245; for τῶν... μαχομένων ("of those fighting") cf. Joseph. *Antiq* 1.78, 335; 14.442; *BJ* 1.349; 4.648.

7.376 ποῦ γέγονεν ἡμῖν ἡ τὸν θεὸν ἔχειν οἰκιστὴν πεπιστευμένη;: trans. the adv. ποῦ as "what": "*what* has happened [to the city] that has been believed...?" The pers. pron. ἡμῖν represents the dat. agent with vbs. in the pf. or plupf. pass. (Smyth §1488–1490): "believed *by us*..." The infin. ἔχειν depends on the idea conveyed by the pf. pass. ptc. πεπιστευμένη: "...believed by us *to have* [ἔχειν] God as its founder." For ὁ οἰκιστής as "founder" cf. Joseph. *BJ* 2.266 (of Herod, the Jewish "founder" of Caesarea); the term does not occur in the LXX or NT.

7.376 πρόρριζος ἐκ βάθρων ἀνήρπασται...: the subj. of the finite vb. ἀνήρπασται is again Jerusalem: "uprooted from her foundations she has been swept away..." Eleazar alludes to the Roman practice of completely razing the foundations of a captured enemy city or fort; this had happened at Jerusalem when the city fell: τὰ τείχη κατέσκαψαν = "they razed the walls to the ground" (Joseph. *BJ* 6.434). For the adj. πρόρριζος, -ον ("root and branch, utterly" LSJ I.1) cf. Joseph. *Antiq* 8.127, 309, 314; 9.109; 11.213; for the vb. ἀνήρπασται (3 pers. sing. pf. pass. of ἀναρπάζω) cf. Joseph. *Antiq* 8.118; *Vita* 381; *BJ* 2.550; 6.110.

7.376 ...καὶ μόνον αὐτῆς μνημεῖον ἀπολείπεται τὸ τῶν ἀνῃρημένων ἔτι τοῖς λειψάνοις ἐποικοῦν: the pron. αὐτῆς refers to Jerusalem: "and a mere monument *of her* is left..." The text of the latter part of the clause is doubtful. Some editors favor ...τὸ τῶν ἀνῃρηκότων αὐτὴν στρατόπεδον (Codex Parisinus Graecus 1425 [cent. x or xi]; Codex Ambrosianus [Mediolanensis, cent. x or xi]; Codex Laurentianus [cent. xi or xii]): "...the camp of those who destroyed her." As the text stands in remaining mss., however, the passage reads: "and a mere monument of those slain ones yet dwelling [ἐποικοῦν] among the ruins remains." Either way, Eleazar plays upon the doubled mng. of the word μνημεῖον which may mean "memorial" (cf. Joseph. *BJ* 1.417; 6.413) or "tomb" (Joseph. *BJ* 2.189; 5.259, 304, 356, 358, 468, 506, 507; 6.169). For ἀπολείπεται ("remains") cf. Aristot. *Top.* 129a; Eur. *Troi.* 603.

7.377 πρεσβῦται δὲ δύστηνοι τῇ σποδῷ τοῦ τεμένους παρακάθηνται καὶ γυναῖκες ὀλίγαι πρὸς ὕβριν αἰσχίστην ὑπὸ τῶν πολεμίων τετηρημέναι: in a descr. sure to arouse his hearers' pity, Eleazar focuses briefly upon the plights of the "wretched" (δύστηνοι, cf. Joseph. *BJ* 7.395) old men (πρεσβῦται, cf. App. *Lib.* 615.1; Aristoph. *Ach.* 179; Eur. *Hec.* 323; Philo *De Conf.* 28; Plato *Leg.* 687c, 712b, 917a; LXX Job 29:8; Jer 38:13; Thuc. 3.67.3) who sat by the still smoking ruin of the Temple and the "few women" (γυναῖκες ὀλίγαι, cf. Aristot. *Hist.* 521a) reserved by the Romans (lit. "by our enemies" = ὑπὸ τῶν πολεμίων, cf. Joseph. *BJ* 2.49; 7.386) for sexual purposes. Eleazar accuses the Romans of violating women (cf. also Joseph. *BJ* 7.382 below), though the only ones guilty of this "most shameful" (αἰσχίστην, cf. τιμωρίαν ταύτην αἰσχίστην, Joseph. *Antiq* 4.238) offense had been the factionalized Zealots in Jerusalem (Joseph. *BJ* 4.560), not the Romans. For the provocative phrase πρὸς ὕβριν ("for outrage") cf. Joseph. *Contra Ap* 2.201; *BJ* 4.344.

7.378 ταῦτα τίς ἐν νῷ βαλλόμενος ἡμῶν καρτερήσει τὸν ἥλιον ὁρᾶν, κἂν δύνηται ζῆν ἀκινδύνως;: even to think about such matters—let alone experience them—was intolerable. Construe the interrog. pron. τίς with the part. gen. ἡμῶν: "who of us...?" For ἐν νῷ ("in his mind") cf. Joseph. *Antiq* 19.321; *BJ* 7.320; for βαλλόμενος ("considering") cf. Joseph. *Antiq* 8.359; *BJ* 7.112. The vb. καρτερήσει means "bear patiently, endure"; here it patterns with the infin. ὁρᾶν: "shall bear to *see* the sun." Κἂν δύνηται ("even if he is able...") constitutes the protasis of a FmoreV cond. (Smyth §2565). For the adv. ἀκινδύνως ("without danger") cf. Joseph. *Antiq* 16.235, 337; 17.102, 153; *BJ* 4.371; 5.539; 7.183.

7.378 τίς οὕτω τῆς πατρίδος ἐχθρός, ἢ τίς οὕτως ἄνανδρος καὶ φιλόψυχος, ὡς μὴ καὶ περὶ τοῦ μέχρι νῦν ζῆσαι μετανοεῖν;: the repeated interrog. prons. τίς... τίς... τίς ("who... who... who...?") repres. anaphora (Smyth §3010). Certainly sugg. of anaphora also are the sim. sounding words οὕτω... οὕτως... ὡς.... The words ὡς μή...

μετανοεῖν ("so as not... to repent [+ infin.]") constitute a pot. res. clause (for ὡς in place of ὥστε cf. Smyth §2260). For the masc. sing. adj. ἐχθρός ("hostile") cf. Joseph. *Antiq* 1.320; 4.319; 8.263; 15.47; 18.96; 19.33, 353; for the adj. ἄνανδρος ("unmanly") cf. Joseph. *Antiq* 6.220; for the adj. φιλόψυχος ("loving one's life," i.e., "cowardly, faint-hearted," LSJ) cf. Eur. *Hec*. 348. Bad citizens, cowards, and persons who prefer base existence to freedom conform to a life that Eleazar believes is not worth living.

7.379 ἀλλ' εἴθε πάντες ἐτεθνήκειμεν πρὶν τὴν ἱερὰν ἐκείνην πόλιν χερσὶν ἰδεῖν κατασκαπτομένην πολεμίων, πρὶν τὸν ναὸν τὸν ἅγιον οὕτως ἀνοσίως ἐξορωρυγμένον: the particle εἴθε + optv. constitutes the optv. of wish (Smyth §1815). After an affirm. clause πρίν + infin. means "before" (Smyth §2431, §2453). Note also the accus. with ptc. after a vb. of percep. (ἰδεῖν; cf. Smyth §2110): "before *seeing* that that holy city had been overthrown by the hands of our enemies..." Since Eleazar and John of Gischala had orchestrated resistance in the Temple complex (cf., Joseph. *BJ* 5.5, 104, 254; 6.249, 251), the Romans razed Jerusalem's foundations following capture of the city (Joseph. *BJ* 6.413, 434; 7.1, 3). Josephus reports that the fire that ended up destroying the Temple broke out accidentally (Joseph. *BJ* 6.252, 258, 266, 281), a further sign of God's displeasure. For the expression τὴν ἱεράν... πόλιν ("the holy city") cf. Joseph. *Antiq* 4.209, 218, 227; 20.118; *Contra Ap* 1.283; *BJ* 2.397; 4.241; for τὸν ναὸν τὸν ἅγιον ("the holy Temple") cf. ἅγιον ναόν (Joseph. *Antiq* 8.71); for οὕτως ἀνοσίως ("so unholy") cf. Joseph. *Contra Ap* 1.284.

BJ 7.380–388

7.380 ἐπεὶ δὲ ἡμᾶς οὐκ ἀγεννὴς ἐλπὶς ἐβουκόλησεν, ὡς τάχα που δυνήσεσθαι τοὺς πολεμίους ὑπὲρ αὐτῆς ἀμύνασθαι...: the clause marker ἐπεί is causal: "but *since* a not ignoble hope beguiled us..." The clause marker ὡς designates the content of the deceptive hope—namely, that the Zealots would quickly be able to "wreak vengeance upon" (ἀμύνασθαι; cf. Joseph. *Antiq* 5.110, 153, 243; 6.281, 366; 9.160; 11.259; 12.274; 13.90, 94; 14.63, 405; 15.212; *BJ* 1.320; 4.23) their "enemies" (τοὺς πολεμίους, cf. Joseph. *BJ* 7.377; 7.379) on behalf of (ὑπέρ) the city. The hope that fanned the rebellion was "not ignoble" (οὐκ ἀγεννής = Litotes)—Eleazar's way of saying that it was valorous, indeed, heroic—but it had consisted in the assumption that the Zealots would be able (δυνήσεσθαι, cf. Joseph. *Antiq* 8.385; 11.259; 15.270; 20.88; *Vita* 177; *BJ* 7.27) to avenge themselves on the enemy "quickly" (τάχα). To be sure, there had been limited successes earlier in the war (e.g., Joseph. *BJ* 2.430, 517–522, 541, 553–555, 562–565; 3.9, 133, 267, etc.) but these were by now only a distant memory. The situation was in fact hopeless.

7.380 φρούδη δὲ γέγονε νῦν καὶ μόνους ἡμᾶς ἐπὶ τῆς ἀνάγκης καταλέλοιπεν...: construe ἐπεί ("since," from the prev clause) with the vbs. γέγονε and καταλέλοιπεν. The fem. sing. adj. φρούδη ("gone away, clean gone") mods. ἐλπίς ("hope") in the prev clause. The expression that hope has "gone away" (φρούδη... γέγονε) seems comparable to ideas conveyed by the Greek dramatists where the adj. φροῦδος, φρούδη, φροῦδον is espec. common, e.g., φροῦδός ἐστιν (Soph. *Antig.* 15); φροῦδος ἐξ οἴκων (Eur. *Alces.* 94); κόρη φρούδη (Eur. *Andr.* 1050); φροῦδος ...σκηνὰς ἐς ἱεράς (Eur. *Ion* 804), etc. Once gone, hope had "abandoned" (καταλέλοιπεν; cf. Joseph. *BJ* 1.289) the Zealots "to their distress" (ἐπὶ τῆς ἀνάγκης, cf. Joseph. *BJ* 3.362, 385).

7.380 σπεύσωμεν καλῶς ἀποθανεῖν, ἐλεήσωμεν ἡμᾶς αὐτοὺς καὶ τὰ τέκνα καὶ τὰς γυναῖκας, ἕως ἡμῖν ἔξεστιν παρ' ἡμῶν αὐτῶν λαβεῖν τὸν ἔλεον: the vbs. σπεύσωμεν ("let us hasten," cf. Joseph. *BJ* 7.388) and ἐλεήσωμεν ("let us pity," cf. Athan. *Exp. in Ps.* vol. 27 pg. 196; *Vita* vol. 28 pg. 1532; LXX 4 Macc 8:20) repres. the delib. subjunct. (Smyth §1805). Here Eleazar uses the expression "children and wives" (τὰ τέκνα καὶ τὰς γυναῖκας; cf. Joseph. *Antiq* 13.141; 20.85), whereas Josephus may be just as inclined to write "wives and children" (τὰς γυναῖκας καὶ τὰ τέκνα, Joseph. *Antiq* 6.360; 10.136; 11.147). The clause marker ἕως + vb. in the pres. indic. ("while") denotes duration of time (Smyth §2422). The expression παρ' ἡμῶν αὐτῶν ("from ourselves") signifies that the radicalism of Eleazar's proposal is not lost on Eleazar himself, an awareness that underscores the heinousness of the suicide. Nevertheless, Eleazar's remarks betray a "logic" that motivated his hearers to do the unthinkable (Judd 1996-97, 383).

7.381 ἐπὶ μὲν γὰρ θάνατον ἐγεννήθημεν καὶ τοὺς ἐξ αὐτῶν ἐγεννήσαμεν, καὶ τοῦτον οὐδὲ τοῖς εὐδαιμονοῦσιν ἔστι διαφυγεῖν: trans. ἐγεννήθημεν (cf. Euseb. *Comm. in Is.* 1.63; Acts 2:8) as "we were born" and τοὺς ἐξ αὐτῶν ἐγεννήσαμεν as "and those [whom] we have begotten." The NT conveys a different view of birth and death, e.g., Jn 1:13; 3:3, 5; 1 Pet 1:23; 1 Jn 3:9; 5:18. Due to the circums. in which he and the Zealots find themselves, Eleazar's thinking is understandably somber. So he takes the long view: that those who were born to die—a fate which not even "the blessed" (οἱ εὐδαίμονες, cf. Joseph. *Antiq* 2.102) can evade—might as well die sooner as opp. to later. For the 2 aor. infin. διαφυγεῖν ("to evade") cf. Joseph. *BJ* 1.208, 212; 2.526; 3.332, 500; 4.288, 488; 5.118, 339; 6.85, 315, 323; 7.7, 208, 251, 277, 410.

7.382 ὕβρις δὲ καὶ δουλεία καὶ τὸ βλέπειν γυναῖκας εἰς αἰσχύνην ἀγομένας μετὰ τέκνων...: for ὕβρις ("outrage," nom. case) cf. Joseph. *Antiq* 6.61; 19.54; *Contra Ap* 2.212; for δουλεία ("slavery," nom. case) cf. Joseph. *BJ* 6.206. The articular infin. τὸ βλέπειν sets off accus. with ptc. after a vb. of percep. (ACP, Smyth §2110): "and *the seeing* of women led off to disgrace with children..." For the alleged (though in reality inaccurate) sexual violation of women by the Romans cf. Joseph. *BJ* 7.377 above. The detail that the women were to be dragged away "with children" (μετὰ τέκνων, cf. Joseph. *Antiq* 7.291; 12.272, 345; 15.145; 20.37; 7.386) may indicate slavery in general, not necessarily sexual exploitation in particular. On the other hand, sexual violation typically attended the Roman sack of cities (cf. Ziolkowski 1993).

7.382 ...οὐκ ἔστιν ἀνθρώποις κακὸν ἐκ φύσεως ἀναγκαῖον: it was no "necessary evil" (κακόν... ἀναγκαῖον, cf. Menand. *Epitrep.* 1105; Philem. Com. Frag. 196.1; John Stoeb. *Anth.* 4.22b.30.2) to see one's wife and children led away to slavery and disgrace. Indeed, Eleazar seems nearly to argue that the holdouts at Masada had "by nature" (ἐκ φύσεως, cf. Joseph. *Antiq* 15.219; 17.47) cert. inalienable rights that the Romans, should they prevail, would surely tread upon. Also quite common in Josephus are the phrases κατὰ φύσιν (*Antiq* 1.54, 323; 2.292, 295; 3.88, 261, 275; 6.283; 7.164, 304; 8.234; 12.76; *Contra Ap* 2.199) and φύσει (95 times in the Josephan corpus).

7.382 ἀλλὰ ταῦτα διὰ τὴν αὐτῶν δειλίαν ὑπομένουσιν οἱ παρὸν πρὸ αὐτῶν ἀποθανεῖν μὴ θελήσαντες: trans. in the same order as the words fall: "but these things [ταῦτα = the things mentioned in the preced clause] according to their cowardice [διὰ τὴν αὐτῶν δειλίαν] they endure, those who [οἱ]—while it is possible [παρόν] to die instead of them [πρὸ αὐτῶν]—they are not willing to." The prep. phrase πρὸ αὐτῶν ("instead of them")—like the earlier ταῦτα—refers to the indignities mentioned in the preced clause. For the vb. ὑπομένουσιν ("they endure") cf. Joseph. *Antiq* 2.208; 11.245; *Contra Ap* 2.234; *BJ* 2.118, 373; 5.486; 7.353.

7.383 ἡμεῖς δὲ ἐπ' ἀνδρείᾳ μέγα φρονοῦντες Ῥωμαίων ἀπέστημεν καὶ τὰ τελευταῖα νῦν ἐπὶ σωτηρίᾳ προκαλουμένων ἡμᾶς οὐχ ὑπηκούσαμεν: note the contr. between ἐπ' ἀνδρείᾳ ("courageously") here and διὰ τὴν αὐτῶν δειλίαν ("by cowardice") in the preced sentence. For the expression μέγα φρονοῦντες ("priding ourselves") cf. Joseph. *Antiq* 3.83; 6.298; 17.41; *Vita* 17, 43, 52; *Contra Ap* 1.99; 2.286. The 1 pers. plur. aor. vb. ἀπέστημεν ("we revolted," cf. Joseph. *BJ* 7.325) patterns with Ῥωμαίων (gen. sep. [Smyth §1392] = "we revolted *from the Romans*"). Trans. the words τὰ τελευταῖα as an adv. accus. (Smyth §1607): "finally." For the prep. phrase ἐπὶ σωτηρίᾳ ("to safety") cf. Joseph. *Antiq* 3.27, 65; 14.402; 17.152; 19.22, 42, 243; *BJ* 1.295; 3.381; 5.262. The 1 pers. plur. aor. vb. ὑπηκούσαμεν ("we hearkened to," cf. Joseph. *Vita* 116) patterns with προκαλουμένων (gen. sep. [Smyth §1392] = "we did not hearken to [the Romans who were] exhorting [us] to safety"). The Zealots had rejected an earlier offer of safety from Titus on grounds that they had sworn never to accept such offers (Joseph. *BJ* 6.351). This rejection had so infuriated Titus that he gave his men permission to burn and sack Jerusalem (Joseph. *BJ* 6.353).

7.384 τίνι τοίνυν οὐκ ἔστιν ὁ θυμὸς αὐτῶν πρόδηλος, εἰ ζώντων ἡμῶν κρατήσουσιν;: the interrog. pron. τίνι ("for whom...?") represents a dat. of ref. (Smyth §1496); the pron. αὐτῶν refers to the Romans: "for whom is *their* [= the Romans'] wrath not manifest, if...?" For the adj. πρόδηλος ("clear," "manifest") cf. Joseph. *Antiq* 17.223; *BJ* 7.182, 236, 283, 326; the vb. κρατήσουσιν (cf. Joseph. *Contra Ap* 1.236) patterns with an obj. gen.: "if *they shall seize* us [when we are] alive." Titus was capable of dealing leniently with deserters during the siege of Jerusalem (e.g., Joseph. *BJ* 5.422), although after a certain point he refused to deal clemently with any of them (Joseph. *BJ* 6.352).

7.384 ἄθλιοι μὲν οἱ νέοι τῆς ῥώμης τῶν σωμάτων εἰς πολλὰς αἰκίας ἀρκέσοντες, ἄθλιοι δὲ οἱ παρηβηκότες φέρειν τῆς ἡλικίας τὰς συμφορὰς οὐ δυναμένης: note the μέν... δέ construction. Equally "wretched" (ἄθλιοι μέν... ἄθλιοι δέ, cf. Joseph. *BJ* 7.393) in Eleazar's opinion were "the young" (οἱ νέοι, cf. Joseph. *BJ* 1.651) and those who, past their prime, "were elderly" (οἱ παρηβηκότες, from παρηβάω). The words τῆς ἡλικίας... οὐ δυναμένης repres. the gen. abs.: "*[since] their age is not able* to endure the misfortunes..." The tallest and handsomest of the youth were reserved for the triumph (Joseph. *BJ* 6.417); the lot of the older prisoners was still worse (Joseph. *BJ* 6.418; 7.24). Eleazar describes the spectacles as a form of "torture" in Joseph. *BJ* 7.369 above.

7.385 ὄψεταί τις γυναῖκα πρὸς βίαν ἀγομένην, φωνῆς ἐπακούσεται τέκνου πατέρα βοῶντος χεῖρας δεδεμένος;: with resp. to τις, text editors have added an enclitic accent to the ultima of ὄψεταί and a quest. mark (...;) to create an odd quest. here ("shall *anyone* see...?"), whereas interrog. prons. in the preced passage have more clearly sustained the rhet. nature of Eleazar's penetrating questions (τίνι...; = "to whom...?," Joseph. *BJ* 7.384; τίς... τίς... τίς...; = "who... who... who...?," Joseph. *BJ* 7.378). The 3 pers. sing. fut. vb. ὄψεται ("he shall see," cf. Joseph. *Antiq* 6.216; 10.141; *Contra Ap* 2.181) initiates accus. with ptc. after a vb. of percep. (ACP, Smyth §2110): "and someone shall see his wife led violently away." For the prep. phrase πρὸς βίαν ("violently") cf. Joseph. *Antiq* 15.281; 18.37; *BJ* 2.264. Note that the vb. ἐπακούσεται ("he shall hearken") construes with the words φωνῆς... τέκνου πατέρα βοῶντος (obj. gen.): "*he shall hearken* to the voice of his son crying 'father!'" The noun χεῖρας represents the accus. resp. (Smyth

§1601.a): "bound *with resp. to* his hands." For the pf. pass. ptc. δεδεμένος ("bound") cf. Joseph. *Antiq* 2.63; 8.140; *BJ* 7.36.

7.386 ἀλλ' ἕως εἰσὶν ἐλεύθεραι καὶ ξίφος ἔχουσιν, καλὴν ὑπουργίαν ὑπουργησάτωσαν: the fem. plur. nom. adj. ἐλεύθεραι ("free") presumes the noun χεῖρες ("hands," cf. χεῖρας in the preced sentence). Trans. ἕως as "while" or "so long as" (Smyth §2422): "but *so long as* they [i.e., the hands, cf. χεῖρας in Joseph. *BJ* 7.385] are free and grasp the sword…" The expression καλὴν ὑπουργίαν ("honorable service"), a cogn. accus. (Smyth §1564), patterns with the vb. ὑπουργησάτωσαν: "let them ply an *honorable service*"— namely, the suicide which shall transpire immediately (cf. τοῖς τὴν δύστηνον ὑπουργίαν ἐκτελοῦσιν = "to those completing the *melancholy office*," Joseph. *BJ* 7.395). For the rule of the cogn. accus. cf. the following examples: πολλὴν φλυαρίαν φλυαροῦντα = "talking *much nonsense*" (Plato *Apol.* 19c); ξυνέφυγε τὴν φυγὴν ταύτην = "he shared in *the recent exile*" (Plato *Apol.* 21a); τὴν ἐν Σαλαμῖνι ναυμαχίαν ναυμαχήσαντες = "having fought *the sea-battle* at Salamis" (Dem. 59.97); ἡ αἰτία ἣν αἰτιῶνται = "*the charge* that they bring" (Antiph. 6.27).

7.386 ἀδούλωτοι μὲν ὑπὸ τῶν πολεμίων ἀποθάνωμεν, ἐλεύθεροι δὲ μετὰ τέκνων καὶ γυναικῶν τοῦ ζῆν συνεξέλθωμεν: note the μέν… δέ construction. The following contr. parallels the μέν… δέ construction: ἀδούλωτοι ("non-enslaved") vs. ἐλεύθεροι ("free," cf. Joseph. *Antiq* 3.282; 11.210; 12.315; 14.313; 17.61 *Contra Ap* 2.134; *BJ* 3.368). The paralleled vbs., however, are synonymous: ἀποθάνωμεν ("let us die") vs. τοῦ ζῆν συνεξέλθωμεν ("let us depart together from life"). The articular infin. τοῦ ζῆν represents the gen. of sep. (Smyth §1392): "*from* life." For the prep. phrase ὑπὸ τῶν πολεμίων ("by our enemies") cf. Joseph. *BJ* 2.49; 7.386; for the prep. phrase μετὰ τέκνων καὶ γυναικῶν ("with our wives and children") cf. Joseph. *Antiq* 7.291; 12.272, 345; 15.145.

7.387 ταῦθ' ἡμᾶς οἱ νόμοι κελεύουσι, ταῦθ' ἡμᾶς γυναῖκες καὶ παῖδες ἱκετεύουσι: the repeated demonstr. prons. ταῦθ'… ταῦθ' (anaphora) refer to what Eleazar has said in prev clauses about dying (ἀποθάνωμεν, Joseph. *BJ* 7.386) and withdrawing from life (τοῦ ζῆν συνεξέλθωμεν, Joseph. *BJ* 7.386). However, Eleazar's statement seems more rhet. than fact.: where do Israel's laws (οἱ νόμοι, cf. Joseph. *Antiq* 12.107; 16.3; 20.16; *Contra Ap* 2.280; *BJ* 3.356; 5.124) enjoin suicide? (Cf. Jacobs 1982 for the ideal of martyrdom in various sources.) And did the wives and children really supplicate their husbands and fathers to be put to death? Josephus states that Eleazar's *hearers* were in a haste to commit the deed (πρὸς τὴν πρᾶξιν ἠπείγοντο, Joseph. *BJ* 7.389), but conspicuously leaves unsaid the resolves of the wives and children (cf. Joseph. *BJ* 7.389, 391, 393). For κελεύουσι ("they command") cf. Joseph. *Antiq* 4.211; 10.94; 11.45; 15.406; *Vita* 62, 233, 317; *BJ* 3.7; 4.274; for ἱκετεύουσι ("they supplicate") cf. Joseph. *BJ* 4.311.

7.387 τούτων τὴν ἀνάγκην θεὸς ἀπέσταλκε, τούτων Ῥωμαῖοι τἀναντία θέλουσι, καὶ μή τις ἡμῶν πρὸ τῆς ἁλώσεως ἀποθάνῃ δεδοίκασι: the prons. τούτων... τούτων (cf. ταῦθ'... ταῦθ' in the preced clause) refer to the prospect of dying and departing from life (ἀποθάνωμεν... τοῦ ζῆν συνεξέλθωμεν, Joseph. *BJ* 7.386). For the idea that Israel's God has sent a "necessity" (τὴν ἀνάγκην, cf. Joseph. *Antiq* 2.60; 3.22; 7.193; 18.148; 20.209; *BJ* 3.271; 4.122, 637; 6.433; 7.53, 196) for suicide cf. Joseph. *BJ* 7.325, 358. But the argument used here flatly contradicts Josephus' own at Jotapata (*BJ* 3.370–370). The Romans, out of a greed for slaves and booty, desire just "the opposite" (τἀναντία = τά + ἐναντία) of what Eleazar and his listeners desire. The vb. δεδοίκασι is one of a category of vbs. in the pf. tense that needs to be trans. as a pres. (Smyth §1946): "they are afraid." Cf. κέκλημαι ("I have received a name" = "I am called"); κέκτημαι ("I have acquired" = "I possess"); τέθνηκα ("I have passed away" = "I am dead"). The clause marker μή after a vb. of fearing sets off a fear clause, prim. seq. (Smyth §§2221–2232): "they fear *lest* any one of us should die before capture." For the vb. ἀπέσταλκε ("he has sent") cf. Joseph. *Antiq* 7.205; for the vb. θέλουσι ("they desire") cf. Joseph. *Antiq* 3.67, 281; 7.156; 9.264; 20.264; *Vita* 31; *BJ* 6.128; for the vb. ἀποθάνῃ ("he die") cf. Joseph. *Antiq* 4.277, 282; 6.204; 8.301, 334; 10.121.

7.388 σπεύσωμεν οὖν ἀντὶ τῆς ἐλπιζομένης αὐτοῖς καθ' ἡμῶν ἀπολαύσεως ἔκπληξιν τοῦ θανάτου καὶ θαῦμα τῆς τόλμης καταλιπεῖν.": Follow this order in trans.: 1) σπεύσωμεν οὖν... καταλιπεῖν... αὐτοῖς...; 2) ἀντὶ τῆς ἐλπιζομένης... καθ' ἡμῶν ἀπολαύσεως; 3) ἔκπληξιν τοῦ θανάτου καὶ θαῦμα τῆς τόλμης. The pers. pron. αὐτοῖς refers to the Romans; the "expected adv. [τῆς ἐλπιζομένης... ἀπολαύσεως] at our expense" refers to the profit the Romans expect to make as a res. of selling the captured Zealots as slaves. Eleazar exhorts the Zealots to die and so create for the Romans an "amazement at our death" (ἔκπληξιν τοῦ θανάτου) and "admiration for our boldness" (θαῦμα τῆς τόλμης)—and indeed the Romans did admire the nobility of the Zealots' death after the suicide (cf. Joseph. *BJ* 7.406). For the vb. σπεύσωμεν ("let us make haste") cf. Joseph. *BJ* 7.380.

BJ 7.389–401

7.389 Ἔτι βουλόμενον αὐτὸν παρακαλεῖν πάντες ὑπετέμνοντο καὶ πρὸς τὴν πρᾶξιν ἠπείγοντο, ἀνεπισχέτου τινὸς ὁρμῆς πεπληρωμένοι...: the pers. pron. αὐτόν refers to Eleazar; πάντες, to the Zealots. The prep. phrase πρὸς τὴν πρᾶξιν ("to the deed," cf. Joseph. *Antiq* 2.21) refers to the suicide. For the vb. ὑπετέμνοντο ("cut off, intercept," in the mid.) cf. Joseph. *BJ* 4.423. The vb. ἐπείγω in the pass. oft means "hurry oneself, haste to do" + infin.; for the vb. ἠπείγοντο cf. Joseph. *Antiq* 7.224; 17.146; 18.332; 19.63; *BJ* 2.213. For ἀνεπισχέτου τινὸς ὁρμῆς πεπληρωμένοι ("full of a cert. unstoppable impulse") cf. πεπληρ. πυρὸς φλεγομένου (Joseph. *Antiq* 3.227); πεπληρ. ...τροφῆς (Joseph. *Antiq* 10.260); κρεῶν πεπληρ. (Joseph. *Antiq* 10.262).

7.389 ...καὶ δαιμονῶντες ἀπῄεσαν ἄλλος πρὸ ἄλλου φθάσαι γλιχόμενος: how else could the Zealots have complied with Eleazar's request unless they were δαιμονῶντες (lit. "god-possessed," cf. Basil *Enarr. in Isaiam* 13.255; *Serm.* vol. 32 pg. 1325; Euseb. *Praep. Ev.* 4.4.1; *De Laud. Const.* 16.5)—i.e., under the influence of an alien, non-rational spirit? For ἀπῄεσαν ("they went away") cf. Joseph. *Antiq* 2.126; 5.56; 8.124; 11.68; 12.106; 14.289; 16.65; 17.218; 19.189; 20.129; *Vita* 280; *BJ* 7.155. The pron. ἄλλος ("other, another") followed by the same pron. derived from itself in a different case (cf. Lat. *alius aliud* = "one... one, another... another") does not require the second half of the statement to be expressed (Smyth §1274). Thus, ἄλλος πρὸ ἄλλου φθάσαι γλιχόμενος means, "each one eager to comply before the other." Cf. the statement, ἄλλος ἄλλα λέγει = "one says one thing, another says another thing" (Xen. *Ana.* 2.1.15). For the pres. mid. ptc. γλιχόμενος ("eager" + infin.) cf. Joseph. *Antiq* 10.210; *BJ* 1.104.

7.389 ...καὶ ταύτην ἐπίδειξιν εἶναι τῆς ἀνδρείας καὶ τῆς εὐβουλίας νομίζοντες, τὸ μή τις ἐν ὑστάτοις γενόμενος ὀφθῆναι: trans. first the ptc. νομίζοντες (cf. Joseph. *BJ* 2.151; 7.49, 61, 64, 191, 271, 338, 394) which sets off accus. with infin. in indir. state. (Smyth §1867): "*supposing* that this [namely, the slaughter!] was the demonstration of courage and prudence." The clause that the def. article τό sets off provides the content of what this "demonstration" consisted—namely, "each man not being seen to be among the last." That is, listener vied with listener to be among the first to comply with Eleazar's request. For the expression ταύτην ἐπίδειξιν... τῆς ἀνδρείας ("this demonstration of manliness") cf. the expressions ἀνδρείας ἐπίδειξιν (Joseph. *Antiq* 13.378; *BJ* 1.321) and ἐπίδειξιν ἀνδρείας (Joseph. *BJ* 6.42); for τῆς εὐβουλίας ("prudence") cf. Joseph. *BJ* 5.320; for ἐν ὑστάτοις ("among the last") cf. Joseph. *BJ* 5.456.

7.389 τοσοῦτος αὐτοῖς γυναικῶν καὶ παιδίων καὶ τῆς αὐτῶν σφαγῆς ἔρως ἐνέπεσεν: the adj. τοσοῦτος mods. ἔρως ("so great a longing"); the pron. αὐτοῖς refers to the listeners; the compound vb. ἐνέπεσεν patterns with the pron. αὐτοῖς in the dat. case (Smyth §1545): "so great a longing for their wives', children's', and their own slaughter *befell them*." For the phrase γυναικῶν καὶ παιδίων ("wives' and children's'") cf. Joseph. *Antiq* 5.29; *BJ* 4.107, 110; 5.448 (cf. γυναικί... καὶ παισί, Joseph. *BJ* 7.395; τὰς γυναῖκας καὶ τὰ τέκνα, Joseph. *Antiq* 6.360; 10.136; 11.147); for the word τῆς... σφαγῆς ("slaughter") cf. Joseph. *Antiq* 1.102, 225, 233; 2.255; 7.39; 17.316; 19.42, 102; *BJ* 3.385; 4.344; for the vb. ἐνέπεσεν ("befell") cf. Joseph. *Antiq* 6.250; 7.316; 13.30; *Vita* 46; *BJ* 3.498; 5.353.

7.390 καὶ μὴν οὐδ' ὅπερ ἄν τις ᾠήθη τῇ πράξει προσιόντες ἠμβλύνθησαν: the expression καὶ μήν (Joseph. *Antiq* 5.30; 16.39;

18.190; *Vita* 100, 256; *Contra Ap* 1.168, 282; 2.140, 181, 257; *BJ* 6.330, 331) oft introduces a new fact or a transition (Smyth §2921). With the neg. particle οὐδέ trans.: "furthermore, they were not even..." (the vb. ἠμβλύνθησαν completes the idea). Here ὅπερ (formed from the rel. pron. ὅ + enclitic –περ, cf. Smyth §338.d) introduces a subordinate idea that intrudes upon the mn. idea to provide a powerful rhet. punch: "furthermore, they were not even blunted [in their resolve] as they went to the task, *the very thing which* [ὅπερ] someone might suppose [they would be]." The particle ἄν + indic. in the past tense = the past pot. (Smyth §1784). In οὐδ'... ἠμβλύνθησαν (lit. "nor did they *become dull*") Josephus has expressed perfectly the Zealots' bitter resolve to comply with Eleazar's request. Speakers of Eng. might say (to express the same idea): "nor did they *lose their nerve*..." For the vb. ᾠήθη ("suppose") cf. Joseph. *Antiq* 1.23; 15.286; 16.76, 355; *Contra Ap* 2.159; *BJ* 1.106; for the expression τῇ πράξει ("the deed") as a ref. to the suicide cf. τὴν πρᾶξιν in Joseph. *BJ* 7.389 above.

7.390 ἀλλ' ἀτενῆ τὴν γνώμην διεφύλαξαν οἵαν ἔσχον τῶν λόγων ἀκροώμενοι: the adj. ἀτενῆ in the accus. case (from ἀτενής, -ές) is in the pred. pos.: "they guarded *as inflex.* the resolve..." The word ἀτενῆ ("inflex.") recalls Eleazar's resolve when he, with an "inflex. gaze," confronted the waverers at an earlier point in the speech (cf. ἀτενὲς ἐμβλέψας, Joseph. *BJ* 7.341). The rel. adj. οἵαν refers to τὴν γνώμην ("the resolve *of the sort* they had..."); the pres. act. ptc. ἀκροώμενοι (cf. Joseph. *Antiq* 8.173) patterns with the obj. gen. τῶν λόγων: "...*as they were listening to* his words." For the vb. διεφύλαξαν ("they guarded") cf. Joseph. *BJ* 2.221; 7.418.

7.390 τοῦ μὲν οἰκείου καὶ φιλοστόργου πάθους ἅπασι παραμένοντος, τοῦ λογισμοῦ δὲ ὡς τὰ κράτιστα βεβουλευκότος τοῖς φιλτάτοις ἐπικρατοῦντος: both clauses feature the gen. abs. Note also the μέν... δέ construction which effects a contr. between τοῦ... πάθους and τοῦ λογισμοῦ—that is, between personal and kindly "affection" and the sort of brute "reason" that, having already made "the best" (τὰ κράτιστα) decision for loved ones, would spare them the indignities Eleazar claims in Joseph. *BJ* 7.382 and 385 above. Trans. τὰ κράτιστα as an adv. accus. (Smyth §1607); the particle ὡς + superl. τὰ κράτιστα means "the best possible." So e.g., ὡς μάλιστα = Lat. *quam maxime*; ὡς ῥᾷστα = Lat. *quam facillime*; ὡς τάχιστα = Lat. *quam celerrime*. In its abs. sense the vb. ἐπικρατέω (cf. ptc. ἐπικρατοῦντος) means simply "prevail in battle, be victorious" (LSJ II.1). For the phrase τοῖς φιλτάτοις ("dearest ones") cf. Joseph. *Antiq* 13.231, 232.

7.391 ὁμοῦ γὰρ ἠσπάζοντο γυναῖκας περιπτυσσόμενοι καὶ τέκνα προσηγκαλίζοντο τοῖς ὑστάτοις φιλήμασιν ἐμφυόμενοι καὶ δακρύοντες...: the adv. ὁμοῦ ("together, at once," repeated in Joseph. *BJ* 7.392) increases the vividness of a scene replete with actions associated with taking leave of loved ones: ἠσπάζοντο... περιπτυσσόμενοι... προσηγκαλίζοντο... τοῖς ὑστάτοις φιλήμασιν ἐμφυόμενοι... δακρύοντες. In the mid. the vb. περιπτύσσω means "embrace" (LSJ I.3; περιπτ. χέρας = "fold the arms round another," LSJ II.1, cf. Eur. *Alces*. 350; *Andr*. 417); the vb. προσαγκαλίζομαι (cf. ἀγκάλισμα ["embrace"]; ἀγκαλίζομαι) means "carry in the arms"; by the expression τοῖς ὑστάτοις φιλήμασιν ἐμφυόμενοι Josephus describes parents who are lit. grown in (or "engrafted," cf. φύω in the mid./pass.) to final kisses exchanged with children; for δακρύοντες ("weeping") cf. Joseph. *Antiq* 2.159; 4.133, 324; *Vita* 210; *BJ* 7.340. By placing such emotionally charged words in close proximity Josephus creates a highly moving scene, one calculated to work powerfully upon the imagination of the reader.

7.392 ὁμοῦ δὲ καθάπερ ἀλλοτρίαις χερσὶν ὑπουργούμενοι συνετέλουν τὸ βούλευμα: at precisely "the same time" (ὁμοῦ) as the holdouts at Masada were taking leave of loved ones—with embraces, final kisses, and tears—they "finalized their plan" (συνετέλουν τὸ βούλευμα), a phrase that recalls Eleazar's earlier "deliberations" (cf. ἐβουλεύσατο, Joseph. *BJ* 7.321) upon the death of so many. Likewise, the seemingly benign statement that the Zealots were "acting" (ὑπουργούμενοι) as if with other peoples' hands recalls Eleazar's earlier exhortation that his listeners should "render an honorable service" (καλὴν ὑπουργίαν ὑπουργησάτωσαν, Joseph. *BJ* 7.386), i.e., perpetrate the suicide (cf. τὴν δύστηνον ὑπουργίαν, Joseph. *BJ* 7.395).

7.392 τὴν ἐπίνοιαν ὧν πείσονται κακῶν ὑπὸ τοῖς πολεμίοις γενόμενοι παραμύθιον τῆς ἐν τῷ κτείνειν ἀνάγκης ἔχοντες: the ptc. ἔχοντες governs both τὴν ἐπίνοιαν and παραμύθιον: "...having the notion [τὴν ἐπίνοιαν] of what evils they would suffer..., a consolation [παραμύθιον] of necessity amid the killing..." Trans. the circumst. ptc. γενόμενοι (cf. Joseph. *BJ* 1.250; 4.135, 431; 6.59, 119; 7.329) conditionally (cf. Smyth §2060): "*if* they should come under the enemies' hands..." For τὴν ἐπίνοιαν ("the notion") cf. Joseph. *Antiq* 2.307; 3.73; 5.170; 15.91; *Vita* 287; *BJ* 3.175, 192, 258; 5.472; for the vb. πείσονται ("they will suffer") cf. Joseph. *Antiq* 2.23; 4.210; 9.265; for the idiom ὑπὸ τοῖς πολεμίοις ("under the enemies' hands") cf. ὑπὸ Ῥωμαίοις in Joseph. *BJ* 7.372 above.

7.393 καὶ πέρας οὐδεὶς τηλικούτου τολμήματος ἥττων εὑρέθη, πάντες δὲ διὰ τῶν οἰκειοτάτων διεξῆλθον: for the adv. πέρας ("finally") cf. Joseph. *BJ* 1.511, 673; 3.47, 51,297; 5.189; 6.73, 147; 7.157, 168, 195, 449, 454. Note the contr. between "no one" (οὐδείς) and "all" (πάντες): so highly affected had been "all" who heard Eleazar's influential speech that "no one" was found "not up to" the brazen act (ἥττων + gen.) Josephus recounts now. For the 3 pers. sing. pass. vb. εὑρέθη ("was found") cf. Joseph. *BJ* 2.357; 5.445; 7.299. Here the vb. διεξῆλθον ("they ran through," cf. Joseph. *Antiq* 8.56; 9.214; 14.442; *Contra Ap* 1.315; *BJ* 3.108; 6.50) has the spec. sense "go through in succession," i.e., "kill them one after another" (cf. Hdt. 3.11; 5.92; Plato *Protag.* 315a).

7.393 ἄθλιοι τῆς ἀνάγκης, οἷς αὐτοχειρὶ γυναῖκας τὰς αὐτῶν καὶ τέκνα κτεῖναι κακῶν ἔδοξεν εἶναι τὸ κουφότατον: for the expression ἄθλιοι τῆς ἀνάγκης ("wretches of necessity") cf. παραμύθιον τῆς ἐν τῷ κτείνειν ἀνάγκης ("refuge of necessity amid the killing," Joseph. *BJ* 7.392). The epithet ἄθλιοι ("wretched") recalls the young captives whose vigorous frames would be able to withstand many tortures (ἄθλιοι... οἱ νέοι, Joseph. *BJ* 7.384) and those more advanced in years who would not be able to bear such calamities (ἄθλιοι... οἱ παρηβηκότες, Joseph. *BJ* 7.384). The anteced. of the rel. pron. οἷς ("to whom") is ἄθλιοι; trans. with the rel. pron. οἷς the impers. vb. ἔδοξεν ("to whom it seemed...").

Likewise, trans. the superl. τὸ κουφότατον ("the slightest") with the part. gen. κακῶν: "to whom it seemed to be *the slightest of evils* to kill by hand their own wives and children." For the adv. αὐτοχειρί ("with one's own hand") cf. App. *Lib.* 499.1; *Bell. Civ.* 2.6.43; Eur. *Med.* 1281; *Orest.* 947, 1040; Paus. *Graec. Desc.* 4.8.8; 7.16.6; Soph. *Antig.* 172; *Elect.* 1019, etc.

7.394 οὔτε δὴ τοίνυν τὴν ἐπὶ τοῖς πεπραγμένοις ὀδύνην ἔτι φέροντες...: in place of οὔτε δή some editors prefer οὗτοι δή: "and these [killers] indeed..." The more accepted version allows the adv. οὔτε to negate the phrase ...ἔτι φέροντες: "nor, accordingly [τοίνυν], could they yet bear..." The perpetrators could scarcely bear the grief (τὴν... ὀδύνην, cf. Joseph. *Antiq* 1.343; 15.62; 16.208) of having put loved ones to death. For the expression ἐπὶ τοῖς πεπραγμένοις ("at what had been done") cf. Joseph. *Antiq* 5.267; 20.178; *Vita* 311.

7.394 ...καὶ τοὺς ἀνῃρημένους νομίζοντες ἀδικεῖν εἰ καὶ βραχὺν αὐτοῖς ἔτι χρόνον ἐπιζήσουσι: the phrase τοὺς ἀνῃρημένους (pf. mid./pass. ptc. of ἀναιρέω = "the slain," cf. Joseph. *Antiq* 7.310; *BJ* 2.34; 4.384) functions as the obj. of ἀδικεῖν; the pres. act. ptc. νομίζοντες (Joseph. *BJ* 2.152; 7.50, 61, 64, 191, 271, 338, 389) sets off accus. with infin. in indir. state. (Smyth §1867): "supposing that they [i.e., the perpetrators] were harming the slain..." The words εἰ... ἐπιζήσουσι comprise the protasis of a fut. most vivid cond. (Smyth §2328); the words βραχὺν... χρόνον constitutes the accus. ext. of time (Smyth §1580): "if they shall outlive them *for even a short time.*"

7.394 ταχὺ μὲν τὴν κτῆσιν ἅπασαν εἰς ταὐτὸ σωρεύσαντες πῦρ εἰς αὐτὴν ἐνέβαλον: the Zealots, under Eleazar's leadership, had been in the habit of plundering Jewish property and setting fire to it (πῦρ ἐνιέντες, Joseph. *BJ* 7.254) on grounds that such unworthy Jews preferred Roman servitude to hard-won "liberty" (τὴν περιμάχητον... ἐλευθερίαν, Joseph. *BJ* 7.255). Here with bitter irony Josephus presents the Zealots doing to themselves what they had done so spitefully to others. For the expression σωρεύσαντες ("having heaped up") cf. ἐσεσώρευντο (Joseph. *BJ* 7.296, of the food "heaped up" in the storage compartments at Masada). For the expression πῦρ... ἐνέβαλον ("they set fire") cf. τοῖς... ἔργοις ἐνέβαλλεν πῦρ

(Joseph. *BJ* 3.205), the subj. of whom is Josephus himself. Josephus himself had "set fire" to the Roman siege instruments at Jotapata during the last, most desperate fighting for that city in AD 67.

7.395 κλήρῳ δ' ἐξ αὐτῶν ἑλόμενοι δέκα τοὺς ἁπάντων σφαγεῖς ἐσομένους: for the expression κλήρῳ ("by lot") cf. Joseph. *Antiq* 5.82; 6.125; 9.210; *BJ* 3.97, 388; for ἑλόμενοι (aor. mid. ptc. of αἱρέω = "having chosen") cf. *Antiq* 4.222; 16.37; *Contra Ap* 2.172; *BJ* 7.324, 336. Here the fut. ptc. ἐσομένους denotes pur. (Smyth §2065): "...*to be* the killers of all." Cf. the comparable expressions κήρυκα πόλεμον προεροῦντα = "herald *to proclaim* war" (Thuc. 1.29); ὁ βάρβαρος ἐπὶ τὴν Ἑλλάδα δουλωσόμενος ἦλθεν = "the Barbarian came against Greece *to enslave* it" (Thuc. 1.18). Inscribed ostraca at Masada possibly provide "physical proof" for the lottery (Huntsman 1996–97, 370).

7.395 καὶ γυναικί τις αὐτὸν καὶ παισὶ κειμένοις παραστρώσας καὶ τὰς χεῖρας περιβαλών: the aor. act. ptc. παραστρώσας patterns with γυναικί... παισὶ κειμένοις: "having laid oneself down beside one's wife and children lying (dead) upon the ground." For the earlier deaths of the Zealots' wives and children cf. Joseph. *BJ* 7.392. For the expression τὰς χεῖρας περιβαλών ("having cast their hands about [their loved ones]") cf. περιβαλών... τὰς χεῖρας (Pseud. Apoll. *Bib.* 2.126); περιβαλών... περὶ τὰς χεῖρας (Iambl. *Babylon.* 97.1); τὰς χεῖρας περιβαλών (Theophyl. *Hist.* 2.18.19). For περιβαλών (aor. act. ptc. of περιβάλλω) cf. Joseph. *Antiq* 1.270; 5.249; 7.168; 8.154; 13.16, 276; 17.251; *BJ* 7.173, 250.

7.395 παρεῖχον ἑτοίμους τὰς σφαγὰς τοῖς τὴν δύστηνον ὑπουργίαν ἐκτελοῦσιν: for the vb. παρεῖχον (impf.: "they kept offering") cf. Joseph. *Antiq* 3.102, 131; 10.71; 11.230; 17.286; *Vita* 113; *BJ* 1.250; 4.27; 5.274; 6.26, 140. The adj. ἑτοίμους (from ἕτοιμος, -ον) mods. τὰς σφαγὰς ("throat," i.e., "the spot where the victim is struck," LSJ II.1). The phrase "those completing the unhappy task" refers to those ten appointed by lot to be the "killers" for the rest (cf. τοὺς ἁπάντων σφαγεῖς, Joseph. *BJ* 7.395). Again, the expression τὴν... ὑπουργίαν ("the task," cf. Joseph. *Antiq* 2.259;

16.186) is here a euphemism for the perpetration of the slaughter (cf. τῇ πράξει, Joseph. *BJ* 7.390; ὑπουργούμενοι, Joseph. *BJ* 7.392).

7.396 οἱ δ' ἀτρέπτως πάντας φονεύσαντες τὸν αὐτὸν ἐπ' ἀλλήλοις τοῦ κλήρου νόμον ὥρισαν: some editors prefer ἀτρέστως ("without trembling," cf. variant ἄτρεστον in Joseph. *BJ* 7.370) to ἀτρέπτως ("inflexibly," "without hesitation"); either adv. captures the almost unbelievable ruthlessness of the Zealots. Having dispatched "all" (πάντας) the others, the remaining Zealots apply the same rule of the lot to each other as that mentioned in Joseph. *BJ* 7.395. For the aor. ptc. φονεύσαντες ("having slaughtered") cf. Joseph. *BJ* 6.358; for the vb. ὥρισαν ("they ordained") cf. Joseph. *Antiq* 18.149.

7.396 ἵν' ὁ λαχὼν τοὺς ἐννέα κτείνας ἑαυτὸν ἐπὶ πᾶσιν ἀνέλῃ: according to the usual rules of syntax, the words ἵνα... ἀνέλῃ ought to set off a pur. clause in prim. seq. (Smyth §2196), e.g., γράφω ἵνα ἐκμάθῃς = "I write in order that you may learn." However, the aorists φονεύσαντες and ὥρισαν in the preced clause ought, by normal rules, set off a pur. clause in sec. seq. (Smyth §2196), thus, ἔγραψα ἵνα ἐκμάθοις = "I wrote in order that you might learn." Josephus' violation of the normal rules of grammar (by substituting the subjunct. ἀνέλῃ for the more normal ἄνελοι in the optv.) makes this pur. clause vivid, a touch that highlights the horrific nature of the action narrated. The rule of the lot mentioned in the prev clause is here revealed more clearly: that the one allotted (ὁ λαχών, cf. Joseph. *BJ* 3.389, 390) to dispatch the other nine "killers" (cf. σφαγεῖς, Joseph. *BJ* 7.395) at length dispatch himself. For the aor. act. ptc. κτείνας cf. Joseph. *BJ* 1.89, 235, 437, 497, 518; 5.162; for the vb. ἀνέλῃ, cf. Joseph. *Antiq* 1.162; 6.157.

7.396 πάντες οὕτως αὐτοῖς ἐθάρρουν μήτ' εἰς τὸ δρᾶν μήτ' εἰς τὸ παθεῖν ἄλλος ἄλλου διαφέρειν: πάντες ("all") seems Ironic. In fact Josephus describes only such few as remained after having killed ninety percent of the other holdouts at Masada (cf. Joseph. *BJ* 7.395)—and those desperados had already dispatched their own wives and children (Joseph. *BJ* 7.393)! Trans. the clause αὐτοῖς ἐθάρρουν... διαφέρειν as follows: "thus they kept encouraging each other to differ the one from another neither in the doing of the deed nor in the suffering of it." In context, τὸ δρᾶν means to perpetrate the slaughter and τὸ παθεῖν, to suffer it. For the vb. ἐθάρρουν ("they were encouraging") cf. Joseph. *BJ* 2.543; 4.307; 5.8, 544; for the expression τὸ παθεῖν ("the suffering") cf. Joseph. *BJ* 2.63; for the pres. act. infin. διαφέρειν ("to differ") cf. Joseph. *BJ* 3.88; 4.134; 7.255.

7.397 καὶ τέλος οἱ μὲν τὰς σφαγὰς ὑπέθεσαν, ὁ δ' εἷς καὶ τελευταῖος τὸ πλῆθος τῶν κειμένων περιαθρήσας, μή πού τις ἔτ' ἐν πολλῷ φόνῳ τῆς αὐτοῦ λείπεται χειρὸς δεόμενος: trans. τέλος as an adv. accus. (Smyth §1607): "finally…" Note the μέν… δέ construction: οἱ μέν ("some," i.e., nine of the ten designated in Joseph. *BJ* 7.395) vs. ὁ δ' εἷς… τελευταῖος ("the last solitary survivor"). For the vb. ὑπέθεσαν ("they bared their necks") cf. Aeschines *in Ctes.* 104; Galen *ad Artes Addisc.* 2; Plato *Polit.* 308a; *Leg.* 682c; for τὰς σφαγάς ("necks"), used of the throat where a victim was struck cf. Joseph. *BJ* 7.395; for the aor. ptc. περιαθρήσας ("looked about") cf. Joseph. *BJ* 1.662. Trans. μή που as "lest perhaps." The vb. δέω/δέομαι, in the expression τῆς αὐτοῦ… χειρὸς δεόμενος ("needing his own hand"), patterns oft with a gen. of Quality, e.g., πολλοῦ γε δέω = "I lack much," i.e., "nothing of the sort" (Plato *Phaed.* 228a); μικροῦ ἔδεον ἐν χερσὶ τῶν ὁπλιτῶν εἶναι = "they were just short of being in the hands of the hoplites" (Xen. *Hiero* 4.6.11); τοῦτο ὑμῶν δέομαι = "I lack this of you," i.e., "I am so far from admiring" (Dem. 8.70).

7.397 ὡς ἔγνω πάντας ἀνῃρημένους, πῦρ μὲν πολὺ τοῖς βασιλείοις ἐνίησιν: trans. the particle ὡς as "when" (Smyth §2383.b). The vb. ἔγνω ("he knew") sets off accus. with ptc. after a vb. of percep. (ACP, Smyth §2110): "when [ὡς] he noticed that everyone was slain." For the pf. pass. ptc. ἀνῃρημένους ("slain") cf. Joseph. *Antiq* 7.310; 12.182; *BJ* 2.34; 4.384; 7.394; for the idiom πῦρ… ἐνίησιν ("enkindle a fire") cf. Joseph. *BJ* 5.469; 6.252; in *BJ* 7.289 Josephus refers to the struct. Herod built at Masada as a βασίλειον (in the sing.), whereas here the plur. τοῖς βασιλείοις contributes to the idea that the fire would destroy individual rooms of the collective whole.

7.397 ἀθρόᾳ δὲ τῇ χειρὶ δι' αὐτοῦ πᾶν ἐλάσας τὸ ξίφος πλησίον τῶν οἰκείων κατέπεσε: trans. the instr. dat. (Smyth §1507) ἀθρόᾳ... τῇ χειρί as "gathering his strength." For the aor. act. ptc. ἐλάσας ("having driven through") cf. Joseph. *Antiq* 13.393; 19.126; *BJ* 2.69; 3.497. Artful placement of the adj. πᾶν ("all"), which mods. τὸ ξίφος ("straight sword"), contributes to the idea that the sword the lone killer used to dispatch himself was quite long. The final assassin "fell dead" (κατέπεσε, cf. Joseph. *Antiq* 5.27; 7.142; 9.88; 12.357; 13.61; *BJ* 1.213; 3.233; 6.64, 176) near family members, just as those had died while holding slain wives and children in their arms (cf. Joseph. *BJ* 7.395 above).

7.398 καὶ οἱ μὲν ἐτεθνήκεσαν ὑπειληφότες οὐδὲν ἔχον ψυχὴν ὑποχείριον ἐξ αὐτῶν Ῥωμαίοις καταλιπεῖν: note the μέν... δέ construction (οἱ μὲν ἐτεθνήκεσαν here) vs. ἔλαθεν δὲ γυνὴ πρεσβῦτις in the next clause (Joseph. *BJ* 7.3.99 below). For the vb. ἐτεθνήκεσαν ("they had died") cf. Appian 1.11.98; 5.11.98; Plut. *Public*. 11.2; *Marcellus* 9.4; Thuc. 7.85.4. The subj. of the 2 aor. infin. καταλιπεῖν is the same as that featured in the pf. ptc. ὑπειληφότες: "and they had died, having supposed that *they* had not left a soul from themselves alive... to be [ἔχον = pres. ptc. neut. of ἔχω] subj. to the Romans." Josephus uses the neut. gender because, at capture, slaves lost personhood and so became mere "things." For the expression ὑποχείριον (cf. Lat. *sub manu*) cf. Joseph. *BJ* 3.144; 4.249; 7.33.

7.399 ἔλαθεν δὲ γυνὴ πρεσβῦτις καὶ συγγενὴς ἑτέρα τις Ἐλεαζάρου: there are two subjs. here—γυνὴ πρεσβῦτις and συγγενὴς ἑτέρα τις Ἐλεαζάρου—though the vb. ἔλαθεν ("escaped notice," cf. Joseph. *Antiq* 9.68; 13.8; 14.277; 15.280; *Vita* 425; *BJ* 4.236; 7.215) occurs in the sing. Vbs. may agree in number with the nearer or more imp. of two or more subjects (Smyth §968), e.g., πάρειμι καὶ ἐγὼ καὶ οὗτος Φρυνίσκος... καὶ Πολυκράτης = "both I and Phryniscus are present here... and Polycrates" (Xen. *Ana.* 7.2.29). The common epithet συγγενὴς ("relative," cf. Joseph. *Antiq* 1.252, 316; 4.14; 5.323, 327; 7.207, 277, 302; 11.36, 58; 13.120; 15.169; 17.167; *Vita* 177; *BJ* 4.568) occurs oft in the NT, e.g., Lk 1:58; 2:44; 14:12; 21:16; Jn 18:26; Acts 10:24; Rom 9:3; 16:7, 11, 21. Some mss. read ἑταίρα ("concubine, courtesan") in place of ἑτέρα ("other"), a version that seems more compatible with Josephus' observation that the second woman surpassed others "in cleverness and training," which are servile descrs.

7.399 φρονήσει καὶ παιδείᾳ πλεῖστον γυναικῶν διαφέρουσα: the vb. διαφέρω freq means to differ—i.e., by excelling or surpassing. Here the quality of excellence occurs in the dat. case ("very much surpassing women *in cleverness and training* [φρονήσει καὶ παιδείᾳ]"), a usage than be attested elsewhere, e.g., πότερον εἴδει διαφέρουσα ἢ γένει (Aristot. *De Anima* 402b); μακαριότητι διαφέρουσα (Arist. *Nich. Eth.* 1178b), but also: διαφέρουσαι δ' ἀλλήλων (Aristot. *Nich. Eth.* 1108a); ἐν μηδενὶ διαφέρουσαν (Basil *Ep.* 189.6.24); μικρὸν διαφέρουσα τὸ εἶδος (Dio Chrys. *Or.* 1.75.1). It was because of this woman's cleverness (φρονήσει, cf. Joseph. *Antiq* 2.9, 46, 299; 6.10; 8.190, 211; *Vita* 192; *Contra Ap* 2.242) and training (παιδείᾳ, cf. Joseph. *Antiq* 12.53, 118; 16.243; 19.213; *Vita* 196; *Contra Ap* 1.181; 2.46) that she had been able to survive the suicide.

7.399 καὶ πέντε παιδία τοῖς ὑπονόμοις, οἳ ποτὸν ἦγον ὕδωρ διὰ γῆς, ἐγκατακρυβῆναι: the text has suffered corruption. Both ἐγκατακρυβῆναι (aor. pass. infin. from ἐγκατακρύπτω: "to hide in") and the variant ἐγκατακρυβεῖσαι (aor. pass. fem. nom. plur. ptc.) seem out of place, though the sense is clear. The anteced. of the rel. pron. οἵ is τοῖς ὑπονόμοις (cf. Joseph. *BJ* 3.336; 6.393, 429, 433; 7.36), the underground passages through which potable water flowed (for the water cisterns at Masada cf. Joseph. *BJ* 7.291).

7.399 τῶν ἄλλων πρὸς τῇ σφαγῇ τὰς διανοίας ἐχόντων: gen. abs.: "as the others were holding their attns. to the slaughter." For the words τῇ σφαγῇ ("the slaughter") cf. Joseph. *Antiq* 18.88, 337; *BJ* 1.472; for τὰς διανοίας ("attns.") cf. Joseph. *Antiq* 2.191; 6.264; 17.204; *BJ* 5.66.

7.400 οἳ τὸν ἀριθμὸν ἦσαν ἑξήκοντα πρὸς τοῖς ἐνακοσίοις γυναικῶν ἅμα καὶ παίδων αὐτοῖς συναριθμουμένων: here the rel. pron. οἵ (the anteced. is τῶν ἄλλων... ἐχόντων, Joseph. *BJ* 7.399) functions like the connecting *qui* construction in Lat.: "and [those who perished] were, with resp. to number, nine hundred and sixty…" For τὸν ἀριθμόν as an accus. resp. (Smyth §1601) cf. μυρία δ' ἦν τὸν ἀριθμόν (Joseph. *BJ* 1.101); ἅπαντας... ὄντας τὸν ἀριθμὸν ὑπὲρ μυρίους καὶ τρισχιλίους (Joseph. *BJ* 2.468); ἑβδομήκοντα τὸν ἀριθμὸν ἄνδρες (Joseph. *BJ* 2.482), etc. The words γυναικῶν... καὶ παίδων... συναριθμουμένων constitute another gen. abs.: "the women and children being counted together with them..." For the pres. mid. ptc. συναριθμουμένων ("being counted") cf. Joseph. *Antiq* 3.284.

7.401 καὶ τὸ πάθος ἐπράχθη πεντεκαιδεκάτῃ Ξανθικοῦ μηνός: trans. τὸ πάθος (Joseph. *BJ* 1.277, 544; 2.234; 3.22, 306, 530; 5.450, 452, 514; 6.186, 190, 213, 214; 7.203) as "disaster": *"the disaster* was perpetrated on the fifteenth [day] of the month Xanthicus"—i.e., 2 May AD 73 (that is, Passover; cf. Eshel 1999, 231). For the vb. ἐπράχθη ("was perpetrated") cf. Joseph. *BJ* 2.440, 555; 3.315; 4.640; 6.67, 159; 7.405. Ξανθικός (alt. Ξανδικός) was a month in the Macedonian calendar (Diod. Sic. 18.56; LXX 2 Macc 11:30).

BJ 7.402–406

7.402 Οἱ δὲ Ῥωμαῖοι μάχην ἔτι προσδοκῶντες, ὑπὸ τὴν ἕω διασκευασάμενοι...: unbeknownst to the Romans (who were still "expecting a fight") the Zealots had all perished. For the temp. expression ὑπὸ τὴν ἕω ("at about dawn") cf. ὑπ' αὐτὸν τὸν χρόνον (Aristoph. *Ach.* 139); ὑπ' αὐτὸν τὸν καιρόν (Polyb. 11.27.4); ὑφ' ἕνα καιρόν (Diogn. Oen. 38); ὑπὸ τὸν αὐτὸν χρόνον (Thuc. 2.26). The aor. ptc. διασκευασάμενοι means "fully armed" (cf. διασκευάσειν Joseph. *BJ* 1.616). For the pres. act. ptc. προσδοκῶντες ("expecting") cf. Joseph. *Antiq* 3.82; 5.176; 6.362; 20.176; *Vita* 140, 219, 271; *Contra Ap* 2.249.

7.402 ...καὶ τὰς ἀπὸ τῶν χωμάτων ἐφόδους ταῖς ἐπιβάθραις γεφυρώσαντες προσβολὴν ἐποιοῦντο: trans. the expression τάς... ἐφόδους ταῖς ἐπιβάθραις γεφυρώσαντες as "having bridged the approaches from the earthworks by means of scaling ladders." Josephus describes the complicated system of earthworks (τὰ χώματα), approaches (αἱ ἔφοδοι), and scaling-ladders (αἱ ἐπιβάθραι) upon which the Romans depended to launch an all-out assault. For the expression προσβολὴν ποιεῖσθαι ("falling upon, attack, assault," LSJ II.1) cf. Hdt. 3.158; 4.128 (plur.); Thuc. 2.4; 5.61; Xen. *Hist. Graec.* 1.3.14; also cf. ῥᾳδίαν... τὴν προσβολὴν τιθέμενος (of Eleazar) Joseph. *BJ* 7.197. For the expression ἀπὸ τῶν χωμάτων ("from the earth works") cf. Joseph. *BJ* 5.275; for the expression τὰς... ἐφόδους ("the approaches") cf. Joseph. *BJ* 3.88; 4.268; 7.294.

7.403 βλέποντες δ' οὐδένα τῶν πολεμίων, ἀλλὰ δεινὴν πανταχόθεν ἐρημίαν καὶ πῦρ ἔνδον καὶ σιωπήν: for βλέποντες ("seeing") cf. Joseph. *BJ* 1.150; 4.171, 172; 5.572; 6.403; for οὐδένα τῶν πολεμίων ("none of the enemies") cf. Joseph. *BJ* 2.471; 7.198; for δεινήν... ἐρημίαν ("dreadful solitude") cf. δεινήν... τὴν ἁρπαγήν (Joseph. *BJ* 6.225).

7.403 ἀπόρως εἶχον τὸ γεγονὸς συμβαλεῖν: for the idiom ἀπόρως ἔχειν ("to be unable") cf. Eur. *Iph. Aul.* 55; Antiph. 1.1; for τὸ γεγονός ("what had happened") cf. Joseph. *BJ* 15.144. The vb. συμβάλλω—in both the mid. and act. voices—can mean "conclude, infer, conjecture, interpret" (LSJ III.3).

7.403 ...καὶ τέλος ὡς εἰς ἄφεσιν βολῆς ἠλάλαξαν: trans. καὶ τέλος as "and finally." The vb. ἀλαλάζω means "shout" (Eur. *Bacch.* 593; *Her. Fur.* 981; LXX Ezek 27:30), particularly in the context of battle, e.g., τῷ Ἐνυαλίῳ ἠλάλαξαν = "raise the war cry" (Xen. *Ana.* 5.2.14; cf. Xen. *Ana.* 6.5.27; Soph. *Antig.* 133). The expression ὡς εἰς ἄφεσιν βολῆς ("as at the release of a cast") links the war cry to the release of javelins that preceded hand-to-hand fighting on the ancient battle line, e.g., *clamore sublato pila in hostes immittunt* (Caes. *BG* 6.8.6). For sim. expressions cf. Caes. *BG* 1.52.4; *BC* 3.46.5; 3.93.1.

7.403 εἴ τινα τῶν ἔνδον προκαλέσαιντο: indir. quest., sec. seq.: "whether they would call forth any of those within."

7.404 τῆς δὲ βοῆς αἴσθησις γίνεται τοῖς γυναίοις: trans. γίνεται τοῖς γυναίοις as a poss. dat. (Smyth §1476): "and the women had a percep. of the shout." Since the war cry indicated that the Romans had gained mastery of Masada, the women deemed it safe to leave their hiding place.

7.404 κἀκ τῶν ὑπονόμων ἀναδῦσαι τὸ πραχθὲν ὡς εἶχε πρὸς τοὺς Ῥωμαίους ἐμήνυον: the nom. fem. plur. ptc. ἀναδῦσαι (from ἀναδύνω: "emerged from the passages") suggs. that the two women and five children were lit. hiding in the water of the storage tanks when they heard the war cry of the Romans which called them forth (ἐκ τῶν ὑπονόμων; cf. τοῖς ὑπονόμοις, *BJ* 7.399). Trans. τὸ πραχθέν (Joseph. *Antiq* 2.34, 130; 7.191; 20.114) as an accus. resp. (Smyth §1600): "and with resp. to what had happened they indicated... how matters stood." For the expression ὡς εἶχε ("how matters stood") cf. Joseph. *Antiq* 7.15; 9.118; for the expression πρὸς τοὺς Ῥωμαίους ("to the Romans") cf. Joseph. *Antiq* 1.4; for the vb. ἐμήνυον ("they indicated") cf. Joseph. *Antiq* 9.81; 13.175; 14.53; 16.337.

7.404 πάντα τῆς ἑτέρας ὡς ἐλέχθη τε καὶ τίνα τρόπον ἐπράχθη σαφῶς ἐκδιηγουμένης: the words τῆς ἑτέρας... ἐκδιηγουμένης constitute a gen. abs.: "the second woman set forth everything clearly..." For the variant ἑταίρας in place of ἑτέρας cf. Joseph. *BJ* 7.399 above. The clause markers ὡς and τίνα τρόπον demarcate indir. quest.: "both *what* was said and *in what manner* it was done"—i.e., she provided for the Romans both what Eleazar had said in his two speeches (Joseph. *BJ* 7.323–336, 341–388) and details pertinent to the suicide (Joseph. *BJ* 7.389–397). For the vb. ἐλέχθη ("it was said") cf. Joseph. *Antiq* 10.130; for the vb. ἐπράχθη ("it was done") cf. Joseph. *Antiq* 1.233; 4.220; 6.80, 142; 10.148; 13.378; 14.56; 15.58, 215; 17.72; 19.78, 111; *BJ* 2.440, 555; 3.315; 4.640; 6.67, 159; 7.401; for the expression τίνα τρόπον ("in what manner") cf. Joseph. *Antiq* 3.17; 7.148; 13.282; *Vita* 236, 258, 342, 385, 412; *Contra Ap* 1.16, 25, 135, 155, 315; *BJ* 1.522; 2.250, 277; 7.2, 454.

7.405 οὐ μὴν ῥᾳδίως αὐτῇ προσεῖχον τῷ μεγέθει τοῦ τολμήματος ἀπιστοῦντες: trans. οὐ μήν with the adv. ῥᾳδίως: "by no means easily" (Litotes). The pron. αὐτῇ refers to the second woman (Eleazar's relative) to whom the Romans "paid heed" (προσεῖχον, Joseph. *Antiq* 8.34; 14.351; *Vita* 124; *BJ* 6.256, 288). The usu. idiom consists of the words προσέχειν τὸν νοῦν τινι = "to dir. one's mind" to someone, "pay attention." So incredible was the woman's account that the Romans could scarcely pay attn. to her. The pres. act. ptc. ἀπιστοῦντες patterns with τῷ μεγέθει: "disbelieving the magnitude of the daring." Cf. the related expressions τῷ μεγέθει τῆς συμφορᾶς (Joseph. *BJ* 1.90); ἐπὶ τῷ μεγέθει τῆς δυνάμεως (Joseph. *BJ* 2.626).

7.405 ἐπεχείρουν τε τὸ πῦρ σβεννύναι καὶ ταχέως ὁδὸν δι' αὐτοῦ τεμόντες τῶν βασιλείων ἐντὸς ἐγένοντο: the pron. αὐτοῦ refers to τὸ πῦρ, the fire. The last man living had set the palace ablaze (cf. πῦρ... τοῖς βασιλείοις ἐνίησιν, Joseph. *BJ* 7.397) before dispatching himself. Most of the killing had taken place in the palace. For the vb. ἐπεχείρουν ("they undertook") cf. Joseph. *Antiq* 3.310; 12.273; 15.351; *BJ* 2.444; 6.371; for the pres. act. ptc. τεμόντες ("cutting") cf. Joseph. *Antiq* 12.156.

7.406 καὶ τῷ πλήθει τῶν πεφονευμένων ἐπιτυχόντες οὐχ ὡς ἐπὶ πολεμίοις ἥσθησαν: oft the vb. ἐπιτυγχάνω ("to encounter τινι") patterns with a dat. obj., e.g., σορῷ (Hdt. 1.68); ναυσί (Thuc. 8.34); βιβλίῳ (Luc. *Dem. Enc.* 27); [ταῖς θύραις] ἀνεῳγμέναις (Plato *Symp.* 223b). For the slaughter cf. espec. Joseph. *BJ* 7.392, 396, 397 above. The vb. ἥσθησαν (cf. Joseph. *Antiq* 2.20; 18.118) represents the 3 pers. plur. aor. indic. pass. of ἥδομαι: "to take pleasure." The Zealots' earnestness in perpetrating the suicides inspired awe on the part of the Romans, not exultation. For the expression ἐπιτυχόντες ("encountering") cf. Joseph. *Antiq* 9.85.

7.406 τὴν δὲ γενναιότητα τοῦ βουλεύματος καὶ τὴν ἐν τοσούτοις ἄτρεπτον ἐπὶ τῶν ἔργων ἐθαύμασαν τοῦ θανάτου καταφρόνησιν: the particle δέ possesses adversative force ("but"), thus effecting a clear distinction between what the Romans did not do (οὐχ... ἥσθησαν) and what they did (ἐθαύμασαν). For the expression τὴν... γενναιότητα τοῦ βουλεύματος ("the nobility of their resolve") cf. γενναιότητα προγόνων (Joseph. *Antiq* 19.122); for the expression ἐν τοσούτοις ("amid so many") cf. Joseph. *Antiq* 6.343; for the word ἄτρεπτον ("unwaveringly") cf. Joseph. *Antiq* 11.57; *BJ* 7.370; for τήν... τοῦ θανάτου καταφρόνησιν ("the despising of death") cf. Joseph. *Antiq* 12.302. There may be Stoic overtones (cf. Ladouceur 1981, 258). The prep. phrase ἐπὶ τῶν ἔργων ("into execution," cf. Joseph. *BJ* 1.344) seems harsh; clearly what amazed the Romans was the Zealots' immovable resolve in actually carrying out (ἐπὶ τῶν ἔργων) the many deaths.

Vocabulary

This list contains all but the easiest words that occur in the text selections contained in this reader, obviating the need for a Greek-English lexicon. Many unusual forms of verbs have been provided to help students with the acquisition of principle parts.

A

ἆ exclamation *ah!*
ἄβατος, -ον adj. *impassable.*
Ἀβραάμ m. *Abraham.*
ἀγαθός, -ή, -όν adj. *good.*
ἀγαθύνω (cf. ἀγαθός): *to make good, exalt; do good.*
ἀγανακτέω, -ήσω: *to be angry at* τινί; *feel irritation.*
ἀγανάκτησις, -εως f. *irritation, anger.*
ἀγαπάω, -ήσω, ἠγάπησα: *to love, be fond of.*
ἄγελλος, -ου m. *messenger; one who is sent; angel.*
ἀγεννής, -ές adj. *low-born, ignoble.*
ἁγιάζω, -άσω, ἡγίασα: *to hallow, sanctify.*
ἁγίασμα, -ματος n.: *that which is hallowed; holy place, sanctuary.*
ἅγιος, -α, -ον adj. *holy; set apart to* or *by God, consecrated; morally pure, upright;* τὸ ἅγιον or τὰ ἅγια: *the sanctuary, holy place* (used of the Temple and the Temple liturgy); *priests* (1 Macc 1:46).
ἀγίρας perhaps replicates Aram. *haggera'* ("lame man").
ἁγνεία, -ας f. *purity.*
ἀγνώμων, -ον adj. *unreasoning; headstrong, reckless.*
ἀγών, -ῶνος m. *contest, struggle.*
ἀδεής, -ές adj. *fearless, secure.*
ἄδεια, -ας f. *freedom from fear; security, safety.*
ἀδελφός, -οῦ m. *brother; fellow countryman.*
Ἀδιαβηνός, -ή, -όν adj. *of Adiabene* (a region of Persia to the northeast of the Tigris and Euphrates rivers).
ἀδιάφθορος, -ον adj. *incorrupt; imperishable.*
ἀδικέω, -ήσω: *to wrong, treat unjustly.*
ἀδίκημα, -ατος n. *injustice, harm.*
ἀδικία, -ας f. *injustice, villainy.*
ἀδόκητος, -ον adj. *unexpected.*
ἀδοξέω, -ήσω: *to hold in no esteem, hold in contempt.*

ἄδοξος, -ον adj. *inglorious; disreputable, disgraceful; obscure.*
ἀδούλωτος, -ον adj. *non-enslaved.*
ἀεί adv. *always.*
Ἀζαρίας m. *Azariah.*
Ἄζωτος, ου f. *Azotus.*
ἀήρ, ἀέρος m. *lower air, atmosphere.*
ἀθανασία, -ας f. *immortality.*
ἀθάνατος, -ου adj. *immortal.*
ἀθέμιτος, -ον adj. *lawless, unholy.*
ἄθλιος, -α, -ον adj. *wretched.*
ἀθροίζω, -σω, ἤθροισα: *to gather together, collect.*
ἄθροισμα, -ματος n. *that which is gathered; gathering, collection.*
ἀθρόος, -α, -ον adj. *in heaps, gathered;* ἀθρόοι ἄνθρωποι *groups of people.*
ἀθυμέω, -ήσω: *to be discouraged, disheartened.*
ἀθυμία, -ας f. *faintheartedness, despondency.*
ἀθῷος, -ον adj. *guiltless, innocent.*
Αἰγύπτιος, -α, -ον adj. *Egyptian.*
Αἴγυπτος, -ου f. *Egypt.*
αἰδέομαι, αἰδέσομαι, ᾐδεσάμην: *to feel shame, be ashamed.*
ἀΐδιος, -ον adj. *eternal.*
αἰδώς, -οῦς f. *regard for others, respect, reverence.*
αἰκία, -ας f. *outrage, insult, affront; torture.*
αἰκίζω, -ίσω: *to torture, torment.*
αἷμα, αἵματος n. *blood.*

αἱμάσσω, -άξω: *to stain with blood.*
αἴνεσις, -εως f. *praise.*
αἰνέω, -έσω, ᾔνεσα: *to praise.*
αἵρεσις, -εως f. *division, faction; relig. party; choice.*
αἱρετίζω, -ιῶ, ᾑρέτισα, ᾑρέτικα: *to choose;* in mid. *to choose.*
αἱρέω, αἱήσω/αἱρεθήσομαι, εἷλον, ᾕρηκα, ᾕρημαι, ᾑρέθην: *to take, grasp, seize;* in mid. *to take for oneself, choose.*
αἴρω, ἀρῶ ἦρα: *to raise, lift up, carry; to put an end to; destroy.*
αἰσθάνομαι, αἰσθήσομαι, ᾐσθόμην: *to perceive.*
αἴσθησις, -εως f. *perception, inkling.*
αἴσχιστος, -η, -ον superl. adj. of αἰσχρός.
αἰσχρός, -ά, -όν adj. *shameful.*
αἰσχρῶς adv. *shamefully.*
αἰσχύνη, -ης f. *shame, disgrace.*
αἰσχύνω, -υνῶ, ᾔσχυνα: *to make ugly, disfigure, mar; to disgrace, dishonor;* in pass. *be put to shame.*
αἰτέω, -ήσω, ᾔτησα, ᾔτηκα: *to ask for, beg.*
αἰτία, -ας f. *cause, ground, reason; charge.*
αἴτιον, -ου n. *a cause.*
αἰχμαλωσία, -ας f. *captivity.*
αἰχμαλωτίζω, -ίσω, ᾐχμαλώτισα: *to take captive, capture.*
αἰχμάλωτα, -ων neut. plur. *booty.*

αἰχμάλωτος, -ον adj. *taken by the spear* or *in war*; substant. noun *prisoner-of-war.*

αἰχμή, -ῆς f. *spear point; spear.*

αἰών, -ῶνος m. *age; eternity.*

αἰώνιος, -ον adj. *eternal.*

ἀκάθαρτος, -ον adj. *unclean, impure; unpurified.*

ἄκαρπος, -ον adj. *fruitless, barren.*

ἀκίνδυνος, -ον adj. *without risk.*

ἀκινδυνῶς adv. *undangerously.*

ἀκίνητος, -ον adj. *unmoved, motionless.*

ἀκμάζω, -άσω: *to flourish, be in full bloom; be at one's prime.*

ἀκμαῖος, -α, -ον adj. *fresh, blooming; in its prime.*

ἀκοή, -ῆς f. *hearing; sense of hearing, the ear.*

ἀκοινώνητος, -η, -ον adj. *not shared in common; unparalleled.*

ἀκολουθέω, -ήσω: *to follow, go after.*

ἀκουσίως adv. *unwillingly.*

ἀκούω, ἀκούσομαι, ἤκουσα, ἀκήκοα, aor. pass. ἠκούσθην: *to hear* (with accus. of thing and gen. of pers.); *hearken to.*

ἄκρα, -ας f. *the end, point* espec. *the highest point, the top* (of the hill, city, etc.); *peak, crest; headland; citadel.*

ἄκρατος, -ον adj. *unmixed, pure.*

ἀκρίβεια, -ας f. *accuracy, precision;* μετὰ ἀκριβείας *accurately.*

ἀκριβέστερον adv. *more precisely.*

ἀκρίτως adv. *undeservedly; without trial.*

ἀκροάομαι, -άσομαι, ἠκροασόμην: *to hearken to* τινός.

ἀκρόασις, -εως f. *a harkening or listening to; lecture, recitation.*

ἀκροβυστία, -ας f. *uncircumcision* (oft of non-Jews); ποιέω ἑαυτῷ ἀκροβυστίας *remove the marks of circumcision.*

ἄκρον, -ου n. *highest or utmost point; tip.*

ἄκρος, -α, -ον adj. *at the end*; thus *top-most, extreme.*

ἀκροτομέω, -ήσω: *to lop off, shave the surface.*

ἀκροώμενοι pres. mid. ptc. of ἀκροάομαι.

ἀκώλυτος, -ον adj. *unhindered.*

ἀλαλάζω, ἀλάξομαι, ἠλάλαξα: *to shout*; espec. *raise the war cry.*

Ἀλβῖνος, -ου m. *Albinus.*

Ἀλεξάνδρεια, -ας f. *Alexandria.*

Ἀλέξανδρος, -ου m. *Alexander,* espec. *Alexander the great (356–323 BC), son of Philip of Macedon.*

ἀληθής, -ές adj. *true*; τἀληθῆ (τά + ἀληθῆ) *true things.*

ἀληθῶς adv. *truly.*

ἁλίσκομαι, ἁλώσομαι, syncop. 2 aor. ἑάλων: *to be taken, conquered, captured.*

ἀλιτήριος, -ον adj. *sinful, guilt-laden.*

ἀλκή, -ῆς f. *bodily strength, prowess, force.*

ἀλλά conj. *but, rather, on the contrary*; ἀλλὰ μήν *well now*.

ἀλλάξητε 2 plur. aor. subjunct. of ἀλλάσσω.

ἀλλάσσω, -άξω, ἤλλαξα, ἤλλαχα, ἤλλαγμαι, ἠλλάχθην: *to make other than it is, to change; give in exchange; to change* and so *leave, quit*.

ἀλλήλων, -οις, -ους recipr. pron. *one another, each other*.

ἀλλογενής, -ές adj. *of another race; foreign*.

ἀλλοιόω, ἀλλοιώσω, ἠλλοίωσα; pf. pass. ἠλλοίωμαι; aor. pass. ἠλλοιώθην (cf. ἄλλος, -η, -ο): *to make different, change, alter*; in pass. *to be different* or *changed; to fade*.

ἄλλος, -η, -ο adj. *other, another*.

ἀλλότριος, -α, -ον (cf. ἄλλος, -η, -ο) adj. *belonging to another; another*; substant. noun ἀλλότριος, -ου m. *stranger;* ἀλλοτρία, -ας f. *a strange (place); stranger*.

ἀλλοφύλος, -ον adj. *of another tribe; foreign, strange;* οἱ ἀλλόφυλοι *foreigners*.

ἀλοῦσα aor. act. ptc., nom. fem. sing. of ἁλίσκομαι.

ἀλῶναι 2 aor. act. infin. of ἁλίσκομαι.

ἀλώσεσθαι fut. mid. infin. of ἁλίσκομαι.

ἄλωσις, -εως f. *capture, conquest*.

ἅμα (1) adv. *at the same time, together*; (2) prep. with dat. *together with*; ἅμα ἡμέρᾳ *at daybreak*.

ἁμαρτία, -ας f. *sin*.

ἁμαρτάνω, -τήσω, ἡμάρτησα: *to miss the mark, err, sin, be mistaken, miss out on* τινός; *to fail of doing something* (+ ptc.).

ἁμαρτάς, ἁμαρτάδος f. Ion. and later Greek for ἁμαρτία.

ἁμάρτημα, -ματος n. *failure, error, sin*.

ἁμαρτωλός, -όν adj. *sinful;* as substant. noun *sinner*.

ἄμαχος, -ον adj. lit. *with whom no one* fights; then *unconquered, invincible*.

ἀμβλύνω, -υνῶ, ἤμβλυνα: *to dull, take the edge off*.

ἀμείνω: accus. sing. (the non-abbrev. form is ἀμείνωνα; cf. ἀμείνων, -ον).

ἀμείνων, -ον irreg. compar. of ἀγαθός: *better; abler, stronger*.

ἀμήχανος, -ον adj. *without means* or *resource; helpless*.

ἀμιγής, -ές adj. *unmixed, pure*.

Ἀμμαους f. *Emmaus*.

ἀμνήμων, -ον adj. *unmindful, forgetful of* τινός.

ἀμοιβή, -ῆς f. *recompense*.

ἀμπελών, -ῶνος m. *vineyard*.

ἄμυνα, -ης f. *a warding off of an attack; self-defense*.

ἀμύνω, ἀμυνῶ: *to keep off, ward off*; in mid. *resist, defend; to avenge oneself upon; requite, repay, punish*.

ἀμφορεύς, -έως m. *amphora.*

ἀμφότερος, -α, -ον adj. *both.*

ἄμφω gen. and dat. ἀμφοῖν *both.*

ἄμωμος, -ον adj. *without blame, blameless.*

ἄν particle denoting contingency in cert. constructions.

ἀνά prep. + gen., dat. and accus. (usually. used distributively with the accus.) *each, each one, apiece.*

ἀναβαίνω, -βήσομαι, 2 aor. ἀνέβην (also 1 aor. mid. ἀνεβησάμην),

ἀναβέβηκα: *to go up; mount; put to sea.*

ἀναβάσις, -εως f. *ascent.*

ἀναγγέλλω: *to bring tidings, report.*

ἀναγκάζω, -άσω: *to force.*

ἀναγκαῖος, -α, -ον adj. *necessary.*

ἀνάγκη, -ης f. *necessity, constraint, compulsion;* κατ' ἀνάγκην *out of necessity.*

ἀναδύνω: *to come to the top of the water.*

ἀναδῦσαι aor. act. ptc., nom. fem. plur. from ἀναδύνω.

ἀναίμακτος, -ον adj. *without bloodshed.*

ἀναιμωτί adv. *bloodlessly.*

ἀναίρεσις, -εως f. *capture; destruction.*

ἀναιρέω, -ήσω: *to take up; to take away, destroy.*

ἀνακμάσασαν aor. act. ptc., fem. sing. accus. of ἀνακμάζω.

ἀνακμάζω, -μάσω: *to break out afresh with renewed vigor* (cf. Joseph. *War* 5.2).

ἀνακομίζω, -ίσω: *to bring back, recover.*

ἀνακράζω, ἀνακράξομαι, ἀνέκραξα (also 2 aor. ἀνέκραγον): *to cry aloud, lift up the voice.*

ἀναλαμβάνω, -λήψομαι, ἀνέλαβον: *to take up.*

ἀναλίσκω, -λώσω, ἀνήλωσα: *to use up, spend, squander; kill, destroy.*

ἀναλούμενον pres. mid./pass. ptc., accus. neut. sing. of ἀναλίσκω.

ἀνάλωτος, -ον adj. *not to be taken, impregnable.*

ἀναμάρτητος, -ον adj. *unfailing, faultless.*

ἀναμένω, -μενῶ: *to wait for, await.*

ἀναμίγνυμι, -μίξω, ἀνέμιξα: *to mix up together, mingle.*

ἀναμιμνήσκω, -ήσω: *to remind;* in pass. *to remember.*

ἀνάμνησις, -εως f. *recollection.*

ἄνανδρος, -ον adj. *unmanly, cowardly.*

Ἀνανίας, -ου m. *Ananias.*

Ἄνανος, -ου m. *Ananos.*

ἀνάξιος, -ον adj. *unworthy.*

ἀνάπαυσις, -εως f. *release; rest, repose, ease.*

ἀναπαύω, -παύσω: *to make stop, cease from a thing;* in mid. *to cease, desist from doing something* (+ ptc.).

ἀναπείθω, -πείσω, ἀνέπεισα: *to persuade; seduce, mislead.*
ἀναπέμπω, -ψω: *to send up; convey.*
ἀναπίμπλημι, -πλήσω, ἀνέπλησα: *to fill full of* τινός.
ἀνάπτετε 2 plur. pres. act. impv. of ἀνάπτω.
ἀνάπτω, -ψω: *to fasten onto* τινί.
ἀναρπάζω, -άξω: *to tear away, snatch up.*
ἀνασκευάζω, -άσω: *to pack up the baggage.*
ἀνάστασις, -εως f. (act.) *awakening*; (pass.) *standing, rising up.*
ἀνασταυρόω, -ώσω: *to impale/crucify.*
ἀναστρέφω, -ψω: intrans. *to turn back around.*
ἀνατείνω, -τενῶ: *to stretch or raise up.*
ἀνατρέπω, -ψω: *to overturn.*
ἀνατρέχω, -θρέξομαι: *to run back.*
ἀναφαίνω, -φανῶ, ἀνέφηνα: *to bring to light*; pass. *to appear.*
ἀναφέρω, ἀνοίσω, ἀνήνεγκα: *to bring* or *carry up; offer* sacrifice; with emotions *to heave up a sigh*; intrans. *to rise up, proceed.*
ἀναχαιτίζω, -ίσω: *to throw back the mane, rear up* (of horses).
ἀναχωρέω, -ήσω: *to retire, retreat.*
ἀνδρεία, -ας f. *manliness; courage.*
ἀνδριάς, -άντος m. *image of a man; statue.*

ἀνδρίζω, -ίσω: *to make a man of*; pass. *to be a man.*
ἀνδρώδης, -ες adj. *manly, like a man.*
ἀνέβην 2 aor. of ἀναβαίνω.
ἀνέδην adv. *indiscriminately, carelessly.*
ἄνειμι: *to go up.*
ἀνειστήκεσαν 3 plur. plupf. indic. act. of ἀνίστημι.
ἀνέλαβον 2 aor. of ἀναλαμβάνω.
ἀνελεῖν 2 aor. infin. of ἀναιρέω.
ἀνέλῃ 3 sing. aor. subjunct. act. of ἀναιρέω.
ἀνελήμφθην 1 aor. pass. of ἀναλαμβάνω.
ἀνέντες aor. act. ptc. of ἀνίημι.
ἀνεπίσχετος, -ον adj. *not to be stopped.*
ἀνεπλήσθη 3 sing. aor. pass. indic. of ἀναπίμπλημι.
ἀνέστην 2 aor. of ἀνίστημι.
ἀνετράπη 3 sing. aor. indic. pass. of ἀνατρέπω.
ἀνήκεστος, -ον adj. *incurable; deadly.*
ἀνήνεγκα 1 aor. of ἀναφέρω.
ἀνήρ, ἀνδρός m. *man* (masculine); *husband.*
ἀνήρουν impf. act. indic. of ἀναιρέω.
ἀνθρώπινος, -η, -ον adj. *human.*
ἄνθρωπος, ου m. *man* (generic), *human being; person.*
ἀνίει 3 sing. impf. of ἀνίημι.

ἀνίημι, ἀνήσω, ἀνῆκα: *to send up or forth; to release* τινά *from* τινός; *to desist, slacken.*

ἀνίκητος, -ον adj. *invincible.*

ἀνίστημι, ἀναστήσω, ἀνέστησα caus. in pres., impf., fut., and 1 aor. *to make to stand; repair, restore*; intrans. in pass. (ἀνίσταμαι), 2 aor. act. (ἀνέστην), pf. (ἀνέστηκα), and plupf. (ἀνεστήκειν): *to stand up, rise; set out for.*

ἀνίσχω: *to go up, rise* (of the sun).

ἄνοδος, -ου f. *way up.*

ἀνόητος, -ον adj. *foolish, unreasonable.*

ἀνοίγνυμι, ἀνοίξω, ἤνοιξα: *to open.*

ἀνομία, -ας f. *lawlessness, wickedness.*

ἄνομος, -ον adj. *lawless*, espec. of someone outside the Jewish law.

ἄνοπλος, -ον adj. *unarmed.*

ἀνταπόδομα, -δόματος n. *requital, recompense.*

ἀνοσίως adv. *unholy, wickedly.*

ἀνταίρω, -αρῶ: *to raise* τι *against.*

ἀνταποδίδωμι, -δώσω: *to give back, repay* τινί; ἀνταποδιδόναι ἀνταπόδομα *to repay in full.*

ἀντέχω, ἀνθέξω, ἄντισχον: *to hold out against, withstand.*

ἀντί prep. + gen. (orig. mng. *opposite) for, in place of, instead of; in behalf of; because of* (ἀνθ ὧν *because; therefore).*

Ἀντίγονος, -ου m. *Antigonos.*

ἀντιγράφω, -ψω: *to write against; write in answer.*

ἀντικρύ prep. + gen. *over against, right opposite.*

ἀντιλαμβάνω, -λήψομαι, -έλαβον, -είληφα: *to receive instead of, receive in one's turn*; in mid. *to lay hold of* τινός; hence *to rescue.*

ἀντίος, -α, -ον adj. *opposite, contrary*; τοὐναντίον *just the opposite.*

ἀντίπαλος, -ον adj. *antagonistic, rival*; substant. noun *rival, adversary.*

Ἀντιοχεία, -ας f. *Antioch.*

Ἀντίοχος, -ου m. *Antiochus*, espec. Antiochus Epiphanes (ca. 215–163 BC), son of Antiochus "the Great" (242–187 BC).

ἀντίπαις, -παιδος m. or f. *like a child; no better than a child.*

Ἀντίπατρος, -ου m. *Antipater.*

ἀντιποιέω, -ήσω: *to do something in return*; mid. *to contend with someone for* τινός.

ἀντίσχοντας aor. act. ptc. of ἀντέχω.

ἀντιτάσσω, -τάξω: *to range in battle against another*; in pass. *to be arranged against.*

Ἀντωνία, -ας f. *Antonia*, espec. the Fortress Antonia.

Ἀντώνιος, -ου m. *Anthony.*

ἀνύβριστος, -ον adj. *unmolested, not insulted.*

ἀνυπέρβλητος, -ον adj. *unsurpassed, not to be outdone.*

ἄνω *above, on high.*

ἀνωθέω, -θήσω: *to push up, push forth;* of a ship *to push off.*

ἄξιος, -α, -ον adj. *worthy, deserving.*

ἀξιόω, -ώσω: *to think* or *deem worthy* of a thing; *to consent, permit.*

ἀξίως adv. *worthily, suitably.*

ἀξίωσις, -εως f. a *thinking oneself worthy;* hence, a *demand, claim.*

ἀοίκητος, -ον adj. *uninhabited.*

ἀόρατος -ον adj. *unseen, invisible.*

ἀοράτως adv. *invisibly.*

ἀπαγγέλλω, -ελῶ, ἀπήγγειλα: *to bear tidings, announce, report.*

ἀπάγω, -άξω: *to lead away, carry off; lead.*

ἀπαθής, -ές adj. *insensible, unsullied.*

ἀπαίρω, -αρῶ, ἀπῆρα: *to lead away* an army or fleet; hence *to sail* or *march away.*

ἀπαλλάσσω, -άξω: intrans. *to get off, get free, escape from* τινός.

ἀπαλλγή, -ῆς f. *deliverance, release, riddance from* τινός.

ἁπανταχοῦ adv. *everywhere.*

ἅπαξ adv. *once, one time.* ἅπαξ καὶ δίς *more than once.*

ἅπας, -πασα, -παν (strength. form of πᾶς, πᾶσα, πᾶν) *all; whole.*

ἀπεθέμην 2 aor. mid. of ἀποτίθημι.

ἀπειλέω, -ησω: *to threaten.*

ἀπειλή, -ῆς f. *threat.*

ἄπειμι (ἀπό + εἶμι): *to go away, depart.*

ἀπείρατος, -ον adj. *unacquainted with* τινός.

ἄπειρος, -ον adj. *boundless, endless, countless.*

ἀπεκρίθην 1 aor. pass. of ἀποκρίνω.

ἀπεκτάνθη 1 aor. pass. of ἀποκτείνω.

ἀπελεύθερος, -ου m. *freedman.*

ἀπελπίζω, ίσω: *to despair of something* + infin.

ἀπερίτμητος, -ον adj. *uncircumcised.*

ἀπέρχομαι, ἀπελεύσομαι, ἀπῆλθον: *to go away, depart from.*

ἀπέστην 2 aor. of ἀφίστημι.

ἀπεχθέω, -σω: *to be hostile, hateful.*

ἀπέχθομαι: *to be hated, be hateful.*

ἀπέχω, ἀφέξω, ἄπεσχον: intrans. *to be away, be distant.*

ἀπῆλθον 2 aor. of ἀπέρχομαι.

ἀπῆρα 1 aor. act. of ἀπαίρω.

ἀπηχθημένος pf. mid./pass. ptc. of ἀπεχθέω.

ἀπήχθην 1 aor. pass. of ἀπάγω.

ἀπιέναι pres. act. infin. of ἄπειμι.

ἀπιστέω, -ήσω, ἠπίστησα: *to disbelieve, distrust.*

ἁπλότης, -ητος f. *sincerity, single-hearted devotion; generosity, liberality.*

ἀπό (ἀφ' before aspirated vowels) prep. with gen. *from, away from;*

Vocabulary

by means of; of; because of, as a res. of; since, ever since; about, for.

ἀποβαίνω, -βήσομαι: *to turn out, issue* in a cert. way.

ἀποβλέπω, -ψω: *to look away.*

ἀπογιγνώσκω, -γνώσομαι, ἀπέγνων: *to depart from a judgment; despair, give up.*

ἀπόγνωσις, -εως f. *despair, desperation.*

ἀποδεκτός, -ή, -όν adj. *acceptable.*

ἀποδειλιάω, -άσω: *to play the coward.*

ἀποδέω, -δεήσω: *to be wanting, to lack, be inferior to* τινός.

ἀποδημία, -ας f. *journey abroad.*

ἀποθαυμάζω, -σω: *to wonder at.*

ἀποθησαυρίζω, -ίσω: *to hoard away.*

ἀποθνήσκω, ἀποθανοῦμαι, ἀπέθανον: *to die; be mortal.*

ἀπόκειμαι, -κείσομαι used as pass. of ἀποτίθημι: *be packed away, laid up in storage.*

ἀποκρίνω, -κρινῶ, pf. mid. ἀπεκέκριμαι, aor. pass. ἀπεκρίθην (depon.): *to part, separate, distinguish; to choose out, select; to render a judgment*; oft in mid. *to give answer* or *make reply* to a quest..

ἀποκτείνω, -κτενῶ, ἀπέκτεινα: *to kill, slay.*

ἀπόκρυφος, -ον adj. *hidden.*

ἀποκωλύω, -σω: *to prevent, hinder.*

ἀπολαμβάνω, -λήψομαι: *to take possession of; to get back.*

ἀπόλαυσις, -εως f. *enjoyment, advantage.*

ἀπολείπω, -ψω, -έλιπον: *to abandon, leave behind.*

ἀπόλλυμαι, ἀπολοῦμαι, ἀπωλάμην, ἀπόλωλα: *to perish, die, be destroyed.*

ἀπόλλυμι, ἀπολέσω/ἀπολῶ, ἀπώλεσα, ἀπώλεκα: *to destroy utter, kill, slay.*

Ἀπολλώνιος, -ου m. *Apollonius.*

ἀπολύω, -λύσω: *to release.*

ἀποπληρόω, -ώσω: *to satisfy, fulfill.*

ἀπορέω, ἀπορήσω, ἠπόρησα: *to be at a loss, not know what to do*; in pass. *to be in doubt.*

ἀπορία, -ας f. *want of means or resources; dearth.*

ἄπορος, -ον adj. *without passage; impossible.*

ἀπόρρητος, -ον adj. *not to be spoken; secret.*

ἀπόρως adv. *unable.*

ἀποστασία, -ας f. *apostasy*; lit. a "standing apart" from the truth or the correct religion.

ἀπόστασις, -εως f. *defection, revolt.*

ἀποστέλλω, ἀποστελῶ, ἀπέστειλα, ἀπέσταλκα; aor. pass. ἀπεστάλην: *to send forth; to send out* or *away.*

ἀποστῆναι 2 aor. act. infin. of ἀφίστημι.

ἀποστολή, -ῆς f. *a sending forth; parting gift* (1 Macc 2:18).

ἀποστρέφω, -στρέψω, 2 aor. ἀπεστράφην: *to turn aside, remove; return;* mid. *turn oneself from, shrink from.*

ἀποσφάζω (or ἀποσφάττω) - άξω: *to cut the throat; slay.*

ἀποτάσσω, -άξω, ἀπέταξα: *to set apart; station.*

ἀποτίθημι, -θήσω, -έθηκα (2 aor. mid. ἀπεθέμην): *to put away, stow away;* in mid. *to put away from oneself; to put away for oneself, to stow away.*

ἀποτρέπω, -ψω: *to turn away from; dissuade, hinder.*

ἀποφαίνω, -φανῶ, -έφηνα: *to show forth, display.*

ἀποφράγνυμι, -φράξω: *to block up.*

ἄπρακτος, -ον adj. *effecting nothing; undone; unmanageable, incurable.*

ἀπρεπής, -ές adj. *ill-befits.*

ἀπρόσιτος, -ον adj. *inapproachable.*

ἅπτω, ἅψω, ἧψα: *to fasten, fix on* a thing; *cling to* τινός.

Ἄπφους m. *Apphus.*

ἀπώλεια, -ας f. *destruction.*

ἄρα *then, therefore, so then.*

ἆρα interrog. pro. that anticipates a neg. answer; equiv. to Lat. *num.*

ἆραι 1 aor. infin. of αἴρω.

ἀργός, -όν adj. *not working; idle; unwrought* (of metal).

ἀργύριον, -ου n. *silver,* espec. *silver coin, money.*

ἀρετή, -ῆς f. *bravery, valor.*

ἀριθμός, -μοῦ m. *number.*

ἀριστερός, -ά, -όν adj. *left* (opp. to *right*).

Ἀριστόβουλος, -ου m. *Aristoboulos.*

ἄριστος, -η, -ον adj. *best.*

ἀρκέω, -έσω, ἤρκεσα: *to be of use, avail* + dat.

ἄρκτος, -ου f. *bear; the north.*

ἅρμα, -τος n. *chariot; carriage.*

ἁρμονία, -ας f. *fitting together; fastening, joint.*

ἀρνέομαι, -ήσομαι: *to deny, refuse.*

ἁρπαγή, -ῆς f. *seizure, robbery; rapacity.* εφ' ἁρπαγήν *for plunder.*

ἁρπάζω, -πάσω: *to seize, plunder; snatch, grab.*

ἅρπαξ, -αγος m. *plunderer, robber.*

ἄρτι adv. *just now.*

ἄρτος, -ου m. *bread, a loaf of bread.*

ἀρχαιότης, -τητος f. *antiquity.*

ἀρχή, -ῆς f. *beginning; supreme power, dominion, rule.*

ἀρχιερεύς, -έως m. *high priest.*

ἄρχω, ἄρχω, ἦρξα, ἦρχα (1) *to begin;* (2) + obj. gen. *to rule, be leader of* τινός; (3) *to hold sway, prevail.*

ἄρχων, -οντος m. *ruler; official, authority; judge.*

ἀσεβέω, -ήσω: to act impiously or outrageously.
ἀσέβεια, -ας f. wickedness, impiety.
ἀσεβής, -ές adj. godless, impious.
ἀσελγής, -ές adj. sensual, brutal.
ἄσημος, -ον adj. unknown, obscure, ignoble.
ἀσθενέω, -ήσω, ἠσθένησα: to be sick or ill; be weak; be faint.
ἀσθενής, -ές adj. weak, ill.
Ἀσία, -ας f. Asia.
Ἀσίδαιος, -ου m. Hasidean.
ἀσιτέω, -ησω: to go without food, to fast.
ἀσκέω, -ήσω: *to practice, exercise.*
ἀσπάζομαι, -άσομαι: *to greet; embrace, kiss, caress.*
ἀσπιδίσκη, -ης f. boss, disk; small shield.
ἄσπορος, -ον adj. unsown.
Ἀσσύριος, -ου m. Assyrian.
ἄστυ, -εος n. town.
ἀσφάλεια, -ας f. firmness, stability; surety; precaution; safety.
ἀσφαλέστερον comp. adv. *more securely.*
ἀσφαλής, -ές adj. *firm, fast, steadfast; safe.*
Ἀσφαλτίτις, -ιδος f. Asphaltitis.
Ἀσωχαῖος, -ου m. Asochaeus.
ἀταμίευτος, -ον adj. *that which cannot be stored; uncontrolled, inordinate.*

ἅτε adv. *inasmuch as, seeing that; since.*
ἄτεγκτος, -ον adj. *not to be softened by water, unsoftened;* hence *relentless.*
ἀτενής, -ές adj. *straight, direct, unwavering;* ἀτενές adv. *unbendingly, steadily.*
ἀτιμία, -ας f. *disgrace, dishonor, shame; humiliation.*
ἀτολμία, -ας f. *faint-heartedness, cowardice.*
ἀτρεκής, -ές adj. *real, true, exact.*
ἄτρεπτος, -ον adj. *unmoved, unwavering, unflappable.*
ἀτρεπτῶς adv. *unswervingly.*
ἀτύχημα, -ατος n. *misfortune.*
Αὐαραν m. *Avaran.*
αὖθις adv. *again; hereafter, at a later period.*
αὐλή, -ῆς f. *court, courtyard.*
αὐλος, -ου m. *flute.*
αὐξάνω, -ήσω, ηὔξησα, ηὔξηκα, ηὔξημαι, ηὐξήθην: *to make grow, increase;* in pass. *to grow, wax, increase.*
αὔριον adv. *tomorrow; the next day.*
αὐτανδρος, -ον adj. *men and all.*
αὐτίκα adv. *immediately.*
αὐτοκράτωρ, -ορος m. *emperor.*
αὐτομάτως adv. *by itself, on its own.*
αὐτομολέω, -ήσω: *to desert.*
αὐτομολία, -ας f. *desertion.*
αὐτόμολος, -ον adj. *going by oneself;* substant. noun *deserter.*

αὐτός, -ή, -ό *self, of oneself, even very*; preceded by the article *the same*; as 3 pers. pron. *he, she, it*; αὐτο μόνον *mere*.

αὐτοχειρί adv. *with one's own hand*.

αὐχήν, -ένος m. *neck*.

ἀφαιρέω, -ήσω: *to take away from*.

ἀφανής, -ές adj. *unseen, invisible*.

ἀφανῶς adv. *invisibly*.

ἀφανίζω, -ίσω: *to hide; to raze to the ground, obliterate*.

ἀφεῖναι aor. act. infin. of ἀφίημι.

ἄφεσις, -εως f. *release, discharge*.

ἀφ' ἧς idiom. expression *from what (time)*.

ἀφῃρέθην 1 aor. pass. of ἀφαιρέω.

ἄφθαρτος, -ον adj. *uncorrupted*.

ἀφθονία, -ας f. *plenty, abundance*.

ἀφίημι, ἀφήσω, ἀφῆκα, ἀφεῖκα, ἀφεῖμαι, ἀφείθην: *to send forth, discharge; let go, release; allow, permit; set free*.

ἀφίστημι, impf. ἀφίστην, fut. ἀποστήσω, 1 aor. ἀπέστησα, 1 aor. mid. ἀπεστησάμην trans. *cause to rebel; cause to withdraw from* τινός; intrans. in pass., with 2 aor. act. ἀπέστην (infin. ἀποστῆναι), pf. ἀφέστηκα, plupf. ἀφεστήκειν: *to stand off, away*, or *aloof from; to revolt, rebel*.

ἄφνω adv. *suddenly*.

ἀφορμή, -ῆς f. *starting place*, i.e., *occasion* or *pretext*; *means* or *resources* for war (money, ships, etc.).

ἀφυλάκτως adv. *unguardedly, without any protection*.

ἀχανής, -ές adj. lit. *not yawning*; thus, *unspeaking*.

ἄχραντος, -ον adj. *undefiled*.

ἄωρος, -ον adj. *untimely, unseasonable*.

B

βαδίζω, -ίσω: *to go on foot, walk, step*.

Βαβυλών, -ῶνος f. *Babylon*.

Βαβυλώνιος, -ου m. *Babylonian*.

βάθος, -εος n. *depth; height*.

βάθρον, -ου n. *base, foundation*.

βαθύς, βαθεῖα, βαθύ adj. *deep; vast*.

Βαιθσουρος m. *Beth-zur*.

Βαιθωρων m. *Beth-Horon*.

βαλανεῖον, -ου n. *bath; bathing establishment*.

βάλλω, βαλῶ, ἔβαλον: *to hurl projectiles at, stone*; in pass. *to be struck, assailed, shot at by arrows*.

Βάννος, -ου m. *Bannus*.

βάπτισις, -εως f. *baptism*.

βαπτιστής, -οῦ m. *Baptist* (surname of John).

βάρος, -εος n. *weight, burden*.

βαρύς, -εῖα, -ύ adj. *heavy; hard, difficult; important, weighty; considerable; serious*.

βασιλεία, -ας f. *reign, rule; kingdom; royalty.*

βασίλειον, -ου n. *palace.*

βασιλεύς, -έως m. king

βασιλεύω *to be king, rule, reign.*

βασίλειον, -ου n. (mostly in plur.) *palace.*

βασιλικός, -ή, -όν adj. *royal, kingly;* the substant. noun βασιλικός, -οῦ m. may mean *courtier, nobleman.*

βασιλίς, -ίδος f. *queen, princess.*

βασίλισσα, -ας f. *queen.*

βάσις, -εως f. *step, tread.*

βδέλυγμα, -ματος n. *something detestable;* βδέλυγμα ἐρημώσεως (1 Macc 1:54) *sacrilegious object* causing the desecration of a sacred place.

βδελύσσω, -ύξω, ἐβδέλυξα: *to cause to stink; to make loathsome.*

βέβαιος, -α, -ον adj. *firm, steady; certain.*

βεβαιόω, -ώσω: *to confirm, establish.*

βεβηλόω, βεβηλώσω, ἐβεβήλωσα: *to desecrate, pollute.*

βεβήλωσις, -εως f. *profanation.*

βέλος, -εος n. *anything thrown; bolt, arrow, dart.*

Βηθεζουβᾶ f. *Bethezuba* (means "House of Hyssop").

βῆμα, βήματος n. *judicial bench.*

βία, -ας f. *violence, force;* βίᾳ adv. *by force.*

βιάζω, -άσω: *to force, constrain;* abs. mid. *to force, force one's way in.*

βιβλίον, -ου n. (oft in plur.) *book, scroll; written statement; decree.*

βιβρώσκω, βρώσομαι, ἔβρωσα: *to eat, eat up.*

βίος, -ου m. *life, course of life, lifetime; world.*

βλασφημέω, -ήσω: *to speak against, slander, insult.*

βλασφημία, -ας f. *blasphemy; speaking against God; slander, insulting talk.*

βλέπω, -έψω: *to see.*

βοάω, βοήσω, ἐβόησα: *to shout.*

βοή, -ῆς f. *cry, outcry, shout.*

βοηθέω, -ήσω: *to help, assist, come to the rescue.*

βοηθός, -οῦ m. *helper, ally.*

βολή, -ῆς f. *throw, cast.*

βουκολέω, -ήσω: *to delude, beguile.*

βούλευμα, -ατος n. *plan, scheme.*

βουλεύω, -εύσω, ἐβουλευσάμην: *to take counsel, consider; to plan* + infin. or articular infin.

βουλή, -ῆς f. *planning, counsel; purpose.*

βούλομαι, βουλήσομαι, ἐβουλήθην (depon.): *to will, wish, be willing.*

βραδύς, -εῖα, -ύ adj. *slow.*

βραδυτής, -τῆτος f. *slowness.*

βραχύς, -εῖα, -ύ adj. *brief, short.*

βρέφος, -ους n. *baby, infant.*

βρῶμα, -ματος n. *food; solid food.*

βωμός, -οῦ m. *altar.*

Γ

Γαδδι m. *Gaddi.*
Γαζηρων f. *Gazara.*
γαζοφυλάκιον, -ου n. *treasury.*
Γάιος, -ου m. *Gaius.*
Γαλιλαία, -ας f. *Galilee.*
γάρ conj. *for, since.*
Γάρις f. *Garis.*
γείσιον, -ου n. *low parapet.*
γέλως, -ωτος m. *laughter.*
γενεά, -ᾶς f. *generation; period, age; family.*
γέννaιος, -α, -ον adj. *noble, free-born.*
γενναιότης, -τητος f. *nobility.*
γενναίως adv. *nobly.*
γεννάω, -ήσω (cf. γένος): *to beget (father); to give birth, bear (mother); pass. to be born.*
γέννημα, γεννήματος n. *offspring.*
γένος, -ους n. *family, race, nation, people; lineage, descendants; offspring; sort, kind.*
γενοῦ 2 sing. aor. act. impv. of γίνομαι/γίγνομαι.
γέρρον, -ου n. *anything made of wicker-work, espec. shields or mantelet covering.*
γεύομαι, γεύσομαι, ἐγευσάμην: *to taste or eat of* τινός; *to experience.*
γεφυρόω, -ώσω: *to make passable by a bridge, bridge over.*
γεώδης, -ες adj. *earth-like, earthly.*

γεωργία, -ας f. *farming.*
γῆ, γῆς f. *the earth; land, country, region; soil; ground.*
γηθέω, -ήσω, ἐγήθησα, γέγηθα: *to be delighted, to rejoice.*
γηραιός, -ά, -όν adj. *old, aged.*
γῆρας, γήρως n. *old age;* ἐπὶ γήρως *in old age.*
γίγας, γίγαντος m. *giant.*
γίνομαι/γίγνομαι, γενήσομαι, ἐγενόμην: *to be, become, come into being; be born.*
γιγνώσκω, γνώσομαι, ἔγνων, ἔγνωκα, ἔγνωσμαι, ἐγνώσθην: *to know; perceive; gain knowledge of.*
γλίχομαι: *to struggle, strive* (oft + infin.).
γλῶσση, -ης f. *tongue, language.*
γνήσιος, -α, -ον adj. *genuine, true; legitimate.*
γνώμη, -ης f. *intention; purpose.*
γνωρίζω, -ίσω: *to know, recognize.*
γνώριμος, -ον adj. *well-known, notable.*
γονεύς, -έως m. *father, ancestor;* in plur. *parent.*
Γοργίας, -ου m. *Gorgias.*
Γορπίαιος, -ου m. *Gorpiaeus (name of a month).*
γοῦν restrict. particle *at least, at any rate; indeed.*

γράμμα, -ατος n. *written character, letter.*

γραμματοφόρος, -ου m. *letter carrier.*

γράφω, γράψω, ἔγραψα, γέγραφα, γέγραμμαι, 2 aor. ἐγράφην (later 1 aor. ἐγράφθην): *to write; record, compose.*

Δ

Δαγών m. *Dagon.*

δαιμονάω: *to be possessed* by an evil spirit.

δαιμόνιος, -α, -ον adj. *of things, proceeding from the Deity; divine, godlike.*

δάκρυον, -ου n. *tear.*

δακρύω, -ύσω: *to weep, shed tears.*

Δαμασκηνός, -ή, -όν adj. *of Damascus;* οἱ Δαμασκηνοί *the men of Damascus.*

Δανιήλ m. *Daniel.*

δαπάνη, -ης f. *cost, expense.*

Δαρεῖος, -ου m. *Darius,* Persian king.

δασμός, -οῦ m. *division, tribute.*

Δαυίδ or Δαυίδης, -ου m. *David.*

δαψιλής, -ές adj. *abundant, plentiful; liberal, profuse.*

δέ *but, to the contrary; and; now, then, so;* μέν... δέ *on the one hand... on the other hand.*

δεδεμέναι pf. pass. ptc., fem. nom. plur. of δέω.

δεδόσθαι pf. pass. infin. of δίδωμι.

γυμνάζω, -σω: *to train, exercise.*

γυμνάσιον, -ίου n. *gymnasium; school; place where exercises were practiced.*

γυμνόω, -ώσω: *to strip naked; unsheathe.*

γύναιον, -ου n. dimin. of γυνή.

γυνή, γυναικός f. *woman; wife.*

δείκνυμι, δείξω, ἔδειξα, δέδειχα, δέδειγμαι, ἐδείχθην: *to show.*

δέησις, -εως f. *entreaty; prayer, petition.*

δεῖ impers. *it is necessary.*

δείδω, δείσομαι, ἔδεισα, δέδοικα: *to fear.*

δείκηλον, -ου n. *representation.*

δείκνυμι, δείξω, ἔδειξα: *to show, point out.*

δειλία, -ας f. *cowardice; fear.*

δειλόομαι: *to be afraid.*

δειλός, -ή, -όν adj. *cowardly, afraid; wretched, miserable, unhappy.*

δειμάμενος aor. mid. ptc. of δέμω.

δεινός, -ή, -όν adj. *dire, dreadful, terrible.*

δείξειεν 3 sing. aor. opt. act. of δείκνυμι.

δείσας nom. masc. sing. aor. ptc. of δείδω.

δεισιδαιμονία, -ας f. *relig. scruple.*

δέκα indecl. *ten.*

δεκάδαρχος, -ου m. *commander of ten.*
δεκάτη, -ης f. *tithe of a tenth; tenth.*
δέδρεσι(ν) dat. plur. of δένδρον.
δέμω 1 aor. ἔδειμα: *to build.*
δένδρον, -ου n. *tree.*
δέομαι, δεήσομαι, ἐδεήθην: *to need, want; owe; to long* or *beg for; ask.*
δέον pres. act. ptc. of δεῖ.
δέος, δέους n. *fear, dread, fright.*
δεσμέω, -ήσω: *to bind, fetter with chains.*
δέσμιος, -ου m. *prisoner.*
δεσμός, -οῦ m. *bonds, imprisonment.*
δεσμωτήριον, -ου n. *prison.*
δεσπότης, -ου m. *lord, master.*
δεύτερος, -α, -ον adj. *second.*
δέχομαι, δέξομαι, ἐδέχθην (depon.): *to take, accept, await;* espec. *to take well, receive kindly.*
δεξιός, -ά, -όν adj. *right* (opp. to *left*).
δέω, δήσω, ἔδησα: *to bind, tie, fetter, chain.*
δή intens. particle *indeed, surely; then, therefore, now.*
δῆθεν or δῆθε adv. *perhaps, I suppose.*
δῆμος, -ου m. *people, crowd; public assembly; populace.*
δημότης, -ου m. *member of the same* δῆμος; *fellow citizen.*
δήποτε adv. *at some time, once;* τί δήποτε in indir. quest. *why, pray?*

διαβαίνω, -βήσομαι, -έβην: *to pass through, cross.*
διάβολος, -ον adj. *slanderous, falsely accusing, calumnious;* as substant. διάβολος, -ου m. *a slanderer;* espec. (in Christian sense) *the devil.*
διαγιγνώσκω, -γνώσομαι: *to resolve, determine; make a decision.*
διάδημα, -τος n. *diadem; crown.*
διαδιδράσκω, -δράσομαι, 2 aor. διέδραν, -δέδρακα: *to run off, escape, get away.*
διαδοχή, -ῆς f. *a succession; a relief* (of a guard).
διάδοχος, -ου m. *successor.*
διαδωρέομαι, -ήσομαι: *to distribute as a gift.*
διαθήκη, -ης f. *covenant;* plur. *ordinances* (of a covenant); *will, testament.*
διαιρέω, -ήσω, διεῖλον: *to divide, part, cleave in twain; divide, distribute.*
δίαιτα, -ης f. *mode of life, way of living.*
διακαλύπτω, -ψω: *to uncover, reveal.*
διακαρτερέω, -ήσω: *to endure to the end; last.*
διακρίνω, -κρινῶ: *to render judgment.*
διακρούω, -σω: *to try* or *prove by knocking;* in mid. *to drive from oneself, elude by delay.*
διαλέγομαι, -λέξομαι: *to converse, communicate.*

διαλογισμός, -οῦ m. *thinking; reasoning; plans.*

διαλύω, -λύσω, διέλυσα: *to dismiss, disband.*

διαμαρτάνω, -τήσομαι, διήμαρτον: *to fail utterly; to be mistaken.*

διαμονή, -ῆς f. *durability.*

διανοία, -ας f. *thought, intention.*

διαπειλέω, -ήσω: *to threaten violently.*

διαπεράω, -άσω, διεπέρασα: *to cross.*

διαπεφοιτηκός pf. act. ptc., nom. neut. sing. of διαφοιτάω.

διαπορεύω, -σω: *to carry across*; in pass. *to go through, pass along.*

διαρκέω, -έσω: *to have full strength; to endure, hold out, prevail; be satisfied in* τινί.

διαρπάζω, -πάσομαι: *to plunder, tear into pieces.*

διαρρήγνυμι, -ήξω, διέρρηξα: *to rip in two, tear apart.*

διασείω, -σω: *to shake violently.*

διασκεδάννυμι, -σκεδάσω, διεσκέδασα: *to scatter abroad, dissipate; reject.*

διασκευάζω, -άσω: *to set in order*; mid./pass. *to arm or equip oneself.*

διάστημα, -ατος n. *distance.*

διασῴζω, -ώσω: *to keep safe; rescue, deliver.*

διατειχίζω, -ίσω: *to fortify by means of a wall; to wall off.*

διατελέω, -έσω: *to fulfill, confirm*; with ptc. *to continue doing something.*

διατιθείς pres. act. ptc., nom. masc. sing. of διατίθημι.

διατίθεμαι, διαθήσομαι, διεθέμην: *to make* (espec. of covenants or wills).

διατίθημι, -θήσω: *to handle, arrange.*

διατρίβω, -ψω: *to rub between; spend time, live.*

διαφέρω, διοίσω, διήνεγκα: *to carry over* or *across*; intrans. *to differ from,* i.e., *to excel, surpass.*

διαφεύγω, -φεύξομαι, -έφυγον: *to flee through, get away, escape.*

διαφθείρω, -φθερῶ: *to destroy utterly, kill.*

διαφίημι, -ήσω: *to disband, dismiss.*

διαφοιτάω, -ήσω: *to wander abroad.*

διαφορά, -ᾶς f. *difference, distinction; dispute.*

διδακτός, -ή, -όν (cf. διδάσκω) adj. *trained; taught, instructed* in τινός.

διδάσκαλος, -ου m. *teacher.*

διδάσκω, διδάξω, ἐδίδαξα: *to teach.*

διδούς pres. act. ptc. of δίδωμι.

δίδωμι, δώσω, ἔδωκα, δέδωκα, δέδομαι, ἐδόθην: *to give; grant, allow, permit; inflict* (punishment).

διεγείρω, -εγερῶ: *to arouse, awake; raise.*

διεγνωκώς pf. act. ptc., nom. masc. sing. of διαγιγνώσκω.
διεῖλον 2 aor. act. of διαιρέω.
διελαύνω, -ασω: *to run through* (with a sword).
διελέχθη 3 sing. aor. pass. indic. of διαλέγομαι.
διέξειμι: *to relate, enumerate.*
διέρρηξα 1 aor. act. of διαρρήγνυμι.
διέρχομαι, -ελεύσομαι: *to pass through, complete.*
διεσκέδασα 1 aor. act. of διασκεδάννυμι.
διῆλθεν 2 aor. act. of διέρχομαι
διέρχομαι, -ελεύσομαι, -ῆλθον: *to go through, traverse.*
διΐστημι, διαστήσω: *to set apart, divide; place at cert. intervals*; in mid. *set oneself apart.*
δικάζω, δικάσω, ἐδίκασα: *to decide, determine.*
δίκαιος, -α, -ον adj. *righteous, just.*
δικαιοσύνη, -ης f. *righteousness, uprightness, justice; what is right.*
δικαίωμα, -ατος n. *act of justice; ordinance; acquittal, act of justification.*
δικαίως adv. *justly, rightly.*
δίκη, -ης f. *justice*; διδόναι δίκην *to pay the penalty.*
διοδεύω, -εύσω: *to travel through.*
διπλούς, -πλῆ, -πλοῦν adj. *double, two-fold.*
δίς adv. *twice.*
δισχίλιοι, -αι, -α *two thousand.*

δίχα prep. with gen. *apart from, without* τινός.
διχοστασία, -ας f. *dissension.*
διώκω, διώξω, ἐδίωξα: *to pursue, chase.*
δοθῆναι aor. pass. infin. of δίδωμι.
δοκέω, -ήσω, ἐδόκησα: *to think, suppose*; intrans. *to seem, appear*; δόκει (impers.) *it seems right to* τινί.
δόλος, -ου m. *guile; deceit, treachery.*
δόμα, δόματος (cf. δίδωμι) n. *gift.*
δόξα, -ης f. *glory, splendor; power; praise, honor; pride.*
δοξάζω, -άσω: *to glorify, exalt.*
Δορυμένης, -ους m. *Dorymenes.*
δορυφόρος, -ον adj. *spear-carrying*; οἱ δορυφόροι *spear carriers, bodyguard.*
δουλεία, -ας f. *bondage, slavery.*
δουλεύω, -σω: *to be a slave to* τινί.
δούλη, -ης f. *female slave.*
δοῦλος, -ου m. *slave, servant.*
δραμών aor. act. ptc., nom. masc. sing. of τρέχω.
δρασμός, -οῦ m. *running away, flight.*
δράσσομαι, δράξομαι, ἐδραξάμην: *to lay hold of* τινός.
δράω, -άσω, ἔδρασα: *to do.*
δρυμός, -οῦ m. *oak coppice; thicket.*
δρύφακτον, -ου n. *railed fence; balustrade*

δύναμαι, δυνήσομαι, ἐδυνησάμην: usu. with a compliment. infin. *be able to do something; be capable* or *strong.*

δύναμις, -εως f. *power, strength; military force; act of power, miracle.*

δυναστεία, -ας f. *power, lordship, sovereignty.*

δυνάστης, -ου m. *lord, master, ruler; prince, chief.*

δυνατός, -ή, -όν adj. *strong, mighty, powerful, able.*

δύο indecl. *two.*

E

ἑάλω 3 sing. 2 aor. of ἁλίσκομαι.

ἑαλώκοτος pf. act. ptc. of ἁλίσκομαι.

ἐάν or ἄν conditional particle *if.*

ἑαυτοῦ, -ῆς, -οῦ (not used in the nom.) reflex. pro. *himself, herself, itself, themselves*; poss. pro. *his, hers*, etc.; reciproc. pron. *one another, each other.*

ἐάω, ἐάσω, εἴασα, εἴακα: *to let, suffer, allow, permit.*

ἑβδομήκοντα indecl. *seventy.*

ἕβδομος, -η, -ον (cf. ἑπτά) *the seventh.*

Ἑβραῖος, -ου m. *a Hebrew pers..*

ἐγγίγνομαι, -γενήσομαι: *to be produced* or *grow in* something else.

ἐγγίζω, -ίσω, ἤγγισα: *to draw near; approach.*

ἐγγύθεν adv. *near; hard by.*

ἐγγύς adv. *near, close to.*

δυσάλωτος, -ον adj. *hard to conquer.*

δυσέξοδος, -ον adj. *hard to get out of.*

δύσις, -εως f. *setting* or *sinking* (of the sun); *west.*

δύστηνος, -ον adj. *wretched, unhappy, unfortunate.*

δώδεκα indecl. *twelve.*

δωμάτιον, -ου n. *room.*

δωρέομαι, -ρήσομαι: *to give* or *present; to gift* τινά *with* τινί.

δῶρον, -ου n. *gift.*

ἐγγώνιος, -ον adj. *angular; forming a right angle.*

ἐγείρω, ἐγερῶ, ἤγειρα, ἐγήγερκα, ἐγήγερμαι, ἠγέρθην: *to rouse, waken; stir up; raise, erect.*

ἐγεννήθην 1 aor. pass. of γεννάω.

ἐγενόμην 2 aor. mid/pass. of γίνομαι/γίγνομαι.

ἐγκάθημαι *to sit in* or *on; lie in ambush.*

ἐγκαθιδρύω, -ύσω: *to set up.*

ἐγκαινίζω, -ίσω: *to renovate, dedicate, consecrate.*

ἐγκαινισμός, -οῦ m. *renovation, dedication.*

ἐγκατακλείω, -σω: *to lock up in* τινί.

ἐγκατακρυβῆναι aor. infin. pass. of ἐγκατακρύπτω.

ἐγκατακρύπτω: *to hide in* τινί.

ἐγκαταλείπω, ἐγκαταλείψω, ἐγκατέλιπον: *to abandon, forsake.*

ἐγκαταμίγνυμι, -μίξω: *to mix or mingle in.*

ἐγκελεύω, -εύσω: *to urge on, cheer on.*

ἐγκρατής, -ές adj. *having control over* τινός.

ἔγνω 3 pers. sing. 2 aor. indic. act. of γιγνώσκω.

ἐγχειρέω, -ήσω: *to take in hand, undertake.*

ἐγχειρίζω: *to place in someone's hands; entrust.*

ἐγχώριος, -α, -ον adj. *native.*

ἐγώ 1 pers. pro. ἐμοῦ (μου), ἐμοί (μοι), ἐμέ (με) *I, me;* plur. ἡμεῖς, ἡμῶν, ἡμῖν, ἡμᾶς *we, us.*

ἔδαφος, -εος n. *flooring; pavement.*

ἔδραμον 2 aor. of τρέχω.

ἔδωκα 1 aor. act. of δίδωμι.

Ἐζεκίας, -ου m. *Ezechias.*

ἐζεύχθην 1 aor. pass. of ζεύγνυμι.

ἔθεντο 3 plur. aor. indic. mid. of τίθημι.

ἔθηκα 1 aor. act. of τίθημι.

ἐθνός, -ους n. *nation, people;* τὰ ἔθνη *non-Jews, Gentiles;* (from the Jewish point of view) *pagans, heathen, unbelievers.*

ἔθος, -ους n. *custom, practice.*

εἰ cond. particle *if; whether;* εἴ τις, εἴ τι *who(ever), what(ever);* εἰ καί *even if.*

εἶ 2 pers. sing., pres. indic. act. of εἰμί.

εἴγε *if at least, if then.*

εἶδον 2 aor. of obsolete *εἴδω which, in pres. act., is suppl. by ὁράω.

εἰδωλεῖον, -ου n. *an idol's temple.*

εἴδωλον, -ου n. *idol, false god.*

εἴθε + vb. in optv. = optv. of Wish: "would that…!"

εἰκάδι = εἴκοσι(ν) *twenty* indecl.

εἰκαῖος, -α, -ον adj. *common, worthless.*

εἰκάς, εἰκάδος *twentieth day* of a month.

εἴκοσι(ν) *twenty* indecl.

εἴκω, -ξω, εἶξα: *to yield, give way to, retire.*

εἰκών, -όνος f. *likeness, image.*

εἴληφα pf. of λαμβάνω.

εἷλκον impf. of ἕλκω.

εἰμί (pres. impv. ἴσθι, ἔστω; 3 plur. ἔστωσαν; inf. εἶναι; impf. ἦν; fut. ἔσομαι): *to be, exist; happen, take place; live.*

εἶναι pres. act. infin. of εἰμί.

εἶπον 2 aor. act. of λέγω.

εἶργον impf. of ἔργω.

εἴρηκα pf. act. of λέγω.

εἰρηνικός, -ή, -όν adj. *of or for peace; peaceful, peaceable.*

εἰς prep. + accus. *into, to; in, at on, upon, by, near; as a.*

εἷς, μία, ἕν gen. ἑνός, μιᾶς, ἑνός *one; a, an; single; only one.*

Vocabulary

εἴσειμι (impf. εἰσῄει): *to enter into; attack.*
εἰσέρχομαι, -ελεύσομαι, -ῆλθον: *to go in.*
εἰσῆλθον 2 aor. of εἰσέρχομαι.
εἰσκομίζω, -κομιῶ: *to bring in, import.*
εἴσοδος, -ου f. *way into, entry.*
εἰσπέμπω, -ψω: *to send to.*
εἰσπηδάω, -ήσω: *to leap into.*
εἰσπορεύομαι, -εύσομαι: *to go in.*
εἰσφέρω, -οίσω, -ήνεγκα: *to bring in, dedicate.*
εἰσχέω, -χεῶ, εἰσέχεα: *to pour into.*
εἰσχυθέντες aor. pass. ptc. of εἰσχέω.
εἴσω adv. *within, inside.*
εἶτα adv. *then; moreover, after all.*
εἶχον impf. indic. act. of ἔχω.
ἐκ (ἐξ before vowels) prep. with gen. *from, out from, away from; by, by means of, by reason of, because; for; on, at; of.*
ἑκατέρωθεν adv. *on both sides.*
ἑκατόν indecl. *hundred.*
ἑκατόναρχος, -ου m. *commander of a hundred.*
ἕκαστος, -η, -ον *each, every.*
ἑκατοστός, -ή, -όν (cf. ἑκατόν) adj. *the hundredth.*
ἐκβαίνω, -βήσομαι, ἐξέβην: *to step out of something; turn out.*
ἐκβάλλω, -βαλῶ, -έβαλον: *to cast out.*

ἐκδιηγέομαι, -γήσομαι: *to tell to the end, recount in full.*
ἐκδικέω, -ήσω: *to avenge, punish*; ἐκδικεῖν ἐκδίκησιν *to exact vengeance.*
ἐκδίκησις, -εως f. *vengeance; punishment.*
ἔκδικος, -ου m. *avenger, punisher.*
ἐκδοχεῖον, -ου n. *reservoir, tank.*
ἐκδρομή, -ῆς f. *sally, charge.*
ἐκεῖ adv. *there, in that place.*
ἐκεκράγεσαν 3 plur. plupf. indic. act. of κράζω.
ἐκεῖνος, -η, -ον demontr. adj. *that; he, she, it.*
ἐκθέω, -θεύσομαι: *to run forth, make a sally.*
ἐκκαίδεκα *sixteen.*
ἐκκαίω, -καύσω: *to burn forth.*
ἐκκλησία, -ας f. *assembly.*
ἐκκλίνω, -κλινῶ: *to bend away.*
ἐκκομίζω, -ίσω: *to carry out.*
ἔκκυπτω, -ψω: *to peep out of; get out.*
ἐκλείπω, -ψω, ἐκέλιπον: *to leave out, omit*; intrans. *to leave off, cease, stop; run out.*
ἐκλεκτός, -ή, -όν adj. *chosen out, selected.*
ἐκλελύμεθα vb. pf. pass. 1 plur. of ἐκλύω.
ἐκλύω, -ύσω, ἐκέλυσα: *to loose, set free*; in pass. *to be faint, exhausted.*
ἐκμηκύνω, -κυνῶ intrans. *to lengthen out.*

ἑκουσιάζομαι: *to offer or be offered willingly.*

ἐκπετάννυμι, -πετάσσω, ἐξεπέτασα: *to unroll, unfurl; stretch out.*

ἔκπληξις, -εως f. *amazement.*

ἐκπλήσσω, -ξω, ἐξέπληξα (cf. 2 aor. pass. ἐξεπλάγην): *to strike out; scare out of one's wits;* in pass. *be amazed, astounded.*

ἐκπολεμέω, -ήσω: *to subdue.*

ἐκπορεύομαι, -εύσομαι: *to go out.*

ἐκπυνθάνομαι, -πεύσομαι, -επυθόμην: *to search out, make full inquiry.*

ἐκραταιώθην 1 aor. pass. of κραταιόω.

ἐκρέμασα 1 aor. of κρεμάννυμι.

ἐκτείνω, -τενῶ: *to stretch out, extend.*

ἐκτελέω, -τελέσω: *to complete, finish.*

ἕκτος, -η, -ον adj. *sixth.*

ἐκτρέχω, -θρέξομαι: *to run forth, make a sally.*

ἐκτρίβω, -ψω, ἐξέτριψα: *to destroy by rubbing, destroy root and branch.*

ἐκφέρω, -οίσω, -ήνεγκα: *to bring out.*

ἐκχέω, ἐκχεῶ, ἐξέχεα: *to pour out; to pour forth in vain, squander.*

ἔλαβον 2 aor. act. of λαμβάνω.

ἔλαιον, -ου n. *olive oil.*

ἐλάσας aor. act. ptc. of ἐλαύνω.

ἐλάσσων, -ον compar. adj. *lesser.*

ἐλαύνω, ἐλάσω, ἤλασα: *to set in motion, drive on* (espec. of horses, chariots, ships); intrans. *to march.*

ἐλάχιστος, -η, -ον adj. *fewest, smallest, least, worst.*

Ἐλεάζαρ, -ου m. *Eleazar.*

ἐλεγμός, -οῦ m. *refutation, confutation; reproach.*

ἐλέγχω, -ξω: *to refute, confute.*

ἐλεεινός, -ή, -όν adj. *pitiable, piteous.*

ἐλεέω, -ήσω: *to have pity on, show mercy to.*

ἑλεῖν 2 aor. act. infin. of αἱρέω.

ἔλεος, -ους n. *mercy, compassion.*

ἑλέπολις, -εως f. *city-destroying* (epithet of Helen and Iphigenia); substant. noun *siege-engine.*

ἐλεύθερα, -ας f. = ἐλευθερία, -ας f. *freedom, liberty.*

ἐλευθέρως adv. *freely.*

ἐλέφας, -φαντος m. *elephant.*

ἐλέχθη 3 sing. aor. pass. infin. of λέγω.

ἐλήφθη 3 sing. aor. pass. indic. of λαμβάνω.

ἔλθω aor. subjunct. of ἔρχομαι.

ἑλιγμός, -οῦ m. *winding, twisting.*

ἕλκω, ἕλξω, εἷλξα: *to draw, drag.*

Ἑλλάς, -άδος f. *Greece.*

ἐλλείπω, -ψω, ἐνέλιπον: intrans. *to lack, stand in need of* τινί.

Ἕλλην, -ηνος m. *Greek; non-Jew, Gentile, pagan.*

Ἑλληνικός, -ή, -όν adj. *Hellenic, Greek*; τὸ Ἑλληνικόν = οἱ Ἕλληνες *the Greeks*.

ἑλόμενοι aor. mid. ptc. of αἱρέω.

ἑλόντες aor. act. ptc. of αἱρέω.

ἐλπίζω, -ίσω, ἤλπισα: *to hope; expect*.

ἑλών 2 aor. ptc. of αἱρέω.

ἐμαυτοῦ, -ῆς reflex. pron. *myself*.

ἐμβάλλω, -βαλῶ, ἐνέβαλον: *to throw, lay, put in*.

ἐμβλέπω, -ψω: *to look at someone*.

ἐμβοάω, -ήσομαι: *to shout aloud*.

ἐμβολή, -ῆς f. *invasion, incursion*.

ἔμοιγε (ἔμοι + γε) *to me, at any rate*.

ἐμπειρία, -ας f. *experience*.

ἐμπίμπλημι, -πλήσω, ἐνέπλησα: *to fill* τι *full of* τινός; mid. *to be full*.

ἐμπίπρημι, ἐνιπρήσω/ἐμπρήσω, ἐνέπρησα: *to set on fire; enkindle*.

ἐμπίπτω, -πεσοῦμαι, ἐνέπεσον: *to fall upon, befall* τινί; + εἰς = *to fall in with*.

ἐμπιστεύω, ἐμπιστεύσω, ἐνεπίστευσα: *to trust in, give credence to* τινί.

ἐμπνέω, -πνεύσομαι, ἐνέπνευσα: *to breathe, live, be alive*.

ἐμπόδιος, -ον adj. *in the way, obstructing*; τὸ ἐμπόδιον *obstacle*.

ἐμποιέω, -ήσω, ἐνεποίησα: *to produce or create in* τινί; *to cause*.

VOCABULARY

ἔμπορος, -ου m. *merchant, trader*.

ἔμπροσθεν (1) prep. with gen. *before, in front of*; (2) adv. *ahead, forward, in front*.

ἐμπυρίζω = ἐμπυρεύω, -σω: *to set on fire*.

ἐμφανίζω, -ίσω: *to show forth, make clear*.

ἐμφράσσω, -ξω, ἐνέφραξα: *to block up, stop up*.

ἐμφύλιος, -ον adj. *native, kindred*.

ἐν prep. with dat. *in, on, at, near, by*; (in Koine, ἐν + dat. is oft equiv. to class. σύν + dat.); *among, within; by, with*; ἐν τῷ + infin.: *during, while, as; by his...* (+ vb.).

ἐμφύω, -σω: *to implant*.

ἐνακόσιοι, -αι, -α *nine hundred*.

ἐνάλλομαι, -αλοῦμαι, -ηλάμην: *to leap at, rush against*.

ἐναντίον prep. with gen. *in the judgment of, before*.

ἐναντίος, -α, -ον adj. *against, contrary, opposed; hostile*; ἐξ ἐναντίας *opposite, in action*.

ἐναργής, -ές adj. *distinct, bright, brilliant*.

ἔνατος, -η, -ον adj. *ninth*.

ἔνδεια, -ας f. *want or lack of* τινός, *dearth; hunger*.

ἐνδείκνυμι, -δείξω, ἐνέδειξα: *to mark out, indict*.

ἔνδειξις, -εως f. *a pointing out; indictment, proof, evidence*.

ἐνδίδωμι, -δώσω, ἐνέδωκα: *to surrender; to give in, give way; relent*.

ἔνδοθεν adv. *from within, within.*

ἔνδον adv. *within;* τὰ ἔδον *the things within, household affairs.*

ἔνδοξος, -ον adj. *glorious, illustrious, splendid; fine expensive* (of clothes); *honored, respected* (of people).

ἐνδότερος, -α, -ον compar. adj. formed from ἔνδον *inner.*

ἐνδοῦναι aor. act. infin. of ἐνδίδωμι.

ἐνδούς 2 aor. ptc. of ἐνδίδωμι.

ἐνδύω, ἐνδύσω, ἐνέδυσα in act.: *to put clothes on* another pers.; intrans. ἐνδύνω and mid. ἐνδύομαι: *to put clothes on oneself; to dress; to wear.*

ἐνεχείρει 3 sing. impf. act. indic. of ἐγχειρέω.

ἐννέα indecl. *nine.*

ἐνεγκεῖν 2 aor. act. infin. of φέρω.

ἔνεδρα, -ας f. *a lying in wait, ambush.*

ἐνεδρεύω, -σω: *to lie in wait, ambush.*

ἔνεδρον, -ου n. = ἔνεδρα, -ων neut. plur. *a lying in wait, ambush.*

ἐνενήκοντα indecl. *ninety.*

ἐνέπρησα 1 aor. act. of ἐμπίπρημι.

ἐνετειλάμην 1 aor. mid. of ἐντέλλω.

ἐνετίναξα 1 aor. of ἐντινάσσω.

ἐνετράπῃν 2 aor. pass. of ἐντρέπω.

ἐνεωκόρουν 3 plur. impf. act. of νεωκορέω.

ἐνήλατο 3 sing. 1 aor. mid. of ἐνάλλομαι.

ἔνθα adv. *where.*

ἔνθεν adv. *from there; thereupon.*

ἐνθρώσκω, -θοροῦμαι, ἐνέθορον: *to leap into, leap among*

ἐνιαυτός, -οῦ m. *year;* ἐνιαυτὸν κατ' ἐνιαυτόν *year after year.*

ἐνίημι, ἐνιήσω: *to send in, throw in.*

ἐνισχύω, ἐνισχύσω, ἐνίσχυσα: trans. *to strengthen;* intrans. *to gain strength.*

ἐννεακαιδέκατος, -η, -ον adj. *nineteenth.*

ἐννοέω, -ήσω, ἐνενόησα: *to think of, hold in mind, consider.*

ἔνοπλος, -ον adj. *armed.*

ἐνσκήπτω, -ψω: *to fall upon someone.*

ἐντάφιον, -ου n. *shroud, winding sheet.*

ἐντέλλω mostly in mid. ἐντέλλομαι: *to enjoin or command* τινί.

ἐντεταλμένων pf. mid./pass. ptc., gen. masc. plur. of ἐντέλλω.

ἐντεῦθεν adv. *from this, from here.*

ἐντινάσσω: *to hurl against; brandish.*

ἐντολή, -ῆς f. *commandment; command, order.*

ἐντός prep. with gen. *within, in the midst of, among.*

ἐντρέπω, ἐντρέψω: *to turn about; respect, heed.*

ἐντυγχάνω, -τεύξομαι: *to happen upon, fall in with.*

ἐνυβρίζω, -ίσω: *to insult one.*
ἐνώπιον prep. with gen. *before, in the presence of, in front of; in the judgment of.*
ἕξ indecl. *six.*
ἐξαιρέτως adv. *specially; to an exceptional degree; exclusively, characteristically.*
ἐξαίρω, ἐξαρῶ, ἐξῆρα: *to lift up; exalt, extol; destroy; take up and away.*
ἐξαναλίσκω, -λώσω: *to consume, spend.*
ἐξανδραποδίζομαι, -ιοῦμαι: *to sell for slaves, reduce to slavery.*
ἐξάπινα adv. *suddenly.*
ἐξαπίνης adv. *suddenly.*
ἐξάπτω, -ψω, ἐξῆψα: *to fasten to; to enkindle, inflame; light.*
ἐξᾶραι aor. infin. of ἐξαίρω.
ἐξέβην 2 aor. of ἐκβαίνω.
ἔξειμι (impf. ἐξῄειν): *to go out.*
ἐξελαύνω, -ελάσω: *to drive out, chase out.*
ἐξενολόγει 3 sing. impf. indic. act. of ξενολογέω.
ἐξεπέτασα 1 sing. aor. act. indic. of ἐκπετάννυμι.
ἐξερευνάω, -ήσω: *to search out, investigate.*
ἐξέρχομαι, ἐξελεύσομαι, ἐξῆλθον, ἐξελήλυθα: *to come forth, go out; get out, escape.*
ἔξεστι(ν) + infin.: *to be possible to do something.*
ἐξέχεα 1 aor. act. of ἐκχέω.

ἐξηγέομαι, -ήσομαι: *to tell at length, narrate.*
ἑξήκοντα indecl. *sixty.*
ἑξηκονταοκτώ indecl. *sixty-eight.*
ἑξηκονταπήχεις *sixty cubits high.*
ἐξῆλθον 2 aor. act. of ἐξέρχομαι.
ἐξήρθην aor. pass. of ἐξαίρω.
ἑξῆς adv. *ensuing;* τῇ ἑξῆς *on the next day.*
ἔξοδος, -ου f. *departure, going out, excursion.*
ἐξολεθρεύω, -εύσω, ἐξωλέθρευσα: *to destroy utterly.*
ἐξομολογέω, -ήσω: *to confess in full, admit.*
ἐξονειδίζω, -ίσω: *to reproach bitterly.*
ἐξορύσσω, -ξω: *to dig up.*
ἐξουδενόω, -ώσω = ἐξουθενέω, -ησω: *to set at naught.*
ἐξουδένωσις, -εως f. *contempt.*
ἐξουσία, -ας f. *authority, right, liberty; ability, capability; ruling power, government.*
ἐξοχή, -ῆς f. *jutting forth; prominence.*
ἐξυβρίζω, -ίσω: *to break out into insolence, run riot, wax wanton.*
ἔξωθεν adv. *outside.*
ἔοικα, -ας, -ε etc., pf. with pres. sense, from εἴκω: *to be like* (+ dat.), *to seem.*
ἑορτάζω, -σω: *to feast.*
ἑορτή, -ῆς f. *feast, festival.*

ἐπάγω, -άξω, ἐπήγαγον: *to bring* or *lead upon*; mid. ἐπηγάγετο: *he won over.*

ἐπεδεξάμην 1 aor. mid./pass. of ἐπιδέχομαι.

ἐπαινέω, -έσω, ἐπήνεσα: *to praise; approve, sanction.*

ἐπαίρω, ἐπαρῶ, ἐπῆρα; pf. mid. ἐπῆρμαι, aor. pass. ἐπήρθην: *to lift up, raise; exalt, magnify.*

ἐπακούω, -ακούσομαι: *to listen, attend to* τινός.

ἐπαληθεύω, -σω: *to prove true, verify.*

ἐπάλληλος, -ον adj. *successive, continuous.*

ἐπανατείνω, -τενῶ: *to hold up towards*; in mid. *to hold over someone else.*

ἐπανατέλλω, -ανατελῶ: *to dawn or rise upon* τινί (of the sun).

ἐπάνω (1) prep. with gen. *on, upon; over, above; more than*; (2) adv. *over; besides.*

ἐπαρθήσομαι fut. pass. of ἐπαίρω.

ἐπαρχία, -ας f. *province.*

ἐπασκέω, -ήσω, -ήσκησα: *to labor at; practice, practice oneself in, cultivate.*

ἐπεγείρω, -γερῶ: *to waken, arouse, excite.*

ἐπεθέμην 2 aor. mid. of ἐπιτίθημι.

ἐπήρθη aor. pass. of ἐπαίρω.

ἐπείγω, -ξω: *to impel, urge on, drive forward.*

ἐπειδάν = ἐπειδή + ἄν *whenever.*

ἔπειτα adv. *then, next.*

ἐπεπήγεσαν 3 plur. plupf. indic. act. of πήγνυμι.

ἐπέρρωσεν 3 sing. aor. act. indic. of ἐπιρρώνυμι.

ἐπέχω, ἐφέξω, ἔπεσχον: *to keep in check, hold back.*

ἐπί prep. with (1) gen *on, upon; over; at, by; before, in the presence of; when, under, at the time of;* (2) dat. *on, at, in; with, by, near; over; because of, on the basis of; to, for; against; in addition to; about, concerning; of, from;* (3) acc. *on, upon; in; against; over; to, for; around, about, concerning; towards; among;* ἐφ᾽ ὅσον χρόνον *while, as long as;* ἐπὶ τοσοῦτον *to such a great degr.;* ἐπὶ τοῦτο *for this purpose.*

ἐπιβάθρα, -ας f. *scaling-ladder, gangway.*

ἐπιβαίνω, -βήσομαι, -έβην: *to set foot on.*

ἐπιβάλλω, -βαλῶ, ἐπέβαλον: *to set against; attack.*

ἐπιβουλεύω, -σω: *to plan, contrive, plot.*

ἐπιβουλή, -ῆς f. *plot, treachery.*

ἐπιγιγνώσκω, -γνώσομαι, -έγνων: *to recognize; find out, discover; know well.*

ἐπιδείκνυμι, -δείξω, -έδειξα: *to show forth, display; exhibit as a pattern.*

ἐπιδεῖν aor. infin. of ἐφοράω, -όψομαι: *to look upon.*

ἐπίδειξις, -εως f. *display, exhibition.*

ἐπιδέχομαι, -δέξομαι, ἐπεδεξάμην (depon.): *to receive, welcome.*

ἐπιδίδωμι, -δώσω: *to give freely, give besides.*

ἐπίδοσις, -εως f. *increase, growth, progress.*

ἐπιδραμόν aor. act. ptc., nom. neut. sing. of ἐπιτρέχω.

ἐπιζάω, -ήσω: *to outlive, survive.*

ἐπίθεσις, -εως f. *setting upon, attack.*

ἐπιθυμέω, -ήσω: *to set one's heart upon something; be greedy for* τινός.

ἐπιθυμία, -ας f. *longing, desire.*

ἐπιθυμητός, -ή, -όν adj. *desired, to be desired.*

ἐπιθυμία, -ας f. *desire.*

ἐπικαλέω, -ήσω: *to call, name; to surname.*

ἐπικαλούμενος pres. pass. ptc., nom. masc. sing. of ἐπικαλέω.

ἐπίκλησις, -εως f. *surname, additional name.*

ἐπικρατέω, -ήσω: *to rule over, govern; begin to rule; get possession of, hold sway over* τινός.

ἐπικρίνω, -κρινῶ: *to pass judgment upon, decide.*

ἐπιλαθέσθαι 2 aor. infin. act. of ἐπιλανθάνομαι.

ἐπιλανθάνομαι, -λήσομαι: *to forget* τινός.

ἐπιλέγω, -λέξω, ἐπέλεξα: *to choose, select.*

ἐπιλείπω, -ψω: *to leave behind; to fail* (as water in a spring).

ἐπίλεκτος, -ον adj. *chosen, picked, selected.*

ἐπίλοιπος, -ον adj. *left over, remaining.*

ἐπινοέω, -ήσω: *to perceive.*

ἐπίνοια, -ας f. *inkling, understanding.*

ἐπίπεδος, -ον adj. *level, flat.*

ἐπιπίπτω, -πεσοῦμαι, -έπεσα, -πέπτωκα: *to fall upon*; in a hostile sense *to attack.*

ἐπιρρώνυμι, -ρώσω: *to add strength to; to strengthen, encourage, cheer on.*

ἐπίσημος, -ον adj. *distinguished, famous, remarkable.*

ἐπίσκοπος, -ου m. *overseer, watcher, guardian.*

ἐπιστάς aor. act. ptc. of ἐφίστημι.

ἐπιστέλλω, -στελῶ: *to send to, send by message* or *letter.*

ἐπιστολή, -ῆς f. *letter*; in plur. *dispatch.*

ἐπιστρατεύω, -σω: *to march against, go on an expedition against.*

ἐπιστρέφω, -ψω, ἐπέστρεψα (2 aor. ἐπεστράφην): *to turn* or *dir. towards*; intrans. in pass. and 2 aor.: *to turn oneself* in any direction; *to return.*

ἐπισυνάγω, -άξω: *to gather together, lead together.*

ἐπισύρω: *to drag* or *trail* after one; also in the mid.

ἐπιτάσσω, -άξω, ἐπέταξα: *to enjoin* or *order* τινί; in pass. *be under orders.*

ἐπιτήδειος, -α, -ον adj. *suitable, appropriate; fit, serviceable, necessary*; neut. plur. τὰ ἐπιτήδεια *provisions.*

ἐπιτίθημι, -θήσω, -έθηκα: *to put* or *lay upon; place, put*; in mid.: *to place upon oneself; launch an attack on* τινί.

ἐπιτιμάω, -ήσω: *to object to one as blame-worthy; find fault with, reprove.*

ἐπιτρέπω, -ψω, ἐπέτρεψα: *to turn to, turn towards; commit, entrust to; give up, yield; permit, allow.*

ἐπιτρέχω, -δραμοῦμαι, ἐπέδραμον: *to rush against, attack suddenly.*

ἐπίτροπος, -ου m. *steward; guardian; procurator.*

ἐπιτυγχάνω, -τεύξομαι, ἐπέτυχον: *to light upon, fall in with, meet* τινί.

ἐπιφανής, -ές adj. *glorious*; cognomen of Antiochus.

ἐπίφθανος, -ον adj. *enviable, liable to jealousy.*

ἐπιφοιτάω, -ήσω: *to go constantly, roam about.*

ἐπιχειρέω, -ήσω: *to put one's hand to something, undertake; attempt, endeavor* to do something.

ἐπιχώριος, -α, -ον adj. *in, of,* or *belonging to the country*; οἱ ἐπιχώριοι *natives, inhabitants.*

ἐποικέω, -ήσω: *to live among.*

ἐπράθην 1 sing. aor. indic. pass. of πιπράσκω.

ἐπράχθη 3 sing. aor. indic. pass. of πράττω.

ἑπτά indecl. *seven.*

ἑπτακαίδεκα *seventeen.*

ἑπτακισχίλιοι, -αι, -α *seven thousand.*

ἐργάζομαι, ἐργάσομαι, εἰργασάμην (depon.): *to work, do, perform, carry out, accomplish.*

ἐργάτης, -ου m. *laborer, worker.*

ἔργον, -ου n. *work, deed; task; occupation*; plur. *works* (i.e., battering rams, siege engines, etc.)

ἔργω, ἔρξω, εἶρξα: *to bar the way; hinder, prevent.*

ἐρεθίζω, ίσω, ἠρέθισα: *to provoke, irritate.*

ἐρείδω, -σω: *to lean*; mid. *to fix, plant firmly.*

ἐρεύγομαι, ἐρεύξομαι: *to roar, bellow.*

ἐρημία, -ας f. *deserted place; wilderness, desert; nothing, desolation.*

ἔρημος, -ον adj. *lonely, deserted, uninhabited; desolate.*

ἔρημος, -ου f. *a deserted place; desert, wilderness.*

ἐρημόω, ἐρημώσω, ἠρήμωσα: *to make solitary* or *desert; to lay waste, desolate.*

ἐρήμωσις, -εως f. *desolation, destruction.*

ἐρίζω, ἐρίσω, ἤρισα: *to rival, strive, vie with.*

ἐρινύς, -ύος f. *avenging fury.*

ἔρις, -ιδος f. *strife, quarreling.*

ἑρμηνεύω, -σω: *to interpret; express, give utterance to.*

ἐρρύσθην aor. pass. of ῥύομαι.

ἐρρωμένος pf. pass. ptc. of ῥώννυμι as adj. *in good health, stout, vigorous.*

ἐρρωμένως adv. *stoutly.*

ἐρυθρός, -ά, -όν adj. *red.*

ἔρυμα, -ατος n. *fence, guard, bulwark.*

ἐρυμνός, -ή, -όν adj. *fenced-off.*

ἔρως, -ωτος m. *love; desire* for a thing.

ἔσῃ 2 pers. sing., fut. indic. act. of εἰμί.

ἐσθής, -ῆτος f. *clothing, apparel.*

ἐσθίω, ἔδομαι, ἔφαγον, ἐδήδοκα, ἐδήδεσμαι, ἠδέσθην: *to eat;* metaphor. *to devour, consume.*

ἐσκορπισμέναι pf. pass. ptc., nom. fem. plur. of σκορπίζω.

ἑσπέρα, -ας f. *evening; west.*

Ἐσρών, -ρῶνος m. *Esron.*

Ἐσσηνός, -οῦ m. *Essene.*

ἐστηρισμένος pf. pass. ptc. of στηρίζω.

ἔστησα 1 aor. act. of ἵστημι.

ἐστράφην 2 aor. of στρέφω.

ἔστω 3 sing. pres. act. impv. of εἰμί.

ἔσχατος, -η, -ον adj. *last, final;* substant. noun ἔσχατος, -ου m. *the end.*

ἑταῖρος, -ου m. *companion, comrade, fellow.*

ἐτάφην 2 aor. of θάπτω.

ἕτερος, -α, -ον adj. *another; one of the.*

ἐτετμήκει 3 sing. plupf. act. indic. of τέμνω.

ἔτι and ἔθ' (before rough breathing) adv. *still, yet* (οὐκ ἔτι *no longer*); *even; further, in addition, moreover.*

ἑτοιμάζω: *to prepare, make ready.*

ἕτοιμος, -η, -ον adj. *ready, prepared.*

ἑτοιμότης, -τητος f. *preparation, readiness.*

ἑτοίμως adv. *preparedly.*

ἔτος, -ους n. *year.*

εὐβουλία, -ας f. *counsel, good prudence.*

εὐγένεια, -ας f. *noble birth.*

εὐγενής, -ές adj. *well-born, of noble descent.*

εὐδαιμονέω, -ήσω: *to be prosperous, well-off, happy.*

εὐδαιμονίζω, -ίσω: *to account happy, felicitate.*

εὐδαίμων, -ον adj. *blessed, happy, fortunate;* οἱ εὐδαίμονες *the blessed.*

εὐδιάλλακτος, -ον adj. *easy to reconcile, placable.*

εὐδοκέω, -ήσω, εὐδόκησα: *to be pleased; take delight/pleasure in* τινί; *choose, will, resolve.*

εὐθέως or εὐθύς adv. *immediately.*

εὐθυμία, -ας f. *cheerfulness.*

εὐκαρδίως adv. *stout-heartedly.*
εὐκλεής, -ές adj. *glorious, noble.*
εὔκοπος, -ον adj. *easy.*
εὐλαβέομαι, -ήσομαι, εὐλαβήθην: *to be cautious; to have a care, beware, fear.*
εὐλογέω, -ήσω, εὐλόγησα: *to bless, offer blessings.*
εὐλογητός, -ή, -όν adj. *blessed.*
εὐλογία, -ας f. *blessing; praise.*
εὔλογος, -ον adj. *reasonable, sensible.*
εὐμαρής, -ές adj. *easy, convenient.*
εὐμενής, -ές adj. *well-disposed, kindly, gracious.*
εὔνοια, -ας f. *kindliness, good will.*
εὐοδόω, -ώσω: *to put in the right way, help* τινί *on the way;* in pass. *to prosper, be successful.*
εὐπλοέω: *to have a good voyage.*
εὐπορέω, -ήσω, εὐπόρησα: *to be prosperous, well off.*
εὑρίσκω, εὑρήσω, εὗρον, εὕρηκα, εὑρέθην; fut. pass. εὑρεθήσομαι): *to find, discover; obtain.*
εὗρον 2 aor. act. of εὑρίσκω.
εὖρος, -εος n. *breadth, width.*
εὐσέβεια, -ας f. *reverence, piety, devotion.*
εὐσεβής, -ές adj. *devout, reverent, pious.*
εὐτολμία, -ας f. *courage, boldness; confidence.*
εὐτρεπίζω, -ίσω: *to make ready, get ready, prepare.*

εὐφραίνω, -ανῶ, εὔφρανα: *to cheer, gladden.*
Εὐφράτης, -ου m. *Euphrates.*
εὐφροσύνη, -ης f. *gladness, joy.*
εὔχομαι, εὔξομαι, εὐξάμην: *to pray.*
ἐφάνη 3 sing. aor. pass. of φαίνω.
ἐφίστημι, -στήσω, -έστησα: *to come upon* τινί or τινός; *to appoint, set over.*
ἔφοδος, -ου f. *onset, attack; approach.*
ἐφοράω: *to look upon.*
ἔφυ 3 sing. 2 aor. of φύω.
ἔχθιστος, -η, -ον superl. adj. of ἐχθρός, -ά, -όν.
ἐχθρός, -ά, -όν adj. *hostile; enemy; hated*; espec. substant. noun ἐχθρός, -οῦ m. *enemy.*
ἐχυρός, -ά, -όν adj. *firm, strong, secure.*
ἔχω (impf. εἶχον), ἕξω/σχήσω, ἔσχον, ἔσχηκα, ἔσχημαι: *to have, hold; possess;* ἔχω + adv. = *"to be" such-and-such.* Thus, ἔχω ἑτοίμως *to be prepared*; ἔχω καλῶς *to be brave;* ἔχω ἀπόρως *to be unable,* etc.
ἑῴκεσαν 3 plur. plupf. of ἔοικα.
ἑῷος, -α, -ον adj. *eastern.*
ἑώρα 3 sing. impf. indic. act. of ὁράω.
ἑωρακώς pf. act. ptc. of ὁράω.
ἕως Attic for Ionic ἠώς, *morn;* ὑπὸ τὴν ἕω *by daybreak.*
ἕως (1) conj. (and ἕως ὅτου or ἕως οὗ) *until* (with any tense); *while*

VOCABULARY

(with pres. indic. only); ἕως ἔτι *as long as*; (2) prep. with gen. *to, until, as far as, to the point of*

Z

Ζαμβρι m. *Zimri.*

ζάω (contracted to ζῶ; impf. ἔζην): *to live, be alive.*

ζεύγνυμι or ζευγνύω, ζεύξω, ἔζευξα; 1 aor. pass. ἐζεύχθην (or more freq) 2 aor. ἐζεύγην: *to join* or *link together, yoke; make fast.*

ζέω, ζέσω, ἔζεσα: *to boil, seethe.*

ζῆλος, -ου m. *zeal; jealousy, envy.*

ζηλόω, -ώσω, ἐζήλωσα: *to be zealous; set one's heart on.*

H

ἤ particle *or* (ἤ... ἤ *either... or*; ἤ καί *or even*; with neg. *nor, or*); *than* (of comp.); πρὶν ἤ *before*; as an interrog. *is it that...?*

ἦ adv. *in truth, verily, indeed.*

ἠβουλόμην impf. of βούλομαι.

ἠγαθύνθη aor. pass. of ἀγαθύνω.

ἡγεμονία, -ας f. *chief command, sovereignty; hegemony.*

ἡγεμών, -όνος m. *leader; commander, captain, chief.*

ἡγέομαι, ἡγήσομαι, ἡγησάμην (depon.): *to guide, conduct, to lead* (espec. an army); *to suppose, believe, think.*

ᾔδειν plupf. (with an impf. sense) of *εἴδω.

ἡδέως adv. *pleasantly, sweetly.*

ἤδη adv. *now, already.*

(ἕως τέλους *to the end, fully*; ἕως τοῦ νῦν *until now;* idiom. *enough of this!*).

ζηλωτής, -οῦ m. *zealot; devoted disciple.*

ζητέω, -ήσω, ἐζήτησα: *to seek, seek after; search out, inquire into; examine, investigate.*

ζωγρέω, -ήσω: *to take alive, take prisoner in war.*

ζωή, -ῆς f. *life.*

ζῷον, -ου n. *living thing; animal.*

ἥδιστος, -η, -ον superl. adj. of ἡδύς.

ἥδομαι, ησθήσομαι, ἥσθην (depon.): *to be pleased, rejoice,* oft with dat.

ἡδονή, -ῆς f. *delight, enjoyment, pleasure.*

ἡδύς, ἡδεῖα, ἡδύ adj. *sweet, pleasant.*

ἥκω, ἥξω: *to have come.*

ἠλέουν impf. act. indic. of ἐλεέω.

ἦλθον 2 aor. act. of ἔρχομαι.

ἤλθοσαν = ἦλθον.

Ἠλίας, -ου m. *Elijah.*

ἡλικία, -ας f. *age, time in life; youth.*

ἡλίκος, -η, -ον in indir. quests. *how great, how strong, how vast; as.*

ἧλιξ, -ικος adj. *of the same age*; as substant. *fellow, comrade, mate.*
ἥλιος, -ου m. *sun.*
ἠλλοιώθην aor. pass. of ἀλλοιόω.
ἥλω 3 sing. aor. indic. act. of ἁλίσκομαι.
ἡμεῖς nom. plur. of ἐγώ.
ἡμέρα, -ας f. *day*; καθ᾽ ἡμέραν *daily*; μεθ᾽ ἡμέραν *after day break.*
ἡμέτερος, -α, -ον adj. *our.*
ἡμίβρωτος, -ον adj. *half-eaten.*
ἥμισυς, -εια, -υ adj. *half.* Oft the substant. is in the gen. but gives its number and gender to the adj., as τὰς ἡμίσεις τῶν δυνάμεων *half of the forces* (1 Macc 3:34).
ἦν 3 sing. impf. of εἰμί.
ἡνίκα adv. *when, at the time when.*
ᾕρει 3 sing. impf. of αἱρέω.

ἠρεμέω, -ήσω: *to be still, keep quiet.*
ᾑρέτισα 1 aor. act. of αἱρετίζω.
ἠρημώθην 1 sing. aor. pass. indic. of ἐρημόω.
ἠρήμωσα 1 aor. act. of ἐρημόω.
ᾑρῆσθαι pf. mid. infin. of αἱρέω.
Ἡρῴδης, -ου m. *Herod.*
ἠσθένησα 1 aor. of ἀσθενέω.
ἥσθησαν 3 plur. aor. pass. indic. of ἥδομαι.
ἡσυχάζω: *to be still, quiet, be at rest.*
ἥττων, ἧσσον adj. *less, weaker, inferior to* τινός.
ηὐξήθην 1 aor. pass. of αὐξάνω.
ᾐχμαλώτισα 1 aor. of αἰχμαλωτίζω.
ἦχος, -ου m. (later form of ἠχή, -ῆς f.) *sound*; tumultuous *noise* of a crowd, *roar* of the sea, etc.

Θ

θάλασσα, -ης f. *sea.*
θαλάσσιος, -α, -ον adj. *marine; like the sea* (in color).
θάλλω, θαλῶ, ἔθαλον, τέθηλα: *to bloom, flourish.*
θάμβος, -εος n. *astonishment, amazement.*
θάνατος, -ου m. *death.*
θανατόω, -ώσω: *to put to death; condemn.*
θάπτω, θάψω, ἔθαψα, τέταφα, τέθαμμαι, ἐτάφθην: *to bury.*

θαρρέω/θαρσέω, -ήσω: *to be of good courage.*
Θασσι m. *Thassi.*
θάτερος, -α, -ον (formed in Attic from the crasis of ὁ + ἕτερος); θάτερον... μέρος *the one part.*
θαῦμα, -ματος n. *astonishment.*
θαυμάζω, -σω: *to be surprised, marvel at* τι.
θαυμάσιος, -α, -ον adj. *wondrous, marvelous.*
θέα, -ας f. *a looking at, view; spectacle.*

θεάομαι, -άσομαι: *to view, behold.*

θέατρον, -ου n. *theater* (for viewing spectacles)

θεῖον, -ου n. *the divinity, deity.*

θεῖος, -α, -ον adj. *of or from the gods; divine; holy, sacred.*

θέλημα, θελήματος n. *will.*

θελητής, -οῦ m. *one who wills.*

θέλω, θελήσω, ἐθέλησα: *to wish, be willing.*

θεμιτός, -ή, -όν adj. *sanctioned by law; lawful.*

θεός, -οῦ m. *god.*

θεοφιλής, -ές adj. *beloved of God.*

θεράπων, -ποντος m. *attendant, servant.*

θεωρέω, -ήσω: *to look at, view, behold.*

θήρα, -ας f. *hunting, the chase;* also in collect. sense *quarry, prey.*

θηρίον, -ου n. *wild animal, beast.*

θησαυρός, -οῦ m. *treasure, store; treasure box, storeroom.*

θνήσκω, θανοῦμαι, ἔθανον: *to die.*

θνητός, -ή, -όν adj. *mortal.*

θολερός, -ά, -όν adj. *muddy, thick, troubled.*

θόρυβος, -ου m. *noise of a crowded assembly; clamor, uproar.*

θράσος, -εος n. *courage, confidence; boldness.*

θρασύνω, -υνῶ: *to make bold, encourage;* pass. *to be bold, courageous.*

θραύω, -σω: *to pierce, shiver, shatter.*

θρῆνος, -ου m. *dirge, song of grief.*

θρησκεία, -ας f. *religion, worship.*

θρίαμβος, -ου m. *triumph.*

θρόνος, -ου m. *throne.*

θυΐσκη, -ης f. *censer.*

θυμίαμα, -ματος n. *incense.*

θυμιάω, -άσω, ἐθυμίασα: *to burn incense.*

θυμός, -οῦ m. *anger, rage, fury; intense feeling.*

θύρα, -ας f. *door, gate; entrance.*

θυρόω, -ώσω: *to furnish with doors.*

θυσία, -ας f. *sacrifice, offering; act of sacrificing.*

θυσιάζω, -άσω: *to sacrifice.*

θυσιαστήριον, -ου n. *altar.*

θύω, θύσω, ἔθυσα: *to sacrifice to* τινί; *to slaughter, kill.*

θωρακίζω, -ίσω: *to arm with a breastplate; to fortify.*

θώραξ, -ακος m. *breastplate.*

I

Ἰακώβ m. *Jacob.*

Ἰάκωβος, -ου m. *James.*

Ἰαμνεία, -ας f. *Jamnia.*

ἰδεῖν 2 aor. infin. of εἶδον; cf. ὁράω.

ἴδιος, -α, -ον adj. *one's own, personal, private;* κατ' ἰδίαν *privately;* ἰδίᾳ *privately, on its own account.*

ἰδιωτικός, -ή, -όν adj. *private or personal,* as opp. to *public.*

ἰδού interjection. *look! see! behold!*

Ἰδουμαία, -ας f. *Idumaea.*

ἰδών 2 aor. ptc. of εἶδον.

ἱεράομαι, -άσομαι: *to serve as priest.*

Ἰερεμίας, ου m. *Jeremiah.*

ἱερεύς, -έως m. *priest.*

ἱερός, -ά, -όν adj. *holy, hallowed, consecrated;* τὸ ἱερόν *holy place.*

Ἱεροσόλυμα neut. plur. and f. sing.; also Ἱερουσαλήμ f. *Jerusalem.*

Ἱεροσολυμίτης, -ου m. *citizen or inhabitant of Jerusalem.*

ἱερωσύνη, -ης f. *priesthood; office of the priest.*

Ἰησοῦς, -οῦ m. *Joshua; Jesus.*

ἴθι 2 sing. of εἶμι.

ἱκανός, -ή, -όν adj. *sufficient, able to do* something; *large, enough.*

ἱκεσία, -ας f. *entreaty, request.*

ἱκετεύω, -σω, ἱκέτευσα: *to beseech, supplicate; to make supplication.*

ἱκέτης, -ου m. *suppliant.*

ἱλάσκομαι, -λάσομαι: *to appease, propitiate.*

ἵλεως, -ων (Attic for ἵλαος, -ον) adj. (of gods) *propitious, gracious;* (of men) *gracious, kindly, gentle;* ἵλεως σοί (sc. ἔστω ὁ Θεός) *God be gracious to thee* (i.e., *may it be far from you to* + infin.).

ἱμάτιον, -ου n. *raiment, clothes* (espec. of outer garments).

ἵνα conjunct. *in order that* (pur.); *so that* (res.); *that* (indir. statement); ἵνα μή *that not, lest;* ἵνα τί *to what end? why?*

Ἰνδοί, -ῶν m. plur. *the Indians; inhabitants of India.*

Ἰορδάνη, -ης f. *river Jordan.*

Ἰουδαῖος, -α, -ον adj. *Jewish; Judean;* espec. Ἰουδαία, -ας f. *Judea* and οἱ Ἰουδαῖοι *the Jews.*

Ἰούδας, -α m. *Judah* (son of Jacob, his tribe or territory); *Judas.*

Ἰούδης m. *Judes.*

ἱππεύς, -έως m. *horseman; knight; charioteer.*

ἵππος, -ου m. and f. *horse; cavalry.*

ἴσος, -η, -ον adj. *equal, the same.*

Ἰσραήλ m. *Israel.*

ἱστάω altern. form of ἵστημι.

ἴστε 2 pers. plur. of οἶδα.

ἵστημι, στήσω, ἔστησα/ἔστην, ἔστηκα, ἔσταμαι, ἐστάθην: *to cause to stand, halt, place;* in

VOCABULARY

mid, 2 aor. and pf. act. *to come to a stand, halt, stop.*

ἱστορία, -ας f. *inquiry, history; a learning by inquiry.*

ἱστῶν pres. act. ptc. of ἱστάω.

ἰσχύω, ἰσχύσω, ἴσχυσα: *to be strong, powerful, mighty.*

ἰσχυρός, ά, όν adj. *strong, mighty, powerful.*

ἰσχύς, -ύος n. *strength, force, violence;* ἐν ἰσχύι... ποιεῖν τινί: *to act violently toward someone.*

ἴσως adv. *probably, perhaps.*

Ἰωάννης, -ου m. *John.*

Ἰωαρίβ m. *Joarib.*

Ἰωναθης, ου m. *Jonathan.*

Ἰώσηπος, -ου m. *Josephus.*

Ἰωσήφ m. *Joseph.*

Ἰωτάπατα, -ων neut. plur. *Jotapata.*

Ἰωταπατηνός, -οῦ m. *citizen of Jotapata.*

Κ

καθαίρεσις, -εως f. *destruction.*

καθαιρέω, καθελῶ, καθεῖλον: *to take down; pull down, drag down; destroy, overthrow.*

καθάπερ conj. or adv. *as, just as.*

καθαρίζω, -ίσω, ἐκαθάρισα: *to purify, cleanse; make purification.*

καθαρός, -ά, -όν adj. *pure.*

καθεῖλον 2 aor. of καθαιρέω.

καθέλκω, -έλξω: *to drag down.*

κάθημαι (2 sing. κάθῃ, impv. κάθου): *to sit; sit down; stay; be.*

καθημένη pres. act. ptc., fem. sing. of κάθημαι.

καθίζω, καθίσω/καθιῶ, ἐκάθισα: caus. *to make to sit down, convene; set, appoint, constitute;* intrans. *to sit down, be seated, sit; dwell.*

καθικιτεύω, -εύσω: *to entreat earnestly.*

καθίστημι, καταστήσω, κατέστησα (2 aor. κατέστην),

καθέστηκα: causal in pres. fut. and 1 aor. *to set down, put down; appoint;* intrans. in 2 aor. and pf. *to be placed, set down.*

καθόλου adv. *in general, generally.*

καθοράω, κατόψομαι, κατεῖδον: *to perceive, behold.*

καθώς adv. *as, just as; inasmuch as, because; in so far as, to the degr. that.*

καί conj. *and, also, but, even; that is, namely;* καὶ... καί *both... and, not only... but also;* frequently used merely to mark the beg. of a sentence.

καὶ γὰρ δή adv. *for in fact.*

καινός, -ή, -όν adj. *new.*

καινοτομέω, -ήσω: *to cut fresh into; innovate, begin something new.*

καιρός, -οῦ m. *time* (viewed more as an occasion than extent); *appointed* or *proper time; opportunity.*

Καῖσαρ, -αρος m. *Caesar.*

Καισάρεος, -α, -ον adj. *Caesarian.*

Καισάρεια, -ας f. *Caesarea.*

καίτοι *although.*

καίω, καύσω, ἔκαυσα: *to burn, kindle, set on fire.*

κακία, -ας f. *wickedness.*

κακός, -ή, -όν adj. *evil, bad, wrong;* as a substant. noun *injury, harm.*

κακόω, -ώσω: *to maltreat, distress.*

κακῶς adv. *badly, basely.*

καλέω (pf. κέκληκα; aor. pass. ἐκλήθην; fut. pass. κληθήσομαι) *call, name, address; invite; summon, call in.*

καλλονή, -ῆς f. (cf. κάλλος) *beauty.*

κάλλος, -ους n. (cf. καλός): *beauty.*

καλός, -ή, -όν adj. *good; beautiful; right, proper, fitting; honorable, honest; fine, noble.*

κάλυμμα, -ματος (cf. καλύπτω) n. *covering, head covering, hood, veil; armor.*

καλύπτω, -ψω, ἐκάλυψα: *to cover.*

καλῶς adv. *bravely.*

κἄν = καί + ἄν *even if.*

κάματος, -ου m. *toil, trouble, labor.*

κάμνω, καμοῦμαι, ἔκαμνον: *to grow weary; suffer, struggle.*

καπνός, -οῦ m. *smoke.*

καρδία, -ας f. *heart, inner self.*

καρπός, -οῦ m. *fruit.*

καρτερέω, -ήσω: *to be steadfast, patient; to persevere or persist* in doing something (+ infin.).

καρτερικόν, -οῦ n. *patience, enduring quality.*

καρτερός, -ά, -όν adj. *strong, stout.*

κατά prep. with (1) accus. *according to, corresponding to, with reference to; in accordance with; on;* used distributively with numerals and places; κατὰ πόλιν καὶ πόλιν (1 Macc 1:51) *city by city;* κατὰ χώραν *throughout their land;* (2) gen. *against; down, down from; throughout; by* (of oaths); *over* (of authority).

καταβαίνω, καταβήσομαι, κατέβην, καταβέβηκα: *to come down, go down.*

καταβάλλω, -βαλῶ, κατέβαλον: *to throw down, cast* or *strike down.*

κατάβασις, -εως f. *descent.*

καταβοάω, -βοήσομαι: *to cry out against.*

καταγγέλλω, -ελῶ: *to announce.*

καταγιγνώσκω, -γνώσομαι: *to observe, discover; pass judgment on, condemn.*

κατάγω, -άξω, -ήγαγον: *to lead* or *carry down;* intrans. *to be drawn down.*

καταγωγή, -ῆς f. a *bringing down; conveyance; aqueduct.*

καταισχύνω, -υνῶ: *to shame, disgrace, dishonor.*

Vocabulary

κατακαίω, -καύσω, κατέκαυσα: *to burn, burn down, consume.*

κατακαλύπτω, -ψω: *to cover up, hide.*

κατακληροδοτέω, -ήσω: *to distribute by lot.*

κατακλουθέω, -ήσω: *to follow closely.*

κατακλύζω, -σω, κατέκλυσα: *to wash over, deluge.*

κατακόπτω, -ψω: *to cut down.*

κατακοσμέω, -ήσω: *to arrange, adorn.*

καταλαμβάνω, -λήψομαι, κατέλαβον, κατείληφα, κατελήφθην: *to seize upon, lay hold of;* in mid. *to seize for oneself; lay hold of; find, discover, come upon.*

κατάλειμμα, -ματος n. *remnant.*

καταλείπω, -ψω: *to leave behind, be left; forsake, abandon;* κατελείπετο impers.: *it remained* + infin.

καταλειφθέντες aor. pass. ptc., nom. masc. plur. of καταλείπω.

κατάλυμα, -λύματος n. *lodging place.*

καταλύω, -λύσω: *to destroy; terminate.*

καταμανθάνω, -μαθήσομαι, -έμαθον: *to learn thoroughly or well.*

κατανακάζω, -άσω: *to force; enforce.*

καταπατέω, -ήσω: *to trample down; tread upon.*

καταπέτασμα, -ματος n. *curtain.*

καταπίπτω, -πεσοῦμαι, κατέπεσον: *to fall down.*

καταπλαγέν aor. pass. ptc., nom. neut. sing. of καταπλήσσω.

καταπλήσσω, -πλήξω, κατέπληξα: *to strike with amazement.*

καταπίμπλημι, -πλήσω: *to fill full of* τινός.

καταπίνω, -πίομαι, κατέπιον: *to gulp down, swallow.*

καταράομαι, -άσομαι: in act. and mid. *to invoke as a curse, to curse;* in pass. *be accursed.*

κατάρχω, -ξω: *to make a beg. of* τινός.

κατασκάπτω, -ψω: *to dig up from below, raze to the ground, demolish.*

κατασκαφή, -ῆς f. *destruction.*

κατασκέπτομαι, -σκέψομαι: *to inspect.*

κατασκευάζω, -άσω: *to prepare, furnish; to cause.*

κατασκευή, -ῆς f. *fixed building on a site.*

καταστέλλω, -στελῶ: *to put in order; to keep down, repress, check.*

καταστενάζω, -άξω: *to sigh over, lament.*

καταστορέννυμι, -στορέσω: *to strew, cover* (as with straw); *to lay low* (an army).

καταστροφή, -ῆς f. *an overturning; down throw.*

κατασφάζω, -ξω: *to slaughter, murder.*

κατασχεδιάζω, -άσω: *to make a rash affirmation of* τινός; *trifle with* τινός.

κατασχίζω, -ίσω: *to cleave asunder, tear apart.*

καταφαίνω, -φανῶ: *to make visible*; pass. *become visible, appear.*

καταφέρω, -οίσω, -ήνεγκα: *to bring down* from above; *to relieve oneself.*

καταφεύγω, -φεύξομαι, -έφυγον: *to flee for refuge.*

καταφθείρω, -φθερῶ: *bring to nothing, ruin.*

καταφονέω, -ήσω: *to slaughter, destroy.*

καταφρονέω, -ήσω: *to scorn, think lightly of* τινός.

καταφρόνησις, -εως f. *disdain.*

κατέβην 2 aor. of καταβαίνω.

κατέγνωστο 3 sing. plupf. indic. mid./pass. of καταγιγνώσκω.

κατέναντι (1) prep. with gen. *opposite, before; in the sight of*; (2) adv. *opposite.*

κατεπείγω, -ξω: *to press down; urge, impel, stimulate, hasten.*

κατερείπω, -ψω: *to throw* or *cast down; totter.*

κατεσθίω, -έδομαι: *to eat, devour.*

κατέστησα 1 aor. of καθίστημι.

κατευοδόω, -ώσω: *to succeed; bring prosperity.*

κατεύχομαι: *to pray earnestly.*

κατέχω, καθέξω/κατασχήσω, κάτεσχον: *to hold/keep back; prevent.*

κατηρορία, -ας f. *accusation, charge.*

κατήπειγεν 3 sing. impf. indic. act. of κατεπείγω.

κατιδών aor. act. ptc. of καθοράω.

κατοικέω, -ήσω, -ᾤκησα: *to dwell, inhabit.*

κατοικία, -ας f. *habitation; place in which one lives.*

κατοικίζω, -ίσω, κατῴκισα: *to cause to dwell; to settle, establish.*

κάτοικος, -ου m. *inhabitant.*

κατοίχομαι, -οιχήσομαι: *to go down*; οἱ κατοιχόμενοι *the departed.*

κατοκνέω, -ήσω: *to shrink* from doing something.

κατορθόω, -ώσω: *to set upright* or *erect; to succeed.*

κάτωθεν adv. *from below.*

κεῖμαι, κείσομαι: *to be laid, to lie.*

κειμήλιον, -ου n. *treasure, precious gift; heirloom.*

κείρω, κερῶ, ἔκειρα: *to cut short, clip.*

κεκραγότας pf. act. ptc., accus. masc. plur. of κράζω.

κεκρατήμενος pf. pass. ptc. of κρατέω.

κελεύω, -εύσω, ἐκέλευσα: *to give an order.*

κενός, -ή, -όν adj. *empty.*

κεραΐζω, ίσω: *to lay waste, ravage; kill, slaughter.*

κέρας, κέρατος n. *horn* of an animal; *wing* of an army or fleet.

κερδαίνω, κερδανῶ/κερδήσω, ἐκέρδανα/ἐκέρδησα: *to gain; profit from.*

κέρδος, -εος n. *gain, profit, advantage.*

κεφαλή, -ῆς f. *head.*

κεχαραγμένας pf. pass. ptc. of χαράσσω.

κῆπος, -ου m. *garden.*

κιθάρα, -ας f. *harp.*

κινδυνεύω, -εύσω: *to be in danger;* + dat. *put at risk.*

κίνδυνος, -ου m. *danger, risk.*

κινέω, -ήσω: *to move; provoke.*

κινύρα, -ας f. Hebr. *kinnor* (a stringed instr. played by the hand).

κίων, -ονος m. and f. *pillar, column.*

κλάω, κλάσω, ἔκλασα: *to break apart;* pass. *is broken.*

Κλεόπατρα, -ας f. *Cleopatra.*

κληδών, -όνος f. *omen, presage, boding.*

κληθείς aor. pass. ptc. from καλέω.

κληρονομέω, -ήσω: *to obtain a portion, obtain by lot; inherit.*

κληρονομία, -ας f. *an allotment; property, possession; what is promised.*

κλῆρος, -ου m. *lot.*

κλοπή, -ῆς f. *theft.*

κνίση, -ης f. *smell or odor of a victim; steam of burnt sacrifice.*

κοινός, -ή, -όν adj. *common, in common; profane; defiled, unclean;* ἐν κοινῷ *publicly.*

κοινωνία, -ας f. *association,* oft with gen.

κοίτη, -ης f. *bed.*

κολάζω, κολάσω, ἐκόλασα: *to chastise, correct, punish.*

κόλασις, -εως f. *pruning, checking; punishment, chastening*

κολλάω, -ήσω, ἐκόλλησα: *to glue, cement; to join together, unite;* in pass. *be joined to, attached to.*

Κομμαγηνός, -ή, -όν adj. *of Commagene* (a petty kingdom on the upper Euphrates).

κονιορτός, -οῦ m. *dust stirred up, cloud of dust.*

κοπετός, -οῦ m. *wailing, mourning.*

κοπιάω, -άσω: *to work hard; grow weary.*

κόπριον, -ου n. = κόπρος, -ου n. *dung, manure.*

κόπτω, κόψω, ἔκοψα, κέκοφα, κέκομμαι: *to beat, strike;* in mid. *to beat* or *strike oneself* as in mourning.

κορβωνᾶς = κορβανᾶς, -οῦ m. *Temple treasury* at Jerusalem.

κορυφή, -ῆς f. *head, top, summit, crown;* κατὰ κορυφήν *over head.*

κοσμέω, -ήσω: *to deck out, adorn, beautify.*

κόσμος, -ου m. *order; ornament, decoration, raiment, dress; the* world or universe.

κοῦφος, -ή, -όν adj. *light, nimble; easy.*

κράζω, κράξω, ἔκραξα, κέκραγα: *to screech, scream; to call out* or *clamor for something.*

κρᾶσις, -εως f. *alloy; crasis.*

κραταιόω, -ώσω = a later form for κρατύνω: act. *to strengthen, confirm*; pass. *to become strong, resolute; become hardened.*

κρατέω, -ήσω: *to be strong and mighty*; with obj. gen. *to lay hold of* τινός, *become master over, conquer*; pass. *to be caught.*

κράτιστος, -η, -ον superl. adj. of ἀγαθός, -ή, -όν: *best.*

κράτος, εος n. *strength, might, force*; ἀνὰ κράτος *up to one's full power.*

κραυγή, -ῆς f. *crying, screaming, shrieking.*

κρείσσων, -ον or κρείττων, -ον: compar. of ἀγαθός, -ή, -όν.

κρεμάννυμι, κρεμάσω, ἐκρέμασα, 1 aor. pass. ἐκρεμάσθην: *to hang, hang up*; pass. *to be suspended.*

κρημνός, -οῦ m. *crag.*

κρημνώδης, -ες adj. *precipitous, steep.*

κρίμα, -ματος n. *judgment; decision, verdict*; κατὰ τὸ κρίμα *in accordance with the (right) judgment; righteously.*

κρίνω, κρινῶ, ἔκρινα: *to judge, decide a contest.*

κριός, -οῦ m. *ram, battering-ram.*

κρίτης, -ου m. *judge.*

κρότος, -ου m. *clapping.*

κρυπτός, -ή, -όν *hidden, secret.*

κρύπτω, -ύψω, ἔκρυψα: *to hide, cover, conceal.*

κρυφός, -οῦ m. *lurking place.*

κτείνω, κτενῶ, ἔκτεινα: *to kill.*

κτῆνος, -ους n. *animal; mount, pack animal.*

κτῆσις, -εως f. *possession, property.*

κτίζω, -ίσω: *to create, make; to found* (a city).

κτίσις, -εως f. *founding, settlement.*

κυκλόθεν (1) prep. with gen. *round, about*; (2) adv. *all around, all about.*

κύκλος, -ου m. *circle, circuit.*

κυκλόω, -ώσω, ἐκύκλωσα: *to encircle, surround.*

κύκλῳ (1) adv. *in a circle, round, round about*, also ἐν κύκλῳ (2) prep. with gen. *around.*

κύμβαλον, -ου n. *cymbal.*

κύριος, -ου m. *lord; master.*

Κῦρος, -ου m. *Cyrus.*

κωλύω, κωλύσω, ἐκώλυσα: *to hinder, prevent, stop; forbid; withhold, keep back.*

κύμβαλον, -ου n. *cymbal.*

κώμη, -ης f. *village.*

Λ

λαβών aor. act. ptc. of λαμβάνω.

λαγχάνω, λάξομαι, ἔλαχον: *to obtain by lot.*

λάκκος, -ου m. *cistern; hole, pit.*

λαλέω, λαλήσω, ἐλάλησα: *to speak, talk, say; tell; proclaim; blather.*

λαμβάνω, λήψομαι, ἔλαβον, εἴληφα, εἴλημμαι, ἐλήφθην: *to take, receive; capture.*

λαμπάς, -άδος f. *torch.*

λαμπρός, -ά, -όν adj. *bright, brilliant, radiant.*

λαμπρότης, -τητος f. *splendor.*

λανθάνω, λήσω, ἔλαθον, λέληθα: *to escape or elude notice;* in mid./pass. λανθάνομαι, λήσομαι, ἐλαθόμην: *to forget, lose the memory of; evade.*

λαός, -οῦ m. *people; nation; crowd*; oft of the Jews as the people of God.

λάρναξ, -ακος f. *coffer, box, chest; ark.*

λατρεία, -ας f. *worship; service.*

λέγω, ἐρῶ, εἶπον, εἴρηκα, εἴρημαι, ἐρρέθην: *to say, speak, tell.*

λείπω, λείψω, ἔλιπον, λέλοιπα, λέλειμμαι, ἐλείθην: *to leave; desert, abandon*; in pass. *to be inferior to* τινί; *come short of* τινός; *fall short of* τινός; *be lacking in* τινός.

λειτουργία, -ας f. *public service.*

λείψανον, -ου n. *relic, remnant; ruins.*

λεπίζω: *to strip* an obj. of its metal covering.

λευκός, -ή, -όν adj. *white.*

λεύω, λεύσω, ἔλευσα: *to stone.*

λέων, λέοντος m. *lion.*

λῄζομαι, λῄσομαι, ἐλῃσάμην: *to seize as booty, make spoil of.*

λῆμα, -ματος n. *spirit, courage; pride, arrogance.*

ληφθέντας aor. pass. ptc. of λαμβάνω.

λῆρος, -ου m. *idle talk, nonsense.*

λῃσαμέναις dat. plur. fem.; aor. pass. participle of λῄζομαι.

λῃστής, -οῦ m. *robber, plunderer; brigand.*

λήσεσθαι fut. mid. infin. of λανθάνω.

λῃστρικός, -ή, -όν adj. *piratical, inclined to rob.*

ληφθείς 1 aor. pass. ptc. of λαμβάνω.

λίθος, -ου m. *stone.*

λίμνη, -ης f. *lake.*

λιμός, -οῦ m. *hunger, famine.*

λιμώττω: *to be famished.*

λογίζομαι, -ίσομαι, ἐλογίσθην: *to reckon, count; impute; calculate.*

λογισμός, -οῦ m. *reason, consideration.*

λόγος, -ου m. *something said* (e.g., *word; saying, message, teaching*;

talk, conversation); *account, settlement of an account; reason, grounds.*
λοιδορέω, -ήσω: *to rail at, abuse, revile.*
λοιδορία, -ας f. *railing, abuse, reproach.*
λοιμώδης, -ες adj. *pestilential.*
λοιπός, -ή, -όν adj. *rest, remaining.*
λούω, -σω, ἔλουσα: *to wash*; in mid. *to wash oneself, bathe.*
λυμαίνομαι, λυμανοῦμαι, ἐλυμηνάμην (depon.): *to treat with indignity or outrageously; despoil.*
λυπέω, λυπήσω: *to pain, distress, aggrieve*; pass. *to suffer pain.*
Λυσίας, -ου m. *Lysias.*
λυσσάω, -ήσω: *to be raging, furious.*
λυσσῆσαν pres. act. ptc., fem. accus. sing. of λυσσάω.
λυτρόω, -ώσω: *to ransom, redeem;* in mid. *to release by payment of ransom.*
λυχνία, -ας f. *lamp stand.*
λύχνος, -ου m. *light, lamp.*

Μ

Μαγάσσαρος, -ου m. *Magassarus.*
μαίνομαι, μανήσομαι: *to rage, be furious.*
μακαρίζω, -ίσω: *to count or esteem as blessed.*
μακάριος, -α, -ον adj. *blessed, happy, fortunate.*
μακαρισμός, -οῦ m. *blessing.*
Μακεδονικός, -ή, -όν adj. *Macedonian.*
Μακεδών, όνος m. *a Macedonian.*
Μακκαβαῖος, -ου m. *Maccabeus* surname of Judas, son of Mattathias, possibly mng. "hammer."
μακρός, -ά, -όν adj. *long; distant, far off*; οὐκ εἰς μακράν *not for a long time.*
μάλα adv. *very, very much, exceedingly.*
μαλακός, -ή, -όν adj. *soft; softened up.*
μάλιστα adv. *especially, most of all.*
μᾶλλον adv. *more*; μᾶλλον ἤ *more than.*
μανέντες aor. pass. ptc. of μαίνομαι.
μανία, -ας f. *madness, insanity.*
μαραίνω, -ανῶ: pass. *to waste away, languish, wither.*
μαρανθέν aor. pass. ptc., nom. neut. sing. of μαραίνω.
Μαρία, -ας f. *Mary.*
Μαριάμμη, -ης f. *Mariamme.*
μαρτυρέω, -ήσω, ἐμαρτύρησα: *to bear witness; be a witness*, oft with dat.
μαρτύρομαι, μαρτυροῦμαι, ἐμαρτυράμην: *to call to witness, invoke.*

Μασάδα, -ας f. *Masada*.

Μασσηφα f. *Mizpah*.

μαστιγόω, -ώσω: *to whip, beat*.

μάστιξ, -ιγος f. *whip, scourge*.

μάταιος, -α, -ον adj. *empty, idle, foolish*.

Ματθίας, -ου m. Matthias

Ματταθίας, -ου m. *Mattathias*.

μάχαιρα, -ας f. *short sword* or *dagger; saber*.

Μαχαιροῦς, Μαχηαιροῦντος m. *Machaerus*.

μάχη, -ης f. *fight, battle*.

μάχιμος, -η, -ον adj. *disposed for battle*; οἱ μάχιμοι *the combatants*.

μάχομαι, μαχέσομαι, ἐμαχεσάμην (depon.): *to fight, contend in battle*.

μέγας, μεγάλη, μέγα adj. *large, great*.

μέγεθος, -εος n. *greatness, magnitude, bulk*.

μέγιστος, -η, -ον superl. adj. of μέγας; τὸ δὲ μέγιστον *and especially*.

μεθίεσαν 3 plur. impf. of μεθίημι.

μεθίημι, μεθήσω, μεθῆκα: *to set loose, let go*.

μεθίστημι, μεταστήσω, μετέστησα: *to put away, remove*.

μειδάω, -ήσω, ἐμείδησα: *to smile*.

μείζων, -ον (compar. of μέγας) *greater*.

μειλικτήριος, -ον adj. *propitiatory*; espec. τὰ μειλικτήρια neut. plur. *atonements*.

μειράκιον, -ου n. *youth, stripling; lad*.

μέλει impers. *there is concern to* τινί about τινός.

μέλειν pres. act. infin. of μέλει.

μέλλω, μελλήσω, ἐμέλλησα: *to be on the point* of doing something; hence, *to intend, design, purpose* (+ infin.) *to do something; slacken, hesitate*.

μέν particle indic. contr., emphasis or continuation; μέν... δέ *on the one hand... on the other hand*.

μέντοι *but, however, nevertheless*.

μένω, μενῶ, ἔμεινα: *to stay, remain*.

μέρος, -ους n. *part, piece; detachment*.

μέσος, -η, -ον adj. *middle, in the middle* of something.

μετά prep. with: (1) gen. *with, in company with, among; by, in; on the side of; against*; (2) acc. *after, behind* (μετά τό + inf. *after*); μετ᾽ ἡμέραν *after daybreak*.

μεταβαλέσθαι aor. mid. infin. of μεταβάλλω.

μεταβάλλω, -βαλῶ, -έβαλον, μεταβέβληκα, -βέβλημαι: *to turn quickly, change, alter*; mid. *to change one's mind or purpose*.

μεταβολή, -ῆς f. *change*, espec. *change in fortune*.

μεταγενέστερος, -η, -ον compar. of μεταγενής, -ές.

μεταγενής, -ές adj. *born after, younger*.

μετακινέω, -ήσω: *to change, alter*; in pass. *be removed*.

μεταλαμβάνω, -λήψομαι: *to partake or share in* τινός.

μεταμέλεια, -ας f. *repentance, regret; change of purpose*.

μετανάστης, -ου m. *a wanderer, migrant*.

μετανοέω, -ήσω: *to repent, be sorry*.

μεταφέρω, μετοίσω, μετήνεγκα: *to carry from one place to another, transfer*.

μετέχω, μεθέξω: *to partake in, share in* τινός.

μετοικία, -ας f. *change of abode; migration*.

μέτριος, -α, -ον adj. *moderate; within means*.

μετρίως adv. *moderately*; οὐ σφόδρα μετρίως *in no measured terms*.

μέτωπον, -ου n. lit. *space between the eyes; I, front*.

μέχρι (1) prep. with gen. *until* (μέχρι τέλους *until the end*); *to the extent, point, as far as*; (2) conj. with finite vb. *until* (μέχρι οὗ *until*).

μή *not* (gen. used with non-indic. verbs); used in quests. when a neg. answer is expected; used with οὐ for emphasis or solemn assertion.

μηδέ neg. particle *nor, and not* (μηδέ... μηδέ *neither... nor*); *not even*.

μηδείς, μηδεμία, μηδέν (1) *no one, nothing*; (2) adj. *no*.

μηδέπω adv. *not as yet*.

Μῆδος, -ου m. *Mede*.

μηκέτι adv. *no longer*.

μήκιστος, -η, -ον superl. adj. of μακρός, -ά, -όν.

μῆκος, -εος n. *length; from end-to-end*.

μακρός, -ά, -όν adj. *long*.

μήν particle strength. affirmation: *yea, indeed, verily*.

μήν, μηνός m. *month*; ἐν παντὶ μηνὶ καὶ μηνὶ (1 Macc 1:58) *month after every month*.

μηνύω, μηνύσω, ἐμήνυσα: *to disclose, make known; inform, betray*.

μήποτε (1) conj. *lest, that... not, otherwise*; (2) interrog. particle *whether perhaps, perhaps*.

μήτηρ, μητρός f. *mother*.

μητρόπολις, -εως f. *mother city, metropolis*.

μηχανάομαι, -ήσομαι: *to construct, devise*.

μηχανή, -ῆς f. *machine, engine of war*.

μιαίνω, μιανῶ, ἐμίανα, μεμίαγκα, μεμίασμαι, ἐμιάνθην: *to stain, defile, soil; to taint, pollute*.

μιανθῶσι(ν) aor. pass. of μιαίνω.

μιαρός, -ά, -όν adj. *polluted, abominable, foul*.

μιασμός, -οῦ m. *corruption, defilement*.

μίγνυμι, μίξω, ἔμιξα: *to mingle, mix*.

μικρός, -ά, -όν adj. *small, little; petty, mean*; κατὰ μικρόν *little by little.*

μιμνήσκομαι (mid. and pass. form of μιμνήσκω), μνήσομαι (also μνησθήσομαι), ἐμνησάμην, μέμνημαι, ἐμνήσθην: act. forms *to remind, put in mind*; mid./pass. forms *to remind oneself, remember.*

Μισαηλ m. *Mishael.*

μῖσος, -εος n. *hatred, hate.*

μνάομαι older form of μιμνήσκομαι.

μνημεῖον, -ου n. *memorial, remembrance, monument.*

μνήμη, -ης f. *memory, faculty of memory.*

μνημόσυνον, -ου n. *remembrance, memorial; fame.*

μνηστεύω, -σω, ἐμνήστευσα: *to promise in marriage, betroth.*

μοῖρα, -ας f. *part* or *portion that falls to someone; lot; division* (of an army).

μοιχεία, -ας f. *adultery.*

μόλιβος, -ου m. *lead.*

μόλις adv. *scarcely, with difficulty.*

μολύνω, μολυνῶ, ἐμόλυνα, pf. pass. μεμόλυσμαι: *to stain, sully, defile, corrupt.*

μονόλιθος, -ον adj. *consisting of one stone.*

μόνος, -η, -ον adj. *only, alone*; μόνον *only*; αὐτὸ μόνον *mere*; μόνον οὐ *well nigh, all but.*

μυελός, -οῦ m. *marrow.*

μῦθος, -ου m. *story; tale.*

μυριάς, -άδος f. *the number 10,000; a myriad.*

μυρίος, -α, -ον adj. *countless, innumerable.*

μύσος, -εος n. *anything that causes disgust; abomination, defilement.*

Μωδεῖν f. *Modein.*

N

Ναβατάταιος, -ου m. *Nabataeus.*

Ναζίραιος, -ου m. *Nazirite.*

ναός, -οῦ m. *temple*, espec. the *inner part of the Jewish Temple, sanctuary.*

ναστός, -ή, -όν adj. *close-pressed, firm, compact.*

νεανίσκος, -ου m. *young man.*

Νεῖλος, -ου m. *Nile.*

νεκρός, -οῦ m. *dead body, corpse.*

νέμω, νεμῶ, ἔνειμα: *to deal out, distribute*; in mid. *dwell in, inhabit, occupy; possess, enjoy.*

νέος, -ον adj. *new, recent, fresh, young; untoward, unusual.*

νεότης, -ητος f. *youth.*

Νέρων, -ωνος m. *Nero.*

νεύω, νεύσω, ἔνευσα: *to nod* or *beckon to* τινί.

νεφρός, -οῦ m. (lit. *kidney*); *mind, thought; heart.*

Νεχαώς m. *Nechaos.*

νεωκορέω, -ήσω: *to have charge of a temple; to keep clean and pure.*

νεωκόρος, -ου m. properly, *one who sweeps a temple; guardian of a shrine.*

νεώς, -ω m. Attic for ναός *temple.*

νεωστί adv. *recently.*

νήπιος, -α, -ον (also νήπιος, -ον) adj. *not speaking*; νήπια, -ων neut. plur. *babies, infants.*

νηστεύω, -εύσω, ἐνήστευσα: *to fast.*

Νικάνωρ, -ορος m. *Nicanor.*

νικάω, -ήσω: *to conquer, prevail.*

νίκη, νίκης f. *victory.*

νοέω, νοήσω: *to think; to reflect.*

νόμιμα, -ίμων neut. plur. *usages, customs; laws.*

νομίζω, νομιῶ, ἐνόμισα: *to think, regard, believe.*

νομοθέτης, -ου m. *lawgiver.*

νόμος, -ου m. *law* (oft of the Jewish sacred tradition).

νόος, -ου m. *mind.*

νόσος, -ου f. *sickness, illness.*

νότος, -ου m. *south wind; south.*

νύκτωρ adv. *during the night.*

νυμφίος, -ου m. *bridegroom.*

νῦν adv. *now.*

νύξ, νυκτός f. *night*; νυκτός gen. of time within which *during the night.*

Ξ

Ξανθικός, -οῦ m. *Xanthicus.*

ξενολογέω, -ήσω: *to enlist foreign troops.*

ξένος, -η, -ον adj. *strange, foreign, unusual.*

ξηραίνω, -ανῶ, ἐξήρανα: *to become* or *be dry.*

ξιφήρης, -ες adj. *sword-in-hand.*

ξίφος, -εος n. *sword.*

ξόανον, -ου n. *image carved of wood; statue of a god.*

ξύλον, -ον n. *cudgel.*

Ο

ὁ, ἡ, τό plur. οἱ, αἱ, τά def. article *the; this, that; he, she, it;* τοῦ + inf. *in order that, so that, with the res. that, that.*

ὄγδοος, -η, -ον adj. *eighth.*

ὅδε, ἥδε, τόδε demonstr. adj. *this; he, she, it.*

ὁδηγέω, -ήσω: *to guide* or *direct.*

ὁδηγός, -οῦ m. *guide.*

ὁδός, οῦ f. *way, road; journey.*

ὀδύνη, -ης f. *pain; grief, distress.*

ὅθεν *whence; where from; for which reason.*

οἶδα (pf. of *εἴδω with pres. mng.; ἴστε may be 2 plur. indic. or impv.; indic. 3 plur. οἴδασι and ἴσασι; subj. εἰδῶ; infin. εἰδέναι; masc. ptc. εἰδώς; fem ptc.

εἰδυῖα; plupf. ᾔδειν; fut. εἰδήσω): *to know, understand; know how to* + infin.

οἰκεῖος, -α, -ον adj. *belonging to a house, domestic; personal*; espec. substant. οἰκεῖος, -ου m. *friend, intimate friend, relation.*

οἰκέω, οἰκήσω, ᾤκησα: *to inhabit; possess, occupy.*

οἴκημα, -ατος n. *apartment, chamber.*

οἰκία, -ας f. *house, dwelling.*

οἰκιστής, -οῦ m. *settler, colonist.*

οἰκοδομέω, οἰκοδομήσω, ᾠκοδόμησα: *to build, erect; to fortify.*

οἴκοθεν adv. *from one's own house, from home.*

οἶκος, -ου m. *house, home; family, household; nation, people; temple, sanctuary.*

οἰκουμένη, -ης f. *civilized world.*

οἰκτείρω, -τερῶ: *to pity, have compassion.*

οἰκτιρμός, -οῦ m. *compassion, mercy, pity.*

οἶκτος, -ου m. *pity, compassion.*

οἰκτρός, -ά, -όν adj. *piteous, mournful.*

οἴμμοι/οἴμοι interjection *woe's me! ah me!, alas!*

οἶνος, -ου m. *wine.*

οἴομαι (impf. ᾤμην), οἰήσομαι, ᾠήθην: *to think, suppose, believe.*

οἷόν τε + infin.: *to be possible.*

οἷος, -α, -ον rel. pron. *such as, as, of what kind.*

ὀκτακισχίλιοι, -αι, -α *eight thousand.*

ὀκτακόσιοι, -αι, -α *eight hundred.*

ὀκτώ indecl. *eight.*

ὀκτωκαίδεκα *eighteen.*

ὀλεθρεύω, -θρεύσω: *to slay, destroy.*

ὄλεθρος, -ου m. *destruction.*

ὀλίγος, -η, -ον adj. *few*; ὀλίγῳ *seldom*; ὀλίγον *a little.*

ὀλιγοστός, -ή, -όν (superl. of ὀλίγος, -η, -ον *few*) *fewest*; technical *with a small force.*

ὀλιγότης, -τητος f. *fewness, paucity.*

ὁλοκαύτωμα, -ατος n. *whole burnt offering.*

ὁλοκαύτωσις, -εως f. *whole burnt offering.*

ὁλόκληρος, -ον adj. *complete in all its parts; whole; uncut.*

ὅλος, -η, -ον adj. *whole, entire, complete*; neut. plur. τὰ ὅλα *one's all.*

ὀλοφύρομαι, ὀλοφυροῦμαι, ὠλοφυράμην (depon.): *to lament, wail, moan, weep.*

ὀλωλέναι pf. act. infin. of ὄλλυμι.

ὅμηρα, -ων neut. plur. Cf. ὅμηρος, -ου m. *pledge, security; hostage.*

ὁμιλέω, -ήσω: *to hold conversation with* τινί; *associate with* τινί.

ὄμμα, -ατος n. *eye.*

ὅμοιος, -α, -ον adj. *like, resembling.*

ὁμοιόω, -ώσω, ὡμοίωσα: *to make like, liken, compare*; in pass. *to be made like, be compared.*

ὁμοίωμα, -ματος n. *image, likeness.*

ὁμοῦ adv. *at the same time, together with.*

ὁμοφύλος, -ον adj. *of the same race.*

ὅμως adv. *nevertheless.*

ὀνειδίζω, -ίσω, ὠνείδισα: *to reproach.*

ὀνειδισμός, -οῦ m. *a reproach.*

ὄνειδος, -ου m. *reproach, blame, disgrace.*

ὀνίνημι, ὀνήσω, ὤνησα: *to profit, benefit, help.*

ὄνομα, -ματος n. *name.*

ὀνομάζω, -άσω, ὠνόμασα, ὠνόμακα, ὠνόμασμαι, ὠνομάσθην: *to name, address by name.*

ὀξυβελής, ές adj. *sharp-pointed*; substant. *"quick-firer,"* a type of catapult.

ὀξύς, -εῖα, -ύ adj. *sharp, keen, pointed.*

ὀπίσω (1) prep. with gen. *after; behind; away from*; (2) adv. *back, behind* (τὰ ὀπίσω *what lies behind*).

ὁπλίζω, -ίσω, ὥπλισα of soldiers: *to train, exercise; to arm* as ὁπλίται.

ὁπλίτης, -ου m. *heavily armed soldier, hoplite.*

ὅπλον, -ου n. *weapon; tool, instrument.*

ὅποι rel. adv. of place *whither, to where.*

ὁπότε adv. *when.*

ὅπου rel. adv. *wherever, where; since.*

ὀπτάω, -ήσω: *to roast or broil meat; to boil.*

ὅπως (or ὅπως ἄν) *that, in order that*; οὐκ ὅπως *to say nothing, let alone.*

ὁράω, (impf. ἑώρων), ὄψομαι, εἶδον (infin. ἰδεῖν), ἑόρακα/ἑώρακα, ἑώραμαι/ὦμμαι, ὤφθην: *to see.*

ὄργανον, -ου n. *instrument, tool, engine; organ.*

ὀργή, -ῆς f. *wrath, anger, rage; retribution, punishment; revenge.*

ὀργίζω, -ίσω, ὤργισα: *to make angry, provoke to anger*; in pass. *to grow angry, be wroth.*

ὀρθρίζω, -σω, ὤρθρισα: *to rise or wake early.*

ὁρίζω, ὁρίσω, ὥρισα: *to lay down, mark out; define.*

ὅριον, -ου n. *boundary, goal*; τὰ ὅρια *the borders.*

ὅρκος, -ου m. *oath, vow.*

ὁρμάω, -ήσω: *to set in motion*; intrans. *to hurry, rush headlong*; pass. *long, be eager to.*

ὁρμή, -ῆς f. *eagerness, passion; attack, assault; impulse.*

ὅρμημα, -ματος n. *a passionate desire; charge.*

ὄρος, -ους n. *mountain; hill; mount*; τὸ ὄρος τοῦ οἴκου *temple mount*.

ὀρρωδέω, -ήσω: *to shudder at* τινί.

ὀρυκτός, -ή, -όν adj. *dug out; formed by digging*.

ὅς, ἥ, ὅ rel. pro. *who, which, what that* (ὅς ἄν or ὅς ἐάν *whoever*; ὅς μέν... ὅς δέ *the one... the other*); *he, she*.

ὀσμή, -ῆς f. *smell, stench*.

ὁσημέραι (for ὅσαι ἡμέραι) adv. *daily, day by day*.

ὅσος, -η, -ον correlative pron. *as much as, how much; as great as, how great; as far as, how far*; ὅσος ἄν or ὅσος ἐάν *whoever*; ἐφ' ὅσον *inasmuch as, while;* καθ' ὅσον *just as, as*.

ὅσπερ, ἥπερ, ὅπερ *who, which*.

ὄσπριον, -ου n. *pulse, bean; vegetable*.

ὅστις, ἥτις, ὅ τι indef. rel. pron. *who, which; whoever, whichever; anyone, someone*.

ὅταν (ὅτε + ἄν) *whenever*.

ὅτε conj. *when, at which time*.

οὐδέτερος, -α, -ον adj. *neither one of two*.

οὖν *therefore, then; thus, so, accordingly*.

οὐδέ *neither, nor, and not*; οὐδέ... οὐδέ... *neither... nor; not even*.

οὐδείς, οὐδεμία, οὐδέν *no one, nothing; no; worth nothing*; οὐδέν *not at all, in no respect*.

οὐδέποτε adv. *never, and not ever*.

Vocabulary

οὔκουν adv. *not therefore, so not*.

οὔτε *not, no, nor*; espec. οὔτε... οὔτε *neither... nor*.

οὗτος, αὕτη, τοῦτο demonstr. pro. and adj. *this, this one; he, she, it*; τοῦτ' ἔστιν *that is, which means*.

ὅτι conj. *that* (oft denotes the beg. of dir. disc.); *because, for, since*.

οὐ (οὐκ, οὐχ) *not*; gen. used with indic. vbs. and in quests. where an affirmative answer is expected.

Οὐεσπασιανός, -οῦ m. *Vespasian*.

οὐκ εἰς μακράν see μακρός.

οὐ μήν adv. *indeed not*.

οὐρανός, -οῦ m. *the sky; heaven* (also used of God to avoid mention of the sacred name).

οὕτω and οὕτως (1) adv. *in this way, thus, so, in the same way*; (2) indecl. adj. *such, of such kind*.

οὐχί (emphatic form of οὐ) *not; no, no indeed*; used in quests. when an affirmative answer is expected.

ὀφθαλμός, -οῦ m. *eye*.

ὄχλος, -ου m. *crowd, multitude*; (common) *people, mob; military force*.

ὀχυρός, -ά, -όν (cf. ἔχω) adj. *firm, lasting, stout, strong; fortified* (of a city or wall).

ὀχυρότης, -τητος f. *firmness, steadfastness*.

ὀχυρόω, -ώσω: *to make fast, fortify;* in pass. *to be fortified*.

337

ὀχύρωμα, -ατος n. *stronghold, fortress.*
ὀφθῆναι aor. infin. pass. of ὀράω.
ὄφις, -εως m. *serpent, snake.*

Π

παγίς, παγίδος f. *snare, trap.*
πάθος, -εος n. *anything that befalls someone; suffering, misfortune, calamity.*
παιανίζω, ίσω: *chant the victory song; sing a song of triumph.*
παίγνιον, -ου n. *a plaything, toy.*
παιδάριον, -ου n. *boy.*
παιδεία, -ας f. *education, training.*
παιδεύω, -σω, ἐπαίδευσα, πεπαίδευκα, πεπαίδευμαι, ἐπαιδεύθην: *to train; teach, educate, instruct.*
παιδίον, -ου n. *young child; young slave.*
παῖς, παιδός m. and f. *servant, slave; child, boy, girl.*
παίω, παίσω, ἔπαισα: *to strike or smite* a pers..
πάλαι adv. *long ago, in olden time;* also, of time *just past.*
Παλαιστίνη, -ης f. *Philistia.*
πάλιν adv. *again.*
πανοικεσίᾳ dat. used adv. *with all the household.*
πανοπλία, -ας f. *full suit of armor.*
πανουργέω, -ήσω: *to play the knave, act like a rouge.*
πανταχόθεν adv. *on all sides.*
πανταχοῦ adv. *everywhere.*

ὀχυρόω, -ώσω: *to make fast, fortify.*
ὄψις, -εως f. *sight, appearance.*
ὀψώνιον, -ου n. *provisions, supply; pay.*

πάντη adv. *in every way, by all means.*
πάντοθεν adv. *from all sides.*
παντοῖος, -α, -ον adj. *of every sort or kind; manifold.*
πάντως adv. *wholly, altogether, completely.*
πάνυ adv. *altogether.*
παράγω, -ξω, -ήγαγον: *to bring beside or in front; bring forward.*
παραδίδωμι, -δώσω, -έδωκα: *to hand over.*
παρέθηκα 1 aor. of παρατίθημι.
παρά prep. with (1) gen. *from beside; from along side of* τινός; (2) dat. *by the side of, beside;* παρά τινι *at someone's house;* παρ' ἡμῖν *in our opinion;* παρ' ὅσον *how great* (3) accus. *along, beside; to, toward; going by, leaving on one side.*
παραβαίνω, -βήσομαι: *to transgress, overstep.*
παράβολος, -ον adj. *reckless, venturesome.*
παραγγέλλω, -αγγελῶ: *to proclaim to specify, designate.*
παραγίγνομαι, -γενήσομαι, -εγενόμην: *to be at hand, be by or near; to come to, arrive at; arise.*
παράδειγμα, -ματος n. *example.*

παράδεισος, -ου m. *park, pleasure ground*; cf. "paradise."

παραδίδωμι, -δώσω, -έδωκα: *to hand over; commit, consign; grant, allow.*

παράδοξος, -ον adj. *unexpected, strange; contr. to opinion.*

παραινέω, -έσω/-έσομαι, παρήνεσα, παρήνεκα: *to advise, counsel; beg.*

παραίτησις, -εως f. *earnest supplication, request.*

παρακάθημαι: *to sit beside* τινί.

παρακαλέω, -καλέσω: *to exhort, encourage.*

παρακέλευσις, -εως f. *exhortation, encouragement.*

παρακινδυνεύω: *to be at risk.*

παρακλίνω, -κλινῶ: *to turn* or *bend aside.*

παραλαμβάνω, -λήψομαι, -έλαβον: *to take possession of, receive; take along with oneself.*

παραλείπω, -ψω: *to leave on one side*, i.e., *overlook, neglect.*

παραλλάξ adv. *alternately, in alternating steps.*

παραλύω, -λύσω: *to forego, detach.*

παραμένω, -μενῶ: *to stand beside; attend, abide, hold out.*

παραμύθιον, -ου n. *consolation, assuagement.*

παρανομέω, -ήσω: *to transgress the law.*

παρανομία, -ας f. *offense, wrongdoing.*

παράνομος, -ον adj. *contr. to the law, lawless; illegal; unjust.*

παραπλήσιος, -α, -ον adj. *close beside; akin to, resembling* τινί.

παρασκευάζω, -σω: *to prepare, get ready.*

παρασκευή, -ῆς f. *preparation, provision.*

παράστημα, -ατος n. *desperate courage; resignation.*

παραστορέννυμι, -στορέσω: *to stretch along side; lie flat.*

παραστρατοπεδεύω, -σω: *to encamp beside* or *opposite.*

παραστρώσας aor. act. ptc. of παραστορέννυμι.

παράταξις, -εως f. *battle array.*

παρατίθημι, -θήσω, παρέθηκα (2 aor. mid. παρεθέμην), pf. pass. παρατέθειμαι: *to place beside, set before; to provide, furnish*; in mid. *to set before oneself, have set before one.*

παρατυγχάνω, -τεύξομαι, -έτυχον: *to be present at* τινί.

παραχρῆμα adv. *forthwith, straight away; instantly.*

παραχωρέω, -ήσω: *to withdraw from* τινός.

παρέδωκα 1 aor. of παραδίδωμι.

παρείκω, -ξω: *to yield; permit, allow.*

πάρειμι, παρέσομαι: *to be present, appear*; παρόν + infin. *to be in one's power to do something.*

παρέκστασις, -εως f. *amazement.*

339

παρελθεῖν 2 aor. act. of παρέρχομαι.

παρεμβάλλω, -εμβαλῶ, παρενέβαλον: *to put in beside* or *between; to draw up troops in battle order; to encamp.*

παρεμβολή, -ῆς f. *a drawing up in battle order; the army so drawn up; any fortified place; castle, camp.*

παρέρχομαι, παρελεύσομαι, παρῆλθον: *to pass by; to enter.*

παρέσχηκε 3 sing. pf. act. indic. of παρέχω.

παρέχω, -έξω: *to offer, supply, provide.*

παρηβάω, -ήσω: *to be past one's prime; be old.*

παρῆν 3 sing. impf. act. indic. of πάρειμι.

παρθένος, -ου f. *unmarried girl, maiden; virgin.*

παρίημι, -ήσω: *to let fall, relax; having done with.*

παρό *wherefore.*

παροξύνω, -υνῶ, παρώξυνα: *to provoke, irritate.*

παρουσία, -ας f. *arrival.*

παρρησία, -ας f. *boldness, confidence.*

παρών pres. act. ptc. of πάρειμι.

πᾶς, πᾶσα, πᾶν; gen. παντός, πάσης, παντός: (1) without the article: *each, every* (plur. *all*); *every kind of; all, full*; (2) with the article: *entire, whole; all* (πᾶς ὁ *every man who*); (3) *everyone, everything* (διὰ παντός *always,* *continually, forever*; κατὰ πάντα *in everything, in every resp.*).

παστός, -οῦ m. = παστάς, -άδος f. *inner chamber; women's chamber; bridal chamber.*

παστοφόριον, -ου n. *priestly chamber.*

πάσχω, πείσομαι, ἔπαθον: *to suffer, experience.*

πατάσσω, -ξω, ἐπάταξα: intr. *to beat, knock, throb*; trans. *to strike, wound, beat, smite; thrash.*

πατέω, -ήσω: *to tread, walk, step; to trample upon.*

πατήρ, πατρός m. *father; forefather, ancestor.*

πάτριος, -α, -ον adj. *ancestral*; neut. plur. τὰ πάτρια *the customs, institutions* of one's ancestors.

πατρίς, -ίδος f. *father land, country.*

παύω, παύσω, ἔπαυσα: *to stop*; mid. *pause*; with infin. or ptc. *to cease* from doing something.

πέδη, -ης f. *fetter.*

πεδινός, -ή, -όν adj. *flat, level; related to a plain.*

πεδίον, -ου n. *plain.*

πείθω, πείσω, ἔπεισα: *to persuade,* oft with dat.; in mid. and pass. *to be persuaded, believe.*

πεῖρα, -ας f. *attempt.*

πειρασμός, -οῦ m. *temptation; period* or *process of testing.*

πειράω, -άσω: *to attempt, undertake, try; experience.*

πέμπτος, -η, -ον (cf. τέντε) *the fifth.*

πέμπω, -ψω, ἔπεμψα: *to send.*

πένης, -ητος m. *poor man*; as adj. *the poor.*

πενθέω, -ήσω, ἐπένθησα: *to bewail, lament, mourn.*

πένθος, -οῦς n. *sorrow, mourning.*

πεντάκις adv. *five times.*

πεντακισχίλιοι, -αι, -α *five thousand.*

πεντακόσιοι, -αι, -α *five hundred.*

πεντεκαιδέκατος, -η, -ον adj. *fifteenth.*

πεντήκοντα *fifty.*

πεντηκονταπήχεις *fifty cubits high.*

πεντηκόνταρχος, -ου m. *commander of fifty.*

Περαία, -ας f. *Peraea* (Transjordan).

περαιτέρω prep. + gen. *further, beyond.*

πέρας adv. *finally.*

περί prep. with (1) gen. *about, concerning, of, with reference to; for, on account of;* (2) accus. *around, about, near; of, with reference to, regarding.*

περιαθρέω: *to look about.*

περιβάλλω, περιβαλῶ, περιέβαλον, περιβέβληκα: *to throw round, about* or *over;* in mid. *to throw about oneself; to put on clothes.*

περίβολος, -ου m. *enclosure, circuit.*

περιεβαλόμην aor. mid. of περιβάλλω.

περίειμι (περί + εἰμί): *to be around; to outnumber; outlive, survive.*

περίειμι (περί + εἶμι): *to go round, make the rounds.*

περιέπω, -έψω: *to be busy about, tend diligently, take care of.*

περιερρώγασι pf. indic. act. of περιρρήγνυμι.

περιέσεσθαι fut. infin. of περίειμι.

περιζώννυμι, -ζώσω: *to gird round about;* in mid. *to gird oneself,* i.e., *dress.*

περιίστημι, -στήσω, -έστησα: *to place* or *set around;* in pass. and intrans. tenses of the act. *to stand around.*

περιιών pres. act. ptc. of περίειμι.

περικαλλής, -ές adj. *very beautiful.*

περικόπτω, -ψω: *to cut* or *clip around; mutilate.*

περιλείπω, -ψω: *to leave remaining;* pass. *to be left, survive.*

περιλειφθέντας pf. pass. ptc. of περιλείπω.

περίοδος, -ου f. *circumference.*

περιοράω, περιόψομαι, περιεῖδον: *to look around; overlook, disregard.*

περιπτύσσω, -ύξω: *to enfold, enwrap;* pass. *to be folded around.*

περιρρήγνυμι, -ρήξω: *to break off round.*

περισπάω, -άσω: *to strip off.*

περισσεύω, -εύσω, ἐπερίσσευσα: *to abound; to be over and above;* in bad sense *to be superfluous.*

περιστρατοπεδεύομαι, -πεδεύσομαι: *to encamp about, invest, besiege.*

περισχίζω, -ίσω: *to split off all around; split apart on all sides.*

περιττεύω see περισσεύω.

περιτείχισμα, -ατος n. *court.*

περιτέμνω, -τεμῶ, περιέτεμον: *to circumcise.*

περιτετμηκυίας pf. act. ptc., fem. accus. plur. of περιτέμνω.

περιφανῶς adv. *obviously, manifestly.*

περιφυλάττω, -άξω: *to guard all around.*

Πέρσης, -ου m. *Persian.*

Περσίς, -ίδος f. *Persis, Persia.*

πέτρα, -ας f. *rock, stone.*

Πετρώνιος, -ου m. *Petronius.*

πηγή, -ῆς f. *spring, well.*

πήγνυμι, πήξω, ἔπηξα: *to stick of fix in, plant;* in plupf. *to be transfixed.*

πηλίκος, -η, -ον interrog. adj. *how great?, how much?*

πῆχυς, -εως m. *cubit.*

πιθανός, -ή, -όν adj. *persuasive, winsome;* the substant. τὸ πιθανόν = *persuasion.*

πικραίνω, -ανῶ: *to embitter; anger.*

πικρῶς adv. *bitterly.*

Πιλᾶτος, -ου m. *Pilate.*

πιπράσκω, πραθήσομαι/πεπράσομαι, pf. pass. πέπραμαι, 1 aor. pass. ἐπράθην: *to sell;* metaphorically *to betray.*

πίπτω, πεσοῦμαι, ἔπεσον, πέπτωκα: *to fall* (oft in battle); *fall ill.*

πιστεύω, -εύσω, ἐπίστευσα: *to believe, be faithful; trust* τινί; in pass. *be trusted.*

πίστις, -εως f. *belief, trust;* ἐπὶ πίστιν *for terms.*

πιστός, -ή, -όν adj. *faithful, trustworthy, reliable.*

πίων, πῖον adj. *fat, plump, rich.*

πλάσσω, πλάσω, ἔπλασα: *to form, mould, fabricate.*

πλατεῖα, -ας f. *street, wide street.*

πλάτος, -εος n. *breadth, width.*

πλατύνω, -υνῶ: *to make broad, widen; to open wide.*

πλείους = πλέονες (nom. plur.).

πλεῖστος, -η, -ον (superl. of πολύς) *most;* πλεῖστον *to the highest degr., quite.*

πλείων/πλέων, πλεῖον/πλέον compar. adj. (from πολύς, πολλή, πολύ) *more.*

πλέον adv. *more;* τὸ πλέον *the majority.*

πλεοναστόν superl. adv. from πλέον, *most fully.*

Vocabulary

πλεονεκτέω, -ήσω: + gen. *to have a greater share of a thing.*

πλευρόν, -οῦ n. *rib*; in plur. *flank.*

πληγή, -ῆς f. *blow, beating; plague, misfortune; disaster.*

πλῆθος, -ους n. *crowd, quantity, number; people, population; congregation, assembly; magnitude, size, bulk.*

πληθύνω, πληθυνῶ, ἐπλήθυνα: *to make full; to increase, multiply.*

πλήθω: *to be* or *become full.*

πλημμέλεια, -ας f. *mistake in music, false note; mistake, error.*

πλημμελέω, -ήσω: *to play the wrong note; to err, offend.*

πλήν (1) conj. *but, yet, nevertheless, however* (πλὴν ὅτι *except that, only that*); (2) prep. with gen. *except, but, besides.*

πλήρης, -ες adj. *full of* τινός.

πληρόω, -ώσω: *to fill, make full; fulfill; finish.*

πλησίον (1) prep. with gen. *near*; (2) ὁ πλησίον *fellow man, neighbor.*

πλούσιος, -α, -ον adj. *rich, abundant.*

πλοῦτος, -ου m. *wealth, riches.*

πόθεν interrog. adv. *from where, whence.*

πόθος, -ου m. *desire; yearning* or *longing for.*

ποιέω, ποιήσω, ἐποίησα: *to make, do, effect*; periphrastic in mid. προσβολὴν ποιεῖσθαι for προσβάλλεσθαι, and ὀργὴν ποιεῖσθαι for ὀργίζεσθαι, etc.

ποιητής, -οῦ m. *one who carries something out; doer; poet.*

ποικίλλω, ποικιλῶ, ἐποίκιλα: *to embroider, diversify, vary.*

ποίκιλος, -η, -ον adj. *diverse, variegated.*

ποινή, -ῆς f. *ransom* paid for the shedding of blood; *price paid, redemption; requital*; also, *the price exacted, vengeance, penalty.*

ποῖος, -α, -ον interrog. adj. *what sort of? what? which?*

πολεμέω, -ήσω, ἐπολέμησα: *to fight, wage war* with τινί.

πολεμικός, -ή, -όν adj. *of* or *for war; martial.*

πολέμιος, -ου m. *enemy, belligerent.*

πολεμιστής, -οῦ m. *warrior; combatant.*

πόλεμος, -ου m. *war, battle; strife, conflict.*

πολιορκέω, -ήσω: *to besiege, blockade.*

πολιορκία, -ας f. *siege.*

πόλις, -εως f. *city.*

πολιτεύομαι, -τεύσομαι: *to be a citizen, take part in government.*

πολίτης, -ου m. *citizen.*

πολλάκις adv. *often, repeatedly, frequently.*

πολύς, πολλή, πολύ gen. πολλοῦ, -ῆς, -οῦ, adj. (1) *much, many* (of *great* crowds; *loud* mourning; *plentiful* harvest; *late*

343

hour, etc.); (2) πολλά neut. plur. *many things*; adv. *often, frequently, strictly, insistently, severely;* πολύ *much, greatly;* πολλῷ μᾶλλον *much more, all the more.*

πολυτελής, -ές adj. *expensive, costly.*

πομπεύω, -σω: *to lead a procession* (cf. Lat. *pompa, -ae* f.)*; to parade about, strut.*

Πομπήιος, -ου m. *Pompey.*

πονέω, -ήσω, ἐπόνησα: intrans. *to toil, suffer pain* or *hardship.*

πονηρός, -ά, -όν adj. *evil, bad, wicked, sinful;* τὸ πονηρόν *that which is evil.*

πόνος, -ου m. *labor, hard work, toil, drudgery.*

πορεύομαι, πορεύσομαι, pf. mid. πεπόρευμαι, 1 aor. pass. ἐπορεύθην (depon.): *to go, proceed; travel, journey, traverse.*

πορθέω, -ήσω: *to destroy, ravage, plunder.*

πόρρωθεν adv. *from afar.*

πορφύρα, -ας f. *purple; purple garment* or *covering.*

πόσος, -η, -ον interrog. adj. *how great?, how much?*

ποταμός, -οῦ m. *river.*

πότε interrog. adv. *when?*

ποτε *perchance.*

ποτνιάομαι, -ιάσομαι: *to shriek, wail.*

ποτός, -ή, -όν adj. *potable, drinkable.*

ποῦ interrog. adv. *where?*

πρᾶγμα, -ματος n. *matter, thing, affair; event, happening, deed; undertaking, task.*

πρᾶξις, -εως f. *deed.*

πράττω, -άξω, ἔπραξα: *to do, achieve, accomplish.*

πραχθέν aor. pass. ptc., accus. neut. sing. of πράττω.

πρέπει impers. *it is fitting, it befits* τινί.

πρεσβυτέρος, -α, -ον adj. *elder* (of the Jewish relig. leaders); *elder* (of two sons).

πρεσβύτης, -ου m. *old man.*

πρεσβῦτις, -ιδος f. *old woman.*

πρηνής, -ές adj. *bent forward, head-foremost.*

πρίν *before, formerly;* πρίν is oft followed by ἤ = *before;* πρίν + infin. *before.*

πρό prep. with gen. *before.*

προάγω, προάξω, προήγαγον: *to lead forward, lead onward.*

προάστειον, -ου n. *space in front of a town, suburb.*

προβάλλω, βαλῶ, -έβαλον: *place something in front of* τινός; pass. *to be shielded, screened.*

προβασανίζω, -ίσω: *to torture before.*

προγιγνώσκω, -γνώσομαι: *to know beforehand.*

πρόγονος, -ου m. *forefather, ancestor.*

προδείκνυμι, -δείξω: *to show before hand, reveal.*

πρόδηλος, -ον adj. *manifest, evident.*

προδηλόω, -ώσω: *to make clear beforehand.*

προδίδωμι, -δώσω: *to betray.*

προεγνωκότων pf. mid./pass. ptc. gen. masc. plur. of προγιγνώσκω.

προεκκαθαίρω: *to purify before.*

προέμενοι aor. mid. ptc., nom. masc. plur. of προΐημι.

προέρχομαι, -ελεύσομαι: *to go forward, advance.*

προήκατο 3 sing. aor. mid. indic. of προΐημι.

πρόθεσις, -εως f. *a placing before, setting forth*; espec. ἄρτοι τῆς προθέσεως the bread *of the setting forth; shew bread* (in Temple).

προθεσπίζω, -ίσω: *to foretell.*

προθυμέομαι, προθυμήσομαι; 1 aor. pass. προὐθυμήθην: *to be ready, willing* and *eager* to do a thing; abs. *to be earnest, zealous.*

προθύω, -θύσω: *to sacrifice first.*

προΐημι, προήσω: *to give up, deliver over.*

προκαλέω, -έσω: *to call forth; to invite.*

προκινδυνεύω, -σω: *to run a risk before others; brave the first danger.*

προκόπτω (impf. προὔκοπτον), -ψω: *to clear the way in front*; intrans. *to make one's way forward, make progress.*

προκρίνω, -κρινῶ: *to prefer.*

προλαμβάνω, -λήψομαι, προὔλαβον, -είληφα: *to take before hand; arrest; outstrip.*

προλέγω, -λέξω, -ειπον, -είηκα: *to state before; foretell, prophesy.*

προμαντεύομαι: *to foretell, prophesy; make a prediction.*

προνοέω, -ήσω: *to take thought for, care for.*

πρόοιδα, προείσομαι: *to know beforehand.*

προπάτωρ, -ορος m. *forefather.*

προπέμπω, -ψω: *to send fort; escort.*

προπηδάω, -δήσομαι: *to spring forward.*

πρόρριζος, -ον adj. *by the roots, roots and branch.*

πρός prep. with (1) accus. *to; toward; for the sake* or *purpose of, in order to; for, against*; (2) dat. *at, on, near; in addition to*; (3) gen. *for, for the sake of.*

προαγκαλίζομαι: *to take in one's arms.*

προσαγορεύω, -σω: *to name, call by name.*

προσάγω, -άξω, προσήγαγον: *to lead up; supply, furnish; induce.*

προσβάλλω, -βαλῶ, ἔβαλον: *to throw forth; attack, assail.*

προσβοηθέω, -ήσω: *to bring aid to, come to the aid of.*

προσβολή, -ῆς f. *a falling upon, attack, assault.*

προσγίγνομαι, -γενήσομαι: *to come up, come on.*

345

προσγινόμενον pres. mid./pass. ptc. of προσγίγνομαι.

προσδέχομαι, -δέξομαι: *to accept, receive favorably.*

προσδιατρίβω, -τρίψω: *to have intercourse with* τινί; *be occupied with.*

προσδοκάω, -ήσω: *to expect, look for, await.*

προσεικάζω, -σω: *to see a resemblance to* τι *in* τινί.

πρόσειμι (πρός + εἰμί): abs. *to be there, be offered.*

πρόσειμι (πρός + εἶμι): *to approach, come into; attack.*

πρόσεισι 3 sing. pres. act. indic. of πρόσειμι.

προσεθόμην 2 aor. mid. of προστίθημι.

προσέρχομαι, προσελεύσομαι, προσῆλθον: *to approach, go to; invade.*

προσετέθην aor. pass. of προστίθημι.

προσευχή, -ῆς f. *prayer.*

προσεύχομαι, -εύξομαι: *to pray.*

προσέχω, -έξω, προσέσχον: *to hold to; attend to.*

προσῆκον (ἐστιν): *it is meet, befitting, beseeming* + infin.

προσῆλθον 2 aor. of προσέρχομαι.

προσηλόω, -ώσω: *to nail to, affix to.*

προσιέμενοι pres. mid. ptc. of προσίημι.

προσιέναι pres. act. infin. of πρόσειμι.

προσίημι, προσήσω, προσῆκα: *to send to*; mid. *let come near to oneself; suffer to approach, admit.*

προσκαθέζομαι, -εδοῦμαι: *to sit down before a town* (in the dat.), i.e., *besiege it.*

προσκαλέω, -έσω: *to call to*; in mid. *to summon*; espec. *summon to court.*

πρόσκειμαι, -κείσομαι: *to be placed or laid beside; lie at hand*; in milit. sense *press hard, pursue closely.*

προσκρεμάννυμι: *to hang on* to something.

προσκυνέω, -ήσω, προσεκύνησα: *to prostrate oneself before, worship.*

προσπίπτω, -πεσοῦμαι: *to fall upon, strike against.*

πρόσταγμα, -ματος (cf. προστάσσω) n. *order, command.*

προστάσσω, -ξω, προσέταξα: *to order, command.*

προστίθημι, -θήσω, -έθηκα: *to put to, add*; in mid. *to take to oneself beside, acquire allies*; in pass. *be added to.*

προστυγχάνω, -τεύξομαι, -έτυχον: *to hit or light upon, fall in with, meet.*

προσυντάσσω: *to arrange beforehand; gather in advance.*

προσφέρω, -οίσω, προσήνεγκα: *to bring to, offer*; προσφέρειν λόγους: *to importune*; in mid. *to take meat or drink to oneself.*

προσφιλονεικέω, -ήσω: *to vie with another in something.*

προσψαύω, -σω: *to touch* τινός.

πρόσωπον, -ου m. *face, countenance; presence; appearance;* τὸ κατὰ πρόσωπον *front;* κατὰ πρόσωπον + gen. *in the direction of* τινός.

προτείνω, -τενῶ, -έτεινα: *to stretch out; proffer; put forward as a pretext or excuse.*

πρότερος, -α, -ον: (1) adj. *former, earlier, past*; (2) adv. πρότερον and τὸ πρότερον *before, previously, formerly; first, first of all; at first, the first time*; καὶ πρότερον *ere now*; πρότερον... ἤ = Lat. *priusquam, before.*

πρόφασις, -εως f. *pretext.*

προφεύγω, προφεύξομαι, προὔφυγον: *to flee forwards,* i.e., *flee for refuge to* τινί.

προφητεία, -ας f. *prophecy.*

προφήτης, -ου m. *prophet.*

Ρ

ῥᾴδιος, -α, -ον adj. *easy.*

ῥᾳδίως adv. *easily.*

ῥᾷον neut. of ῥᾴων.

ῥᾴων, -ον irreg. compar. of ῥᾴδιος.

ῥέω, ῥυήσομαι, ἐρρύην: *to flow.*

ῥίζα, -ης f. *root; descendant; source, cause* (of evil).

πρωί adv. *early morning, in the morning;* εἰς πρωί *in the morning;* τὸ πρωί *early.*

πρωτογένημα, -γενήματος n. *first fruits.*

πρῶτος, -η, -ον adj. *first; leading, foremost, prominent, most important;* τὸ πρῶτον adv. *at first.*

πταῖσμα, -ατος n. *blunder, mistake.*

πταίω, πταίσω, ἔπταισα intr. *to strike the foot, stumble; fail.*

πτόη, -ης f. *terror, fright.*

Πτολεμαῖος, -ου m. *Ptolemy.*

Πτολεμαΐς, -μαΐδος f. *Ptolemais.*

πτῶμα, -ατος n. *corpse.*

πυνθάνομαι, πεύσομαι, ἐπυθόμην: *to inquire; to learn* (by inquiry).

πῦρ, πυρός n. *fire.*

πύργος, -ου m. *tower, watch tower.*

πωλέω, -ήσω: *to sell.*

πῶς interrog. partic. *how?, in what way?*

ῥίπτω, ῥίψω, ἔρριψα: *to throw, throw away.*

ῥομφαία, -ας f. *sword; large sword, scimitar.*

ῥοπή, -ῆς f. *the turn of the scale, the critical moment.*

ῥύομαι, ῥύσομαι, ἐρρυσάμην (aor. pass. ἐρρύσθην): *to draw to* oneself, draw out of harm's way; hence *to rescue, save*.

Ῥωμαῖος, -ου m. *Roman*.

Ῥώμη, -ης f. *Rome*.

Σ

σάββατον, -ου n. (oft in plur.; Jewish sacred day of worship and rest) *the seventh day; Sabbath*.

Σαδδουκαῖος, -ου m. *Sadducee*.

σάκκος, -ου m. *sackcloth* (worn by those in mourning).

σαλεύω, -σω, ἐσάλευσα: *to shake*.

σαλπίζω, -ίξω, ἐσάλπισα: *to sound the trumpet*.

σάλπιγξ, -ιγγος f. *trumpet; trumpet blast*.

Σαλωμ m. *Salu*.

Σαμαρεία, -ας f. *Samaria*.

Σαουλ m. *Saul*.

σάρξ, σαρκός f. *flesh*.

Σάρρα, -ας f. *Sarah*.

σαφῶς adv. *clearly, plainly*.

σβέννυμι, σβέσω, ἔσβεσα: *to quench, put out*.

σεαυτοῦ, -ῆς reflex. pron. in the 2d pers. sing. *yourself*.

Σεδεκίας m. *Zedekiah*.

σείω, σείσω, ἔσεισα, σέσεισμαι; 1 aor. pass. ἐσείσθην: *to shake, brandish, move to and fro*.

σεσωρευμένων pf. pass. ptc. of σωρεύω.

σημαία, -ας = σημεία f. *military standard*.

ῥώμη, -ης f. *bodily strength, might*.

ῥώννυμι, ῥώσω, ἔρρωσα: *to strengthen, make strong*.

Σενναχηρείμ m. *Sennacherib*.

σημαία, -ας f. = σημεία, -ας f. *military standard*; Lat. *vexillum, -I* n.

σημαίνω, σημανῶ, ἐσήμανα: *to show by sign or token; signal*.

σημασία, -ας f. *the giving of a signal* or *command; indication, meaning*.

σημεῖον, -ου n. *sign, signal*.

σήμερον adv. *today*.

σήπω, σήψω, ἔσηψα: *to make rotten or putrid*; in pass. *to rot, molder, ulcerate*.

Σήρων, -ονος m. *Seron*.

σιγάω, σιγήσομαι: *to be silent, keep silent*.

σιδήρεος, -α, -ον adj. *made of iron*.

σίδηρος, -ου m. *iron*.

σικάριος, -ου m. *assassin*.

Σιλωάμ f. *Siloam*.

Σίμων, -ωνος m. *Simon*.

σιτία, -ων neut. plur. *food, victuals, provisions*.

σιτίον, -ου n. *morsel of food*.

σῖτος, -ου m. *corn, grain*.

Σιών f. *Zion*.

σιωπάω, -ήσομαι, ἐσιώπησα: *to keep silent*.

σιωπή, -ῆς f. *silence*.

σκεπάζω, -άσω: *to cover; protect, shelter*.

σκεῦος, -ους n. *object, thing* (in plur. oft *goods, property; vessel, container, dish; instruments; weaponry; armor*.

σκῆπτρον, -ου n. *staff, scepter*.

σκιά, -ᾶς f. *shadow, shade*.

σκληραγωγέω: *harden*.

σκληρύνω, σκληρυνῶ, ἐσκλήρυνα, pf. mid. ἐσκλήρυμμαι, aor. pass. ἐσκληρύνθην: *to harden*; in pass. *to become thick, hard; press upon*.

σκορπίζω, -ίσω: *to scatter, disperse*.

Σκυθόπολις, -εως f. *Scythopolis*.

σκυλεία, -ας f. *despoiling, plundering*.

σκυλεύω, -εύσω, ἐσκύλευσα: *to strip* or *spoil a slain enemy*.

σκῦλον, -ου n. usually in plur. σκῦλα *the arms* stripped off a slain enemy; *spoils*.

σκύμνος, -ου m. *young animal*; espec. *lion's cub*.

σκώληξ, -ηκος m. *worm*.

σκώπτω: *to hoot, mock, jeer*.

Σόλυμα n. *Solyma*.

Σόσσιος, -ου m. *Sossius*.

σοφίζομαι, -ίσομαι, σεσόφισμαι: *to devise, contrive*.

σοφός, -ή, -όν adj. *wise, learned, skilled; clever*.

σπάω, σπάσω, ἔσπασα: *to draw in, suck in, quaff*.

σπεύδω, σπεύσω, ἔσπευσα: intrans. *to press on, hasten*; + infin. *to be eager to do something*.

σπλάγχνον, -ου n. *inner part* of the body; *bowels, entrails*.

σποδός, -οῦ f. *ashes; embers*.

σπονδεῖος, -α, -ον adj. *of* or *belonging to a drink-offering* or *libation*; τὰ σπονδεῖα neut. plur. *cups* used in the drink offering.

σπονδή, -ῆς f. *drink-offering, libation*.

σπόρος, -ου m. *seed-time, sowing*.

σπουδή, -ῆς f. *eagerness; zeal, pains, earnestness*.

στάδιοι, -ων m. *stades, furlongs* (about 607 feet).

στάδιον, -ου n. *stadium*.

στασιαστής, -οῦ m. *rebel; one who stirs up a sedition*.

στάσις, -εως f. *sedition, rebellion*.

στασιώδης, -ες adj. *seditious*.

στασιώτης, -ου m. *one of a party* or *faction, partisan*.

σταυρός, -οῦ m. *cross; crucifixion*.

στενάζω, στενάξω, ἐστέναξα: *to sigh, groan; complain, grumble; rue*.

στενός, -ή, -όν adj. *narrow, strait*.

στενοχωρία, -ας f. *distress, difficulty*.

στενωπός, -όν adj. *made narrow, straitened*; subst. noun *alley-way*.

στερέω, στερήσω, ἐστέρησα: *to deprive* or *rob someone of* τινός.

στερρότης, -τητος f. *hardness, firmness.*

στεφάνος, -ου m. *crown, chaplet.*

στήλη, -ης f. *upright stone; boundary stone.*

στήριγμα, -ματος n. *support, prop, stay.*

στηρίζω, -ίσω, ἐστήριξα pf. pass. ἐστήριγμαι, aor. pass. ἐστηρίχθην: *to set fast, make firm*; metaph. *to confirm, establish.*

στῖφος, -εος n. *body of men in close array; compact body.*

στοά, -ᾶς f. *stoa; portico.*

στόλος, -ου m. *equipment* for warlike purposes; an *expedition* by land or sea; *journey, voyage.*

στόμα, στόματος n. *mouth; word(s), utterance*; κατὰ στόμα *in the face.*

στοχάζομαι, -άσομαι: *to take aim at* τινός.

στρατηγέω, -ήσω: *to accomplish something as a general.*

στρατηγός, -οῦ m. *general.*

στρατιά, -ᾶς f. *army.*

στρατιώτης, -ου m. *soldier.*

στρατολογέω, -ήσω: *to levy* or *enlist soldiers.*

στατόπεδον, -ου n. *the ground* on which soldiers are encamped; *encampment, camp.*

στενότης, -τητος f. *narrowness, straitness.*

στρατός, -οῦ m. *camp* (of an army), *host; army.*

στρεβλόω, -ώσω: *to tighten with a windlass*; pass. *to be racked, stretched out on a wheel.*

στρέφω, στρέψω, ἔστρεψα, ἔστροφα, ἔστραμμαι, ἐστρέφθην (2 aor. ἐστράφην): intrans. (mostly in pass.) *to turn, turn around*; trans. *to turn, offer.*

στρῶσις, -εως f. *spreading, covering*; λίθου στρῶσις *mosaic.*

στυγέω, -ήσω: *to hate, abhor.*

Στωικός, -ή, -όν adj. *Stoic.*

συγγένεια, -ας f. *kinship, family relationship.*

συγγενής, -ές adj. *congenital, natural, in-born*; οἱ συγγενεῖς *kinsfolk, kinsmen.*

συγκαθιδρύω, -δρύσω: *to erect with* τινί.

συγκαθίστημι, -στήσω: *to establish with someone; join in settling, managing.*

συγκαλέω, -έσω: *to call* or *summon together; call to council.*

συγκινδυνεύω, -εύσω: *to incur danger together with* τινί.

συγκλεισθῆναι aor. pass. infin. of συγκλείω.

συγκλείω, -κλείσω: *to shut up, hem in; to surround.*

συγκομιδή, -ῆς f. *a gathering together; ingathering* (of food or timber).

σύγκριμα, -ματος n. *decree.*

συγκρίσις, -εως f. *a putting together; comparison.*

συγχέω, -χεῶ, συνέχεα, -κέχυκα, aor. pass. -εχύθην: *to pour together, mix; to confound.*

συζώννυμι, -ζώσω: *to gird together, gird up*; in mid. *to gird oneself, gird one's loins.*

συλλέγω, -λέξω: *to gather, collect.*

συλλοχάω, -ήσω, συνελόχησα: *to collect* or *requisition soldiers.*

συμβαίνω, -βήσομαι, συνέβην, -βέβηκα: *to stand with the feet together*; of events *to happen, come to pass, befall.*

συμβάλλω, -βαλῶ, συνέβαλον: *to throw together; interpret*; also συμβάλλειν (μάχην) *engage in battle, join battle.*

συμβέβηκα pf. of συμβαίνω.

συμβουλεύω, -εύσω: *to advise, counsel.*

συμβουλή, -ῆς f. *advice, counsel.*

σύμβουλος, -ου m. *advisor, counselor.*

Συμεών m. *Simeon.*

συμμαχία, -ας f. *alliance.*

σύμμαχος, -ον adj. *allied; auxiliary*; as substant. noun in sing. *ally*; in plur. *auxiliaries.*

συμπαθής, -ές adj. *sympathetic.*

συμπαιδεύω, -εύσω: *to teach together*; in pass. *to be educated together with* τινί.

συμπάρειμι: *to be present along with.*

συμπλέκω, -ξω, συνέπλεξα: *to twist or twin together*; in pass. *to be plaited together; to be locked in combat.*

συμπολιορκέω, -ήσω: *to besiege together with others.*

συμφεύγω, -φεύξομαι: *to flee with someone else.*

συμφορά, -ᾶς f. *event, circumstance; misfortune, calamity; fate.*

σύν prep. with dat. *with, in company with, along with, together with.*

συνάγω, -άξω, 1 aor. σύνηξα, 2 aor. συνήγαγον: *to gather together, bring together, assemble.*

συναγωγή, -ῆς f. *assembly, company.*

συναθροίζω, -σω: *to gather together, assemble.*

συναίρω, -αρῶ: *to raise, lift, take up together*; mid. *to take part in* τινός.

συναναπίμπλημι: *to infect with* τινός.

συναντάω, -ήσω: *to meet.*

συνάντησις, -εως f. *meeting, encounter.*

συνάπτω, -άψω, συνῆψα: *to tie/join together; to engage* or *encounter*; συνάπτειν μάχην *to engage in battle.*

συναριθμέω: *to count with* τινί.

συνδεδεμένη pf. pass. ptc., nom. fem. sin. of συνδέω.

συνδέω, -δήσω: *to bind together with* τινί.

συνδιατίθημι: *to help in arranging; compose, put together; bring over to one's way of thinking.*

συνέδριον, -ου n. *Sanhedrin* (high Jewish council in relig. and civic matters).

συνεζωσάμην aor. mid. of συζώννυμι.

*συνείδω, 2 aor. συνεῖδον, pf. σύνοιδα in pres. sense: *to perceive.*

σύνειμι *to go/come together, assemble.*

συνεκθηλύνω, -λυνῶ: *to help to make womanish; to*

συνεκτρέφω, -θρέψω: *to rear up along with*; pass.: *to grow up with.*

συνελαύνω, -ελάσω, -ήλασα: *to drive together.*

συνεξέρχομαι, -ελεύσομαι: *to go forth from something together with* τινί.

συνεργέω: *to work together with, cooperate with; assist.*

συνερύω, -σω, συνέρρευσα: *to draw together.*

σύνεσις, -εως f. *understanding; power of comprehension, insight, intelligence.*

συνεστάλην 2 aor. pass. of συστέλλω.

συνέστην 2 aor. of συνίστημι.

συνευδοκέω, -ήσω: *to approve of* τινί; *to be well pleased with; consent to* τινί.

συνεχής, -ές adj. *continuous, unceasing.*

συνεχύθην 1 aor. pass. of συγχέω.

συνήθης, -ες adj. *customary, usual.*

συνῆκται pf. pass. of συνάγω.

συνήχθην 1 sing. aor. pass. indic. of συνάγω.

συνθέω, -θεύσομαι: *to run along with, run together.*

σύνθημα, -ματος n. *an agreed-upon signal; anything agreed upon.*

συνθλίβω, -ψω: *to press together, compress.*

συνιδεῖν 2 aor. infin. of *συνείδω.

συνιέναι pre. act. infin. of συνίημι.

συνίημι, συνήσω, συνῆκα, συνεῖκα: *to send, bring, or set together.*

συνίστημι, -στήσω, -έστησα: *to put together, arrange; organize, compose*; pass. with 2 aor. act. συνέστην and pf. συνέστηκα: *to stand*; in middle: *to organize; be engaged in, involved in, implicated in* a thing.

συννοέω, -ήσω: *to think upon, reflect.*

σύνταγμα, -ματος n. *that which is put together in order; the troops thus arranged;* ἐκ συντάγματος adv. *by arrangement.*

σύνταξις, -εως f. *order, arrangement* (espec. of troops in battle).

συνταράσσω, -ταράξω: *to throw into confusion; to confound.*

συντέλεια, -ας f. *completion, end, consummation.*

συντελέω, -έσω: *to bring to conclusion, to complete.*
συντρέχω, -δραμοῦμαι, -έδραμον: *to run* or *rush together; gather together.*
συντριβή, -ῆς f. *destruction.*
συντρίβω, -ψω, συνέτριψα: *to crush.*
σύντριμμα, -ματος n. *destruction, fracture; stumbling block, offence.*
Συρία, -ας f. *Syria.*
Σύρος, -ου m. *Syrian.*
σύρω, συρῶ, ἐσυρά, σέσυρκα, σέσυρμαι, 2 aor. ἐσύρην: *to draw, drag; sweep away.*
συστέλλω, -στελῶ, -έστειλα, -έσταλκα, -έσταλμαι: *to draw together, draw in;* pass. *to be contracted, get smaller; shrink.*
συστρατιῶτις, -ιδος f. *ally.*
συστρέφω, -ψω: *to gather together, collect.*
συχνός, -ή, -όν adj. *many, much, frequent, great.*
σφαγεύς, -έως m. *killer, butcher.*
σφαγή, -ῆς f. *slaughter, sacrifice; throat.*

σφάζω, σφάξω, ἔσφαξα: *to slay, slaughter, sacrifice.*
σφόδρα, adv. *very much, exceedingly, very, greatly.*
σφεῖς, σφῶν, σφισι(ν), σφᾶς reflex. pron. 3 plur. *themselves*; κατὰ σφᾶς *by themselves.*
σχεδόν adv. *almost, nearly.*
σχετλιάζω, -άσω: *to complain, inveigh bitterly.*
σχῆμα, -ατος n. *form, shape, appearance.*
σῴζω, σώσω, ἔσωσα, σέσωκα, σέσωσμαι, ἐσώθην: *to save, preserve.*
σωθῆναι aor. pass. infin. of σῴζω.
σωθήσεσθαι fut. pass. infin. of σῴζω.
σῶμα, σώματος n. *body.*
σωρεύω, -σω: *to heap up.*
σωτήρ, σωτῆρος m. *savior, deliverer.*
σωτηρία, -ας f. *salvation, safety; preservation.*
σωτήριος, -ον adj. *saving, delivering.*
σωφρονέω, -ήσω: *to be of sound mind, practice self-control, be wise.*

T

τάγμα, -ματος n. *order, directive; division; legion.*
ταλαιπωρέω, -ήσω: *to endure hardship, do hard work.*
τἀληθές = τὸ ἀληθές *the truth.*

τἀληθέστατον = τὸ ἀληθέστατον *the truest.*
τἄνδον = τὰ ἔδον *the things within.*
τάξις, -εως f. *an arrangement, rank; drawing up in order* (of soldiers).

ταπείνωσις, -εως f. *humbleness, humiliation.*

ταράσσω, ταράξω, ἐτάραξα: *to stir up, disturb, disquiet.*

ταραχή, -ῆς f. *disquiet, unrest.*

τἆργα = τὰ ἔργα.

ταύτῃ adv. *this way; here.*

τάφος, -ου m. *grave, tomb.*

τάχα adv. *perhaps, probably.*

ταχέως adv. *quickly.*

τάχιον adv. (compar. of ταχέως) *quickly, at once, soon; sooner, more quickly.*

ταχύ adv. *quickly.*

ταχύνω, -υνῶ, ἐτάχυνα: *to make quick, hasten; urge on.*

τέ enclitic particle *and;* τέ... τέ or τέ... δέ *both... and; not only... but also.*

τεθαρρηκότες pf. act. ptc. of θαρσέω.

τέθηλεν 3 sing. pf. act. indic. of θάλλω.

τεθνάναι pf. infin. act. of θνήσκω.

τεκμαίρομαι, τεκμαροῦμαι, ἐτεκμηράμην: *to perceive by signs or tokens; infer, conclude, judge.*

τεκμήριον, -ου n. *proof.*

τέκνον, -ου n. *child.*

τελειόω, -ώσω: *to complete, bring to accomplishment.*

τελευταῖον adv. *finally;* also in plur., τὰ τελευταῖα *finally.*

τελευταῖος, -α, -ον adj. *final, last.*

τελευτάω, -ήσω: *to come to an end, die.*

τελευτή, -ῆς f. *end; death.*

τελέω, τελέσω, ἐτέλεσα: *to complete, fulfill, accomplish.*

τέλος, -ους n. *end, termination; outcome, issue; fate.*

τέμενος, -εος/ους n. *sacred precinct, sanctuary; a piece of land sacred to a god.*

τέμνω, τεμῶ, ἔτεμον, τέτμηκα: *to cut, hew.*

τεμόντες aor. act. ptc., nom. masc. plur. of τέμνω.

τέρας, τέρατος n. *sign, portent, marvel, miracle.*

τέρμα, -ατος n. *end, boundary; base.*

τέρψις, -εως f. *enjoyment; gladness, delight.*

τεσσεράκοντα *forty.*

τεσσαρακοστός, -ή, -όν (cf. τεσσεράκοντα) adj. *fortieth.*

τεσσαρεσκαιδέκατος, -η, -ον adj. *fourteenth.*

τεῖχος, -ους n. *wall.*

τέκνον, -ου n. *child.*

τετηρηκέναι pf. act. ptc. of τηρέω.

τετρακόσιοι, -αι, -α *four hundred.*

τέτταρες, τέτταρα *four.*

Τεφθέος, -ου m. *Tephtheos.* Some mss. read Γεφθέος.

τήκω, τήξω, ἔτηξα: *to melt.*

τηλικοῦτος, -αύτη, -οῦτον interrog. adj. *so very much, so great.*

τηνικαῦτα adv. *at this particular time.*

τηρέω, -ήσω, ἐτήρησα: *to take care of, keep, guard, preserve.*

Τιβεριάς, -άδος f. *Tiberias.*

Τιβέριος, -ου m. *Tiberius.*

τίθημι, θήσω, ἔθηκα, τέθεικα, τέθειμαι, ἐτέθην: *to put, place, set; to fix, settle, determine;* in mid. *to establish for oneself; set in motion, drive.*

τιμή, -ῆς f. *honor, respect, recognition; price, value.*

τιμωρία, -ας f. *vengeance, retribution; punishment.*

τίνω, τίσω, ἔτισα, τέτικα, τέτισμαι, ἐτείσθην: *to pay, expiate;* in mid. *to take payment, avenge.*

τίς, τί gen. τίνος dat. τίνι accus. τίνα, τί interrog. pro. and adj. *who?, which? what? what sort of?* τί, διὰ τί, εἰς τί, τί ὅτι *why? for what reason* or *purpose?* τί γάρ, τί οὖν *why then?*

τὶς, τὶ gen. τινός dat. τινί accus. τινά, τὶ enclitic pro. and adj. *anyone, anything; someone, something; any, some, a certain, several.*

Τίτος, -ου m. *Titus.*

τὸ γε μήν conj. *and as to the fact that…*

τοιγαροῦν adv. *therefore, indeed.*

τοίνυν adv. *so then, therefore.*

τοιοῦτος, τοιαύτα, τοιοῦτον correlative pron. and adj. *such, of such kind; similar, like.*

τοῖχος, -ου m. *internal wall* (cf. τεῖχος, -ους n.).

τολμάω, -ήσω: *to venture, dare.*

τόλμη, -ης f. *courage; boldness, daring, recklessness.*

τόλμημα, -ατος n. *brazen act.*

τολμηρός, -ά, -όν adj. *daring, bold.*

τονόω, -ώσω: *to brace up, support.*

τοξεύω, -σω: *to shoot the bow.*

τόπος, -ου m. *place, location, region, spot; station, position, office.*

τοσόσδε, -ήδε, -όνδε adj. *so great, so large, so wide,* etc.

τοσοῦτος, -αύτη, -οῦτον correl. adj. *so much, so great, so large,* etc.; in plur. *so many, many;* ἐπὶ τοσοῦτον *to such a great degree.*

τότε adv. *then, at that time; erstwhile.*

τοὐναντίον = τό + ἀντίον.

τράπεζα, -ας f. *table.*

τραπέντων aor. pass. ptc. of τρέπω.

τραυματίας, -ου m. *wounded man.*

τράχηλος, -ου m. *throat, neck.*

τρεῖς, τρία *three.*

τρέμω (used only in the pres. and impf.): *to tremble, quake.*

τρέπω, τρέψω, ἔτρεψα, τέτροφα, τέτραμμαι, ἐτρέφθην: *to turn; to rout* (an army).

τρέφω, θρέψω, ἔθρεψα, τέτροφα, τέθραμμαι, ἐθρέφθην: *to nourish, feed, rear.*

τρέχω, δραμοῦμαι, ἔδραμον, δεδράμηκα, δεδράμημαι: *to run*; τρέχειν ὀπίσω τινός: *to run behind someone*; i.e., *pursue*.

τριάκοντα indecl. *thirty*.

τριακόσιοι, -αι, -α *three hundred*.

τριακοστός, -ή, -όν (cf. τριάκοντα) adj. *the thirtieth*.

τριμερής, -ές adj. *tripartite, threefold*.

τριστιχεί adv. *in triple row, three deep*.

τρισχίλιοι, -αι, -α *three thousand*.

τρίτος, -η, -ον (cf. τρίς, τρεῖς) adj. *third*.

τρομέω, -ήσω, ἐτρόμησα: intrans. *to tremble, quiver, quake*.

τροπή, -ῆς f. *turn, turning around*; espec. *turning about* of a force in battle, *flight*.

τρόπος, -ου m. *manner, fashion, way*; ὃν προειρήκαμεν τρόπον *in the manner described above*; κατὰ τρόπον *fitly, duly*.

τροφή, -ῆς f. *food, nourishment; living, keep*; plur. *provisions, rations*.

τυγχάνω, τεύξομαι, ἔτυχον: *to meet with, get, obtain* τινός; espec. οἱ τυχόντες *the ordinary run-of-the-mill men; ordinary men*.

τύμπανον, -ου n. *drum*.

τύπτω, τύψω, ἔτυψα: *to beat, strike*.

τυραννέω, -ήσω: *to rule as a tyrant*; in pass. *to be ruled absolutely*.

τύραννος, -ου m. *lord, master*; abs. *sovereign; tyrant*.

τύχη, -ης f. *chance, fortune, luck*.

Υ

ὑάκινθος, -ου m. *blue color; blue stuff*.

ὑβρίζω, -ίσω: *to outrage, insult, affront*.

ὕβρις, -εως f. *insolence; insult, outrage*.

ὑβριστής, -ου m. *a wanton, violent man; a ravisher*.

ὕδωρ, ὕδατος n. *water*.

ὕειος, -α, -ον (cf. ὗς): *of* or *pertaining to swine*; subst. noun ὕειον: *pig*.

υἱός, -οῦ m. *son; descendant, offspring, heir*.

ὕλη, -ης f. *wood, forest; timber, logs*.

ὑμνέω, -ήσω, ὕμνησα: *to sing praise, sing hymns*.

ὕμνος, -ου m. *hymn*.

ὑπάγω, -άξω, ὑπήγαγον: *to lead* or *bring down; to draw, lead by degrees*.

ὑπακούω, -κούσομαι: *to hearken, give ear to* τινί; *to obey*.

ὕπαρχος, -ου m. *commanding under another; lieutenant-governor*.

ὑπάρχω, -ξω: *to begin, be*; espec. impers. ὑπάρχει μοι : *it belongs to me*.

ὑπέρ (1) prep. with gen. *for, in behalf of, for the sake of; of, about, concerning; from*; (2) prep. with accus. *over and above, beyond; more than, than*; (3) adv. *even more.*

ὑπερβαίνω, -βήσομαι: *to step over.*

ὑπερβάλλω, -βαλῶ: *to exceed, surpass.*

ὑπερβάντας accus. plur. masc.; aor. act. ptc. of ὑπερβαίνω.

ὑπερβολή, -ῆς f. *excess.*

ὑπερέχω (impf. ὑπερεῖχον), -έξω, ὑπέρεσχον: *to be above, stand out above; to excel, surpass, be the better.*

ὑπερηφανία, -ας f. *arrogance, pride.*

ὑπερθαυμάζω, -άσω: *to be exceedingly surprised.*

ὑπερπαθέω, -ήσω: *to be grievously distressed.*

ὑπέχω, ὑφέξω, ὑπέσχον: *to hold underneath; to supply, afford.* ὑπέχειν δίκην: *to pay the penalty.*

ὑπηρέτης, -ου m. *rower*; of any *laborer; servant.*

ὑπῆρξε 3 sing. aor. act. indic. of ὑπάρχω.

ὑπισχνέομαι, ὑποσχήσομαι, ὑπεσχόμην: *to take upon oneself, undertake; to promise.*

ὕπνος, -ου m. *sleep.*

ὑπό prep. with (1) gen. *by; by means of; at the hands of*; (2) accus. *under, below, under the authority of.*

ὑποκάτω *below, underneath.*

ὑποκέχηνε pf. indic. act. of ὑποχάσχω.

ὑποκλάω, -άσω: *to break underneath; break by degrees.*

ὑπολαμβάνω, ὑπολήψομαι, ὑπέλαβον, ὑπείληφα, ὑπείλημμαι: *to take up from below, take on one's back; to take up* a notion, *assume, understand, suppose; suspect*; in a conversation *to take up the discourse, retort, offer a rejoinder.*

ὑποληπτέον: impers. vb. adj. from ὑπολαμβάνω: *one must assume that...* (+ accus. and infin. in indir. state.).

ὑπομάσθιος, -ον adj. *under the breast, sucking.*

ὑπομένω, -μενῶ, -έμεινα: *to stay behind, survive; to abide or await* τι; with infin. *to endure, abide.*

ὑπόμνησις, -εως f. *reminder, remembrance.*

ὑπόνοια, -ας f. *suspicion.*

ὑπόνομος, -ου m. *underground passage, water pipe.*

ὑποπίμπρημι, -πρήσω: *to set on afire, enkindle underneath.*

ὑποπίπτω, -πεσοῦμαι, ὑπέπεσον: *to fall down before, succumb to* τινί.

ὑποπτήσσω, -ήξω: *to crouch* or *cower down in fear.*

ὑποστρέφω, -ψω: *to return.*

ὑπόσχεσις, -εως f. *promise; engagement.*

ὑποστῆναι 2 aor. infin. of ὑφίστημι.

ὑποτάσσω, -άξω: *to set under someone else; to make subj.*; in pass. *become subj. to* τινί.

ὑποτέμνω, -τεμῶ: *to cut away; to cut off, interrupt.*

ὑποτίθημι, -θήσω, ὑπέθηκα: *to set underneath, place under.*

ὑπουργέω, -ήσω: *render service, perform a duty.*

ὑπουργία, -ας f. *service, duty.*

ὑποφυγή, -ῆς f. *refuge.*

ὑποχάσχω: *to gape or yawn open.*

ὑποχείριος, -ον adj. *under one's control, subj. to.*

ὑποχωρέω, -ήσομαι: *to withdraw.*

ὑποψία, -ας f. *suspicion, jealousy.*

Ὑρκανός, -οῦ m. *Hyrcanus.*

ὕσσωπος –ου f. *hyssop.*

ὕστατος, -η, -ον adj. *last, utmost, hindmost*; ἐν ὑστάτοις *at the last.*

ὑστερέω, -ήσω, ὑστέρησα, ὑστέρηκα: *to be behind, come later*; metaphor. *come short of, be inferior to* τινός.

ὑφάπτω, -ψω, ὕφηψα: *to set on fire from underneath.*

ὑφεστηκότων pf. act. ptc., gen. masc. plur. of ὑφίστημι.

ὑφίστημι, ὑποστήσω, ὑπέστησα (2 aor. ὑπέστην), ὑφέστηκα: *to place or set under; to withstand, endure.*

ὑφοράομαι, ὑπόψομαι: *to look at from below; to suspect.*

ὑψηλός, -ή, -όν adj. *high, lofty; tall.*

ὕψος, -ους n. *height; loftiness; exaltation.*

ὑψόω, -ώσω, ὕψωσα, fut. pass. ὑψωθήσομαι, 1 aor. pass. ὑψώθην: *to heighten, raise, elevate, exalt.*

Φ

φαγεῖν infin. of 2 aor. ἔφαγον of ἐσθίω.

φάγετε 2 plur. aor. impv. act. of ἐσθίω.

φαίνω, φανῶ, ἔφηνα, πέφαγκα, πέφασμαι, ἐφάνθην: *to shine, bring to light*; in pass. and 2 aor. *to appear.*

φάλαγξ, -αγγος f. *phalanx.*

φανερός, -ά, -όν adj. *visible, evident.*

φάντασμα, -ματος n. *vision, dream.*

φάραγξ, -αγγος n. *ravine, gully; chasm.*

Φαραώ m. *Pharaoh.*

Φαρισσαῖος, -ου m. *Pharisee.*

φάσκω only pres. and impf. = φημί.

φαυλίζω, -ίσω: *to hold cheap; disparage; despise.*

φείδομαι, φείσομαι, ἐφεισάμην: *to spare* τινός.

φέρω, οἴσω, ἤνεγκα/ἤνεγκον, ἐνήνοχα, ἐνήνεγμαι, ἠνέχθην: *to bear, carry, bring*; intrans. *lead to.*

φεύγω, φεύξομαι/φευξοῦμαι, ἔφυγον, πέφευγα: *to flee; become an exile.*

φήμη, -ης f. *rumor, report.*

φημί, φήσω, ἔφησα: *to say, speak.*

Φῆστος, -ου m. *Festus.*

φθάνω, φθήσομαι: *to outstrip, precede* τινός; oft with suppl. ptc.

φθείρω, φθερῶ, ἔφθειρα: *to corrupt, spoil, ruin*; pass. *to perish.*

φθονέω, -ήσω: *to begrudge* τινί *something.*

φιάλη, -ης f. *shallow bowel* used in a drink offering, *bowel* for libations.

φίλημα, -ατος n. *kiss.*

φίλιος, -α, -ον adj. *of or from a friend; friendly, kindly.*

Φίλιππος, ου m. *Philip, king of Macedon, father of Alexander the Great.*

φιλογράμματος, -ον adj. *book-loving, letter-loving.*

φίλος, -η, -ον adj. *loved, beloved, dear*; espec. substant. noun φίλος, -ου m. *friend; associate.*

φιλόστοργος, -ον adj. *affectionate.*

φιλοφρονέομαι: *to deal with affectionately.*

Vocabulary

φιλόψυχος, -ον adj. *loving one's life too much.*

φίλτατος, -η, -ον superl. of φίλος, -η, -ον.

Φινεες m. *Phinehas.*

φλέγω, φλέξω, ἔφλεξα: *to burn, scorch*; pass. *become hot, blaze up.*

φλογίζω, -ίσω: *to set on fire, burn up.*

φλόξ, φλογός f. *flame.*

φοβέομαι, φοβήσομαι, ἐφοβήθην: *to fear, be afraid, take fright.*

φοβερός, -ά, -όν adj. *fearful; frightful, formidable.*

φοβερότης, -τητος f. *frightfulness.*

φοβέω, -ήσω, ἐφόβησα: *to frighten.*

φοῖνιξ, -ικος m. *date.*

φονεύω, -σω: *to slaughter, kill.*

φονοκτονία, -ας f. *deed of murder.*

φόνος, -ου m. *slaughter, carnage; blood and gore.*

φονόω, -ώσω: *stain with blood, perpetrate murder.*

φορολογία, -ας f. *the leveling of tribute; tribute.*

φόρος, -ου m. *tax, tribute.*

φρενοβλάβεια, -ας f. *damaged understanding.*

φρίκη, -ης f. *shuddering; fright.*

φρικώδης, -ες adj. *something that causes one to shudder; horrible, awful.*

φρίττω, φρίξω: *to shudder* with fear.

359

φρονέω, -ήσω: *to think.*

φρόνημα, -ματος n. *mind, will, spirit.*

φρόνησις, -εως f. *purpose, intention.*

Φρόντων, -ονος m. *Fronto.*

φροῦδος, -η, -ον adj. *gone away, departed.*

φρουρά, -ᾶς f. *watch, imprisonment.*

φρουρέω, -ήσω: *to keep watch, guard.*

φρούριον, -ίου n. *watch post; fort, citadel.*

φρουρός, -οῦ m. *watcher, guard.*

φυγαδευτήριον, -ου n. *city of refuge.*

φυγαδεύω, -σω: trans. *to make one an exile, banish*; intrans. *to be an exile, live in banishment.*

φυγή, -ῆς f. *flight, rout.*

φυλακή, -ῆς f. *watching, guarding.*

φυλακτήρ, -ῆρος m. = φύλαξ.

φύλαξ, -ακος m. *guardian, watcher, sentinel.*

φυλάσσω, φυλάξω, ἐφύλαξα, πεφύλακα, πεφύλαγμαι, ἐφυλάχθην: *to guard, keep; watch.*

φυλάττω see φυλάσσω.

Φυλιστιιμ indecl. noun in the plur. *Philistines.*

φῦλον, -ου n. *stock, race, kind; tribe.*

φύρω, φύρσω, ἔφυσα: *to mix, mingle* with something wet; hence *to wet, soil, defile.*

φύσις, -εως f. *nature; inborn quality.*

φυτεύω, φυτεύσω, ἐφύτευσα: *to plant.*

φυτόν, -οῦ n. *plant, bush.*

φύω, φύσω, ἔφυσα (2 aor. ἔφυ), πέφυκα: *to plant, sow*; in the pass., mid., and pf. tense *to grow, spring forth.*

φωνή, -ῆς f. *voice.*

φωράω, -άσω: *trace, detect, discover.*

φῶς, φωτός n. *light* (oft with relig. connotations).

Χ

Χαλεβ m. *Caleb.*

χαλεπός, -ή, -όν adj. *hard to bear; severe, grievous, serious.*

χαλκός, -οῦ m. *brass, bronze.*

Χαναναῖος, -α, -ον adj. *Canaanite.*

χαρά, -ᾶς f. *joy, gladness, happiness.*

χαρίζομαι, χαριοῦμαι, ἐχαρισάμην: *to show favor* or *kindness to* τινί.

χαρίζομαι, -ίσομαι: *to give* τι *as a gift.*

χάριν prep. with gen. *for the sake of, because of, by reason of.*

χάρις, χάριτος f. *favor.*

Χασελευ m. *Chislev* ninth month in the Hebr. calendar, correspond. to Nov.–Dec.

χειμάζω, -μάσω: *to pass the winter*; in pass. *to be tempest-tossed.*

χείρ, χειρός f. *hand; power, authority; band, host*; κατὰ χεῖρα *hand-to-hand.*

χειροκοπέω, -ήσω: *to cut off the hand.*

χεῖρον adv. accus. *worse.*

χειροποιήτως adv. *made by hand; artificially.*

χείρων, -ον compar. of κακός; ἐπὶ τὸ χεῖρον *for the worse.*

Χέλικας, -α m. *Chelicas.*

Χεττιιμ indecl. noun in the plur. *the Greeks, sea people.*

χιλίαρχος, -ου m. *the commander of a thousand.*

χιλιάς, χιλιάδος f. *one thousand.*

χίλιοι, -αι, -α *thousand.*

χλευάζω, -άσω: *to joke, jest, scoff*; trans. *to scoff at* τι.

χλεύη, -ης f. *joke, jest*; πρὸς χλεύην *as a jest.*

χόλος, -ου m. *gall bile; bitter anger, wrath.*

χορηγία, -ας f. *abundance of means; wealth, plenty.*

χοῦς, χοός (accus. χοῦν) m. *dust.*

χράομαι, χρήσομαι, ἐχρησάμην: *to use or experience* τινί.

χρεία, -ας f. *need, necessity.*

χρή impers. vb. + infin. *it is necessary, one may.*

χρῆμα, -ματος n. (mostly plur.) *possessions, wealth, money.*

χρήσιμος, -η, -ον adj. *serviceable.*

Χριστιανός, -οῦ m. *Christian.*

χριστός, -ή, -όν vb. adj. from χρίω *rubbed on, anointed*; espec. ὁ Χριστός *the Christ.*

χρόνος, -ου m. *time.*

χρυσίον, -ου n. dimin. of χρυσός: *gold; piece of gold, gold coin; money.*

χρυσός, -οῦ m. *gold.*

χρυσοῦς, -ῆ, -οῦν adj. *made of gold, golden.*

Χωβαρεύς, -έως m. *Chobareus.*

χωλός, -ή, -όν adj. *lame.*

χῶμα, -ματος n. *embankment, mound* (such as besiegers throw up against the wall of a city).

χώρα, -ας f. *country, region, territory; countryside; land, field*; κατὰ χώραν *throughout their land.*

χωρέω, -ήσω, ἐχώρησα: *to make room for, contain, give way; to march; to spread abroad, become current.*

χωρίζω: *to separate*; pass. *be separated from; to retire.*

χωρίον, -ου n. (dimin. of χῶρος and χώρα) *a particular place, spot.*

χῶρος, -ου m. *space; place, land, country; region.*

Ψ

ψαύω, -σω: *to touch* τινός; ψαύει τοῦ πρόσω lit. *it touches the going forth*, i.e., *it makes progress.*

ψεύδομαι, ψεύσομαι, ἐψευσάμην: *to play false, lie; to be deceived.*

ψῆφος, -ου f. *small stone, pebble* used in voting; hence, *resolution, decree.*

ψυχή, -ῆς f. *soul; life; heart.*

ψυχρός, -ά, -όν adj. *cold.*

Ω

ὦ *oh!* expresses anger or joy.

ᾠδή, -ῆς f. *song, song of praise.*

ᾠήθη 3 sing. aor. pass. indic. of οἴομαι.

ὠλοφύρατο 3 sing. plupf. indic. pass. of ὀλοφύρομαι.

ὡμοιώθη aor. pass. of ὁμοιόω.

ὤν pres. act. ptc., nom. masc. sing. of εἰμί.

ὠνέομαι, -ήσομαι, ἐωνησάμην: *to buy, purchase.*

ὤνησεν 3 sing. aor. act. indic. of ὀνίνημι.

ὥρα, -ας f. *moment, occasion; time.*

ὡρμημένους pf. mid./pass. ptc. of ὁμάω.

ὡς (1) particle of comp. *as, like; as though, as if, on the grounds that; on the pretext of*; with numerals *about* (ὡς ἀπὸ σταδίων δεκαπέντε *about fifteen stades away*); (2) introduces disc. *how, that*; (3) intensifies an adv. or adj. *very, how* (ὡς τάχιστα *as soon as possible*; ὡς ὡραῖοι οἱ πόδες *how beautiful/lovely are the feet*); (4) temp. and conseq. particle *as, as long as, while, when* (with pres. or impf.); *when, after* (with aor.); *so that, in order that, because* (after pur. clause).

ὥσπερ adv. *as, just as.*

ὥστε adv. and clause marker *that, so that.*

ὠφελέω, -ήσω: *to help, aid, assist; be of use or service to someone.*

ὠφέληκεν 3 sing. pf. act. indic. of ὠφελέω.

ὤφθην 1 aor. pass. of ὁράω.

ὠχυρώθην 1 aor. pass. of ὀχυρόω.

ὠχύρωτο plupf. indic. pass. of ὀχυρόω.

CREDITS AND ACKNOWLEDGMENTS

This work uses the Cardo font developed by David J Perry and released under the SIL Open Font License. See http://www.scholarsfonts.net

Septuaginta, edited by Alfred Rahlfs, 2nd revised edition ed. by Robert Hanhart © 2006 Deutsche Bibelgesellschaft, Stuttgart. Used by permission.

Texts from *Flavii Iosephi Opera,* edited by Benedikt Niese, copyright 1895 Weidmann, Berlin, used by permission of the Perseus Digital Library, http://www.perseus.tufts.edu/hopper/

Josephus and the New Testament, 2nd edition by Steve Mason, copyright 2003 by Hendrickson Publishers, Peabody, Massachusetts. Used by permission. All rights reserved.

Herod: King of the Jews and Friend of the Romans by Peter Richardson, copyright 1996 by University of South Carolina Press, Columbia SC. Used by permission. All rights reserved.

From the Maccabees to the Mishnah by Shaye Cohen, copyright 1987 by Westminster John Knox Press, Philadelphia. Used by permission. All rights reserved.

"Eleazar Ben Yair's Sanction for Martyrdom" by I. Jacobs in *Journal for the Study of Judaism* 13:183–86 copyright 1982 by Koninklijke Brill NV, Leiden, The Netherlands. Used by permission. All rights reserved.

"Ananus, James, and Earliest Christianity: Josephus' Account of the Death of James." by James S. McLaren in *Journal of Theological Studies* 52:1–25 copyright 2001 by Oxford University Press. Used by permission of Oxford University Press. All rights reserved.

The Jews from Alexander to Herod by David S. Russell copyright 1967 by Oxford University Press. Used by permission of Oxford University Press. All rights reserved.

G.W. Bowersock, "Foreign Elites at Rome," pages 53–62 and Tessa Rajak, "Josephus in the Diaspora," pages 79–97 in *Flavius Josephus and Flavian Rome,* edited by Jonathan Edmondson, Steve Mason, and James Rives copyright 2005 by Oxford University Press. Used by permission of Oxford University Press. All rights reserved.

A Greek-English Lexicon, edited by Henry G. Liddell, Robert Scott, and Henry S. Jones copyright 1966 by Clarendon Press. Used by permission of Oxford University Press. All rights reserved.

Reprinted by permission of the publishers and the Trustees of the Loeb Classical Library from JOSEPHUS: VOLUME I, Loeb Classical Library Volume 186, translated by H. St. J. Thackeray, Cambridge, Mass.: Harvard University Press, Copyright © 1926, by the President and Fellows of Harvard College. Loeb Classical Library ® is a registered trademark of the President and Fellows of Harvard College.

Reprinted by permission of the publishers and the Trustees of the Loeb Classical Library from JOSEPHUS: VOLUME II, Loeb Classical Library Volume 203, translated by H. St. J. Thackeray, Cambridge, Mass.: Harvard University Press, Copyright © 1927, by the President and Fellows of Harvard College. Loeb Classical Library ® is a registered trademark of the President and Fellows of Harvard College.

Reprinted by permission of the publishers and the Trustees of the Loeb Classical Library from JOSEPHUS: VOLUME III, Loeb Classical Library Volume 210, translated by H. St. J. Thackeray, Cambridge, Mass.: Harvard University Press, Copyright © 1928, by the President and Fellows of Harvard College. Loeb Classical Library ® is a registered trademark of the

President and Fellows of Harvard College.

Reprinted by permission of the publishers and the Trustees of the Loeb Classical Library from JOSEPHUS: VOLUME VII, Loeb Classical Library Volume 365, translated by Ralph Marcus, Cambridge, Mass.: Harvard University Press, Copyright © 1943, by the President and Fellows of Harvard College. Loeb Classical Library ® is a registered trademark of the President and Fellows of Harvard College.

Reprinted by permission of the publishers and the Trustees of the Loeb Classical Library from JOSEPHUS: VOLUME IX, Loeb Classical Library Volume 433, translated by Louis H. Feldman, Cambridge, Mass.: Harvard University Press, Copyright © 1965, by the President and Fellows of Harvard College. Loeb Classical Library ® is a registered trademark of the President and Fellows of Harvard College.

Reprinted by permission of the publisher from GREEK GRAMMAR by Herbert Weir Smyth, revised by Gordon G. Messing, Cambridge, Mass.: Harvard University Press, Copyright © 1920 by Herbert Weir Smyth, Copyright © 1956 by the President and Fellows of Harvard College. Copyright © renewed 1984 by the President and Fellows of Harvard College.

Peer Reviewed

Concordia Publishing House

Similar to the peer review or "refereed" process used to publish professional and academic journals, the Peer Review process is designed to enable authors to publish book manuscripts through Concordia Publishing House. The Peer Review process is well-suited for smaller projects and textbook publication.

We aim to provide quality resources for congregations, church workers, seminaries, universities, and colleges. Our books are faithful to the Holy Scriptures and the Lutheran Confessions, promoting the rich theological heritage of the historic, creedal Church. Concordia Publishing House (CPH) is the publishing arm of The Lutheran Church—Missouri Synod. We develop, produce, and distribute (1) resources that support pastoral and congregational ministry, and (2) scholarly and professional books in exegetical, historical, dogmatic, and practical theology.

**For more information, visit:
www.cph.org/PeerReview.**

www.ingramcontent.com/pod-product-compliance
Lightning Source LLC
Chambersburg PA
CBHW031959220426
43664CB00005B/77